R

Richmond upon Thames Libraries

Renew online at www.richmond.gov.uk/libraries

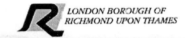

The Great Divide

JOSEPH E. STIGLITZ

The Great Divide

ALLEN LANE
an imprint of
PENGUIN BOOKS

ALLEN LANE

UK | USA | Canada | Ireland | Australia

India | New Zealand | South Africa

Penguin Books is part of the Penguin Random House group of companies
whose addresses can be found at global.penguinrandomhouse.com.

First published in the United States of America by W. W. Norton and Company, Inc. 2015
First published in Great Britain by Allen Lane 2015

004

Printed in Great Britain by Clays Ltd, St Ives plc

A CIP catalogue record for this book is available from the British Library

ISBN: 978–0–241–20290–6

MIX
Paper from
responsible sources
FSC® C018179

Penguin Random House is committed to a
sustainable future for our business, our readers
and our planet. This book is made from Forest
Stewardship Council® certified paper.

To my many readers, who have responded with such enthusiasm
to my writings on inequality and opportunity.

To my children, Siobhan, Michael, Jed, and Julia,
and my wife, Anya, all of whom, in their own way,
are striving to create a fairer and better world.

And to the scholars and activists everywhere who work with
such dedication for social justice.

Thank you for the inspiration and encouragement you have provided.

Contents

═══

Part V

CONSEQUENCES OF INEQUALITY

Part VI

POLICY

Part VII

REGIONAL PERSPECTIVES

INTRODUCTION

N O ONE TODAY CAN DENY THAT THERE IS A GREAT DIVIDE in America, separating the very richest—sometimes described as the 1 percent—and the rest. Their lives are different: they have different worries, different aspirations, and different lifestyles.

Ordinary Americans worry about how they will pay for the college education of their children, about what happens if someone in the family has a serious illness, about how they are to manage their retirement. In the depths of the Great Recession, tens of millions worried whether they would be able to keep their house. Millions weren't able to do so.

Those in the 1 percent—and even more the upper .1 percent—debate other issues: what kind of jet airplane to buy, the best way to shelter their income from taxes (What happens if the United States forces the end to bank secrecy in Switzerland—will the Cayman Islands be next? Is Andorra safe?). On the beaches of Southampton they complain about the noise their neighbors make as they helicopter in from New York City. They worry, too, about what would happen if they fell off their perch—there is so far to fall, and on rare occasions it does happen.

Not long ago I found myself at a dinner party hosted by a bright and concerned member of the 1 percent. Aware of the great divide, our host had brought together leading billionaires, academics, and others who were worried about inequality. As the evening's early chitchat burbled on, I overheard one billionaire—who had gotten his start in life by inheriting a fortune—discuss with another the problem of lazy Americans who were trying to free ride on the rest. Soon thereafter, they seamlessly transitioned into a discussion of tax shelters, apparently unaware of the irony. Several times in the evening, Marie Antoinette and the guillotine were invoked as the gathered plutocrats reminded each other of the risks of allowing inequality to grow to excess: "Remember the guillotine" set the tone for the evening. And in that refrain they confessed a central message of this book: the level of inequality in America is not inevitable; it is not the result of inexorable laws of economics. It is a matter of policies and politics. It was, they seemed to be saying, possible for these powerful men to do something about inequality.

This is but one of the reasons why concern about inequality has become urgent even among the 1 percent: increasing numbers of them realize that sustained economic growth, upon which their prosperity depends, can't happen when the vast majority of citizens have stagnant incomes.

Oxfam forcefully brought home the extent of the world's growing inequality to the annual gathering of the world's elite in Davos in 2014, pointing out that a bus with some 85 of the world's billionaires had as much wealth as the bottom half of its population, some three billion people.[1] By a year later the bus had shrunk—it required only 80 seats. Just as dramatic, Oxfam found that the top 1 percent of the world now owned nearly half the world's wealth—and are on track to own as much of the rest of the 99 percent combined by 2016.

The great divide has been a long time in coming. In the decades after World War II the country grew at its fastest pace, and the country grew together. While all segments saw an increase in their incomes, it was shared prosperity. Incomes of those at the bottom grew faster than the incomes of those at the top.

It was a golden age in America, but to my young eyes there appeared darker edges. Growing up on the southern shore of Lake Michigan, in one of the country's iconic industrial towns, Gary, Indiana, I saw poverty, inequality, racial discrimination, and episodic unemployment as one recession after another battered the country. Labor strife was common as workers struggled to get a fair share of America's deservedly lauded prosperity. I heard rhetoric about America being a middle-class society, but for the most part, the people I saw occupied the lower rungs of that supposed middle-class society, and their voices were not among those that were shaping the country.

We were not rich, but my parents had adjusted their lifestyle to their incomes—and in the end that is a big part of the battle. I wore hand-me-down clothes from my brother that my mother had always bought on sale, with an eye toward durability rather than saving money in the short run: penny wise but pound foolish, she would say. When I was growing up, my mother, who had graduated from the University of Chicago in the midst of the Great Depression, helped my father in his insurance business. When she was working, we were left in the care of our "help," Minnie Fae Ellis, a loving, hardworking, and bright woman. Even as a 10-year-old, I was disturbed: I wondered, Why did she have only a sixth-grade education, in a country that was supposedly so rich and that supposedly offered opportunities for all? Why was she taking care of me rather than her own children?

After I graduated from high school, my mother pursued her life's ambition—going back to school to get teacher certification and teach elementary school. She taught in the Gary public schools; as white flight set in, she became one of the few white teachers in what had turned into a de facto segregated school. After she was forced to retire at the age of 67, she started teaching on the northwest Indiana campus of Purdue University, working to make sure that there was access for as many as possible. In her 80s, she eventually retired.

Like so many of my contemporaries, I was impatient for change. We were told that changing society was difficult, that it took time. Even though I had not suffered the kinds of hardships that my peers faced in Gary (apart from a small amount of discrimination), I identified with those who had. It would be decades before I studied in detail the statistics concerning income, but I sensed that America was not the land of opportunity that it claimed to be: there was remarkable opportunity for some, but little for others. Horatio Alger, at least in part, was a myth: many hardworking Americans would never make it. I was one of the lucky ones for whom America did offer opportunity: a National Merit Scholarship to Amherst College. More than anything else, *that* opportunity opened up a world of other opportunities over time.

As I explain in "The Myth of America's Golden Age," in my junior year at Amherst, I switched my major from physics to economics. I was driven to find out why our society worked the way it did. I became an economist not just to understand inequality, discrimination, and unemployment but also, I hoped, to do something about these problems plaguing the country. The most important chapter of my Ph.D. thesis at MIT, written under the supervision of Robert Solow and Paul Samuelson (both of whom were later to receive Nobel Prizes), focused on the determinants of the distribution of income and wealth. Presented in a meeting of the Econometric Society (the international association of economists focusing on mathematics and statistical applications to economics) in 1966 and published in its journal, *Econometrica*, in 1969, it still often serves half a century later as a framework for thinking about the subject.

Readership for an analysis of inequality was limited, both among the general public and even among economists. People were not interested in the subject. Within the economics profession, there sometimes was outright hostility. This remained true even as the country's inequality began to increase markedly, beginning around the time Reagan became president. One noted economist, a University of Chicago Nobel Prize winner, Robert Lucas, put it forcefully: "Of the tendencies that are harmful to sound economics, the most seductive and . . . poisonous is to focus on questions of distribution."[2]

Like so many conservative economists, he argued that the best way to help the poor was to increase the size of the nation's economic pie, and he believed that focusing attention on the small slice of the pie given to the poor would detract attention from the more fundamental issue of how to enlarge the pie. There is in fact a long tradition in economics that holds that the two issues (of efficiency and distribution, of the size of the pie and how it is divided) can be separated, and that the job of the economist was narrow, important, but hard: it was only to figure out how to maximize the size of the pie. The division of the pie was a matter of politics, something that economists should stay well clear of.

With stances like Lucas's so fashionable in the economics profession, it was little wonder that economists paid almost no attention to growing inequality in the country. They didn't pay much attention to the fact that while GDP was growing, the incomes of most Americans were stagnating. This neglect meant that ultimately they couldn't provide a good explanation of what was going on in the economy, they couldn't grasp the implications of growing inequality, and they couldn't devise policies that might put the country on a different course.

That was why I so welcomed in 2011 the offer of *Vanity Fair* to bring the issues to a wider audience. The resulting article, "Of the 1 Percent, by the 1 Percent, for the 1 Percent," did have a far wider readership than my *Econometrica* article decades earlier. The new social order that my *Vanity Fair* article discussed—the 99 percent of Americans who were in the same stagnating boat—became the slogan of the Occupy Wall Street movement: "We are the 99 percent." It presented the thesis that reverberates through the articles here and my subsequent writing: almost all of us, including many in the 1 percent, would actually be better off if there were less inequality. It was in the enlightened self-interest of the 1 percent to help construct a less divided society. I was not seeking to wage a new class war, but rather to establish a new sense of national cohesion, one that had waned as a great divide had opened up in our society.

The article zeroed in on the question of *why we should care about the large increase in inequality*: it was a matter not only of values and morality but also of economics, the nature of our society, and our sense of national identity. There were even broader strategic interests. Though we remain the largest military power—spending almost half of what is spent around the world—our long wars in Iraq and Afghanistan revealed the limits of that power: we were unable to win clear control of even small swaths of land in countries far, far weaker than the United States. The strength of the United States has always been its "soft power" and, most notably, its moral and economic influence, the example it gives for others and the influence of its ideas, including those concerning its form of economics and politics.

Unfortunately, because of growing inequality, the American economic model has not been delivering for large fractions of the population—the typical American family is worse off than it was a quarter-century ago, adjusted for inflation. Even the fraction in poverty has increased. While a rising China is marked by high levels of inequality and a democratic deficit, its economy has delivered more for most of its citizens—it moved some 500 million out of poverty over the same period that stagnation seized America's middle class. An economic model that doesn't serve a majority of its citizens is unlikely to become a role model for other countries to emulate.

The *Vanity Fair* article led to my book *The Price of Inequality*, in which I expanded on many of the themes that I had raised, and this in turn led to the invitation from the *New York Times* in 2013 to curate a series of articles on inequality that we called The Great

Divide. It was my hope that, through this series, I could further awaken the country to the problem confronting us: We were not the land of opportunity that we believed we were—and that so many others believed as well. We had become the advanced country with the highest level of inequality, and we had among the lowest levels of equality of opportunity. Our inequalities manifested themselves in numerous ways. But they were not inevitable, the inexorable workings out of the laws of economics: rather, they were the result of our policies and politics. Different policies could lead to different outcomes: better economic performance (however measured) and lower levels of inequality.

The original *Vanity Fair* article and the series of articles I wrote for The Great Divide constitute the core of this book. For some fifteen years, I have also written a monthly syndicated column for *Project Syndicate*. Originally dedicated to bringing modern economic thinking to countries in transition to a market economy after the fall of the Iron Curtain, *Project Syndicate* in time became so successful that its articles are now published in papers all over the world, including in most of the advanced countries. Not surprisingly, many of the articles I wrote for *Project Syndicate* were concerned with one aspect of inequality or another, and a selection of these—as well as articles published in various other newspapers and periodicals—is included here.

While the focus of these essays is on inequality, I have decided to include several on the Great Recession—articles written in the run-up to the financial crisis of 2007–08 and in the aftermath, as the country and the world entered the *great malaise*. Those articles deserve a place in this volume because the financial crisis and inequality are intricately intertwined: inequality helped lead to the crisis, the crisis exacerbated already extant inequalities, and the worsening of these inequalities has created a significant downdraft in the economy, making a *robust* recovery all the more difficult. Like inequality itself, there was nothing inevitable about either the depth or the duration of the crisis. Indeed, the crisis was not an act of God, like a once-in-a-hundred-years flood or earthquake. It was something that we did to ourselves; as with outsized inequality, it was the result of our policies and politics.

THIS BOOK IS mostly about the *economics* of inequality. But as I have just suggested, one cannot neatly separate out politics and economics. In various essays in this volume, and in my earlier book *The Price of Inequality*, I describe the nexus between politics and economics: the vicious circle by which more economic inequality gets translated into political inequality, especially in America's political system, which gives such unbridled power to money. Political inequality in turn increases economic inequality. But this process has been reinforced as many ordinary Americans have become disillusioned with the political process: in the aftermath of the 2008 crisis, hundreds of billions went to save the banks, and little went to help homeowners. Under the influence of Treasury Secretary Timothy Geithner and the National Economic Council chairman Larry Summers—who were among the architects of deregulation policies that helped to foment the crisis—the Obama administration initially did not support, or even opposed, efforts to restructure home mortgages, to relieve millions of Americans who had suffered from predatory and discriminatory lending by the banks. No wonder, then, that so many people cast a pox on both houses.

I HAVE RESISTED the temptation to revise or expand the articles gathered here, or even to update them. Nor have I restored the many "cuttings" of the original pieces, important ideas that had to be left out as I struggled to meet assigned word limits.[3] The journalistic format has much to commend itself: its pieces are short and punchy, responding to the issues of the moment, without all the qualifications and caveats that surround so much academic writing. As I wrote these articles, engaging in the often heated debates at the time, I kept in mind the deeper messages that I wanted to convey. I hope this book succeeds in conveying these broad themes.

As chairman of the Council of Economic Advisers and as chief economist of the World Bank, I had occasionally written op-eds, but it was not until *Project Syndicate* invited me to write a monthly column in 2000 that I did so on a regular basis. The challenge enormously increased my respect for those who have to write a column once or twice a week. By contrast, one of the main challenges in writing a column once a month is selectivity: Of the myriad economic issues that arise around the world each month, which one would be of greatest interest and provide the context of delivering a message of broader import?

During the past decade, four of the central issues facing our society have been the great divide—the huge inequality that is emerging in the United States and many other advanced countries—economic mismanagement, globalization, and the role of the state and the market. As this book shows, those four themes are interrelated. The growing inequality has been both cause and consequence of our macroeconomic travails, the 2008 crisis and the long malaise that followed. Globalization, whatever its virtues in spurring growth, has almost surely increased inequality—and especially so, given the way we have been mismanaging globalization. The mismanagement of our economy and the mismanagement of globalization are, in turn, related to the role of special interests in our politics—a politics that increasingly represents the interests of the 1 percent. But while politics has been part of the cause of our current troubles, it will only be through politics that we will find solutions: the market by itself won't do it. Unfettered markets will lead to more monopoly power, more abuses of the financial sector, more unbalanced trade relations. It will only be through reform of our democracy—making our government more accountable to *all* of the people, more reflective of their interests—that we will be able to heal the great divide and restore the country to shared prosperity.

———

THE ESSAYS IN this book are grouped into eight parts, each preceded by a short introductory essay, which attempts to explain the context in which the articles were written or touch upon a few of the topics that I was unable to address in the short confines of the articles reprinted here.

I begin with "Prelude: Showing Cracks." In the years before the crisis our economic leaders, including the Federal Reserve chairman Alan Greenspan, could boast of a new economy in which economic fluctuations that had been the scourge of the past would be put behind us; the so-called great moderation was bringing a new era of low inflation and seemingly high growth. But those who looked even a little bit more closely saw all of this as merely a thin veneer, masking economic mismanagement and political corruption on a massive scale (some of which had come to light in the Enron scandal); even worse, the growth that was occurring was not being shared *by most Americans*. The great divide was growing larger. The chapters describe the making of the crisis and its consequences.

After presenting in Part I an overview of some of the key issues in inequality (including my "Of the 1 Percent, by the 1 Percent, for the 1 Percent" *Vanity Fair* article, and my inaugural article for The Great Divide series in the *New York Times*), I turn in Part II to two articles providing personal reminiscences on the early awakening of my interest in the subject. Parts III, IV, and V deal with the dimensions, causes, and consequences of inequality; Part VI presents some discussions of key policy ideas. Part VII looks at inequality and policies designed to address it in other countries. Finally, in Part VIII I turn to one of the core causes of inequality in America today—the prolonged weakness in our labor market. I ask how we can best put America back to work, at decent jobs paying livable wages. An afterword contains a short interview with *Vanity Fair*'s editor Cullen Murphy that touches on some of the questions that have been raised repeatedly during discussions of inequality: When did America make the wrong turn? Aren't the 1 percent the job creators, so won't making a more equal society wind up hurting the 99 percent?

Acknowledgments

This is not a standard academic book, but a collection of articles and essays written for an assortment of periodicals and newspapers over the last few years on the subject of inequality—the yawning divide that has opened up especially in America, but to a lesser extent in many other countries around the world. But the articles are based on a long history of academic research, begun when I was a graduate student at M.I.T. and a Fulbright scholar at Cambridge, UK, in the mid-1960s. Back then—and until recently—there was little interest among the American economics profession in the subject. And so, I owe a great deal to my thesis supervisors, two of the great economists of the twentieth century, Robert Solow (whose own dissertation was on the subject) and Paul Samuelson, for encouraging me in this line of research, as well as for their great insights.[4] And an especial thanks to my first co-author, George Akerlof, who shared the 2001 Nobel Prize with me.

At Cambridge, we often discussed the determinants of the distribution of income, and I benefited enormously from conversations with Frank Hahn, James Meade, Nicholas Kaldor, James Mirrlees, Partha Dasgupta, David Champernowne, and Michael Farrell. It was there that I tutored and then began my collaboration with Anthony Atkinson, the leading scholar on inequality in the past half century. Ravi Kanbur, Arjun Jayadev, Karla Hoff, and Rob Johnson are other former students and colleagues who taught me much about the subjects discussed in this book.

Rob Johnson currently heads the Institute for New Economic Thinking (INET), founded in the aftermath of the Great Recession. Amidst the wreckage of the economy, it was increasingly recognized that standard economic models had not served the country or the world well; new economic thinking—including a greater focus on inequality and the limitations of markets—was needed. I wish to acknowledge the support of INET for some of the research that underlies the essays here.[5]

While the link between inequality and macroeconomic performance has long been a concern in my theoretical research and
policy work, there is, at last, a growing recognition of the importance
of this connection (including by the International Monetary Fund).
Here, I want to acknowledge the collaboration with my Columbia
colleagues Bruce Greenwald and Jose Antonio Ocampo, and the
work of the Commission of Experts on Reforms of the International
Monetary and Financial System appointed by the President of the
United Nations General Assembly, which I chaired.[6]

Anyone working in the area of inequality today also owes a great
debt to Emmanuel Saez and Thomas Piketty, whose painstaking
work has produced so much of the data that reveals the extent of
inequality at the top in the U.S. and many other advanced countries. Other leading scholars whose influence will be seen here
include Francois Bourgignon, Branko Milanovic, Paul Krugman,
and James Galbraith.[7]

When Cullen Murphy, then an editor at *The Atlantic Monthly*,
persuaded me to write an article on some of my experiences at the
White House (in an article, "The Roaring Nineties," which eventually
led to my second book for a more popular audience),[8] it provided not
only an opportunity to articulate ideas I had been pondering for some
years but also a new challenge: Could I address complex ideas in a
succinct way that would make them widely accessible? I had written
many of my academic papers with a co-author; the close relationship
between an editor and a writer is similar in some ways, but different
in others. We each had distinct roles. He knew the audience, in a
way I could barely fathom. I came to appreciate the role that a great
editor plays in shaping an article. Great editors allow the voice of the
author to come through, even as they improve the exposition—and in
some cases, make the topic more tantalizing.

After "The Roaring Nineties" I wrote several other pieces for *The
Atlantic Monthly,* and when Cullen Murphy moved to *Vanity Fair,*
he continued to solicit articles from me. One of these, "Capitalist
Fools" (included in this volume), written in the lead-up to and the

aftermath of the Great Recession, won a prestigious Gerald Loeb Award for outstanding journalism. Evidently, under the tutelage of Cullen, I had made strides in my writing.

He has worked closely with me on all of the articles I have written for *Vanity Fair,* of which four are included here. Most importantly for this volume, he solicited and worked diligently with me in writing the article "Of the 1 Percent, by the 1 Percent, for the 1 Percent," which, in turn, gave rise to my book *The Price of Inequality* and this book. Graydon Carter suggested the title for that article. "We are the 99%" became the slogan of the Occupy Wall Street movement, symbolizing America's Great Divide.

The arrangements I made with *Project Syndicate, Vanity Fair, The New York Times,* and a host of other media, reflected in the articles collected here, gave me the opportunity to express my views on what was happening in the world—to be a pundit, perhaps more thoughtful than those who are forced to offer their opinions on a huge range of topics on the Sunday morning shows, because I could both choose my topics and mull over the answers.

The editors of each of these articles made invaluable contributions to the essays collected here. In particular, I want to thank Sewell Chan and Aaron Retica, who edited the *New York Times Great Divide* series (which provides the title of this volume). Even before we had strategized together in late 2012 on how to bring the issues of America's growing inequality, in all of its dimensions and with all of its consequences, before the American people, Sewell had worked with me in editing the essay published here (with Mark Zandi), "The One Housing Solution Left: Mass Mortgage Refinancing." Aaron and Sewell did an amazing job editing the sixteen articles from *The New York Times* included here. I have a proclivity for writing too long, and it is always sad to see so much of one's writing end up on the cutting floor; but getting across a set of ideas in 750 words, or even 1,500 words, is one of the real challenges in journalism. Aaron and Sewell always added great insights as they cut away excess verbiage.

Among the many other editors to whom I am greatly indebted are Andrzej Rapaczynski, Kevin Murphy, and the other staff at *Project Syndicate,* Allison Silver (now at Thomson Reuters), Michael Hirsh at *Politico,* Rana Foroohar at *Time,* Philip Oltermann at *The Guardian,* Christopher Beha at *Harper's,* Joshua Greenman at the *New York Daily News,* Glen Nishimura at *USA Today,* Fred Hiatt at the *Washington Post,* and Ed Paisley at the *Washington Monthly.* I should also acknowledge the encouragement and support of Aaron Edlin at the *Economists' Voice,* Roman Frydman at *Project Syndicate,* and Felicia Wong, Cathy Harding, Mike Konczal, and Nell Abernathy at the Roosevelt Institute, for which I wrote a policy brief that I partly describe in my essay "Phony Capitalism."

The Roosevelt Institute and Columbia University have provided unparalleled institutional backing. The Roosevelt Institute, which grew out of the Roosevelt Presidential Library, has developed into one of the country's leading think-tanks, advancing the ideals of social and economic justice for which the Roosevelts stood. The Ford and MacArthur Foundations and Bernard Schwartz have provided generous support for the Roosevelt/Columbia research program on inequality.

For the past fifteen years, Columbia University has been my intellectual home. It has given me the freedom to pursue my research, gifted me with bright students enthusiastic about engaging in debates about ideas, and brilliant colleagues from whom I have learned so much. Columbia has provided an environment that has enabled me to flourish, to do what I love to do: research, teach, and advocate ideas and principles that I hope will make the world a better place.

Once again, I am indebted to Drake McFeely, president of W. W. Norton, and my long time friend and editor Brendan Curry, who once again did a superb job in editing this book and benefitted in turn from the help of Sophie Duvernoy. I am indebted too, as usual, to Elizabeth Kerr and Rachel Salzman at Norton—for this book and for their support over the years. I have also benefitted enormously over the years from the close editing of Stuart Proffitt, my editor at Penguin in the UK.

I could not have completed this book without a smooth-running office, headed by Hannah Assadi and Julia Cunico, with the support of Sarah Thomas and Jiaming Ju.

Eamon Kircher-Allen not only managed the whole process of producing the book, but served as an editor as well. I owe him a double thanks: he also edited each of the articles in the book at the time they were originally published.

As always, my biggest debt is to my wife, Anya, who strongly believes in the subjects that I discuss here and in the importance of bringing them to a wider public, who provided such encouragement and help in my doing so, who has repeatedly discussed the ideas behind all of my books and has helped shape and reshape them.

Notes

1. Oxfam, "Working for the Few: Political Capture and Inequality," Briefing Paper 178, January 20, 2014.
2. Robert Lucas, "The Industrial Revolution: Past and Present," 2003 Annual Report Essay, Federal Reserve Bank of Minneapolis, May 1, 2014. He went on to say, "Of the vast increase in the well-being of hundreds of millions of people that has occurred in the 200-year course of the industrial revolution to date, virtually none of it can be attributed to the direct redistribution of resources from rich to poor. The potential for improving the lives of poor people by finding different ways of distributing current production is *nothing* compared to the apparently limitless potential of increasing production."
3. In a few cases, where inadvertently the headline writers choose leads that were too similar, I changed the title of the article. This decision also meant that there is inevitably some overlap in the themes discussed in the different essays. Some small edits have been made to avoid duplication.
4. I later co-authored a paper with Solow touching on some of the macroeconomic aspects of inequality and demand. See, R. M. Solow and J. E. Stiglitz, "Output, Employment, and Wages in the Short Run." *Quarterly Journal of Economics*, 82 (November 1968): 537–560.
5. In particular, the essay "The Book of Jobs," originally published in *Vanity Fair*, was based on research jointly done with Bruce Greenwald and other co-authors,

supported by INET. See, e.g., D. Delli Gatti, M. Gallegati, B. C. Greenwald, A. Russo, and J. E. Stiglitz, "Sectoral Imbalances and Long Run Crises," in F. Allen, M. Aoki, J.-P. Fitoussi, N. Kiyotaki, R. Gordon, and J. E. Stiglitz, eds., *The Global Macro Economy and Finance*, IEA Conference Volume No. 150-III (Houndmills, UK, and New York: Palgrave, 2012), pp. 61–97; and D. Delli Gatti, M. Gallegati, B. C. Greenwald, A. Russo, and J. E. Stiglitz, "Mobility Constraints, Productivity Trends, and Extended Crises," *Journal of Economic Behavior & Organization*, 83(3): 375–393.

6. The Commission included among its members Jose Antonio Ocampo, Rob Johnson, and Jean Paul Fitoussi. The report of the Commission is available as *The Stiglitz Report: Reforming the International Monetary and Financial Systems in the Wake of the Global Crisis* (New York: The New Press, 2010). I co-chaired with Jean Paul Fitoussi and Amartya Sen an International Commission on the Measurement of Economic Performance and Social Progress, emphasizing the many dimensions of well-being that are not well captured in GDP. Many of the ideas of the Commission are reflected in the essays contained in this book. The work of the Commission is now being carried on at the OECD. The report of the Commission is available as J. E. Stiglitz, J. Fitoussi, and A. Sen, *Mismeasuring Our Lives: Why GDP Doesn't Add Up* (New York: The New Press, 2010).

7. A fuller list of acknowledgments is contained in the paperback edition of *The Price of Inequality*.

8. "The Roaring Nineties," *Atlantic Monthly*, October 1992, gave rise to *The Roaring Nineties: A New History of the World's Most Prosperous Decade* (New York: W. W. Norton, 2003).

PRELUDE:

SHOWING CRACKS

THE BOOK BEGINS WITH THE ONSET OF THE GREAT Recession, several years before the start of the *Times's* Great Divide series. The first selection was published in *Vanity Fair* in December 2007, the very month the U.S. economy slipped into a downturn that would prove to be the worst since the Great Depression.

For the preceding three years, I, together with a small band of other economists, had been warning of the impending implosion. Warning signs were, in fact, there for anyone to see—but too many people were making too much money: it was more convenient to close their eyes. There was a party going on—only a few at the top were invited, but the rest of us would be asked to pay the bill. Unfortunately, however, those who were supposed to make sure that the economy was kept on an even keel were too closely connected to those who were throwing the party and who were having all the fun (and making all the money). And that's why these chapters are included here, as a prelude. The making of the Great Recession is intimately connected with the making of America's great divide.

First, let's set the scene: there was a major economic boom during the 90s, fueled by a tech bubble in which technology stocks soared in price, but after that bubble broke, the economy slid into recession in 2001. The George W. Bush administration's all-purpose remedy for any problem was a tax cut—and especially a tax cut aimed at the wealthy.

For those in the Clinton administration who had worked hard to reduce the fiscal deficit, this was troubling for many reasons. It brought back the deficits—undoing all the work that had been done over the preceding eight years. The Clinton administration had put off investments in infrastructure and education and programs to help the poor, all in the name of deficit reduction. I had not agreed with some of these actions—I thought borrowing to make invest-ments in the country's future made economic sense, and I was wor-ried that a later administration might squander these hard-fought gains for less noble purposes.

As the economy sank into the 2001 recession, there was con-sensus among policymakers that the economy needed a stimulus. A far better way of providing that stimulus than Bush's tax cuts for the rich would have involved making the investments we had postponed.[1] I was already concerned about the country's growing inequality, and these inequitable tax cuts only made matters worse. I began my *New York Review of Books* article, "Bush's Tax Plan— The Dangers" (March 13, 2003) as follows: "Seldom have so few gotten so much from so many."

Worse still, I thought the tax cuts would be *relatively* ineffective. And that proved correct. This is a theme I return to frequently in this book. *Inequality weakens aggregate demand and the economy.* America's growing inequality was moving money from the bottom of the pyramid to the top, and since those at the top spent less of their money than those at the bottom, this weakened overall demand. During the 90s we masked the deficiency by creating the tech bubble—a boom in investment. But with the breaking of the tech bubble, the economy fell into recession. Bush responded with a tax cut aimed at the rich. With consumers worried about their future, the hoped-for stimulus to the economy from Bush's tax cuts was weak. Piling on a further capital-gains tax cut—on top of one that had been given a few years before by President Clinton—only encouraged more speculation. Since its benefits went overwhelmingly to the very top, this tax cut was particularly ineffective and also strongly increased inequality.

The most effective tools for strengthening demand and improving equality are fiscal policies—tax and expenditure policies decided by Congress and the administration. Inadequate fiscal policies put an undue burden on monetary policies, which are the responsibility of the Federal Reserve. The Fed can (sometimes) stimulate the economy by lowering interest rates and making regulations more lax. But these monetary policies are dangerous. Their prescriptions should come with a big label: Use only with caution, and under the close supervision of adults who understand the full risks. Unfortunately, those in charge of monetary policy had not read any such label; and they were naïve market fundamentalists—believing that markets are always efficient and stable. While they underestimated the risks that their policies posed to the economy—and even to the government's budget—they didn't seem to care about the inequality that was growing day by day. The result is now well known: they unleashed a bubble, and their policies led to an unprecedented growth in inequality.

The Fed kept the economy churning with a policy of low interest rates and lax regulations. But it worked only by creating a housing bubble. It should have been apparent to all that the housing bubble and the consumption boom to which it led could only be a temporary palliative. Bubbles always break. Our consumption binge meant that the bottom 80 percent of Americans were *on average* spending 110 percent of their income. By 2005 as a country we were borrowing more than $2 billion a day from abroad. It was not sustainable, and, quoting one of my predecessors as chairman of the Council of Economic Advisers, in my speeches and writings I repeatedly warned that that which is not sustainable wouldn't be sustained.

When the Fed started to raise interest rates in 2004 and 2005, I anticipated that the housing bubble would break. It did not, in part because we were given a kind of reprieve: long-term interest rates failed to rise in tandem. By January 1, 2006, I predicted that this could not continue.[2] The bubble did break not long thereafter, but it would take a year and a half to two years for the full effects to be realized. As I wrote soon afterward, "Just as the collapse of the real estate bubble was predictable, so are its consequences . . . ."[3] With "by some reckonings, more than two-thirds of the increase in output and employment over the [preceding] six years . . . [being] real estate–related, reflecting both new housing and households borrowing against their homes to support a consumption binge," it should have been no surprise that the subsequent downturn would be deep and long.[4]

The articles included in this first section describe the policies that laid the groundwork for the Great Recession: What did we do wrong? Who is to blame? While those in the financial market, at the Fed, and at Treasury would like to pretend it was just something that happened—an unpreventable, once-in-a-hundred-years flood—I believed then, and believe even more strongly now, that the crisis was man-made. It was something that the 1 percent (indeed, a sliver of that 1 percent) did to the rest of us. The fact that it could happen was itself a manifestation of the great divide.

THE MAKING OF A CRISIS

That the Great Recession had created victims is clear. But who were the perpetrators of this "crime"? If we were to believe the Justice Department, which brought charges against none of the leaders of the big banks that played a central role in this drama, this was a crime without *any* perpetrator. I don't believe that, nor do most Americans. In three of the articles reprinted here, I attempt to find out who killed America's economy, to trace out the historical arc that led us to this juncture.[5] I wanted to dig deeper and go back further: there was more to the story than the stock response "The bankers lent too much and homeowners borrowed too much."

What, I asked, had brought us to this juncture? There was incompetence and bad judgment. The ill-conceived and poorly executed war in Iraq, whose eventual costs would amount to trillions,[6] was the most telling example. But the main blame I assign to a combination of ideology and special-interest pressure—the same combination that has led to the country's growing inequality. I point a finger particularly at the belief that unfettered markets are necessarily efficient and stable. We should know otherwise: major economic fluctuations have marked capitalism from the start. Some have suggested that *all* that needs to be done is for the government to ensure macrostability—as if market failures occur only in big macrodoses. I suggest otherwise: the macrocrises are only the tip of the iceberg; less noticeable are myriad inefficiencies. The crisis itself provides ample evidence: the market collapse was a result of a host of failures in the management of risk and the allocation of capital, mistakes made by mortgage originators, investment banks, credit-rating agencies—indeed by millions throughout the financial sector and elsewhere in the economy.[7]

But I suggest also that there was more than a small dose of hypocrisy on the part of those who advocated free markets, again evidenced in the Great Recession: the *seeming* advocates of free-market economics were more than willing to accept government assistance—including massive bailouts. Such policies distort the economy, of course, and lead to poorer economic performance; but reflecting the theme of this book, they also have distributive consequences—with more money going to those at the top, with everyone else picking up the tab.

As I thought about *who killed the economy*, No. 1 on the list of suspects was the president at the time. "The Economic Consequences of Mr. Bush" details *some* of the *economic* consequences of the president. Though conservatives rail against deficits, they seem to have a particular knack for creating them. Large deficits first began to characterize the American economy with President Reagan, and it was not until President Clinton that the deficits turned into surpluses. But in short order Bush reversed this—the largest turnaround (in the wrong direction) in the nation's history— partly as a result of paying for two wars on the credit card, partly as a result of tax cuts for the rich, partly as a result of his largesse to drug companies and the expansion of other forms of corporate welfare—the increased "dole-out" to the rich corporations across a wide range of sectors, some hidden in the tax system or through guarantees, some brazenly open. And all this even as we cut back on the safety net for the poor, on the grounds that we couldn't afford it.

As I have written repeatedly,[8] deficits are not necessarily a problem: not if the money is spent to make investments, and especially not if this spending occurs when the economy is weak. But the Bush deficits were especially problematic: they occurred during a time of seeming prosperity, even if that prosperity reached only a few. The money was spent not to strengthen the economy but to strengthen the coffers of a few corporations and the pocketbooks of the 1 percent. Most troublesome was that I saw storms ahead— Would we have the wherewithal to weather the storms? Would the conservatives at that point again demand fiscal prudence, imposing austerity at the moment the economy desperately needed the opposite medicine?

Most importantly for this book, the Bush years were marked by growing inequality, which he neither recognized nor did anything about—except to make it worse. This was a short article, and I could not provide a full litany of what had gone wrong. I didn't note that while inequality had mildly improved during the Clinton years, the income of a *typical* American (median income) adjusted for inflation actually fell under Bush—and this was true even before the recession made things so much worse. More Americans lacked health coverage. And they faced more insecurity—a greater risk of losing their jobs.[9]

But perhaps his most grievous failure was setting up the conditions for the Great Recession, topics that I delve into at greater length in the next two chapters. Bush's tax cuts for the rich, which

I discussed above, play prominent roles in the drama—while they did not provide much stimulus, they exacerbated the country's already large inequality. They illustrate a second theme to which I will return later in the book, and which has now been taken up by the International Monetary Fund (IMF), an organization not known for taking "radical" positions: inequality is associated with instability.[10] The making of the 2008 crisis exemplifies how this happens: central banks create bubbles in response to a weakened economy born of growing inequality. The bubble eventually breaks and wreaks havoc on the economy. (Of course, the Fed should have been aware of this risk. But its leadership evinced an almost blind faith in markets and, like Bush, who had reappointed the Fed chair Alan Greenspan and later appointed the Fed chair Ben Bernanke— he had been his chief economic adviser—the institution appeared to pay little attention to the inequality that was growing day by day in the country.)

At the same time, this illustrates a third theme: the role of politics. It is policies and politics that matter. The United States could have responded to the weakened economy by investing in America, or by undertaking policies that reduce inequality. Both of these would have led to a stronger economy and a fairer society. But economic inequality inevitably leads to political inequality. What happened in America is what one comes to expect of a polity with a divided society. Rather than more investment, we got tax cuts and corporate welfare for the rich. Rather than regulations that would stabilize the economy and protect ordinary citizens, we got deregulation that led to instability and left Americans prey to the bankers.

Deregulation

To understand the makings of the Great Recession, one has to go back in time, to the deregulatory movement that was given such a boost by President Reagan. In "Capitalist Fools" I identify five critical "mistakes," which both reflected broader trends in our society and reinforced each other—culminating in the worst economic downturn in three-quarters of a century. Several of them illustrate the new power of finance—the appointment of Greenspan because he supported deregulation, the deregulation itself, begun under Reagan, but continuing under Clinton, including the destruction of regulatory walls between investment and commercial banks.[11]

The regulators didn't do what they should have done, but the crimes themselves were committed by the financial sector. At the time I wrote these articles, we had only a partial glimpse of how bad things had become. We knew that the banks had mismanaged risk and misallocated capital—all the time offering huge bonuses to their leaders for the wonderful job that they were doing. We knew that the bonus system itself had created incentives for excessive risk-taking and shortsighted behavior. We knew that the credit-rating agencies had failed miserably in their job of assessing risk. We knew that securitization, long vaunted for its ability to manage risk, had provided incentives for mortgage originators to weaken standards (what was called the moral hazard problem). We knew that the banks had engaged in predatory lending.

But we didn't know the full extent of the moral depravity of the banks, of their willingness to engage in exploitive practices, or their recklessness. We didn't know, for instance, just how widely they engaged in discriminatory lending. We didn't know of their manipulation of the foreign exchange and other markets. We didn't know of the sloppiness in their record keeping, in their race to write an ever larger number of bad mortgages. And we didn't know the full extent of fraudulent behavior, on the part not just of the banks but of the credit-rating agencies and other market participants. Competition among rating agencies to provide a high rating (they were paid only if the investment banks "used" their ratings, and they used only the ratings that were most favorable) had led them to deliberately ignore relevant information that might have yielded a less favorable rating.

The chapters published here do provide, however, a good description of where the financial sector went wrong.

Financial Markets and the Growth
of Inequality

In these articles and elsewhere in this volume, I dwell extensively on the financial sector, and for good reason. As Jamie Galbraith of the University of Texas has so persuasively shown,[12] there is a clear link between the increasing financialization of the world's economies and the growth of inequality. The financial sector is emblematic of what has gone wrong in our economy—a major contributor to the growth of inequality, the major source of instability in our economy, and an important cause of the economy's poor performance over the last three decades.

This isn't, of course, the way it was supposed to be. Liberalization of financial markets ("deregulation") was *supposed* to allow financial experts to allocate scarce capital and manage risk better; the result was *supposed* to be faster and more stable growth. The proponents of a strong financial sector were right about one thing: it is hard to have a well-performing economy without a well-performing financial sector. But, as we have seen repeatedly, the financial sector doesn't perform well on its own; it requires strong regulations, effectively enforced, both to prevent it from imposing harm on the rest of the society and to make sure that it actually performs the functions it is *supposed* to perform. Sadly, recent discussions on financial sector reform have focused only on the first half of this task—how to prevent the banks and other financial institutions from *harming* the rest of society, by exposing it to excessive risk-taking or some other form of exploitation—and given little attention to the second.

The crisis confronting the United States and the world in 2008 was, as noted earlier, a man-made disaster. I had seen this movie before: how a combination of powerful (if wrong) ideas and powerful interests can combine to produce calamitous results. As chief economist of the World Bank, I had observed how, after the end of colonialism, the West managed to push ideas of free-market fundamentalism—many of which reflected the perspectives and interests of Wall Street—on developing countries. Of course, the developing countries didn't have much choice: colonial powers had ravaged these countries, exploiting them ruthlessly, extracting their resources, but doing little to develop their economies. They needed assistance from the advanced countries, and as a condition of that assistance, officials at the IMF and elsewhere imposed conditions— that the developing countries liberalize their financial markets and open up their domestic markets to a flood of goods from the advanced countries, even as the advanced countries refused to open their markets to the agricultural goods of the South.

The policies failed: Africa saw its per capita income fall; Latin America saw stagnation, with the benefits of the limited growth going to a small sliver at the top. Meanwhile, East Asia took a different course; with governments leading the development effort ("the developmental state," as it was called), incomes per capita rapidly doubled, tripled—eventually increasing eightfold. In the third of a century that Americans saw their incomes stagnate, China went from being an impoverished country, with a per capita income less than 1 percent that of the United States and a GDP that was less than 5 percent that of the United States, to being the largest economy in the world (measured in what economists called purchasing power parities). By the end of the next quarter-century, it was slated to be twice the size of the U.S. economy.

But ideologies are often more influential than evidence. Free-market economists seldom looked at the success of the managed-market economies of East Asia. They preferred to talk about the failures of the Soviet Union, which eschewed the use of the market altogether. With the fall of the Berlin Wall and the collapse of Communism, it *seemed* that free markets had triumphed. Though this was the wrong lesson to be drawn, the United States used its sway as the sole remaining superpower to advance its economic interests—or, more accurately, to advance the interests of its large and powerful corporations. And among these, perhaps the most influential was the financial sector. The United States pushed countries to liberalize their financial markets. The result: country after country faced crises—including some of the very countries that had been doing so well *before* they liberalized their markets.

In a sense, though, we were no worse to these other countries than we were to ourselves. Under both Clinton and Bush we pursued policies at home and abroad that were demanded by the financial sector. In "The Anatomy of a Murder" I touch on how these policies led to a crisis. (In my book *Freefall* I discuss these issues more extensively.)

Here my concern is how the financial sector contributes to growing inequality. There are several channels by which financialization has had these effects. The financial sector excels in rent seeking, in wealth appropriation. There are two ways of getting wealthy: increasing the size of the national pie, and attempting to get a larger size of a preexisting pie—and in the process, the size of the pie may actually be diminished. Incomes at the top of the financial sector are more related to the latter than to the former. While some of the wealth of those in the financial sector comes at the expense of other wealthy people, including much of what they acquire through market manipulation, much of it comes from siphoning money from the bottom of the economic pyramid. This is true of the billions generated through abusive credit card practices and predatory and discriminatory lending. But it is even true of their abuses of monopoly power in credit and debit cards: the excessive charges they impose on merchants act like a tax on every transaction—a tax that enriches the coffers of the bankers rather than the well-being of society; in competitive markets, the charges inevitably get passed on in the form of higher prices paid by ordinary citizens.

At least before the crisis, those in the financial sector boasted that they were the engine of economic growth, that their "innovativeness" had led to the country's outstanding economic performance.

The real measure of the performance of an economy is how well the typical family does, and in those terms there has been zero growth over the past quarter-century. But even if one uses GDP as the yardstick, performance has been anemic—far worse than in the decades before financial liberalization and the financialization of the economy—and it's hard to attribute what growth there has been to the financial sector. But though it's hard to show any positive effect on growth, it's easy to establish the connection between the financial sector's shenanigans and the economy's instability, evidenced most strongly by the 2008 crisis.

Data on GDP and profits tell us a great deal about how the financial sector helped lead the economy astray. In the years before the crisis, the financial sector absorbed an increasing share of the economy—8 percent of GDP, 40 percent of all corporate profits—with little to show for it. There was, of course, a credit bubble, but rather than leading to higher levels of *real* investment, which would have led to higher wages and sustained growth, it went toward speculation and to higher real estate prices. A higher price for real estate on the French Riviera, or for Manhattan apartments for billionaires, doesn't translate into a more productive economy. And that helps explain why, in spite of the enormous increase in the wealth-to-income ratio, average wages stagnated and real returns on capital did not decline. (The standard law of economics—the law of diminishing returns—should have meant that the return to capital should have fallen, and wages should have risen. Improvements in technology would have reinforced the conclusion that *average* wages should have increased, even if wages for some types of labor would have decreased.)

The excessive risk-taking in the financial sector, combined with its success in curbing regulation, led, in a way that was predictable and predicted, to the most severe crisis in three-quarters of a century. As always, it is the poor who suffer the most from such crises, as they lose their jobs and face protracted unemployment. In this case, the effects on ordinary Americans were particularly grave, given that more than 14 million homes were foreclosed from 2007 to 2013, and given the magnitude of the cutbacks in government spending, including for education. Aggressive monetary policy (so-called quantitative easing) focused more on restoring prices in the stock market than on restoring lending to small and medium-size enterprises, and as a result was much more effective in restoring wealth to the rich than in benefiting average Americans or in creating jobs for them. That's why in the first three years of the so-called recovery, some 95 percent of the increases in income went to the top 1 percent, and why six years after the start of the crisis, median wealth was down 40 percent relative to precrisis levels.

There is a final role that the financial sector has played in the creation of America's, and the world's, growing inequality (and poor economic performance): I noted earlier that the country's outsize inequality is a result of the policies it has pursued. The financial sector pushed inequality-increasing policies and developed an ideology to support them. Of course, some participants in financial markets have been important voices of opposition; there are many who embrace "enlightened self-interest." But, by and large, the financial sector has pushed the idea that markets on their own lead to efficient and stable outcomes, and on that assumption governments should liberalize and privatize; it has argued that progressive taxation should be limited because of its adverse effects on incentives; it has contended that monetary policy should focus on inflation and not job creation. And after these policies brought about the Great Recession, a single-minded focus on fiscal deficits led to cutbacks in government spending that hurt ordinary citizens. These policies in turn prolonged the economic downturn.

Transparency

There is a broad understanding that market economies work best with transparency—it is only with good information that resources can be well allocated. But while markets—especially financial markets—may preach transparency *for others*, they do what they can to limit it for themselves; after all, with transparent and competitive markets, profits are driven to zero. Ask any businessperson: it's no fun to be in such markets. One has to struggle to survive. There's little upside potential. That's why they make such a big deal over business secrets and confidentiality. All of this is natural and well understood. But government is supposed to weigh in on the other side, to countervail these tendencies, to make markets more competitive and transparent. But this won't happen if government is captured by businesses, and especially by financial markets. And that's where I felt special disappointment with what happened in the Clinton administration. One somehow expects this of administrations on the right, but not of one that claimed to be "putting people first." In "Capitalist Fools" I explain how the Clinton and Bush administrations had put in place incentives to "fake the numbers." Unfortunately, the Obama administration failed to use the 2008 crisis to force more transparency—allowing trade in nontransparent over-the-counter derivatives, the source of so much havoc in the crisis—to go on, though with some restrictions.

The Role of the Economist

In its list of who is to be blamed, the chapter on the anatomy of a murder adds one more category: economists—the many economists who claimed that markets were self-regulating, who provided the so-called intellectual underpinnings to the deregulatory movement, in spite of the long history of the failure of unregulated and under-regulated financial markets, and in spite of important advances in economic theory, which had explained why financial markets *need to be* and *should be* regulated. These advances focused on the importance of information imperfections and imperfections of competition, important in all sectors of the economy, but especially in the financial system. Moreover, when an ordinary business fails, there are consequences for its owners and their families, but typically not for the entire economy. As our political leaders and the banks themselves said, we cannot allow any of the big banks to fail.

But if that is the case, then they *must* be regulated. For if they are too big to fail, and they know it, excessive risk-taking is a one-sided bet: if they win, they keep the profits; if they lose, taxpayers pick up the tab.

Dodd-Frank, the financial sector reform bill, did nothing to address the too-big-to-fail problem. Indeed, the way we addressed the crisis made it worse: we encouraged, in some cases forced, banks to merge, so that today concentration of market power is even greater than it was before the crisis. This concentration has one further consequence: it leads to a concentration of political power, so evident in the ongoing struggle to pass effective bank regulation. One area where progress was made in Dodd-Frank was to circumscribe the ability of federally insured financial institutions from writing derivatives—those risky products that had led to the collapse of AIG and the largest bailout in the history of the planet. While there is disagreement about whether these financial products are gambling instruments or insurance, there is no justifiable reason that they should be provided by *lending* institutions, and especially those insured by the government. But Congress, with language written by Citibank itself, repealed even this provision in 2014, without even any hearings!

The influential documentary *Inside Job* threw light on what may have been going on within the economics profession. Economists are wont to say that incentives matter: indeed, that is the one thing that economists seemingly agree on. The financial sector provides ample rewards for those who agree with them: lucrative consultancies, research grants, and the like. The documentary raises a question: Could this have influenced some economists' judgments?

RESPONSES TO THE CRISIS

Just as the "making of the crisis" illustrates several of the themes of this book, so do the articles I wrote in 2008 and 2009 on the responses, of which one, "How to Get Out of the Financial Crisis," published in *Time* magazine a month after the collapse of Lehman Brothers, is included here. The disparity between what was needed and what was done illustrates the great divide.

Even though the crisis had long been in the making, and even though there had been ample warnings, those in charge, both at the Fed and in the administration, *seemed* surprised, and I believe genuinely were—a remarkable testament to the ability to close one's senses to information that one finds unpleasant and contradicts one's preconceptions. After all, the housing bubble had broken in 2006, the economy had plunged into recession in 2007, the Fed had been supplying unprecedented funds to banks in 2007 and 2008, and there had been a very expensive rescue of Bear Stearns in March 2008. Virtually any economist who did not blindly believe in the virtues of the free and unregulated markets, their efficiency and stability, saw the writing on the wall. Yet the Fed chair Ben Bernanke would blithely claim that the risks were "contained."[13]

The precipitating event that plunged the country from the recession that began in December 2007 (which Bush's policies—another tax cut for the rich in February 2008—had done little to end) into a *deep* recession, the worst since the Great Depression, was the collapse of Lehman Brothers on September 15, 2008. After confidently asserting that letting it collapse would have only a limited effect on the economy—and would teach banks an important lesson—the Fed and Treasury took a 180-degree turn and bailed out AIG, the most expensive bailout in human history, an amount of corporate welfare to one firm that exceeded that given to the millions of poor Americans over years and years. Later we were to learn why—and why they did everything they could to hide what they were doing from the American people: the money passed quickly from AIG to Goldman Sachs and other banks. It was when these banks were in jeopardy that the Fed and Treasury came to the rescue.

In my *Time* article, I put forward a simple agenda. Regrettably, what was done reflected more the interests and perspectives of the banks and the 1 percent than it did the agenda I laid forth, as I feared at the time. And so too, the recovery has been anemic. The Obama administration may claim that it stopped the economy from falling into another Great Depression. Whether or not that is true, it is clear that it didn't engineer a robust recovery. As this book goes to press, seven years later, most Americans' incomes are still below what they were before the crisis. Wealth in the middle is almost back to the level of 1992, some two decades ago.[14] The recovery was designed by the 1 percent, for the 1 percent. President Obama may have claimed in his State of the Union address on January 20, 2015, that the crisis is over. But not even he would suggest that all is well. GDP is some 15 percent below what it would have been had there not been the crisis, and the gap between where we are and where we would have been is barely closing. Trillions have been unnecessarily lost by following the 1 percent's agenda.

There were five items on my agenda. The first was a recapitalization of the banks—in a way that ensured that they return to lending and that gave American taxpayers a fair deal for bearing the risks that they bore. We did recapitalize the banks. Bailing out the banks, however, didn't mean bailing out the shareholders, the bondholders, and the bankers. But that's what we did.

When the IMF, the World Bank, or the U.S. government lends money to other countries, we impose conditions—we want to make sure that the money is spent in the way intended. The irony is that the U.S. Treasury is among those most insistent on such conditionality. But when it came to imposing conditions on U.S. banks, Treasury demurred.

Here the intent was clear: to save the banks so that they could continue to provide funds to make our economy function. But because we imposed no conditions, the money went instead to pay mega-bonuses—clearly undeserved—to the bankers. Years after the crisis, lending to small and medium-size businesses was still far below what it had been before the crisis.

The administration claims that the government was repaid, but it was largely a shell game, repaid from one pocket with money the government put into another. The Fed lent money to the banks at a zero interest rate, which they then lent out to the government and big businesses at far higher interest rates. (Even a 12-year-old could make money this way; one didn't need to be a financial wizard—though the bankers received bonuses as if they were.) The government stealthily arranged for the bad mortgages to move off the banks' books and onto the government balance sheet. Even then, what the government got was but a fraction of that received by private investors, like Warren Buffett, who had put money into the banks at the time of the crisis.

Put baldly, ordinary Americans were cheated. A huge gift was given to the banks by providing them money at much more favorable terms than those given to others—and at rates much lower than others were willing to extend to the banks. Doing so redistributed money from ordinary citizens to the wealthy bankers. Had the banks been charged what they should have been, our national debt would be lower and we would have more money to invest in education, technology, infrastructure—investments that would have led to a stronger economy with more shared prosperity.

Like so many of the economic policies designed by the 1 percent and for the 1 percent, it relied on trickle-down economics: throw enough money at the banks, and everyone will benefit. It didn't work out that way, and predictably so.[15] I had argued, by contrast, that we should have tried a bit of trickle-up economics—help those in the middle and the bottom, and the entire economy will benefit.

The crisis had begun in housing, and so it was natural to suggest that a robust recovery would require stemming the tide of foreclosures. Even before he became president, I warned Obama that bailing out the banks would not be enough. He had to help America's homeowners. But his secretary of treasury Tim Geithner, who had been the head of the New York Fed as the banks engaged in their reckless behavior, thought mostly about the banks. The result was that literally millions and millions of Americans lost their homes.

While hundreds of billions went to the banks, a fraction of this was allocated to help homeowners, and even then only something like $10 billion was actually spent—Treasury's report to Congress didn't bother to give the amount of support provided—as the administration struggled with one poorly designed program after another. Wasting money on banks might be necessary to save the economy, and any fine-tuning of the bank rescue programs apparently was viewed as a luxury we could not afford. But exactly the opposite attitude was taken in regard to homeowners and ordinary citizens: we had to proceed carefully, so as not to make any mistakes. Terms like "moral hazard" were thrown around glibly—the risk that a bailout to homeowners would encourage reckless borrowing—even though the real moral hazard issue was that of the banks, which had been rescued time after time.

Standard economics—taught in virtually every textbook—calls for a fiscal stimulus when the economy is weak. But we had learned from the Bush 2008 tax cut for the rich that a poorly designed stimulus would be relatively ineffective. Those in the Obama administration, however, including several who bore considerable responsibility for the creation of the crisis, both in their active support of deregulation and in their failure to engage in responsible supervision of the banks, believed that essentially all that was needed was a modest measure: the banks were sick, they required an admittedly massive (money) transfusion, but after a short period in the infirmary, they and the economy would recover. What was needed was a temporary stimulus, while the banks were still sick; and because the recovery was anticipated to be quick, the size, design, and duration of the plan didn't matter much.

I argued, to the contrary, that the economy had been sick before the crisis—sustained only by an artificial bubble; that the crisis was likely to be long and deep, especially if the right policies weren't followed (which they weren't). Moreover, the politics was ugly: one had but a single bite of the apple. If the economy didn't recover, conservatives would claim that the stimulus didn't work, and it would be hard to get a second stimulus package. So I argued we needed a large stimulus[16]—far larger than that asked for by the administration and passed by Congress; it needed to be well designed—not the kind of tax cuts for the rich that marked Bush's so-called stimulus. As it was, about a third of the stimulus consisted of tax cuts. To make matters worse, the administration, not understanding the depth of the downturn, forecast that with the stimulus unemployment would peak at 7 to 8 percent; when it peaked at 10 percent, this claim provided easy fodder for critics. What they should have said was that the stimulus would reduce unemployment by some 2 to 3 percent from what it otherwise would have been—and that, the stimulus succeeded in doing.

The last items on the *Time* agenda were domestic regulatory reform and the creation of a multilateral agency to coordinate regulation across national jurisdictions. By the time I wrote the article, it was already clear that this was going to be a global crisis, and that bad banking practices (not just in the United States, but in several countries in Europe as well) had large repercussions elsewhere. Our own toxic mortgages (those mortgages that eventually exploded, bringing on the global crisis) had polluted international financial markets.

These last two items have occasioned the greatest disappointment. Even when it passed in 2010, two years after the crisis, the regulatory reform bill (Dodd-Frank) was recognized to be at most a cup half full. But no sooner was it passed than the banks began efforts to water it down. They resisted attempts to implement regulations. They initiated efforts in Congress to repeal key provisions—and finally, in December 2014, they were successful in rolling back a key provision regulating derivatives, restricting government-insured banks from creating these risky financial products.

Globally, no international agency has been created. An international Financial Stability Board was established (replacing the Financial Stability Forum, which had been established in the aftermath of the East Asian crisis at the end of the 1990s and proven itself ineffective). As with Dodd-Frank, what has emerged is a halfway house: things are, in some ways, better than they were before the crisis, but few outside the financial sector believe that we have really eliminated a significant risk of another meltdown.

What is so striking, though. is that all of the discussions have centered on how to prevent the banks from doing harm to the rest of society; almost no attention has focused on how to make banks actually perform the critical functions that they need to perform if our economy is to function well. For purposes of this book, that is important for at least two reasons. When there is a crisis, it is always ordinary citizens who bear the brunt—workers who lose their jobs, homeowners who lose their homes, ordinary citizens who see their retirement accounts vanish, who are unable to send their children to college, and who cannot live out their dreams. Small businesses go into bankruptcy in droves.

By contrast, big businesses not only survive; some even prosper as wages are forced down and they maintain sales abroad. The bankers who caused the crisis also manage to do quite well, thank you. They might not be quite as well off as they would have been if the unsustainable bubbles that they helped create had been sustained. They might have to scale down from a ski chalet in the Swiss Alps to one in Colorado, from a home on the Riviera to one in the Hamptons.[17]

The need for regulation should have been particularly clear because the banks and others in the financial sector have a long-established proclivity for exploitation—for taking advantage of others, whether it's in the form of market manipulation, insider trading, abusive credit card practices, monopolistic anticompetitive practices, discriminatory and predatory lending, . . . the list is endless. It seems easier to make money in these ways than by more honest activity, say, by lending to small businesses, which would create new jobs. When banks focus on exploitation, they increase inequality; when they focus on job creation, they promote equality, both by reducing unemployment and by leading to higher wages, which naturally follow from lowered unemployment.

Thus, bank regulations that restrict their bad behavior can help doubly: they inhibit their ability to exploit, and encourage them to do what they should be doing—simply by reducing the profits to be made in alternative ways.

The Failures of the Obama and Bush Responses

In short, just as the crisis itself was the predictable and predicted consequence of our economic policies in the preceding decades, what happened in the years after the crisis was the predictable and predicted consequence of the policies taken in response.

What can we say almost eight years after the beginning of the recession, nine years after the breaking of the bubble? Who has been proven right? The administration and the Fed like to claim that they saved us from another Great Depression. That may be the case, but they failed utterly in restoring the economy to prosperity.

The banking system has largely healed. The recession officially ended, and fairly quickly. But the economy has clearly not been restored to health. Even as growth is restored, it will be years and years, if ever, before the damage of the Great Recession is repaired, years and years, if ever, before the incomes of most Americans are back to where they would have been without the crisis. Indeed, the damage appears to be long-lasting.

Notes

1. President Bush enacted two sets of tax cuts for the rich—the first, in 2001, as the economy slipped into recession. When that didn't do the trick, he decided to double down and offer even more tax cuts for the rich, in 2003.
2. In "Global Malaise in 2006," *Project Syndicate*, January 1, 2006.
3. In "America's Day of Reckoning," *Project Syndicate*, August 6, 2007.
4. I elaborated on this theme in "America's Houses of Cards," *Project Syndicate*, October 9, 2007.
5. The article "The Anatomy of a Murder: Who Killed America's Economy?" was reprinted in *Best American Political Writing, 2009*, ed. Royce Flippin (New York: PublicAffairs, 2009).

6. See Joseph E. Stiglitz and Linda J. Bilmes, *The Three Trillion Dollar War: The True Cost of the Iraq Conflict* (New York: W. W. Norton, 2008). Though some challenged our numbers at the time, we were deliberately conservative in our estimates, and history has proved us right. The numbers have turned out worse. Indeed, the cost of disability payments and health care through the middle of the century is now estimated by itself to be as much as a trillion dollars, in part because almost 50 percent of troops returning file disability claims, often with multiple disabilities. (See the Web site of Costs of War at http://www.costsofwar.org/article/caring-us-veterans.)

7. I had developed this perspective with my co-author Bruce Greenwald almost three decades earlier, in "Keynesian, New Keynesian and New Classical Economics," *Oxford Economic Papers* 39 (March 1987): 119–33.

8. See, for example, my articles "Why I Didn't Sign Deficit Letter," *Politico*, March 28, 2011; "The Dangers of Deficit Reduction," *Project Syndicate*, March 5, 2010; and "Obama Must Resist 'Deficit Fetish,'" *Politico*, February 10, 2010.

9. These failings, clear already at the end of his first term, had become even clearer by the end of the second. I noted, for instance, in "Bush's Four Years of Failure," *Project Syndicate*, October 4, 2004, "Median real income has fallen by over $1,500 in real terms." The growth that occurred "benefited only those at the top of the income distribution. the same group that had done so well over the previous thirty years and that benefited most from Bush's tax cut."

10. Andrew G. Berg and Jonathan D. Ostry, "Inequality and Unsustainable Growth: Two Sides of the Same Coin?," IMF Staff Discussion Note 11/08, April 8, 2011.

11. For a discussion of the role of the Clinton administration and how what was done then helped "seed" the problems that were to emerge, see Joseph E. Stiglitz, *The Roaring Nineties: A New History of the World's Most Prosperous Decade* (New York: W. W. Norton, 2003).

12. James Galbraith, *Inequality and Instability: A Study of the World Economy Just before the Great Crisis* (New York: Oxford University Press, 2012).

13. In March 2007 Bernanke claimed that "the impact on the broader economy and financial markets of the problems in the subprime market seems likely to be contained." Statement of Ben S. Bernanke, Chairman, Board of Governors of the Federal Reserve System, before the Joint Economic Committee, U.S. Congress, Washington, DC, March 28, 2007.

14. Median household wealth was $81,400 in 2013, almost back to the $80,800 figure of 1992. Poor Americans—defined as those with a size-adjusted household income less than 67% of the median—have fared much worse: their median wealth declined from $11,400 in 1983 to $9,300 in 2013. See "America's Wealth Gap between Middle-Income and Upper-Income Families Is Widest on Record," Pew Research Center, available at http://www.pewresearch.org/fact-tank/2014/12/17/wealth-gap-upper-middle-income/.

15. I elaborated on this in a brief article, "Bail-out Blues," *Guardian*, September 30, 2008.

16. A little after my *Time* article, I expanded on the need for a large and well-designed stimulus in an op-ed, "A Trillion Dollar Answer," *New York Times*, November 30, 2008. I reflected on the inadequacy of the Obama stimulus further in another op-ed, "Stimulate or Die," *Project Syndicate*, August 6, 2009.

17. I wrote about this in the context of the East Asian crisis in my *Globalization and Its Discontents* (New York: W. W. Norton, 2002); Jason Furman (later one of my successors as chairman of the Council of Economic Advisers) and I showed that there was a regular pattern to this, in our 1998 paper "Economic Consequences of Income Inequality," in *Income Inequality: Issues and Policy Options* (Proceedings of a Symposium at Jackson Hole, Wyoming) (Kansas City, MO: Federal Reserve Bank of Kansas City, 1998), pp. 221–63.

THE ECONOMIC
CONSEQUENCES OF
MR. BUSH[*]

W HEN WE LOOK BACK SOMEDAY AT THE CATASTROPHE
that was the Bush administration, we will think of many
things: the tragedy of the Iraq war, the shame of Guantánamo and
Abu Ghraib, the erosion of civil liberties. The damage done to the
American economy does not make front-page headlines every day,
but the repercussions will be felt beyond the lifetime of anyone
reading this page.

I can hear an irritated counterthrust already. The president has
not driven the United States into a recession during his almost
seven years in office. Unemployment stands at a respectable 4.6
percent. Well, fine. But the other side of the ledger groans with
distress: a tax code that has become hideously biased in favor of
the rich; a national debt that will probably have grown 70 percent
by the time this president leaves Washington; a swelling cascade of
mortgage defaults; a record near-$850 billion trade deficit; oil prices
that are higher than they have ever been; and a dollar so weak that
for an American to buy a cup of coffee in London or Paris—or even
the Yukon—becomes a venture in high finance.

---

[*] *Vanity Fair*, December 2007. Anya Schiffrin and Izzet Yildiz assisted with research
for this article.

And it gets worse. After almost seven years of this president, the United States is less prepared than ever to face the future. We have not been educating enough engineers and scientists, people with the skills we will need to compete with China and India. We have not been investing in the kinds of basic research that made us the technological powerhouse of the late 20th century. And although the president now understands—or so he says—that we must begin to wean ourselves from oil and coal, we have on his watch become more deeply dependent on both.

Up to now, the conventional wisdom has been that Herbert Hoover, whose policies aggravated the Great Depression, is the odds-on claimant for the mantle "worst president" when it comes to stewardship of the American economy. Once Franklin Roosevelt assumed office and reversed Hoover's policies, the country began to recover. The economic effects of Bush's presidency are more insidious than those of Hoover, harder to reverse, and likely to be longer-lasting. There is no threat of America's being displaced from its position as the world's richest economy. But our grandchildren will still be living with, and struggling with, the economic consequences of Mr. Bush.

REMEMBER THE SURPLUS?

The world was a very different place, economically speaking, when George W. Bush took office, in January 2001. During the Roaring 90s, many had believed that the Internet would transform everything. Productivity gains, which had averaged about 1.5 percent a year from the early 1970s through the early 90s, now approached 3 percent. During Bill Clinton's second term, gains in manufacturing productivity sometimes even surpassed 6 percent. The Federal Reserve chairman, Alan Greenspan, spoke of a New Economy marked by continued productivity gains as the Internet buried the old ways of doing business. Others went so far as to predict an end to the business cycle. Greenspan worried aloud about how he'd ever be able to manage monetary policy once the nation's debt was fully paid off.

This tremendous confidence took the Dow Jones index higher and higher. The rich did well, but so did the not-so-rich and even the downright poor. The Clinton years were not an economic Nirvana; as chairman of the president's Council of Economic Advisers during part of this time, I'm all too aware of mistakes and lost opportunities. The global-trade agreements we pushed through were often unfair to developing countries. We should have invested more in infrastructure, tightened regulation of the securities markets, and taken additional steps to promote energy conservation. We fell short because of politics and lack of money—and also, frankly, because special interests sometimes shaped the agenda more than they should have. But these boom years were the first time since Jimmy Carter that the deficit was under control. And they were the first time since the 1970s that incomes at the bottom grew faster than those at the top—a benchmark worth celebrating.

By the time George W. Bush was sworn in, parts of this bright picture had begun to dim. The tech boom was over. The NASDAQ fell 15 percent in the single month of April 2000, and no one knew for sure what effect the collapse of the Internet bubble would have on the real economy. It was a moment ripe for Keynesian economics, a time to prime the pump by spending more money on education, technology, and infrastructure—all of which America desperately needed, and still does, but which the Clinton administration had postponed in its relentless drive to eliminate the deficit. Bill Clinton had left President Bush in an ideal position to pursue such policies. Remember the presidential debates in 2000 between Al Gore and George Bush, and how the two men argued over how to spend America's anticipated $2.2 trillion budget surplus? The country could well have afforded to ramp up domestic investment in key areas. In fact, doing so would have staved off recession in the short run while spurring growth in the long run.

But the Bush administration had its own ideas. The first major economic initiative pursued by the president was a massive tax cut for the rich, enacted in June of 2001. Those with incomes over a million got a tax cut of $18,000—more than 30 times larger than the cut received by the average American. The inequities were compounded by a second tax cut, in 2003, this one skewed even more heavily toward the rich. Together these tax cuts, when fully implemented and if made permanent, mean that in 2012 the average reduction for an American in the bottom 20 percent will be a scant $45, while those with incomes of more than $1 million will see their tax bills reduced by an average of $162,000.

The administration crows that the economy grew—by some 16 percent—during its first six years, but the growth helped mainly people who had no need of any help, and failed to help those who need plenty. A rising tide lifted all yachts. Inequality is now widening in America, and at a rate not seen in three-quarters of a century. A young male in his 30s today has an income, adjusted for inflation, that is 12 percent less than what his father was making 30 years ago. Some 5.3 million more Americans are living in poverty now than were living in poverty when Bush became president. America's class structure may not have arrived there yet, but it's heading in the direction of Brazil's and Mexico's.

THE BANKRUPTCY BOOM

In breathtaking disregard for the most basic rules of fiscal propriety, the administration continued to cut taxes even as it undertook expensive new spending programs and embarked on a financially ruinous "war of choice" in Iraq. A budget surplus of 2.4 percent of gross domestic product (GDP), which greeted Bush as he took office, turned into a deficit of 3.6 percent in the space of four years. The United States had not experienced a turnaround of this magnitude since the global crisis of World War II.

Agricultural subsidies were doubled between 2002 and 2005. Tax expenditures—the vast system of subsidies and preferences hidden in the tax code—increased more than a quarter. Tax breaks for the president's friends in the oil-and-gas industry increased by billions and billions of dollars. Yes, in the five years after 9/11, defense expenditures did increase (by some 70 percent), though much of the growth wasn't helping to fight the War on Terror at all, but was being lost or outsourced in failed missions in Iraq. Meanwhile, other funds continued to be spent on the usual high-tech gimcrackery—weapons that don't work, for enemies we don't have. In a nutshell, money was being spent everyplace except where it was needed. During these past seven years the percentage of GDP spent on research and development outside defense and health has fallen. Little has been done about our decaying infrastructure—be it levees in New Orleans or bridges in Minneapolis. Coping with most of the damage will fall to the next occupant of the White House.

Although it railed against entitlement programs for the needy, the administration enacted the largest increase in entitlements in four decades—the poorly designed Medicare prescription-drug benefit, intended as both an election-season bribe and a sop to the pharmaceutical industry. As internal documents later revealed, the true cost of the measure was hidden from Congress. Meanwhile, the pharmaceutical companies received special favors. To access the new benefits, elderly patients couldn't opt to buy cheaper medications from Canada or other countries. The law also prohibited the U.S. government, the largest single buyer of prescription drugs, from negotiating with drug manufacturers to keep costs down. As a result, American consumers pay far more for medications than people elsewhere in the developed world.

You'll still hear some—and, loudly, the president himself—argue that the administration's tax cuts were meant to stimulate the economy, but this was never true. The bang for the buck—the amount of stimulus per dollar of deficit—was astonishingly low. Therefore, the job of economic stimulation fell to the Federal Reserve Board, which stepped on the accelerator in a historically unprecedented way, driving interest rates down to 1 percent. In real terms, taking inflation into account, interest rates actually dropped to negative 2 percent. The predictable result was a consumer spending spree. Looked at another way, Bush's own fiscal irresponsibility fostered irresponsibility in everyone else. Credit was shoveled out the door, and subprime mortgages were made available to anyone this side of life support. Credit card debt mounted to a whopping $900 billion by the summer of 2007. "Qualified at birth" became the drunken slogan of the Bush era. American households took advantage of the low interest rates, signed up for new mortgages with "teaser" initial rates, and went to town on the proceeds.

All of this spending made the economy look better for a while; the president could (and did) boast about the economic statistics. But the consequences for many families would become apparent within a few years, when interest rates rose and mortgages proved impossible to repay. The president undoubtedly hoped the reckoning would come sometime after 2008. It arrived 18 months early. As many as 1.7 million Americans are expected to lose their homes in the months ahead. For many, this will mean the beginning of a downward spiral into poverty.

Between March 2006 and March 2007 personal-bankruptcy rates soared more than 60 percent. As families went into bankruptcy, more and more of them came to understand who had won and who had lost as a result of the president's 2005 bankruptcy bill, which made it harder for individuals to discharge their debts in a reasonable way. The lenders that had pressed for "reform" had been the clear winners, gaining added leverage and protections for themselves; people facing financial distress got the shaft.

AND THEN THERE'S IRAQ

The war in Iraq (along with, to a lesser extent, the war in Afghanistan) has cost the country dearly in blood and treasure. The loss in lives can never be quantified. As for the treasure, it's worth calling to mind that the administration, in the run-up to the invasion of Iraq, was reluctant to venture an estimate of what the war would cost (and publicly humiliated a White House aide who suggested that it might run as much as $200 billion). When pressed to give a number, the administration suggested $50 billion—what the United States is actually spending every few months. Today, government figures officially acknowledge that more than half a trillion dollars total has been spent by the U.S. "in theater." But in fact the overall cost of the conflict could be quadruple that amount—as a study I did with Linda Bilmes of Harvard has pointed out—even as the Congressional Budget Office now concedes that total expenditures are likely to be more than double the spending on operations. The official numbers do not include, for instance, other relevant expenditures hidden in the defense budget, such as the soaring costs of recruitment, with reenlistment bonuses of as much as $100,000. They do not include the lifetime of disability and health care benefits that will be required by tens of thousands of wounded veterans, as many as 20 percent of whom have suffered devastating brain and spinal injuries. Astonishingly, they do not include much of the cost of the equipment that has been used in the war, and that will have to be replaced. If you also take into account the costs to the economy from higher oil prices and the knock-on effects of the war—for instance, the depressing domino effect that war-fueled uncertainty has on investment, and the difficulties U.S. firms face overseas because America is the most disliked country in the world—the total costs of the Iraq war mount, even by a conservative estimate, to at least $2 trillion. To which one needs to add these words: so far.

It is natural to wonder, What would this money have bought if we had spent it on other things? U.S. aid to all of Africa has been hovering around $5 billion a year, the equivalent of less than two weeks of direct Iraq-war expenditures. The president made a big deal out of the financial problems facing Social Security, but the system could have been repaired for a century with what we have bled into the sands of Iraq. Had even a fraction of that $2 trillion been spent on investments in education and technology, or improving our infrastructure, the country would be in a far better position economically to meet the challenges it faces in the future, including threats from abroad. For a sliver of that $2 trillion we could have provided guaranteed access to higher education for all qualified Americans.

The soaring price of oil is clearly related to the Iraq war. The issue is not *whether* to blame the war for this but simply how much to blame it. It seems unbelievable now to recall that Bush-administration officials before the invasion suggested not only that Iraq's oil revenues would pay for the war in its entirety—hadn't we actually turned a tidy profit from the 1991 Gulf War?—but also that war was the best way to ensure low oil prices. In retrospect, the only big winners from the war have been the oil companies, the defense contractors, and al-Qaeda. Before the war, the oil markets anticipated that the then price range of $20 to $25 a barrel would continue for the next three years or so. Market players expected to see more demand from China and India, sure, but they also anticipated that this greater demand would be met mostly by increased production in the Middle East. The war upset that calculation, not so much by curtailing oil production in Iraq, which it did, but rather by heightening the sense of insecurity everywhere in the region, suppressing future investment.

The continuing reliance on oil, regardless of price, points to one more administration legacy: the failure to diversify America's energy resources. Leave aside the environmental reasons for weaning the world from hydrocarbons—the president has never convincingly embraced them, anyway. The economic and national-security arguments ought to have been powerful enough. Instead, the administration has pursued a policy of "drain America first"—that is, take as much oil out of America as possible, and as quickly as possible, with as little regard for the environment as one can get away with, leaving the country even more dependent on foreign oil in the future, and hope against hope that nuclear fusion or some other miracle will come to the rescue. So many gifts to the oil industry were included in the president's 2003 energy bill that John McCain referred to it as the "No Lobbyist Left Behind" bill.

CONTEMPT FOR THE WORLD

America's budget and trade deficits have grown to record highs under President Bush. To be sure, deficits don't have to be crippling in and of themselves. If a business borrows to buy a machine, it's a good thing, not a bad thing. During the past six years, America—its government, its families, the country as a whole—has been borrowing to sustain its consumption. Meanwhile, investment in fixed assets—the plants and equipment that help increase our wealth— has been declining.

What's the impact of all this down the road? The growth rate in America's standard of living will almost certainly slow, and there could even be a decline. The American economy can take a lot of abuse, but no economy is invincible, and our vulnerabilities are plain for all to see. As confidence in the American economy has plummeted, so has the value of the dollar—by 40 percent against the euro since 2001.

The disarray in our economic policies at home has parallels in our economic policies abroad. President Bush blamed the Chinese for our huge trade deficit, but an increase in the value of the yuan, which he has pushed, would simply make us buy more textiles and apparel from Bangladesh and Cambodia instead of China; our deficit would remain unchanged. The president claimed to believe in free trade but instituted measures aimed at protecting the American steel industry. The United States pushed hard for a series of bilateral trade agreements and bullied smaller countries into accepting all sorts of bitter conditions, such as extending patent protection on drugs that were desperately needed to fight AIDS. We pressed for open markets around the world but prevented China from buying Unocal, a small American oil company, most of whose assets lie outside the United States.

Not surprisingly, protests over U.S. trade practices erupted in places such as Thailand and Morocco. But America has refused to compromise—refused, for instance, to take any decisive action to do away with our huge agricultural subsidies, which distort international markets and hurt poor farmers in developing countries. This intransigence led to the collapse of talks designed to open up international markets. As in so many other areas, President Bush worked to undermine multilateralism—the notion that countries around the world need to cooperate—and to replace it with an America-dominated system. In the end, he failed to impose American dominance—but did succeed in weakening cooperation.

The administration's basic contempt for global institutions was underscored in 2005 when it named Paul Wolfowitz, the former deputy secretary of defense and a chief architect of the Iraq war, as president of the World Bank. Widely distrusted from the outset, and soon caught up in personal controversy, Wolfowitz became an international embarrassment and was forced to resign his position after less than two years on the job.

Globalization means that America's economy and the rest of the world have become increasingly interwoven. Consider those bad American mortgages. As families default, the owners of the mortgages find themselves holding worthless pieces of paper. The originators of these problem mortgages had already sold them to others, who packaged them, in a nontransparent way, with other assets, and passed them on once again to unidentified others. When the problems became apparent, global financial markets faced real tremors: it was discovered that billions in bad mortgages were hidden in portfolios in Europe, China, and Australia, and even in star American investment banks such as Goldman Sachs and Bear Stearns. Indonesia and other developing countries—innocent bystanders, really—

suffered as global risk premiums soared, and investors pulled money out of these emerging markets, looking for safer havens. It will take years to sort out this mess.

Meanwhile, we have become dependent on other nations for the financing of our own debt. Today, China alone holds more than $1 trillion in public and private American IOUs. Cumulative borrowing from abroad during the six years of the Bush administration amounts to some $5 trillion. Most likely these creditors will not call in their loans—if they ever did, there would be a global financial crisis. But there is something bizarre and troubling about the richest country in the world not being able to live even remotely within its means. Just as Guantánamo and Abu Ghraib have eroded America's moral authority, so the Bush administration's fiscal housekeeping has eroded our economic authority.

THE WAY FORWARD

Whoever moves into the White House in January 2009 will face an unenviable set of economic circumstances. Extricating the country from Iraq will be the bloodier task, but putting America's economic house in order will be wrenching and take years.

The most immediate challenge will be simply to get the economy's metabolism back into the normal range. That will mean moving from a savings rate of zero (or less) to a more typical savings rate of, say, 4 percent. While such an increase would be good for the long-term health of America's economy, the short-term consequences would be painful. Money saved is money not spent. If people don't spend money, the economic engine stalls. If households curtail their spending quickly—as they may be forced to do as a result of the meltdown in the mortgage market—this could mean a recession; if done in a more measured way, it would still mean a protracted slowdown. The problems of foreclosure and bankruptcy posed by excessive household debt are likely to get worse before they get better. And the federal government is in a bind: any quick restoration of fiscal sanity will only aggravate both problems.

And in any case there's more to be done. What is required is in some ways simple to describe: it amounts to ceasing our current behavior and doing exactly the opposite. It means not spending money that we don't have, increasing taxes on the rich, reducing corporate welfare, strengthening the safety net for the less well off, and making greater investment in education, technology, and infrastructure.

When it comes to taxes, we should be trying to shift the burden away from things we view as good, such as labor and savings, to things we view as bad, such as pollution. With respect to the safety net, we need to remember that the more the government does to help workers improve their skills and get affordable health care the more we free up American businesses to compete in the global economy. Finally, we'll be a lot better off if we work with other countries to create fair and efficient global trade and financial systems. We'll have a better chance of getting others to open up their markets if we ourselves act less hypocritically—that is, if we open our own markets to their goods and stop subsidizing American agriculture.

Some portion of the damage done by the Bush administration could be rectified quickly. A large portion will take decades to fix—and that's assuming the political will to do so exists both in the White House and in Congress. Think of the interest we are paying, year after year, on the almost $4 trillion of increased debt burden—even at 5 percent, that's an annual payment of $200 billion. Think of the taxes that future governments will have to levy to repay even a fraction of the debt we have accumulated. And think of the widening divide between rich and poor in America, a phenomenon that goes beyond economics and speaks to the very future of the American dream.

In short, there's a momentum here that will require a generation to reverse. Decades hence we should take stock, and revisit the conventional wisdom. Will Herbert Hoover still deserve his dubious mantle? I'm guessing that George W. Bush will have earned one more grim superlative.

CAPITALIST FOOLS*

T HERE WILL COME A MOMENT WHEN THE MOST URGENT
threats posed by the credit crisis have eased and the larger
task before us will be to chart a direction for the economic steps
ahead. This will be a dangerous moment. Behind the debates over
future policy is a debate over history—a debate over the causes of
our current situation. The battle for the past will determine the
battle for the present. So it's crucial to get the history straight.

What were the critical decisions that led to the crisis? Mistakes
were made at every fork in the road—we had what engineers call a
"system failure," when not a single decision but a cascade of decisions produce a tragic result. Let's look at five key moments.

No. 1: Firing the Chairman

In 1987 the Reagan administration decided to remove Paul Volcker as chairman of the Federal Reserve Board and appoint Alan
Greenspan in his place. Volcker had done what central bankers are
supposed to do. On his watch, inflation had been brought down

* *Vanity Fair*, January 2009.

from more than 11 percent to under 4 percent. In the world of central banking, that should have earned him a grade of A+++ and assured his reappointment. But Volcker also understood that financial markets need to be regulated. Reagan wanted someone who did not believe any such thing, and he found him in a devotee of the objectivist philosopher and free market-zealot Ayn Rand.

Greenspan played a double role. The Fed controls the money spigot, and in the early years of this decade, he turned it on full force. But the Fed is also a regulator. If you appoint an anti-regulator as your enforcer, you know what kind of enforcement you'll get. A flood of liquidity combined with the failed levees of regulation proved disastrous.

Greenspan presided over not one but two financial bubbles. After the high-tech bubble popped, in 2000–2001, he helped inflate the housing bubble. The first responsibility of a central bank should be to maintain the stability of the financial system. If banks lend on the basis of artificially high asset prices, the result can be a meltdown—as we are seeing now, and as Greenspan should have known. He had many of the tools he needed to cope with the situation. To deal with the high-tech bubble, he could have increased margin requirements (the amount of cash people need to put down to buy stock). To deflate the housing bubble, he could have curbed predatory lending to low-income households and prohibited other insidious practices (the no-documentation—or "liar"—loans, the interest-only loans, and so on). This would have gone a long way toward protecting us. If he didn't have the tools, he could have gone to Congress and asked for them.

Of course, the current problems with our financial system are not solely the result of bad lending. The banks have made mega-bets with one another through complicated instruments such as derivatives, credit-default swaps, and so forth. With these, one party pays another if certain events happen—for instance, if Bear Stearns goes bankrupt, or if the dollar soars. These instruments were originally created to help manage risk—but they can also be used to gamble.

Thus, if you felt confident that the dollar was going to fall, you could make a big bet accordingly, and if the dollar indeed fell, your profits would soar. The problem is that, with this complicated intertwining of bets of great magnitude, no one could be sure of the financial position of anyone else—or even of one's own position. Not surprisingly, the credit markets froze.

Here too Greenspan played a role. When I was chairman of the Council of Economic Advisors, during the Clinton administration, I served on a committee of all the major federal financial regulators, a group that included Greenspan and Treasury Secretary Robert Rubin. Even then, it was clear that derivatives posed a danger. And yet, for all the risk, the deregulators in charge of the financial system—at the Fed, at the Securities and Exchange Commission, and elsewhere—decided to do nothing, worried that any action might interfere with "innovation" in the financial system. But innovation, like "change," has no inherent value. It can be bad (the "liar" loans are a good example) as well as good.

No. 2: Tearing Down the Walls

The deregulation philosophy would pay unwelcome dividends for years to come. In November 1999, Congress repealed the Glass-Steagall Act—the culmination of a $300 million lobbying effort by the banking and financial-services industries, and spearheaded in Congress by Senator Phil Gramm. Glass-Steagall had long separated commercial banks (which lend money) and investment banks (which organize the sale of bonds and equities); it had been enacted in the aftermath of the Great Depression and was meant to curb the excesses of that era, including grave conflicts of interest. For instance, without separation, if a company whose shares had been issued by an investment bank, with its strong endorsement, got into trouble, wouldn't its commercial arm, if it had one, feel pressure to lend it money, perhaps unwisely? An ensuing spiral of bad judgment is not hard to foresee. I had opposed repeal of Glass-Steagall. The proponents said, in effect, Trust us: we will create Chinese walls to make sure that the problems of the past do not recur. As an economist, I certainly possessed a healthy degree of trust, trust in the power of economic incentives to bend human behavior toward self-interest—toward short-term self-interest, at any rate, rather than Tocqueville's "self interest rightly understood."

The most important consequence of the repeal of Glass-Steagall was indirect—it lay in the way repeal changed an entire culture. Commercial banks are not supposed to be high-risk ventures; they are supposed to manage other people's money very conservatively. It is with this understanding that the government agrees to pick up the tab should they fail. Investment banks, on the other hand, have traditionally managed rich people's money—people who can take bigger risks in order to get bigger returns. When repeal of Glass-Steagall brought investment and commercial banks together, the investment-bank culture came out on top. There was a demand for the kind of high returns that could be obtained only through high leverage and big risk taking.

There were other important steps down the deregulatory path. One was the decision in April 2004 by the Securities and Exchange Commission, at a meeting attended by virtually no one and largely overlooked at the time, to allow big investment banks to increase their debt-to-capital ratio (from 12:1 to 30:1, or higher) so that they could buy more mortgage-backed securities, inflating the housing bubble in the process. In agreeing to this measure, the SEC argued for the virtues of self-regulation: the peculiar notion that the banks can effectively police themselves. Self-regulation is preposterous, as even Alan Greenspan now concedes, and as a practical matter it can't, in any case, identify systemic risks—the kinds of risks that arise when, for instance, the models used by each of the banks to manage their portfolios tell all the banks to sell some security all at once.

As we stripped back the old regulations, we did nothing to address the new challenges posed by 21st-century markets. The most important challenge was that posed by derivatives. In 1998 the head of the Commodity Futures Trading Commission, Brooksley Born, had called for such regulation—a concern that took on urgency after the Fed, in that same year, engineered the bailout of Long-Term Capital Management, a hedge fund whose trillion-dollar-plus failure threatened global financial markets. But Secretary of the Treasury Robert Rubin, his deputy Larry Summers, and Greenspan were adamant—and successful—in their opposition. Nothing was done.

No. 3: Applying the Leeches

Then along came the Bush tax cuts, enacted first on June 7, 2001, with a follow-on installment two years later. The president and his advisers seemed to believe that tax cuts, especially for upper-income Americans and corporations, were a cure-all for any economic disease—the modern-day equivalent of leeches. The tax cuts played a pivotal role in shaping the background conditions of the current crisis. Because they did very little to stimulate the economy, real stimulation was left to the Fed, which took up the task with unprecedented low-interest rates and liquidity. The war in Iraq made matters worse, because it led to soaring oil prices. With America so dependent on oil imports, we had to spend several hundred billion more to purchase oil—money that otherwise would have been spent on American goods. Normally this would have led to an economic slowdown, as it had in the 1970s. But the Fed met the challenge in the most myopic way imaginable. The flood of liquidity made money readily available in mortgage markets, even to those who would normally not be able to borrow. And, yes, this succeeded in forestalling an economic downturn; America's household saving rate plummeted to zero. But it should have been clear that we were living on borrowed money and borrowed time.

The cut in the tax rate on capital gains contributed to the crisis in another way. It was a decision that turned on values: those who speculated (read: gambled) and won were taxed more lightly than wage earners who simply worked hard. But more than that, the decision encouraged leveraging, because interest was tax-deductible. If, for instance, you borrowed a million to buy a home or took a $100,000 home-equity loan to buy stock, the interest would be fully deductible every year. Any capital gains you made were taxed lightly—and at some possibly remote day in the future. The Bush administration was providing an open invitation to excessive borrowing and lending—not that American consumers needed any more encouragement.

No. 4: Faking the Numbers

Meanwhile, on July 30, 2002, in the wake of a series of major scandals—notably the collapse of WorldCom and Enron—Congress passed the Sarbanes-Oxley Act. The scandals had involved every major American accounting firm, most of our banks, and some of our premier companies, and made it clear that we had serious problems with our accounting system. Accounting is a sleep-inducing topic for most people, but if you can't have faith in a company's numbers, then you can't have faith in anything about a company at all. Unfortunately, in the negotiations over what became Sarbanes-Oxley a decision was made not to deal with what many, including the respected former head of the SEC Arthur Levitt, believed to be a fundamental underlying problem: stock options. Stock options have been defended as providing healthy incentives toward good management, but in fact they are "incentive pay" in name only. If a company does well, the CEO gets great rewards in the form of stock options; if a company does poorly, the compensation is almost as substantial but is bestowed in other ways. This is bad enough. But a collateral problem with stock options is that they provide incentives for bad accounting: top management has every incentive to provide distorted information in order to pump up share prices.

The incentive structure of the rating agencies also proved perverse. Agencies such as Moody's and Standard & Poor's are paid by the very people they are supposed to grade. As a result, they've had every reason to give companies high ratings, in a financial version of what college professors know as grade inflation. The rating agencies, like the investment banks that were paying them, believed in financial alchemy—that F-rated toxic mortgages could be converted into products that were safe enough to be held by commercial banks and pension funds. We had seen this same failure of the rating agencies during the East Asia crisis of the 1990s: high ratings facilitated a rush of money into the region, and then a sudden reversal in the ratings brought devastation. But the financial overseers paid no attention.

No. 5: Letting it Bleed

The final turning point came with the passage of a bailout package on October 3, 2008—that is, with the administration's response to the crisis itself. We will be feeling the consequences for years to come. Both the administration and the Fed had long been driven by wishful thinking, hoping that the bad news was just a blip, and that a return to growth was just around the corner. As America's banks faced collapse, the administration veered from one course of action to another. Some institutions (Bear Stearns, AIG, Fannie Mae, Freddie Mac) were bailed out. Lehman Brothers was not. Some shareholders got something back. Others did not.

The original proposal by Treasury Secretary Henry Paulson, a three-page document that would have provided $700 billion for the secretary to spend at his sole discretion, without oversight or judicial review, was an act of extraordinary arrogance. He sold the program as necessary to restore confidence. But it didn't address the underlying reasons for the loss of confidence. The banks had made too many bad loans. There were big holes in their balance sheets.

No one knew what was truth and what was fiction. The bailout package was like a massive transfusion to a patient suffering from internal bleeding—and nothing was being done about the source of the problem, namely all those foreclosures. Valuable time was wasted as Paulson pushed his own plan, "cash for trash," buying up the bad assets and putting the risk onto American taxpayers. When he finally abandoned it, providing banks with money they needed, he did it in a way that not only cheated America's taxpayers, but failed to ensure that the banks would use the money to restart lending. He even allowed the banks to pour out money to their shareholders as taxpayers were pouring money into the banks.

The other problem not addressed involved the looming weaknesses in the economy. The economy had been sustained by excessive borrowing. That game was up. As consumption contracted, exports kept the economy going, but with the dollar strengthening and Europe and the rest of the world declining, it was hard to see how that could continue. Meanwhile, states faced massive drop-offs in revenues—they would have to cut back on expenditures. Without quick action by government, the economy faced a downturn. And even if banks had lent wisely—which they hadn't—the downturn was sure to mean an increase in bad debts, further weakening the struggling financial sector.

The administration talked about confidence building, but what it delivered was actually a confidence trick. If the administration had really wanted to restore confidence in the financial system, it would have begun by addressing the underlying problems—the flawed incentive structures and the inadequate regulatory system.

WAS THERE ANY single decision which, had it been reversed, would have changed the course of history? Every decision—including decisions not to do something, as many of our bad economic decisions have been—is a consequence of prior decisions, an interlinked web stretching from the distant past into the future. You'll hear some on the right point to certain actions by the government itself—such as the Community Reinvestment Act, which requires banks to make mortgage money available in low-income neighborhoods. (Defaults on CRA lending were actually much lower than on other lending.) There has been much finger-pointing at Fannie Mae and Freddie Mac, the two huge mortgage lenders, which were originally government-owned. But in fact they came late to the subprime game, and their problem was similar to that of the private sector: their CEOs had the same perverse incentive to indulge in gambling.

The truth is most of the individual mistakes boil down to just one: a belief that markets are self-adjusting and that the role of government should be minimal. Looking back at that belief during hearings this fall on Capitol Hill, Alan Greenspan said out loud, "I have found a flaw." Congressman Henry Waxman pushed him, responding, "In other words, you found that your view of the world, your ideology, was not right; it wasn't working." "Absolutely, precisely," Greenspan said. The embrace by America—and much of the rest of the world—of this flawed economic philosophy made it inevitable that we would eventually arrive at the place we are today.

THE ANATOMY OF A MURDER: WHO KILLED AMERICA'S ECONOMY?[*]

THE SEARCH IS ON FOR WHOM TO BLAME FOR THE GLOBAL economic crisis. It is not just a matter of vindictiveness; it is important to know who or what caused the crisis if one is to figure out how to prevent another, or perhaps even to fix this one.

The notion of causation is, however, complex. Presumably, it means something like, "If only the guilty party had taken another course of action, the crisis would not have occurred." But the consequences of one party changing its actions depend on the behavior of others; presumably the actions of other parties, too, may have changed.

Consider a murder. We can identify who pulled the trigger. But somebody had to sell that person the gun. Somebody may have paid the gunman. Somebody may have provided inside information about the whereabouts of the victim. All of these people are party to the crime. If the person who paid the gunman was determined to have his victim shot, then even if the particular gunman who ended up pulling the trigger had refused the job, the victim would have been shot: Someone else would have been found to pull the trigger.

There are many parties to this crime—both people and institutions. Any discussion of "who is to blame" conjures up names like Robert Rubin, co-conspirator in deregulation and a senior official in

_____

* *Critical Review*, July 2009.

one of the two financial institutions into which the American government has poured the most money. Then there was Alan Greenspan, who also pushed the deregulatory philosophy; who failed to use
the regulatory authority that he had; who encouraged homeowners
to take out highly risky adjustable mortgages; and who supported
President Bush's tax cut for the rich,[1]—making lower interest rates,
which fed the bubble, necessary to stimulate the economy. But if
these people hadn't been there, others would have occupied their
seats, arguably doing similar things. There were others equally willing and able to perpetrate the crimes. Moreover, the fact that similar problems arose in other countries—with different people playing
the parts of the protagonists—suggests that there were more fundamental economic forces at play.

The list of institutions that must assume considerable responsibility for the crisis includes the investment banks and the investors;
the credit-rating agencies; the regulators, including the SEC and
the Federal Reserve; the mortgage brokers; and a string of administrations, from Reagan to Bush II, that pushed financial-sector
deregulation. Some of these institutions contributed to the crisis
in multiple roles—most notably the Federal Reserve, which failed
in its role as regulator, but which also may have contributed to the
crisis by mishandling interest rates and credit availability. All of
these—and some others discussed below—share some culpability.

THE MAIN PROTAGONISTS

But I would argue that blame should be centrally placed on the
banks (and the financial sector more broadly) and the investors.

The banks were supposed to be the experts in risk management.
They not only didn't manage risk; they created it. They engaged
in excessive leverage. At a 30-to-1 leverage ratio, a mere 3 percent
change in asset values wipes out one's net worth. (To put matters
in perspective, real estate prices have fallen some 20 percent and,

as of March 2009, are expected to fall another 10–15 percent, at least.) The banks adopted incentive structures that were designed to induce shortsighted and excessively risky behavior. The stock options that they used to pay some of their senior executives, moreover, provided incentives for bad accounting, including incentives to engage in extensive off-balance-sheet accounting.

The bankers seemingly didn't understand the risks that were being created by securitization—including those arising from information asymmetries: The originators of the mortgages did not end up holding on to them, so the originators didn't bear the consequences of any failure at due diligence. The bankers also misestimated the extent of correlation among default rates in different parts of the country—not realizing that a rise in the interest rate or an increase in unemployment might have adverse effects in many parts of the country—and they underestimated the risk of real estate price declines. Nor did the banks assess with any degree of accuracy the risks associated with some of the new financial products, such as low- or no-documentation loans.

The only defense that the bankers have—and it's admittedly a weak defense—is that their investors made them do it. Their investors didn't understand risk. They confused high returns brought on by excessive leverage in an up market with "smart" investment. Banks that didn't engage in excessive leverage, and so had lower returns, were "punished" by having their stock values beaten down. The reality, however, is that the banks exploited this investor ignorance to push their stock prices up, getting higher short-term returns at the expense of higher risk.

ACCESSORIES TO THE CRIME

If the banks were the main perpetrators of the crime, they had many accomplices.

Rating agencies played a central role. They believed in financial alchemy, and converted F-rated subprime mortgages into A-rated securities that were safe enough to be held by pension funds. This was important, because it allowed a steady flow of cash into the housing market, which in turn provided the fuel for the housing bubble. The rating agencies' behavior may have been affected by the perverse incentive of being paid by those that they rated, but I suspect that even without these incentive problems, their models would have been badly flawed. Competition, in this case, had a perverse effect: It caused a race to the bottom—a race to provide ratings that were most favorable to those being rated.

Mortgage brokers played a key role: They were less interested in originating good mortgages—after all, they didn't hold the mortgages for long—than in originating *many* mortgages. Some of the mortgage brokers were so enthusiastic that they invented new forms of mortgages: The low- or no-documentation loans to which I referred earlier were an invitation to deception, and came to be called liar loans. This was an "innovation," but there was a good reason that such innovations hadn't occurred before.

Other new mortgage products—low- or no-amortization, variable-rate loans—snared unwary borrowers. Home-equity loans, too, encouraged Americans to borrow against the equity in their homes, increasing the (total) loan-to-value ratios and thereby making the mortgages riskier.

The mortgage originators didn't focus on risk, but rather on transactions costs. But they weren't trying to minimize transactions costs; they were trying to maximize them—devising ways that they could increase them, and thereby their revenues. Short-term loans that had to be refinanced—and left open the risk of not being able to be refinanced—were particularly useful in this respect.

The transactions costs generated by writing mortgages provided a strong incentive to prey on innocent and inexperienced borrowers—for instance, by encouraging more short-term lending and borrowing, entailing repeated loan restructurings, which helped generate high transactions costs.

The regulators, too, were accomplices in crime. They should have recognized the inherent risks in the new products; they should have done their own risk assessments, rather than relying on self-regulation or on the credit-rating agencies. They should have realized the risks associated with high leverage, with over-the-counter derivatives, and especially the risks that were compounding as these were not netted out.

The regulators deceived themselves into thinking that if only they ensured that each bank managed its own risk (which they had every incentive, presumably, to do), then the system would work. Amazingly, they did not pay any attention to *systemic risk*, though concerns about systemic risk constitute one of the primary rationales for regulation in the first place. Even if every bank were, "on average," sound, they could act in a correlated way that generated risks to the economy as a whole.

In some cases, the regulators had a defense: They had no legal basis for acting, even had they discovered something was wrong. They had not been given the power to regulate derivatives. But that defense is disingenuous, because some of the regulators—most notably Greenspan—had worked hard to make sure that appropriate regulations were not adopted.

The repeal of the Glass-Steagall Act played an especial role, not just because of the conflicts of interest that it opened up (made so evident in the Enron and WorldCom scandals), but also because it transmitted the risk-taking culture of investment banking to commercial banks, which should have acted in a far more prudential manner.

It was not just *financial* regulation and regulators that were at fault. There should have been tougher enforcement of antitrust laws. Banks were allowed to grow to be too big to fail—or too big to be managed. And such banks have perverse incentives. When it's heads I win, tails you lose, too-big-to-fail banks have incentives to engage in excessive risk taking.

Corporate governance laws, too, are partly to blame. Regulators and investors should have been aware of the risks that the peculiar incentive structures engendered. These did not even serve share-holder interests well. In the aftermath of the Enron and WorldCom scandals, there was much discussion of the need for reform, and the Sarbanes-Oxley Act represented a beginning. But it didn't attack perhaps the most fundamental problem: stock options.

Bush's and Clinton's capital-gains tax cuts, in conjunction with the deductibility of interest, provided enhanced incentives for leverage—for homeowners to take out, for instance, as large a mortgage as they could.

CREDENTIALED ACCOMPLICES

There is one other set of accomplices—the economists who pro-vided the arguments that those in the financial markets found so convenient and self-serving. These economists provided models—based on unrealistic assumptions of perfect information, per-fect competition, and perfect markets—in which regulation was unnecessary.

Modern economic theories, particularly those focusing on imper-fect and asymmetric information and on systematic irrationali-ties, especially with respect to risk judgments, had explained how flawed those earlier "neoclassical" models were. They had shown that those models were not robust—even slight deviations from the extreme assumptions destroyed the conclusions. But these insights were simply ignored.

Some important strands in recent economic theory, moreover, encouraged central bankers to focus solely on fighting inflation. They seemed to argue that low inflation was necessary, and almost sufficient, for stable and robust growth. The result was that cen-tral bankers (including the Fed) paid little attention to the financial structure.

In short, many of the most popular microeconomic and macro-economic theories aided and abetted regulators, investors, bankers, and policymakers—they provided the "rationale" for their policies and actions. They made the bankers believe that in pursuing their self-interest, they were, in fact, advancing the well-being of society; they made the regulators believe that in pursuing their policies of benign neglect, they were allowing the private sector to flourish, from which all would benefit.

REBUTTING THE DEFENSE

Alan Greenspan has tried to shift the blame for low interest rates to China, because of its high savings rate.[2] Clearly, Greenspan's defense is unpersuasive· The Fed had enough control, at least in the short run, to have raised interest rates in spite of China's willingness to lend to America at a relatively low interest rate. Indeed, the Fed did just that in the middle of the decade, which contributed—predictably—to the popping of the housing bubble.

Low interest rates did feed the bubble. But that is not the necessary consequence of low interest rates. Many countries yearn for low interest rates to help finance needed investment. The funds could have been channeled into more productive uses. Our financial markets failed to do that. Our regulatory authorities allowed the financial markets (including the banks) to use the abundance of funds in ways that were not socially productive. They allowed the low interest rates to feed a housing bubble. They had the tools to stop this. They didn't use the tools that they had.

If we are to blame low interest rates for "feeding" the frenzy, then we have to ask what induced the Fed to pursue low interest rates. It did so, in part, to maintain the strength of the economy, which was suffering from inadequate aggregate demand as a result of the collapse of the tech bubble.

In that regard, Bush's tax cut for the rich was perhaps pivotal. It was not designed to stimulate the economy and did so only to a limited extent. His war in Iraq, too, played an important role. In its aftermath, oil prices rose from $20 a barrel to $140 a barrel. (We don't have to parse out here what fraction of this increase is due to the war; but there is little doubt that it played a role.[3]) Americans were now spending hundreds of billions of dollars a year more to import oil. This was money not available to be spent at home.

In the 1970s, when oil prices soared, most countries faced recessions because of the transfer of purchasing power abroad to finance the purchase of oil. There was one exception: Latin America, which used debt finance to continue its consumption unabated. But its borrowing was unsustainable. Over the last decade, America took the Latin American route. To offset the negative effect of higher spending on oil, the Fed kept interest rates *lower than they otherwise would have been*, and this fed the housing bubble more than it otherwise would have. The American economy, like the Latin American economies of the 70s, seemed to be doing well, because the housing bubble fed a consumption boom, as household savings fell all the way down to zero.

Given the war and the consequent soaring oil prices and given Bush's poorly designed tax cuts, the burden of maintaining economic strength fell to the Fed. The Fed could have exercised its authority as a regulator to do what it could do to direct the resources into more productive uses. Here, the Fed and its chairman have a double culpability. Not only did they fail in their regulatory role, they became cheerleaders for the bubble that eventually consumed America. When asked about a possible bubble, Greenspan suggested there was none—only a little froth. That was clearly wrong. The Fed argued that you could not tell a bubble until after it broke. That, too, was not fully correct. You can't be *sure* there is a bubble until after it breaks, but one can make strong probabilistic statements.

All policy is made in the context of uncertainty. House prices, especially at the lower end, soared, yet the real incomes of most Americans stagnated: There was a clear problem. And it was clear that the problem would get worse once interest rates rose. Greenspan had encouraged people to take out variable-rate mortgages when interest rates were at historically low levels. And he allowed them to borrow up to the hilt—assuming interest rates would remain at the same low level. But because interest rates were so low—real interest rates were negative—it was unreasonable to expect them to remain at that level for long. When they rose, it was clear that many Americans would be in trouble—and so would the lenders who had lent to them.

Apologists for the Fed sometimes try to defend this irresponsible and shortsighted policy by saying they had no choice: Raising interest rates would have killed the bubble, but also would have killed the economy. But the Fed has more tools than just the interest rate. There were, for instance, a number of regulatory actions that would have dampened the bubble. It chose not to employ these tools. It could have reduced maximum loan-to-value ratios as the likelihood of a bubble increased; it could have lowered the maximum house payment-to-income ratios allowed. If it believed it did not have the requisite tools, it could have gone to Congress and requested them.

This doesn't provide a *fully* satisfactory counterfactual. True, perhaps the money could have been deployed by financial markets more productively, to support, for instance, more innovation, or important projects in developing countries. But perhaps the financial markets would have found another scam to support irresponsible borrowing—for instance, a new credit card boom.

DEFENDING THE INNOCENT

Just as all of the accomplices are not equally culpable, some suspects should be acquitted.

In the long list of possible culprits, there are two that many Republicans often name. They find it difficult to accept that markets fail, that market participants could act in such an irresponsible manner, that the wizards of finance didn't understand risk, that capitalism has serious flaws. It is government, they are sure, which is to blame.

I have suggested government is indeed to blame, but for doing too little. The conservative critics believe that government is to blame for doing too much. They criticize the Community Reinvestment Act (CRA) requirements imposed on banks, which required them to lend a certain fraction of their portfolio to underserved minority communities. They also blame Fannie Mae and Freddie Mac, the peculiar government-sponsored enterprises, which, though privatized in 1968, play a very large role in mortgage markets. Fannie and Freddie were, according to conservatives, "under pressure" from Congress and the president to expand homeownership (President Bush often talked about the "ownership society").

This is clearly just an attempt to shift blame. A recent Fed study showed that the default rate among CRA mortgagors is actually *below* average.[4] The problems in America's mortgage markets began with the subprime market, while Fannie Mae and Freddie Mac primarily financed "conforming" (prime) mortgages.

It is America's fully private financial markets that invented all the bad practices that played a central role in this crisis. When government encouraged homeownership, it meant *permanent* homeownership. It didn't intend for people to buy homes beyond their ability to afford them. That would generate ephemeral gains, and contribute to impoverishment: The poor would lose their life savings as they lost their home.

There is always a home that is of an appropriate cost to an individual's budget. The irony is that because of the bubble, many of the impoverished wound up owning a home no bigger than they would have if more prudent lending policies had been enforced—which would have dampened the bubble. To be sure, Fannie Mae and Freddie Mac did get into the high-risk high-leverage "games" that were the fad in the private sector, though rather late, and rather ineptly. Here, too, there was regulatory failure; the government-sponsored enterprises have a special regulator which should have constrained them, but evidently, amidst the deregulatory philosophy of the Bush administration, did not. Once they entered the game, they had an advantage, because they could borrow somewhat more cheaply because of their (ambiguous at the time) government guarantee. They could arbitrage that guarantee to generate bonuses comparable to those that they saw were being "earned" by their counterparts in the fully private sector.

POLITICS AND ECONOMICS

There is one more important culprit, which, in fact, has played a key behind-the-scenes role in many various parts of this story: America's political system, and especially its dependence on campaign contributions. This allowed Wall Street to exercise the enormous influence that it has had, to push for the stripping of regulations and to the appointment of regulators who didn't believe in regulations—with the predictable and predicted consequences that we have seen.[5] Even today, that influence is playing a role in the design of effective means of addressing the financial crisis.

Any economy needs rules and referees. Our rules and referees were shaped by special interests; ironically, it is not even clear whether those rules and referees served those special interests well. It is clear that they did not serve the national interests well.

In the end, this is a crisis of our economic and political system. Each of the players was, to a large extent, doing what they thought they should do. The bankers were maximizing their incomes, given the rules of the game. The rules of the game said that they should use their political influence to get regulations and regulators that allowed them, and the corporations they headed, to walk away with as much money as they could. The politicians responded to the rules of the game: They had to raise money to get elected, and to do that, they had to please powerful and wealthy constituents. There were economists who provided the politicians, the bankers, and the regulators with a convenient ideology: According to this ideology, the policies and practices that they were pursuing would supposedly benefit all.

There are those who now would like to reconstruct the system as it was prior to 2008. They will push for regulatory reform, but it will be more cosmetic than real. Banks that are too big to fail will be allowed to continue little changed. There will be "oversight," whatever that means. But the banks will continue to be able to gamble, and they will continue to be too big to fail. Accounting standards will be relaxed, to give them greater leeway. Little will be done about incentive structures or even risky practices. If so, then, another crisis is sure to follow.

Notes

1. Greenspan supported the 2001 tax cut even though he should have known that it would lead to the deficits which previously he has treated as such an anathema. His argument that, unless we acted now, the surpluses that were accumulating as a result of Clinton's prudent fiscal policies would drain the economy of all its T-bills, which would make the conduct of monetary policy difficult, was one of the worst arguments from a respected government official I have ever heard; presumably, if the contingency he imagined—the wiping out of the national debt—was imminent, Congress had the tools and incentives with which to correct the situation in short order.

2. Alan Greenspan."The Fed Didn't Cause the Housing Bubble," *Wall Street Journal,* March 11, 2009.

3. Joseph E. Stiglitz and Linda Bilmes. *The Three Trillion Dollar War: The True Costs of the Iraq Conflict* (New York: W. W. Norton, 2008).

4. Randall S. Kroszner. "The Community Reinvestment Act and the Recent Mortgage Crisis," Speech to the Confronting Concentrated Poverty Policy Forum, Board of Governors of Federal Reserve System, Washington, D.C., December 3, 2008.

5. Joseph E. Stiglitz. *The Roaring Nineties* (New York: W. W. Norton, 2003).

HOW TO GET OUT OF THE
FINANCIAL CRISIS*

T HE AMOUNT OF BAD NEWS OVER THE PAST WEEKS HAS
been bewildering for many people in the world. Stock markets have plunged, banks have stopped lending to one another, and central bankers and treasury secretaries appear daily on television looking worried. Many economists have warned that we are facing the worst economic crisis the world has seen since 1929. The only good news is that oil prices have finally started to come down.

While these times are scary and strange for many Americans, a number of people in other countries feel a sense of déjà vu. Asia went through a similar crisis in the late 1990s, and various other countries (including Argentina, Turkey, Mexico, Norway, Sweden, Indonesia, and South Korea) have suffered through banking crises, stock market collapses, and credit crunches.

Capitalism may be the best economic system that man has come up with, but no one ever said it would create stability. In fact, over the past 30 years, market economies have faced more than 100 crises. That is why I and many other economists believe that government regulation and oversight are an essential part of a functioning market economy. Without them, there will continue to be

---

*   *Time*, October 17, 2008.

frequent severe economic crises in different parts of the world. The market on its own is not enough. Government must play a role.

It's good news that Treasury Secretary Henry Paulson seems to finally be coming around to the idea that the U.S. government needs to help recapitalize our banks and should receive stakes in the banks that it bails out. But more must be done to prevent the crisis from spreading around the world. Here's what it will take.

How We Got Here

The troubles we now face were caused largely by the combination of deregulation and low interest rates. After the collapse of the tech bubble, the economy needed a stimulus. But the Bush tax cuts didn't provide much stimulus to the economy. This put the burden of keeping the economy going on the Fed, and it responded by flooding the economy with liquidity. Under normal circumstances, it's fine to have money sloshing around in the system, since that helps the economy grow. But the economy had already overinvested, and so the extra money wasn't put to productive use. Low interest rates and easy access to funds encouraged reckless lending, the infamous interest-only, no-down-payment, no-documentation ("liar") subprime mortgages. It was clear that if the bubble got deflated even a little, many mortgages would end up underwater—with the price of the house less than the value of the mortgage. That has happened—12 million so far, and more every hour. Not only are the poor losing their homes, but they are also losing their life savings.

The climate of deregulation that dominated the Bush-Greenspan years helped the spread of a new banking model. At its core was securitization: mortgage brokers originated mortgages that they sold on to others. Borrowers were told not to worry about paying the ever-mounting debt, because house prices would keep rising and they could refinance, taking out some of the capital gains to buy a car or pay for a vacation. Of course, this violated the first law of economics—that there is no such thing as a free lunch. The assumption that house prices could continue to go up at a rapid pace looked particularly absurd in an economy in which most Americans were seeing their real incomes declining.

The mortgage brokers loved these new products because they ensured an endless stream of fees. They maximized their profits by originating as many mortgages as possible, with frequent refinancing. Their allies in investment banking bought them, sliced and diced the risk, and then passed them on—or at least as much as they could. Our bankers forgot that their job was to prudently manage risk and allocate capital. They became gambling casinos—gambling with other people's money, knowing that the taxpayer would step in if the losses were too great. They misallocated capital, with massive amounts going into housing that was ultimately unaffordable. Loose money and light regulation were a toxic mixture. It exploded.

A Global Crisis

What made America's recklessness truly dangerous is that we exported it. A few months ago, some talked about decoupling—that Europe would carry on even as the U.S. suffered a downturn. I always thought that decoupling was a myth, and events have proven that right. Thanks to globalization, Wall Street was able to sell off its toxic mortgages around the world. It appears that about half the toxic mortgages were exported. Had they not been, the U.S. would be in even worse shape. Moreover, even as our economy went into a slowdown, exports kept the U.S. going. But the weaknesses in America weakened the dollar and made it more difficult for Europe to sell its goods abroad. Weak exports meant a weak economy, and so the U.S. exported our downturn just as earlier we had exported our toxic mortgages.

But now the problems are ricocheting back. The bad mortgages are contributing to forcing many European banks into bankruptcy. (We exported not only bad loans but also bad lending and regulatory practices; many of Europe's bad loans are to European borrowers.) And as market participants realized that the fire had spread from America to Europe, there was panic. Part of the concern is psychological. But part of it is because our financial and economic systems are closely intertwined. Banks all over the world lend and borrow from each other; they buy and sell complicated financial instruments—which is why bad regulatory practices in one country, leading to bad loans, can infect the global system.

How to Fix It

We are now facing a liquidity problem, a solvency problem, and a macroeconomic problem. We are in the first phase of a downward spiral. It is, of course, part of the inevitable process of adjustment: returning housing prices to equilibrium levels and getting rid of the excessive leverage (debt) that had kept our phantom economy going.

Even with the new capital provided by the government, banks won't want to, or be able to, lend as much as they did in their reckless past. Homeowners won't want to borrow so much. Savings, which have been near zero, will go up—good for the economy in the long run but bad for an economy going into recession. While some large firms may be sitting on a bundle of cash, small firms depend on loans not just for investment but even for the working capital to keep going. That's going to be harder to come by. And the investment in real estate, which played such an important role in our modest growth of the past 6 years, has reached lows not seen in 20 years.

The administration has veered from one half-baked solution to another. Wall Street panicked, but so did the White House, and in that panic, they had a hard time figuring out what to do. The weeks that Paulson and Bush spent pushing Paulson's orignal bailout plan—in the face of massive opposition—were weeks that could have been spent actually fixing the problem. At this point, we need a comprehensive approach. Another failed faint attempt could be disastrous. Here's a five-step, comprehensive approach:

1. Recapitalize banks. With all the losses, banks have insufficient equity. Banks will have a hard time raising this equity under current circumstances. The government needs to provide equity. In return, it should have voting stakes in the banks it helps. But equity injections also bail out bondholders. Right now the market is discounting these bonds, saying there is a high probability of default. There needs to be a forced conversion of this debt to equity. If this is done, the amount of government assistance that will be required will be much reduced.

It's good news that Treasury Secretary Paulson seems to finally realize that his original proposal of buying what he euphemistically called distressed assets was flawed. That Secretary Paulson took so long to figure this out is worrying. He was so bound by the idea of a free-market solution that he was unable to accept what economists of all stripes were telling him: that he needed to recapitalize the banks and provide new money to make up for the losses they incurred on their bad loans.

The administration is now doing this, but three questions are raised: Was it a fair deal to the taxpayer? The answer to that seems fairly clear: taxpayers got a raw deal, evident by comparing the terms of Warren Buffet's injection of $5 billion into Goldman Sachs, and the terms extracted by the administration. Second, is there enough oversight and restrictions to make sure that the bad practices of the past do not recur and that new lending does occur? Again, comparing the terms demanded by the UK and by the U.S. Treasury, we got the short end of the stick. For instance, banks can continue to pay out money to shareholders, as the government pours money in. Third, is it enough money? The banks are so nontransparent that no one can fully answer the question, but what we do know is that the gaps in the balance sheet are likely to get bigger. That is because too little is being done about the underlying problem.

2. Stem the tide of foreclosures. The original Paulson plan is like a massive blood transfusion to a patient with severe internal hemorrhaging. We won't save the patient if we don't do something about the foreclosures. Even after congressional revisions, too little is being done. We need to help people stay in their homes, by converting the mortgage-interest and property-tax deductions into cashable tax credits; by reforming bankruptcy laws to allow expedited restructuring, which would bring down the value of the mortgage when the price of the house is below that of the mortgage; and even government lending, taking advantage of the government's lower cost of funds and passing the savings on to poor and middle-income homeowners.

3. Pass a stimulus that works. Helping Wall Street and stopping the foreclosures are only part of the solution. The U.S. economy is headed for a serious recession and needs a big stimulus. We need increased unemployment insurance; if states and localities are not helped, they will have to reduce expenditures as their tax revenues plummet, and their reduced spending will lead to a contraction of the economy. But to kick-start the economy, Washington must make investments in the future. Hurricane Katrina and the collapse of the bridge in Minneapolis were grim reminders of how decrepit our infrastructure has become. Investments in infrastructure and technology will stimulate the economy in the short run and enhance growth in the long run.

4. Restore confidence through regulatory reform. Underlying the problems are banks' bad decisions and regulatory failures. These must be addressed if confidence in our financial system is to be restored. Corporate governance structures that lead to flawed incentive structures designed to generously reward CEOs should be changed and so should many of the incentive systems themselves. It is not just the level of compensation; it is also the form—nontransparent stock options that provide incentives for bad accounting to bloat up reported returns.

5. Create an effective multilateral agency. As the global economy becomes more interconnected, we need better global oversight. It is unimaginable that America's financial market could function effectively if we had to rely on 50 separate state regulators. But we are trying to do essentially that at the global level.

The recent crisis provides an example of the dangers: as some foreign governments provided blanket guarantees for their deposits, money started to move to what looked like safe havens. Other countries had to respond. A few European governments have been far more thoughtful than the U.S. in figuring out what needs to be done. Even before the crisis turned global, French President Nicolas Sarkozy, in his address to the UN last month, called for a world summit to lay the foundations for more state regulation to replace the current laissez-faire approach. We may be at a new "Bretton Woods moment." As the world emerged from the Great Depression and World War II, it realized there was need for a new global economic order. It lasted more than 60 years. That it was not well adapted for the new world of globalization has been clear for a long time. Now, as the world emerges from the Cold War and the Great Financial Crisis, it will need to construct a new global economic order for the 21st century, and that will include a new global regulatory agency.

This crisis may have taught us that unfettered markets are risky. It should also have taught us that unilateralism can't work in a world of economic interdependence.

GOING FORWARD

The next U.S. president will have a very hard time of it. Even the most well-thought-out plans may not work as intended. But I am confident that a comprehensive program along the lines I have suggested—stemming foreclosures, recapitalizing banks, stimulating the economy, protecting the unemployed, shoring up state finances, providing guarantees where needed and appropriate, reforming regulations and regulatory structures and replacing regulators and those with responsibility to protect the economy with those focused more on rescuing the economy than on rescuing Wall Street—will not only restore confidence but in due time also enable America to live up to its full potential. Halfway approaches, on the other hand, by continually bringing disappointment, are sure to fail.

In a country where money is respected, Wall Street's leaders used to have our respect. They had our trust. They were believed to be a font of wisdom, at least on economic matters. Times have changed. Gone is the respect and trust. Too bad, because financial markets are necessary for a well-functioning economy. But most Americans believe that Wall Streeters are more likely to put their interests ahead of those of the rest of the country, dressing it up in as fancy language as necessary. If the next president is seen to have his policies unduly shaped by Wall Street and those policies don't do the trick, his honeymoon will be short. That will be bad news for him, for the country, and for the world.

PART I

BIG THINK

I OPEN THIS PART OF THE BOOK WITH MY *VANITY FAIR* article "Of the 1 Percent, by the 1 Percent, for the 1 Percent," evoking the lines of President Lincoln's famous Gettysburg Address, arguing that the real issue of the Civil War was to ensure "that government of the people, by the people, for the people, shall not perish from the earth." Democracy, we now know, is more than periodic elections: in some countries, such elections have been used to legitimize essentially authoritarian regimes and deprive large parts of the citizenry of basic rights.

Perhaps the most important aspect of inequality is inequality of political rights—when America's Declaration of Independence said that "all men are created equal," it didn't mean that all were of equal ability; it meant especially that all men should be equal in their political rights.[1] But even the meaning of "political rights" is not obvious, as debates in recent years in the United States have made clear. Though every citizen has the *right* to vote,[2] the rules of the game affect the ability and likelihood of exercising that right. Making it more difficult to register to vote, or even to vote, for certain groups (e.g., those without a driver's license, the usual piece of identification in the United States, where there is no national identity card) discourages them from voting. The poll tax (imposing a tax on everyone who votes) affects the "economics" of voting. It creates a de facto disenfranchisement of the poor. This was one of the tried-and-true ways used in America's South. Some countries try to make it easy for the working poor to vote, by having elections on Sunday. Other countries (like Australia) have actively sought to make sure that the voices of all citizens are heard. Australia's rule of mandatory voting—charging a penalty on everyone who does not show up at the voting booth—affects the economics of voting in precisely the opposite way that a poll tax does.

Voice is even more important: the ability to influence the political process, either by affecting voting patterns or, more directly, by affecting the actions of key decision makers. If the rich can use their money to control the press or to influence (a gentler, but perhaps less accurate word than "buy") politicians, then their voice will be heard far more loudly. It is almost inevitable that the rich will be, in this sense, more influential than others; but the rules of the game affect the extent to which this is so. And that's why America's laws and regulations governing lobbying, campaign contributions, and revolving doors are so invidious: other Western democracies take the notion of political equality more seriously, and have curbed these abuses; some have gone so far as to enhance equality of voice (e.g., through public support of media or ensuring equal candidate access to all media). And that's why so many Americans see *Citizens United*, the Supreme Court decision that paved the way for unbridled spending by corporations, as having such an adverse effect on equality of voice—and contributing to the country's endemic disease, "process American style." It is a corruption that occurs not via cash-stuffed envelopes handed to politicians, but via an equally invidious process, using campaign contributions to buy "policies" that bring riches to a few.

Those themes are elaborated in many of the essays to follow: economic inequality (especially of the magnitude found in the United States) leads to political inequality (particularly when the rules of the *political game* facilitate this—as in the United States). Economic inequality is not *just* or even *so much* the result of inexorable laws of economics, as it is of our policies and politics. It is, in this sense, a matter of *choice*. But here we have a vicious circle, as economic inequality leads to and reinforces political inequality, which simply reinforces our economic inequality.

I argue, too, that inequality—again at least in the extreme form in the United States—is not even in the interests of the 1 percent. "The 1 Percent's Problem" explains further some of the reasons that inequality is bad for the economy. If those in the 1 percent were pursuing their *enlightened* self-interest, they would worry about inequality and try to do something about it. As I suggest in "Inequality Is Not Inevitable," at least in some parts of the world, that is beginning to happen.

The Conservative Response

In the years since these pieces were published, a few critics have said that inequality was not quite as bad as the statistics suggested; changes in tax laws meant that there was now less incentive to engage in tax evasion and avoidance. Of course, if these critics were right, their arguments implied only that the current outrageously high levels of inequality—where the top 1 percent gets between a quarter and a fifth of national income—have prevailed in America for much longer than we had thought. It would also imply that America's economic performance is even weaker than we thought—for the only people in America who have been doing well are those at the very top. These conservative critics seem to be arguing that even the very top has not seen a real increase in income, only an increase in *reported income*. But the careful work of Emmanuel Saez and his co-authors actually took into account the effects of the tax changes;[3] in any case, even with subsequent tax changes—which would have restored the incentive for tax avoidance—the share of the top continued to rise.

Others have argued that what mattered was not inequality of outcomes but inequality of opportunity. However, as a later chapter in Part III ("Equal Opportunity: Our National Myth") points out, America is no longer the land of opportunity that it (and others) like to think it is. To a large extent, the American dream is a myth. Of course, some very talented immigrants do make it to the top. But when social scientists refer to equality of opportunity, they mean the likelihood that someone at the bottom will make it to the top. For a young American today, the chances are far lower than for young persons in other advanced countries.

Enlightened Self-Interest

The essay "The 1 Percent's Problem" (also originally published in *Vanity Fair*) was, in a sense, addressed to members of the 1 percent— to explain to them why the level of inequality that characterized the United States was *not* in their enlightened self-interest.

In the space of a few pages, I summarize why it is that inequality is so bad for economic performance. This is perhaps the most profound change in our thinking about inequality in recent decades. It used to be thought that even if one were opposed to inequality, the cost of doing anything about it—in terms of overall economic performance—would be too great. Most discussions focused on *redistribution*, or at least asking those at the top to contribute more to the support of public goods, like national defense, not only absolutely but as a percentage of income. Redistribution was characterized as a leaky bucket: because of the leak, a $100 taken from the top would be worth half as much by the time it was given to the middle or bottom. But in this article I argue that there may not be a trade-off: we can have both more equality and a higher GDP; that there are policies that can increase the equality of before-tax and transfer income, as well as policies that redistribute, and do so in ways that strengthen overall performance. Indeed, some tax policies—taxing the rich on their capital gains on land—could actually lead to more *productive* investments (instead of real estate speculation) and more job creaticn. Curbing the outsize incomes of the financial sector might divert more of our most talented people into activities that would increase the productivity of the economy. And by increasing overall economic performance, not only would society as a whole benefit, but so would at least many of the 1 percent. They would benefit not just from being part of a more cohesive society but even economically.

Inequality as a Political Choice

The next chapter picks up where this chapter leaves off. Observing that our higher inequality has been partially responsible for our slow growth, I argue that slow growth and inequality are political choices and that we can choose otherwise. The article "Phony Capitalism" was written three years into the debate about inequality that my first *Vanity Fair* article had helped launch. The *Washington Monthly* organized a special edition to describe the way that America's inequality plays out at each stage of life. There was an emphasis on education—one of the main ways that the advantaged pass on their privileged position to their children. I discuss briefly America's health inequities, which result in large disparities—even in life expectancy. These are hardly a surprise, given the magnitude of the country's income inequality, combined with a reliance on an expensive, private health insurance and medical system. America is unique among the advanced countries in not recognizing access to health care as a basic human right.

I counter a popular conservative argument that we can't afford to do more, to do a better job in promoting equality and equality of opportunity. Quite the contrary: our economy pays a high price for our failure to do so. We make *political* choices about how we spend our money—whether on tax breaks for the rich or on education for ordinary Americans; whether on weapons that don't work against enemies that don't exist or on health care for the poor; whether on subsidies for rich cotton farmers or on food stamps to reduce hunger among the poor. We could even raise tax revenues by simply making companies like General Electric and Apple pay the taxes they already should be paying. By taxing pollution, we could have a cleaner environment and more money to spend, both to reduce the inequities in our society and to promote our economy's growth.

Global Perspectives

While America may have more inequality than any other advanced country, there has been an increase in inequality in most—but not all—countries. Sometimes this inequality has played a central role in the evolution of political events.

I was in Egypt on that fateful day, January 14, 2011, when Ben Ali, the dictator of Tunisia, was overthrown. At a dinner at the American University in Cairo, as news almost instantaneously traveled across North Africa, I remember being told: Egypt is next. In less than two weeks, the predictions I heard that night would come to pass.

During my visit to Egypt, I could see why: though the country had been growing, the benefits had not reached most Egyptians. Socialism under Gamal Abdel Nassar had failed them. Neoliberalism under Hosni Mubarak had also failed them. The desperation to try something else was palpable. Mustapha Nabli, later the central bank governor of Tunisia, helped explain to me what was behind the unrest. It was not just the high level of unemployment. It was the unfairness of the system, the inequities. Those with political connections, those who were willing to be corrupted by the system, were the ones who did well, not those who worked hard, did well in school, and played by the *supposed* rules.

I returned to Egypt and Tunisia several times in the ensuing years, and I became quite close to some of the young revolutionaries, as well as to some of the older, more established people who welcomed the revolution. I admired the enthusiasm of the former, their idealism, but I worried about their naïveté, their conviction that simply because they had right on their side, they would prevail. Matters have not gone well in Egypt; but as this book goes to press, it appears that at least in one country, Tunisia, the seeds sown in the Arab Spring may actually have taken root.

Growing awareness of the role that inequality had played in the Arab Spring—and growing inequality around the world—moved concerns about inequality front and center. "Inequality Goes Global"[4] was written after I returned from the 2013 meeting at Davos, Switzerland, of the World Economic Forum. This is the annual gathering of the world's elite—entertained and instructed by a few academics and complemented by a few people from civil society and social entrepreneurs. The meeting is a good place to feel the world's pulse—or at least the pulse of this rarefied group. Before the crisis there was unbridled euphoria about globalization and technology. This optimism sank with the economy. But with the faltering, and unequal, recovery, attention turned to some long-standing problems. What was notable about the 2013 meeting was that inequality had risen to the top of the attendees' concerns.

"Inequality Is a Choice" was written for the inaugural issue of the international edition of the *New York Times* (really, simply a change in the name, from the *International Herald Tribune*). I chose to focus on a striking aspect of global inequality: though inequality was increasing in most countries around the world, in some countries it was not increasing; in some countries inequality was much, much lower than in the United States. It's not simply economic laws that determine the degree of inequality in a country, but, as I have repeatedly said, politics and policies.

The effects of globalization on *global inequality* have in fact been complex. India and China, two countries with some 45 percent of the world's population, whose share of global GDP had shrunk to less than 10 percent, are in resurgence. With growth rates that are so much larger than those of the advanced countries, the gap between them and the advanced countries is narrowing—though there is still a long way to go. China has now become the world's largest economy—which simply means that because it has roughly five times the population, its income per head is only one-fifth that of the United States (based on standard statistics, called "purchasing power parities," designed to convert the income in one country into an equivalent income in another). Still, that's much better than it was even 25 years ago, when purchasing-power-parity income per capita was less than 5 percent that of the United States. But at the same time there has been an enormous growth of inequality in China—more millionaires, more billionaires. Although India's growth spurt has not been as long or as fast as China's, it did peak at 9 percent per year. But while fewer people and a smaller percentage of the population moved out of poverty, the increase in millionaires and even billionaires was equally impressive. At the same time, while Africa has finally started to grow, creating an increasing number of middle-class African families, the number of people in poverty has remained very high, with some 415 million people living on less than $1.25 per day. Putting all of this together, one reaches a disappointing result: *overall inequality*, in the way it is conventionally measured (the Gini coefficient, a number ranging from zero, with perfect equality, to one, with perfect *in*equality), has barely budged.

The Piketty Phenomenon

The final two articles of this section are, in part, a response to the enormous success of the economist Thomas Piketty's book *Capitalism in the Twenty-First Century*. The success of that book echoed the growing concern about inequality, a concern expressed in Davos by the world's elite, and consistent with the way my own article "Of the 1 percent, by the 1 Percent, for the 1 Percent" had gone viral. President Obama had in 2013 declared that inequality would in fact be the focus of his attention for the remaining three years of his office. There is, he said, "a dangerous and growing inequality and lack of upward mobility that has jeopardized middle-class America's basic bargain—that if you work hard, you have a chance to get ahead."

Piketty assembled a wealth of data reinforcing what I and others had pointed out about increasing inequality since around 1980, especially at the top. His great contribution was to put this into historical context, showing that the period in which I had grown up, the period after World War II, was an aberration. This was the one period in which all groups in the United States saw an increase in incomes, but those at the bottom saw their incomes grow more than those at the top. The country grew together, and it grew more rapidly than in any other period. Piketty showed that this was, by and large, true of other countries as well. More importantly, he showed that this was historically unusual.

We had come to think of a new *middle-class capitalism*, but the division of society into "classes" (fashionable at least since Marx)—workers and capitalists—seemed quaint and out-of-date. We were *all* middle class.

My "1 Percent" article suggested a new classification: almost everyone was in the *same* boat, but that boat was very different from that on which the 1 percent was traveling. The 99 percent's boat was sinking, or at least not doing very well. Meanwhile, the other ship was sailing magnificently. Piketty showed that the United States was not alone: similar patterns could be seen elsewhere. Economists had misinterpreted what was happening in the aftermath of World War II. Simon Kuznets, one of the founders of our system of national accounts (by which we measure the size of the economy), who received a Nobel Prize in 1971, had suggested that after an initial period of growth, in which there was an increase in inequality, as economies became richer they became more equal. Experiences since 1980 have showed that this was not true. The conclusion that Piketty reached was thus perhaps a natural one: capitalism was characterized by a high degree of inequality. More disturbing was his argument that as capitalists reinvested most of their wealth, their wealth would grow at the rate of interest—and if the rate of interest was greater than the rate of growth of the economy, that meant that the ratio of their capital to national income would rise forever.

I welcomed Piketty's work and the attention it received: we were comrades in arms trying to change the global discourse, to recognize the seriousness of the problem posed by inequality. His work was particularly disturbing because its main policy recommendation, a global tax on capital, seemed well beyond anything attainable in the near (or even distant) future. Did that mean we would simply have to accept ever-increasing inequality? I wrote two articles in part to give an emphatic negative answer to that question. Inequality—at least in the extremes that the United States and some other countries were experiencing it—was not inevitable.

I had, in fact, worried about the question of whether there was a tendency in capitalist economies for ever-increasing inequality in my Ph.D. thesis, completed at MIT in 1966, to which I referred in the introduction. I argued that there was a presumption that the economy would eventually move toward an *equilibrium* degree of inequality of wealth and income, where inequality was neither increasing nor decreasing. Changes in the economy, in social patterns, and in policies could, of course, move the economy from one equilibrium to another—they could result, for instance, in the economy's having *more* inequality.

In that and subsequent work, a number of *centrifugal* and *centripetal* forces have been identified—forces leading to greater inequality, on the one hand, or less inequality, on the other. I had argued that there was typically over the long run a *balance* between these forces. For instance, the fact that the children or grandchildren of very rich people often tend not to do so well, dissipating the family fortune, limits the extent to which inequalities build up. (As the expression goes, from rags to riches and back to rags in three generations.)

The fact that the suburban rich spend more on the education of their children than is spent on the education of the poor is an example of a centrifugal force—the rich transmit their economic advantage to their children. The reality that America is getting more economically segregated means that the strength of this centrifugal force is increasing, and implies that the distribution of wealth and income in the future is likely to be more unequal than it is today (unless something else happens).

Piketty's book posed a puzzle for standard economic theory. Wealth (or "capital") was increasing faster than incomes or the labor supply. Normally, one might expect such an increase in wealth to lead to a diminution in the return to capital—one of the most long-standing principles in economics, learned by every student of the subject, is the law of diminishing returns. Piketty seemed to have quietly *repealed* this law. If the law of diminishing returns worked (as I had assumed in my work), as capital increased (relative to the supply of labor), the interest rate would fall. It would have to fall to the point where capital increased only at the pace of income. There would then not be this ever-increasing inequality of wealth. Piketty is an empiricist. He simply observed that the rate of return on capital was not falling and inferred that there was no reason to believe that it would fall in the future.

As I puzzled over this, it became clear that both of us had not adequately emphasized a key aspect of growing inequality and the seemingly anomalous behavior of the wealth-to-income ratio and the return to capital. Traditionally, wealth had grown as families and firms put aside savings, year after year. But the increase in measured wealth was far greater than could be accounted for by such savings. A careful look at the data showed that much of the increase in wealth was capital gains.

Economists refer to income derived from land as rents; it is income based not on hard work but simply on the ownership of a fixed asset. Larger rents will give rise to a higher price, but a higher price for that asset won't elicit a greater supply. But economists now apply the term "rents" more generally, not only to land rents but also to the returns, say to a monopolist ("monopoly rents"). If rents—not only land rents or the returns to monopoly power and other forms of market exploitation—increase, there will be corresponding capital gains. Much of the increase in inequality in incomes and wealth is associated with an increase in rents and capital gains, reflecting an increased value of real estate and increased market power (exploitation) in many sectors of the economy. But this means that "wealth" and "capital" (as conventionally understood) are distinct concepts. Indeed, it is even possible that *wealth* could be increasing, even as *"capital"* was decreasing. In Piketty's home country of France, the value of land in the Riviera was increasing. But that didn't mean that there was *more* land. The land in the Riviera is the same today as it was fifty years ago. Only the price of land was increasing.

Loose money (for instance, associated with quantitative easing, where the U.S. Fed tripled its balance sheet by buying large amounts of medium- and long-term debt, increasing it by some two trillion dollars over a short time) had led to a flood of credit. Textbook economics suggested that this should increase the quantity of lending and reduce the cost of lending, and both would have helped the American economy. But in a world of globalization, money created by the Fed doesn't have to stay in the United States; it can go anywhere in the world it wants; and it naturally went to economies that were booming—and that wasn't here at home. Money went to where it wasn't needed or wanted; it didn't go to where it was intended to go. But even when money stayed here, it did not stimulate the economy much.

Money can be used to purchase two kinds of things: *produced objects* and *fixed objects* (like land). When money goes to the former, the demand for those objects increases, and output is likely to increase (unless there is a temporary bottleneck in production). But when money goes to fixed objects, there is only a price effect: the *value* of the asset increases, not the quantity. Monetary authorities have, in recent years, done a poor job in steering money. Small businesses that desperately needed cash remained starved, as money increased stock market values at home and asset prices globally. As a result, large fractions of supposedly stimulative monetary policies go into asset price bubbles, like an increase in the price of land. An increase in credit then shows up as an increase in wealth, but one shouldn't confuse what has happened: the country isn't, as a result, *wealthier*. The amount of the assets is just the same.

There is a real danger that in the irrational exuberance concerning the growth of the prices in the fixed assets (the real estate bubble), investments in real capital—the plant and equipment that make the economy function and grow—might even diminish. This focus on land offers a resolution of the conundrums discussed earlier: with *real* capital down or not significantly up (relative to the supply of labor), no wonder that the rate of return to capital has not diminished and average wages have not increased. Asset price bubbles can go on for a *very* long time—though eventually such bubbles break, and prices come down. But even when they come down, they may still be too high—and a new asset price bubble can easily form. For years the world has, in fact, been going from one asset price bubble to another, from the tech bubble to the housing bubble.

Of course, even a bubble can have *some* positive effects for a while—the people who feel wealthy may spend more than they otherwise would, and this may give a boost to the economy. Still, every bubble comes to an end, and it is foolish for policymakers to try to base the recovery from a downturn on the creation of a new bubble—something that the Fed seems to have made into a regular policy since Alan Greenspan assumed office in 1987.[5]

Here's how I attempt to square the circle posed by Piketty's argument: *if* we can avoid a bubble, returns to capital will *eventually* diminish enough that there will not be ever-increasing inequality—but the equilibrium inequality the economy arrives at may well be larger than today's already high and unacceptable level. There are a number of policies—practical policies that can be implemented by individual countries, even without international cooperation—

that can lead to a lower level of equilibrium inequality. Many of these policies will actually result not only in lower inequality but in higher growth, because they will result in more *real* investment.

Moreover, land rents are not the only source of "rents" in our economy. As we observed, much of the wealth of the top is a result of wealth appropriation or other kinds of rent seeking.

When there is an increase in such rent seeking, it can *appear* as if there is an increase in the wealth of the economy—even though the productivity of the economy decreases as a result. For rents, like monopoly rents, can be bought and sold. They are "capitalized." They show up in an increase in stock market value. But such increases in wealth do not mean the economy is wealthier; quite the contrary. Monopoly power reflects an underlying inefficiency. There is a redistribution from consumers to those with market power. Indeed, because of the distortion associated with market power, the productivity of the economy is actually lowered, even though *measured* wealth has increased.

Thus, much of the increase in wealth in our economy is an increase in the *value* (but not the amount) of fixed assets, like land; some of it is the capitalization of increases in monopoly power. Many changes in our economy have given rise to new opportunities for the exercise of monopoly power. At the end of the 19th century, there was a range of such possibilities, as economies of scale led to a few firms' dominating key industries, like steel. But much of this dominance, as in oil and tobacco, had little to do with economies of scale or scope; it was just a matter of brute economic power. Teddy Roosevelt led the charge to break up these monopolies, and he worried as much about the concentration of political power as about the concentration of economic power. It is a lesson that we should today bear more in mind.

In subsequent years we didn't achieve a *perfectly* competitive market in many industrial goods, but it was a far cry from the monopoly capitalism that some feared we were headed toward.[6] In the latter part of the 20th century new sources of market power arose, associated with network externalities. It made life easier if everyone used Microsoft's operating system, and it became the dominant platform for personal computers. It leveraged that market dominance to fend off competitors in other areas and to become dominant in office products like word processing and spread sheets, even though it was not the innovator in any of these areas.

In 1982 the United States broke up the telephone monopoly, AT&T, into seven "Baby Bells." But the incentive to become a monopolist—or at least large enough to exercise market power—is irresistible in the absence of government curbs; and those weren't working very well in this era where so many believed in unfettered markets. The result is that today two telephone companies control about two-thirds of the market. If the Comcast merger with Time Warner goes through, a single company will dominate the "information highway."

As an economist, I understand the drive to get market power. Competitive markets are ruthless, it's hard to survive. Still, standard theory has it that in competitive markets profits are driven down to zero—and that's no fun for an entrepreneur—while in less competitive markets, there can be sustained profits.

There are many other instances where measured wealth can go up, but the underlying economy can be worse off. Consider banks. If we weaken regulation (as we did after Reagan took office), the expected value of their profits can increase, taking into account the bailout money that they can be expected to receive. But those gains come, of course, at the expense of taxpayers. Again, it's a negative-sum game: because of the distortions in the financial sector, our economy is left worse off. Nonetheless, the "market" shows an increase in the value of banks, and no note is made of the losses to taxpayers—the costs that they would have to bear down the line if and when the banks need yet another bailout. Seemingly, wealth has increased as a result of deregulation; in reality, the economy is in worse shape.

We cannot think of wealth as capital. They are distinct concepts.

They can change in markedly different ways. If we think, as suggested earlier, that a variety of centrifugal and centripetal forces are pulling the economy and our society apart—making the great divide larger—or pulling it together, either increasing or decreasing inequality, we can attempt to identify forces that we can change—increasing the strength of the centripetal forces and reducing the strength of the centrifugal forces.

The fact that capital gains are taxed at very low rates is one of the reasons that the rich get richer. They can open up corporate accounts in some offshore center, letting money accumulate there like an unlimited IRA without paying taxes, so long as they don't bring the money back to the United States. These are easy policies to change—policies that almost surely, over the long run, would reduce the extent of inequality of wealth. So too, since so much of the increase in wealth—and wealth inequality—is associated with an increase in the value of land, high land taxes might contribute to lowering inequality—but because the supply of land is (relatively) fixed, there wouldn't be any significant effect on the amount of land in the country.

As these essays point out, much of the inequality that we see today is the result not of true market forces but of "ersatz capitalism" or, as I also refer to it there, "phony capitalism." Making markets act like *true* markets would increase efficiency and economic performance. I also explain that there are many tax policies that can lead to a more efficient and more equitable economy. Many other social and economic policies would do the same. We know what to do to achieve a more egalitarian society.

Inequality is a matter not so much of *capitalism* in the 20th century as of *democracy* in the 20th century. The worry is that our ersatz capitalism—socializing losses while we privatize gains—and our imperfect democracy—closer to a system of one dollar one vote than to one person one vote—will interact to produce disappointment in both the economic and the political spheres.

Notes

1. Danielle Allen, *Our Declaration: A Reading of the Declaration of Independence in Defense of Equality* (New York: Liveright, 2014).
2. This is not quite accurate. Convicted felons in some U.S. states lose their voting rights—a provision that is unusual in democracies.
3. See "Income Inequality in the United States, 1913–1998," with Thomas Piketty, *Quarterly Journal of Economics* 118, no. 1 (2003): 1–39. A longer, updated version is published in A. B. Atkinson and T. Piketty, eds., *Top Incomes over the Twentieth Century* (Oxford: Oxford University Press, 2007). Tables and figures updated to 2012 in Excel format, September 2013, and related materials are available at http://eml.berkeley.edu/~saez/.
4. Originally published as "Complacency in a Leaderless World," *Project Syndicate*, February 6, 2013.
5. For a discussion of this, see George Soros, *The New Paradigm for Financial Markets: The Credit Crisis of 2008 and What It Means* (New York: Public Affairs, 2008).
6. See Joan Robinson, *The Economics of Imperfect Competition* (London: Macmillan, 1933); and Paul Sweezy, *The Theory of Capitalist Development* (London: D. Dobson, 1946).

OF THE 1 PERCENT,
BY THE 1 PERCENT,
FOR THE 1 PERCENT*

IT'S NO USE PRETENDING THAT WHAT HAS OBVIOUSLY HAP-
pened has not in fact happened. The upper 1 percent of Americans are now taking in nearly a quarter of the nation's income
every year. In terms of wealth rather than income, the top 1 percent control 40 percent. Their lot in life has improved considerably.
Twenty-five years ago, the corresponding figures were 12 percent
and 33 percent. One response might be to celebrate the ingenuity
and drive that brought good fortune to these people, and to contend
that a rising tide lifts all boats. That response would be misguided.
While the top 1 percent have seen their incomes rise 18 percent
over the past decade, those in the middle have actually seen their
incomes fall. For men with only high-school degrees, the decline
has been precipitous—12 percent in the last quarter-century alone.
All the growth in recent decades—and more—has gone to those
at the top. In terms of income equality, America lags behind any
country in the old, ossified Europe that President George W. Bush
used to deride. Among our closest counterparts are Russia with its
oligarchs and Iran. While many of the old centers of inequality in
Latin America, such as Brazil, have been striving in recent years,

---

rather successfully, to improve the plight of the poor and reduce gaps in income, America has allowed inequality to grow.

Economists long ago tried to justify the vast inequalities that seemed so troubling in the mid-19th century—inequalities that are but a pale shadow of what we are seeing in America today. The justification they came up with was called "marginal-productivity theory." In a nutshell, this theory associated higher incomes with higher productivity and a greater contribution to society. It is a theory that has always been cherished by the rich. Evidence for its validity, however, remains thin. The corporate executives who helped bring on the recession of the past three years—whose contribution to our society, and to their own companies, has been massively negative—went on to receive large bonuses. In some cases, companies were so embarrassed about calling such rewards "performance bonuses" that they felt compelled to change the name to "retention bonuses" (even if the only thing being retained was bad performance). Those who have contributed great positive innovations to our society, from the pioneers of genetic understanding to the pioneers of the Information Age, have received a pittance compared with those responsible for the financial innovations that brought our global economy to the brink of ruin.

SOME PEOPLE LOOK at income inequality and shrug their shoulders. So what if this person gains and that person loses? What matters, they argue, is not how the pie is divided but the size of the pie. That argument is fundamentally wrong. An economy in which *most* citizens are doing worse year after year—an economy like America's—is not likely to do well over the long haul. There are several reasons for this.

First, growing inequality is the flip side of something else: shrinking opportunity. Whenever we diminish equality of opportunity, it means that we are not using some of our most valuable assets—our people—in the most productive way possible. Second, many of the distortions that lead to inequality—such as those associated with monopoly power and preferential tax treatment for special interests—undermine the efficiency of the economy. This new inequality goes on to create new distortions, undermining efficiency even further. To give just one example, far too many of our most talented young people, seeing the astronomical rewards, have gone into finance rather than into fields that would lead to a more productive and healthy economy.

Third, and perhaps most important, a modern economy requires "collective action"—it needs government to invest in infrastructure, education, and technology. The United States and the world have benefited greatly from government-sponsored research that led to the Internet, to advances in public health, and so on. But America has long suffered from an underinvestment in infrastructure (look at the condition of our highways and bridges, our railroads and airports), in basic research, and in education at all levels. Further cutbacks in these areas lie ahead.

None of this should come as a surprise—it is simply what happens when a society's wealth distribution becomes lopsided. The more divided a society becomes in terms of wealth, the more reluctant the wealthy become to spend money on common needs. The rich don't need to rely on government for parks or education or medical care or personal security—they can buy all these things for themselves. In the process, they become more distant from ordinary people, losing whatever empathy they may once have had. They also worry about strong government—one that could use its powers to adjust the balance, take some of their wealth, and invest it for the common good. The top 1 percent may complain about the kind of government we have in America, but in truth they like it just fine: too gridlocked to redistribute, too divided to do anything but lower taxes.

ECONOMISTS ARE NOT sure how to fully explain the growing inequality in America. The ordinary dynamics of supply and demand have certainly played a role: labor-saving technologies have reduced the demand for many "good" middle-class, blue-collar jobs. Glo-balization has created a worldwide marketplace, pitting expensive unskilled workers in America against cheap unskilled workers overseas. Social changes have also played a role—for instance, the decline of unions, which once represented a third of American workers and now represent about 12 percent.

But one big part of the reason we have so much inequality is that the top 1 percent want it that way. The most obvious exam-ple involves tax policy. Lowering tax rates on capital gains, which is how the rich receive a large portion of their income, has given the wealthiest Americans close to a free ride. Monopolies and near monopolies have always been a source of economic power—from John D. Rockefeller at the beginning of the last century to Bill Gates at the end. Lax enforcement of antitrust laws, especially during Republican administrations, has been a godsend to the top 1 percent. Much of today's inequality is due to manipulation of the financial system, enabled by changes in the rules that have been bought and paid for by the financial industry itself—one if its best investments ever. The government lent money to financial institu-tions at close to zero percent interest and provided generous bail-outs on favorable terms when all else failed. Regulators turned a blind eye to a lack of transparency and to conflicts of interest.

When you look at the sheer volume of wealth controlled by the top 1 percent in this country, it's tempting to see our growing inequality as a quintessentially American achievement—we started way behind the pack, but now we're doing inequality on a world-class level. And it looks as if we'll be building on this achievement for years to come, because what made it possible is self-reinforcing. Wealth begets power, which begets more wealth. During the savings-and-loan scan-dal of the 1980s—a scandal whose dimensions, by today's stan-dards, seem almost quaint—the banker Charles Keating was asked by a congressional committee whether the $1.5 million he had spread among a few key elected officials could actually buy influ-ence. "I certainly hope so," he replied. The Supreme Court, in its recent *Citizens United* case, has enshrined the right of corporations to buy government, by removing limitations on campaign spending. The personal and the political are today in perfect alignment. Virtually all U.S. senators, and most of the representatives in the House, are members of the top 1 percent when they arrive, are kept in office by money from the top 1 percent, and know that if they serve the top 1 percent well they will be rewarded by the top 1 percent when they leave office. By and large, the key executive-branch policymakers on trade and economic policy also come from the top 1 percent. When pharmaceutical companies receive a trillion-dollar gift—through legislation prohibiting the government, the largest buyer of drugs, from bargaining over price—it should not come as cause for wonder. It should not make jaws drop that a tax bill cannot emerge from Congress unless big tax cuts are put in place for the wealthy. Given the power of the top 1 percent, this is the way you would *expect* the system to work.

America's inequality distorts our society in every conceivable way. There is, for one thing, a well-documented lifestyle effect—people outside the top 1 percent increasingly live beyond their means. Trickle-down economics may be a chimera, but trickle-down behaviorism is very real. Inequality massively distorts our foreign policy. The top 1 percent rarely serve in the military—the reality is that the "all-volunteer" army does not pay enough to attract their sons and daughters, and patriotism goes only so far. Plus, the wealthiest class feels no pinch from higher taxes when the nation goes to war: borrowed money will pay for all that. Foreign policy, by definition, is about the balancing of national interests and national resources. With the top 1 percent in charge, and paying no price, the notion of balance and restraint goes out the window. There is no limit to the adventures we can undertake; corporations and contractors stand only to gain. The rules of economic globalization are likewise designed to benefit the rich: they encourage competition among countries for *business*, which drives down taxes on corporations, weakens health and environmental protections, and undermines what used to be viewed as the "core" labor rights, which include the right to collective bargaining. Imagine what the world might look like if the rules were designed instead to encourage competition among countries for *workers*. Governments would compete in providing economic security, low taxes on ordinary wage earners, good education, and a clean environment—things workers care about. But the top 1 percent don't need to care.

Or, more accurately, they think they don't. Of all the costs imposed on our society by the top 1 percent, perhaps the greatest is this: the erosion of our sense of identity, in which fair play, equality of opportunity, and a sense of community are so important. America has long prided itself on being a fair society, where everyone has an equal chance of getting ahead, but the statistics suggest otherwise: the chances of a poor citizen, or even a middle-class citizen, making it to the top in America are smaller than in many countries of Europe. The cards are stacked against them. It is this sense of an unjust system without opportunity that has given rise to the conflagrations in the Middle East: rising food prices and growing and persistent youth unemployment simply served as kindling. With youth unemployment in America at around 20 percent (and in some locations, and among some socio-demographic groups, at twice that); with one out of six Americans desiring a full-time job not able to get one; with one out of seven Americans on food stamps (and about the same number suffering from "food insecurity")—given all this, there is ample evidence that something has blocked the vaunted "trickling down" from the top 1 percent to everyone else. All of this is having the predictable effect of creating alienation—voter turnout among those in their 20s in the last election stood at 21 percent, comparable to the unemployment rate.

In recent weeks we have watched people taking to the streets by the millions to protest political, economic, and social conditions in the oppressive societies they inhabit. Governments have been toppled in Egypt and Tunisia. Protests have erupted in Libya, Yemen, and Bahrain. The ruling families elsewhere in the region look on nervously from their air-conditioned penthouses—will they be next? They are right to worry. These are societies where a minuscule fraction of the population—less than 1 percent—controls the lion's share of the wealth; where wealth is a main determinant of power; where entrenched corruption of one sort or another is a way of life; and where the wealthiest often stand actively in the way of policies that would improve life for people in general.

As we gaze out at the popular fervor in the streets, one question to ask ourselves is this: When will it come to America? In important ways, our own country has become like one of these distant, troubled places.

Alexis de Tocqueville once described what he saw as a chief part of the peculiar genius of American society—something he called "self-interest properly understood." The last two words were the key. Everyone possesses self-interest in a narrow sense: I want what's good for me right now! Self-interest "properly understood" is different. It means appreciating that paying attention to everyone else's self-interest—in other words, the common welfare—is in fact a precondition for one's own ultimate well-being. Tocqueville was not suggesting that there was anything noble or idealistic about this outlook—in fact, he was suggesting the opposite. It was a mark of American pragmatism. Those canny Americans understood a basic fact: looking out for the other guy isn't just good for the soul—it's good for business.

The top 1 percent have the best houses, the best educations, the best doctors, and the best lifestyles, but there is one thing that money doesn't seem to have bought: an understanding that their fate is bound up with how the other 99 percent live. Throughout history, this is something that the top 1 percent eventually do learn. Too late.

THE 1 PERCENT'S
PROBLEM*

Let's start by laying down the baseline premise: inequality in America has been widening for decades. We're all aware of the fact. Yes, there are some on the right who deny this reality, but serious analysts across the political spectrum take it for granted. I won't run through all the evidence here, except to say that the gap between the 1 percent and the 99 percent is vast when looked at in terms of annual income, and even vaster when looked at in terms of wealth—that is, in terms of accumulated capital and other assets. Consider the Walton family: the six heirs to the Walmart empire possess a combined wealth of some $90 billion, which is equivalent to the wealth of the entire bottom 30 percent of U.S. society. (Many at the bottom have zero or negative net worth, especially after the housing debacle.) Warren Buffett put the matter correctly when he said, "There's been class warfare going on for the last 20 years and my class has won."

So, no: there's little debate over the basic fact of widening inequality. The debate is over its meaning. From the right, you sometimes hear the argument made that inequality is basically a good thing: as the rich increasingly benefit, so does everyone else. This argument

---

* *Vanity Fair*, May 31, 2012.

is false: while the rich have been growing richer, most Americans (and not just those at the bottom) have been unable to maintain their standard of living, let alone to keep pace. A typical full-time male worker receives the same income today he did a third of a century ago.

From the left, meanwhile, the widening inequality often elicits an appeal for simple justice: why should so few have so much when so many have so little? It's not hard to see why, in a market-driven age where justice itself is a commodity to be bought and sold, some would dismiss that argument as the stuff of pious sentiment.

Put sentiment aside. There are good reasons why plutocrats should care about inequality anyway—even if they're thinking only about themselves. The rich do not exist in a vacuum. They need a functioning society around them to sustain their position. Widely unequal societies do not function efficiently and their economies are neither stable nor sustainable. The evidence from history and from around the modern world is unequivocal: there comes a point when inequality spirals into economic dysfunction for the whole society, and when it does, even the rich pay a steep price.

Let me run through a few reasons why.

THE CONSUMPTION PROBLEM

When one interest group holds too much power, it succeeds in getting policies that help itself in the short term rather than help society as a whole over the long term. This is what has happened in America when it comes to tax policy, regulatory policy, and public investment. The consequence of channeling gains in income and wealth in one direction only is easy to see when it comes to ordinary household spending, which is one of the engines of the American economy.

It is no accident that the periods in which the broadest cross sections of Americans have reported higher net incomes—when inequality has been reduced, partly as a result of progressive taxation—have been the periods in which the U.S. economy has grown the fastest. It is likewise no accident that the current recession, like the Great Depression, was preceded by large increases in inequality. When too much money is concentrated at the top of society, spending by the average American is necessarily reduced—or at least it will be in the absence of some artificial prop. Moving money from the bottom to the top lowers consumption because higher-income individuals consume, as a fraction of their income, less than lower-income individuals do.

In our imaginations, it doesn't always seem as if this is the case, because spending by the wealthy is so conspicuous. Just look at the color photographs in the back pages of the weekend *Wall Street Journal* of houses for sale. But the phenomenon makes sense when you do the math. Consider someone like Mitt Romney, whose income in 2010 was $21.7 million. Even if Romney chose to live a much more indulgent lifestyle, he would spend only a fraction of that sum in a typical year to support himself and his wife in their several homes. But take the same amount of money and divide it among 500 people—say, in the form of jobs paying $43,400 apiece—and you'll find that almost all of the money gets spent.

The relationship is straightforward and ironclad: as more money becomes concentrated at the top, aggregate demand goes into a decline. Unless something else happens by way of intervention, total demand in the economy will be less than what the economy is capable of supplying—and that means that there will be growing unemployment, which will dampen demand even further. In the 1990s that "something else" was the tech bubble. In the first decade of the 21st century, it was the housing bubble. Today, the only recourse, amid deep recession, is government spending—which is exactly what those at the top are now hoping to curb.

THE "RENT SEEKING" PROBLEM

Here I need to resort to a bit of economic jargon. The word "rent" was originally used, and still is, to describe what someone received for the use of a piece of his land—it's the return obtained by virtue of ownership, and not because of anything one actually does or produces. This stands in contrast to "wages," for example, which connotes compensation for the labor that workers provide. The term "rent" was eventually extended to include monopoly profits—the income that one receives simply from the control of a monopoly. In time, the meaning was expanded still further to include the returns on other kinds of ownership claims. If the government gave a company the exclusive right to import a certain amount of a certain good, such as sugar, then the extra return was called a "quota rent." The acquisition of rights to mine or drill produces a form of rent. So does preferential tax treatment for special interests. In a broad sense, "rent seeking" defines many of the ways by which our current political process helps the rich at the expense of everyone else, including transfers and subsidies from the government, laws that make the marketplace less competitive, laws that allow CEOs to take a disproportionate share of corporate revenue (though Dodd-Frank has made matters better by requiring a nonbinding shareholder vote on compensation at least once every three years), and laws that permit corporations to make profits as they degrade the environment.

The magnitude of rent seeking in our economy, while hard to quantify, is clearly enormous. Individuals and corporations that excel at rent seeking are handsomely rewarded. The financial industry, which now largely functions as a market in speculation rather than a tool for promoting true economic productivity, is the rent-seeking sector par excellence. Rent seeking goes beyond speculation. The financial sector also gets rents out of its domination of the means of payment—the exorbitant credit and debit card fees and also the less well-known fees charged to merchants and passed on, eventually, to consumers. The money it siphons from poor and middle-class Americans through predatory lending practices can be thought of as rents. In recent years, the financial sector has accounted for some 40 percent of all corporate profits. This does not mean that its social contribution sneaks into the plus column, or comes even close. The crisis showed how it could wreak havoc on the economy. In a rent-seeking economy such as ours has become, private returns and social returns are badly out of whack.

In their simplest form, rents are nothing more than redistributions from one part of society to the rent seekers. Much of the inequality in our economy has been the result of rent seeking, because, to a significant degree, rent seeking redistributes money from those at the bottom to those at the top.

But there is a broader economic consequence: the fight to acquire rents is at best a zero-sum activity. Rent seeking makes nothing grow. Efforts are directed toward getting a larger share of the pie rather than increasing the size of the pie. But it's worse than that: rent seeking distorts resource allocations and makes the economy weaker. It is a centripetal force: the rewards of rent seeking become so outsize that more and more energy is directed toward it, at the expense of everything else. Countries rich in natural resources are infamous for rent-seeking activities. It's far easier to get rich in these places by getting access to resources at favorable terms than by producing goods or services that benefit people and increase productivity. That's why these economies have done so badly, in spite of their seeming wealth. It's easy to scoff and say: We're not Nigeria, we're not Congo. But the rent-seeking dynamic is the same.

THE FAIRNESS PROBLEM

People are not machines. They have to be motivated to work hard. If they feel that they are being treated unfairly, it can be difficult to motivate them. This is one of the central tenets of modern labor economics, encapsulated in the so-called efficiency-wage theory, which argues that how firms treat their workers—including how much they pay them—affects productivity. It was, in fact, a theory elaborated nearly a century ago by the great economist Alfred Marshall, who observed that "highly paid labour is generally efficient and therefore not dear labour." In truth, it's wrong to think of this proposition as just a theory: it has been borne out by countless economic experiments.

While people will always disagree over the precise meaning of what constitutes "fair," there is a growing sense in America that the current disparity in income, and the way wealth is allocated in general, is profoundly unfair. There's no begrudging the wealth accrued by those who have transformed our economy—the inventors of the computer, the pioneers of biotechnology. But, for the most part, these are not the people at the top of our economic pyramid. Rather, to a too large extent, it's people who have excelled at rent seeking in one form or another. And, to most Americans, that seems unfair.

People were surprised when the financial firm MF Global, headed by Jon Corzine, suddenly collapsed into bankruptcy last year, leaving victims by the thousands as a result of actions that may prove to have been criminal; but given Wall Street's recent history, I'm not sure people were all that surprised to learn that several MF Global executives would still be getting their bonuses. When corporate CEOs argue that wages have to be reduced or that there must be layoffs in order for companies to compete—and simultaneously increase their own compensation—workers rightly consider what is happening to be unfair. This in turn affects their efforts on the job, their loyalty to the firm, and their willingness to invest in its future. The widespread sense by workers in the Soviet Union that they were being mistreated in exactly this way—exploited by managers who lived high on the hog—played a major role in the hollowing out of the Soviet economy, and in its ultimate collapse.

As the old Soviet joke had it, "They pretend to pay us, and we pretend to work."

In a society in which inequality is widening, fairness is not just about wages and income, or wealth. It's a far more generalized perception. Do I seem to have a stake in the direction society is going, or not? Do I share in the benefits of collective action, or not? If the answer is a loud "no," then brace for a decline in motivation whose repercussions will be felt economically and in all aspects of civic life.

For Americans, one key aspect of fairness is opportunity: everyone should have a fair shot at living the American dream. Horatio Alger stories remain the mythic ideal, but the statistics paint a very different picture: in America, the chances of someone's making it to the top, or even to the middle, from a place near the bottom are lower than in the countries of old Europe or in any other advanced industrial country. Those at the top can take comfort from knowing that their chances of becoming downwardly mobile are lower in America than they are elsewhere.

There are many costs to this lack of opportunity. A large number of Americans are not living up to their potential; we're wasting our most valuable asset, our talent. As we slowly grasp what's been happening, there will be an erosion of our sense of identity, in which America is seen as a fair country. This will have direct economic effects—but also indirect ones, fraying the bonds that hold us together as a nation.

THE MISTRUST PROBLEM

One of the puzzles in modern political economy is why anyone bothers to vote. Very few elections actually turn on the ballot of a single individual. There is a cost to voting—no state has an explicit penalty for staying home, but it takes time and effort to get to the polls—and there is seemingly almost never a benefit. Modern political and economic theory assumes the existence of rational, self-interested actors. On that basis, why anyone would vote is a mystery.

The answer is that we've been inculcated with notions of "civic virtue." It is our responsibility to vote. But civic virtue is fragile. If the belief takes hold that the political and economic systems are stacked, individuals will feel released from their civic obligations. When that social contract is abrogated—when trust between a government and its citizens fails—disillusionment, disengagement, or worse is sure to follow. In the United States today, and in many other democracies around the world, mistrust is on the ascendant.

It's even built in. The head of Goldman Sachs, Lloyd Blankfein, made it perfectly clear: sophisticated investors don't, or at least shouldn't, rely on trust. Those who bought the products his bank sold were consenting adults who should have known better. They should have known that Goldman Sachs had the means, and the incentive, to design products that would fail; that they had the means and the incentive to create asymmetries of information—where they knew more about the products than the buyers did—and the means and the incentive to take advantage of those asymmetries. The people who fell victim to the investment banks were, for the most part, well-off investors. But deceptive credit card practices and predatory lending have left Americans more broadly with a sense that banks are not to be trusted.

Economists often underestimate the role of trust in making our economy work. If every contract had to be enforced by one party taking the other to court, our economy would be in gridlock. Throughout history, the economies that have flourished are those where a handshake is a deal. Without trust, business arrangements based on an understanding that complex details will be worked out later are no longer feasible. Without trust, each participant looks around to see how and when those with whom he is dealing will betray him.

Widening inequality is corrosive of trust: in its economic impact, think of it as the universal solvent. It creates an economic world in which even the winners are wary. But the losers! In every transaction—in every encounter with a boss or business or bureaucrat—they see the hand of someone out to take advantage of them.

Nowhere is trust more important than in politics and the public sphere. There, we have to act together. It's easier to act together when most individuals are in similar situations—when most of us are, if not in the same boat, at least in boats within a range of like sizes. But growing inequality makes it clear that our fleet looks different—it's a few mega-yachts surrounded by masses of people in dugout canoes, or clinging to flotsam—which helps explain our vastly differing views of what the government should do.

Today's widening inequality extends to almost everything—police protection, the condition of local roads and utilities, access to decent health care, access to good public schools. As higher education becomes more important—not just for individuals but for the future of the whole U.S. economy—those at the top push for university budget cuts and tuition hikes, on the one hand, and cutbacks in guaranteed student loans, on the other. To the extent that they advocate student loans at all, it's as another opportunity for rent seeking: loans to for-profit schools, without standards; loans that are non-dischargeable even in bankruptcy; loans designed as another way for those at the top to exploit those aspiring to get out of the bottom.

THE "BE SELFISH" SOLUTION

Many, if not most, Americans possess a limited understanding of the nature of the inequality in our society. They know that something has gone wrong, but they underestimate the harm that inequality does even as they overestimate the cost of taking action. These mistaken beliefs, which have been reinforced by ideological rhetoric, are having a catastrophic effect on politics and economic policy.

There is no good reason why the 1 percent, with their good educations, their ranks of advisers, and their much-vaunted business acumen, should be so misinformed. The 1 percent in generations past often knew better. They knew that there would be no top of the pyramid if there wasn't a solid base—that their own position was precarious if society itself was unsound. Henry Ford, not remembered as one of history's softies, understood that the best thing he could do for himself and his company was to pay his workers a decent wage, because he wanted them to work hard and he wanted them to be able to buy his cars. Franklin D. Roosevelt, a purebred patrician, understood that the only way to save an essentially capitalist America was not only to spread the wealth, through taxation and social programs, but to put restraints on capitalism itself, through regulation. Roosevelt and the economist John Maynard Keynes, while reviled by the capitalists, succeeded in saving capitalism from the capitalists. Richard Nixon, known to this day as a manipulative cynic, concluded that social peace and economic stability could best be secured by investment—and invest he did, heavily, in Medicare, Head Start, Social Security, and efforts to clean up the environment. Nixon even floated the idea of a guaranteed annual income.

So, the advice I'd give to the 1 percent today is: Harden your hearts. When invited to consider proposals to reduce inequality— by raising taxes and investing in education, public works, health care, and science—put any latent notions of altruism aside and reduce the idea to one of unadulterated self-interest. Don't embrace it because it helps other people. Just do it for yourself.

SLOW GROWTH AND INEQUALITY ARE POLITICAL CHOICES. WE CAN CHOOSE OTHERWISE.*

A RICH COUNTRY WITH MILLIONS OF POOR PEOPLE. A country that prides itself on being the land of opportunity, but in which a child's prospects are more dependent on the income and education of his or her parents than in other advanced countries. A country that believes in fair play, but in which the richest often pay a smaller percentage of their income in taxes than those less well off. A country in which children every day pledge allegiance to the flag, asserting that there is "justice for all," but in which, increasingly, there is only justice for those who can afford it. These are the contradictions that the United States is gradually and painfully struggling to come to terms with as it begins to comprehend the enormity of the inequalities that mark its society—inequities that are greater than in any other advanced country.

Those who strive not to think about this issue suggest that this is just about the "politics of envy." Those who discuss the issue are accused of fomenting class warfare. But as we have come to grasp the causes and consequences of these inequities we have come to understand that this is not about envy. The extreme to which inequality has grown in the United States and the manner in which

---

* *Washington Monthly*, December 2014.

these inequities arise undermine our economy. Too much of the wealth at the top of the ladder arises from exploitation—whether from the exercise of monopoly power, from taking advantage of deficiencies in corporate governance laws to divert large amounts of corporate revenues to pay CEOs' outsized bonuses unrelated to true performance, or from a financial sector devoted to market manipulation, predatory and discriminatory lending, and abusive credit card practices. Too much of the poverty at the bottom of the income spectrum is due to economic discrimination and the failure to provide adequate education and health care to the nearly one out of five children growing up poor.

The growing debate about inequality in America today is, above all, about the nature of our society, our vision of who we are, and others' vision of us. We used to think of ourselves as a middle-class society, where each generation was better off than the last. At the foundation of our democracy was the middle class—the modern-day version of the small, property-owning American farmer whom Thomas Jefferson saw as the backbone of the country. It was understood that the best way to grow was to build out from the middle—rather than trickle down from the top. This commonsense perspective has been verified by studies at the International Monetary Fund, which demonstrate that countries with greater equality perform better—higher growth, more stability. It was one of the main messages of my book *The Price of Inequality*. Because of our tolerance for inequality, even the quintessential American dream has been shown to be a myth: America is less of a land of opportunity than even most countries of "old Europe."

The articles in this special edition of the *Washington Monthly* describe the way that America's inequality plays out at each stage of one's life, with several articles focusing in particular on education. We now know that there are huge disparities even as children enter kindergarten. These grow larger over time, as the children of the rich, living in rich enclaves, get a better education than the one received by those attending schools in poorer areas. Economic segregation has become the order of the day, so much so that even those well-off and well-intentioned selective colleges that instituted programs of economic affirmative action—explicitly trying to increase the fraction of their student body from lower socioeconomic groups—have struggled to do so. The children of the poor can afford neither the advanced degrees that are increasingly required for employment nor the unpaid internships that provide the alternative route to "good" jobs.

Similar stories could be told about each of the dimensions of America's outsized inequality. Take health care. America is unique among the advanced countries in not recognizing access to health care as a basic human right. And that means if you are a poor American, your prospects of getting adequate, let alone good, medical care are worse than in other advanced countries. Even after passage of the Affordable Care Act (ACA), almost two dozen states have rejected expanding vitally needed Medicaid, and more than forty million Americans still lacked health insurance at the beginning of 2014. The dismal statistics concerning America's health care system are well known: while we spend more—far more—on health care (both per capita and as a percentage of gross domestic product) than other countries, health outcomes are worse. In Australia, for instance, spending on health care per capita is just over two-thirds that in the United States, yet health outcomes are better—including a life expectancy that is a remarkable three years longer.

Two of the reasons for our dismal health statistics are related to inequalities at the top and the bottom of our society—monopoly profits reaped by drug companies, medical device makers, health insurers, and highly concentrated provider networks drive prices, and inequality, up while the lack of access to timely care for the poor, including preventive medicine, makes the population sicker and more costly to treat. The ACA is helping on both accounts. The health insurance exchanges are designed to promote competition. And the whole act is designed to increase access. The numbers suggest it's working. As for costs, the widespread predictions that Obamacare would cause massive health care inflation have proven false, as the rate of increase in health care prices has remained comparatively moderate over the last several years, showing once again that there is no necessary trade-off between fairness and efficiency. The first year of the ACA showed significant increases in coverage—far more significant in those states that implemented the Medicaid expansion than in those that refused to do so. But the ACA was a compromise, leaving out dental and long-term extended care insurance.

Inequities in health care, then, are still with us, beginning even before birth. The poor are more likely to be exposed to environmental hazards, and mothers have less access to good prenatal care. The result is infant mortality rates that are comparable to those in some developing countries alongside a higher incidence of low birth weight (systemically correlated with poor lifetime prospects) than in other advanced countries. Lack of access to comprehensive health care for the 20 percent of American children growing up in poverty, combined with lack of access to adequate nutrition, makes success in school even less likely. With the cheapest form of food often being unhealthy carbohydrates, the poor are more likely to face problems of childhood diabetes and obesity. The inequities continue throughout life—culminating in dramatically different statistics on life expectancy.

All well and good, you might say: it would be nice if we could give free health care to all, free college education to all, but these are dreams that have to be tamed by the harsh realities of what we can afford. Already the country has a large deficit. Proposals to create a more equal society would make the large deficit even larger—so the argument goes. America is especially constrained because it has assumed the costly mission of ensuring peace and security for the world.

This is nonsense, on several counts.

The real strength of the United States is derived from its "soft power," not its military power. But growing inequality is sapping our standing in the world from within. Can an economic system that provides so little opportunity—where real median household income (half above, half below, after adjusting for inflation) is lower today than it was a quarter-century ago—provide a role model that others seek to emulate, even if a few at the very top have done very well?

Moreover, what we can afford is as much a matter of priorities as anything else. Other countries, such as the nations of Scandinavia, have, for instance, managed to provide good health care to all, virtually free college education for all, and good public transportation, *and* have done just as well, or even better, on standard metrics of economic performance: incomes per head and growth are at least comparable. Even some countries that are far poorer than the United States (such as Mauritius, in the Indian Ocean east of Africa) have managed to provide free college education and better access to health care. A nation must make choices, and these countries have made different ones: they may spend less on their military, they may spend less on prisons, they may tax more.

Besides, many of the distributional issues are related not to how much we spend but whom we spend it on. If we include within our expenditures the "tax expenditures" buried in our tax system, we effectively spend a lot more on the housing of the rich than is generally recognized. Interest deductability on a mega-mansion could easily be worth $25,000 a year. And alone among advanced economies, the United States tends to invest more in schools with richer student bodies than in those with mostly poor students—an effect of U.S. school districts' dependence on local tax bases for funding. Interestingly, according to some calculations, the entire deficit can be attributed to our inefficient and inequitable health care system: if we had a better health care system—of the kind that provided more equality at lower cost, such as those in so many European countries—we arguably wouldn't even have a federal budget deficit today.

Or consider this: if we provided more opportunity to the poor, including better education and an economic system that ensured access to jobs with decent pay, then perhaps we would not spend so much on prisons—in some states spending on prisons has at times exceeded that on universities. The poor instead would be better able to seize new employment opportunities, in turn making our economy more productive. And if we had better public transportation systems that made it easier and more affordable for working-class people to commute to where jobs are available, then a higher percentage of our population would be working and paying taxes. If, like the Scandinavian countries, we provided better child care and had more active labor market policies that assisted workers in moving from one job to another, we would have a higher labor-force participation rate—and the enhanced growth would yield more tax revenues. It pays to invest in people.

This brings me to the final point: we could impose a fair tax system, raising more revenue, improving equity, and boosting economic growth while reducing distortions in our economy and our society. (That was the central finding of my 2014 Roosevelt Institute white paper, "Reforming Taxation to Promote Growth and Equity.") For instance, if we just imposed the same taxes on the returns to capital that we impose on those who work for a living, we could raise some $2 trillion over ten years. "Loopholes" does not adequately describe the flaws in our tax system; "gaps" might be better. Closing them might end the specter of the very rich almost proudly disclosing that they pay a tax rate on their disclosed income at half the rate of those with less income, and that they keep their money in tax havens like the Cayman Islands. No one can claim that the inhabitants of these small islands know how to manage money better than the wizards of Wall Street; but it seems as though that money grows better in the sunshine of these beach resorts!

One of the few advantages of there being so much money at the top of the income ladder, with close to a quarter of all income going to the top 1 percent, is that slight increases in taxes at the top can now raise large amounts of money. And because so much of the money at the top comes from exploitation (or, as economists prefer to call it, "rent seeking"—that is, seizing a larger share of the national pie rather than increasing its size), higher taxes at the top do not seem to have much of an adverse effect on economic performance.

Then there's our corporate tax rate. If we actually made corporations pay what they are supposed to pay and eliminated loopholes, we would raise hundreds of billions of dollars. With the right redesign, we could even get more employment and investment in the United States. True, U.S. corporations face one of the higher *official* corporate tax rates among the advanced countries; but the reality is otherwise—as a share of corporate income actually paid, our federal corporate taxes are just 13 percent of reported worldwide income. By most accounts, the amount of taxes actually paid (as a percentage of profits) is no higher than the average of other advanced countries. Apple Inc., Google Inc., and General Electric Co. have become the poster children of American ingenuity—making products that are the envy of the rest of the world. But they are using too much of that ingenuity to figure out how to avoid paying their fair share of taxes. Yet they and other U.S. corporations make full use of ideas and innovations produced with the support of the U.S. government, starting with the Internet itself. At the same time they rely on the talent produced by the country's first-rate universities, all of which receive extensive support from the federal government. They even turn to the U.S. government to demand better treatment from our trading partners.

Corporations argue that they would not engage in so much despicable tax avoidance if tax rates were lower. But there is a far better solution, and one that the individual U.S. states have discovered: have corporations pay taxes based on the economic activity they conduct in the United States, on the basis of a simple formula reflecting their sales, their production, and their research activities here, and tax corporations that invest in the United States at lower rates than those that don't. In this way we could increase investment and employment here at home—a far cry from the current system, in which we in effect encourage even U.S. corporations to produce elsewhere. (Even if U.S. taxes are no higher than the average, there are some tax havens—like Ireland—that are engaged in a race to the bottom, trying to recruit companies to make their country their tax home.) Such a reform would end the corporate stampede toward "inversions," changing a corporation's tax home to avoid taxes. Where they claim their home office is would make little difference; only where they actually do business would.

Other sources of revenue would benefit our economy and our society. Two basic principles of taxation are that it is better to tax bad things than good; and it is better to tax factors in what economists call "inelastic supply"—meaning that the amounts produced and sold won't change when taxes are imposed on them. Thus, if we taxed pollution in all of its forms—including carbon emissions—we could raise hundreds of billions of dollars every year, and have a better environment. Similarly, appropriately designed taxes on the financial sector would not only raise considerable amounts of money but also discourage banks from imposing costs on others—as when they polluted the global economy with toxic mortgages.

The $700 billion bank bailout pales in comparison to what the bankers' fecklessness has cost our economy and our society—trillions of dollars in lost GDP, millions of Americans thrown out of their homes and jobs. Yet few in the financial world have been held accountable.

If we required the banks to pay but a fraction of the costs they have imposed on others, we would then have further funds to undo some of the damage that they caused by their discriminatory and predatory lending practices, which moved money from the bottom of the economic pyramid to the top. And by imposing even slight taxes on Wall Street's speculative activities via a financial transactions tax, we would raise much-needed revenue, decrease speculation (thus increasing economic stability), and encourage more productive use of our scarce resources, including the most valuable one: talented young Americans.

Similarly, by taxing land, oil, and minerals more, and forcing those who extract resources from public land to pay the full values of these resources, which rightly belong to *all* the people, we could then spend those proceeds for public investments—for instance, in education, technology, and infrastructure—without resulting in less land, less oil, fewer minerals. (Even if they are taxed more, these resources won't go on strike; they won't leave the country!) The result: increased long-term investments in our economy would pay substantial future dividends in higher economic productivity and growth—and if the money was spent right, we could have more shared prosperity. The question is not whether we can afford to do more about our inequality; it is whether we can afford *not* to do more. The debate in America is not about eliminating inequality. It is simply about moderating it and restoring the American dream.

INEQUALITY GOES GLOBAL*

THE WORLD ECONOMIC FORUM'S ANNUAL MEETING IN Davos has lost some of its precrisis panache. After all, before the meltdown in 2008, the captains of finance and industry could trumpet the virtues of globalization, technology, and financial liberalization, which supposedly heralded a new era of relentless growth. The benefits would be shared by all, if only they would do "the right thing."

Those days are gone. But Davos remains a good place to get a sense of the global zeitgeist.

It goes without saying that developing and emerging-market countries no longer look at the advanced countries as they once did. But a remark by one mining company executive from a developing country caught the spirit of change. In response to one development expert's heartfelt despair that unfair trade treaties and unfulfilled promises of aid have cost the developed countries their moral authority, he retorted: "The West never had any moral authority." Colonialism, slavery, the splintering of Africa into small countries, and a long history of resource exploitation may be matters of the

* *Project Syndicate*, February 6, 2013.

distant past to the perpetrators, but not so to those who suffered as a result.

If there is a single topic that concerned the assembled leaders the most, it is economic inequality. The shift in the debate from just a year ago seems dramatic: no one even mentions the notion of trickle-down economics anymore, and few are willing to argue that there is a close congruence between social contributions and private rewards.

While the realization that America is *not* the land of opportunity that it has long claimed to be is as disconcerting to others as it is to Americans, inequality of opportunity at the global scale is even greater. One cannot really claim that the world is "flat" when a typical African receives investment in his or her human capital of a few hundred dollars, while rich Americans get a gift from their parents and society in excess of a half-million dollars.

A high point of the meeting was the speech by Christine Lagarde, the International Monetary Fund's managing director, who stressed the marked change in her institution, at least at the top: deep concern about women's rights; renewed emphasis on the link between inequality and instability; and recognition that collective bargaining and minimum wages could play an important role in reducing inequality. If only the IMF programs in Greece and elsewhere fully reflected these sentiments!

The Associated Press organized a sobering session on technology and unemployment: Can countries (particularly in the developed world) create new jobs—especially good jobs—in the face of modern technology that has replaced workers with robots and other machines in any task that can be routinized?

Overall, the private sector in Europe and America has been unable to create many good jobs since the beginning of the current century. Even in China and other parts of the world with growing manufacturing sectors, productivity improvements—often related to job-killing automated processes—account for most of the growth in output. Those suffering the most are the young, whose life prospects will be badly hurt by the extended periods of unemployment that they face today.

But most of those in Davos put aside these problems to celebrate the euro's survival. The dominant note was one of complacency—or even optimism. The "Draghi put"—the notion that the European Central Bank, with its deep pockets, would and could do whatever necessary to save the euro and each of the crisis countries—seemed to have worked, at least for a while. The temporary calm provided some support for those who claimed that what was required, above all, was a restoration of confidence. The hope was that Draghi's promises would be a *costless* way of providing that confidence, because they would never have to be fulfilled.

Critics repeatedly pointed out that the fundamental contradictions had not been resolved, and that if the euro was to survive in the long run, there would have to be a fiscal and banking union, which would require more political unification than most Europeans are willing to accept. But much of what was said in and around the meetings reflected a deep lack of solidarity. One very senior government official of a northern European country did not even put down his fork when interrupted by an earnest dinner companion who pointed out that many Spaniards now eat out of garbage cans. They should have reformed earlier, he replied, as he continued to eat his steak.

IMF growth forecasts released during the Davos meeting highlight the extent to which the world has become decoupled: GDP growth in the advanced industrial countries is expected to be 1.4 percent this year, while developing countries continue to grow at a robust 5.5 percent annual rate.

While Western leaders talked about a new emphasis on growth and employment, they offered no concrete policies backing these aspirations. In Europe, there was continued emphasis on austerity, with self-congratulations on the progress made so far, and a reaffirmation of resolve to continue along a course that has now plunged

Europe as a whole into recession—and the United Kingdom into a triple-dip downturn.

Perhaps the most optimistic note came from the emerging markets: while the risk of globalization was that it implied a new interdependence, so that flawed economic policies in the U.S. and Europe could torpedo developing countries' economies, the more successful emerging markets have managed globalization well enough to sustain growth in the face of failures in the West.

With the U.S. politically paralyzed by the Republicans' infantile political tantrums, and Europe focused on ensuring the survival of the ill-conceived euro project, the lack of global leadership was a major complaint at Davos. In the last 25 years, we have moved from a world dominated by two superpowers to one dominated by one, and now to a leaderless, multi-polar world. While we may talk about the G-7, or G-8, or G-20, the more apt description is G-0. We will have to learn how to live, and thrive, in this new world.

INEQUALITY IS A CHOICE*

I T'S WELL KNOWN BY NOW THAT INCOME AND WEALTH inequality in most rich countries, especially the United States, have soared in recent decades and, tragically, worsened even more since the Great Recession. But what about the rest of the world? Is the gap between countries narrowing, as rising economic powers like China and India have lifted hundreds of millions of people from poverty? And within poor and middle-income countries, is inequality getting worse or better? Are we moving toward a more fair world, or a more unjust one?

These are complex questions, and new research by a World Bank economist named Branko Milanovic, along with other scholars, points the way to some answers.

Starting in the 18th century, the industrial revolution produced giant wealth for Europe and North America. Of course, inequality within these countries was appalling—think of the textile mills of Liverpool and Manchester, England, in the 1820s, and the tenements of the Lower East Side of Manhattan and the South Side of Chicago in the 1890s—but the gap between the rich and the rest, as a global phenomenon, widened even more, right up through

---

* *New York Times*, October 13, 2013.

about World War II. To this day, inequality between countries is far greater than inequality within countries.

But starting around the fall of Communism in the late 1980s, economic globalization accelerated and the gap between nations began to shrink. The period from 1988 to 2008 "might have witnessed the first decline in global inequality between world citizens since the Industrial Revolution," Mr. Milanovic, who was born in the former Yugoslavia and is the author of *The Haves and the Have-Nots: A Brief and Idiosyncratic History of Global Inequality*, wrote in a paper published last November. While the gap between some regions has markedly narrowed—namely, between Asia and the advanced economies of the West—huge gaps remain. Average global incomes, by country, have moved closer together over the last several decades, particularly on the strength of the growth of China and India. But overall equality across humanity, considered as individuals, has improved very little. (The Gini coefficient, a measurement of inequality, improved by just 1.4 points from 2002 to 2008.)

So while nations in Asia, the Middle East, and Latin America, as a whole, might be catching up with the West, the poor everywhere are left behind, even in places like China where they've benefited somewhat from rising living standards.

From 1988 to 2008, Mr. Milanovic found, people in the world's top 1 percent saw their incomes increase by 60 percent, while those in the bottom 5 percent had no change in their income. And while median incomes have greatly improved in recent decades, there are still enormous imbalances: 8 percent of humanity takes home 50 percent of global income; the top 1 percent alone takes home 15 percent. Income gains have been greatest among the global elite— financial and corporate executives in rich countries—and the great "emerging middle classes" of China, India, Indonesia, and Brazil. Who lost out? Africans, some Latin Americans, and people in post-Communist Eastern Europe and the former Soviet Union, Mr. Milanovic found.

The United States provides a particularly grim example for the world. And because, in so many ways, America often "leads the world," if others follow America's example, it does not portend well for the future.

On the one hand, widening income and wealth inequality in America is part of a trend seen across the Western world. A 2011 study by the Organization for Economic Cooperation and Development found that income inequality first started to rise in the late '70s and early '80s in America and Britain (and also in Israel). The trend became more widespread starting in the late '80s. Within the last decade, income inequality grew even in traditionally egalitarian countries like Germany, Sweden, and Denmark. With a few exceptions—France, Japan, Spain—the top 10 percent of earners in most advanced economies raced ahead, while the bottom 10 percent fell further behind.

But the trend was not universal, or inevitable. Over these same years, countries like Chile, Mexico, Greece, Turkey, and Hungary managed to reduce (in some cases very high) income inequality significantly, suggesting that inequality is a product of political and not merely macroeconomic forces. It is not true that inequality is an inevitable byproduct of globalization, the free movement of labor, capital, goods and services, and technological change that favors better-skilled and better-educated employees.

Of the advanced economies, America has some of the worst disparities in incomes and opportunities, with devastating macroeconomic consequences. The gross domestic product of the United States has more than quadrupled in the last 40 years and nearly doubled in the last 25, but as is now well known, the benefits have gone to the top—and increasingly to the very, very top.

Last year, the top 1 percent of Americans took home 22 percent of the nation's income; the top 0.1 percent, 11 percent. Ninety-five percent of all income gains since 2009 have gone to the top 1 percent. Recently released census figures show that median income in America hasn't budged in almost a quarter-century. The typical American man makes less than he did 45 years ago (after adjusting for inflation);

men who graduated from high school but don't have four-year college degrees make almost 40 percent less than they did four decades ago.

American inequality began its upswing 30 years ago, along with tax decreases for the rich and the easing of regulations on the financial sector. That's no coincidence. It has worsened as we have underinvested in our infrastructure, education and health care systems, and social safety nets. Rising inequality reinforces itself by corroding our political system and our democratic governance.

And Europe seems all too eager to follow America's bad example. The embrace of austerity, from Britain to Germany, is leading to high unemployment, falling wages, and increasing inequality. Officials like Angela Merkel, the newly reelected German chancellor, and Mario Draghi, president of the European Central Bank, argue that Europe's problems are a result of a bloated welfare spending. But that line of thinking has only taken Europe into recession (and even depression). That things may have bottomed out—that the recession may be "officially" over—is little comfort to the 27 million out of a job in the EU. On both sides of the Atlantic, the austerity fanatics say, march on: these are the bitter pills that we need to take to achieve prosperity But prosperity for whom?

Excessive financialization—which helps explain Britain's dubious status as the second-most-unequal country, after the United States, among the world's most advanced economies—also helps explain the soaring inequality. In many countries, weak corporate governance and eroding social cohesion have led to increasing gaps between the pay of chief executives and that of ordinary workers—not yet approaching the 500-to-1 level for America's biggest companies (as estimated by the International Labor Organization) but still greater than prerecession levels. (Japan, which has curbed executive pay, is a notable exception.) American innovations in rent seeking—enriching oneself not by making the size of the economic pie bigger but by manipulating the system to seize a larger slice—have gone global.

Asymmetric globalization has also exerted its toll around the globe. Mobile capital has demanded that workers make wage concessions and governments make tax concessions. The result is a race to the bottom. Wages and working conditions are being threatened. Pioneering firms like Apple, whose work relies on enormous advances in science and technology, many of them financed by government, have also shown great dexterity in avoiding taxes. They are willing to take, but not to give back.

Inequality and poverty among children are a special moral disgrace. They flout right-wing suggestions that poverty is a result of laziness and poor choices; children can't choose their parents. In America, nearly one in four children lives in poverty; in Spain and Greece, about one in six; in Australia, Britain, and Canada, more than one in ten. None of this is inevitable. Some countries have made the choice to create more equitable economies: South Korea, where a half-century ago just one in ten people attained a college degree, today has one of the world's highest university completion rates.

For these reasons, I see us entering a world divided not just between the haves and have-nots, but also between those countries that do nothing about it, and those that do. Some countries will be successful in creating shared prosperity—the only kind of prosperity that I believe is truly sustainable. Others will let inequality run amok. In these divided societies, the rich will hunker in gated communities, almost completely separated from the poor, whose lives will be almost unfathomable to them, and vice versa. I've visited societies that seem to have chosen this path. They are not places in which most of us would want to live, whether in their cloistered enclaves or their desperate shantytowns.

DEMOCRACY IN THE
21ST CENTURY*

THE RECEPTION IN THE UNITED STATES, AND IN OTHER advanced economies, of Thomas Piketty's recent book *Capital in the Twenty-First Century* attests to growing concern about rising inequality. His book lends further weight to the already overwhelming body of evidence concerning the soaring share of income and wealth at the very top.

Piketty's book, moreover, provides a different perspective on the 30 or so years that followed the Great Depression and World War II, viewing this period as a historical anomaly, perhaps caused by the unusual social cohesion that cataclysmic events can stimulate. In that era of rapid economic growth, prosperity was widely shared, with all groups advancing, but with those at the bottom seeing larger percentage gains.

Piketty also sheds new light on the "reforms" sold by Ronald Reagan and Margaret Thatcher in the 1980s as growth enhancers from which all would benefit. Their reforms were followed by slower growth and heightened global instability, and what growth did occur benefited mostly those at the top.

---

* *Project Syndicate*, September 1, 2014.

But Piketty's work raises fundamental issues concerning both economic theory and the future of capitalism. He documents large increases in the wealth/output ratio. In standard theory, such increases would be associated with a fall in the return to capital and an increase in wages. But today the return to capital does not seem to have diminished, and wages have not increased as one could have expected. (In the U.S., for example, average wages have stagnated over the past four decades.)

The most obvious explanation is that the increase in measured wealth does not correspond to an increase in productive capital— and the data seem consistent with this interpretation. Much of the increase in wealth stemmed from an increase in the value of real estate. Before the 2008 financial crisis, a real estate bubble was evident in many countries; even now, there may not have been a full "correction." The rise in value also can represent competition among the rich for "positional" goods—a house on the beach or an apartment on New York City's Fifth Avenue.

Sometimes an increase in measured financial wealth corresponds to little more than a shift from "unmeasured" wealth to measured wealth—shifts that can actually reflect deterioration in overall economic performance. If monopoly power increases, or firms (like banks) develop better methods of exploiting ordinary consumers, it will show up as higher profits and, when capitalized, as an increase in financial wealth.

But when this happens, of course, societal well-being and economic efficiency fall, even as officially measured wealth rises. We simply do not take into account the corresponding diminution of the value of human capital—the wealth of workers.

Moreover, if banks succeed in using their political influence to socialize losses and retain more and more of their ill-gotten gains, the *measured* wealth in the financial sector increases. We do not measure the corresponding diminution of taxpayers' wealth. Likewise, if corporations convince the government to overpay for their products (as the major drug companies have succeeded in doing), or are given access to public resources at below-market prices (as mining companies have succeeded in doing), reported financial wealth increases, though the wealth of ordinary citizens does not.

What we have been observing—wage stagnation and rising inequality, even as wealth increases—does not reflect the workings of a normal market economy, but of what I call "ersatz capitalism." The problem may not be with how markets *should* work, but with our political system, which has failed to ensure that markets are competitive, and has designed rules that sustain distorted markets in which corporations and the rich can (and unfortunately do) exploit everyone else.

Markets, of course, do not exist in a vacuum. There *have* to be rules of the game, and these are established through political processes. High levels of economic inequality in countries like the U.S. and, increasingly, in those that have followed its economic model lead to political inequality. In such a system, opportunities for economic advancement become unequal as well, reinforcing low levels of social mobility.

Thus, Piketty's forecast of still higher levels of inequality does not reflect the inexorable laws of economics. Simple changes—including higher capital-gains and inheritance taxes, greater spending to broaden access to education, rigorous enforcement of anti-trust laws, corporate-governance reforms that circumscribe executive pay, and financial regulations that rein in banks' ability to exploit the rest of society—would reduce inequality and increase equality of opportunity markedly.

If we get the rules of the game right, we might even be able to restore the rapid and *shared* economic growth that characterized the middle-class societies of the mid-20th century. The main question confronting us today is not really about capitalism in the 21st century. It is about democracy in the 21st century.

PHONY CAPITALISM*

AMERICANS ARE FINALLY BEGINNING TO APPRECIATE THE magnitude of the inequalities in income and wealth that mark our society. Lately, this realization has been helped along by an unexpected source: the French economist Thomas Piketty, whose *Capital in the Twenty-First Century* is the surprise bestseller of the year. Piketty has collected the most extensive evidence available of the increases in economic inequality and inherited wealth over the past forty years, which are creating a new plutocracy. But while Piketty is right about the severity of the problem, he is not completely right about its cause—and how to fix it. If Americans take the wrong lessons from his work, we may fail to make the changes that could actually address our inequality problem.

Bluntly put, Piketty argues that inequality is the natural outcome of capitalism. In his view, the long period of shared prosperity that characterized the middle of the 20th century was a historical anomaly, while the disparities of the Gilded Age and our own time are the norm. But what is practiced in the United States today is perhaps best described as an ersatz capitalism designed to create inequalities. This fact was made abundantly clear during the finan-

---

* *Harper's Magazine*, September 2014.

cial crisis, when we socialized losses but allowed the banks to privatize profits, extended largesse to the victimizers but did little to help
the victims who were losing their homes and jobs.

Of course, there is no such thing as a "purely" capitalist system.
We have always had a mixed economy, relying on the government
for investment in education, technology, and infrastructure. The
most innovative and successful industries in the U.S. economy
(tech and biotech) rest on foundations provided by government
research. A well-functioning economy requires a balance between
the public and private sectors, with essential public investments
and an adequately funded system of social protection. All this
requires taxation.

A well-designed tax system can do more than just raise money—
it can be used to improve economic efficiency and reduce inequality. Our current system does just the opposite. Piketty's proposal for
addressing inequality through taxation—a global wealth tax—is a
political nonstarter, whatever one thinks of its merits. But there are
steps the United States—home to the worst inequality among the
advanced countries—can take on its own. With a sensible reform of
our domestic tax code, we can simultaneously raise money, improve
the performance of our economy, and address some of our biggest
social problems—not just inequality but joblessness and looming
environmental catastrophe.

AT THE TOP of the list of concerns in assessing any tax proposal
should be its impact on the distribution of income. But three broad
principles should also help guide thinking. First, it is better to tax
bad things than good things—to tax pollution and speculation, say,
than work and savings. Second, it is better to tax things like land,
oil, and other natural resources, which don't disappear when they
are taxed (factors in inelastic supply, as economists put it). These
two principles reflect a more general third principle: incentives
matter. Taxes should encourage activities that are of widespread

benefit and discourage those that are costly to our society. There are a host of reforms that would increase equity while conforming to these principles.

To begin with, corporate taxation should encourage firms to invest and create jobs in America by lowering taxes on those that do so relative to those that do not. Taxing multinational firms on their global income would close what might be called the Apple–Google loophole. Globalization has given these companies new opportunities to dodge taxes by claiming that their immense profits originate not from the ingenuity of their American researchers or the seemingly limitless demand from American consumers for their products but from a few employees scattered across low-tax jurisdictions, such as Ireland. By taxing all corporations on the basis of production and sales here, we can raise significant revenues to create jobs and spur growth.

In addition, there ought to be a special set of taxes on the financial sector. Given the role this sector played in the financial crisis, it is natural that it should pay some of the costs. Well-designed financial-sector taxes would increase the sector's performance and efficiency and induce it to do better what it's *supposed* to do.

While Piketty tells us that market capitalism naturally creates obscene levels of inequality, I believe we have a different problem: our markets don't act like competitive markets. We learn in the most elementary economics courses that competitive markets, which promote efficiency and innovation, drive profits down. Wealth winds up in the hands of a few multibillionaires because we don't have a truly competitive economy. The most successful "entrepreneurs" have figured out how to create barriers to competition, behind which they can earn huge profits. It is not a surprise that the world's richest person, Bill Gates, earned his fortune through a company that has engaged in anticompetitive practices in Europe, America, and Asia. Nor that the world's second richest, Carlos Slim, made his fortune by taking advantage of a poorly designed privatization process, creating a virtual monopoly in Mexico's telecom industry, and by charging prices a multiple of what they would be in competitive markets.

To the extent that we fail in our efforts to make markets truly competitive, we should tax monopoly profits, which are a form of what economists call rents. Just as the taxation of land doesn't lead to less land, so too for a tax on other forms of rent. Other sources of rents include revenues received by the owners of natural resources. In many cases, oil, gas, and mineral companies don't actually own these resources; they simply extract them from publicly owned land while paying just a fraction of their true value. The best solution to this inequity would be a fair and efficient auction, which would guarantee to the public the full return on these assets. In cases where corporations have already managed to get these resources while paying the public a fraction of their worth, we need to recoup that value by taxing the resulting profits at a higher rate.

MOVING FROM CORPORATE to personal taxes, we must enact a fair income tax so that those who work for a living aren't forced to pay a larger portion of their income in taxes than those who enjoy the fruits of inherited wealth or manage private equity funds. While most Americans accept the general principle that the rich should pay a larger fraction of their income in taxes, our system departs markedly from this principle in practice. The very richest pay a lower percentage of their reported income than do the merely rich—and their reported income is often a fraction of their actual income.

Many of the commonly discussed proposals for reform of the personal tax code focus on eliminating provisions designed to help the middle class—most notably deductions for mortgage interest and the tax exemption of employer-provided health insurance. Such provisions narrow the tax base and make the economy less efficient, so there is some virtue to eliminating them, if done carefully. In practice, the deduction in mortgage interest provides more assistance to rich homeowners than to the middle class—indeed, by some estimates, the government provides more housing assistance to the rich through the tax system than it does to the poor through public housing. The deduction encourages excessive housing consumption and excessive borrowing (not surprising, given the political clout of our banks). But our real estate sector is still struggling after the housing collapse, when millions of Americans lost a substantial portion of their wealth. Eliminating all subsidies now would make matters worse. A phaseout of the deduction should be gradual, and we should use some of the savings to encourage equity in housing—for instance, through a provision of extended assistance for first-time homebuyers.

Given how hard-pressed the middle class is—incomes, adjusted for inflation, have barely budged in decades—deduction reforms should not be viewed as ways of raising revenue. Instead, the resulting savings should be given back in the form of a reduction of the marginal income-tax rates that hit the middle class. Some would respond that there is no way to achieve significant deficit reduction while raising taxes only on the rich: they don't have *that* much money. That was once true, but no longer. One upside of growing inequality is that we can raise enormous amounts of money while increasing tax burdens only at the very top of the scale.

Taxing carbon emissions is another way we could raise substantial amounts of money while improving the overall performance of our economy. The most basic principle in economics is that firms should pay the costs that are incurred in their production processes. This is what enables the price system to guide the economy toward efficiency. When production is subsidized, it creates distortions in the market. Our environment is one of our scarcest resources—those who damage it through pollution are imposing serious costs. Forcing firms with high carbon emissions to pay those costs will make the economy more efficient and at the same time raise revenue.

Taken together, these proposals would make real inroads into reducing inequality, returning us to an economy more like that of the postwar years. Those were the years when America was becoming the middle-class society it had long professed to be, with decades of rapid growth and widely shared prosperity, when those at the bottom saw their incomes grow faster than those at the top. They are also the years that Thomas Piketty views as an anomaly in the history of capitalism. But getting back to that time doesn't require eliminating capitalism; it requires eliminating the market distortions of the ersatz capitalism practiced in this country today. This is less about economics than it is about politics. We don't have to choose between capitalism and fairness. We must choose both.

Part II

PERSONAL REFLECTIONS

THE TWO CHAPTERS IN THIS SHORT PART LOOK BACK at my youth from today's vantage point. The first was written on the occasion of the fiftieth anniversary of the March on Washington for Jobs and Freedom on August 28, 1963. It was there, at the Washington Mall, that the Reverend Martin Luther King gave his memorable "I have a dream" speech. I was lucky to be there. Of course, it was not just luck: like so many of my classmates, I was engaged in the fight for racial equality. Discrimination was a scar on our body politic. Growing up, I had seen all around me how discrimination was destroying lives. It was against *everything* I was taught America stood for. And yet the United States had lived with this poison even from before its founding.

Later I would (with other economists) ask whether discrimination could persist in a market economy. It was easy to show that the answer was yes—how could it be otherwise, given that discrimination was a persistent feature of market economies all over the world. Yet some economists had tried to argue the contrary. In "How Dr. King Shaped My Work in Economics" I make a brief allusion to this work—an illustration (like the work on macroeconomics that said that crises couldn't happen) of how far out of touch with reality some economic models get.[1]

By contrast, I wrote "The Myth of America's Golden Age" after reading Thomas Piketty's book *Capitalism in the Twenty-First Century* and reflecting back on my youth. Piketty had described this period of my youth as the golden age of capitalism—the one period in which capitalism had not been marked by extremes of inequality. My memories were different: Growing up in dirty, industrial America, marked by high levels of discrimination, inequality, labor strife, episodic unemployment, I hardly thought of it as the golden age of capitalism.

President Kennedy had said that "a rising tide lifts all boats"; while there may have been a grain of truth in that statement when he uttered those words in the 60s,[2] it was clearly not true half a century later.

What had upset me most about the Obama administration's response to the economic crisis was that it, too, seemed wedded to trickle-down economics: throw enough money at the banks, and the economy will recover. I had argued for a greater dose of trickle-up economics—give money to American homeowners, who were losing their homes by the millions, and that will help the economy. It will even help the banks, because of the positive effects on the real estate market, the reduced defaults on home mortgages, and the increased strength of the overall economy.

"The Myth of America's Golden Age" was also written soon after the publication of former treasury secretary Timothy Geitner's book, *Stress Test*, where he valiantly, but in my view unsuccessfully, attempt to defend his and the administration's policies during the crisis period. They worried that helping homeowners who were underwater would be unfair to those homeowners who had managed their funds well and didn't need assistance. Going forward, it would discourage prudence on the part of homeowners—the "moral hazard problem" well-known to economists.

I never understood how he (like so many in the banking community) could embrace such a double standard. Bailing out bad banks was, in these terms, not only unfair to other banks; it was unfair to the millions of Americans who were suffering because of the misdeeds of the banks. It was going to the assistance of the victimizer, and leaving the victims to take care of themselves. If there was ever need for proof of the relevance of moral hazard, the bankers had provided it: the savings-and-loan bailout, and the Mexican, Korean, Thai, and Indonesian bailouts, which were all really bailouts of Western financial institutions. But here we were, bailing them out one more time. By contrast, for the most part, the homeowners had been *misled* by those in the financial sector, advised to take large mortgages beyond their capacity to pay. They had learned their lesson and were unlikely to ever repeat such behavior. Besides, among the proposals for dealing with the massive number of foreclosures were those that provided for debt restructuring, but which would have required the homeowners to give up much of the equity in their homes. It wasn't the virtual free pass that the administration gave the banks.

Notes

1. My own more theoretical work in this area includes "Approaches to the Economics of Discrimination," *American Economic Review* 62, no. 2 (May 1973): 287–95, and "Theories of Discrimination and Economic Policy," in *Patterns of Racial Discrimination*, ed. G. von Furstenberg et al. (Lexington, MA: Lexington Books, 1974), pp. 5–26. Work with Andy Weiss established the theoretical foundations for red-lining, banks' practice of excluding loans from those living in some locales. See J. E. Stiglitz and A. Weiss, "Credit Rationing in Markets with Imperfect Information," *American Economic Review* 71, no. 3 (June 1981): 393–410. The basic work setting forth the alternative perspective, that market forces would militate against discrimination, was that of the late Nobel Prize–winning economist Gary Becker, in his book *The Economics of Discrimination*, 2d ed. (Chicago: University of Chicago Press, 1971). Not surprisingly, he was upset with my article and sent me an e-mail saying so.
2. President Kennedy actually said this on more than one occasion, including in 1960 when praising the building of the St. Lawrence Seaway.

HOW DR. KING SHAPED MY
WORK IN ECONOMICS*

I HAD THE GOOD FORTUNE TO BE IN THE CROWD IN WASH-
ington when the Rev. Dr. Martin Luther King Jr. gave his thrill-
ing "I Have a Dream" speech on Aug. 28, 1963. I was 20 years old,
and had just finished college. It was just a couple of weeks before
I began my graduate studies in economics at the Massachusetts
Institute of Technology.

The night before the March on Washington for Jobs and Freedom, I had stayed at the home of a college classmate whose father,
Arthur J. Goldberg, was an associate justice of the Supreme Court
and was committed to bringing about economic justice. Who would
have imagined, 50 years later, that this very body, which had once
seemed determined to usher in a more fair and inclusive America,
would become the instrument for preserving inequalities: allowing
nearly unlimited corporate spending to influence political cam-
paigns, pretending that the legacy of voting discrimination no longer
exists, and restricting the rights of workers and other plaintiffs to
sue employers and companies for misconduct?

Listening to Dr. King speak evoked many emotions for me. Young
and sheltered though I was, I was part of a generation that saw the

*   *New York Times*, August 27, 2013.

inequities that had been inherited from the past, and was committed to correcting these wrongs. Born during World War II, I came of age as quiet but unmistakable changes were washing over American society.

As president of the student council at Amherst College, I had led a group of classmates down South to help push for racial integration. We couldn't understand the violence of those who wanted to preserve the old system of segregation. When we visited an all-black college, we felt intensely the disparity in educational opportunities that had been given to the students there, especially when compared with those that we had received in our privileged, cloistered college. It was an unlevel playing field, and it was fundamentally unfair. It was a travesty of the idea of the American dream that we had grown up with and believed in.

It was because I hoped that something could be done about these and the other problems I had seen so vividly growing up in Gary, Indiana—poverty, episodic and persistent unemployment, unending discrimination against African-Americans—that I decided to become an economist, veering away from my earlier intention to go into theoretical physics. I soon discovered I had joined a strange tribe. While there were a few scholars (including several of my teachers) who cared deeply about the issues that had led me to the field, most were unconcerned about inequality; the dominant school worshiped at the feet of (a misunderstood) Adam Smith, at the miracle of the efficiency of the market economy. I thought that if this was the best of all possible worlds, I wanted to construct and live in another world.

In that odd world of economics, unemployment (if it existed) was the fault of workers. One Chicago School economist, the Nobel Prize winner Robert E. Lucas Jr., would later write: "Of the tendencies that are harmful to sound economics, the most seductive, and in my opinion the most poisonous, is to focus on questions of distribution." Another Nobel laureate of the Chicago School, Gary S. Becker, would attempt to show how in truly competitive labor markets discrimination couldn't exist. While I and others wrote multiple papers explaining the sophistry in the argument, his was an argument that fell on receptive ears.

Like so many looking back over the past 50 years, I cannot but be struck by the gap between our aspirations then and what we have accomplished.

True, one "glass ceiling" has been shattered: we have an African-American president.

But Dr. King realized that the struggle for social justice had to be conceived broadly: it was a battle not just against racial segregation and discrimination, but for greater economic equality and justice for all Americans. It was not for nothing that the march's organizers, Bayard Rustin and A. Philip Randolph, had called it the March on Washington for Jobs and Freedom.

In so many respects, progress in race relations has been eroded, and even reversed, by the growing economic divides afflicting the entire country.

The battle against outright discrimination is, regrettably, far from over: 50 years after the march, and 45 years after the passage of the Fair Housing Act, major United States banks, like Wells Fargo, still discriminated on the basis of race, targeting the most vulnerable of our citizens with their predatory lending activities. Discrimination in the job market is pervasive and deep. Research suggests that applicants with names that sound African-American get fewer calls for interviews. Discrimination takes new forms; racial profiling remains rampant in many American cities, including through the stop-and-frisk policies that became standard practice in New York. Our incarceration rate is the world's highest, although there are signs, finally, that fiscally strapped states are starting to see the folly, if not the inhumanity, of wasting so much human capital through mass incarceration. Almost 40 percent of prisoners are black. This tragedy has been documented powerfully by Michelle Alexander and other legal scholars.

The raw numbers tell much of the story: There has been no significant closing of the gap between the income of African-Americans (or Hispanics) and white Americans the last 30 years. In 2011, the median income of black families was $40,495, just 58 percent of the median income of white families.

Turning from income to wealth, we see gaping inequality, too. By 2009, the median wealth of whites was 20 times that of blacks. The Great Recession of 2007–9 was particularly hard on African-Americans (as it typically is on those at the bottom of the socioeconomic spectrum). They saw their median wealth fall by 53 percent between 2005 and 2009, more than three times that of whites: a record gap. But the so-called recovery has been little more than a chimera—with more than 100 percent of the gains going to the top 1 percent—a group where, needless to say, African-Americans cannot be found in large numbers.

Who knows how Dr. King's life would have unfolded had it not been cut short by an assassin's bullet? Just 39 when he was killed, he would be 84 today. While he would have likely embraced President Obama's efforts to reform our health care system and to defend the social safety net for the elderly, the poor, and the disabled, it is difficult to imagine that someone of such acute moral acumen would look at the America of today with anything short of despair.

Despite rhetoric about the land of opportunity, a young person's life prospects are in America more dependent on the income and education of his parents than in almost any other advanced country. And thus, the legacy of discrimination and lack of educational and job opportunity is perpetuated, from one generation to the next.

Given this lack of mobility, the fact that even today, 65 percent of African-American children live in low-income families does not bode well for their future, or the nation's.

Men with just a high school education have seen enormous drops in their real incomes over the past two decades, a decline that has disproportionately affected African-Americans.

While outright race-based segregation in schools was banned, in reality, educational segregation has worsened in recent decades, as Gary Orfield and other scholars have documented.

Part of the reason is that the country has become more economically segregated. Poor black children are more likely to live in communities with concentrated poverty—some 45 percent do so, as opposed to 12 percent for poor white children, as the Economic Policy Institute has pointed out.

I turned 70 earlier this year. Much of my scholarship and public service in recent decades—including my service at the Council of Economic Advisers during the Clinton administration, and then at the World Bank—has been devoted to the reduction of poverty and inequality. I hope I've lived up to the call Dr. King issued a half-century ago.

He was right to recognize that these persistent divides are a cancer in our society, undermining our democracy and weakening our economy. His message was that the injustices of the past were not inevitable. But he knew, too, that dreaming was not enough.

THE MYTH
OF AMERICA'S
GOLDEN AGE[*]

I HADN'T REALIZED WHEN I WAS GROWING UP IN GARY, INDI-
ana, an industrial town on the southern shore of Lake Michigan
plagued by discrimination, poverty, and bouts of high unemployment, that I was living in the golden era of capitalism. It was a company town, named after the chairman of the board of U.S. Steel. It
had the world's largest integrated steel mill and a progressive school
system designed to turn Gary into a melting pot fed by migrants
from all over Europe. But by the time I was born, in 1943, cracks
in the pot were already appearing. To break strikes—to ensure that
workers did not fully share in the productivity gains being driven
by modern technology—the big steel companies brought African-
American workers up from the South who lived in impoverished,
separate neighborhoods.

Smokestacks poured poisons into the air. Periodic layoffs left
many families living hand to mouth. Even as a kid, it seemed clear
to me that the free market as we knew it was hardly a formula for
sustaining a prosperous, happy, and healthy society.

So when I went off to college to study, I was astonished by what
I read. The standard economic texts of the time seemed to be

---

* *Politico*, July/August 2014.

unrelated to the reality I had witnessed growing up in Gary. They said that unemployment shouldn't exist and that the market led to the best of all possible worlds. But if that were the case, I decided, I wanted to live in a different world. While other economists were obsessed with extolling the virtues of the market economy, I focused a lot of my work on why markets fail, and I devoted much of my Ph.D. thesis at MIT to understanding the causes of inequality.

Nearly half a century later, the problem of inequality has reached crisis proportions. John F. Kennedy, in the spirit of optimism that prevailed at the time I was a college student, once declared that a rising tide lifts all boats. It turns out today that almost all of us now are in the same boat—the one that holds the bottom 99 percent. It is a far different boat, one marked by more poverty at the bottom and a hollowing out of the middle class, from the one occupied by the top 1 percent.

Most disturbing is the realization that the American dream— the notion that we are living in the land of opportunity—is a myth. The life chances of a child in America are today more dependent on the income and education of his parents than in many other advanced countries, including "old Europe."

Now comes Thomas Piketty, who warns us in his justly cele- brated new book, *Capital in the Twenty-first Century*, that matters are only likely to get worse. Above all, he argues that the natural state of capitalism seems to be one of great inequality. When I was a graduate student, we were taught the opposite. The economist Simon Kuznets optimistically wrote that after an initial period of development in which inequality grew, it would begin to decline. Although data at the time were scarce, it might have been true when he wrote it: The inequalities of the 19th and early 20th cen- turies seemed to be diminishing. This conclusion appeared to be vindicated during the period from World War II to 1980, when the fortunes of the wealthy and the middle class rose together.

But the evidence of the last third of a century suggests this

period was an aberration. It was a time of war-induced solidarity
when the government kept the playing field level, and the GI Bill
of Rights and subsequent civil rights advances meant that there
was something to the American dream. Today, inequality is growing dramatically again, and the past three decades or so have
proved conclusively that one of the major culprits is trickle-down
economics—the idea that the government can just step back and
if the rich get richer and use their talents and resources to create
jobs, everyone will benefit. It just doesn't work; the historical data
now prove that.

But it has taken us far too long as a country to understand this
danger. Changes in the distribution of income and wealth occur
slowly, which is why it requires a grand historical perspective of the
kind that Piketty provides to get a feel for what is happening.

Ironically enough, the final proof debunking this very Republican idea of trickle-down economics has come from a Democratic
administration. President Barack Obama's banks-first approach
to saving the nation from another Great Depression held that by
giving money to the banks (rather than to homeowners who had
been preyed upon by the banks), the economy would be saved. The
administration poured billions into the banks that had brought the
country to the brink of ruin, without setting conditions in return.
When the International Monetary Fund and the World Bank engage
in a rescue, they virtually always impose requirements to ensure
the money is used in the way intended. But here, the government
merely expressed the hope that the banks would keep credit, the
lifeblood of the economy, flowing. And so the banks shrank lending, and paid their executives mega-bonuses, even though they had
almost destroyed their businesses. Even then, we knew that much
of the banks' profits had been earned not by increasing the efficiency of the economy but by exploitation—through predatory lending, abusive credit card practices, and monopolistic pricing. The full
extent of their misdeeds—for instance, the illegal manipulation of
key interest rates and foreign exchange rates, affecting derivatives

and mortgages in the amount of hundreds of trillions of dollars—
was only just beginning to be fathomed.

Obama promised to stop these abuses, but so far only a single
senior banker has gone to jail (along with a very few mid- and low-
level employees). The president's former Treasury secretary, Timothy Geithner, in his recent book, *Stress Test*, made a valiant but
unsuccessful attempt to defend the administration's actions, suggesting that there were no alternatives. But Geithner clearly worried
excessively about the "moral hazard" of helping underwater homeowners—in other words, encouraging lax borrowing habits—while
seeming to care far less about the moral hazard of helping banks, or
the culpability of the banks in encouraging excessive indebtedness
and in marketing mortgages that put unbearable risks on the poor
and middle classes.

In fact, Geithner's attempts to justify what the administration did
only reinforce my belief that the system is rigged. If those who are
in charge of making the critical decisions are so "cognitively captured" by the 1 percent, by the bankers, that they see that the only
alternative is to give those who caused the crisis hundreds of billions of dollars while leaving workers and homeowners in the lurch,
the system is unfair.

This approach also exacerbated one of the country's most pressing problems: its growing inequality. Only with a vibrant middle
class can the economy fully recover and grow faster. The more
inequality, the slower the growth—a conclusion now endorsed even
by the IMF. Because the less wealthy consume a greater share of
their income than do the rich, they expand demand when they have
more income. When demand is expanded, jobs are created: In this
sense, it is ordinary Americans who are the real job creators. So
inequality commands a high price: a weaker economy, marked by
lower growth and more instability. It is not very complicated.

None of this is the outcome of inexorable economic forces, either;
it's the result of policies and politics—what we did and didn't do. If
our politics leads to preferential taxation of those who earn income

from capital; to an education system in which the children of the
rich have access to the best schools, but the children of the poor go
to mediocre ones; to exclusive access by the wealthy to talented tax
lawyers and offshore banking centers to avoid paying a fair share
of taxes—then it is not surprising that there will be a high level of
inequality and a low level of opportunity. And if these policies continue, these conditions will grow even worse.

And now it's also clear that the high level of economic inequality has translated into gross new forms of political inequality—
to the point where we can more aptly be described as having a
political system with "one dollar, one vote" than "one person, one
vote." The Supreme Court's *Citizens United* decision in January
2010 gave corporations more rights to influence politics than ordinary individuals—without making them, or their officers, really
accountable. This year's follow-on *McCutcheon* decision eliminated
aggregate limits on individual contributions to national candidates
and parties. So today, the richer you are, the more you are able to
influence the political process and the economic decisions that
stem from it, and to rig it all in favor of the 1 percent. Is it any
wonder the rich keep getting richer?

CAUTIOUSLY AND BELATEDLY, some six years after the fact, the
Obama administration has now begun to revise its views about
the Great Recession. Even Geithner, in his book, agrees that more
should have been done. But hey, resources were scarce, and one
had to make bets where they would be most effective. That's the
point: Listening to the bankers, it's not a surprise that he placed his
money on the bankers. Even before Obama took office, I urged a
greater emphasis on homeowners: that we should combine at least a
little trickle-up economics with trickle-down economics. But those
of my persuasion were given short shrift, as the administration
sought counsel from the vested interests in the financial sector.

The Obamians seem bewildered that the country is not more

thankful to its government for having prevented another Great Depression. They saved the banks, and in doing so, they saved the economy from a once-in-a-hundred-year storm. And they proudly point out that all the money given to the financial sector has been more than repaid. But in making such claims, they ignore some critical realities: It was not something that just happened. It was the result of reckless behavior, the predictable and predicted consequences of deregulation and the inadequate enforcement of the regulations that remained, of buying into the mind-set of the 1 percent and the bankers—for which Geithner and his mentor, former White House economic adviser Larry Summers, had more than a little culpability. It was as if, after an accident caused by drunk driving, in which the last drink was served by the police officer on duty, the drunk driver was put back into the driver's seat, his car rushed to the repair shop, while the victim was left to languish at the scene of the crime.

The repayment itself is, at least in part, the result of a game that would do any con man proud. The government, under the auspices of the Federal Reserve, lends money to the bank at a near-zero interest rate. The bank then lends it back to the government at 2 or 3 percent, and the "profit" is paid back to the government in repayment of the "investment" the government made. Bank officials, meanwhile, get a bonus for the hefty returns they have "earned" for the bank—something a 12-year-old could have done. This is capitalism? In a true rule-of-law world, a drunk driver would have to pay for not only his own repair costs but also the damage he has inflicted—in this case, the cumulative loss of GDP, which now amounts to more than $8 trillion, and which is mounting at the rate of $2 trillion a year. The banks recover, while the typical American's income plummets to levels not seen in two decades. It is understandable why there might be some anger in the body politic.

What we have here is not, as administration officials would have it, a failure to communicate. The problem was that Americans saw what they were doing. There was a healthy debate in the country about alternative courses of action—before, during, and after the bailouts. The reason critics like Sheila Bair, Elizabeth Warren, Neil Barofsky, Simon Johnson, Paul Krugman, and others (left, right, and center) won the day—at least the intellectual debate and the war over public perceptions—was not that they were better communicators. It was that they had a more convincing message: There were alternative ways of rescuing the economy that were fairer and that would have resulted in a stronger economy. Instead, our politics and economics are now locked into a vicious circle: Economic inequality leads to political inequality, and this political inequality then leads to rewriting the rules to increase the level of economic inequality even further, and so on. The result? Ever greater disillusionment with our democracy.

Matters may well get worse. Recent research has uncovered a variety of other vicious cycles. Poverty traps mean those in the bottom remain there. The fortunes of a child of poor parents who does well in school are far bleaker than those of a child of rich parents who does much more poorly in school. About a quarter of U.S. college freshmen from the bottom income half finish college by age 24, compared with 90 percent of the upper quartile. And with wages of those who have only a high school diploma at 62 percent of the typical college grad's earnings—compared with 81 percent in 1965—the prospects are they will be poorer than their parents.

Meanwhile, lower taxes on capital and lower inheritance taxes are allowing the accumulation of inherited wealth—in effect, the creation of a new American plutocracy. It is even possible, as I pointed out long ago in my Ph.D. thesis and as Piketty has emphasized, that wealth will be increasingly concentrated among a select few. The shared prosperity that marked the country in that golden age of my youth—in which every group saw its income growing but those at the bottom saw it rise the fastest—is long gone.

Yet I am, perhaps, naïve enough to believe it is not capitalism alone that is at fault: It is, even more, the paralysis of our politics and the banishing of any progressive thought from a debate that still pretends the No. 1 problem is government. I have spent my career as an economist second-guessing markets, demonstrating their imperfections, and yet markets can be a powerful force for increasing standards of living for all. But we need a balance of the kind we achieved in the middle of the 20th century, when government was afforded a progressive role. Otherwise, I fear, we will permanently scar ourselves with the rigged economic and political system that already has done so much to create today's inequality.

When I was growing up in Gary during its own smog-choked "golden age," it was impossible to see where the city was going. We didn't know, or talk, about the deindustrialization of America, which was about to occur. I didn't realize, in other words, that the rather grim reality I was leaving behind as I went to college was actually as good as Gary was ever going to get.

I fear America could be at the same place today.

PART III

DIMENSIONS OF INEQUALITY

I NEQUALITY—IN AMERICA, AS IN OTHER COUNTRIES— has many dimensions. Each has its own story. Some countries are worse in one dimension, better in others. There is inequality at the top—the share of income grabbed by the top 1 percent or .1 percent—and inequality at the bottom—the number of people in poverty, and the depth of their poverty. There are inequalities in health and in access to education, in political voice, and in insecurity. There are gender inequities, and childhood deprivations. And perhaps most important is *equality of opportunity*.

The inequalities are, of course, related: childhood deprivations, inequality of access to education and health care, essentially ensure that there will not be equality of opportunity. Growing evidence that countries (or areas) where there is more inequality of income are places where there is less equality of opportunity helps us understand why the United States, with the highest level of inequality of outcomes among the advanced countries, has become one of the advanced countries with the least equality of opportunity. A young American's life prospects are more dependent on the income and education of his parents than are those of young people in other advanced countries.

The articles in this part of the book provide a selective exploration of some key aspects of these inequalities, beginning with "Equal

Opportunity, Our National Myth." Many of the aspects of the issue that are noted there are echoed in later essays. For instance, childhood deprivation seems so morally wrong, simply because children cannot be in any sense responsible for their plight; but we will not be able to do anything about our inequality of opportunity unless we address childhood deprivation. But, as I note in a UNICEF article, written in commemoration of the 25th anniversary of the Convention on the Rights of the Child, one out of five children in America grows up in poverty.

"Student Debt and the Crushing of the American Dream" addresses one of America's more serious inequities: access to higher education. Inequities in access to education in turn are among the reasons that the United States is no longer the land of opportunity. Whereas it used to have the largest fraction of its population graduating from college, it is now down in the league tables. Even more devastating is how education perpetuates advantages and disadvantages: of Americans born around 1980, only about 9 percent of those from the bottom quarter of the income distribution graduated from college.

One reason for this is the cost of higher education. Other countries provide free education, or subsidize it more heavily. Matters were bad before the 2008 crisis, but that made them worse. As incomes deteriorated, states cut back on support, and colleges were forced to raise tuition. Just as Americans became overleveraged in their purchase of housing, now they are becoming overindebted to finance education—with student debt well over a trillion dollars, and the average student graduating with a debt of nearly $30,000. The macroeconomic consequences of this trend are parsed later—it has implications for young people's decisions to buy a car or a house, or even to marry. But the micro consequences are pervasive—stress as young people feel caught between a rock and a hard place, knowing that if they don't get an advanced education, their prospects are bleak, but that if they do, they will graduate with crushing debt.

In this short essay, I don't address an obvious question: Is there an alternative, especially in a country facing severe budget restraints? There are two approaches. Countries much poorer than the United States have decided that education for all is a priority, and are providing free (or much more subsidized) university education. President Obama's 2015 initiative to make community colleges free for qualifying students is an example. This was a major issue in Scotland's 2014 referendum on independence: while England has been following the American model, raising tuition markedly over the last 15 years, Scotland has been providing free education to its young people. The other approach is that of Australia. There the government lends students money at low interest rates, and then collects from them on the basis of their income. Those with higher income pay back more. This not only avoids the enormous stress put on young people by the U.S. system—and exploitation by private lenders—but also enables young people to choose a profession that corresponds to their interests and abilities. They can go into ministry or teaching without worrying about their loans. Law students can decide to go into public interest law, rather than corporate law. The benefits to society should be obvious.

"Justice for Some" discusses a particularly unsavory aspect of U.S. inequality—the lack of equal access to justice. Young Americans start the day by pledging allegiance to the flag. A key phrase in that pledge is "with justice for all." Yet increasingly, America is more aptly described as offering "justice for those who can afford it." Nowhere is this more evident than in our criminal justice system. America sends a larger fraction of its citizens to prison than any other country, including China: with less than 5 percent of the world's population, it has 25 percent of the world's prisoners. But it is the poor, and African-Americans, who are most likely to spend their late teens and early twenties in prison, rather than at school.[1]

The article takes up the issue in the context of America's housing crisis, and one aspect of it in particular: the "robo-signing crisis." In their rush to issue bad mortgages, banks didn't pay attention to record keeping. When the inevitable housing crisis arrived, and it came time to throw people out of the homes for which banks had gladly lent them money only a few years earlier, the banks' records of who had repaid what were a mess. Many states have a system in which banks can simply sign an affidavit that they have examined the records and that the individual who is being declared in foreclosure does in fact owe the money alleged. The poor person who is being accused can spend money to try to defend himself—but that's the problem with being poor in America: obtaining justice is expensive. The banks essentially lied to the courts, not once, but repeatedly. People were thrown out of their homes who didn't owe money.

The article raises a troubling question: Americans believe that one of their country's strengths is the rule of law, but is it really? The rule of law is supposed to protect the weak against the strong. And it is supposed to mean that the law is impartially enforced. We have laws against perjury. We have laws that are designed to protect people from unjust takings of their property. But we didn't enforce the laws against the bankers—not a single one went to jail for this gross miscarriage of justice. We could have prevented the mortgage crisis, if we had only more effectively enforced laws already on the books, regarding predatory and discriminatory lending—and if the Fed had lived up to its responsibilities in enforcing standards of lending in the mortgage market.

"The One Housing Solution Left," written with Mark Zandi, chief economist of Moody's, argues that there were alternative ways of handling the housing crisis, after it emerged—borrowing an idea that had worked in the Great Depression and that would have cost the government nothing. Senator Jeff Merkley of Oregon introduced a bill, Rebuilding American Homeownership, which would have accomplished this. And there was even a strategy for doing this within the political constraints of the time. But we couldn't get the Obama administration on board.

Later the administration recognized its failure to do more for housing as one of its critical mistakes, both economically and politically. Money was being thrown at the banks, while almost nothing was going to ordinary Americans who were losing their homes. There were a few small programs, involving a few billion dollars, announced with great fanfare, each of which in turn would prove to be a disappointment. Few homeowners were rescued. The administration never explained adequately why it didn't get behind this cost-effective proposal, or alternatives that I and others had advocated.[2] Perhaps it was because they never fathomed the depth of the crisis that was emerging; perhaps because they were so obsessed with rescuing the banks that they thought attention—and money—spent anywhere else would be a mistake; perhaps because they listened too much to the bankers, who were more inclined to blame the borrowers than their own lending practices; perhaps because many of the proposals (but not this one) required the banks to recognize the losses; or perhaps because the bankers hoped to continue to exploit homeowners, and this proposal would have limited their scope for doing so, by giving them an option for refinancing.

The final two articles in this part touch on two of the most disturbing aspects of America's inequality: poverty among children and inequities in health care. Childhood poverty in America, among the worst within the advanced countries, has lifelong consequences. Because a large fraction of Americans are not living up to their potential, it also has significant consequences for the overall performance of the economy. Children have been particularly hard hit by the country's growing inequality among adults and the gutting of public programs providing not just a safety net but benefits that ordinary citizens rely upon. Indeed, matters have become so bad that, simply looking at the statistics, if a hypothetical unborn person—not knowing where he would wind up, whether at the bottom or the top, whether the child of a millionaire, of a plumber, of a schoolteacher—were to be asked in which country his best chances would be, he would not choose the United States. Of course, he would, if he knew that he would be born into a rich and well-educated family, if he could be assured that he entered the fray at the top. But not otherwise.

The last article in this part was written as the Ebola epidemic raged in West Africa, creating fears that it would spread to the United States. There were two key points: the disease took root where poverty was high and health services limited. And we turn to the government—not the private sector—to manage such a crisis; but underfunding of public agencies at the national and global level had undermined their capacity to do so. The article concludes by arguing that we—the United States and the world—are paying a high price for our ideological commitment to privately provided and financed health care and for our failure to do enough to lessen health care inequality in particular.

Before moving on from this section, I should emphasize that I have touched on only some of the many dimensions of America's great divide. I haven't written, in particular, about the gender or racial divide; although disparities in gender have been reduced, they remain large, and improvements in racial disparities have been disappointing. Of course, there are iconic successes—a few CEOs and President Obama himself. But income differences between whites and African-Americans have actually worsened, and wealth differentials have increased, particularly in the aftermath of the Great Recession.

Nor have I described how America's middle class has been eviscerated.

The essays in this part prepare the way to those in the next, where we look at the *causes* of this growing inequality.

Notes

1. Some have suggested that this is not just an accident but a continuation of policies of discrimination that have long plagued the United States. See, in particular, Michelle Alexander, *The New Jim Crow: Mass Incarceration in the Age of Colorblindness*, rev. ed. (New York: New Press, 2012).

2. See, for instance, Joseph E. Stiglitz, *Freefall: America, Free Markets, and the Sinking of the World Economy* (New York: W. W. Norton, 2010).

EQUAL OPPORTUNITY, OUR NATIONAL MYTH[*]

P RESIDENT OBAMA'S SECOND INAUGURAL ADDRESS USED
soaring language to reaffirm America's commitment to the
dream of equality of opportunity: "We are true to our creed when
a little girl born into the bleakest poverty knows that she has the
same chance to succeed as anybody else, because she is an American; she is free, and she is equal, not just in the eyes of God but
also in our own."

The gap between aspiration and reality could hardly be wider.
Today, the United States has less equality of opportunity than almost
any other advanced industrial country. Study after study has exposed
the myth that America is a land of opportunity. This is especially
tragic: While Americans may differ on the desirability of equality of outcomes, there is near-universal consensus that inequality of
opportunity is indefensible. The Pew Research Center has found that
some 90 percent of Americans believe that the government should do
everything it can to ensure equality of opportunity.

Perhaps a hundred years ago, America might have rightly claimed
to be the land of opportunity, or at least a land where there was
more opportunity than elsewhere. But not for at least a quarter of a

---

* *New York Times*, February 16, 2013.

century. Horatio Alger–style rags-to-riches stories were not a deliberate hoax, but given how they've lulled us into a sense of complacency, they might as well have been.

It's not that social mobility is impossible, but that the upwardly mobile American is becoming a statistical oddity. According to research from the Brookings Institution, only 58 percent of Americans born into the bottom fifth of income earners move out of that category, and just 6 percent born into the bottom fifth move into the top. Economic mobility is lower in the United States than in most of Europe and lower than in all of Scandinavia.

Another way of looking at equality of opportunity is to ask to what extent the life chances of a child are dependent on the education and income of his parents. Is it just as likely that a child of poor or poorly educated parents gets a good education and rises to the middle class as someone born to middle-class parents with college degrees? Even in a more egalitarian society, the answer would be no. But the life prospects of an American are more dependent on the income and education of his parents than in almost any other advanced country for which there is data.

How do we explain this? Some of it has to do with persistent discrimination. Latinos and African-Americans still get paid less than whites, and women still get paid less than men, even though they recently surpassed men in the number of advanced degrees they obtain. Though gender disparities in the workplace are less than they once were, there is still a glass ceiling: women are sorely underrepresented in top corporate positions and constitute a minuscule fraction of CEOs.

Discrimination, however, is only a small part of the picture. Probably the most important reason for lack of equality of opportunity is education: both its quantity and quality. After World War II, Europe made a major effort to democratize its education systems. We did, too, with the GI Bill, which extended higher education to Americans across the economic spectrum.

But then we changed, in several ways. While racial segregation decreased, economic segregation increased. After 1980, the poor grew poorer, the middle stagnated, and the top did better and better. Disparities widened between those living in poor localities and those living in rich suburbs—or rich enough to send their kids to private schools. A result was a widening gap in educational performance— the achievement gap between rich and poor kids born in 2001 was 30 to 40 percent larger than it was for those born 25 years earlier, the Stanford sociologist Sean F. Reardon found.

Of course, there are other forces at play, some of which start even before birth. Children in affluent families get more exposure to reading and less exposure to environmental hazards. Their families can afford enriching experiences like music lessons and summer camp. They get better nutrition and health care, which enhance their learning, directly and indirectly.

Unless current trends in education are reversed, the situation is likely to get even worse. In some cases it seems as if policy has actually been designed to reduce opportunity: government support for many state schools has been steadily gutted over the last few decades—and especially in the last few years. Meanwhile, students are crushed by giant student loan debts that are almost impossible to discharge, even in bankruptcy. This is happening at the same time that a college education is more important than ever for getting a good job.

Young people from families of modest means face a Catch-22: without a college education, they are condemned to a life of poor prospects; with a college education, they may be condemned to a lifetime of living at the brink. And increasingly even a college degree isn't enough; one needs either a graduate degree or a series of (often unpaid) internships. Those at the top have the connections and social capital to get those opportunities. Those in the middle and bottom don't. The point is that no one makes it on his or her own. And those at the top get more help from their families than do those lower down on the ladder. Government should help to level the playing field.

Americans are coming to realize that their cherished narrative of social and economic mobility is a myth. Grand deceptions of this magnitude are hard to maintain for long—and the country has already been through a couple of decades of self-deception.

Without substantial policy changes, our self-image, and the image we project to the world, will diminish—and so will our economic standing and stability. Inequality of outcomes and inequality of opportunity reinforce each other—and contribute to economic weakness, as Alan B. Krueger, a Princeton economist and the chairman of the White House Council of Economic Advisers, has emphasized. We have an economic, and not only moral, interest in saving the American dream.

Policies that promote equality of opportunity must target the youngest Americans. First, we have to make sure that mothers are not exposed to environmental hazards and get adequate prenatal health care. Then, we have to reverse the damaging cutbacks to preschool education, a theme Mr. Obama emphasized on Tuesday. We have to make sure that all children have adequate nutrition and health care—not only do we have to provide the resources, but if necessary, we have to incentivize parents, by coaching or training them or even rewarding them for being good caregivers. The right says that money isn't the solution. They've chased reforms like charter schools and private-school vouchers, but most of these efforts have shown ambiguous results at best. Giving more money to poor schools would help. So would summer and extracurricular programs that enrich low-income students' skills.

Finally, it is unconscionable that a rich country like the United States has made access to higher education so difficult for those at the bottom and middle. There are many alternative ways of providing universal access to higher education, from Australia's income-contingent loan program to the near-free system of universities in Europe. A more educated population yields greater innovation, a robust economy, and higher incomes—which mean a higher tax base. Those benefits are, of course, why we've long been committed to free public education through 12th grade. But while a 12th-grade education might have sufficed a century ago, it doesn't today. Yet we haven't adjusted our system to contemporary realities.

The steps I've outlined are not just affordable but imperative. Even more important, though, is that we cannot afford to let our country drift farther from ideals that the vast majority of Americans share. We will never fully succeed in achieving Mr. Obama's vision of a poor girl's having exactly the same opportunities as a wealthy girl. But we could do much, much better, and must not rest until we do.

STUDENT DEBT AND
THE CRUSHING OF THE
AMERICAN DREAM[*]

A CERTAIN DRAMA HAS BECOME FAMILIAR IN THE UNITED States (and some other advanced industrialized countries): Bankers encourage people to borrow beyond their means, preying especially on those who are financially unsophisticated. They use their political influence to get favorable treatment of one form or another. Debts mount. Journalists record the human toll. Then comes bewilderment: How could we let this happen again? Officials promise to fix things. Something is done about the most egregious abuses. People move on, reassured that the crisis has abated, but suspecting that it will recur soon.

The crisis that is about to break out involves student debt and how we finance higher education. Like the housing crisis that preceded it, this crisis is intimately connected to America's soaring inequality, and how, as Americans on the bottom rungs of the ladder strive to climb up, they are inevitably pulled down—some to a point even lower than where they began.

This new crisis is emerging even before the last one has been resolved, and the two are becoming intertwined. In the decades

---

[*] *New York Times*, May 12, 2013.

after World War II, homeownership and higher education became signs of success in America.

Before the housing bubble burst in 2007, banks persuaded low-and moderate-income homeowners that they could turn their houses and apartments into piggy banks. They seduced them into taking out home equity loans—and in the end, millions lost their homes. In other cases, the banks, mortgage brokers, and real estate agents pushed aspiring homeowners to borrow beyond their means. The wizards of finance, who prided themselves on risk management, sold toxic mortgages that were designed to explode. They bundled the dubious loans into complex financial instruments and sold them to unsuspecting investors.

Everyone recognizes that education is the only way up, but as a college degree becomes increasingly essential to making one's way in a 21st-century economy, education for those not to the manner born is increasingly unaffordable. Student debt for seniors graduating with loans now exceeds $26,000, about a 40 percent increase (not adjusted for inflation) in just seven years. But an "average" like this masks huge variations.

According to the Federal Reserve Bank of New York, almost 13 percent of student-loan borrowers of all ages owe more than $50,000, and nearly 4 percent owe more than $100,000. These debts are beyond students' ability to repay (especially in our nearly jobless recovery); this is demonstrated by the fact that delinquency and default rates are soaring. Some 17 percent of student-loan borrowers were 90 days or more behind in payments at the end of 2012. When only those in repayment were counted—in other words, not including borrowers who were in loan deferment or forbearance—more than 30 percent were 90 days or more behind. For federal loans taken out in the 2009 fiscal year, three-year default rates exceeded 13 percent.

America is distinctive among advanced industrialized countries in the burden it places on students and their parents for financing higher education. America is also exceptional among comparable countries for the high cost of a college degree, including at public universities. Average tuition, and room and board, at four-year colleges is just short of $22,000 a year, up from under $9,000 (adjusted for inflation) in 1980–81.

Compare this more-than-doubling in tuition with the stagnation in median family income, which is now about $50,000, compared to $46,000 in 1980 (adjusted for inflation).

Like much else, the problem of student debt worsened during the Great Recession: tuition costs at public universities increased by 27 percent in the past five years—partly because of cutbacks in government support—while median income shrank. In California, inflation-adjusted tuition more than doubled in public two-year community colleges (which for poorer Americans are often the key to upward mobility), and by more than 70 percent in four-year public schools, from 2007–8 to 2012–13.

With costs soaring, incomes stagnating, and little help from government, it was not surprising that total student debt, around $1 trillion, surpassed total credit card debt last year. Responsible Americans have learned how to curb their credit card debt—many have forsaken them for debit cards, or educated themselves about usurious interest rates, fees, and penalties charged by card issuers—but the challenge of controlling student debt is even more unsettling.

Curbing student debt is tantamount to curbing social and economic opportunity. College graduates earn $12,000 more per year than those without college degrees; the gap has almost tripled just since 1980. Our economy is increasingly reliant on knowledge-related industries. No matter what happens with currency wars and trade balances, the United States is not going to return to making textiles. Unemployment rates among college graduates are much lower than among those with only a high school diploma.

America—home of the land-grant university, the GI Bill, and world-class public universities from California to Michigan to Texas—has fallen from the top in terms of university education. With strangling student debt, we are likely to fall further. What economists call "human capital"—investing in people—is a key to long-term growth. To be competitive in the 21st century is to have a highly educated labor force, one with college and advanced degrees. Instead, we are foreclosing on our future as a nation.

Student debt also is a drag on the slow recovery that began in 2009. By dampening consumption, it hinders economic growth. It is also holding back recovery in real estate, the sector where the Great Recession started.

It's true that housing prices seem to be on the upswing, but home construction is far from the levels reached in the years before the bubble burst of 2007.

Those with huge debts are likely to be cautious before undertaking the additional burdens of a family. But even when they do, they will find it more difficult to get a mortgage. And if they do, it will be smaller, and the real estate recovery will consequently be weaker. (One study of recent Rutgers University graduates showed that 40 percent had delayed making a major home purchase, and for a quarter, the high level of debt had an effect on household formation or getting further education. Another recent study showed that homeownership among 30-year-olds with a history of student debt fell by more than 10 percentage points during the Great Recession and in its aftermath.)

It's a vicious cycle: lack of demand for housing contributes to a lack of jobs, which contributes to weak household formation, which contributes to a lack of demand for housing.

As bad as things are, they may get worse. With budgetary pressures mounting—along with demands for cutbacks in "discretionary domestic programs" (read: K–12 education subsidies, Pell Grants for poor kids to attend college, research money)—students and families are left to fend for themselves. College costs will continue to rise far faster than incomes. As has been repeatedly observed, *all* of the economic gains since the Great Recession have gone to the top 1 percent.

Consider another dubious distinction: student debt is almost impossible to discharge in bankruptcy proceedings.

We're a long way from the debtors' prisons Dickens described. We don't send debtors to penal colonies or put them in bonded labor. Although personal bankruptcy laws have been tightened, the principle that bankrupt individuals should be allowed a fresh start, and a chance to discharge excessive debt, is an established principle. This helps debt markets work better, and also provides incentives for creditors to assess the creditworthiness of borrowers.

Yet education loans are almost impossible to write off in bankruptcy court—even when for-profit schools didn't deliver what they promised and didn't provide an education that would let the borrower get a job that paid enough to pay back the loan.

We should cut off federal support for these for-profit schools when they fail to graduate students, who don't get jobs and then default on their loans.

To its credit, the Obama administration tried to make it tougher for these predatory schools to lure students with false promises. Under the new rules, schools had to meet one of three tests, or lose their eligibility for federal student aid: at least 35 percent of graduates had to be repaying their loans; the typical graduate's estimated annual loan payments could not exceed 12 percent of earnings; or the payments could not exceed 30 percent of discretionary income. But in 2012, a federal judge struck down the rules as arbitrary; the rules remain in legal limbo.

The combination of predatory for-profit schools and predatory lenders is a leech on America's poor. These schools have even gone after young veterans who served in Iraq and Afghanistan. There are heart-rending stories of parents who co-signed student loans—only to see their child killed in an accident or die of cancer or another disease—and, like students, can't easily discharge these debts.

Interest rates on federal Stafford loans were set to double in July, to 6.8 percent. Good news came on Friday: it appears that there is a temporary reprieve, as Republicans have come around. But the stay would be temporary and would not address a more fundamental issue: if the Federal Reserve is willing to lend to the banks that caused the crisis at just 0.75 percent, shouldn't it be willing to lend to students, who will be crucial to our long-term recovery, at an appropriately low rate? The government shouldn't be profiting from our poorest while subsidizing our richest. A proposal by Senator Elizabeth Warren, Democrat of Massachusetts, for lower student-loan interest rates is a step in the right direction.

Along with tougher regulation of for-profit schools and the banks they connive with, and more humane bankruptcy laws, we must give more support to middle-class families struggling to send their children to college, to ensure that they have a standard of living at least equal to that of their parents.

But a real long-term solution requires rethinking how we finance higher education. Australia has designed a system of publicly provided income-contingent loans that all students must take out. Repayments vary according to individual income after graduation. This aligns the incentives of the providers of education and the receivers. Both have an incentive to see that students do well. It means that if an unfortunate event happens, like an illness or an accident, the loan obligation is automatically reduced. It means that the burden of the debt is always commensurate with an individual's ability to repay. The repayments are collected through the tax system, minimizing the administrative costs.

Some wonder how the American ideal of equality of opportunity has eroded so much. The way we finance higher education provides part of the answer. Student debt has become an integral part of the story of American inequality. Robust higher education, with healthy public support, was once the linchpin in a system that promised opportunity for dedicated students of any means. We now have a pay-to-play, winner-take-all game where the wealthiest are assured a spot, and the rest are compelled to take a gamble on huge debts, with no guarantee of a payoff.

Even if compassion isn't a factor—even if we focus just on recovery now and growth and innovation tomorrow—we must do something about student debt. Those concerned about the damage America's growing divide is doing to our ideals and our moral character should put student debt at the top of any reform agenda.

JUSTICE FOR SOME*

THE MORTGAGE DEBACLE IN THE UNITED STATES HAS
raised deep questions about "the rule of law," the universally
accepted hallmark of an advanced, civilized society. The rule of law
is supposed to protect the weak against the strong, and ensure that
everyone is treated fairly. In America in the wake of the subprime
mortgage crisis, it has done neither.

Part of the rule of law is security of property rights—if you owe
money on your house, for example, the bank can't simply take it
away without following the prescribed legal process. But in recent
weeks and months, Americans have seen several instances in which
individuals have been dispossessed of their houses *even when they
have no debts.*

To some banks, this is just collateral damage: millions of Americans—in addition to the estimated four million in 2008 and
2009—still have to be thrown out of their homes. Indeed, the pace
of foreclosures would be set to increase—were it not for government intervention. The procedural shortcuts, incomplete documen-
tation, and rampant fraud that accompanied banks' rush to generate

* *Project Syndicate*, November 4, 2010.

millions of bad loans during the housing bubble has, however, complicated the process of cleaning up the ensuing mess.

To many bankers, these are just details to be overlooked. Most
people evicted from their homes have not been paying their mortgages, and, in most cases, those who are throwing them out have
rightful claims. But Americans are not supposed to believe in justice *on average*. We don't say that most people imprisoned for life
committed a crime worthy of that sentence. The U.S. justice system
demands more, and we have imposed procedural safeguards to
meet these demands.

But banks want to short-circuit these procedural safeguards.
They should not be allowed to do so.

To some, all of this is reminiscent of what happened in Russia,
where the rule of law—bankruptcy legislation in particular—was
used as a legal mechanism to replace one group of owners with
another. Courts were bought, documents forged, and the process
went smoothly.

In America, the venality is at a higher level. It is not particular
judges that are bought, but the laws themselves, through campaign
contributions and lobbying, in what has come to be called "corruption, American-style."

It was widely known that banks and mortgage companies were
engaged in predatory lending practices, taking advantage of the
least educated and most financially uninformed to make loans that
maximized fees and imposed enormous risks on the borrowers. (To
be fair, the banks tried to take advantage of the more financially
sophisticated as well, as with securities created by Goldman Sachs
that were designed to fail.) But banks used all their political muscle
to stop states from enacting laws to curtail predatory lending.

When it became clear that people could not pay back what
was owed, the rules of the game changed. Bankruptcy laws were
amended to introduce a system of "partial indentured servitude."
An individual with, say, debts equal to 100 percent of his income
could be forced to hand over to the bank 25 percent of his gross,

pretax income for the rest of his life, because, the bank could add on, say, 30 percent interest each year to what a person owed. In the end, a mortgage holder would owe far more than the bank ever received, even though the debtor had worked, in effect, one-quarter time for the bank.

When this new bankruptcy law was passed, no one complained that it interfered with the sanctity of contracts: at the time borrowers incurred their debt, a more humane—and economically rational—bankruptcy law gave them a chance for a fresh start if the burden of debt repayment became too onerous.

That knowledge should have given lenders incentives to make loans only to those who could repay. But lenders perhaps knew that, with the Republicans in control of government, they could make bad loans and then change the law to ensure that they could squeeze the poor.

With one out of four mortgages in the U.S. underwater—more owed than the house is worth—there is a growing consensus that the only way to deal with the mess is to write down the value of the principal (what is owed). America has a special procedure for corporate bankruptcy, called Chapter 11, which allows a speedy restructuring by writing down debt, and converting some of it to equity.

It is important to keep enterprises alive as going concerns, in order to preserve jobs and growth. But it is also important to keep families and communities intact. So America needs a "homeowners' Chapter 11."

Lenders complain that such a law would violate their property rights. But almost all changes in laws and regulations benefit some at the expense of others. When the 2005 bankruptcy law was passed, lenders were the beneficiaries; they didn't worry about how the law affected the rights of debtors.

Growing inequality, combined with a flawed system of campaign finance, risks turning America's legal system into a travesty of justice. Some may still call it the "rule of law," but it would not be a rule of law that protects the weak against the powerful. Rather, it would enable the powerful to exploit the weak.

In today's America, the proud claim of "justice for all" is being replaced by the more modest claim of "justice for those who can afford it." And the number of people who can afford it is rapidly diminishing.

THE ONE HOUSING SOLUTION LEFT: MASS MORTGAGE REFINANCING*

with Mark Zandi

MORE THAN FOUR MILLION AMERICANS HAVE LOST THEIR homes since the housing bubble began bursting six years ago. An additional 3.5 million homeowners are in the foreclosure process or are so delinquent on payments that they will be soon. With 13.5 million homeowners underwater—they owe more than their home is now worth—the odds are high that many millions more will lose their homes.

Housing remains the biggest impediment to economic recovery, yet Washington seems paralyzed. While the Obama administration's housing policies have fallen short, Mitt Romney hasn't offered any meaningful new proposals to aid distressed or underwater homeowners.

Late last month, the top regulator overseeing Fannie Mae and Freddie Mac blocked a plan backed by the Obama administration to let the companies forgive some of the mortgage debt owed by stressed homeowners. While half a million homeowners could be helped with a principal writedown, the regulator, Edward J. DeMarco, argued (we believe incorrectly) that helping some home-

* *New York Times*, August 12, 2012.

owners might cause others who are paying on their loans to stop so that they also could get their mortgages reduced.

With principal writedown no longer an option, the government needs to find a new way to facilitate mass mortgage refinancings. With rates at record lows, refinancing would allow homeowners to significantly reduce their monthly payments, freeing up money to spend on other things. A mass refinancing program would work like a potent tax cut.

Refinancing would also significantly reduce the chance of default for underwater homeowners. With fewer losses from past loans burdening their balance sheets, lenders could make more new loans, and communities plagued by mass foreclosures might see relief from blight.

Well over half of all American homeowners with mortgages are paying rates that would appear to make them excellent candidates to refinance. Many of those with stable jobs, good credit scores, and even a modest amount of home equity have already done so, taking out 30-year loans at rates around 3.5 percent, some of the lowest rates since the 1950s. But many others can't refinance because the collapse in house prices has wiped out their home equity.

Senator Jeff Merkley, an Oregon Democrat, has proposed a remedy. Under his plan, called Rebuilding American Homeownership, underwater homeowners who are current on their payments and meet other requirements would have the option to refinance to either lower their monthly payments or pay down their loans and rebuild equity.

A government-financed trust would be used to buy the mortgages of homeowners who had refinanced at an interest rate that was about 2 percentage points more than the record-low Treasury rates at which the government borrows. This would generate enough interest income to cover the costs of any defaults, administration of the trust, and other expenses. Families would have three years to refinance; after that, the trust would stop buying loans and eventually wind itself down as homeowners repaid their loans.

Homeowners would see lower mortgage payments and rebuild equity more quickly. Taxpayers would get their money back, with interest, and would gain further as a stronger economy lifted tax revenues. Banks and other mortgage investors would get potentially troubled loans off their books. Some banks won't like losing the large amounts of interest income they are earning on their current mortgages, but if the refinancing market were working properly these loans would have been refinanced long ago.

If the program was very successful, we envisage that two million outstanding loans could be placed in a Rebuilding American Homeownership trust at its peak. If the average mortgage balance was $150,000, then at the peak there would be $300 billion outstanding.

The federal government could finance the plan directly, through the Federal Housing Administration, or indirectly, through the Federal Home Loan Banks, which offer government-backed credit. Or the Federal Reserve could underwrite the plan; the central bank's chairman, Ben S. Bernanke, recently talked about the Fed's doing something akin to the Bank of England's new Funding for Lending program, which offers incentives to banks to increase lending to households and nonfinancial businesses.

Opponents of additional borrowing or Fed lending will say that a program like this is an unacceptable risk, but the greater risk is to do nothing and let the housing market continue to hold back the economy.

Mr. Merkley's plan resembles the Obama administration's Home Affordable Refinance Plan, or HARP, which was designed to help underwater homeowners refinance loans backed by Fannie and Freddie. It has made possible 1.4 million refinancings, far fewer than the goal set in 2009 of 3 million to 4 million. The administration has made some improvements to HARP and proposed others. But the Merkley plan has the potential to go further, reaching the 20 million households with mortgages that aren't backed by Fannie or Freddie.

The Merkley plan has a successful precedent in the Home Owners' Loan Corporation, established in 1933. It swept more than a million Americans out of foreclosure and into the long-term, stable mortgages that would become the hallmark of the middle class during the 1950s and '60s It's time to revive this idea.

Since the Great Recession began almost five years ago, housing has been at the heart of our economic woes. If we do nothing, the problem will eventually resolve itself, but only with significant pain and a long wait. Mr. Merkley's plan would speed the healing.

INEQUALITY AND THE
AMERICAN CHILD*

C HILDREN, IT HAS LONG BEEN RECOGNIZED, ARE A SPE-
cial group. They do not choose their parents, let alone the
broader conditions into which they are born. They do not have the
same abilities as adults to protect or care for themselves. That is
why the League of Nations approved the Geneva Declaration on
the Rights of the Child in 1924, and why the international community adopted the Convention on the Rights of the Child in 1989.

Sadly, the United States is not living up to its obligations. In
fact, it has not even ratified the Convention on the Rights of the
Child. The U.S., with its cherished image as a land of opportunity,
should be an inspiring example of just and enlightened treatment of
children. Instead, it is a beacon of failure—one that contributes to
global sluggishness on children's rights in the international arena.

Though an average American childhood may not be the worst in
the world, the disparity between the country's wealth and the condition of its children is unparalleled. About 14.5 percent of the American population as a whole is poor, but 19.9 percent of children—some
15 million individuals—live in poverty. Among developed countries,
only Romania has a higher rate of child poverty. The U.S. rate is

* *Project Syndicate*, December 11, 2014.

two-thirds higher than that in the United Kingdom, and up to four times the rate in the Nordic countries. For some groups, the situation is much worse: more than 38 percent of black children and 30 percent of Hispanic children, are poor.

None of this is because Americans don't care about their children. It is because America has embraced a policy agenda in recent decades that has caused its economy to become wildly unequal, leaving the most vulnerable segments of society further and further behind. The growing concentration of wealth—and a significant reduction in taxes on it—has meant less money to spend on investments for the public good, like education and the protection of children.

As a result, America's children have become worse off. Their fate is a painful example of how inequality not only undermines economic growth and stability—as economists and organizations like the International Monetary Fund are finally acknowledging—but also violates our most cherished notions of what a fair society should look like.

Income inequality is correlated with inequalities in health, access to education, and exposure to environmental hazards, all of which burden children more than other segments of the population. Indeed, nearly one in five poor American children are diagnosed with asthma, a rate that is 60 percent higher than that for nonpoor children. Learning disabilities occur almost twice as frequently among children in households earning less than $35,000 a year than they do in households earning more than $100,000. And some in the U.S. Congress want to cut food stamps—on which some 23 million American households depend, threatening the poorest children with hunger.

These inequalities in outcomes are closely tied to inequalities in opportunities. Inevitably, in countries where children have inadequate nutrition, insufficient access to health care and education, and higher exposure to environmental hazards, the children of the poor will have far different life prospects from those of the rich.

And, partly because in America a child's lifetime prospects are more dependent on his or her parents' income and education than in other advanced countries, the U.S. now has the least equality of opportunity of any advanced country. At America's most elite universities, for example, only around 9 percent of students come from the bottom half of the population, while 74 percent come from the top quarter.

Most societies recognize a moral obligation to help ensure that young people can live up to their potential. Some countries even impose a constitutional mandate for equality of educational opportunities.

But in America, more is spent on the education of rich students than on the education of the poor. As a result, the U.S. is wasting some of its most valuable assets, with some young people—bereft of skills—turning to dysfunctional activities. American states like California spend about as much on prisons as on higher education—and sometimes more.

Without compensatory measures—including preschool education, ideally beginning at a very young age—unequal opportunities translate to unequal lifelong outcomes. That should be a spur to policy action.

Indeed, while inequality's harmful effects are wide-reaching, and impose huge costs on our economies and societies, they are largely avoidable. The *extremes* of inequality observed in some countries are not the inexorable result of economic forces and laws. The right policies—stronger social safety nets, progressive taxation, and better regulation (especially of the financial sector), to name a few—can reverse these devastating trends.

To generate the political will that such reforms require, we must confront policymakers' inertia and inaction with the grim facts of inequality and its devastating effects on our children. We *can* reduce childhood deprivation and increase equality of opportunity, thereby laying the groundwork for a more just and prosperous future—one that reflects our own avowed values. So why don't we?

Of the harm that inequality inflicts on our economies, politics, and societies, the damage done to children demands special concern. Whatever responsibility poor adults may bear for their lot in life—they may not have worked hard enough, saved enough, or made good decisions—children's circumstances are thrust upon them without any sort of choice. Children, perhaps more than anyone else, need the protection that rights afford—and the U.S. should be providing the world with a shining example of what that means.

EBOLA AND INEQUALITY[*]

THE EBOLA CRISIS REMINDS US, ONCE AGAIN, OF THE downside of globalization. Not only good things—like principles of social justice and gender equality—cross borders more easily than ever before; so do malign influences like environmental problems and disease.

The crisis also reminds us of the importance of government and civil society. We do not turn to the private sector to control the spread of a disease like Ebola. Rather, we turn to institutions—the Centers for Disease Control and Prevention (CDC) in the United States, the World Health Organization (WHO), and Médecins Sans Frontières, the remarkable group of doctors and nurses who risk their lives to save those of others in poor countries around the world.

Even right-wing fanatics who want to dismantle government institutions turn to them when facing a crisis like that caused by Ebola. Governments may not do a perfect job in addressing such crises, but one of the reasons that they have not done as well as we would hope is that we have underfunded the relevant agencies at the national and global level.

The Ebola episode holds further lessons. One reason that the dis-

---
*   *Project Syndicate*, November 10, 2014.

ease spread so rapidly in Liberia and Sierra Leone is that both are war-ravaged countries, where a large proportion of the population is malnourished and the health care system has been devastated.

Moreover, where the private sector does play an essential role— vaccine development—it has little incentive to devote resources to diseases that afflict the poor or poor countries. It is only when advanced countries are threatened that there is sufficient impetus to invest in vaccines to confront diseases like Ebola.

This is not so much a criticism of the private sector; after all, drug companies are not in business out of the goodness of their hearts, and there is no money in preventing or curing the diseases of the poor. Rather, what the Ebola crisis calls into question is our reliance on the private sector to do the things that governments perform best. Indeed, it appears that with more public funding, an Ebola vaccine could have been developed years ago.

America's failures in this regard have drawn particular attention— so much so that some African countries are treating visitors from the U.S. with special precautions. But this just echoes a more fundamental problem: America's largely private health care system is failing.

True, at the top end, the U.S. has some of the world's leading hospitals, research universities, and advanced medical centers. But, though the U.S. spends more per capita and as a percentage of its GDP on medical care than any other country, its health outcomes are truly disappointing.

American male life expectancy at birth is the worst of 17 high-income countries—almost four years shorter than that in Switzerland, Australia, and Japan. And it is the second worst for women, more than five years below life expectancy in Japan.

Other health metrics are equally disappointing, with data indicating poorer health outcomes for Americans throughout their lives. And, for at least three decades, matters have been getting worse.

Many factors contribute to America's health lag, with lessons that are relevant for other countries as well. For starters, access to medicine matters. With the U.S. among the few advanced countries that does not recognize access as a basic human right, and more reliant than others on the private sector, it is no surprise that many Americans do not get the medicines they need. Though the Patient Protection and Affordable Care Act (Obamacare) has improved matters, health-insurance coverage remains weak, with almost half of the 50 U.S. states refusing to expand Medicaid, the health care financing program for America's poor.

Moreover, the U.S. has one of the highest rates of childhood poverty among the advanced countries (which was especially true before austerity policies dramatically increased poverty in several European countries), and lack of nutrition and health care in childhood has lifelong effects. Meanwhile, America's gun laws contribute to the highest incidence of violent deaths among advanced countries, and its dependence on the automobile underpins a high rate of highway fatalities.

America's outsize inequality, too, is a critical factor in its health lag, especially combined with the factors mentioned above. With more poverty, more childhood poverty, more people without access to health care, decent housing, and education, and more people facing food insecurity (often consuming cheap foods that contribute to obesity), it is no surprise that U.S. health outcomes are bad.

But health outcomes are also worse in the U.S. than elsewhere for those with higher incomes and insurance coverage. Perhaps this, too, is related to higher inequality than in other advanced countries. Health, we know, is related to stress. Those striving to climb the ladder of success know the consequences of failure. In the U.S., the rungs of the ladder are farther apart than elsewhere, and the distance from the top to the bottom is greater. That means more anxiety, which translates into poorer health.

Good health is a blessing. But how countries structure their health care system—and their society—makes a huge difference in terms of outcomes. America and the world pay a high price for excessive reliance on market forces and an insufficient attention to broader values, including equality and social justice.

PART IV

CAUSES OF AMERICA'S GROWING INEQUALITY

THERE HAS ALWAYS BEEN INEQUALITY. THERE ALWAYS will be. The question posed by these articles is why inequality—in virtually all of its dimensions—has increased so much in the last 35 years. The Great Recession, of course, contributed greatly to inequality (though, as we comment in the next section, it was also partly a consequence of inequality). The trends were, however, apparent well before then.

Each aspect of inequality—the increasing share of the very top, the growth in poverty, the weakening of the middle—has its own explanations. At the top, the larger share of capital and the high level of capital gains are critical—the rich own a disproportionate share of capital and receive the overwhelming share of capital gains. But that only pushes the question back a little: Why has this occurred? Earlier in the book we explained the concept of rent seeking—there are two ways to get wealthy, making the size of the nation's economic pie larger and increasing the size of one's own slice relative to that of others (and in the fight over getting a larger slice, the pie may even get smaller). The increase in the wealth at the top is overwhelmingly associated with an increase in rent seeking. Corporate executives are seizing a larger share of the corporate pie, but not because they have suddenly become more productive.

Financialization—the increased importance of the financial sector in the economy—has been central, not only in the increased instability of the economy, evidenced by the Great Recession, but in the increased inequality. Monopoly power has expanded, too, with the growth of firms with global market power (like Apple, Google, and Microsoft) and, in some cases, even the growth of firms with more local market power (like Walmart and Amazon).

In the preceding section we noted a number of aspects of America's inequality, including inequality in access to health care and education and poverty among children. The result of these inequities is that inequalities get transmitted across generations: the children of the advantaged begin life with a major head start. Inequalities of opportunity are both cause and consequence of inequalities in incomes. It is not surprising that inequality would grow over time, as America is becoming *more* economically segregated—with the children of the rich going to well-funded schools, the children of the poor going to schools that often hardly function.

The increase in inequality in before-tax and transfer income in the United States, while large, is not that much larger than in some other advanced countries. What distinguishes America's growing inequality from that of other countries is that we do so little about it: others have made a greater effort to ameliorate the inequalities.

In earlier sections of this book, we emphasized that inequality was a matter of choice: the laws of economics are the same in different countries, but how they play out is markedly different. Every law and regulation, every government expenditure, every policy, can have an effect on inequality. In the next section, we illustrate this with several of the heated policy debates in which America has been engaged. The preceding section also provided a number of illustrations: we have chosen to finance higher education in a way that is markedly different from that of other countries, and this makes access to higher education more difficult for the poor and even the middle. In *The Price of Inequality* I discuss other examples: how our bankruptcy laws—the laws that specify what happens when a firm or an individual can't pay all that is owed—favor the financial sector and discriminate against the poor trying to make their way up by borrowing to get an education.

The articles in this part take up only a small part of the story. They don't discuss how inequality in access to and achievement in education is both a consequence and cause of our ever-increasing income and wealth inequality; how inadequate nutrition and access to health care for the poor (and increasingly even middle America) can also perpetuate inequality; or how poor children's greater exposure to environmental hazards can do likewise. Nor do they consider how inequality in access to justice can do the same.

Instead, the articles focus on just two issues—corporate welfare and our tax system. The title of the first essay, written soon after America's bailouts for the banks, says it all: "America's Socialism for the Rich." "Socialism" has, of course, become a dirty word in America, just like "welfare." But how else should one describe the mega-bailouts for America's banks. We didn't play by the rules of capitalism, which would have made the bankers, the bank shareholders, and the bondholders pay for their mistakes. Critics of my view say that we *had* to bail out the banks. That's true. But we didn't have to bail out the bankers, the shareholders, and the bondholders.

The essay not only illustrates that the tax system is unfair; it also shows how it distorts our economy—and leads to higher levels not only of after-tax inequality but even of before-tax inequality. If speculators are taxed at lower rates than those who work for a living, then speculation is encouraged. In April 2014 I testified to the Senate about America's growing inequality. One senator asked how he could explain to his constituents why a plumber should pay a higher tax rate than someone with a comparable income reaping the returns from (long-term) speculation. The question was, of course, rhetorical, and none of the panel—either Republican, Democrat, or Independent—could give an answer.

More generally, earlier chapters explained how inequality at the top is associated with exploitation and rent seeking; and here I explain how our tax system encourages these activities, weakening the economy and increasing inequality.

As Americans face the deadline for filing their tax returns every April 15, there is always a rash of articles about our tax system. "A Tax System Stacked against the 99 Percent" shows how our tax system is not just a little unfair—it's stacked against the 99 percent. Because those at the top don't pay their fair share of taxes, the burden on the rest is increased; and it means the rich get to keep—and reinvest—their profits, getting richer and richer in the process. Warren Buffett famously pointed out that it was unfair that he paid a lower tax rate than his secretary. What he didn't point out is that when he said that, he was presumably referring to the ratio of his taxes to his *realized* income. Every year, he gets a small salary (relative to his overall income), receives dividends and interest, and realizes *some* capital gains. But normally he has enormous *unrealized* capital gains. The assets he owns increase in value, and so long as he doesn't sell his stock or other ownership claims, no taxes are due. So if the very rich just hold on to their assets, they can increase in value, year after year, without paying *any* taxes. And then they can pass the assets on to their children; and the children can pass them on to their children. So long as the assets are not sold, no income taxes will ever have to be paid. And if they are sold, the great-grandchild has to pay taxes only on the increase in value since he inherited them; the entire capital gains over the previous generations totally escape taxation. (True, there may be inheritance taxes, though clever estate tax management can often avoid, or at least minimize, these taxes.)

These articles were written before the scandals of tax avoidance on a global scale were exposed. At that time, GE was the shining example of a corporate leader that had managed to avoid paying its fair share of taxes. But then the Apple and Google scandals broke out—these Silicon Valley companies, long noted for their ingenuity in technology, had displayed the same ingenuity in tax avoidance. They took advantage of globalization—the ability to move money around the world. Apple claimed that its profits could really be attributed to a few people working in Ireland! Honesty—let alone a sense of fair play—seems a rarer commodity than ingenuity. These companies were willing to take but not to give back: after all, their success depends on the Internet, which was created by government spending. If we don't replenish the stock of ideas upon which companies can draw through basic research, the flow of innovations won't be sustained. But that requires money, tax dollars. Google and Apple have shown that the same shortsighted and selfish behavior that was endemic in America's financial sector can manifest itself in Silicon Valley.

"Fallacies of Romney's Logic" was written amid the fury that followed the release of a video of a speech by Mitt Romney, then the Republican candidate for the presidency (he intended the remarks to be private). He claimed that 47 percent of American's didn't pay income taxes, and he derided them as free riders. The irony was, of course, that Romney himself had managed to avoid paying his fair share of taxes, taking advantage of a loophole in the tax law that allowed those in the private equity business to pay low taxes—much lower than that of a plumber who earned a comparable income. (There was another issue that I didn't have time to raise in the article. He admitted that he kept much of his wealth in the Cayman Islands. America has, presumably, the best financial markets in the world—at least for serving the interests of the rich. Surely, he wasn't keeping his money in the Cayman Islands because they provided unique services—other than a lack of transparency—that Wall Street could not provide. He never deigned to provide Americans with an explanation.) This article explains more narrowly what the flaw was in Romney's logic—why his castigating "the 47 percent" was simply wrongheaded.

AMERICA'S SOCIALISM
FOR THE RICH*

WITH ALL THE TALK OF "GREEN SHOOTS" OF ECONOMIC recovery, America's banks are pushing back on efforts to regulate them. While politicians talk about their commitment to regulatory reform to prevent a recurrence of the crisis, this is one area where the devil really is in the details—and the banks will muster what muscle they have left to ensure that they have ample room to continue as they did in the past.

The old system worked well for the bankers (if not for their shareholders), so why should they embrace change? Indeed, the efforts to rescue them devoted so little thought to the kind of post-crisis financial system we want that we will end up with a banking system that is less competitive, with the large banks that were too big to fail even larger.

It has long been recognized that America's banks that are too big to fail are also too big to be managed. That is one reason that the performance of several of them has been so dismal. Because government provides deposit insurance, it plays a large role in restructuring (unlike other sectors). Normally, when a bank fails, the government engineers a financial restructuring; if it has to put

---

* *Project Syndicate*, June 8, 2009.

in money, it, of course, gains a stake in the future. Officials know that if they wait too long, zombie or near-zombie banks—with little or no net worth, but treated as if they were viable institutions—are likely to "gamble on resurrection." If they take big bets and win, they walk away with the proceeds; if they fail, the government picks up the tab.

This is not just theory; it is a lesson we learned, at great expense, during the savings-and-loan crisis of the 1980s. When the ATM machine says, "insufficient funds," the government doesn't want this to mean that the bank, rather than your account, is out of money, so it intervenes before the till is empty. In a financial restructuring, shareholders typically get wiped out, and bondholders become the new shareholders. Sometimes the government must provide additional funds; sometimes it looks for a new investor to take over the failed bank.

The Obama administration has, however, introduced a new concept: too big to be financially restructured. The administration argues that all hell would break loose if we tried to play by the usual rules with these big banks. Markets would panic. So, not only can't we touch the bondholders, we can't even touch the shareholders— even if most of the shares' existing value merely reflects a bet on a government bailout.

I think this judgment is wrong. I think the Obama administration has succumbed to political pressure and scaremongering by the big banks. As a result, the administration has confused bailing out the bankers and their shareholders with bailing out the banks.

Restructuring gives banks a chance for a new start: new potential investors (whether in equity or debt instruments) will have more confidence, other banks will be more willing to lend to them, and they will be more willing to lend to others. The bondholders will gain from an orderly restructuring, and if the value of the assets is truly greater than the market (and outside analysts) believe, they will eventually reap the gains.

But what is clear is that the Obama strategy's current and future costs are very high—and so far, it has not achieved its limited objective of restarting lending. The taxpayer has had to pony up billions, and has provided billions more in guarantees—bills that are likely to come due in the future.

Rewriting the rules of the market economy—in a way that has benefited those that have caused so much pain to the entire global economy—is worse than financially costly. Most Americans view it as grossly unjust, especially after they saw the banks divert the billions intended to enable them to revive lending to payments of outsized bonuses and dividends. Tearing up the social contract is something that should not be done lightly.

But this new form of ersatz capitalism, in which losses are socialized and profits privatized, is doomed to failure. Incentives are distorted. There is no market discipline. The too-big-to-be-restructured banks know that they can gamble with impunity—and, with the Federal Reserve making funds available at near-zero interest rates, there are ample funds to do so.

Some have called this new economic regime "socialism with American characteristics." But socialism is concerned about ordinary individuals. By contrast, the United States has provided little help for the millions of Americans who are losing their homes. Workers who lose their jobs receive only 39 weeks of limited unemployment benefits, and are then left on their own. And, when they lose their jobs, most lose their health insurance, too.

America has expanded its corporate safety net in unprecedented ways, from commercial banks to investment banks, then to insurance, and now to automobiles, with no end in sight. In truth, this is not socialism, but an extension of long-standing corporate welfarism. The rich and powerful turn to the government to help them whenever they can, while needy individuals get little social protection.

We need to break up the too-big-to-fail banks; there is no evidence that these behemoths deliver societal benefits that are commensurate with the costs they have imposed on others. And, if we don't break them up, then we have to severely limit what they do. They can't be allowed to do what they did in the past—gamble at others' expenses.

This raises another problem with America's too-big-to-fail, too-big-to-be-restructured banks: they are too politically powerful. Their lobbying efforts worked well, first to deregulate, and then to have taxpayers pay for the cleanup. Their hope is that it will work once again to keep them free to do as they please, regardless of the risks for taxpayers and the economy. We cannot afford to let that happen.

A TAX SYSTEM STACKED
AGAINST THE 99 PERCENT[*]

Leona Helmsley, the hotel chain executive who was convicted of federal tax evasion in 1989, was notorious for, among other things, reportedly having said that "only the little people pay taxes."

As a statement of principle, the quotation may well have earned Mrs. Helmsley, who died in 2007, the title Queen of Mean. But as a prediction about the fairness of American tax policy, Mrs. Helmsley's remark might actually have been prescient.

Today, the deadline for filing individual income-tax returns, is a day when Americans would do well to pause and reflect on our tax system and the society it creates. No one enjoys paying taxes, and yet all but the extreme libertarians agree, as Oliver Wendell Holmes said, that taxes are the price we pay for civilized society. But in recent decades, the burden for paying that price has been distributed in increasingly unfair ways.

About 6 in 10 of us believe that the tax system is unfair—and they're right: put simply, the very rich don't pay their fair share. The richest 400 individual taxpayers, with an average income of more

---

[*] *New York Times*, April 14, 2013.

than $200 million, pay less than 20 percent of their income in taxes—far lower than mere millionaires, who pay about 25 percent of their income in taxes, and about the same as those earning a mere $200,000 to $500,000. And in 2009, 116 of the top 400 earners—almost a third—paid less than 15 percent of their income in taxes.

Conservatives like to point out that the richest Americans' tax payments make up a large portion of total receipts. This is true, as well it should be in any tax system that is progressive—that is, a system that taxes the affluent at higher rates than those of modest means. It's also true that as the wealthiest Americans' incomes have skyrocketed in recent years, their total tax payments have grown. This would be so even if we had a single flat income-tax rate across the board.

What should shock and outrage us is that as the top 1 percent has grown extremely rich, the effective tax rates they pay have markedly decreased. Our tax system is much less progressive than it was for much of the 20th century. The top marginal income tax rate peaked at 94 percent during World War II and remained at 70 percent through the 1960s and 1970s; it is now 39.6 percent. Tax fairness has gotten much worse in the 30 years since the Reagan "revolution" of the 1980s.

Citizens for Tax Justice, an organization that advocates for a more progressive tax system, has estimated that, when federal, state, and local taxes are taken into account, the top 1 percent paid only slightly more than 20 percent of all American taxes in 2010—about the same as the share of income they took home, an outcome that is not progressive at all.

With such low effective tax rates—and, importantly, the low tax rate of 20 percent on income from capital gains—it's not a huge surprise that the share of income going to the top 1 percent has doubled since 1979, and that the share going to the top 0.1 percent has almost tripled, according to the economists Thomas Piketty and Emmanuel Saez. Recall that the wealthiest 1 percent of Americans own about 40 percent of the nation's wealth, and the picture becomes even more disturbing.

If these numbers still don't impress you as being unfair, consider them in comparison with other wealthy countries.

The United States stands out among the countries of the Organization for Economic Cooperation and Development, the world's club of rich nations, for its low top marginal income-tax rate. These low rates are not essential for growth—consider Germany, for instance, which has managed to maintain its status as a center of advanced manufacturing, even though its top income-tax rate exceeds America's by a considerable margin. And in general, our top tax rate kicks in at much higher incomes. Denmark, for example, has a top tax rate of more than 60 percent, but that applies to anyone making more than $54,900. The top rate in the United States, 39.6 percent, doesn't kick in until individual income reaches $400,000 (or $450,000 for a couple). Only three OECD countries—South Korea, Canada, and Spain—have higher thresholds.

Most of the Western world has experienced an increase in inequality in recent decades, though not as much as the United States has. But among most economists there is a general understanding that a country with excessive inequality can't function well; many countries have used their tax codes to help "correct" the market's distribution of wealth and income. The United States hasn't— or at least not very much. Indeed, the low rates at the top serve to exacerbate and perpetuate the inequality—so much so that among the advanced industrial countries, America now has the highest income inequality and the least equality of opportunity. This is a gross inversion of America's traditional meritocratic ideals—ideals that our leaders, across the spectrum, continue to profess.

Over the years, some of the wealthy have been enormously successful in getting special treatment, shifting an ever greater share of the burden of financing the country's expenditures—defense, education, social programs—onto others. Ironically, this is especially true of some of our multinational corporations, which call on the federal government to negotiate favorable trade treaties that allow them easy entry into foreign markets and to defend their commercial interests around the world, but then use these foreign bases to avoid paying taxes.

General Electric has become the symbol for multinational corporations that have their headquarters in the United States but pay almost no taxes—its effective corporate-tax rate averaged less than 2 percent from 2002 to 2012—just as Mitt Romney, the Republican presidential nominee last year, became the symbol for the wealthy who don't pay their fair share when he admitted that he paid only 14 percent of his income in taxes in 2011, even as he notoriously complained that 47 percent of Americans were freeloaders. Neither G.E. nor Mr. Romney has, to my knowledge, broken any tax laws, but the sparse taxes they've paid violate most Americans' basic sense of fairness.

In looking at such statistics, one has to be careful: they typically reflect taxes as a percentage of reported income. And the tax laws don't require the reporting of all kinds of income. For the rich, hiding such assets has become an elite sport. Many avail themselves of the Cayman Islands or other offshore tax shelters to avoid taxes (and not, you can safely assume, because of the sunny weather). They don't have to report income until it is brought back ("repatriated") to the United States. So, too, capital gains have to be reported as income only when they are realized.

And if the assets are passed on to one's children or grandchildren at death, no taxes are ever paid, in a peculiar loophole called the "step-up in cost basis at death." Yes, the tax privileges of being rich in America extend into the afterlife.

As Americans look at some of the special provisions in the tax code—for vacation homes, racetracks, beer breweries, oil refineries, hedge funds, and movie studios, among many other favored assets or industries—it is no wonder that they feel disillusioned with a tax system that is so riddled with special rewards. Most of these tax-code loopholes and giveaways did not materialize from thin air, of course—usually, they were enacted in pursuit of, or at least in response to, campaign contributions from influential donors. It is estimated that these kinds of special tax provisions amount to some $123 billion a year, and that the price tag for offshore tax loopholes is not far behind. Eliminating these provisions alone would go a long way toward meeting deficit-reduction targets called for by fiscal conservatives who worry about the size of the public debt.

Yet another source of unfairness is the tax treatment on so-called carried interest. Some Wall Street financiers are able to pay taxes at lower capital-gains tax rates on income that comes from managing assets for private equity funds or hedge funds. But why should managing financial assets be treated any differently from managing people, or making discoveries? Of course, those in finance say they are essential. But so are doctors, lawyers, teachers, and everyone else who contributes to making our complex society work. They say they are necessary for job creation. But in fact, many of the private equity firms that have excelled in exploiting the carried interest loophole are actually job destroyers; they excel in restructuring firms to "save" on labor costs, often by moving jobs abroad.

Economists often eschew the word "fair"—fairness, like beauty, is in the eye of the beholder. But the unfairness of the American tax system has gotten so great that it's dishonest to apply any other label to it.

Traditionally, economists have focused less on issues of equality than on the more mundane issues of growth and efficiency. But here again, our tax system comes in with low marks. Our growth was higher in the era of high top marginal tax rates than it has been since 1980. Economists—even at traditional, conservative international institutions like the International Monetary Fund—have come to realize that excessive inequality is bad for growth and stability. The tax system can play an important role in moderating the degree of inequality. Ours, however, does remarkably little about it.

One of the reasons for our poor economic performance is the large distortion in our economy caused by the tax system. The one thing economists agree on is that incentives matter—if you lower taxes on speculation, say, you will get more speculation. We've drawn our most talented young people into financial shenanigans, rather than into creating real businesses, making real discoveries, providing real services to others. More efforts go into "rent seeking"—getting a larger slice of the country's economic pie—than into enlarging the size of the pie.

Research in recent years has linked the tax rates, sluggish growth, and rising inequality. Remember, the low tax rates at the top were supposed to spur savings and hard work, and thus economic growth. They didn't. Indeed, the household savings rate fell to a record level of near zero after President George W. Bush's two rounds of cuts, in 2001 and 2003, on taxes on dividends and capital gains. What low tax rates at the top did do was increase the return on rent seeking. It flourished, which meant that growth slowed and inequality grew. This is a pattern that has now been observed across countries. Contrary to the warnings of those who want to preserve their privileges, countries that have increased their top tax bracket have not grown more slowly. Another piece of evidence is here at home: if the efforts at the top were resulting in our entire economic engine's doing better, we would expect everyone to benefit. If they were engaged in rent seeking, as their incomes increased, we'd expect that of others to decrease. And that's exactly what's been happening. Incomes in the middle, and even the bottom, have been stagnating or falling.

Aside from the evidence, there is a strong intuitive case to be made for the idea that tax rates have encouraged rent seeking at the expense of wealth creation. There is an intrinsic satisfaction in creating a new business, in expanding the horizons of our knowledge, and in helping others. By contrast, it is unpleasant to spend one's days fine-tuning dishonest and deceptive practices that siphon money off the poor, as was common in the financial sector before the 2007–8 financial crisis. I believe that a vast majority of Americans would, all things being equal, choose the former over the latter. But our tax system tilts the field. It increases the net returns from engaging in some of these intrinsically distasteful activities, and it has helped us become a rent-seeking society.

It doesn't have to be this way. We could have a much simpler tax system without all the distortions—a society where those who clip coupons for a living pay the same taxes as someone with the same income who works in a factory; where someone who earns his income from saving companies pays the same tax as a doctor who makes the income by saving lives; where someone who earns his income from financial innovations pays the same taxes as a some- one who does research to create real innovations that transform our economy and society. We could have a tax system that encourages good things like hard work and thrift and discourages bad things, like rent seeking, gambling, financial speculation, and pollution. Such a tax system could raise far more money than the current one—we wouldn't have to go through all the wrangling we've been going through with sequestration, fiscal cliffs, and threats to end Medicare and Social Security as we know it. We would be in sound fiscal position, for at least the next quarter-century.

The consequences of our broken tax system are not just eco- nomic. Our tax system relies heavily on voluntary compliance. But if citizens believe that the tax system is unfair, this voluntary com- pliance will not be forthcoming. More broadly, government plays an important role not just in social protection, but in making invest- ments in infrastructure, technology, education, and health. Without such investments, our economy will be weaker, and our economic growth slower.

Society can't function well without a minimal sense of national solidarity and cohesion, and that sense of shared purpose also rests on a fair tax system. If Americans believe that government is unfair—that ours is a government of the 1 percent, for the 1 per- cent, and by the 1 percent—then faith in our democracy will surely perish.

GLOBALIZATION ISN'T JUST ABOUT PROFITS. IT'S ABOUT TAXES TOO.*

T HE WORLD LOOKED ON AGOG AS TIM COOK, THE HEAD OF Apple, said his company had paid all the taxes owed—seeming to say that it paid all the taxes it should have paid. There is, of course, a big difference between the two. It's no surprise that a company with the resources and ingenuity of Apple would do what it could to avoid paying as much tax as it could within the law. While the Supreme Court, in its *Citizens United* case, seems to have said that corporations are people, with all the rights attendant thereto, this legal fiction didn't endow corporations with a sense of moral responsibility; and they have the Plastic Man capacity to be everywhere and nowhere at the same time—to be everywhere when it comes to selling their products, and nowhere when it comes to reporting the profits derived from those sales.

Apple, like Google, has benefited enormously from what the U.S. and other Western governments provide: highly educated workers trained in universities that are supported both directly by government and indirectly (through generous charitable deductions). The basic research on which their products rest was paid for by taxpayer-supported developments—the Internet, without

---

* *The Guardian*, May 27, 2013.

which they couldn't exist. Their prosperity depends in part on our legal system—including strong enforcement of intellectual property rights; they asked (and got) government to force countries around the world to adopt our standards, in some cases, at great costs to the lives and development of those in emerging markets and developing countries. Yes, they brought genius and organizational skills, for which they justly receive kudos. But while Newton was at least modest enough to note that he stood on the shoulders of giants, these titans of industry have no compunction about being free riders, taking generously from the benefits afforded by our system, but not willing to contribute commensurately. Without public support, the wellspring from which future innovation and growth will come will dry up—not to say what will happen to our increasingly divided society.

It is not even true that higher corporate tax rates would necessarily significantly decrease investment. As Apple has shown, it can finance anything it wants to with debt—including paying dividends, another ploy to avoid paying their fair share of taxes. But interest payments are tax deductible—which means that to the extent that investment is debt-financed, the cost of capital and returns are both changed commensurately, with no adverse effect on investment. And with the low rate of taxation on capital gains, returns on equity are treated even more favorably. Still more benefits accrue from other details of the tax code, such as accelerated depreciation and the tax treatment of research and development expenditures.

It is time the international community faced the reality: we have an unmanageable, unfair, distortionary global tax regime. It is a tax system that is pivotal in creating the increasing inequality that marks most advanced countries today—with America standing out in the forefront and the UK not far behind. It is the starving of the public sector which has been pivotal in America no longer being the land of opportunity—with a child's life prospects more dependent on the income and education of its parents than in other advanced countries.

Globalization has made us increasingly interdependent. These international corporations are the big beneficiaries of globalization—it is not, for instance, the average American worker and those in many other countries, who, partly under the pressure from globalization, has seen his income fully adjusted for inflation, including the lowering of prices that globalization has brought about, fall year after year, to the point where a full-time male worker in the U.S. has an income lower than four decades ago. Our multinationals have learned how to exploit globalization in every sense of the term—including exploiting the tax loopholes that allow them to evade their global social responsibilities.

The U.S. could not have a functioning corporate income tax system within the country if we had elected to have a transfer price system (where firms "make up" the prices of goods and services that one part buys from another, allowing profits to be booked to one state or another). The U.S. has developed a formulaic system, where global profits are allocated on the basis of employment, sales, and capital goods. But there is plenty of room to further fine-tune the system in response to the easier ability to shift profits around when a major source of the real "value added" is intellectual property.

Some have suggested that while the sources of production (value added) are difficult to identify, the destination is less so (though with reshipping, this may not be so clear); they suggest a destination-based system. But such a system would not necessarily be fair—providing no revenues to the countries that have borne the costs of production. But a destination system would clearly be better than the current one.

Even if the U.S. were not rewarded for its global publicly supported scientific contributions and the intellectual property built on them, at least the country would be rewarded for its unbridled consumerism, which provides incentives for such innovation. It would be good if there could be an international agreement on the taxation of corporate profits. In the absence of such an agreement, any country that threatened to impose fair corporate taxes based on production would be punished—production (and jobs) would be taken elsewhere. In some cases, countries can call their bluff. Others may feel the risk is too high. But what cannot be escaped are customers.

The U.S. by itself could go a long way to moving reform along: any firm selling goods there could be obliged to pay a tax on its global profits, at say a rate of 30 percent, based on a consolidated balance sheet, but with a deduction for corporate profits taxes paid in other jurisdictions (up to some limit). In other words, the U.S. would set itself up as enforcing a global minimum-tax regime. Some might opt out of selling in the U.S., but I doubt that many would.

The problem of multinational corporate tax avoidance is deeper, and requires more profound reform, including dealing with tax havens that shelter money for tax evaders and facilitate money-laundering. Google and Apple hire the most talented lawyers, who know how to avoid taxes staying within the law. But there should be no room in our system for countries that are complicitous in tax avoidance. Why should taxpayers in Germany help bail out citizens in a country whose business model was based on tax avoidance and a race to the bottom—and why should citizens in any country allow their companies to take advantage of these predatory countries?

To say that Apple or Google simply took advantage of the current system is to let them off the hook too easily: the system didn't just come into being on its own. It was shaped from the start by lobby-ists from large multinationals. Companies like General Electric lob-bied for, and got, provisions that enabled them to avoid even more taxes. They lobbied for, and got, amnesty provisions that allowed them to bring their money back to the U.S. at a special low rate, on the promise that the money would be invested in the country; and then they figured out how to comply with the letter of the law, while avoiding the spirit and intention. If Apple and Google stand for the opportunities afforded by globalization, their attitudes towards tax avoidance have made them emblematic of what can go, and is going, wrong with that system.

FALLACIES OF
ROMNEY'S LOGIC*

M ITT ROMNEY'S ACERBIC ATTACK AGAINST THE 47 PER-
cent of Americans who allegedly don't pay income taxes
and are dependent on government has rightly given rise to a storm.
It suggests that large numbers—Barack Obama's supporters—are
freeloaders.

The irony is that it is people such as Romney who are freeload-
ing: The taxes that he has said he is paying (as a percentage of his
reported income) are far less than those of people with substantially less income. And contrary to what some of them would like
to believe, no one makes it on his own. Even if they don't inherit
their wealth, success in business requires a rule of law, an educated
workforce, a public infrastructure, all of which are provided by
government.

Even "innovators" such as Google have done what they did only
by building on the work of others. Before Google could create the
Internet's most popular search engine, someone had to create the
Internet—and it was government that did that.

---

* *USA Today*, September 20, 2012.

DISPELLING MYTHS

But the fallacies in Romney's logic run deeper.

First, even those who don't pay income taxes pay a host of other taxes, including payroll, sales, excise, and property taxes. Many of those receiving "benefits" paid for them—through Social Security and Medicare contributions. They're not free riders. Government has done a better job providing these benefits than the private sector. Let's remember why these programs were started: The private sector left most elderly bereft of support, the market for annuities essentially didn't exist, and the elderly couldn't get health insurance.

Even today, the private sector doesn't provide the kind of security that Social Security provides—including protection against market volatility and inflation. And transaction costs of the Social Security Administration are markedly lower than those in the private sector—not a surprise, since their objective is to maximize these costs. Transaction costs are their profits.

Second, many of those receiving benefits are our young—providing them education and healthcare (even if they or their parents don't pay taxes) are investments in our future. America is the country with the least equality of opportunity of any of the advanced countries for which there is data. While the American dream may have become a myth, it doesn't have to be that way. Children shouldn't have to depend on the wealth of their parents to get the education or health care they need to live up to their potential.

Third, an efficient system of social protection is an important part of any modern society—necessary to enable individuals to take risks. Again, the market failed to provide adequate insurance; for instance, for unemployment or disability. That's why the government stepped in. Those receiving those benefits typically paid for them, either directly or indirectly, through contributions they or their employer made on their behalf to these insurance funds. But providing social protection against these risks too can make for a more productive society. Individuals can take on more high-return, high-risk activities if they know there is a safety net protecting them if things don't work out. It's one of the reasons that some economies with better social protection have been growing much more rapidly than the United States, even during the recent recession.

GOVERNMENT FAILURE

Fourth, many of those at the bottom—who have become so dependent on government—are there partly because government has failed in one way or the other. It has failed to provide them with skills that would make them productive, so they could earn an adequate living. It has failed to stop banks from taking advantage of them through predatory lending and abusive credit card practices. It has failed to stop for-profit schools from taking advantage of their aspirations to move up in the world through education.

Finally, we are a community—and all communities help those who are less fortunate among them. If our economic system results in so many without jobs, dependent on the government for food, then government has to step in. Our economic system has not worked in the way it should: It has not created jobs for all those who would like to work. Many of the jobs that have been created do not pay a livable wage.

We do have a divided society. But it is not divided, as Romney has suggested, between those who are freeloaders and the rest, even if some of those who are paying taxes are not paying their fair share, and are free riding on those who do.

Rather, it is divided between those who see America as a community, and who recognize that the only way to have sustained prosperity is to have shared prosperity, and those who don't.

PART V

CONSEQUENCES OF INEQUALITY

THE THRUST OF MY BOOK *THE PRICE OF INEQUALITY* was that inequality weakens our economy, undermines our democracy, and divides our society. The series The Great Divide elaborated on various aspects. The articles reprinted here again can touch on only a few of the topics. Some of the articles included in the prelude (and the introduction to that section) discuss how inequality undercuts economic performance, lowering demand and increasing instability. In an essay in the last part ("Inequality Is Holding Back the Recovery"), I explain how the country's ever-increasing inequality was part of the explanation for the extraordinarily slow recovery from the 2008 crisis—a crisis that inequality itself helped create.

Earlier I described America's high level of inequality of opportunity. A large fraction of Americans—those that weren't lucky enough to be born of parents of means—have little chance of living up to their potential. This is, of course, a disaster for these individuals, but it is also bad for the economy: we are not using fully our most important resource, our people.

As a government of the 1 percent, for the 1 percent, and by the 1 percent works to enrich the 1 percent, through corporate welfare and tax benefits, fewer resources are available for investments in infrastructure, education, and technology, investments that are needed to keep the economy strong and growing.

But the real cost of inequality is to our democracy and our society. Basic values for which the country has stood—equality of opportunity, equal access to justice, a sense of a system that is fair—have been eroded, as I explain in earlier essays ("Equal Opportunity, Our National Myth" and "Justice for Some"). Bonds of shared sacrifice that hold a country together in times of war are undermined when the rich get a tax cut at the same time that we have a "voluntary" armed forces, disproportionately consisting of poor individuals whose alternative job prospects seem bleak—and then, instead of rewarding them as we did those who served in the armed forces in World War II, with the GI Bill of Rights, we forced them to return time and time again to the battlefield, to the point where nearly half of those returning had one or more disabilities. Making matters still worse, we (or, more accurately, the Bush administration) then underfunded the veterans' hospitals to which they turn.[1]

There are many ways in which our society starts to fray as a sense of fair play diminishes. As I point out in "A Tax System Stacked against the 99 Percent," a tax system such as ours, based largely on voluntary compliance, works only if there is a belief that the system is fair—but it is now evident to all that ours is not, that those at the top get a far better deal than those in the middle.

The two articles reprinted here take up two consequences of inequality that have been given insufficient attention. The first focuses on what's happening to our inner cities, in which so many of the country's poor live. Detroit's bankruptcy is emblematic. Like so many American families, it was hurt by following the advice of the exploitive financial sector, buying risky derivatives, which Warren Buffett referred to as financial weapons of mass destruction. In the case of Detroit, they did explode. As in so many other instances, when troubles emerged, the financial sector demanded to be paid back first—putting the welfare of ordinary citizens, including workers with contracts promising them retirement benefits, in the backseat.

The other article in this section, "In No One We Trust," discusses a further casualty of America's growing inequality—a loss of trust, without which no society can function. Although economists typically don't use words like "trust," in fact, our economy simply can't function without trust. I explain why this is so, how inequality has eroded this most precious thing, and why, once eroded, it may prove hard to restore.

Note

1. See Linda J. Bilmes and Joseph E. Stiglitz, *The Three Trillion Dollar War: The True Cost of the War in Iraq* (New York: W. W. Norton, 2008); Linda J. Bilmes and Joseph E. Stiglitz, "Estimating the Costs of War: Methodological Issues, with Applications to Iraq and Afghanistan," in *Oxford Handbook of the Economics of Peace and Conflict*, ed. Michelle R. Garfinkel and Stergios Skaperdas (New York: Oxford University Press, 2012), pp. 275–317; and Witness testimony to the House Committee on Veterans' Affairs, September 30, 2010.

THE WRONG LESSON FROM
DETROIT'S BANKRUPTCY*

WHEN I WAS GROWING UP IN GARY, INDIANA, NEARLY A quarter of American workers were employed in the manufacturing sector. There were plenty of jobs at the time that paid well enough for a single breadwinner, working one job, to fulfill the American dream for his family of four. He could earn a living on the sweat of his brow, afford to send his children to college, and even see them rise to the professional class.

Cities like Detroit and Gary thrived on that industry, not just in terms of the wealth that it produced but also in terms of strong communities, healthy tax bases, and good infrastructure. From the stable foundation of Gary's excellent public schools, influenced by the ideas of the progressive reformer John Dewey, I went on to Amherst College and then to MIT for graduate school.

Today, fewer than 8 percent of American workers are employed in manufacturing, and many Rust Belt cities are skeletons. The distressing facts about Detroit are by now almost a cliché: 40 percent of streetlights were not working this spring, tens of thousands of buildings are abandoned, schools have closed, and the population declined 25 percent in the last decade alone. The violent crime rate

* *New York Times*, August 11, 2013.

last year was the highest of any big city. In 1950, when Detroit's population was 1.85 million, there were 296,000 manufacturing jobs in the city; as of 2011, with a population of just over 700,000, there were fewer than 27,000.

So much is packed into the dramatic event of Detroit's fall—the largest municipal bankruptcy in American history—that it's worth taking a pause to see what it says about our changing economy and society, and what it portends for our future.

Failures of national and local policy are by now well known: underinvestment in infrastructure and public services, geographic isolation that has marginalized poor and African-American communities in the Rust Belt, intergenerational poverty that has stymied equality of opportunity and the privileging of moneyed interests (like those of corporate executives and financial services companies) over those of workers.

At one level, one might shrug: companies die every day; new ones are born. That is part of the dynamics of capitalism. So, too, for cities. Maybe Detroit and cities like it are just in the wrong location for the goods and services that 21st-century America demands.

But such a diagnosis would be wrong, and it's extremely important to recognize that Detroit's demise is not simply an inevitable outcome of the market.

For one, the description is incomplete: Detroit's most serious problems are confined to the city limits. Elsewhere in the metropolitan area, there is ample economic activity. In suburbs like Bloomfield Hills, Mich., the median household income is more than $125,000. A 45-minute drive from Detroit is Ann Arbor, home of the University of Michigan, one of the world's preeminent hubs of research and knowledge production.

Detroit's travails arise in part from a distinctive aspect of America's divided economy and society. As the sociologists Sean F. Reardon and Kendra Bischoff have pointed out, our country is becoming vastly more economically segregated, which can be even more pernicious than being racially segregated. Detroit is the example par excellence of the seclusion of affluent (and mostly white) elites in suburban enclaves. There is a rationale for battening down the hatches: the rich thus ensure that they don't have to pay any share of the local public goods and services of their less well-off neighbors, and that their children don't have to mix with those of lower socioeconomic status.

The trend toward self-reinforcing inequality is especially apparent in education, an ever shrinking ladder for upward mobility. Schools in poorer districts get worse, parents with means move out to richer districts, and the divisions between the haves and have-nots—not only in this generation, but also in the next—grow ever larger.

Residential segregation along economic lines amplifies inequality for adults, too. The poor have to somehow manage to get from their neighborhoods to part-time, low-paying, and increasingly scarce jobs at distant work sites. Combine this urban sprawl with inadequate public transportation systems and you have a blueprint for transforming working-class communities into depopulated ghettos.

Adding to the problems that would inevitably arise from such poorly designed urban agglomerations is the fact that the Detroit metropolitan area is divided into separate political jurisdictions. The poor are thus not only geographically isolated, but politically ghettoized as well. The result is a separate, poorer inner city with a dearth of resources, made even worse because the industrial plants that had provided the core of the tax base are shut down.

The decision to file for Chapter 9 municipal bankruptcy protection was made by Kevyn D. Orr, the nonelected emergency manager appointed by Gov. Rick Snyder, a Republican, to run the city's finances. The incumbent mayor, Dave Bing, a Democrat, has decided not to seek a second term, which is hardly surprising given that he and other local officials have been left on the sidelines as their city's future—and the accumulated debts owed its creditors—is being hashed out in court.

As historians like Thomas J. Sugrue have demonstrated, the disintegration of Detroit precedes the conflicts over social-welfare programs and race relations (including riots in 1967) and reaches back into the postwar decades, a time when the roots of deindustrialization, racial discrimination, and geographic isolation were planted. We've reaped what we've sown.

Lacking regional political unity, there is no overall structure to improve the infrastructure and public services between poorer inner cities and affluent suburbs. So the poor fall back on what means they have, which is not good enough. Cars inevitably break down and buses are late, making workers appear to be "unreliable." But what is really unreliable is the iniquitous design of the city. No wonder America is becoming the advanced industrial country with the least equality of opportunity.

The same skewed priorities that have gutted Detroit at the local level are echoed in a void at the level of national policy. Every country, every society, has regions and industries whose stars are rising, and others that are in decline. Silicon Valley has, for some time, been America's rising star—just as the upper Midwest was a hundred years ago. With technological change and globalization, though, the Midwest's comparative advantage as a global manufacturing hub has ebbed, for reasons too well known to list here. Markets, however, often don't do a good job of self-rejuvenation.

Rather than deal purposefully with this changing economic landscape with useful policies encouraging the growth of other industries, our government spent decades papering over the growing weaknesses by allowing the financial sector to run amok, creating "growth" based on bubbles. We didn't just let the market run its course. We made an active choice to embrace short-term profits and large-scale inefficiency.

There may be something inevitable about the structural changes that have made American manufacturing less central to our economy, but there is nothing inevitable about the waste, pain, and human despair in cities that have accompanied that change. There are policy alternatives that can soften such transitions in ways that preserve wealth and promote equality. Just four hours from Detroit, Pittsburgh, too, grappled with white flight. But it more rapidly shifted its economy from one dependent on steel and coal to one that emphasizes education, health care, and legal and financial services. Manchester, the center of Britain's textile industry for more than a century, has been transformed into a center of education, culture, and music. America does have an urban renewal program, but it is aimed more at restoring buildings and gentrification than at maintaining and restoring communities, and even at that, it is languishing. American workers were sold "free" trade policies on the promise that the winners could compensate the losers. The losers are still waiting.

Of course, the Great Recession and the policies that created it have made this, like so many other things, much worse. The mortgage bankers marched into large sections of some of our cities and found them good subjects for their predatory and discriminatory lending. Once the bubble burst, those cities were abandoned by all but the debt collectors and foreclosure sheriffs. Rather than saving our communities, our politicians focused more on saving the bankers, their shareholders, and their bondholders.

The situation may be grim, but all is not lost for Detroit and other cities facing similar problems. The question facing Detroit now is how to manage bankruptcy.

But here, too, we must be wary of the influence of the "wisdom" of wealthy interests. In recent years, our financial "wizards" at private banks—whose skill is supposed to be managing risk—sold Detroit some fancy financial products (derivatives) that have worsened its financial plight by hundreds of millions of dollars.

In a conventional bankruptcy, derivatives would get priority as creditors before current and retired municipal workers. Fortunately, the rules governing Chapter 9 of the bankruptcy code put greater emphasis on the public good. When a public body goes into bankruptcy, there is always some ambiguity about its assets and liabilities. Its obligations include an unwritten "social contract," including social services for its residents. Its ability to increase revenues is limited: higher taxes can accelerate a death spiral, driving out more businesses and homeowners.

The banks, not surprisingly, would like other priorities. With nearly $300 million of outstanding derivatives at stake, they may connive to be first in line for repayment. The Chapter 9 proceeding provides the opportunity to place the banks where they ought to be—at the back of the queue. It was bad enough that these non-transparent financial instruments were used to confuse and deceive investors. It would add insult to injury to reward the banks' behavior. The priority in the bankruptcy proceedings must be restoring Detroit to vitality as a city, not just getting it out of the red. The basic principle of Chapter 11 of our bankruptcy code (focusing on corporations) is that bankruptcy should provide a fresh start: doing so is vital to preserving jobs and our economy. But when cities go bankrupt, it's even more important to preserve our communities.

Banks and bondholders will argue that pension payments for city workers are an undue burden, and should be limited or canceled to reduce the banks' losses. But the high priority that workers are typically given in municipal bankruptcies is entirely justified. After all, they have performed their services on the understanding that they would be paid, and pensions are nothing but "deferred compensation." Workers are not engaged in the complicated business of risk assessment, as investors are. And unlike investors, they can't really diversify their portfolios to manage their risk. So it should be unconscionable to tell workers that, sorry, we aren't paying you what we promised for work you've already done. Especially because their pensions, unlike those of corporate chieftains, are far from generous. Most of the retired city employees receiving checks get about $1,600 a month.

This means that much of the burden of bankruptcy will have to fall on those who lent Detroit money, and those who insured those lenders. This is as it should be. They got a return, reflecting their subjective estimate of the risk that they faced. Of course, they would like to get high returns, and somehow not bear the risk. But this is not the way markets work, or should work.

Ensuring that bankruptcy proceeds in a way that is good for Detroit will require vigilance, and is only the first step in recovery. In the longer term, we will need to change the way we run our metropolitan areas. We need to provide better public transportation, an education system that promotes a modicum of equality of opportunity, and a system of metropolitan "governance" that works not just for the 1 percent, nor even for the top 20 percent, but for all citizens.

And on the national level, we need policies—investment in education, training, and infrastructure—that smooth America's transition away from a dependency on manufacturing for jobs. If we don't, post–Great Recession bankruptcies like those in Jefferson County, Ala., Vallejo, Calif., Central Falls., R.I., and now Detroit will become far too common.

Detroit's bankruptcy is a reminder of how divided our society has become and how much has to be done to heal the wounds. And it provides an important warning to those living in today's boom-towns: it could happen to you.

IN NO ONE WE TRUST[*]

I N AMERICA TODAY, WE ARE SOMETIMES MADE TO FEEL that it is naïve to be preoccupied with trust. Our songs advise against it, our TV shows tell stories showing its futility, and incessant reports of financial scandal remind us we'd be fools to give it to our bankers.

That last point may be true, but that doesn't mean we should stop striving for a bit more trust in our society and our economy. Trust is what makes contracts, plans, and everyday transactions possible; it facilitates the democratic process, from voting to law creation, and is necessary for social stability. It is essential for our lives. It is trust, more than money, that makes the world go round.

We do not measure trust in our national income accounts, but investments in trust are no less important than those in human capital or machines.

Unfortunately, however, trust is becoming yet another casualty of our country's staggering inequality: As the gap between Americans widens, the bonds that hold society together weaken. So, too, as more and more people lose faith in a system that seems inexorably stacked against them, and the 1 percent ascend to ever more distant

---

* *New York Times*, December 21, 2013.

heights, this vital element of our institutions and our way of life is eroding.

The undervaluing of trust has its roots in our most popular economic traditions. Adam Smith argued forcefully that we would do better to trust in the pursuit of self-interest than in the good intentions of those who pursue the general interest. If everyone looked out for just himself, we would reach an equilibrium that was not just comfortable but also productive, in which the economy was fully efficient. To the morally uninspired, it's an appealing idea: selfishness as the ultimate form of selflessness. (Elsewhere, in particular in his *Theory of Moral Sentiments*, Smith took a much more balanced view, though most of his latter-day adherents have not followed suit.)

But events—and economic research—over the past 30 years have shown not only that we cannot rely on self-interest, but also that no economy, not even a modern, market-based economy like America's, can function well without a modicum of trust—and that unmitigated selfishness inevitably diminishes trust.

Take banking, the industry that spawned the crisis that has cost us dearly.

That industry in particular had long been based on trust. You put your money into the bank, trusting that when you wanted to take it out in the future, it would be there. This is not to say that bankers never tried to deceive one another or their clients. But a vast majority of their business was conducted on the basis of assumed mutual accountability, sufficient levels of transparency, and a sense of responsibility. At their best, banks were stalwart community institutions that made judicious loans to promising small businesses and prospective homeowners.

In the years leading up to the crisis, though, our traditional bankers changed drastically, aggressively branching out into other activities, including those historically associated with investment banking. Trust went out the window. Commercial lenders hard-sold mortgages to families who couldn't afford them, using false assurances. They could comfort themselves with the idea that no matter how much they exploited their customers and how much risk they had undertaken, new "insurance" products—derivatives and other chicanery—insulated their banks from the consequences. If any of them thought about the social implications of their activities, whether it was predatory lending, abusive credit card practices, or market manipulation, they might have taken comfort that, in accordance with Adam Smith's dictum, their swelling bank accounts implied that they must be boosting social welfare.

Of course, we now know this was all a mirage. Things didn't turn out well for our economy or our society. As millions lost their homes during and after the crisis, median wealth declined nearly 40 percent in three years. Banks would have done badly, too, had it not been for the Bush-Obama mega-bailouts.

This cascade of trust destruction was unrelenting. One of the reasons that the bubble's bursting in 2007 led to such an enormous crisis was that no bank could trust another. Each bank knew the shenanigans it had been engaged in—the movement of liabilities off its balance sheets, the predatory and reckless lending—and so knew that it could not trust any other bank. Interbank lending froze, and the financial system came to the verge of collapse, saved only by the resolute action of the public, whose trust had been the most abused of all.

There had been earlier episodes when the financial sector showed how fragile trust was. Most notable was the crash of 1929, which prompted new laws to stop the worst abuses, from fraud to market manipulation. We trusted regulators to enforce the law, and we trusted the banks to obey the law: The government couldn't be everywhere, but banks would at least be kept in line by fearing the consequences of bad behavior.

Decades later, however, bankers used their political influence to eviscerate regulations and install regulators who didn't believe in them. Officials and academics assured lawmakers and the public that banks could self-regulate.

But it all turned out to be a scam. We had created a system of rewards that encouraged shortsighted behavior and excessive risk-taking. In fact, we had entered an era in which moral values were given short shrift and trust itself was discounted.

THE BANKING INDUSTRY is only one example of what amounts to a broad agenda, promoted by some politicians and theoreticians on the right, to undermine the role of trust in our economy. This movement promotes policies based on the view that trust should never be relied on as motivation, for any kind of behavior, in any context. Incentives, in this scheme, are all that matter.

So CEOs must be given stock options to induce them to work hard. I find this puzzling: If a firm pays someone $10 million to run a company, he should give his all to ensure its success. He shouldn't do so only if he is promised a big chunk of any increase in the company's stock market value, even if the increase is only a result of a bubble created by the Fed's low interest rates.

Similarly, teachers must be given incentive pay to induce them to exert themselves. But teachers already work hard for low wages because they are dedicated to improving the lives of their students. Do we really believe that giving them $50 more, or even $500 more, as incentive pay will induce them to work harder? What we should do is increase teacher salaries generally because we recognize the value of their contributions and trust in their professionalism. According to the advocates of an incentive-based culture, though, this would be akin to giving something for nothing.

In practice, the right's narrow focus on incentives has proved inimical to long-term thinking and so rife with opportunities for greed that it was bound to promote distrust, both in society and within companies. Bank managers and corporate executives search out creative accounting devices to make their enterprises look good in the short run, even if their long-run prospects are compromised.

Of course, incentives are an important component of human

behavior. But the incentive movement has made them into a sort of religion, blind to all the other factors—social ties, moral impulses, compassion—that influence our conduct.

This is not just a coldhearted vision of human nature. It is also implausible. It is simply impossible to pay for trust every time it is required. Without trust, life would be absurdly expensive; good information would be nearly unobtainable; fraud would be even more rampant than it is; and transaction and litigation costs would soar. Our society would be as frozen as the banks were when their years of dishonesty came to a head and the crisis broke in 2007.

AMERICA FACES ANOTHER formidable hurdle if it wants to restore a climate of trust: our out-of-control inequality. Not only did the actions of the bankers and government policies influenced by the right directly undermine trust: both contributed greatly to this inequality.

When 1 percent of the population takes home more than 22 percent of the country's income—and 95 percent of the increase in income in the post-crisis recovery—some pretty basic things are at stake. Reasonable people, even those ignorant of the maze of unfair policies that created this reality, can look at this absurd distribution and be pretty certain that the game is rigged.

But for our economy and society to function, participants must trust that the system is reasonably fair. Trust between individuals is usually reciprocal. But if I think that you are cheating me, it is more likely that I will retaliate, and try to cheat you. (These notions have been well developed in a branch of economics called the "theory of repeated games.") When Americans see a tax system that taxes the wealthiest at a fraction of what they pay, they feel that they are fools to play along. All the more so when the wealthiest are able to move profits offshore. The fact that this can be done without breaking the law simply shows Americans that the financial and legal systems are designed by and for the rich.

As the trust deficit persists, a deeper rot takes hold: Attitudes and norms begin to change. When no one is trustworthy, it will be only fools who trust. The concept of fairness itself is eroded. A study published last year by the National Academy of Sciences suggests that the upper classes are more likely to engage in what has traditionally been considered unethical behavior. Perhaps this is the only way for some to reconcile their worldview with their outlandish financial success, often achieved through actions that reveal a kind of moral deprivation.

It's hard to know just how far we've gone down the path toward complete trust disintegration, but the evidence is not encouraging.

Economic inequality, political inequality, and an inequality-promoting legal system all mutually reinforce one another. We get a legal system that provides privileges to the rich and powerful. Occasionally, individual egregious behavior is punished (Bernard L. Madoff comes to mind); but none of those who headed our mighty banks are held accountable.

As always, it is the poor and the unconnected who suffer most from this, and who are the most repeatedly deceived. Nowhere was this more evident than in the foreclosure crisis. The sub-prime mortgage hawkers, putting themselves forward as experts in finance, assured unqualified borrowers that repayment would be no problem. Later millions would lose their homes. The banks figured out how to get court affidavits signed by the thousands (in what came to be called robo-signing), certifying that they had examined their records and that these particular individuals owed money— and so should be booted out of their homes. The banks were lying on a grand scale, but they knew that if they didn't get caught, they would walk off with huge profits, their officials' pockets stuffed with bonuses. And if they did get caught, their shareholders would be left paying the tab. The ordinary homeowner simply didn't have the resources to fight them. It was just one example among many in the wake of the crisis where banks were seemingly immune to the rule of law.

I've written about many dimensions of inequality in our society—inequality of wealth, of income, of access to education and health, of opportunity. But perhaps even more than opportunity, Americans cherish equality before the law. Here, inequality has infected the heart of our ideals.

I suspect there is only one way to really get trust back. We need to pass strong regulations, embodying norms of good behavior, and appoint bold regulators to enforce them. We did just that after the Roaring 20s crashed; our efforts since 2007 have been sputtering and incomplete. Firms also need to do better than skirt the edges of regulations. We need higher norms for what constitutes acceptable behavior, like those embodied in the United Nations' Guiding Principles on Business and Human Rights. But we also need regulations to enforce these norms—a new version of trust but verify. No rules will be strong enough to prevent every abuse, yet good, strong regulations can stop the worst of it.

Strong values enable us to live in harmony with one another. Without trust, there can be no harmony, nor can there be a strong economy. Inequality in America is degrading our trust. For our own sake, and for the sake of future generations, it's time to start rebuilding it. That this even requires pointing out shows how far we have to go.

PART VI

POLICY

A CENTRAL MESSAGE OF THIS BOOK IS THAT INEQUAL-
ity is affected by virtually every policy that the government
undertakes. Economists are wont to discuss how a policy affects
efficiency, how incentives might be distorted. But especially in our
divided society, policies that increase that divide should be looked
at carefully. I wrote these articles in response to particular policy
debates that emerged in the country at various times, debates in
which the distributive consequences of the policy were often given
short shrift.

"How Policy Has Contributed to the Great Economic Divide"
provides an overview of ways in which policies—especially the
country's macroeconomic policies, which determine output and
employment—have widened the great divide.

"Why Janet Yellen, Not Larry Summers, Should Lead the Fed"
is one of several articles I have written highlighting the relationship
between monetary policy and inequality. (I also devoted chapter 9
of *The Price of Inequality* to the subject.) It was the most pointed.
In the summer of 2013, the country became divided over who
should lead the Fed after Ben Bernanke's term came to an end.
Bernanke had had a mixed record—the Fed's policies before the
crisis—including the period in which he was chairman, from 2006

on, and an earlier period, 2002 to 2005, when he was an active member of the Federal Reserve Board—were central to its creation; the unprecedented actions the Fed took as the crisis developed are often credited with saving the economy from a Great Depression. But it was clear that the Fed was more interested in saving the big Wall Street banks than in helping the local and regional banks that provide loans to small and medium-size enterprises, more interested in saving the bankers and their shareholders and bondholders than in helping ordinary homeowners save their homes. It was also demonstrably uninterested in democratic transparency, as it, for instance, funneled money to AIG, money that eventually went to Goldman Sachs and other big banks. For obvious reasons, the Fed didn't want American citizens to know where the money was going.

The battle was more complex and multifaceted than these choices often are. There were two main candidates, Larry Summers and Janet Yellen. I knew both well. I had worked in the White House closely with the former. Janet had been one my earliest Ph.D. students at Yale. Both were smart. Both were experienced. Most of those who had worked closely with both strongly thought Yellen was more suited to the difficult tasks of managing perhaps the most important financial institution in the world. I wrote an early article[1] explaining what was needed in the job, and hinting that Yellen was the right candidate. A large group of senators thought likewise, and in a letter to President Obama urged him to make her his choice. No one wanted to make the battle personal. But, somehow, Obama did not get the hint. He seemingly felt more comfortable with the "old boys club" approach, appointing someone he knew well and who had served him as head of the National Economic Council. A quiet battle became less so, and this article may have helped turn the tide.[2] A critical number of senators on the Senate Banking Committee (which has to approve such nominations) made it clear that they would not support his nomination, and so the battle ended.

Part of what was at issue was the glass ceiling—another aspect of America's inequality, reflected in differences in incomes and opportunities across gender. Yellen had distinguished herself, not only in managing the San Francisco Fed and serving as vice chair of the Fed, but in making forecasts that were more accurate than others. (The administration's forecasts, in which Summers played a central role, were notoriously off the mark. He was constantly seeing greenshoots: a revival of the economy that would not occur until years later. Earlier, we noted the major political and economic mistake of the administration in underestimating the severity of the downturn.) Yellen's evenhandedness and her acumen had generated enormous respect on Wall Street.

But the deeper battle was about economic philosophy and values. Summers had become synonymous with financial deregulation. He boasted of his role in passing the legislation that ensured that derivatives—the financial products that had played such a large role in the making of the crisis, and were responsible for the $180 billion AIG bailout—were not regulated. The administration's strategy for saving the economy focused on saving the banks, with little help for homeowners. Its stimulus had been too small, too poorly designed, and too short.

I thought that Yellen might bring about some real changes in central banking, not only in the United States, but elsewhere as well. Central bank governors have long been generous with opinions about matters going well beyond monetary policy. While Greenspan made a mess of the financial sector, he freely gave advice on fiscal policy (supporting the tax cut for the rich, on the truly remarkable grounds that without such a tax cut, the country risked paying off the entire national debt, and that would make the conduct of monetary policy difficult!). In Europe the head of the European Central Bank similarly mismanaged the eurozone's financial system, but he freely offered advice on labor market policy, arguing that there was a need for more wage flexibility—code words for saying that wages should be cut, increasing the economic divide in Europe.

Central banks typically focus single-mindedly on inflation. Even though in the United States the central bank is *supposed* to look also at unemployment and growth (and now, belatedly, at financial stability), de facto it focused on inflation. Yellen helped change that. In recent years, the Fed has announced that it won't raise interest rates until the *labor market* improves.

More dramatic was the speech that Yellen gave at a conference at the Boston Fed on October 17, 2014, on inequality and inequality of opportunity. In a debate in the *New York Times*[3] some suggested that this was going beyond the remit of the Fed—no matter that when other central bank governors opined on other aspects of economic policy, no such criticism was levied. I believe strongly that Yellen was right to talk about inequality because the Fed has such a big impact. If it tightens monetary policy too much—raising interest rates too high or restricting credit availability too severely—unemployment will be higher than it otherwise would be, hurting workers both directly and indirectly, through the resulting downward pressure on wages. If it tightens prematurely—as soon as inflation seems nascent—it is likely that the share of wages will be ratcheted downward, for during the downturn, workers fare badly, and they have to be allowed to make up for what they lost.

While the main thrust of the Fed's policy has been to restore the economy to full employment—a policy that would be an enormous boon to workers—some of what it has done may have contributed to inequality. One of the main effects of quantitative easing, the policy of buying long-term bonds to lower the long-term interest rate, has been to bolster the stock market—of benefit disproportionately to the rich. Meanwhile, its failure to do what it could and should have done to make the financial market work better for ordinary Americans—to ensure competition, to restrict the excessive fees that credit and debit cards charge to merchants that ultimately get paid by consumers, to restore lending to small and medium-size enterprises, to create a mortgage market that serves Americans rather than the interests of the banks—has hurt those in the middle and bottom at the same time that it has enriched the coffers of the banks.

Yellen is right, too, to point out (as I have done in this book) the limits to monetary policy. It is hard-pressed to restore the economy to full employment on its own. Indeed, it may be contributing to the jobless recovery that we are experiencing (the percentage of the working-age population that is employed, though it has rebounded slightly since the crisis, is still lower than at any time since 1984). Low interest rates encourage firms, when they invest, to invest in very capital intensive technologies—replacing unskilled workers with machines makes no sense in an era in which so many unskilled workers are striving to find jobs.

In some areas of policy the impacts on the poor are almost obvious. "The Insanity of Our Food Policy" discusses one such area— our food programs, upon which close to one out of seven Americans depend. At the time, Congress was debating major cutbacks to this program. But the Republicans in the House of Representatives who argued for such cutbacks were simultaneously supporting the continuation of massive agricultural subsidies for rich farmers. Seldom does one see so starkly the contradictions associated with government of the 1 percent, by the 1 percent, and for the 1 percent. Rhetoric about free markets is uncloaked for what it is: just rhetoric. The Republican-controlled House sustains a safety net for the rich as it renews the corporate welfare largesse for agro-business, even as it hacks away at the safety net for the poor.

Workers have often blamed globalization for their declining fortunes, and in several earlier books I explained how mismanaged globalization can increase inequality in both developed and developing countries.[4] Trade agreements have always been sold on the grounds that they create jobs—and if that were true, workers should be among the loudest champions of these agreements. The reality is often otherwise, and the fact that our political leaders (not only Republicans but Clinton and Obama as well) have tried to misrepresent these trade agreements in this way undermines confidence in them, and again reminds citizens of the extent to which our government reflects the interests of those at the top.

There are at least three key flaws in the "logic" that trade agreements create jobs. Administrations across the political spectrum rightly point to the jobs created by the increased exports. But trade balance requires imports to roughly equal exports—and our trading partners would not sign an imbalanced agreement, in which our exports increased but theirs (our imports) did not do so commensurately. But if exports create jobs, imports destroy them. And then there is the careful and complex calculation: Are more jobs created or destroyed? Since our imports tend to be in labor-intensive industries (industries where many workers are required to produce a given value of output) and our exports (like airplanes) are high-technology industries requiring relatively little labor—and what labor is required is highly skilled—on net, it is plausible that balanced trade agreements destroy jobs.

The analysis I have just given assumes that markets are working well. But in recent years the American economy has not been working well: there is a high level of open and disguised unemployment. It is easier to destroy jobs than to create new ones. Competition from imports can destroy jobs overnight. Expanding exports requires expansion of existing firms and the creation of new firms. But when financial markets do not work well—and ours have not been working well—often firms that would like to expand can't get the capital to do so. Entrepreneurs who would like to start a new business can't get the funding they need.

Perhaps the most important point is that responsibility for maintaining the economy should lie not with trade but with monetary and fiscal authorities, with the Federal Reserve and the administration. Admittedly, they haven't done a good job. But it is unlikely that trade will correct for their failures. Indeed, if the Fed were doing its job well, and the economy were at full employment, and the administration were correct that a trade agreement created net new jobs, then the Fed would respond by increasing interest rates, fully offsetting the alleged job creation benefits of the trade agreement.

Dishonesty is never the best policy, and the dishonest selling of trade agreements stands as a low point in public policy.

"On the Wrong Side of Globalization" and "The Free-Trade Charade" were written as President Obama promoted new trade agreements across the Pacific and Atlantic. While trade agreements may not create jobs—and arguably they destroy them—their real effects lie elsewhere. Among those effects is the exacerbation of the country's already high level of inequality. That this might be so has long been recognized—but politicians have been loath to mention this, and, ironically, some of the strongest advocates of free trade have been among those least willing to support policies that might mitigate some of these adverse effects.

The reasoning for why trade agreements increase inequality is simple. The effects are seen most clearly in a world of perfect markets—the kind of world imagined as the ideal by many of the advocates of globalization. In such a world, goods, capital, and, yes, even labor would move freely across boundaries. It should be obvious then that unskilled labor (or, for that matter, any factor of production) would have the same price anywhere in the world. And that means that unskilled workers in the United States would get paid the same wage as unskilled workers in China or India. And the level of that wage would almost surely be closer to that of India and China than to that of the United States. The big insight of modern economics was that trade in goods and services was effectively a substitute for the free movement of labor and capital: when China sells labor-intensive goods to the United States, it increases the demand for China's labor and lowers the demand for that in America, raising wages there and lowering them here. Trade liberalization moves the wages of unskilled labor in the two countries closer together. And the wages of our workers is likely to go down more than theirs is likely to go up.

While economists have long debated the relative importance of this effect—compared with others that increase income inequality—there is a growing consensus that today the impact of trade on wages and inequality can be significant. Places in the country that used to produce goods that are now imported from China have seen a decline in employment and wages.

Unfortunately, our trade agreements are unbalanced in ways that make the inequality-generating effects worse. Advocates of these agreements have worked hard to promote the free flow of not only goods and services but also capital. But that has changed in a fundamental way the bargaining position of workers. If they demand decent wages, the employer can easily threaten to move the factory abroad—knowing that there are no barriers to the movement of his firm and the reverse flow of goods. This too undoubtedly weakens wages.

Ironically, many of the advocates of globalization not only propose to do nothing to help those who are being hurt by it, but say that workers should accept cutbacks in job protections and public services: globalization demands it, if we are to remain competitive, so goes the argument. In effect, they are *admitting* that workers have to take a hit with globalization. But if globalization does benefit the country *as a whole*, and if workers *as a whole* are worse off, what does that mean? It means that all the benefits of globalization—and more—go to the top, to the corporations and their owners.

These two essays argue, however, that the proposed *new* trade agreements are even more pernicious. Presumably, that's one of the reasons that the negotiations have been conducted with such secrecy. Since tariffs are already very low, the new agreements are really about strengthening intellectual property rights—driving drug prices higher as the agreements try to put generic drugs at more of a competitive disadvantage—and undermining regulations that protect the environment, workers, consumers, and even the economy.

Most disturbing are the provisions that go euphemistically under the label of "investment provisions," seemingly designed to protect property rights. Who could be against that? But when the United States proposed essentially the same provisions in an agreement across the Atlantic with Europeans, eyebrows were raised. It became clear that something else was going on. For Europe has good property rights—every bit as good as those in the United States. And if there was something wrong with Europe's system of property rights, why should one want to correct it only for foreign firms and not for

Europe's own firms? Europe, too, has a good regulatory and judicial system. Why would one seek to replace a system for adjudicating disputes (in this case between firms and states) that is well established and well thought through (with good protections for both sides in the dispute, with transparent proceedings based on strong legal precedents) with arbitration proceedings, held in secret, with arbitrators who often have conflicts of interests with positions in other cases, without adequate provisions for appeal and judicial review? If the peculiar form of judicial proceedings called for by these agreements is really superior, why don't we employ them more widely? And if so, shouldn't there be a national debate in Congress, with the attorney general and the judiciary committees leading the deliberations—not the U.S. Trade Representative and the congressional committees involving trade?

The articles contend that the new trade agreements are simply an end run by corporate interests, to try to get through a trade agreement the kind of regulatory regime that they could never hope to get through open democratic debate. The agreements attempt to undermine safeguards that have been put into place over 50 years—and even the more recent safeguards meant to restrict the excesses of the financial sector. For these agreements seem to have the power even to restrict our ability and that of our trading partners to regulate the financial sector.

The other noxious set of provisions of these trade agreements are about intellectual property (IP). Intellectual property rights are important, but as I saw so clearly when I first became involved in these issues during the Clinton administration in discussions over the Uruguay Round trade negotiations, the provisions contained in our trade agreements are *not* those designed to advance the progress of science. They are designed to fatten the coffers of corporations, particularly in the pharmaceutical and entertainment industries. Indeed, there is a real concern that current provisions *retard* scientific progress.

The IP provisions of the new trade agreements are particularly aimed against generics. There is a bitter irony in Obama's having fought so hard for a bill to create a more efficient health care sector—that would lower the cost of health care—now undermining his own efforts with an agreement that would almost surely drive prices of pharmaceuticals up.

In "How Intellectual Property Reinforces Inequality" I continue the discussion of the role that intellectual property plays in worsening the great divide, focusing on the dramatic case in which a private company attempted to patent a set of genes closely related to breast cancer—and then forcing anybody who wished to find out whether she was exposed to this risk to use its tests (which were not as good as those offered by others), paying an exorbitant price. Perhaps the worst inequality of all is the deprivation of life—and that's what our IP system did. Fortunately, in this case, the Supreme Court ruled the patents invalid. Remarkably, even after the ruling, firms attempting to provide more affordable tests for these genes were sued.

Intellectual property law is not God given. It is man-made. It is a social construction supposedly designed to encourage innovation and the dissemination of knowledge. But there are many details that go into the law, and if one doesn't get these details right, IP can inhibit innovation. For instance, one is supposed to obtain a patent only for *new* ideas, and that's why patent laws embrace a standard of novelty. It has to be *sufficiently* novel. So too, patents are for a limited period only, 20 years. Drug companies try to extend their monopoly power by coming up with a minor improvement of their drugs. This is called evergreening. India took a tough stance—refusing to grant a patent for an obvious minor variant of a drug that would have simply extended the patent. "India's Patently Wise Decision" explains why India was right to do so. Since then, the U.S. government has been putting pressure on India to change its policies, hoping that its new, business friendly government, headed by Prime Minister Narendra Modi, will be more receptive to doing a deal.

Bad as inequality in the United States is—and its level in the

United States (after taxes and transfers) is the worst among the advanced countries—in some developing countries and emerging markets it is worse. (I talk about many of those countries in the next part of the book.) And just as there are many forms of inequality (inequalities of wealth, income, health, and opportunity), some may have more invidious societal effects than others. "Eliminating Extreme Inequality" was written with my Columbia political science colleague, and former assistant secretary-general of the UN, Michael Doyle, to promote the idea that some measure of reduction in extreme inequality be included in the sustainable development goals that were then under discussion at the UN. At the turn of the century, the UN had formulated a set of *millennium development goals*, to focus the world's attention on achievable targets over the succeeding 15 years, including reducing poverty by half by 2015. The goals were more successful than even its most ardent advocates had hoped, not only in centering attention on the importance of reducing poverty, in all of its manifestations, but even in achieving these goals.

Not surprisingly, as 2015 approached, the consensus was that a new set of goals should be formulated. But there has been extensive debate about the list of objectives to be included. Given my belief that inequality—especially the extremes of inequality being observed in many countries—was so bad for both the economy and society, it was natural that I would advocate including doing something about that in our global goals. I teamed up with Professor Doyle, because I wanted to highlight not just the economic consequences of inequality but also the political and broader societal consequences. One aspect of inequality that we draw attention to is inequality across ethnic groups. In developing countries this kind of inequality is systematically related to civil conflict. America, of course, has enormous inequalities of this form—differences between African-Americans, Hispanics, and other groups are very large. Disturbingly, while there has been progress at the very top, disparities in averages have improved little. Indeed, the Great Recession worsened wealth disparities.

The penultimate article in this section, "The Postcrisis Crises," was motivated by my concern that, as so much attention was being focused on the Great Recession and its aftermath, we were doing too little about long-festering problems. If we didn't begin to address them, we would inevitably face a series of other crises, such as climate change.

In some cases, the crisis represented a lost opportunity—we could and should have used the crisis to make investments that would have helped us meet the challenges of climate change. If we had done that, our downturn would have been shallower, growth and employment would have been higher, and we would have emerged from the crisis in a stronger position to deal with global warming.

In others, the crisis made matters worse. That was the case with inequality, which had been growing markedly over the past third of a century, and especially since the new millennium. Because the Fed and the administration focused on helping the banks and engineering a stock market boom—but did little about housing—wealth inequality continued to expand.[5]

The final article in this section, "Inequality Is Not Inevitable," was written as the last article for the *New York Times* Great Divide series; it harks back to my earlier article "Inequality Is a Choice" and was intended to recap the central messages and insights of the series that I had curated. Among the most important is that the high level of inequality in the United States is not just or mostly the result of underlying economic forces; rather, it is the result of how we shape those forces, through our *policies*, through our laws and regulations, our monetary, tax, and expenditure policies. Indeed, some other countries have as much, or almost as much, before-tax and transfer inequality; but those countries that have allowed market forces to play out in this way then trim back the inequality through taxes and transfer and the provision of public services. There are many other countries, however, that have managed to have a much lower level of market income inequality—and, as I have noted elsewhere, these countries have just as good overall economic performance as the United States. So not only is inequality not inevitable, but there are policies that would enable us to have a more shared prosperity; indeed, with more sharing, we could have more prosperity.

Notes

1. Another is "The Changing of the Monetary Guard," *Project Syndicate*, August 5, 2013.
2. For a more extensive discussion of the battle, see Nicholas Lemann, "The Hand on the Lever," *New Yorker*, July 21, 2014.
3. The "Room for Debate" published October 28, 2014, to which I contributed, asked, "Should central bank policies attempt to offset inequality in economic outcome? Or should that be left exclusively to the political process?"
4. See Joseph E. Stiglitz, *Globalization and Its Discontents* (New York: W. W. Norton, 2002), Joseph E. Stiglitz, *Making Globalization Work* (New York: W. W. Norton, 2006), and Andrew Charlton and Joseph E. Stiglitz, *Fair Trade for All* (New York: Oxford University Press, 2005).
5. See the Federal Reserve's October 2014 Survey of Consumer Finances for a summary of the expansion in wealth inequality since the recession. Median wealth is down 40 percent since the start of the crisis, from $135,400 in 2007 to $81,200 in 2013 (adjusted for inflation).

HOW POLICY HAS CONTRIBUTED TO THE GREAT ECONOMIC DIVIDE*

THE UNITED STATES IS IN THE MIDST OF A VICIOUS CYCLE of inequality and recession: Inequality prolongs the downturn, and the downturn exacerbates inequality. Unfortunately, the austerity agenda advocated by conservatives will make matters worse on both counts.

The seriousness of America's growing problem of inequality was highlighted by Federal Reserve data released this month showing the recession's devastating effect on the wealth and income of those at the bottom and in the middle. The decline in median wealth, down almost 40 percent in just three years, wiped out two decades of wealth accumulation for most Americans. If the average American had actually shared in the country's seeming prosperity the past two decades, his wealth, instead of stagnating, would have increased by some three-fourths.

In some ways the data confirmed what was already known, but the numbers still shocked. We knew that house prices—the principal source of saving for most Americans—had declined precipitously and that trillions of dollars in home equity had been wiped

---

* *Washington Post*, June 22, 2012.

out. But unless we understand the link between inequality and economic performance, we risk pursuing policies that will worsen both.

America has "excelled" in inequality since at least the beginning of the millennium. Inequality is greater here than in any other advanced country. The data remind us how a combination of monetary, fiscal, and regulatory policies have contributed to these outcomes. Market forces play a role, but they are at play in other countries, too. Politics has much to do with the difference in outcomes.

The Great Recession has made this inequality worse, which is likely to prolong the downturn. Those at the top spend a smaller fraction of their income than do those in the bottom and middle—who have to spend everything today just to get by. Redistribution from the bottom to the top of the kind that has been going on in the United States lowers total demand. And the weakness in the U.S. economy arises out of deficient aggregate demand. The tax cuts passed under President George W. Bush in 2001 and 2003, aimed especially at the rich, were a particularly ineffective way of filling the gap; they put the burden of attaining full employment on the Fed, which filled the gap by creating a bubble, through lax regulations and loose monetary policy. And the bubble induced the bottom 80 percent of Americans to consume beyond their means. The policy worked, but it was a temporary and unsustainable palliative.

The Fed has consistently failed to understand the links between inequality and macroeconomic performance. Before the crisis, the Fed paid too little attention to inequality, focusing more on inflation than on employment. Many of the fashionable models in macroeconomics said that the distribution of income didn't matter. Fed officials' belief in unfettered markets restrained them from doing anything about the abuses of the banks. Even a former Fed governor, Ed Gramlich, argued in a forceful 2007 book that something should be done, but nothing was. The Fed refused to use the authority to regulate the mortgage market that Congress gave it in 1994. After the crisis, as the Fed lowered interest rates—in a predictably futile attempt to stimulate investment—it ignored the devastating effect that these rates would have on those Americans who had behaved prudently and invested in short-term government bonds, as well as the macroeconomic effects from their reduced consumption. Fed officials hoped that low interest rates would lead to high stock prices, which would in turn induce rich stock owners to consume more. Today, persistent low interest rates encourage firms that do invest to use capital-intensive technologies, such as replacing low-skilled checkout clerks with machines. In this way, the Fed may still be contributing to a jobless recovery, when we finally do recover.

Matters may get worse. The austerity advocated by some Republicans will lead to higher unemployment, which will lead to lower wages as workers compete for jobs. Less growth will mean lower state and local tax revenue, leading to cutbacks in services important to most Americans (including the jobs of teachers, police officers, and firefighters). It will force further increases in tuition— data published this month show that the average tuition for a four-year public university climbed 15 percent between 2008 and 2010, while most Americans' incomes and wealth were falling. This will lead to more student debt, more profits for bankers—but more pain at the bottom and middle. Some, seeing the consequences of their parents' debts, won't be willing to take on the levels of debt necessary to get a college education, condemning them to a life of lower wages. Even in the middle, incomes have been doing miserably; for male workers, inflation-adjusted median incomes are lower today than they were in 1968. Opportunity in America—already the country with the least equality of opportunity among the world's advanced nations, where a child's prospects depend more on the income and education of his parents than even in ossified Europe— will decline still further.

If we want recovery, there is no choice but to rely on fiscal policy. Fortunately, well-designed spending can lead simultaneously to more employment, growth, and equality. Further investments in education, especially aimed at the poor and middle class, from pre-school to Pell Grants, would stimulate the economy, improve opportunity, and increase growth. Spending a fraction of the money the federal government gave to the banks to help underwater home-owners—or extending unemployment benefits for those who have long searched but failed to find a job—would simultaneously ease the burden of those suffering from the recession and help bring the recession to an end. This higher growth would, in turn, lead to higher tax revenue, improving our fiscal position. Plenty of investments would pay for themselves.

By contrast, if we go down the path of austerity, we risk entering a double-dip recession, especially if the European crisis worsens. At the very least, our downturn would be likely to last years longer than it otherwise would. Our growth in the future will be weaker. But perhaps most important, our country will increasingly become divided, and we will pay a high economic price for our growing inequality and declining opportunity. The consequences will be even harder on our democracy, our identity as a nation of opportunity and fair play, and our society.

WHY JANET YELLEN, NOT LARRY SUMMERS, SHOULD LEAD THE FED[*]

THE CONTROVERSY OVER THE CHOICE OF THE NEXT HEAD of the Federal Reserve has become unusually heated. The country is fortunate to have an enormously qualified candidate: the Fed's current vice chairwoman, Janet L. Yellen. There is concern that the president might turn to another candidate, Lawrence H. Summers. Since I have worked closely with both of these individuals for more than three decades, both inside and outside of government, I have perhaps a distinct perspective.

But why, one might ask, is this a matter for a column usually devoted to understanding the growing divide between rich and poor in the United States and around the world? The reason is simple: What the Fed does has as much to do with the growth of inequality as virtually anything else. The good news is that both of the leading candidates talk as if they care about inequality. The bad news is that the policies that have been pushed by one of the candidates, Mr. Summers, have much to do with the woes faced by the middle and the bottom.

The Fed has responsibilities both in regulation and in macroeconomic management. Regulatory failures were at the core of Amer-

* *New York Times*, September 6, 2013.

ica's crisis. As a Treasury Department official during the Clinton administration, Mr. Summers supported banking deregulation, including the repeal of the Glass-Steagall Act, which was pivotal in America's financial crisis. His great "achievement" as secretary of the Treasury, from 1999 to 2001, was passage of the law that ensured that derivatives would not be regulated—a decision that helped blow up the financial markets. (Warren E. Buffett was right to call these derivatives "financial weapons of mass financial destruction." Some of those who were responsible for these key policy mistakes have admitted the fundamental "flaws" in their analyses. Mr. Summers, to my knowledge, has not.)

Regulatory failures have been at the center of previous crises as well. At Treasury in the 1990s, Mr. Summers encouraged countries to quickly liberalize their capital markets, to allow capital to flow in and out without restrictions—indeed insisted that they do so—against the advice of the White House Council of Economic Advisers (which I led from 1995 to 1997), and this more than anything else led to the Asian financial crisis. Few policies or actions have greater culpability for that Asian crisis and the global financial crisis of 2008 than the deregulatory policies that Mr. Summers advocated.

Supporters of Mr. Summers argue that he is exceptionally qualified to manage crises—and that, while we hope that there won't be a crisis in the next four years, prudence requires someone who excels at those critical moments. To be fair, Mr. Summers has been involved in several crises. What matters, however, is not just "being there" during a crisis, but showing good judgment in its management. Even more important is a commitment to taking actions to make another crisis less likely—in sharp contrast to measures that almost ensure the inevitability of another one.

Mr. Summers's conduct and judgment in the crises was as flawed as his lack of commitment in that regard. In both Asia and the United States, he seemed to me to underestimate the severity of the downturns, and with forecasts that were so off, it was not a surprise that the policies were inappropriate. The performance of those in the Treasury who were responsible for managing the Asian crisis was, to say the least, disappointing—converting downturns into recessions and recessions into depressions. So, too, while the banking system was saved, and the United States avoided another depression, those responsible for managing the 2008 crisis cannot be credited with creating a robust, inclusive recovery. Botched efforts at mortgage restructuring, a failure to restore the flow of credit to small and medium-size enterprises, and the mishandling of the bailouts have all been well documented—as was the failure to foresee the severity of the economic collapse.

These issues are important to anyone concerned with inequality for four reasons. First, crises and how they are managed are real creators of poverty and inequality. Just look at what havoc this crisis wrought: median wealth fell by 40 percent, those in the middle still have not seen their incomes recover to precrisis levels, and those in the upper 1 percent enjoyed all the fruits of the recovery (and then some). It is ordinary workers who have suffered most: they are the ones who face high unemployment, who see their wages cut, and who bear the brunt of cutbacks in public services as a result of the budget austerity. They are the ones who lost their homes in the millions. The Obama administration could have done more, far more, to help homeowners, and to help localities maintain public services (for instance, through the kind of revenue sharing with states and localities that I urged at the beginning of the crisis).

Second, deregulation contributed to the financialization of the economy. It distorted our economy. It provided greater scope for those who manipulate the rules of the game for their benefit. As James K. Galbraith has forcefully argued, as we look around the world, bloated and underregulated financial sectors are closely linked with greater inequality. Those, like Britain, that emulated America's deregulation have seen inequality soar, too.

Third, the most invidious aspect of this deregulation-induced inequality is that associated with the abusive practices of the financial sector—which prospers at the expense of ordinary Americans, through predatory lending, market manipulation, abusive credit card practices, or taking advantage of its monopoly power in the payments system. The Fed has enormous powers to prevent these abuses, and even more since the passage of the Dodd-Frank Act of 2010. Yet the central bank has repeatedly failed at this, systematically focusing on strengthening the banks' balance sheets, at the expense of ordinary Americans.

Fourth, it is not only the case that America's financial sector did what it shouldn't have done, but it also didn't do what it was supposed to do. Even today, there is a dearth of loans to small and medium-size enterprises. Good regulation would shift banks away from speculation and market manipulation, back to what should be their core business: making loans.

Whoever succeeds Ben S. Bernanke as the Fed's leader will have to make repeated judgment calls about when to raise or lower interest rates, the levers of monetary policy.

Two elements enter into these judgments. The first is forecasting. Wrong forecasts lead to wrong policies. Without a good sense of direction of where the economy is going, one can't take appropriate policies. Ms. Yellen has a superb record in forecasting where the economy is going—the best, according to the *Wall Street Journal*, of anyone at the Fed. As I noted earlier, Mr. Summers's leaves something to be desired.

Ms. Yellen's superlative performance should not come as a surprise. Janet Yellen, whom I taught at Yale, was one of the best students I have had, in 47 years of teaching at Columbia, Princeton, Stanford, Yale, MIT, and Oxford. She is an economist of great intellect, with a strong ability to forge consensus, and she has proved her mettle as chairwoman of the president's Council of Economic Advisers (she succeeded me in that role), as president of the Federal Reserve Bank of San Francisco, from 2004 to 2010, and in her current role, as the Fed's No. 2.

Ms. Yellen brings to bear an understanding not just of financial markets and monetary policy, but also of labor markets—which is essential at a time when unemployment and wage stagnation are primary concerns.

The second element of Fed policy making is risk assessment: if one steps on the brakes too hard, one risks excessively high unemployment; too gently, one risks inflation. Ms. Yellen has shown herself to be not only excellent in forecasting, but balanced. Legitimate questions have been raised: Would Mr. Summers, with his close connections with Wall Street, reflect financiers' single-minded focus on inflation, and be more worried about the effects on bond prices than on ordinary Americans? In the past, central banks have focused excessively on inflation. Indeed, this single-minded focus, with little regard to financial stability, not only has contributed to the crisis, but, as I argued in my book *Freefall*, it has also contributed to the declining share of total income that is earned by ordinary workers.

Though the willingness to take actions to prevent crises, and good judgments in a crisis, are undoubtedly critical in the choice of the next Fed chair, there are other important considerations. The Fed is a large organization that has to be managed—and Ms. Yellen demonstrated her management skills at the San Francisco Fed. One has to obtain consensus among a diverse group of strong-minded individuals, some more worried about inflation, some more worried about unemployment. We need someone who knows how to build consensus, not someone who excels in bullying, who knows how to listen to and respect the views of others. When I was chairman of Economic Policy Committee of the Organization for Economic Cooperation and Development, I saw how effectively Ms. Yellen represented the United States, and the respect in which she was held. In the ensuing years, she has gained in stature, and today has the enormous respect of central bank governors around the world. She has the judgment, wisdom, and gravitas one should expect of the leader of the Fed.

Finally, the Fed is an enormously important institution, but regrettably, its conduct in the years before Ms. Yellen took up her role in Washington—both its failures in dealing with the bubble and certain aspects of its conduct in the immediate aftermath of the crisis (like the lack of transparency)—has undermined confidence in it. It is important that President Obama's nominee not be—or even be seen to be—acting at the behest of financial markets. That person cannot be someone who can be tainted even by an accusation of conflict of interest, which is inevitable with the "revolving door" that has too often been associated with the regulation of this sector. Nor should it be someone who suffers from "cognitive capture" by Wall Street. At the same time, the person has to have the confidence of the financial markets, and a deep understanding of those markets. Ms. Yellen has managed to do this—an impressive achievement in its own right.

One might say that the country is fortunate to have two candidates who, as the Harvard economist Kenneth S. Rogoff, a former chief economist at the International Monetary Fund, writes, are "brilliant scholars with extensive experience in public service." But brilliance is not the only determinant of performance. Values, judgment, and personality matter, too.

The choices have seldom been so stark, the stakes so large. No wonder that the choice of the Fed leader has stirred such emotion. Ms. Yellen has a truly impressive record in each of the jobs she has undertaken. The country has before it one candidate who played a pivotal role in creating the economic problems that we confront today, and another candidate of enormous stature, experience, and judgment.

THE INSANITY OF OUR
FOOD POLICY*

AMERICAN FOOD POLICY HAS LONG BEEN RIFE WITH HEAD-scratching illogic. We spend billions every year on farm subsidies, many of which help wealthy commercial operations to plant more crops than we need. The glut depresses world crop prices, harming farmers in developing countries. Meanwhile, millions of Americans live tenuously close to hunger, which is barely kept at bay by a food stamp program that gives most beneficiaries just a little more than $4 a day.

So it's almost too absurd to believe that House Republicans are asking for a farm bill that would make all of these problems worse. For the putative purpose of balancing the country's books, the measures that the House Republican caucus is pushing for in negotiations with the Senate, as Congress attempts to pass a long-stalled extension of the farm bill, would cut back the meager aid to our country's most vulnerable and use the proceeds to continue fattening up a small number of wealthy American farmers.

The House has proposed cutting food stamp benefits by $40 billion over 10 years—that's on top of $5 billion in cuts that already came into effect this month with the expiration of increases to the

---

* *New York Times*, November 16, 2013.

food stamp program that were included in the 2009 stimulus law. Meanwhile, House Republicans appear satisfied to allow farm subsidies, which totaled some $14.9 billion last year, to continue apace. Republican proposals would shift government assistance from direct payments—paid at a set rate to farmers every year to encourage them to keep growing particular crops, regardless of market fluctuations—to crop insurance premium subsidies. But this is unlikely to be any cheaper. Worse, unlike direct payments, the insurance premium subsidies carry no income limit for the farmers who would receive this form of largesse.

The proposal is a perfect example of how growing inequality has been fed by what economists call rent seeking. As small numbers of Americans have grown extremely wealthy, their political power has also ballooned to a disproportionate size. Small, powerful interests—in this case, wealthy commercial farmers—help create market-skewing public policies that benefit only themselves, appropriating a larger slice of the nation's economic pie. Their larger slice means everyone else gets a smaller one—the pie doesn't get any bigger—though the rent seekers are usually adept at taking little enough from individual Americans that they are hardly aware of the loss. While the money that they've picked from each individual American's pocket is small, the aggregate is huge for the rent seeker. And this in turn deepens inequality.

The nonsensical arrangement being proposed in the House Republicans' farm bill is an especially egregious version of this process. It takes real money, money that is necessary for bare survival, from the poorest Americans, and gives it to a small group of the undeserving rich, in return for their campaign contributions and political support. There is no economic justification: The bill actually distorts our economy by promoting the kind of production we don't need and shrinking the consumption of those with the smallest incomes. There is no moral justification either: It actually increases misery and precariousness of daily life for millions of Americans.

FARM SUBSIDIES WERE much more sensible when they began eight decades ago, in 1933, at a time when more than 40 percent of Americans lived in rural areas. Farm incomes had fallen by about a half in the first three years of the Great Depression. In that context, the subsidies were an antipoverty program.

Now, though, the farm subsidies serve a quite different purpose. From 1995 to 2012, 1 percent of farms received about $1.5 million each, which is more than a quarter of all subsidies, according to the Environmental Working Group. Some three-quarters of the subsidies went to just 10 percent of farms. These farms received an average of more than $30,000 a year—about 20 times the amount received by the average individual beneficiary last year from the federal Supplemental Nutrition Assistance Program, or SNAP, commonly called food stamps.

Today, food stamps are one of the main support beams in our antipoverty efforts. More than 80 percent of the 45 million or so Americans who participated in SNAP in 2011, the last year for which there is comprehensive data from the United States Department of Agriculture, had gross household incomes below the poverty level. (Since then, the total number of participants has expanded to nearly 48 million.) Even with that support, many of them experience food insecurity, that is, they had trouble putting food on the table at some point during the year.

Historically, food stamp programs and agricultural subsidies have been tied together. The two may seem strange bedfellows, but there is a rationale: There is a need to address both sides of the economics of food—production and consumption. Having a bounteous supply within a country does not ensure that the citizens of that country are well fed. The radical imbalance between farm subsidies to the wealthy and nutritional assistance to the neediest—an imbalance that the farm bill proposals would directly promote—is a painful testament to this established economic fact.

The Nobel Prize–winning economist Amartya Sen has reminded us that even famines are not necessarily caused by a lack of supply, but by a failure to get the food that exists to the people who need it. This was true in the Bengal famine of 1943 and in the Irish potato famine a century earlier: Ireland, controlled by its British masters, was exporting food even as its citizens died of starvation.

A similar dynamic is playing out in the United States. American farmers are heralded as among the most efficient in the world. Our country is the largest producer and exporter of corn and soybeans, to name just two of its biggest crops. And yet millions of Americans still suffer from hunger, and millions more would, were it not for the vital programs that government provides to prevent hunger and malnutrition—the programs that the Republicans are now seeking to cut back.

And there is an extra layer of irony to America's food policies: While they encourage overproduction, they pay little attention to the quality and diversity of foods our farms produce. The heavy subsidization of corn, for instance, means that many unhealthful foods are relatively cheap. So grocery shopping on a tight budget often means choosing foods that are not nutritious. This is part of the reason that Americans face the paradox of hunger out of proportion to their wealth, along with some of the world's highest obesity rates, and a high incidence of Type 2 diabetes. Poor Americans are especially at risk for obesity.

A few years ago, I was in India, a country of 1.2 billion, in which tens of millions face hunger on a daily basis, when a front-page headline blared that one in seven Americans faced food insecurity because they couldn't afford the basic necessities of life. Indian friends I met that day and in the following week were puzzled by this news: How could it be that in the richest country of the world there was still hunger?

Their puzzlement was understandable: Hunger in this rich land is unnecessary. What my Indian friends didn't understand is that 15 percent of Americans—and 22 percent of America's children—live in poverty. Someone working full-time (2,080 hours a year) at the minimum wage of $7.25 would earn about $15,000 a year, far less than the poverty threshold for a family of four ($23,492 in 2012), and even less than the poverty level of a family of three.

This grim picture is a result of political decisions made in Washington that have helped create an economic system in which the undereducated must work exceptionally hard simply to remain in poverty.

This is not how America is supposed to work. In his famous 1941 "four freedoms" speech, Franklin D. Roosevelt enunciated the principle that all Americans should have certain basic economic rights, including "freedom from want." These ideas were later embraced by the international community in the Universal Declaration of Human Rights, which also enshrined the right to adequate food. But while the United States was instrumental in advocating for these basic economic human rights on the international scene— and getting them adopted—America's performance back home has been disappointing.

It is, of course, no surprise that with the high level of poverty millions of Americans have had to turn to the government to meet the basic necessities of life. And those numbers increased drastically with the onset of the Great Recession. The number of Americans on food stamps went up by more than 80 percent between 2007 and 2013.

To say that most of these Americans are technically poor only begins to get at the depth of their need. In 2012, for example, two in five SNAP recipients had gross incomes that were less than half of the poverty line. The amount they get from the program is very small—$4.39 a day per recipient. This is hardly enough to survive on, but it makes an enormous difference in the lives of those who get it: The Center on Budget and Policy Priorities estimates that SNAP lifted four million Americans out of poverty in 2010.

Given the inadequacies of the existing programs to combat hunger and poor nutrition, and given the magnitude of poverty in the aftermath of the Great Recession, one might have thought that the natural response of our political leaders would be to expand programs enhancing food security. But the members of the Republican caucus in the House of Representatives see things differently. They seem to want to blame the victims—the poor who have been provided an inadequate public education and so lack marketable skills, and those who earnestly seek work, but can't find any, because of an economic system that has stalled, with almost one out of seven Americans who would like to find full-time employment still unable to obtain it. Far from alleviating the impacts of these problems, the Republicans' proposal would reinforce privation and inequalities.

And the calamitous effects of the Republicans' proposal will reach even beyond our borders.

Viewed from a larger perspective, the farming subsidies, combined with the cutbacks in food stamps, increase global poverty and hunger. This is because, with American consumption diminished from what it otherwise would be and production increased, food exports will inevitably increase. Greater exports drive down global prices, hurting poor farmers around the world. Agriculture is the main source of livelihood for the 70 percent of the world's poor living in rural areas, who overwhelmingly reside in developing countries.

The adoption of the House Republicans' plan will reverberate in our economy through several channels. One is simply that poor families with diminished resources will tamp down growth. More pernicious is that the Republicans' farm bill would deepen inequality—and not just through the immediate giveaways to wealthy farmers and corresponding cuts to the poor. Children with poor nutrition—whether they are hungry or ill because of bad diets—do not learn as well as those who are better fed.

By cutting back on food stamps, we are ensuring the perpetuation of inequality, and at that, one of its worst manifestations: the inequality of opportunity. When it comes to opportunity, America is doing an alarmingly bad job, as I've written before in this series. We are endangering our future because there will be a large coterie of people at the bottom who will not live up to their potential, who will not be able to make the contribution that they could have made, to the prosperity of the country as a whole.

All of this exposes the Republicans' argument in favor of these food policies—a concern for our future, particularly the impact of the national debt on our children—as a dishonest and deeply cynical pretense. Not only has the intellectual undergirding of debt fetishism been knocked out (with the debunking of work by the Harvard economists Carmen M. Reinhart and Kenneth S. Rogoff that tied slowed growth to debt-to-GDP ratios above 90 percent). The Republicans' farm bill also clearly harms both America's children and the world's in a variety of ways.

For these proposals to become law would be a moral and economic failure for the country.

ON THE WRONG SIDE
OF GLOBALIZATION*

TRADE AGREEMENTS ARE A SUBJECT THAT CAN CAUSE THE eyes to glaze over, but we should all be paying attention. Right now, there are trade proposals in the works that threaten to put most Americans on the wrong side of globalization.

The conflicting views about the agreements are actually tearing at the fabric of the Democratic Party, though you wouldn't know it from President Obama's rhetoric. In his State of the Union address, for example, he blandly referred to "new trade partnerships" that would "create more jobs." Most immediately at issue is the Trans-Pacific Partnership, or TPP, which would bring together 12 countries along the Pacific Rim in what would be the largest free-trade area in the world.

Negotiations for the TPP began in 2010, for the purpose, according to the United States Trade Representative, of increasing trade and investment, through lowering tariffs and other trade barriers among participating countries. But the TPP negotiations have been taking place in secret, forcing us to rely on leaked drafts to guess at the proposed provisions. At the same time, Congress introduced a bill this year that would grant the White House filibuster-proof fast-track

* *New York Times*, March 15, 2014.

authority, under which Congress simply approves or rejects whatever trade agreement is put before it, without revisions or amendments.

Controversy has erupted, and justifiably so. Based on the leaks—and the history of arrangements in past trade pacts—it is easy to infer the shape of the whole TPP, and it doesn't look good. There is a real risk that it will benefit the wealthiest sliver of the American and global elite at the expense of everyone else. The fact that such a plan is under consideration at all is testament to how deeply inequality reverberates through our economic policies.

Worse, agreements like the TPP are only one aspect of a larger problem: our gross mismanagement of globalization.

Let's tackle the history first. In general, trade deals today are markedly different from those made in the decades following World War II, when negotiations focused on lowering tariffs. As tariffs came down on all sides, trade expanded, and each country could develop the sectors in which it had strengths and as a result, standards of living would rise. Some jobs would be lost, but new jobs would be created.

Today, the purpose of trade agreements is different. Tariffs around the world are already low. The focus has shifted to "nontariff barriers," and the most important of these—for the corporate interests pushing agreements—are regulations. Huge multinational corporations complain that inconsistent regulations make business costly. But most of the regulations, even if they are imperfect, are there for a reason: to protect workers, consumers, the economy, and the environment.

What's more, those regulations were often put in place by governments responding to the democratic demands of their citizens. Trade agreements' new boosters euphemistically claim that they are simply after regulatory harmonization, a clean-sounding phrase that implies an innocent plan to promote efficiency. One could, of course, get regulatory harmonization by strengthening regulations to the highest standards everywhere. But when corporations call for harmonization, what they really mean is a race to the bottom.

When agreements like the TPP govern international trade—when every country has agreed to similarly minimal regulations—

multinational corporations can return to the practices that were common before the Clean Air and Clean Water Acts became law (in 1970 and 1972, respectively) and before the latest financial crisis hit. Corporations everywhere may well agree that getting rid of regulations would be good for corporate profits. Trade negotiators might be persuaded that these trade agreements would be good for trade and corporate profits. But there would be some big losers—namely, the rest of us.

These high stakes are why it is especially risky to let trade negotiations proceed in secret. All over the world, trade ministries are captured by corporate and financial interests. And when negotiations are secret, there is no way that the democratic process can exert the checks and balances required to put limits on the negative effects of these agreements.

The secrecy might be enough to cause significant controversy for the TPP. What we know of its particulars only makes it more unpalatable. One of the worst is that it allows corporations to seek restitution in an international tribunal, not only for unjust expropriation, but also for alleged diminution of their potential profits as a result of regulation. This is not a theoretical problem. Philip Morris has already tried this tactic against Uruguay, claiming that its antismoking regulations, which have won accolades from the World Health Organization, unfairly hurt profits, violating a bilateral trade treaty between Switzerland and Uruguay. In this sense, recent trade agreements are reminiscent of the Opium Wars, in which Western powers successfully demanded that China keep itself open to opium because they saw it as vital in correcting what otherwise would be a large trade imbalance.

Provisions already incorporated in other trade agreements are being used elsewhere to undermine environmental and other regulations. Developing countries pay a high price for signing on to these provisions, but the evidence that they get more investment in return is scant and controversial. And though these countries are the most obvious victims, the same issue could become a problem for the United States, as well. American corporations could conceivably create a subsidiary in some Pacific Rim country, invest in the United States through that subsidiary, and then take action against the United States government—getting rights as a "foreign" company that they would not have had as an American company. Again, this is not just a theoretical possibility: There is already some evidence that companies are choosing how to funnel their money into different countries on the basis of where their legal position in relation to the government is strongest.

There are other noxious provisions. America has been fighting to lower the cost of health care. But the TPP would make the introduction of generic drugs more difficult, and thus raise the price of medicines. In the poorest countries, this is not just about moving money into corporate coffers: thousands would die unnecessarily. Of course, those who do research have to be compensated. That's why we have a patent system. But the patent system is supposed to carefully balance the benefits of intellectual protection with another worthy goal: making access to knowledge more available. I've written before about how the system has been abused by those seeking patents for the genes that predispose women to breast cancer. The Supreme Court ended up rejecting those patents, but not before many women suffered unnecessarily. Trade agreements provide even more opportunities for patent abuse.

The worries mount. One way of reading the leaked negotiation documents suggests that the TPP would make it easier for American banks to sell risky derivatives around the world, perhaps setting us up for the same kind of crisis that led to the Great Recession.

In spite of all this, there are those who passionately support the TPP and agreements like it, including many economists. What makes this support possible is bogus, debunked economic theory, which has remained in circulation mostly because it serves the interests of the wealthiest.

Free trade was a central tenet of economics in the discipline's early years. Yes, there are winners and losers, the theory went, but the winners can always compensate the losers, so that free trade (or even freer trade) is a win-win. This conclusion, unfortunately, is based on numerous assumptions, many of which are simply wrong.

The older theories, for instance, simply ignored risk, and assumed that workers could move seamlessly between jobs. It was assumed that the economy was at full employment, so that workers displaced by globalization would quickly move from low-productivity sectors (which had thrived simply because foreign competition was kept at bay through tariffs and other trade restrictions) to high-productivity sectors. But when there is a high level of unemployment, and especially when a large percentage of the unemployed have been out of work long-term (as is the case now), there can't be such complacency.

Today, there are 20 million Americans who would like a full-time job but can't get one. Millions have stopped looking. So there is a real risk that individuals moved from low productivity-employment in a protected sector will end up zero-productivity members of the vast ranks of the unemployed. This hurts even those who keep their jobs, as higher unemployment puts downward pressure on wages.

We can argue over why our economy isn't performing the way it's supposed to—whether it's because of a lack of aggregate demand, or because our banks, more interested in speculation and market manipulation than lending, are not providing adequate funds to small and medium-size enterprises. But whatever the reasons, the reality is that these trade agreements do risk increasing unemployment.

One of the reasons that we are in such bad shape is that we have mismanaged globalization. Our economic policies encourage the out-sourcing of jobs: Goods produced abroad with cheap labor can be cheaply brought back into the United States. So American workers understand that they have to compete with those abroad, and their bargaining power is weakened. This is one of the reasons that the real median income of full-time male workers is lower than it was 40 years ago.

American politics today compounds these problems. Even in the best of circumstances, the old free-trade theory said only that the winners could compensate the losers, not that they would. And they haven't—quite the opposite. Advocates of trade agreements often say that for America to be competitive, not only will wages have to be cut, but so will taxes and expenditures, especially on programs that are of benefit to ordinary citizens. We should accept the short-term pain, they say, because in the long run, all will benefit. But there is little evidence that the trade agreements will lead to faster or more profound growth or that in the long run most workers will benefit.

Critics of the TPP are so numerous because both the process and the theory that undergird it are bankrupt. Opposition has blossomed not just in the United States, but also in Asia, where the talks have stalled.

By leading a full-on rejection of fast-track authority for the TPP, the Senate majority leader, Harry Reid, seems to have given us all a little respite. Those who see trade agreements as enriching corporations at the expense of the 99 percent seem to have won this skirmish. But there is a broader war to ensure that trade policy—and globalization more generally—is designed so as to increase the standards of living of most Americans. The outcome of that war remains uncertain.

In this series, I have repeatedly made two points: The first is that the high level of inequality in the United States today, and its enormous increase during the past 30 years, is the cumulative result of an array of policies, programs, and laws. Given that the president himself has emphasized that inequality should be the country's top priority, every new policy, program, or law should be examined from the perspective of its impact on inequality. Agreements like the TPP have contributed in important ways to this inequality. Corporations may profit, and it is even possible, though far from assured, that gross domestic product as conventionally measured will increase. But the well-being of ordinary citizens is likely to take a hit.

And this brings me to the second point that I have repeatedly emphasized: Trickle-down economics is a myth. Enriching corporations—as the TPP would—will not necessarily help those in the middle, let alone those at the bottom.

THE FREE-TRADE CHARADE*

THOUGH NOTHING HAS COME OF THE WORLD TRADE Organization's Doha Development Round of global trade negotiations since they were launched almost a dozen years ago, another round of talks is in the works. But this time the negotiations will not be held on a global, multilateral basis; rather, two huge regional agreements—one transpacific, and the other transatlantic—are to be negotiated. Are the coming talks likely to be more successful?

The Doha round was torpedoed by the United States' refusal to eliminate agricultural subsidies—a sine qua non for any true development round, given that 70 percent of those in the developing world depend on agriculture directly or indirectly. The U.S. position was truly breathtaking, given that the WTO had already judged that America's cotton subsidies—paid to fewer than 25,000 rich farmers—were illegal. America's response was to bribe Brazil, which had brought the complaint, not to pursue the matter further, leaving in the lurch millions of poor cotton farmers in sub-Saharan Africa and India, who suffer from depressed prices because of America's largesse to its wealthy farmers.

Given this recent history, it now seems clear that the nego-

* *Project Syndicate*, July 4, 2013

tiations to create a free-trade area between the U.S. and Europe, and another between the U.S. and much of the Pacific (except for China), are not about establishing a true free-trade system. Instead, the goal is a managed trade regime—managed, that is, to serve the special interests that have long dominated trade policy in the West.

There are a few basic principles that those entering the discussions will, one hopes, take to heart. First, any trade agreement has to be symmetrical. If, as part of the Trans-Pacific Partnership (TPP), the U.S. demands that Japan eliminate its rice subsidies, the US should, in turn, offer to eliminate its production (and water) subsidies, not just on rice (which is relatively unimportant in the U.S.) but on other agricultural commodities as well.

Second, no trade agreement should put commercial interests ahead of broader national interests, especially when non-trade-related issues like financial regulation and intellectual property are at stake. America's trade agreement with Chile, for example, impedes Chile's use of capital controls—even though the International Monetary Fund now recognizes that capital controls can be an important instrument of macro-prudential policy.

Other trade agreements have insisted on financial liberalization and deregulation as well, even though the 2008 crisis should have taught us that the absence of good regulation can jeopardize economic prosperity. America's pharmaceutical industry, which wields considerable clout with the office of the U.S. Trade Representative (USTR), has succeeded in foisting on other countries an unbalanced intellectual-property regime, which, designed to fight generic drugs, puts profit ahead of saving lives. Even the U.S. Supreme Court has now said that the U.S. Patent Office went too far in granting patents on genes.

Finally, there must be a commitment to transparency. But those engaging in these trade negotiations should be forewarned: the U.S. is committed to a *lack* of transparency. The USTR's office has been reluctant to reveal its negotiating position even to members of the U.S. Congress; on the basis of what has been leaked, one can understand why. The USTR's office is backtracking on principles—for example, access to generic medicines—that Congress had inserted into earlier trade agreements, like that with Peru.

In the case of the TPP, there is a further concern. Asia has developed an efficient supply chain, with goods flowing easily from one country to another in the process of producing finished goods. But the TPP could interfere with that if China remains outside of it.

With formal tariffs already so low, negotiators will focus largely on nontariff barriers—such as regulatory barriers. But the USTR's office, representing corporate interests, will almost surely push for the lowest common standard, leveling *downward* rather than upward. For example, many countries have tax and regulatory provisions that discourage large automobiles—not because they are trying to discriminate against U.S. goods, but because they worry about pollution and energy efficiency.

The more general point, alluded to earlier, is that trade agreements typically put commercial interests ahead of other values—the right to a healthy life and protection of the environment, to name just two. France, for example, wants a "cultural exception" in trade agreements that would allow it to continue to support its films— from which the whole world benefits. This and other broader values should be nonnegotiable.

Indeed, the irony is that the social benefits of such subsidies are enormous, while the costs are negligible. Does anyone really believe that a French art film represents a serious threat to a Hollywood summer blockbuster? Yet Hollywood's greed knows no limit, and America's trade negotiators take no prisoners. And that's precisely why such items should be taken off the table *before* negotiations begin. Otherwise, arms will be twisted, and there is a real risk that an agreement will sacrifice basic values to commercial interests.

If negotiators created a genuine free-trade regime that put the public interest first, with the views of ordinary citizens given at least as much weight as those of corporate lobbyists, I might be optimistic that what would emerge would strengthen the economy and improve social well-being. The reality, however, is that we have a managed trade regime that puts corporate interests first, and a process of negotiations that is undemocratic and nontransparent.

The likelihood that what emerges from the coming talks will serve ordinary Americans' interests is low; the outlook for ordinary citizens in other countries is even bleaker.

HOW INTELLECTUAL
PROPERTY REINFORCES
INEQUALITY*

I N THE WAR AGAINST INEQUALITY, WE'VE BECOME SO USED
to bad news that we're almost taken aback when something
positive happens. And with the Supreme Court having affirmed
that wealthy people and corporations have a constitutional right
to buy American elections, who would have expected it to bring
good news? But a decision in the term that just ended gave ordinary
Americans something that is more precious than money alone—the
right to live.

At first glance, the case, *Association for Molecular Pathology v.
Myriad Genetics*, might seem like scientific arcana: the court ruled,
unanimously, that human genes cannot be patented, though syn-
thetic DNA, created in the laboratory, can be. But the real stakes
were much higher, and the issues much more fundamental, than is
commonly understood. The case was a battle between those who
would privatize good health, making it a privilege to be enjoyed in
proportion to wealth, and those who see it as a right for all—and a
central component of a fair society and well-functioning economy.
Even more deeply, it was about the way inequality is shaping our
politics, legal institutions, and the health of our population.

---

* *New York Times*, July 14, 2013.

Unlike the bitter battles between Samsung and Apple, in which the referees (American courts), while making a pretense at balance, seem to consistently favor the home team, this was a case that was more than just a battle between corporate giants. It is a lens through which we can see the pernicious and far-reaching effects of inequality, what a victory over self-serving corporate behavior looks like and—just as important—how much we still risk losing in such fights.

Of course, the court and the parties didn't frame the issues that way in their arguments and decision. A Utah firm, Myriad Genetics, had isolated two human genes, BRCA1 and BRCA2, that can contain mutations that predispose women who carry them to breast cancer—crucial knowledge for early detection and prevention. The company had successfully obtained patents for the genes. "Owning" the genes gave it the right to prevent others from testing for them. The core question of the case was seemingly technical: Are isolated, naturally occurring genes something that can be patented?

But the patents had devastating real-world implications, because they kept the prices for the diagnostics artificially high. Gene tests can actually be administered at low cost—a person can in fact have all 20,000 of her genes sequenced for about $1,000, to say nothing of much cheaper tests for a variety of specific pathologies. Myriad, however, charged about $4,000 for comprehensive testing on just two genes. Scientists have argued that there was nothing inherently special or superior about Myriad's methods—it simply tested for genes that the company claimed to own, and did so by relying on data that was not available to others because of the patents.

Hours after the Supreme Court's ruling in favor of the plaintiffs—a group of universities, researchers, and patient advocates, represented by the American Civil Liberties Union and the Public Patent Foundation—other laboratories quickly announced that they would also begin offering tests for the breast cancer genes, underlining the fact that Myriad's "innovation" was identifying existing genes, not developing the test for them. (Myriad is not done fighting, though, having filed two new lawsuits this month that seek to block the companies Ambry Genetics and Gene by Gene from administering their own BRCA tests, on the grounds that they violate other patents that Myriad holds.)

It should not be very surprising that Myriad has done everything it can to prevent its tests' revenue stream from facing competition—indeed, after recovering somewhat from a 30 percent drop in the wake of the court ruling, its share price is still nearly 20 percent below what it was beforehand. It owned the genes, and didn't want anybody trespassing on its property. In obtaining the patent, Myriad, like most corporations, seemed motivated more by maximizing profits than by saving lives—if it really cared about the latter, it could and would have done better at providing tests at lower costs and encouraged others to develop better, more accurate, and cheaper tests. Not surprisingly, it made labored arguments that its patents, which allowed monopolistic prices and exclusionary practices, were essential to incentivize future research. But when the devastating effects of its patents became apparent, and it remained adamant in exerting its full monopoly rights, these pretensions of interest in the greater good were woefully unconvincing.

The drug industry, as always, claimed that without patent protection, there would be no incentives for research and all would suffer. I filed an expert declaration with the court (pro bono), explaining why the industry's arguments were wrong, and why this and similar patents actually impeded rather than fostered innovation. Other groups that filed amicus briefs supporting the plaintiffs, like AARP, pointed out that Myriad's patents prevented patients from obtaining second opinions and confirmatory tests. Recently, Myriad pledged it would not block such tests—a pledge it made even as it filed the lawsuits against Ambry Genetics and Gene by Gene.

Myriad denied the test to two women in the case by rejecting their Medicaid insurance—according to the plaintiffs, because the reimbursement was too low. Other women, after one round of Myriad's testing, had to make agonizing decisions about whether to have a single or double mastectomy, or whether to have their ovaries removed, with severely incomplete information—either Myriad's testing for additional BRCA mutations was unaffordable (Myriad charges $700 extra for information that national guidelines say should be provided to patients), or second opinions were unattainable because of Myriad's patents.

The good news coming from the Supreme Court was that in the United States, genes could not be patented. In a sense, the court gave back to women something they thought they already owned. This had two enormous practical implications: one is it meant that there could now be competition to develop better, more accurate, less expensive tests for the gene. We could once again have competitive markets driving innovation. And the second is that poor women would have a more equal chance to live—in this case, to conquer breast cancer.

But as important a victory as this is, it is ultimately only one corner of a global intellectual property landscape that is heavily shaped by corporate interests—usually American. And America has attempted to foist its intellectual property regime on others, through the World Trade Organization and bilateral and other multilateral trade regimes. It is doing so now in negotiations as part of the so-called Trans-Pacific Partnership. Trade agreements are supposed to be an important instrument of diplomacy: closer trade integration brings closer ties in other dimensions. But attempts by the office of the United States Trade Representative to persuade others that, in effect, corporate profits are more important than human lives undermines America's international standing: if anything, it reinforces the stereotype of the crass American.

Economic power often speaks louder, though, than moral values; and in the many instances in which American corporate interests prevail in intellectual property rights, our policies help increase inequality abroad. In most countries, it's much the same as in the United States: the lives of the poor are sacrificed at the altar of corporate profits. But even in those where, say, the government would provide a test like Myriad's at affordable prices for all, there is a cost: when a government pays monopoly prices for a medical test, it takes money away that could be spent for other lifesaving health expenditures.

THE MYRIAD CASE was an embodiment of three key messages in my book *The Price of Inequality*. First, I argued that societal inequality was a result not just of the laws of economics, but also of how we shape the economy—through politics, including through almost every aspect of our legal system. Here, it's our intellectual property regime that contributes needlessly to the gravest form of inequality. The right to life should not be contingent on the ability to pay.

The second is that some of the most iniquitous aspects of inequality creation within our economic system are a result of "rent seeking": profits, and inequality, generated by manipulating social or political conditions to get a larger share of the economic pie, rather than increasing the size of that pie. And the most iniquitous aspect of this wealth appropriation arises when the wealth that goes to the top comes at the expense of the bottom. Myriad's efforts satisfied both these conditions: the profits the company gained from charging for its test added nothing to the size and dynamism of the economy, and simultaneously decreased the welfare of those who could not afford it.

While all of the insured contributed to Myriad's profits—premiums had to go up to offset its fees, and millions of uninsured middle-income Americans who had to pay Myriad's monopoly prices were on the hook for even more if they chose to get the test—it was the uninsured at the bottom who paid the highest price. With the test unaffordable, they faced a higher risk of early death.

Advocates of tough intellectual property rights say that this is simply the price we have to pay to get the innovation that, in the long run, will save lives. It's a trade-off: the lives of a relatively few poor women today, versus the lives of many more women sometime in the future. But this claim is wrong in many ways. In this particular case, it is especially wrong, because the two genes would likely have been isolated ("discovered," in Myriad's terminology) soon anyway, as part of the global Human Genome Project. But it is wrong on other counts, as well. Genetic researchers have argued that the patent actually prevented the development of better tests, and so interfered with the advancement of science. All knowledge is based on prior knowledge, and by making prior knowledge less available, innovation is impeded. Myriad's own discovery—like any in science—used technologies and ideas that were developed by others. Had that prior knowledge not been publicly available, Myriad could not have done what it did.

And that's the third major theme. I titled my book to emphasize that inequality is not just morally repugnant but also has material costs. When the legal regime governing intellectual property rights is designed poorly, it facilitates rent seeking—and ours is poorly designed, though this and other recent Supreme Court decisions have led to one that is better than it otherwise would have been. And the result is that there is actually less innovation and more inequality.

Indeed, one of the important insights of Robert W. Fogel, a Nobel Prize–winning economic historian who died last month, was that a synergy between improved health and technology accounts for a good part of the explosive economic growth since the 19th century. So it stands to reason that intellectual property regimes that create monopoly rents that impede access to health both create inequality and hamper growth more generally.

There are alternatives. Advocates of intellectual property rights have overemphasized their role in promoting innovation. Most of the key innovations—from the basic ideas underlying the computer, to transistors, to lasers, to the discovery of DNA—were not motivated by pecuniary gain. They were motivated by the quest for knowledge. Of course, resources have to be made available. But the patent system is only one way, and often not the best way, of providing these resources. Government-financed research, foundations, and the prize system (which offers a prize to whoever makes a discovery, and then makes the knowledge widely available, using the power of the market to reap the benefits) are alternatives, with major advantages, and without the inequality-increasing disadvantages of the current intellectual property rights system.

Myriad's effort to patent human DNA was one of the worst manifestations of the inequality in access to health, which in turn is one of the worst manifestations of the country's economic inequality. That the court decision has upheld our cherished rights and values is a cause for a sigh of relief. But it is only one victory in the bigger struggle for a more egalitarian society and economy.

INDIA'S PATENTLY
WISE DECISION*

with Arjun Jayadev

THE INDIAN SUPREME COURT'S REFUSAL TO UPHOLD THE patent on Gleevec, the blockbuster cancer drug developed by the Swiss pharmaceutical giant Novartis, is good news for many of those in India suffering from cancer. If other developing countries follow India's example, it will be good news elsewhere, too: more money could be devoted to other needs, whether fighting AIDS, providing education, or making investments that enable growth and poverty reduction.

But the Indian decision also means less money for the big multinational pharmaceutical companies. Not surprisingly, this has led to an overwrought response from them and their lobbyists: the ruling, they allege, destroys the incentive to innovate, and thus will deal a serious blow to public health globally.

These claims are wildly overstated. In both economic and social-policy terms, the Indian court's decision makes good sense. Moreover, it is only a localized effort at rebalancing a global intellectual property (IP) regime that is tilted heavily toward pharmaceutical interests at the expense of social welfare. Indeed, there is a growing

---

* *Project Syndicate*, April 8, 2013.

consensus among economists that the current IP regime actually stifles innovation.

The impact of strong IP protection on social welfare has long been considered ambiguous. The promise of monopoly rights can spur innovation (though the most important discoveries, like that of DNA, typically occur within universities and government-sponsored research labs, and depend on other incentives). But there often are serious costs as well: higher prices for consumers, the dampening effect on further innovation of reducing access to knowledge, and, in the case of life-saving drugs, death for all who are unable to afford the innovation that could have saved them.

The weight given to each of these factors depends on circumstances and priorities, and should vary by country and time. Advanced industrialized countries in earlier stages of their development benefited from faster economic growth and greater social welfare by explicitly adopting weaker IP protection than is demanded of developing countries today. Even in the United States, there is growing concern that so-called hold-up patents and me-too patents—and the sheer *thicket* of patents, in which any innovation is likely to become entangled in someone else's IP claims—are diverting scarce research resources away from their most productive uses.

India represents only about 1–2 percent of the global pharmaceutical market. But it has long been a flashpoint in battles over expansion of pharmaceutical companies' global IP rights, owing to its dynamic generics industry and its willingness to challenge patent provisions both domestically and in foreign jurisdictions.

The revocation of patent protection for medicines in 1972 greatly expanded access to essential medicines, and led to the growth of a globally competitive domestic industry that is often called the "pharmacy of the developing world." For example, production of antiretroviral drugs by Indian generic manufacturers such as Cipla has reduced the cost of life-saving AIDS treatment in sub-Saharan Africa to just 1 percent of the cost a decade ago.

Much of this globally valuable capacity was built under a regime of weak—in fact, non-existent—protection for pharmaceutical patents. But India is now bound by the World Trade Organization's TRIPS agreement, and has revised its patent laws accordingly, causing widespread anxiety in the developing world about the implications for global provision of affordable medicines.

Indeed, the Gleevec decision is still only a small reversal for Western pharmaceuticals. Over the last two decades, lobbyists have worked to harmonize and strengthen a far stricter and globally enforceable IP regime. As a result, there are now numerous overlapping protections for pharmaceutical companies that are very difficult for most developing countries to contest, and that often pit their global obligations against their domestic obligations to protect their citizens' lives and health.

According to the Indian Supreme Court, the country's amended patent law still places greater weight on social objectives than in the U.S. and elsewhere: the standards of non-obviousness and novelty required to obtain a patent are stricter (especially as they pertain to medicines), and no "evergreening" of existing patents—or patent protection for incremental follow-up innovations—is allowed. The court thus reaffirmed India's primary commitment to protecting its citizens' lives and health.

The decision also highlighted an important fact: Despite its severe limitations, the TRIPS agreement does have some (rarely used) safeguards that give developing countries a certain degree of flexibility to limit patent protection. That is why the pharmaceutical industry, the U.S., and others have pushed since its inception for a wider and stronger set of standards through add-on agreements.

Such agreements would, for example, limit opposition to patent applications; prohibit national regulatory authorities from approving generic medicines until patents have expired; maintain data exclusivity, thereby delaying the approval of biogeneric drugs; and require new forms of protection, such as anticounterfeiting measures.

There is a curious incoherence in the argument that the Indian decision undermines property rights. A critical institutional foundation for well-functioning property rights is an independent judiciary to enforce them. India's Supreme Court has shown that it is independent, interprets the law faithfully, and does not easily succumb to global corporate interests. It is now up to the Indian government to use the TRIPS agreement's safeguards to ensure that the country's intellectual property regime advances both innovation and public health.

Globally, there is growing recognition of the need for a more balanced IP regime. But the pharmaceutical industry, trying to consolidate its gains, has been pushing instead for an ever stronger and more imbalanced IP regime. Countries considering agreements like the Trans-Pacific Partnership or bilateral "partnership" agreements with the U.S. and Europe need to be aware that this is one of the hidden objectives. What are being sold as "free-trade agreements" include IP provisions that could stifle access to affordable medicines, with a potentially significant impact on economic growth and development.

ELIMINATING EXTREME INEQUALITY: A SUSTAINABLE DEVELOPMENT GOAL, 2015–2030[*]

with Michael Doyle

A T THE UNITED NATIONS MILLENNIUM SUMMIT IN SEP-
tember 2000, UN member states took a dramatic step by putting people rather than states at the center of the UN's agenda. In
their Millennium Declaration,[1] the assembled world leaders agreed
to a set of breathtakingly broad goals touching on peace through
development, the environment, human rights, the protection of the
vulnerable, the special needs of Africa, and reforms of UN institutions. Particularly influential was the codification of the declaration's development related objectives, which emerged in the summer
of 2001 as the now familiar eight Millennium Development Goals
(MDGs), to be realized by 2015:[2]

1. Eradicate extreme poverty and hunger.[3]
    *   Halve the proportion of people living on less than a dollar a
        day and those who suffer from hunger.
2. Achieve universal primary education.

---

[*]   *Ethics and International Affairs*, March 20, 2014. The authors have
benefited from the research assistance of Alicia Evangelades, Eamon
Kircher-Allen, and Laurence Wilse-Samson.

- Ensure that all boys and girls complete primary school.
3. Promote gender equality and empower women.
   - Eliminate gender disparities in primary and secondary education preferably by 2005, and at all levels by 2015.
4. Reduce child mortality.
   - Reduce by two-thirds the mortality rate among children under five.
5. Improve maternal health.
   - Reduce by three-quarters the ratio of women dying in childbirth.
6. Combat HIV/AIDS, malaria, and other diseases.
   - Halt and begin to reverse the spread of HIV/AIDS and the incidence of malaria and other major diseases.
7. Ensure environmental sustainability.
   - Integrate the principles of sustainable development into country policies and programs and reverse the loss of environmental resources.
   - By 2015, reduce by half the proportion of people without access to safe drinking water.
   - By 2020, achieve significant improvement in the lives of at least 100 million slum dwellers.
8. Develop a global partnership for development.
   - Develop further an open trading and financial system that includes a commitment to good governance, development, and poverty reduction—nationally and internationally.
   - Address the special needs of the least developed countries, and the special needs of landlocked and small island developing states.
   - Deal comprehensively with the debt problems of developing countries.
   - Develop decent and productive work for youth.
   - In cooperation with pharmaceutical companies, provide access to affordable essential drugs in developing countries.

- In cooperation with the private sector, make available the benefits of new technologies—especially information and communications technologies.

As UN Secretary-General Kofi Annan later described them, the MDGs were a remarkable effort in international coordination. They established common ground among competitive development agencies, inspired concerted action by international organizations and national governments, and offered an opportunity for citizens to insist that governments focus on the "we the peoples" they claimed to represent. In short, they transformed the agenda of world leaders.[4]

Fourteen years later, the MDG record has been mixed. Some goals, such as halving the proportion of people living in extreme poverty, have been met at the global level, but none have been fulfilled in all countries. Others, such as universal access to primary education, are unlikely to be achieved by 2015.[5]

However, while the accomplishment of these goals would have been an impressive achievement, even taken together they do not represent a complete or comprehensive vision of human development. They were constrained by what the member states could agree upon in 2000 and, in particular, they lacked a vision of *equitable* development.[6] As the international community thinks about the set of goals that will follow the MDGs, it is time to address that shortcoming by adding the goal of "eliminating extreme inequality" to the original eight.

WHY INEQUALITY MATTERS

Every country has a distinct political economy that shapes the extent and effects of inequalities; each requires separate assessment. The marked differences in the extent and nature of inequality across countries demonstrate that inequality is not just determined by economic forces; it is shaped by politics and policies.

Full equality is not the goal. Some economic inequalities may be conducive to economic growth. Other inequalities may not be worth addressing because doing so infringes on cherished liberties. While the precise point at which inequalities turn harmful may differ from country to country, once inequality becomes extreme, harmful social, economic, and political effects become evident. Extreme inequalities tend to hamper economic growth and undermine both political equality and social stability. And because inequalities have cumulative economic, social, and political effects, each of these contributing factors requires separate and concerted attention. We turn first to the economic arguments for reducing extreme inequalities, and then to the political and social arguments.

Economic Arguments[7]

Economists of widely differing philosophical outlooks agree that inequalities of incomes and assets have harmful economic effects. Increasing inequalities, with top-heavy income distributions, lessen aggregate demand (the rich tend to spend a smaller fraction of their income than the poor), which can slow economic growth. The attempt of monetary authorities to offset these effects can contribute to credit bubbles, and these bubbles in turn lead to economic instability. That is why inequality is often associated with economic instability. In this perspective, it is not a surprise that inequality reached high levels before the Great Recession of 2008 and before the Great Depression of the 1930s.[8] Recent International Monetary Fund research shows that high inequality is associated with shorter growth cycles.[9]

Much of the inequality observed around the world is associated with rent seeking (for example, the exercise of monopoly power), and such inequality manifestly undermines economic efficiency. But perhaps the worse dimension of inequality is inequality of opportunity, which is both the cause and the consequence of inequality of outcomes, and causes economic inefficiency and reduced development, as large numbers of individuals are not able to live up to their potential.[10] Countries with high inequality tend to invest less in public goods, such as infrastructure, technology, and education, which contribute to long-term economic prosperity and growth.

Reducing inequality, on the other hand, has clear economic as well as social benefits. It strengthens people's sense that society is fair; improves social cohesion and mobility, making it more likely that more citizens live up to their potential; and broadens support for growth initiatives. Policies that aim for growth but ignore inequality may ultimately be self-defeating, whereas policies that decrease inequality by, for example, boosting employment and education have beneficial effects on the human capital that modern economies increasingly need.[11]

Political and Social Arguments

Gaps between the rich and the poor are partly the result of economic forces, but equally, or even more, they are the result of public policy choices, such as taxation, the level of the minimum wage, and the amount invested in health care and education. This is why countries whose economic circumstances are otherwise similar can have markedly different levels of inequality. These inequalities in turn affect policy making because even democratically elected officials respond more attentively to the views of affluent constituents than they do to the views of poor people.[12] The more that wealth is allowed unrestricted roles in funding elections, the more likely it is that economic inequality will get translated into political inequality.

As noted, extreme inequalities undermine not only economic stability but also social and political stability. But there is no simple causal relation between economic inequality and social stability, as measured by crime or civil violence. Neither form of violence correlates with Gini indices or Palma ratios (the top 10 percent of the population's share of gross national income [GNI] divided by the poorest 40 percent of the population's share of GNI).[13] There are, however, substantial links between violence and "horizontal inequalities" that combine economic stratification with race, ethnicity, religion, or region. When the poor are from one race, ethnicity, religion, or region, and the rich are from another, a lethal, destabilizing dynamic often emerges.

Drawing on 123 national surveys in 61 developing countries, one study carefully documents the effects of inequalities in assets among ethnicities. For a typical country with average values on all the variables accounting for violence, the probability of civil conflict in a given year is 2.3 percent. If the level of horizontal asset inequality among ethnic groups is increased to the 95th percentile (and the other variables remain at their average values), the probability of conflict increases to 6.1 percent—more than a twofold increase. A similar comparison focused on differences in income among religious groups shows an increase from 2.9 percent to 7.2 percent—again, more than twofold.[14] Another study using similar methods finds regional disparities in wealth to be correlated with an especially high risk of conflict onset in sub-Saharan Africa.[15]

Using a different methodology that focuses on geographical disparities in income that are linked with ethnic differentiation, rather than surveys to measure inequalities, other authors confirm the dangers of large horizontal inequalities. Focusing on the post–Cold War period (1991–2005), Lars-Erik Cederman, Nils Weidmann, and Kristian Gleditsch divide the total sum of economic production in a given ethnic settlement area by the group's population size to get ethnic group–specific measures of per capita economic production. They find that both relatively poorer and relatively richer ethnic groups have higher likelihoods of experiencing civil war. Demonstrating that not just ethnographic factors are at work, they show that the richer (or the poorer) the ethnographic group is, the greater the likelihood of the extreme groups experiencing civil war with other ethnographic groups.[16]

THE MANY DIMENSIONS
OF INEQUALITY

Just as discussions of poverty and poverty reduction expanded from a single-minded focus on *income* to many other dimensions of deprivation—including health and the environment—so too did they evolve in the case of inequality.[17] Indeed, in most countries it appears that inequalities in wealth exceed those in income. Especially in countries without adequate public health systems, a Palma ratio reflecting health status would almost surely show even greater inequalities than a Palma ratio for income. A Palma ratio based on exposures to environmental hazards would likely demonstrate a similar trend.

One of the most pernicious forms of inequality relates to inequality of opportunity, reflected in a lack of socioeconomic mobility, condemning those born into the bottom of the economic pyramid to almost surely remain there. Alan Krueger, former chairman of the U.S. Council of Economic Advisers, has pointed to this link between inequality and opportunity.[18] Inequality of income tends to be associated with less economic mobility and fewer opportunities across generations. The fact that those born into the bottom of the economic pyramid are condemned to never reach their potential reinforces the correlation between inequality and slower long-term economic growth.[19]

That these dimensions of inequality are related suggests that focusing on one dimension at a time may underestimate the true magnitude of societal inequalities and provide an inadequate basis for policy. For example, health inequality is both a cause and consequence of income inequality. Inequalities in education are a primary determinant of inequalities in income and opportunity. In turn, as we have emphasized, when there are distinct social patterns of these multiple inequalities (for example, those associated with race or ethnicity), the consequences for society (including social instability) are increased.

Measuring the Goal

We propose that the following goal—call it "Goal Nine"—be added to revisions and updates of the original eight: *Eliminate extreme inequality at the national level in every country*. For this goal, we propose the following targets:

- By 2030, reduce extreme income inequalities in all countries such that the post-tax income of the top 10 percent is no more than the post-transfer income of the bottom 40 percent.
- By 2020, establish a public commission in every country that will assess and report on the effects of national inequalities.

There is a growing consensus that the best indicator for these targets is the Palma ratio, which effectively focuses on extremes of inequality—the ratio of incomes at the very top to those at the bottom.[20] In many countries around the world it is changes in these extremes that are most noticeable and most invidious, while the share of income in the middle is relatively stable.[21] All countries should focus on their "extreme" inequalities, that is, the inequalities that do most harm to equitable and sustainable economic growth and that undermine social and political stability. A Palma ratio of 1 is an ideal reached in only a few countries. For example, countries in Scandinavia, with Palma ratios at 1 or less,[22] do not seem to suffer from the liabilities associated with extreme inequalities. Indeed, in some accounts they seem to benefit from a positive "equality multiplier" across the various aspects of their socioeconomic development, making them efficient and flexible as well as equitable and stable.[23]

But countries differ not just in how unequal they are now but also in their culture, tolerance of inequality of various kinds, and capacity for social change. Hence, the more important target is the second one: a national dialogue by 2020 on what should be done to address the inequalities of most relevance to the particular country. Such a dialogue would draw attention to the policies in each country that exacerbate inequality (for example, deficiencies in the education system, the legal system, or the tax and transfer system); those that simultaneously distort the economy and contribute to economic, political, and social instability; and those that might most easily be altered.[24]

Support for reducing extreme inequalities is widespread.[25] In a letter to Dr. Homi Kharas, lead author and executive secretary of the secretariat supporting the High-Level Panel of Eminent Persons on the Post-2015 Development Agenda, 90 economists, academics, and development experts urged that reduction in inequality in the post-2015 development framework be made a priority, and suggested that inequality be measured using the Palma ratio.[26] They argue—consistent with our analysis—that inequality threatens poverty eradication, sustainable development, democratic processes, and social cohesion.[27]

Awareness of the adverse effects of inequality has moved beyond academics and social activists. A July 2013 speech by U.S. President Barack Obama outlined the role of inequality in creating credit bubbles (like the one that precipitated the Great Recession) and the way it deprives people of opportunity, which in turn fosters an inefficient economy in which the talents of many cannot be mobilized for the good of all.[28] And Pope Francis, in his address in the Varginha slum of Rio de Janeiro on World Youth Day 2013, emphasized the need for greater solidarity, greater social justice, and special attention to the circumstances of youth. And, again consistent with the studies cited earlier, he declared that peace cannot be maintained in unequal societies with marginalized communities.[29]

There are many dimensions to inequality—some with more

invidious effects than others—and many ways to measure these inequalities. One thing is certain, however: sustainable development cannot be achieved while ignoring extreme disparities. It is imperative that the post-MDG agenda have as one of its central points a focus on inequality.

Notes

1. *General Assembly Resolution 55/2,* "United Nations Millennium Declaration," UN document A/RES/55/2, September 8, 2000, www.un.org/millennium/declaration/ares552e.pdf.

2. As announced in the appendix to the "Roadmap Report," UN document A/56/326 of September 6, 2001. The UN member states tasked the UN secretary-general with preparing a "roadmap" that would develop and monitor "results and benchmarks" ("Follow-up to the Outcome of the Millennium Summit," UN document A/RES/55/162, December 18 2000). For an analysis of the origins and significance of the MDGs, see Michael Doyle, "Dialectics of a Global Constitution: The Struggle over the UN Charter," *European Journal of International Relations* 18, no. 4 (2012), pp. 601–24.

3. The original indicator was $1 a day, which has since been raised to $1.25 to reflect inflation.

4. Kofi Annan, with Nader Mousavizadeh, *Interventions: A Life in War and Peace* (New York: Penguin, 2012), pp. 244–50.

5. United Nations, *The Millennium Development Goals Report 2013,* pp. 4–5. For more information on the status of the Millennium Development Goals, see the full 2013 report: www.un.org/millenniumgoals/pdf/report-2013/mdg-report-2013-english.pdf.

6. The original goals did not include access to reproductive rights, which was corrected in 2005. See *General Assembly Resolution 60/1,* "2005 World Summit Outcome," UN document A/RES/60/1, paragraphs 57(g) and 58(c): mdgs.un.org/unsd/mdg/Resources/Attach/Indicators/ares60_1_2005summit_eng.pdf. These goals also lacked the governance goals being considered today. See the Report of the High-Level Panel of Eminent Persons on the Post-2015 Development Agenda, *A New Global Partnership: Eradicate Poverty and Transform Economies through Sustainable Development,* Annex II, p. 50: www.un.org/sg/management/pdf/HLP_P2015_Report.pdf.

7. For a more thorough discussion of the adverse economic consequences of inequality, see Joseph Stiglitz, *The Price of Inequality* (New York: W. W. Norton, 2012), pp. 83–117, and the references cited there

8. Ibid.

9. A. Berg, J. Ostry, and J. Zettelmeyer, "What Makes Growth Sustained?" *Journal of Development Economics* 98, no. 2 (2012). For a more theoretical treatment of the links between inequality, instability, and human development, see Stiglitz, "Macroeconomic Fluctuations, Inequality, and Human Development," *Journal of Human Development and Capabilities* 13, no. 1 (2012), pp. 31–58. Reprinted in Deepak Nayyar, ed., *Macroeconomics and Human Development* (London: Routledge, Taylor & Francis Group, 2013).

10. William Easterly, "Inequality Does Cause Underdevelopment: Insights from a New Instrument," *Journal of Development Economics* 84, no. 2 (2007). The Council on Foreign Relations reported this year that there are enormous gaps in American students' achievement depending on their socioeconomic background, and found that parental wealth exerts a stronger influence on achievement in the United States than in almost any other developed country. See Council on Foreign Relations, *Remedial Education: Federal Education Policy*, June 2013, www.cfr.org/united-states/remedial-education-federal-education-policy/p30141.

11. Easterly, "Inequality Does Cause Underdevelopment."

12. Larry Bartels, *Unequal Democracy* (Princeton, N.J.: Princeton University Press, 2008).

13. We would prefer a measure of post-tax (after all income and other taxes) and post-transfer incomes (after housing, child care, social security, and other subsidies), but this is not yet widely available. Unofficial Palma ratios by country available upon request. To request this unofficial data, please contact Alicia Evangelides at ame2148@columbia.edu.

14. Gudrun Østby, "Inequalities, the Political Environment and Civil Conflict: Evidence from 55 Developing Countries," in Frances Stewart, ed., *Horizontal Inequalities and Conflict: Understanding Group Violence in Multiethnic Societies* (Basingstoke: Palgrave Macmillan, 2008), pp. 136–57, p. 149.

15. Gudrun Østby and Håvard Strand, "Horizontal Inequalities and Internal Conflict: The Impact of Regime Type and Political Leadership Regulation," in K. Kalu, U. O. Uzodike, D. Kraybill, and J. Moolakkattu, eds., *Territoriality, Citizenship, and Peacebuilding: Perspectives on Challenges to Peace in Africa* (Pietermaritzburg, South Africa: Adonis & Abbey, 2013).

16. Lars-Erik Cederman, Nils B. Weidmann, and Kristian Skrede Gleditsch, "Horizontal Inequalities and Ethnonationalist Civil War: A Global Comparison," *American Political Science Review* 105, no. 3 (2011), pp. 487–89.

17. The World Bank's classic study *Voices of the Poor* highlighted that the poor suffered not just from a lack of income but from insecurity and a lack of voice. This was subsequently reflected in the decennial World Bank's *World Development Report on Poverty* in 2000. The International Commission on the Measurement of Economic Performance and Social Well-Being (2010) emphasized that metrics of performance (including output and inequality) had to be expanded

beyond just conventional measures of GDP and/or income. The OECD has carried on this work in their *Better Living Initiative*, including the construction of the Better Life Index. An important part of the agenda of the OECD High Level Expert Group on the Measurement of Economic Performance and Social Well-Being is the construction/evaluation of alternative measures of inequality.

18. Alan B. Krueger, "Land of Hope and Dreams: Rock and Roll, Economics, and Rebuilding the Middle Class" (remarks, Rock and Roll Hall of Fame and Museum, Cleveland, Ohio, June 12, 2013), www.whitehouse.gov/blog/2013/06/12/rock-and-roll-economics-and-rebuilding-middle-class#fulltext.

19. Miles Corak, "Income Inequality, Equality of Opportunity, and Intergenerational Mobility," *Journal of Economic Perspectives* 27, no. 3 (2013), pp. 79–102.

20. Alex Cobham and Andy Sumner, "Putting the Gini Back in the Bottle? 'The Palma' as a Policy-Relevant Measure of Inequality," King's College London, March 15, 2013, www.kcl.ac.uk/aboutkings/worldwide/initiatives/global/intdev/people/Sumner/Cobham-Sumner-15March2013.pdf.

21. This is not true, however, for all countries. In the United States, for instance, there has been a hollowing out of the middle class, with a declining fraction of the population between, say, twice and half median income and a declining fraction of income going to this group. It has long been thought that a stable democracy depends on a thriving middle class. If so, the decline of the middle class should be of special concern. (For a fuller discussion of these issues, see Stiglitz, *The Price of Inequality*.) Part of the national dialogues on inequality that we recommend below would focus on the nature of the inequality that is emerging in various countries.

22. José Gabriel Palma, "Homogenous Middles vs. Heterogeneous Tails, and the End of the 'Inverted-U': The Share of the Rich Is What It's All About," Cambridge Working Papers in Economics (CWPE) 1111, January 2011, www.econ.cam.ac.uk/dae/repec/cam/pdf/cwpe1111.pdf.

23. Karl Ove Moene, "Scandinavian Equality: A Prime Example of Protection without Protectionism," in Joseph E. Stiglitz and Mary Kaldor, eds., *The Quest for Security: Protection without Protectionism and the Challenge of Global Governance* (New York: Columbia University Press, 2013), pp. 48–74.

24. For instance, in the United States, such a dialogue would note inequalities in access to education and health; a bankruptcy code that gives first priority to derivatives and makes student loans difficult to discharge, even in bankruptcy; a tax system that taxes income of the rich derived from speculation at much lower rates than wage income; a minimum wage that, adjusted for inflation, has not increased in half a century; and a system of social protection that does a much poorer job in "correcting" inequalities in income than systems in other advanced industrial countries. It would analyze the extent to which disparities in income are a result of differences in productivities, with differences in productivity in

turn partly explained by disparities in access to quality education; the extent to which disparities in income are related to rent seeking; and the extent to which such disparities can be accounted for by inheritances.

25. Alex Cobham and Andy Sumner, "Is It All About the Tails? The Palma Measure of Income Inequality," Center for Global Development, Working Paper 343, September 2013, www.cgdev.org/sites/default/files/it-all-about-tails-palma-measure-income-inequality.pdf.

26. See the letter to Dr. Homi Kharas of the Brookings Institution from 90 economists, academics, and development experts supporting the use of the Palma ratio as a measure of inequality at www.post2015hlp.org/wp-content/uploads/2013/03/Dr-Homi-Kharas.pdf.

27. Ibid.

28. Michael Shear and Peter Baker, "Obama Focuses on Economy, Vowing to Help Middle Class," *New York Times*, July 24, 2013, www.nytimes.com/2013/07/25/us/politics/obama-to-restate-economic-vision-at-knox-college.html?_r=0.

29. Pope Francis, "WYD 2013: Full text of Pope Francis's address in Rio slum," *Catholic Herald*, July 25, 2013, www.catholicherald.co.uk/news/2013/07/25/wyd-2013-full- text-of-pope-franciss-address-in-rio-slum/.

THE POSTCRISIS CRISES[*]

IN THE SHADOW OF THE EURO CRISIS AND **A**MERICA'S FISCAL cliff, it is easy to ignore the global economy's long-term problems. But, while we focus on immediate concerns, they continue to fester, and we overlook them at our peril.

The most serious is global warming. While the global economy's weak performance has led to a corresponding slowdown in the *increase* in carbon emissions, it amounts to only a short respite. And we are far behind the curve: Because we have been so slow to respond to climate change, achieving the targeted limit of a two-degree (centigrade) rise in global temperature will require sharp reductions in emissions in the future.

Some suggest that, given the economic slowdown, we should put global warming on the backburner. On the contrary, retrofitting the global economy for climate change would help to restore aggregate demand and growth.

At the same time, the pace of technological progress and globalization necessitates rapid structural changes in both developed and developing countries alike. Such changes can be traumatic, and markets often do not handle them well.

---

[*] *Project Syndicate*, January 7, 2013.

Just as the Great Depression arose in part from the difficulties in moving from a rural, agrarian economy to an urban, manufacturing one, so today's problems arise partly from the need to move from manufacturing to services. New firms must be created, and modern financial markets are better at speculation and exploitation than they are at providing funds for new enterprises, especially small and medium-size companies.

Moreover, making the transition requires investments in human capital that individuals often cannot afford. Among the services that people want are health care and education, two sectors in which government naturally plays an important role (owing to inherent market imperfections in these sectors and concerns about equity).

Before the 2008 crisis, there was much talk of global imbalances, and the need for the trade-surplus countries, like Germany and China, to increase their consumption. That issue has not gone away; indeed, Germany's failure to address its chronic external surplus is part and parcel of the euro crisis. China's surplus, as a percentage of GDP, has fallen, but the long-term implications have yet to play out.

America's overall trade deficit will not disappear without an increase in domestic savings and a more fundamental change in global monetary arrangements. The former would exacerbate the country's slowdown, and neither change is in the cards. As China increases its consumption, it will not necessarily buy more goods from the United States. In fact, it is more likely to increase consumption of nontraded goods—like health care and education—resulting in profound disturbances to the global supply chain, especially in countries that had been supplying the inputs to China's manufacturing exporters.

Finally, there is a worldwide crisis in inequality. The problem is not only that the top income groups are getting a larger share of the economic pie, but also that those in the middle are not sharing in economic growth, while in many countries poverty is increasing. In the U.S., equality of opportunity has been exposed as a myth.

While the Great Recession has exacerbated these trends, they were apparent long before its onset. Indeed, I (and others) have argued that growing inequality is one of the reasons for the economic slowdown, and is partly a consequence of the global economy's deep, ongoing structural changes.

An economic and political system that does not deliver for most citizens is one that is not sustainable in the long run. Eventually, faith in democracy and the market economy will erode, and the legitimacy of existing institutions and arrangements will be called into question.

The good news is that the gap between the emerging and advanced countries has narrowed greatly in the last three decades. Nonetheless, hundreds of millions of people remain in poverty, and there has been only a little progress in reducing the gap between the least developed countries and the rest.

Here, unfair trade agreements—including the persistence of unjustifiable agricultural subsidies, which depress the prices upon which the income of many of the poorest depend—have played a role. The developed countries have not lived up to their promise in Doha in November 2001 to create a pro-development trade regime, or to their pledge at the G-8 summit in Gleneagles in 2005 to provide significantly more assistance to the poorest countries.

The market will not, on its own, solve any of these problems. Global warming is a quintessential "public goods" problem. To make the structural transitions that the world needs, we need governments to take a more active role—at a time when demands for cutbacks are increasing in Europe and the U.S.

As we struggle with today's crises, we should be asking whether we are responding in ways that exacerbate our long-term problems. The path marked out by the deficit hawks and austerity advocates both weakens the economy today and undermines future prospects. The irony is that, with insufficient aggregate demand the major source of global weakness today, there is an alternative: invest in our future, in ways that help us to address simultaneously the problems of global warming, global inequality and poverty, and the necessity of structural change.

INEQUALITY IS NOT
INEVITABLE*

AN INSIDIOUS TREND HAS DEVELOPED OVER THIS PAST third of a century. A country that experienced shared growth after World War II began to tear apart, so much so that when the Great Recession hit in late 2007, one could no longer ignore the fissures that had come to define the American economic landscape. How did this "shining city on a hill" become the advanced country with the greatest level of inequality?

One stream of the extraordinary discussion set in motion by Thomas Piketty's timely, important book, *Capital in the Twenty-First Century*, has settled on the idea that violent extremes of wealth and income are inherent in capitalism. In this scheme, we should view the decades after World War II—a period of rapidly falling inequality—as an aberration.

This is actually a superficial reading of Mr. Piketty's work, which provides an institutional context for understanding the deepening of inequality over time. Unfortunately, that part of his analysis received somewhat less attention than the more fatalistic-seeming aspects.

Over the past year and a half, The Great Divide, a series in the *New York Times* for which I have served as moderator, has also pre-

---

* *New York Times*, June 27, 2014.

sented a wide range of examples that undermine the notion that there are any truly fundamental laws of capitalism. The dynamics of the imperial capitalism of the 19th century needn't apply in the democracies of the 21st. We don't need to have this much inequality in America.

Our current brand of capitalism is an ersatz capitalism. For proof of this go back to our response to the Great Recession, where we socialized losses, even as we privatized gains. Perfect competition should drive profits to zero, at least theoretically, but we have monopolies and oligopolies making persistently high profits. CEOs enjoy incomes that are on average 295 times that of the typical worker, a much higher ratio than in the past, without any evidence of a proportionate increase in productivity.

If it is not the inexorable laws of economics that have led to America's great divide, what is it? The straightforward answer: our policies and our politics. People get tired of hearing about Scandinavian success stories, but the fact of the matter is that Sweden, Finland, and Norway have all succeeded in having about as much growth in per capita incomes as, or even faster growth than, the United States and with far greater equality.

So why has America chosen these inequality-enhancing policies? Part of the answer is that as World War II faded into memory, so too did the solidarity it had engendered. As America triumphed in the Cold War, there didn't seem to be a viable competitor to our economic model. Without this international competition, we no longer had to show that our system could deliver for most of our citizens.

Ideology and interests combined nefariously. Some drew the wrong lesson from the collapse of the Soviet system. The pendulum swung from much too much government there to much too little here. Corporate interests argued for getting rid of regulations, even when those regulations had done so much to protect and improve our environment, our safety, our health, and the economy itself.

But this ideology was hypocritical. The bankers, among the strongest advocates of laissez-faire economics, were only too willing to accept hundreds of billions of dollars from the government in the bailouts that have been a recurring feature of the global economy since the beginning of the Thatcher-Reagan era of "free" markets and deregulation.

The American political system is overrun by money. Economic inequality translates into political inequality, and political inequality yields increasing economic inequality. In fact, as he recognizes, Mr. Piketty's argument rests on the ability of wealth-holders to keep their after-tax rate of return high relative to economic growth. How do they do this? By designing the rules of the game to ensure this outcome; that is, through politics.

So corporate welfare increases as we curtail welfare for the poor. Congress maintains subsidies for rich farmers as we cut back on nutritional support for the needy. Drug companies have been given hundreds of billions of dollars as we limit Medicaid benefits. The banks that brought on the global financial crisis got billions while a pittance went to the homeowners and victims of the same banks' predatory lending practices. This last decision was particularly foolish. There were alternatives to throwing money at the banks and hoping it would circulate through increased lending. We could have helped underwater homeowners and the victims of predatory behavior directly. This would not only have helped the economy, it would have put us on the path to robust recovery.

OUR DIVISIONS ARE DEEP. Economic and geographic segregation have immunized those at the top from the problems of those down below. Like the kings of yore, they have come to perceive their privileged positions essentially as a natural right. How else to explain the recent comments of the venture capitalist Tom Perkins, who suggested that criticism of the 1 percent was akin to Nazi fascism, or those coming from the private equity titan Stephen A. Schwarzman, who compared asking financiers to pay taxes at the same rate as those who work for a living to Hitler's invasion of Poland.

Our economy, our democracy, and our society have paid for these gross inequities. The true test of an economy is not how much wealth its princes can accumulate in tax havens, but how well off the typical citizen is—even more so in America, where our self-image is rooted in our claim to be the great middle-class society. But median incomes are lower than they were a quarter-century ago. Growth has gone to the very, very top, whose share has almost quadrupled since 1980. Money that was meant to have trickled down has instead evaporated in the balmy climate of the Cayman Islands.

With almost a quarter of American children younger than five living in poverty, and with America doing so little for its poor, the deprivations of one generation are being visited upon the next. Of course, no country has ever come close to providing complete equality of opportunity. But why is America one of the advanced countries where the life prospects of the young are most sharply determined by the income and education of their parents?

Among the most poignant stories in The Great Divide were those that portrayed the frustrations of the young, who yearn to enter our shrinking middle class. Soaring tuitions and declining incomes have resulted in larger debt burdens. Those with only a high school diploma have seen their incomes decline by 13 percent over the past 35 years.

Where justice is concerned, there is also a yawning divide. In the eyes of the rest of the world and a significant part of its own population, mass incarceration has come to define America—a country, it bears repeating, with about 5 percent of the world's population but around a fourth of the world's prisoners.

Justice has become a commodity, affordable to only a few. While Wall Street executives used their high-retainer lawyers to ensure that their ranks were not held accountable for the misdeeds that the crisis in 2008 so graphically revealed, the banks abused our legal system to foreclose on mortgages and evict people, some of whom did not even owe money.

More than a half-century ago, America led the way in advocating for the Universal Declaration of Human Rights, adopted by the United Nations in 1948. Today, access to health care is among the most universally accepted rights, at least in the advanced countries. America, despite the implementation of the Affordable Care Act, is the exception. It has become a country with great divides in access to health care, life expectancy, and health status.

In the relief that many felt when the Supreme Court did not overturn the Affordable Care Act, the implications of the decision for Medicaid were not fully appreciated. Obamacare's objective—to ensure that all Americans have access to health care—has been stymied: 24 states have not implemented the expanded Medicaid program, which was the means by which Obamacare was supposed to deliver on its promise to some of the poorest.

We need not just a new war on poverty but a war to protect the middle class. Solutions to these problems do not have to be new-fangled. Far from it. Making markets act like markets would be a good place to start. We must end the rent-seeking society we have gravitated toward, in which the wealthy obtain profits by manipulating the system.

The problem of inequality is not so much a matter of technical economics. It's really a problem of practical politics. Ensuring that those at the top pay their fair share of taxes—ending the special privileges of speculators, corporations, and the rich—is both pragmatic and fair. We are not embracing a politics of envy if we reverse a politics of greed. Inequality is not just about the top marginal tax rate but also about our children's access to food and the right to justice for all. If we spent more on education, health, and infrastructure, we would strengthen our economy, now and in the future. Just because you've heard it before doesn't mean we shouldn't try it again.

We have located the underlying source of the problem: political inequities and policies that have commodified and corrupted our democracy. It is only engaged citizens who can fight to restore a fairer America, and they can do so only if they understand the depths and dimensions of the challenge. It is not too late to restore our position in the world and recapture our sense of who we are as a nation. Widening and deepening inequality is not driven by immutable economic laws, but by laws we have written ourselves.

PART VII

REGIONAL
PERSPECTIVES

I NEQUALITY HAS BECOME AN INTERNATIONAL ISSUE. There is a general pattern here: those countries that have followed the U.S. economic model, including the heavy financialization of the economy, have wound up with similar results. Thus the UK, which has followed the U.S. model most closely (and in some cases was its inspiration: there were many similarities between the policies and ideologies of Prime Minister Thatcher and those of President Reagan), has, not surprisingly, the highest level of inequality among the advanced countries, next to that of the United States. Countries pay a high price for this inequality; at stake is not just inequality of incomes but also inequality of opportunity.

Over the past quarter century, I have had the good fortune to be able to travel around the world, talking to governments, students, fellow economists, labor groups, civic societies, and business people. I have been particularly interested in how economics and politics interact differently in different countries: how some countries have been able to achieve more equal societies and societies with greater equality of opportunity.

The articles presented in this section sample these different developments around the world. I begin with "The Mauritius Miracle." One can never predict when an article will hit a resonant chord, but this one did. Tiny Mauritius, in the Indian Ocean east of Africa, has long been viewed as one of the real success cases of development. Its economy has grown rapidly. One of the reasons for my visit was to understand better why. The not-surprising answer, told to me by the president, who had been prime minister in the early days of the country's rapid growth, was that they had been greatly influenced by the model of East Asia's development, where the state played a central role in promoting development (giving rise to the term "developmental state").[1]

But what especially intrigued me about Mauritius was how this relatively poor country managed to provide free health care and free college education for all of its citizens—when the United States seemingly says it can't afford them. It even provides free transportation to its youth and elderly—the former because they are the country's future, the latter because of what they have done for society. The point I made was a simple one: we *could* afford to provide these services to all Americans. The investments in our young people would make our country stronger. Most countries view access to basic health care as a basic human right. The fact that we don't is a matter of *choice*, a reflection of priorities—priorities set by a political process where disproportionate weight is given to the interests and views of the top.

Nothing made this so clear as the events surrounding the recent financial crisis. Shortly before then, President Bush had vetoed a bill providing health insurance for poor children, *saying that we couldn't afford it*. Somehow, though, we suddenly found $700 billion to bail out banks—and more than $150 billion to rescue one wayward company. We had money to provide a safety net for the rich, but not for the poor. The argument was that, in doing so, the economy would be saved and everyone would benefit. This was, of course, nothing more than a naked version of trickle-down economics. It didn't work that way—those at the top did very well, while the typical American is worse off than he was a quarter-century ago.

The experience of Mauritius shows that, on the contrary, investing in people does pay off.

East Asia, as I noted earlier, is the region of the world that has been most successful in development—with per capita incomes increasing by as much as eightfold in 30 years. Indeed, previously no one, not even the most optimistic economist, had thought such rapid growth was possible. No wonder, then, that what happened in these countries has been a subject of intense study. What is clear is that these countries did not follow the market fundamentalist model; markets played a critical role in their success, but it was managed markets, managed for the benefits of society as a whole, not for that of a few shareholders or managers; it was a market economy in which the government played the role of an orchestra conductor. It catalyzed growth, investing heavily in technology, education, and infrastructure.

A central feature of most of these countries was a shared prosperity—inequality, as conventionally measured, was low; there was heavy investment in female education. They created the middle-class society that America had thought of itself as being—back in the years after World War II.

Among the most successful *economically* of the East Asian countries was Singapore, a small island state with today some five and a half million people. When it was thrown out of what was then called Malaya in 1969, it was a desperately poor country, with an unemployment rate of 25 percent. Its leader, Prime Minister Lee Kuan Yew, famously cried on television as he thought about the country's bleak prospects. But the developmental state worked for Singapore, so much so that per capita income today is more than $55,000, ninth among the highest-income countries of the world. And (putting aside those wealthy people who have moved to Singapore because it is viewed by many as a safe haven in a turbulent part of the world) it has relatively low inequality.

There were strong reactions to the article on Singapore, as to the one about Mauritius. Many Americans evidently don't like to see their country placed in a bad light. The idea that *in some dimensions* others were doing better (particularly given their limited resources) than the United States was anathema. In the case of Singapore there was another problem. Deficiencies in its democracy have long been pointed out, and I carefully made note of them in my article. Increasingly, though, those in other countries have commented on the deficiencies in our democracy, which have given such scope to the power of money.

The next two articles deal with Japan. Its economic miracle was ending just at the time I was doing my study of East Asia's miracle at the end of the 80s and beginning of 90s.[2] It has now gone through more than a quarter-century of near stagnation—often referred to as the Japanese malaise. But somehow, even as it passed through those difficult times, it managed to keep unemployment low (typically, around 5 percent, half of the peak hit by the United States in its downturn). Its inequality was lower and its safety net much better than that of the United States (including its provision of health care), so that one has the sense that there was much less suffering. Still, "Japan Should Be Alert" points to the dangers of increasing inequality.[3] Large changes in Japan's economy have occurred over the past quarter-century, and Japan has been under pressure to make some of the "market reforms" that contributed to the growth of inequality elsewhere. There are signs of a troubling increase in inequality—and matters could get worse.

Nonetheless, on balance, I believe "Japan is a model—not a cautionary tale." The image of Japan's lackluster growth is distorted by the decline of its labor force (working-age population). If one takes that into account, in the past decade or so Japan has been toward the top of the league tables—hard as that is for many to believe, given the criticisms that have been leveled at Japan. Even more, as I mentioned earlier, it has so far been able to manage more inclusive growth than America has.

This article was written not long after Shinzo Abe became prime minister. I went to Tokyo twice in the early months of his administration, to discuss with him and his advisers the policies that have come to be called Abenomics. I was impressed with their recognition that one couldn't rely on monetary policy; one also needed to stimulate the economy with fiscal policy (expenditures and/or tax cuts) and with pro-growth structural policies. These were the three arrows of Abenomics. Monetary policy (under my good friend Haruhiko Kuroda) was remarkably successful. Fiscal policy unfortunately wavered. Initial expansionary policies were followed by a tax increase; and the tax increase had the predicted effect: growth was thrown off track. Other policies might have worked far better—a carbon tax would have raised money and stimulated firms to make energy-saving investments, thus actually helping the macroeconomy. But the politics seemingly did not allow this.

The structural policies were far slower to get off the ground. Some of them were perhaps more symbolic than real (though they might have real effects on particular industries). For instance, Prime Minister Abe proposed joining discussions over the creation of the Trans-Pacific Partnership, a trade agreement that the United States was pushing among several countries around the Pacific Rim. One of the reasons for doing so was allegedly his hope that it would help facilitate the restructuring of Japan's highly subsidized agricultural sector. The irony, of course, was that the United States itself highly subsidizes its agricultural sector—indeed, how else could one grow rice in the middle of what otherwise would be a desert? But even if he succeeded in restructuring agriculture, the sector is so small that it would have only a small effect on the economy.

Interestingly, one of the most promising structural reforms is one that would simultaneously promote equity. We noted above the country's declining workforce, caused by a decrease in population combined with a resistance to immigration. Abe proposed tapping into an important part of the country's labor force that has been long underutilized—its highly educated women.

The next two chapters deal with China. I have been actively involved in China's development since early on in its transition from Communism to a market economy. My first extended visit to the country was in 1981. A second extended visit was part of my research project on the East Asia Miracle. Beginning in the mid-1990s, I had the opportunity to go to China once or more every year, with annual meetings with the premier and other senior officials, first as a member of the U.S. government, then as chief economist of the World Bank, and then as a participant in the annual China Development Forum, where I was often asked to reflect on the new economic strategies as they evolved.

"China's Roadmap" was written in 2006, shortly after the announcement of the 11th five-year plan. (Every five years, China formulates a "roadmap" to provide guidance for the coming period.) As I discuss in the article, central to that plan was creating a harmonious society—trying to *avoid* the divides that have come to characterize America's society. In the case of China, the concern is not just the divide between rich and poor but between the urban and the rural areas, and between the coastal areas—where the country's transition to a market economy began—and the western regions.

"Reforming China's State–Market Balance" was written some eight years later, shortly after a new government had taken over and begun to formulate the economic strategy that would guide the country over the coming decade. China had a mixed record of ensuring that its citizens widely shared in the country's growing prosperity. It succeeded in moving some 500 million people out of poverty—the most successful antipoverty program in the world, *ever.* At the same time, when I wrote this article, the level of inequality, as measured by the standard metrics (the Gini coefficient), was comparable to that of the United States. In some ways, it was impressive: 30 years earlier, the country had been relatively equal. It had taken America a long time to achieve the same level of inequality that China had achieved in 30 years!

But it is important to understand the difference between developed and developing countries. In the initial stages of development, some parts of the country start to grow more than others. Almost always, development is about industrialization and urbanization; with urban incomes so much higher than those in the rural areas, early on inequality grows. But as the rural sector diminishes in importance, inequality diminishes. That's one of the reasons that Simon Kuznets had anticipated that the widely observed increases in inequality in early stages of development would be reversed. China is so far no exception to this pattern. The United States (and increasingly other advanced countries) are. The diminution of inequality did mark the United States in the first three-fourths of the last century, but beginning with the Reagan era, matters reversed.

My message to China in this article was a note of caution, especially regarding how its leaders saw the continuing transition to a market economy. Yes, in many sectors that should be welcome. But many of the pressing problems confronting their economy—including inequality and pollution—were largely the making of the private sector, and it would take active government policies to reverse the disturbing trends.

As I travel around the world, every once in a while I experience something almost totally unexpected, something that provides hope, a source of inspiration. My visit to Mauritius produced one such experience. A visit to Medellín, Colombia, in April 2014 yielded another. I had gone there to participate in a meeting of the World Urban Forum, an event that occurs every three years. This meeting was the largest ever—some 22,000 people, some 7,000 of whom listened enthusiastically to my address. In "A Light unto Cities" I describe the turnaround in this city once notorious for its drug gangs. At the heart of its success was its fight against inequality. Although the brunt of the struggle to create a fairer and more egalitarian society, where there is shared prosperity and all live with a modicum of dignity, has to occur at the national level, Medellín shows that much can be done at the local level, especially since so many of the essential services that are vital to the living standards of all individuals are provided locally—housing, public transportation, amenities like parks, and education. This is an important message for the United States, where political gridlock means that progress at the national level will be minimal; indeed, the concern is that national politics will lead to an increase in inequality in the coming years. If there is to be progress, then, on these issues, it will have to be at the local level.

The battles between those trying to create a more equal society and those opposing such changes are being fought all over the world. I often got drawn into these fights, even during my more academic lecture tours. This occurred during my visits to Australia in 2011 and 2014. "American Delusions Down Under" was written after my return from Australia in early July 2014.[4] Tony Abbott had assumed the prime ministership the preceding September and was determined to reverse the policies undertaken by previous administrations that had led to enormous success for that country—to the point that its per capita income was some $67,000 (among the highest in the world, and well above that of the United States). Those policies had resulted in a more shared prosperity: a minimum wage that was twice that of the United States, with an unemployment rate (at the time) that was much lower, a national debt that was a fraction of that of the United States, a way of financing higher education that provided opportunity for all (loans where payments were adjusted according to the individual's income), and a health care system that led to higher life expectancy and better health at a fraction of the cost of that of the United States. In spite of these successes, Abbott was somehow trying to push Australia to follow the American model—an example of blind ideology dominating all else.

That same year I got drawn into the debate over Scottish independence. I had served (with Sir James Mirrlees, my good friend and fellow Nobel laureate) on an advisory council to the Scottish government. Scotland had been active in implementing ideas I had been promoting about how to measure economic performance better. I had chaired the international Commission on the Measurement of Economic Performance and Social Progress, and we had unanimously agreed that GDP was an inadequate—sometimes misleading—measure of economic performance.[5] I was enthusiastic about countries that were interested in implementing our ideas, and Scotland was one. There were other innovative ideas, like policies to promote a better environment and active industrial policies to create jobs and foster innovation.

In September 2014 Scotland voted on independence. There had been much scaremongering by the opponents, portraying the disastrous effects that might follow independence. Although I was concerned about a world of increasing national fragmentation, I was unconvinced by the scaremongering, and I was impressed with the tone of the discussion on the part of the advocates of independence—it was positive, about the possibilities that might be opened up, far different from the parochial nationalism that characterized many similar movements. This small country had been the birthplace of the Enlightenment, the intellectual movement to which we all owe a great debt both in terms of our democratic values and the advances in science and technology to which it gave rise. Most importantly for purposes of this book, while England was following the American economic model—with inequality increasing as a result in the expected way—Scotland saw itself as following the Scandinavian model, with greater equality of opportunity. "Scottish Independence" was published in Scotland in the days before the election.

Independence was rejected in the referendum, though a remarkable 45 percent of the voters in a very high turnout voted to sever the 300-year-old union. Interestingly, in the aftermath, there was a surge of support for the Scottish Independence Party, and the increased devolution of powers that was promised meant that Scotland would almost surely pursue policies promoting more equality.

While Scotland provides a note of optimism in a world of increasing inequality, Spain does just the opposite. I visit Spain often. Among the protests that marked the spring of 2011, those in Spain were particularly large, and understandably so, given the hardship that that country was going through. I spoke to the young protesters in Retiro Park, in Madrid. I agreed with them that something was wrong with our economic and political systems: we had unemployed workers and homeless people, in a world in which there were vast unmet needs and empty homes; while ordinary citizens were suffering, those who had brought on the crisis—the bankers and their cronies—were doing very well.

"Spain's Depression" was written as the preface to the Spanish edition of *The Price of Inequality*. Spain was one of the countries that had actually managed to reduce inequality in the years before the Great Recession—just the opposite of the trend in the United States. But all of the progress was being lost in the Great Recession. While most in Europe—and especially its political leaders—are hesitant to call what was going on in Spain a depression, that's what it was—with a huge decline in incomes and with a youth unemployment rate in excess of 50 percent. I argue here that the problems lie squarely with the structure of the eurozone and the policies of austerity that have been imposed on that country—and not so much with the policies of Spain or its economic structure.

Notes

1. I had done an extensive study for the World Bank in the late 1980s and early 1990s on the reasons for East Asia's success, subsequently published as *The East Asian Miracle: Economic Growth and Public Policy* (Washington, DC: World Bank, 1993) and as a shorter journal article, "Some Lessons from the East Asian Miracle," *World Bank Research Observer* 11, no. 2 (August 1996): 151–77.
2. See J. E. Stiglitz, "Some Lessons from the East Asian Miracle," *World Bank Research Observer* 11, no. 2 (August 1996): 151–77; J. E. Stiglitz and M. Uy, "Financial Markets, Public Policy, and the East Asian Miracle," ibid., 249–76; and World Bank, *The East Asian Miracle: Economic Growth and Public Policy* (Washington, DC: World Bank, 1993).
3. Reprinted from the introduction to the Japanese edition of *The Price of Inequality*.
4. I also wrote an article, "Australia, You Don't Know How Good You've Got It," for the *Sydney Morning Herald*, published in September 2013.
5. The report of the commission is available as *Mismeasuring Our Lives: Why GDP Doesn't Add Up*, with Jean-Paul Fitoussi and Amartya Sen (New York: New Press, 2010).

THE MAURITIUS MIRACLE*

S UPPOSE SOMEONE WERE TO DESCRIBE A SMALL COUNTRY that provided free education through university for all of its citizens, transportation for schoolchildren, and free health care—including heart surgery—for all. You might suspect that such a country is either phenomenally rich or on the fast track to fiscal crisis.

After all, rich countries in Europe have increasingly found that they cannot pay for university education, and are asking young people and their families to bear the costs. For its part, the United States has never attempted to give free college for all, and it took a bitter battle just to ensure that America's poor get access to health care—a guarantee that the Republican Party is now working hard to repeal, claiming that the country cannot afford it.

But Mauritius, a small island nation off the east coast of Africa, is neither particularly rich nor on its way to budgetary ruin. Nonetheless, it has spent the last decades successfully building a diverse economy, a democratic political system, *and* a strong social safety net. Many countries, not least the U.S., could learn from its experience.

---

* *Project Syndicate*, March 7, 2011.

In a recent visit to this tropical archipelago of 1.3 million people, I had a chance to see some of the leaps Mauritius has taken— accomplishments that can seem bewildering in light of the debate in the U.S. and elsewhere. Consider homeownership: while American conservatives say that the government's attempt to extend homeownership to 70 percent of the U.S. population was responsible for the financial meltdown, 87 percent of Mauritians own their own homes—without fueling a housing bubble.

Now comes the painful number: Mauritius's GDP has grown faster than 5 percent annually for almost 30 years. Surely, this must be some "trick." Mauritius must be rich in diamonds, oil, or some other valuable commodity. But Mauritius has no exploitable natural resources. Indeed, so dismal were its prospects as it approached independence from Britain, which came in 1968, that the Nobel Prize–winning economist James Meade wrote in 1961: "It is going to be a great achievement if [the country] can find productive employment for its population without a serious reduction in the existing standard of living . . .[T]he outlook for peaceful development is weak."

As if to prove Meade wrong, the Mauritians have increased per capita income from less than $400 around the time of independence to more than $6,700 today. The country has progressed from the sugar-based monoculture of 50 years ago to a diversified economy that includes tourism, finance, textiles, and, if current plans bear fruit, advanced technology.

During my visit, my interest was to understand better what had led to what some have called the Mauritius Miracle, and what others might learn from it. There are, in fact, many lessons, some of which should be borne in mind by politicians in the U.S. and elsewhere as they fight their budget battles.

First, the question is not whether we can afford to provide health care or education for all, or ensure widespread homeownership. If Mauritius can afford these things, America and Europe—which are several orders of magnitude richer—can, too. The question, rather, is how to organize society. Mauritians have chosen a path that leads to higher levels of social cohesion, welfare, and economic growth—and to a lower level of inequality.

Second, unlike many other small countries, Mauritius has decided that most military spending is a waste. The U.S. need not go as far: just a fraction of the money that America spends on weapons that don't work against enemies that don't exist would go a long way toward creating a more humane society, including provision of health care and education to those who cannot afford them.

Third, Mauritius recognized that without natural resources, its people were its only asset. Maybe that appreciation for its human resources is also what led Mauritius to realize that, particularly given the country's potential religious, ethnic, and political differences—which some tried to exploit in order to induce it to remain a British colony—education for all was crucial to social unity. So was a strong commitment to democratic institutions and cooperation between workers, government, and employers—precisely the opposite of the kind of dissension and division being engendered by conservatives in the U.S. today.

This is not to say that Mauritius is without problems. Like many other successful emerging-market countries, Mauritius is confronting a loss of exchange-rate competitiveness. And, as more and more countries intervene to weaken their exchange rates in response to America's attempt at competitive devaluation through quantitative easing, the problem is becoming worse. Almost surely, Mauritius, too, will have to intervene.

Moreover, like many other countries around the world, Mauritius worries today about imported food and energy inflation. To respond to inflation by increasing interest rates would simply compound the difficulties of high prices with high unemployment and an even less competitive exchange rate. Direct interventions, restrictions on short-term capital inflows, capital-gains taxes, and stabilizing prudential banking regulations will all have to be considered.

The Mauritius Miracle dates to independence. But the country still struggles with some of its colonial legacies: inequality in land and wealth, as well as vulnerability to high-stakes global politics. The U.S. occupies one of Mauritius's offshore islands, Diego Garcia, as a naval base without compensation, officially leasing it from the United Kingdom, which not only retained the Chagos Islands in violation of the UN and international law, but expelled its citizens and refuses to allow them to return.

The U.S. should now do right by this peaceful and democratic country: recognize Mauritius's rightful ownership of Diego Garcia, renegotiate the lease, and redeem past sins by paying a fair amount for land that it has illegally occupied for decades.

SINGAPORE'S LESSONS FOR AN UNEQUAL AMERICA*

I NEQUALITY HAS BEEN RISING IN MOST COUNTRIES AROUND the world, but it has played out in different ways across countries and regions. The United States, it is increasingly recognized, has the sad distinction of being the most unequal advanced country, though the income gap has also widened, to a lesser extent, in Britain, Japan, Canada, and Germany. Of course, the situation is even worse in Russia, and some developing countries in Latin America and Africa. But this is a club of which we should not be proud to be a member.

Some big countries—Brazil, Indonesia, and Argentina—have become more equal in recent years, and other countries, like Spain, were on that trajectory until the economic crisis of 2007–8.

Singapore has had the distinction of having prioritized social and economic equity while achieving very high rates of growth over the past 30 years—an example par excellence that inequality is not just a matter of social justice but of economic performance. Societies with fewer economic disparities perform better—not just for those at the bottom or the middle, but over all.

It's hard to believe how far this city-state has come in the half-

---

* *New York Times*, March 18, 2013.

century since it attained independence from Britain, in 1963. (A short-lived merger with Malaysia ended in 1965.) Around the time of independence, a quarter of Singapore's workforce was unemployed or underemployed. Its per capita income (adjusted for inflation) was less than a tenth of what it is today.

There were many things that Singapore did to become one of Asia's economic "tigers," and curbing inequalities was one of them. The government made sure that wages at the bottom were not beaten down to the exploitative levels they could have been.

The government mandated that individuals save into a "provident fund"—36 percent of the wages of young workers—to be used to pay for adequate health care, housing, and retirement benefits. It provided universal education, sent some of its best students abroad, and did what it could to make sure they returned. (Some of my brightest students came from Singapore.)

There are at least four distinctive aspects of the Singaporean model, and they are more applicable to the United States than a skeptical American observer might imagine.

First, individuals were compelled to take responsibility for their own needs. For example, through the savings in their provident fund, around 90 percent of Singaporeans became homeowners, compared to about 65 percent in the United States since the housing bubble burst in 2007.

Second, Singaporean leaders realized they had to break the pernicious, self-sustaining cycle of inequality that has characterized so much of the West. Government programs were universal but progressive: while everyone contributed, those who were well off contributed more to help those at the bottom, to make sure that everyone could live a decent life, as defined by what Singaporean society, at each stage of its development, could afford. Not only did those at the top pay their share of the public investments; they were asked to contribute even more to helping the neediest.

Third, the government intervened in the distribution of pretax income—to help those at the bottom, rather than, as in the United

States, those at the top. It weighed in, gently, on the bargaining between workers and firms, tilting the balance toward the group with less economic power—in sharp contrast to the United States, where the rules of the game have shifted power away from labor and toward capital, especially during the past three decades.

Fourth, Singapore realized that the key to future success was heavy investment in education—and more recently, scientific research—and that national advancement would mean that all citizens—not just the children of the rich—would need access to the best education for which they were qualified.

Lee Kuan Yew, Singapore's first prime minister, who was in power for three decades, and his successors took a broader perspective on what makes for a successful economy than a single-minded focus on gross domestic product, though even by that imperfect measure of success, it did splendidly, growing 5.5 times faster than the United States has since 1980.

More recently, the government has focused intensively on the environment, making sure that this packed city of 5.3 million retains its green spaces, even if that means putting them on the tops of buildings.

In an era when urbanization and modernization have weakened family ties, Singapore has realized the importance of maintaining them, especially across generations, and has instituted housing programs to help its aging population.

Singapore realized that an economy could not succeed if most of its citizens were not participating in its growth or if large segments lacked adequate housing, access to health care, and retirement security. By insisting that individuals contribute significantly toward their own social welfare accounts, it avoided charges of being a nanny state. But by recognizing the different capacities of individuals to meet these needs, it created a more cohesive society. By understanding that children cannot choose their parents—and that all children should have the right to develop their innate capacities—it created a more dynamic society.

Singapore's success is reflected in other indicators, as well. Life expectancy is 82 years, compared with 78 in the United States. Student scores on math, science, and reading tests are among the highest in the world—well above the average for the Organization of Economic Cooperation and Development, the world's club of rich nations, and well ahead of the United States.

The situation is not perfect: In the last decade, growing income inequality has posed a challenge for Singapore, as it has for many countries in the world. But Singaporeans have acknowledged the problem, and there is a lively conversation about the best ways to mitigate adverse global trends.

Some argue that all of this was possible only because Mr. Lee, who left office in 1990, was not firmly committed to democratic processes. It's true that Singapore, a highly centralized state, has been ruled for decades by Mr. Lee's People's Action Party. Critics say it has authoritarian aspects: limitations on civil liberties; harsh criminal penalties; insufficient multiparty competition; and a judiciary that is not fully independent. But it's also true that Singapore is routinely rated one of the world's least corrupt and most transparent governments, and that its leaders have taken steps toward expanding democratic participation.

Moreover, there are other countries, committed to open, democratic processes, that have been spectacularly successful in creating economies that are both dynamic and fair—with far less inequality and far greater equality of opportunity than in the United States.

Each of the Nordic countries has taken a slightly different path, but each has impressive achievements of growth with equity. A standard measure of performance is the United Nations Development Program's inequality-adjusted Human Development Index, which is less a measure of economic output than it is of human well-being. For each country, it looks at citizens' income, education, and health, and makes an adjustment for how access to these is distributed among the population. The Northern European countries (Sweden, Denmark, Finland, and Norway) stand towards the top. In comparison—and especially considering its No. 3 ranking in the non-inequality-adjusted index—the United States is further down the list, at No. 16. And when other indicators of well-being are considered in isolation, the situation is even worse: the United States ranks 33rd on the United Nations Development Program's inequality-adjusted life expectancy index, just behind Chile.

Economic forces are global; the fact that there are such differences in outcomes (both levels of inequality and opportunity) suggests that what matters is how local forces—most notably, politics—shape these global economic forces. Singapore and Scandinavia have shown that they can be shaped in ways to ensure growth with equity.

Democracy, we now recognize, involves more than periodic voting. Societies with a high level of economic inequality inevitably wind up with a high level of political inequality: the elites run the political system for their own interests, pursuing what economists call rent-seeking behavior, rather than the general public interest. The result is a most imperfect democracy. The Nordic democracies, in this sense, have achieved what most Americans aspire toward: a political system where the voice of ordinary citizens is fairly represented, where political traditions reinforce openness and transparency; where money does not dominate political decision-making; where government activities are transparent.

I believe the economic achievements of the Nordic countries are in large measure a result of the strongly democratic nature of these societies. There is a positive nexus not just between growth and equality, but between these two and democracy. (The flip side is that greater inequality not only weakens our economy; it also weakens our democracy.)

A measure of the social justice of a society is the treatment of children. Many a conservative or libertarian in the United States asserts that poor adults are responsible for their own plight—having brought their situation on themselves by not working as hard as they could. (That assumes, of course, that there are jobs to be had—an increasingly dubious assumption.)

But the well-being of children is manifestly not a matter for which children can be blamed (or praised). Only 7.3 percent of children in Sweden are poor, in contrast to the United States, where a startling 23.1 percent are in poverty. Not only is this a basic violation of social justice, but it does not bode well for the future: these children have diminished prospects for contributing to their country's future.

Discussions of these alternative models, which seem to deliver more for more people, often end by some contrarian assertion or other about why these countries are different, and why their model has few lessons for the United States. All of this is understandable. None of us likes to think badly of ourselves or of our economic system. We want to believe that we have the best economic system in the world.

Part of this self-satisfaction, though, comes from a failure to understand the realities of the United States today. When Americans are asked what is the ideal distribution of income, they recognize that a capitalist system will always yield some inequality—without it, there would be no incentive for thrift, innovation, and industry. And they realize that we do not live up to what they view as their "ideal." The reality is that we have far more inequality than they believe we have, and that their view of the ideal is not too different from what the Nordic countries actually manage to achieve.

Among the American elite—that sliver of Americans who have seen historic gains in wealth and income since the mid-1970s even as most Americans' real incomes have stagnated—many look for rationalizations and excuses. They talk, for instance, about these countries' being homogeneous, with few immigrants. But Sweden has taken in large numbers of immigrants (roughly 14 percent of the population is foreign-born, compared with 11 percent in Britain and 13 percent in the United States). Singapore is a city-state with multiple races, languages, and religions. What about size? Germany has 82 million people and has substantially greater equality of opportunity than the United States, a nation of 314 million (although inequality has been rising there, too, though not as much as in the United States).

It is true that a legacy of discrimination—including, among many things, the scourge of slavery. America's original sin—makes the task of achieving a society with more equality and more equality of opportunity, on a par with the best-performing countries around the world, particularly tricky. But a recognition of this legacy should reinforce our resolve, not diminish our efforts, to achieve an ideal that is within our reach, and is consistent with our best ideals.

JAPAN SHOULD BE ALERT*

I NEQUALITY IS A GLOBAL PROBLEM. IT PLAGUES RICH AND poor countries, and countries in every continent. There are many dimensions to the changing face of inequality—greater excesses at the top, a hollowing out of the middle, an increase in poverty at the bottom. One thesis of this book is that societies pay a high price for this inequality—poorer economic performance, a weakening of democracy, compromises in other fundamental values, such as the rule of law. A corollary is that there can be large dividends from curbing the growth of inequality and creating a more equal society: not just economic returns, but an increase in a sense of fairness and fair play, important in all cultures. This book shows that this can be done, and describes the economic policies that can bring these improvements in the functioning of our economy and society.

But while there are many similarities among countries, there are some important differences. There are a few countries for which inequality is not increasing, in the standard overall summary statistic (the Gini coefficient, described in chapter 1). The United States, upon which I focus much of the analysis of this book, has the most inequality of any of the advanced industrial countries. And con-

---

* Preface to the Japanese edition of *The Price of Inequality*.

trary to a widely held belief—and contrary to America's own self-image—it is the country with the least equality of opportunity. Of course, there are famous instances of individuals who made it by dint of hard work from the bottom to the top. But these are exceptions. What matters are the statistics: What are the life prospects of someone born to a family with poor education and low income? And life prospects in the U.S. are more dependent on the income and education of one's parents than elsewhere.

Inevitably, there will be inequalities in outcomes and opportunities, but I argue here that those inequities don't have to be as large as they've become in the U.S. Other countries do far better. The fact that others do better, and others have managed to keep inequality from increasing, should give us hope: today's inequalities are not *just* the inevitable consequence of market forces. Markets do not exist in a vacuum. They are shaped by public policy. The successes of other countries in tempering inequality—in creating a *more* shared prosperity—show that the kinds of policies that I describe here can actually work to limit the growth of inequality and increase fairness in the economic system.

Over the last forty years, the countries with the most rapid growth have been the countries of East Asia. The increases in income that have occurred were beyond the imagination a half-century ago. There are many factors which have contributed to that success, such as a high savings rate. But one factor, I and others have argued, has been central, at least in most of the countries: the high level of equality, and especially the investments in education, which have extended opportunity far more broadly. Historically, there has been a strong social contract, limiting, for instance, the excesses at the top—the ratio of CEO pay to that of the typical worker is but a fraction of that in the U.S. There has not always been this social contract. Labor relations in Japan in the prewar period were far more fractious. The fact that matters could change so dramatically provides hope.

Many Americans worry that the path that the U.S. is on, with a nexus of ever-increasing economic and political inequality, will be near to impossible to reverse. But in other periods when the U.S. faced high levels of inequality, it pulled back from the brink and reversed course: the Gilded Age was followed by the Progressive Era, the unprecedented inequality of the Roaring 20s was followed by the landmark social legislation of the 30s. That Japan, Brazil, and the U.S. have, at various times in their histories, changed course, undertaking policies that have brought their citizens closer together, should provide a counterweight to the growing sense of despair.

But if America does not change course, it will pay a high price for its high and worsening inequality. This book explains why societies with greater equality are likely to get better economic performance. Unfortunately, there can be vicious as well as virtuous circles: higher economic inequality can lead to a weakening of the social contract, an increase in the imbalances of political power, which in turn can lead to laws, regulations, and policies that increase economic inequality still further.

The experiences of the U.S. should be an important warning to other countries, including Japan. Even as Japanese growth has weakened, it has managed to avoid some of the extremes exposed by recent U.S. data. For instance, even those in the middle lost almost 40 percent of their wealth in the period 2008–10, wiping out two decades of wealth accumulation for the typical American. In the recovery year of 2010, 93 percent of the gains accrued to the top 1 percent. While the U.S. labor market remains anemic— with almost one out of six Americans who would like a full-time job unable to find one—even the long slump in Japan has resulted in relatively low unemployment. America's system of social protection is among the worst in the advanced industrial countries. But as tax revenues have declined, the already inadequate system of social protection is becoming even more frayed. There have been major cutbacks in public services that are essential to the well-being of ordinary Americans. The inevitable result is that the economic downturn leads to increasing poverty.

There is, in the United States, another vicious circle: high inequality leads to a weaker economy, and the weak economy leads in turn to more inequality. High unemployment, for instance, leads to downward pressure on wages, hurting the middle class. As I explain in the book, high inequality lowers total demand, and it is lack of demand that is inhibiting growth in the U.S. and many other countries.

While all the other countries can claim some satisfaction in performing better than the U.S.—at least in this dimension—there is a risk of smugness. Success at one moment of time does not guarantee success at later dates.

Although inequality in Japan is still markedly less than that in the U.S., it has been increasing in Japan—just as it has been in the U.S. Could Japan revert to the fractiousness that marked the prewar period?

This book thus provides an important set of warnings and lessons for Japan: It should not take for granted its past successes in creating a more equal and fair society and economy. It should worry about increasing in equality. It should worry about the economic consequences. It should worry about the consequences for politics and society.

Even more than the U.S., Japan faces a problem of a large debt and an aging society. Its economy has been growing even more slowly than that of the U.S. It may be tempted to resort to cutbacks in investments in the common good or to undermining the system of social protections. But such policies would put at risk basic values and future economic prospects.

There are policies available (described in the last chapter) that would simultaneously increase growth and equality—creating a shared prosperity. For Japan, as for the U.S., the question is more one of politics than of economics. Will Japan be able to curb its rent seekers, in their pursuit of their own narrow interests, which inevitably harms the economy as a whole? Will it be able to construct a social contract for the 21st century, ensuring that the benefits of what growth that occurs will be fairly shared?

The answers to these questions are crucial to Japan's future—both as a society and as an economy.

JAPAN IS A MODEL, NOT A
CAUTIONARY TALE*

I N THE FIVE YEARS SINCE THE FINANCIAL CRISIS CRIPPLED
the American economy, a favorite warning of those who have
urged forceful government action, myself included, has been that
the United States risked entering a long period of "Japanese-style
malaise." Japan's two decades of anemic growth, which followed a
crash in 1989, have been the quintessential cautionary tale about
how not to respond to a financial crisis.

Now, though, Japan is leading the way. The recently elected
prime minister, Shinzo Abe, has embarked on a crash course of
monetary easing, public works spending, and promotion of entrepreneurship and foreign investment to reverse what he has called "a
deep loss of confidence." The new policies look to be a major boon
for Japan. And what happens in Japan, which is the world's third-
largest economy and was once seen as America's fiercest economic
rival, will have a big impact in the United States and around the
world.

Of course, not everyone is convinced: though Japan reported a
robust 3.5 percent annualized growth rate for the first quarter of
this year, the stock market has dipped from a five-year high amid

* *New York Times*, June 9, 2013.

doubts about whether "Abenomics" will go far enough. But we shouldn't read anything into short-term stock fluctuations. Abenomics is, without a doubt, a huge step in the right direction.

To really understand why things look good for Japan requires not only looking closely at Mr. Abe's platform, but also reexamining the popular narrative of Japanese stagnation. The last two decades are hardly a one-sided story of failure. On the surface, it does look as if there's been sluggish growth. In the first decade of this century, Japan's economy grew at a measly average annual rate of 0.78 percent from 2000 to 2011, compared with 1.8 percent for the United States.

BUT JAPAN'S SLOW growth does not look so bad under close examination. Any serious student of economic performance needs to look not at overall growth, but at growth related to the size of the working-age population. Japan's working-age population (ages 15 to 64) shrank 5.5 percent from 2001 to 2010, while the number of Americans of that age increased by 9.2 percent—so we should expect to see slower GDP growth. But even before Abenomics, Japan's real economic output, per member of the labor force, grew at a faster rate over the first decade of the century than that of the United States, Germany, Britain, or Australia.

Still, Japan's growth is far lower than it was before its crisis, in 1989. From our own recent experience in America, we know the devastating effects of even a short (albeit much deeper) recession: in America, we've had soaring inequality (with the top 1 percent securing all of the gains of the "recovery," and even more income), increased joblessness, and a middle that has been falling farther and farther behind. Japan's example shows that full recovery doesn't happen on its own. Luckily for Japan, its government took steps to ensure that the extremes in inequality that happened in the United States weren't manifest there, and now is finally being proactive about its growth.

And if we broaden the range of metrics we consider, we see that even after two decades of "malaise," Japan's performance is far superior to that of the United States.

Consider, for instance, the Gini coefficient, the standard measure of inequality. Zero represents perfect equality, and 1 stands for perfect inequality. While Japan's Gini coefficient stands today at around 0.33, the number for the United States is 0.38, according to the Organization for Economic Cooperation and Development. (Other data sources put the United States' level of inequality at even higher levels.) In the United States, the average income of the top 10 percent is 15.9 times that of the bottom 10 percent—compared with 10.7 times for Japan.

The reasons for these differences are political choices, not economic inevitability. Also according to the OECD, the Gini coefficient before taxes and transfer payments is about the same in the two countries: 0.499 for the United States, and 0.488 for Japan. But the United States does only a little to modulate its inequality, bringing it down to .38. Japan does much more, reducing the Gini coefficient to 0.33.

To be sure, Japan's situation is not perfect. The country needs to do better in caring for its "older old," those over 75. This cohort constitutes a growing share of the world's aging population. In 2008, the OECD estimated that 25.4 percent of Japan's "older old" lived in relative poverty—that is, with incomes less than half the national median—a figure only marginally better than the United States' (27.4 percent), and far above the OECD average of 16.1 percent. While neither we nor Japan may be as rich as we once thought we were, it is unconscionable that such a large fraction of our elderly should face such hardship.

But if Japan has a problem with poverty among the very aged, it does much better on another front, one that has important implications for any country's future: Some 14.9 percent of Japan's children are poor, compared to a disheartening 23.1 percent of American children.

Broader measures of performance are equally indicative. Life expectancy at birth (a good measure of the health of the economy) is a world-leading 83.6 years in Japan, versus 78.7 years for Americans. And even this data does not expose the full scope of inequality in life expectancies. It's been estimated that the longest-living 10th of Americans—who tend to be the wealthiest Americans—live almost as long as the average Japanese person. But those in our bottom 10th live about as long as the average person in Mexico or Argentina. The United Nations Development Program estimates that the effect of inequality on life expectancy in America is nearly twice as strong as it is in Japan.

Other measures also show Japan's strengths. It is second-highest in the world for attainment of university education, well ahead of the United States. And even in periods of slow growth, Japan has run its economy in a way that has kept a lid on the unemployment rate. During the global financial crisis, the rate peaked at 5.5 percent; in the two decades of its malaise, it never surpassed 5.8 percent. This low unemployment is one of the reasons Japan has fared so much better than the United States.

Those are numbers we now look on with envy. American unemployment, and an overall weak labor market, hurts those in the middle and bottom in four ways.

First, those who lose their jobs obviously suffer—and in America, especially so, because until Obamacare, they overwhelmingly depended on their employers for health insurance. The combination of the loss of a job and an illness sends many Americans to the brink of bankruptcy, or over it. Second, a weak labor market means that even those who have a job are likely to see their hours cut short. The official unemployment rate hides the huge numbers of Americans who have accepted part-time work, not because that's what they wanted, but because that's all there was. But even those who are supposed to be working full-time see their incomes erode when their hours are cut back. Third, with so many seeking work and not getting it, employers are under no pressure to raise wages; wages do not even keep up with inflation. Real incomes decline—and that's what's been happening to most middle-class American families. Finally, public expenditures of all sorts—so important to those in the middle and bottom—are cut back.

WITH HIS THREE-PRONGED approach—structural, monetary, and fiscal policies—Mr. Abe, who took office last December, has done what America should have done long ago. Though the structural policies have not been fully fleshed out, they are likely to include measures aimed at increasing labor-force participation, especially among women, and hopefully by facilitating employment for the large number of healthy elderly. Some have suggested encouraging immigration as well. These are areas in which the United States has done well in the past, and are crucial for Japan to address, for the sake of both growth and inequality.

Though Japan has long prioritized equal access to education for women—with a result that Japanese girls score higher in science than boys, and are not as far behind boys in math as American girls are—it still has a relatively low labor-force participation rate for women (49 percent, according to the World Bank, compared with 58 percent for the United States). And an astonishingly small portion of Japanese women—7 percent, according to one—occupy senior positions in management.

Achieving better labor participation by Japan's highly educated female population is of course as much a matter of social mores and customs as it is of government policy. And while governments can have only a limited role in changing social mores, they can tilt the playing field—making it easier for woman to participate actively in the labor market through pro-family policies (like pregnancy leaves and child-care facilities) and strongly enforced antidiscrimination laws. National statistics typically assess inequality among households or families—they don't get into what happens within the family. Yet inequalities within families can be marked, and differ markedly across countries.

Other likely reforms address the fact that Japan, like other advanced industrial countries, needs to go through some major structural transformations—moving from a manufacturing economy to a service-sector economy, and adapting to the dramatic changes in global comparative advantage, to the realities of climate change, and to the challenges of an aging population. While its powerful manufacturing sector has long showed good productivity growth, other sectors have lagged. Japan has the potential to extend its demonstrated innovativeness to the service sector.

With an aging population, increased efficiencies in the health care sector will be crucial; combining its manufacturing and technological prowess with new diagnostic devices is an example of an arena in which it can make global breakthroughs. Investments in research and higher education will help ensure that young Japanese have the skills and mind-set needed to succeed in globalization. Markets don't make these structural transformations easily on their own. And that's why government cutbacks in such situations are particularly foolish.

In fact, that is one reason the second pillar of Abenomics, its fiscal stimulus, is so important. Stimulus is needed, as we should have all learned, to increase aggregate demand. But it's also needed to complete the structural transformation. Investments in infrastructure, research, and education promise high dividends. Yet just as deficit hawks blocked stronger action in the United States, critics claim that Japan, with a debt that is more than twice the size of its GDP, is not in a position to pursue this critical aspect of the new policies. They point to the fact that Japan's indebtedness coincides with its long period of low growth. But even here, the data tell a more nuanced story. It is not the debt that caused the slow growth, but the slow growth that caused the deficit. Growth would have been even slower had the government not stimulated the economy.

What's more, the foundation of austerity advocates' logic—that high levels of debt-spending always slow growth, anywhere in the world—has been debunked. Europe is providing ever more evidence that austerity breeds austerity, which brings on recession and depression.

The final facet of Abenomics is its monetary policy, which reinforces stimulus with monetary stimulus. We should have learned that monetary stimulus—even strong and unprecedented actions like quantitative easing—has, at most, limited effects. Attention is focused on reversing deflation, which I believe is mainly a concern because it is a symptom of underutilization. While weakening the yen's exchange rate will make Japanese goods more competitive and thus stimulate the economy's growth, this is the reality of the international interdependence of monetary policy. It is equally true that the Federal Reserve's policy of "quantitative easing" weakens the dollar. We can look forward to a day when global coordination improves in this area.

AS THE PIECES of evidence fall into place, the pressing issue turns out to be not whether Abenomics is a good plan, but how the United States could achieve a similarly integrated plan, and what the consequences would be if it fails. The obstacle is not economic science but, as usual, America's raging political battles. For example, despite austerity advocates' dubious intellectual foundation, we have allowed public expenditures to slip in all sorts of areas, including those necessary for ensuring a future of shared prosperity. As a result, even as some states' financial situations start to edge toward improvement, public employment is still some 500,000 lower than it was before the crisis; the decrease in jobs has occurred almost completely at the state and local level. To regain the prerecession levels of employment and public services is a tremendous task, to say nothing of bringing them to where they would have been without a recession. (If the economy had been expanding normally, public employment would have increased significantly.) With inequality still high, the burdens are being felt, disproportionately, by our country's most vulnerable.

A major theme of my research has been that any country pays a high price for its inequality. Societies can have higher growth and more equality—the two are not mutually exclusive. Abenomics has already laid out some policies aimed to produce both. And one hopes that as further details are worked out, there will be more policies that promote greater gender equality in the labor market and tap into one of that country's underutilized resources. It will enhance growth, efficiency, and equality. Mr. Abe's plan also reflects an understanding that monetary policy can only go so far. One needs to have coordinated monetary, fiscal, and structural policies.

Those who see Japan's performance over the last decades as an unmitigated failure have too narrow a conception of economic success. Along many dimensions—greater income equality, longer life expectancy, lower unemployment, greater investments in children's education and health, and even greater productivity relative to the size of the labor force—Japan has done better than the United States. It may have quite a lot to teach us. If Abenomics is even half as successful as its advocates hope, it will have still more to teach us.

CHINA'S ROADMAP[*]

C HINA IS ABOUT TO ADOPT ITS 11TH FIVE-YEAR PLAN, SET-
ting the stage for the continuation of probably the most
remarkable economic transformation in history, while improving
the well-being of almost a quarter of the world's population. Never
before has the world seen such sustained growth; never before has
there been so much poverty reduction.

Part of the key to China's long-run success has been its almost
unique combination of pragmatism and vision. While much of the
rest of the developing world, following the Washington Consensus,
has been directed at a quixotic quest for higher GDP, China has
once again made clear that it seeks sustainable and more equitable
increases in real living standards.

China realizes that it has entered a phase of economic growth
that is imposing enormous—and unsustainable—demands on the
environment. Unless there is a change in course, living standards
will eventually be compromised. That is why the new five-year plan
places great emphasis on the environment.

Even many of the more backward parts of China have been growing at a pace that would be a marvel, were it not for the fact that

---

* *Project Syndicate*, April 6, 2006.

other parts of the country are growing even more rapidly. While this has reduced poverty, inequality has been increasing, with growing disparities between cities and rural areas, and between coastal regions and the interior. This year's World Bank *World Development Report* explains why inequality, not just poverty, should be a concern, and China's 11th five-year plan attacks the problem head-on. The government has for several years talked about a more harmonious society, and the plan describes ambitious programs for achieving this.

China recognizes, too, that what separates less developed from more developed countries is not only a gap in resources, but also a gap in knowledge. So it has laid out bold plans not only to reduce that gap, but to create a basis for independent innovation.

China's role in the world and the world's economy has changed, and the plan reflects this, too. Its future growth will have to be based more on domestic demand than on exports, which will require increases in consumption. Indeed, China has a rare problem: excessive savings. People save partly because of weaknesses in government social-insurance programs; strengthening social security (pensions) and public health and education will simultaneously reduce social inequalities, increase citizens' sense of well-being, and promote current consumption.

If successful—and, so far, China has almost always surpassed even its own high expectations—these adjustments may impose enormous strains on a global economic system that is already unbalanced by America's huge fiscal and trade imbalances. If China saves less—and if, as officials have announced, it pursues a more diversified policy of investing its reserves—who will finance America's more than $2 billion a day trade deficit? This is a topic for another day, but that day may not be far off.

With such a clear vision of the future, the challenge will be implementation. China is a large country, and it could not have succeeded as it has without widespread decentralization. But decentralization raises problems of its own.

Greenhouse gases, for example, are global problems. While America says that it cannot afford to do anything about it, China's senior officials have acted more responsibly. Within a month of the adoption of the plan, new environmental taxes on cars, gasoline, and wood products were imposed: China was using market-based mechanisms to address its and the world's environmental problems. But the pressures on local government officials to deliver economic growth and jobs will be enormous. They will be sorely tempted to argue that if America cannot afford to produce in a way that preserves our planet, how can we? To translate its vision into action, the Chinese government will need strong policies, such as the environmental taxes already imposed.

As China has moved toward a market economy, it has developed some of the problems that have plagued the developed countries: special interests that clothe self-serving arguments behind a thin veil of market ideology.

Some will argue for trickle-down economics: don't worry about the poor, eventually everybody will benefit from growth. And some will oppose competition policy and strong corporate governance laws: let Darwinian survival work its wonders. Growth arguments will be advanced to counter strong social and environmental policies: higher gasoline taxes, for example, will kill our nascent auto industry.

Such allegedly pro-growth policies would not only fail to deliver growth; they would threaten the entire vision of China's future. There is only one way to prevent this: open discussion of economic policies in order to expose fallacies and provide scope for creative solutions to the many challenges facing China today. George W. Bush has shown the dangers of excessive secrecy and confining decision-making to a narrow circle of sycophants. Most people outside China do not fully appreciate the extent to which its leaders, by contrast, have engaged in extensive deliberations and broad consultations (even with foreigners) as they strive to solve the enormous problems they face.

Market economies are *not* self-regulating. They cannot simply be left on autopilot, especially if one wants to ensure that their benefits are shared widely. But managing a market economy is no easy task. It is a balancing act that must constantly respond to economic changes. China's 11th five-year plan provides a roadmap for that response. The world watches in awe, and hope, as the lives of 1.3 billion people continue to be transformed.

REFORMING CHINA'S
STATE–MARKET BALANCE*

N O COUNTRY IN RECORDED HISTORY HAS GROWN AS fast—and moved as many people out of poverty—as China over the last 30 years. A hallmark of China's success has been its leaders' willingness to revise the country's economic model when and as needed, despite opposition from powerful vested interests. And now, as China implements another series of fundamental reforms, such interests are already lining up to resist. Can the reformers triumph again?

In answering that question, the crucial point to bear in mind is that, as in the past, the current round of reforms will restructure not only the economy, but also the vested interests that will shape *future* reforms (and even determine whether they are possible). And today, while high-profile initiatives—for example, the government's widening anti-corruption campaign—receive much attention, the deeper issue that China faces concerns the appropriate roles of the state and the market.

When China began its reforms more than three decades ago, the direction was clear: the market needed to play a far greater role in resource allocation. And so it has, with the private sector far more

* *Project Syndicate*, April 2, 2014.

important now than it was. Moreover, there is a broad consensus that the market needs to play what officials call a "decisive role" in many sectors where state-owned enterprises (SOEs) dominate. But what should its role be in other sectors, and in the economy more generally?

Many of China's problems today stem from too *much* market and too *little* government. Or, to put it another way, while the government is clearly doing some things that it should not, it is also not doing some things that it should.

Worsening environmental pollution, for example, threatens living standards, while inequality of income and wealth now rivals that of the United States and corruption pervades public institutions and the private sector alike. All of this undermines trust within society and in government—a trend that is particularly obvious with respect to, say, food safety.

Such problems could worsen as China restructures its economy away from export-led growth toward services and household consumption. Clearly, there is room for growth in private consumption; but embracing America's profligate materialist lifestyle would be a disaster for China—and the planet. Air quality in China is already putting people's lives at risk; global warming from even higher Chinese carbon emissions would threaten the entire world.

There is a better strategy. For starters, Chinese living standards could and would increase if more resources were allocated to redress large deficiencies in health care and education. Here, government *should* play a leading role, and does so in most market economies, for good reason.

America's privately based health care system is expensive, inefficient, and achieves far worse outcomes than those in European countries, which spend far less. A more market-based system is *not* the direction in which China should be going. In recent years, the government has made important strides in providing basic health care, especially in rural areas, and some have likened China's approach to that of the United Kingdom, where private provision is layered atop a public base. Whether that model is better than, say, French-style government-dominated provision may be debated. But if one adopts the UK model, the level of the base makes all the difference; given the relatively small role of private health care provision in the UK, the country has what is essentially a public system.

Likewise, though China has already made progress in moving away from manufacturing toward a service-based economy (the GDP share of services exceeded that of manufacturing for the first time in 2013), there is still a long way to go. Already, many industries are suffering from overcapacity, and efficient and smooth restructuring will not be easy without government help.

China is restructuring in another way: rapid urbanization. Ensuring that cities are livable and environmentally sustainable will require strong government action to provide sufficient public transport, public schools, public hospitals, parks, and effective zoning, among other public goods.

One major lesson that should have been learned from the post-2008 global economic crisis is that markets are not self-regulating. They are prone to asset and credit bubbles, which inevitably collapse—often when cross-border capital flows abruptly reverse direction—imposing massive social costs.

America's infatuation with deregulation was the cause of the crisis. The issue is *not* just the pacing and sequencing of liberalization, as some suggest; the end result also matters. Liberalization of deposit rates led to America's savings-and-loan crisis in the 1980s. Liberalization of lending rates encouraged predatory behavior that exploited poor consumers. Bank deregulation led not to more growth, but simply to more risk.

China, one hopes, will not take the route that America followed, with such disastrous consequences. The challenge for its leaders is to devise effective regulatory regimes that are appropriate for its stage of development.

That will require the government to raise more money. Local governments' current reliance on land sales is a source of many of the economy's distortions—and much of the corruption. Instead, the authorities should boost revenue by imposing environmental taxes (including a carbon tax), a more comprehensive progressive income tax (including capital gains), and a property tax. Moreover, the state should appropriate, through dividends, a larger share of SOEs' value (some of which might be at the expense of these firms' managers).

The question is whether China can maintain rapid growth (though somewhat slower than its recent breakneck pace), even as it reins in credit expansion (which could cause an abrupt reversal in asset prices), confronts weak global demand, restructures its economy, and fights corruption. In other countries, such daunting challenges have led to paralysis, not progress.

The economics of success is clear: higher spending on urbanization, health care, and education, funded by increases in taxes, could simultaneously sustain growth, improve the environment, and reduce inequality. If China's politics can manage the implementation of this agenda, China and the entire world will be better off.

MEDELLÍN:
A LIGHT UNTO CITIES*

L AST MONTH, A REMARKABLE GATHERING OCCURRED in Medellín, Colombia. Some 22,000 people came together to attend the World Urban Forum and discuss the future of cities. The focus was on creating "cities for life"—that is, on promoting equitable development in the urban environments in which a majority of the world's citizens already live, and in which two-thirds will reside by the year 2050.

The location itself was symbolic: Once notorious for its drug gangs, Medellín now has a well-deserved reputation as one of the most innovative cities in the world. The tale of the city's transformation holds important lessons for urban areas everywhere.

In the 1980s and 1990s, cartel bosses like the infamous Pablo Escobar ruled Medellín's streets and controlled its politics. The source of Escobar's power was not just the hugely profitable international cocaine trade (fueled by demand in the United States), but also extreme inequality in Medellín and Colombia. On the steep Andean slopes of the valley that cradles the city, vast slums, virtually abandoned by the government, provided a ready supply of recruits for the cartels. In the absence of public services, Escobar

* *Project Syndicate*, May 7, 2014.

won the hearts and minds of Medellín's poorest with his largesse—
even as he terrorized the city.

One can hardly recognize those slums today. In the poor neighborhood of Santo Domingo, the city's new Metrocable system, consisting of three lines of aerial gondolas, serves residents hundreds of
vertical feet up a mountainside, ending their isolation from the city
center. The commute is now minutes, and the social and economic
barriers between the informal settlements and the rest of the city
are on their way to being broken down.

The problems of the city's poor neighborhoods have not been
erased, but the benefits that the infrastructure improvements have
brought are brilliantly evident in the well-kept houses, murals, and
soccer fields perched near the gondola stations. The cable cars are
only the most iconic of the projects for which Medellín last year
won Harvard University's Veronica Rudge Green Prize in Urban
Design, the most prestigious award in the field.

Beginning with the mayoralty of Sergio Fajardo (now the governor of Medellín's department, Antioquia), who took office in 2004,
the city has made major efforts to transform its slums, improve
education, and promote development. (The current mayor, Aníbal
Gaviria, has affirmed his commitment to continuing on this path.)

Medellín constructed avant-garde public buildings in areas that
were the most run-down, provided house paint to citizens living in
poor districts, and cleaned up and improved the streets—all in the
belief that if you treat people with dignity, they will value their surroundings and take pride in their communities. And that faith has
been more than borne out.

Throughout the world, cities are both the locus and the focus
of society's major debates, and for good reason. When individuals
live in close quarters, they cannot escape major societal problems:
growing inequality, environmental degradation, and inadequate
public investment.

The forum reminded participants that livable cities require planning—a message at odds with prevailing attitudes in much of the

world. But without planning and government investment in infra-structure, public transportation and parks, and the provision of clean water and sanitation, cities won't be livable. And it is the poor who inevitably suffer the most from the absence of these public goods.

Medellín holds some lessons for America, too. Indeed, recent research shows how inadequate planning has fueled economic seg-regation in the United States, and how poverty traps have formed in cities without public transportation, owing to a shortage of acces-sible jobs.

The conference went beyond this, emphasizing that "livable cities" are not enough. We need to create urban areas in which individuals can flourish and innovate. It is no accident that the Enlightenment—which led in turn to the fastest and largest increases in living stan-dards in human history—unfolded in cities. New thinking is a natural consequence of high population density, provided the right conditions are met—conditions that include public spaces in which people can interact and culture can thrive, and a democratic ethos that welcomes and encourages public participation.

A key theme of the forum was the emerging consensus on the need for environmentally, socially, and economically sustainable development. All of these aspects of sustainability are intertwined and complementary, and cities provide the context in which this is most clear.

One of the biggest obstacles to achieving sustainability is inequal-ity. Our economies, our democracies, and our societies pay a high price for the growing gap between the rich and poor. And perhaps the most invidious aspect of the widening income and wealth gap in so many countries is that it is deepening inequality of opportunity.

Some cities have shown that these widely observed patterns are not the result of immutable economic laws. Even in the advanced country with the most inequality—the U.S.—some cities, like San Francisco and San Jose, are comparable to the best-performing economies in terms of equality of opportunity.

With political gridlock afflicting so many national governments around the world, forward-thinking cities are becoming a beacon of hope. A divided U.S. seems incapable of addressing its alarming increase in inequality. But in New York City, Mayor Bill de Blasio was elected on the promise of doing something about it.

While there are limits to what can be done at the local level—national taxation, for instance, is far more important than municipal taxes—cities can help ensure the availability of affordable housing. And they have a special responsibility to provide high-quality public education and public amenities for all, regardless of income.

Medellín and the World Urban Forum have shown that this is not just a pipe dream. Another world is possible; we need only the political will to pursue it.

AMERICAN DELUSIONS
DOWN UNDER*

FOR BETTER OR WORSE, ECONOMIC-POLICY DEBATES IN THE United States are often echoed elsewhere, regardless of whether they are relevant. Australian Prime Minister Tony Abbott's recently elected government provides a case in point.

As in many other countries, conservative governments are arguing for cutbacks in government spending, on the grounds that fiscal deficits imperil their future. In the case of Australia, however, such assertions ring particularly hollow—though that has not stopped Abbott's government from trafficking in them.

Even if one accepts the claim of the Harvard economists Carmen Reinhart and Kenneth Rogoff that very high public debt levels mean lower growth—a view that they never really established and that has subsequently been discredited—Australia is nowhere near that threshold. Its debt-to-GDP ratio is only a fraction of that of the U.S., and one of the lowest among the OECD countries.

What matters more for long-term growth are investments in the future—including crucial public investments in education, technology, and infrastructure. Such investments ensure that *all* citizens, no matter how poor their parents, can live up to their potential.

---

* *Project Syndicate*, July 9, 2014.

There is something deeply ironic about Abbott's reverence for the American model in defending many of his government's proposed "reforms." After all, America's economic model has not been working for most Americans. Median income in the U.S. is lower today than it was a quarter-century ago—not because productivity has been stagnating, but because wages have.

The Australian model has performed far better. Indeed, Australia is one of the few commodity-based economies that has not suffered from the natural-resource curse. Prosperity has been relatively widely shared. Median household income has grown at an average annual rate above 3 percent in the last decades—almost twice the OECD average.

To be sure, given its abundance of natural resources, Australia should have far greater equality than it does. After all, a country's natural resources should belong to all of its people, and the "rents" that they generate provide a source of revenue that could be used to reduce inequality. And taxing natural-resource rents at high rates does not cause the adverse consequences that follow from taxing savings or work (reserves of iron ore and natural gas cannot move to another country to avoid taxation). But Australia's Gini coefficient, a standard measure of inequality, is one-third higher than that of Norway, a resource-rich country that has done a particularly good job of managing its wealth for the benefit of *all* citizens.

One wonders whether Abbott and his government really understand what has happened in the U.S. Does he realize that since the era of deregulation and liberalization began in the late 1970s, GDP growth has slowed markedly, and that what growth has occurred has primarily benefited those at the top? Does he know that prior to these "reforms," the U.S. had not had a financial crisis—now a regular occurrence around the world—for a half-century, and that deregulation led to a bloated financial sector that attracted many talented young people who otherwise might have devoted their careers to more productive activities? Their financial innovations made them extremely rich but brought America and the global economy to the brink of ruin.

Australia's public services are the envy of the world. Its health care system delivers better outcomes than that of the U.S., at a fraction of the cost. It has an income-contingent education-loan program that permits borrowers to spread their repayments over more years if necessary, and in which, if their income turns out to be particularly low (perhaps because they chose important but low-paying jobs, say, in education or religion), the government forgives some of the debt.

The contrast with the U.S. is striking. In the U.S., student debt, now in excess of $1.2 trillion (more than all credit card debt), is becoming a burden for graduates and the economy. America's failed financial model for higher education is one of the reasons that, among the advanced countries, America now has the least equality of opportunity, with the life prospects of a young American more dependent on his or her parents' income and education than are those of a young person in other advanced countries.

Abbott's notions about higher education also suggest that he clearly does not understand why America's best universities succeed. It is not price competition or the drive for profit that has made Harvard, Yale, or Stanford great. None of America's great universities are for-profit institutions. They are all not-for-profit institutions, either public or supported by large endowments, contributed largely by alumni and foundations.

There is competition, but of a different sort. They strive for inclusiveness and diversity. They compete for government research grants. America's underregulated for-profit universities excel in two dimensions: the ability to exploit young people from poor backgrounds, charging them high fees without delivering anything of value, and the ability to lobby for government money *without regulation* and to continue their exploitative practices.

Australia should be proud of its successes, from which the rest of the world can learn a great deal. It would be a shame if a misunderstanding of what has happened in the U.S., combined with a strong dose of ideology, caused its leaders to fix what is not broken.

SCOTTISH INDEPENDENCE[*]

A S SCOTLAND CONTEMPLATES INDEPENDENCE, SOME, SUCH as Paul Krugman, have questioned the "economics."

Would Scotland, going it alone, risk a decline in standards of living or a fall in GDP? There are, to be sure, risks in any course of action: should Scotland stay in the UK, and the UK leave the EU, the downside risks are, by almost any account, significantly greater. If Scotland stays in the UK, and the UK continues in its policies that have resulted in growing inequality, even if GDP were slightly larger, the standards of living of most Scots could fall.

Cutbacks in UK public support to education and health could force Scotland to face a set of unpalatable choices—even with Scotland having considerable discretion over what it spends its money on.

But there is, in fact, little basis for any of the forms of fear-mongering that have been advanced. Krugman, for instance, suggests that there are significant economies of scale: a small economy is likely, he seems to suggest, not to do well. But an independent Scotland will still be part of Europe, and the great success of the EU is the creation of a large economic zone.

Besides, small political entities like Sweden, Singapore, and Hong

---

*   *Herald* (Glasgow), September 13, 2014.

Kong have prospered, while much larger entities have not. By an order of magnitude, far more important is pursuit of the right policies.

Another example of a nonissue is the currency. There are many currency arrangements that would work. Scotland could continue using sterling—with or without England's consent.

Because the economies of England and Scotland are so similar, a common currency is likely to work far better than the euro—even without shared fiscal policy. But many small countries have managed to have a currency of their own—floating, pegged, or "managed."

The fundamental issue facing Scotland is different. It is clear that there is, within Scotland, more of a shared vision and values—a vision of the country, the society, politics, the role of the state; values like fairness, equity, and opportunity. Not everyone in the country agrees on the precise policies, on the delicate balance.

But the Scottish vision and values are different from those dominant south of the border. Scotland has free university education for all; England has increased student fees, forcing students with parents of limited means to take out loans.

Scotland has repeatedly stressed its commitment to the National Health Service. England has repeatedly made moves toward privatization. Some differences are of long standing: even 200 years ago, male literacy in Scotland was 50 percent higher than in England, and Scottish universities charged one-tenth of the fees for Cambridge and Oxford.

Differences in these and other related policies can, over time, lead not only to markedly different growth rates, and thus to markedly different levels of GDP per capita—swamping any slight short-run impact—but also, and more importantly, to differences in the distribution of income and wealth. If the UK continues on its current course, imitating the American model, it is likely that the results will be like those of the U.S.—where the typical family has seen its income stagnate for a quarter-century, even as the rich get richer.

Independence may have its costs, although these have yet to be demonstrated convincingly, but it will also have its benefits.

Scotland can make investments in tidal energy, or in its young people; it can strive to increase female labor-force participation and provide for early-years education—both essential for creating a fairer society. It can make these investments, knowing that the country will recapture more of the benefits from them through taxation.

Under current arrangements, while Scotland bears the cost of these social investments, the extra tax revenue resulting from the additional growth from these investments will go overwhelming south of the border.

The difficult question that Scotland has to face is thus not about arcane issues about monetary arrangements or economies of scope, about the minutiae of the short-run gains and losses, but whether Scotland's future—its shared vision and values, which have increasingly deviated from those dominant south of the border—will be better achieved through independence.

SPAIN'S DEPRESSION*

S PAIN IS IN DEPRESSION. THAT'S THE ONLY WORD THAT ONE
can use to describe the economy, with close to one out of four
workers unemployed, and a youth unemployment rate of 50 percent
(as of the time this book goes to press). The prognosis for the immediate future is more of the same, perhaps a little worse. This is in
spite of promises from the government and international official-
dom that prescribed the austerity packages on Spain that growth
would, by now, have been restored. They have repeatedly underestimated the magnitude of the downturn that their policies would
bring about, and as a result they have consistently overestimated
the fiscal benefit that would be derived: deeper downturns inevitably result in lower revenues and more expenditures for unemployment and social programs. Though they then try to shift the blame
back onto Spain for missing the fiscal targets, it is their misdiagno-
sis of the problem and the resulting wrong prescription that should
be held accountable.

This book explains how flawed economic policies can lead to
both more inequality and lower growth—and the policies being
adopted in Spain and Europe more broadly provide a perfect illus-

---

* Foreword to the Spanish edition of *The Price of Inequality*.

tration. In the years before the crisis (especially between 1985 and 2000), Spain was fairly unusual in that inequality in net labor earnings and household net disposable income fell.[1] Even as before-tax inequality was reduced, government "corrected" the distribution of income through important social policies and measures directed at improving public health, and continued to do so through the early years of the crisis.[2] But by now the prolonged recession has caused a dramatic increase in inequality.[3]

But as we explain in chapter 1, downturns, especially a depression such as Spain is going through now, are bad for inequality. Those who are unemployed, especially the long-term unemployed, are more likely to move into poverty. The high unemployment rate puts downward pressure on wages, and wages at the bottom are especially sensitive. And as austerity has tightened, social programs essential to the well-being of those in the middle and bottom get cut back. As in the United States, compounding these effects is the decline in real estate prices, the most important asset for those at the bottom and in the middle.

The implications of Spain's growing inequality and its deep depression should be profoundly worrying for its future. It's not just that resources are being wasted; the country's human capital is deteriorating. Those who are skilled and can't get a job in Spain are migrating: there is a global market for the country's talents. Whether they will come back when and if recovery sets in will depend, in part, on how long the depression lasts.

Spain's problems today are largely a result of the same mix of ideology and special interests that (as this book describes) led to financial market liberalization and deregulation and other "market fundamentalist" policies in the United States—policies that contributed to the high level of inequality and instability in the U.S., and which have resulted in growth rates far lower than those in the preceding decades. (These "market fundamentalist" policies are also referred to as "neoliberalism." As I explain, they rest not on a deep understanding of modern economic theory, but on a naïve reading of economics, based on assumptions of perfect competition and perfect markets.)

In some cases, the ideology did little more than masquerade the attempt by some vested interests to garner more for themselves. A nexus developed between banks, property developers, and some politicians: environmental and zoning regulations were set aside and/or not effectively enforced; banks were not only inadequately regulated, but what regulations existed were not tightly enforced. There was a party. Money flowed everywhere. Some of it flowed back to the politicians who allowed this to happen, either in campaign contributions or in lucrative jobs after serving their time in office. Even tax revenues increased, and the politicians could pride themselves both on the growth that the real estate bubble had brought about and on the improvement in the country's fiscal position. But it was all a chimera: the economy was based on shaky, unsustainable foundations.

In Europe, the neoliberal, market fundamentalist ideas get encoded into basic economic structure underlying the European Union, and especially the eurozone. These principles were supposed to lead to greater efficiency and stability; and everybody, it was presumed, would benefit from the enhanced growth, so little attention was paid to what the new rules would imply for inequality.

In fact, they have led to lower growth, more instability. And in most countries in the European Union, already before the crisis but even more so afterwards, those at the bottom and in the middle have not done well. This book lays out many of the fallacies in the market fundamentalist ideology, and explains why policies based on that have repeatedly failed. But it is worth looking more closely at how these issues have played out in Europe.

Take the principle of free labor mobility. That was supposed to lead to an efficient allocation of labor, and there are circumstances in which that may be the case. With debt burdens in several countries so high, however, young people can escape repaying the debts of their parents simply by moving; taxes to repay these debts induce inefficient migration. But it also creates an adverse dynamic: as young people move out, the tax burden on the rest increases, providing even more incentives for inefficient migration.

Or take the principle of free movement of goods, combined with the failure to have tax harmonization. Companies (and individuals) have an incentive to move to low-taxed jurisdictions, from which they can ship their goods anywhere within the EU. Location is not based on where production is most efficient, but on where taxes are lowest. This in turn sets off a race to the bottom: creating pressure not only to lower taxes on capital and corporations but also to lower wages and working conditions. The burden of taxation is shifted to workers. And with so much inequality associated with the inequality of capital and corporate profits, overall inequality in (after-tax and transfer) income inevitably increases.

The so-called single-market principle, whereby a bank regulated by any European government can operate anywhere else in the EU, combined with the free mobility of capital, has been perhaps the worst of the neoliberal policies. In the years before the crisis, we saw one aspect of that: financial products and deposits from under-regulated countries caused havoc in other countries; the host countries failed to fulfill their responsibilities of protecting their citizens and their economies. By the same token, the doctrine that markets are efficient—and that governments should not interfere with their wondrous workings—led to the decision not to interfere with real estate bubbles as they formed in Ireland, Spain, and the United States. But markets have repeatedly been subject to bouts of irrational optimism and pessimism: they were excessively optimistic in the years after the beginning of the euro, and money flowed into real estate in Spain and Ireland; today they are excessively pessimistic, and money is flowing out. The outflow weakens the economy further. And the single-market principle exacerbates the problem: it's relatively easy for someone in Greece or Spain or Portugal to shift his or her euros into a German bank account.

But the banking system, like the other aspects of the euro economy, is distorted. It's not a level playing field. Confidence in a bank rests on the ability of the government to rescue the bank's depositors should things go wrong, and this is especially the case as we have allowed banks to become bigger and to trade in complex, non-transparent, hard-to-value financial products. German banks are advantaged over Spanish banks simply because there is greater confidence in Germany's ability to rescue its banks. There is a hidden subsidy. But this again creates a downward spiral: as money leaves the country, the economy weakens, undermining confidence in the ability of the government to rescue the country's banks, enhancing an outflow of money.

There are other aspects of Europe's economic framework that contribute to its problems now: the European Central Bank has a single-minded focus on inflation (in contrast with the U.S., where the mandate includes growth, employment, and financial stability). Chapter 9 explains why a focus on inflation contributes to more inequality. But the *disparity* in mandates is especially disadvantageous for Europe now. As the U.S. has lowered its interest rates essentially to zero and Europe has not, the euro is stronger than it otherwise would have been, and this makes exports weaker, imports stronger, destroying still more jobs.

The fundamental problem with the euro was that it took away two of the critical mechanisms for adjustment in the face of a shock that affected some countries differently from others—the interest rate and exchange rate mechanisms—and put nothing in its place. The eurozone was not what economists call an "optimal currency area," a group of countries that could viably share the same currency. When countries face a shock, one way they adjust is to change the exchange rate. This is true even for similar countries, like the United States and Canada; the exchange rate between the two has varied markedly. But the euro imposes a constraint on adjustment.

Some suggest that an alternative to adjusting the exchange rate is to lower all wages and prices within the country. This is called *internal devaluation*. If internal devaluation were easy, the gold standard would not have posed a barrier to adjustment in the Great Depression. It is easier for countries like Germany to adjust through a real appreciation of their currency (as China is now doing) than it is for its trading partners to adjust through a real depreciation of their currency. Real appreciation can be accomplished through inflation. It is easier to get moderate inflation than a corresponding level of deflation. But Germany has been resistant.

The consequence of Germany's *real* exchange rate being too low is just like that of China's: Germany has a surplus (like China), and its trading partners (like Spain) have a trade deficit. When there are imbalances, it is the surplus country as much as the deficit country that is to blame, and the burden of adjustment should be assigned to where the adjustment is easiest. This is the doctrine that the rest of the world has enunciated in discussions with China. China has responded, with a remarkably large increase in its real exchange rate since 2005. The necessary adjustment has not occurred within Europe.

Not every country can have a surplus, and so the view of some of those in Germany that others should imitate its policy is, in a sense, simply incoherent. For every surplus, there has to be a deficit. And particularly today, the surplus countries are imposing costs on others: the global problem today is a lack of global aggregate demand, a problem to which surpluses contribute.

It is instructive to compare Europe with the U.S. The 50 states of the United States have a common currency. Some contrasts between the U.S., where there is a common currency, which works, and Europe, may be illustrative. In the U.S., two-thirds of all public expenditures occur at the federal level. The federal government bears the brunt of welfare payments, unemployment insurance, and capital investments, such as roads and R&D. The locus of counter-cyclical policies lies with the federal government. The federal government backs the banks—even most of the state banks—through the Federal Deposit Insurance Corporation (FDIC). There is free mobility, but in the U.S., no one cares if some state, like North Dakota, becomes devoid of population as a result of out-migration. Indeed, it lowers the cost of buying that state's congressmen.

The euro was a political project, but one where the politics was not strong enough to "complete" the project, to do what had to be done to make a currency area bringing together such a diverse group of countries work. The hope was that, with time, the project would be completed as the euro would bring the countries together. In practice, its effect has been just the opposite. Old wounds have been reopened, and new enmities have developed.

When things were going well, no one thought of these problems. I was hopeful that the Greek debt crisis that broke out in January 2010 would provide the impetus for more fundamental reforms. But little was done. As this book goes to press, interest rates faced by Spain are at levels that are not sustainable, and there is no prospect of recovery anytime soon.

The major mistake that Europe, prodded by Germany, has made is that it ascribed the difficulties of the periphery countries, like Spain, to profligate spending. Though it is true that Greece had run large deficits in the years before the crisis, both Spain and Ireland had surpluses and low debt levels (relative to their GDP). Thus, the focus on austerity would not even have prevented a recurrence of a crisis, let alone solved the crisis confronting Europe.

Earlier I described how the high level of unemployment is increasing inequality. But because those at the top spend a smaller fraction of their income than those at the bottom—who have no choice but to spend everything—inequality leads to a weaker economy. There is a downward vicious circle. And austerity exacerbates all of this. Today, the problem in Europe is inadequate overall demand. As the depression continues, banks are less willing to lend, housing prices decline, and households become poorer and poorer, and more uncertain of the future, depressing consumption further.

No large economy—and Europe is a large economy—has ever emerged from a crisis at the same time that it has imposed austerity. Austerity always, inevitably, and predictably makes matters worse. The only examples where fiscal stringency has been associated with recovery are small countries, typically with flexible exchange rates, and whose trading partners were growing robustly, so exports filled in the gap created by the cutbacks in government spending. But that is hardly the situation confronting Spain today: its major trading partners are in recession, and it has no control over its exchange rate.

European leaders have recognized that its problems will not be solved without growth. But they have failed to explain how growth can be achieved with austerity. So too, they assert that what is needed is a restoration of confidence. Austerity will not bring about either growth or confidence. The failed policies of the last two years on the part of Europe, as it has tried, repeatedly, patchwork solutions, misdiagnosing Europe's problems, have undermined confidence. Because austerity has destroyed growth, it has also destroyed confidence, and will continue to do so, no matter how many speeches are given about the importance of confidence and growth.

The austerity measures have been particularly ineffective, because the market understood that they would bring with them recessions, political turmoil, and disappointing improvements in the fiscal position, as tax revenues declined. Rating agencies downgraded countries undertaking austerity measures, and rightly so. Spain was downgraded as the first austerity measures were passed: the rating agency believed that Spain would do what it promised, and it knew that that meant low growth and an increase in its economic problems.

While austerity was designed to resolve the "sovereign debt" crisis, to save the banking system, Europe has resorted to a series of equally ineffective temporary measures. For the past year, Europe has been engaged in a costly, fruitless bootstrap operation: providing more money to banks to buy sovereigns helped support the sovereigns; and providing more money to the sovereigns that helped support the banks. But it was nothing but voodoo economics, a hidden gift to the banks in the tens of billions of dollars, but one that the markets quickly saw through. Each measure was but a short-term palliative, the effects disappearing faster than even the pundits had warned. With the inefficacy of the bootstrap operations fully exposed, the financial system of the crisis countries has been put into jeopardy. Finally, almost two and a half years after the beginning of the crisis, it seemed to recognize the folly of this strategy. But even then, it couldn't devise an effective alternative.

There is a second prong (besides getting their fiscal house in order) to Europe's strategy: structural reforms to make the afflicted economies more competitive. Structural reforms are important, but they take time, and they are supply-side measures; but it is demand that is limiting production today. The wrong so-called supply-side measures—those that lead to lower incomes today—may exacerbate the lack of aggregate demand. Thus, measures to improve the labor market won't lead to more hiring if there is no demand for the goods produced by firms. So too, weakening unions and job protections may well result in lower wages, weaker demand, and higher unemployment. Neoliberal doctrines held that moving workers away from subsidized sectors to more productive uses would increase growth and efficiency. But in situations such as that of Spain, where unemployment is already high, and especially so when the financial sector is weak, what happens is that workers move from low-productivity, subsidized sectors to unemployment; and the economy is further weakened by the resulting reduced consumption.

For years, now, Europe has struggled, and the only result is that, as this book goes to press, not just the crisis countries but Europe as a whole has slid into recession. There is an alternative set of policies that might work—might at least end the depression, end the corrosive increase in poverty and inequality, and perhaps even restore growth.

A long-recognized principle is that a balanced expansion of taxes and spending stimulates the economy, and if the program is well designed (taxes at the top, spending on education) the increase in GDP and employment can be significant.

But what Spain can do is limited. Europe must act if the euro is to survive. Europe as a whole is not in a bad fiscal position—its debt-to-GDP ratio compares favorably with that of the U.S. If each state in the U.S. were totally responsible for its own budget, including paying for all unemployment benefits, the U.S., too, would be in fiscal crisis. The lesson is obvious: the whole is more than the sum of the parts. There are a variety of ways in which Europe could act together, beyond the measures already taken.

There are already institutions within Europe, such as the European Investment Bank, that could help finance needed investments in the cash-starved economies. It should expand its lending. So too, funds available to support small and medium-size enterprises should be enhanced, while large firms can turn to capital banks. Credit contraction by banks hits these enterprises particularly hard, and in all economies these firms are the source of job creation. Those measures are already on the table, but they are unlikely to suffice.

What is required is much more akin to a common treasury: a larger European solidarity fund for stabilization or Eurobonds. If Europe (and the ECB in particular) were to borrow, and relend the proceeds, the costs of servicing Europe's debt would decrease, and that would make room for the kinds of expenditure that promote growth and employment.

But the common policies currently being discussed are little more than a suicide pact—an agreement to limit spending to revenues, even in a recession, without a commitment from the countries that are in a strong position to help the weaker. One of the victories of the Clinton administration was the defeat of a similar attempt by the Republicans to force a balanced budget amendment to the U.S. Constitution. We had not, of course, anticipated the fiscal profligacy of the Bush administration, the irresponsible deregulatory policies, the inadequate supervision, that led to a ballooning of the federal debt. But even if we had, I believe we would have come to the same conclusion. It is wrong not to use tools in a country's toolkit; a primary obligation in modern economy is to maintain full employment, and monetary policy alone often cannot suffice.

Some in Germany say Europe is not a transfer union. Many economic relationships are not transfer unions—a free-trade zone is an example. But the system of a single currency sought to go beyond that. Europe and Germany will have to face the reality—if they are not willing to change the economic framework beyond an agreement of fiscal stringency, the euro will not work. It may survive for a little longer, causing untold pain in its death throes. But it will not survive.

So too, there is only one way out of the banking crisis—a common banking framework, a Europe-wide backing of the financial system. Not surprisingly, the banks receiving the implicit subsidies of the governments in a better financial position don't want this. They enjoy their competitive advantage. And bankers everywhere have undue sway over their governments.

The consequences will be deep and long-lasting. Young people long deprived of a decent job become alienated. When they eventually get a job, it will be at a much lower wage. Normally, youth is a time when skills get built up. Now it's a time when they atrophy. Society's most valuable asset, the talents of its people, is being wasted and even destroyed.

There are so many natural disasters in the world—earthquakes, floods, typhoons, hurricanes, tsunamis. It's a shame to add to these a man-made disaster. But that's what Europe is doing. Indeed, the willful ignorance of the lessons of the past is criminal. The pain that Europe is experiencing, especially its poor and its young people, is so unnecessary.

There is, I have suggested, an alternative. But Spain cannot act alone. The policies that are required are European policies. Delay in grasping this alternative will be very costly.

Right now, unfortunately, the kind of reform that would make the euro work is not being discussed, at least not openly. As I noted earlier, all that we have is platitudes about fiscal responsibility, and restoring growth and confidence. Quietly, academics and others are beginning to discuss a Plan B: what happens if the lack of political will that was evidenced at the founding of the euro—a political will to create the institutional structures that would make a common currency work—continues. As the widely used metaphor puts it, unscrambling a scrambled egg is costly. But so is maintaining the current flawed institutional arrangements. Flawed currency arrangements have collapsed before. There is a price to be paid. But life continues after debt and devaluation. And that life can be far better than the depression confronting some of the countries in Europe today. If there were light at the end of this tunnel, that would be one thing. But austerity provides no promise of a better world anytime in the foreseeable future. History and experience provide no basis for reassurance.

And if the depression does continue, it is those at the bottom and in the middle who will suffer the most.

Notes

1. Josep Pijoan-Mas and Virginia Sanchez-Marcos ascribe that to a falling premium associated with a college education and falling unemployment rates in "Spain Is Different: Falling Trends of Inequality," *Review of Economic Dynamics* 13, no. 1 (January 2010), pp. 154–78.
2. For a description of some of these efforts, see *OECD Perspectives: Spain Policies for a Sustainable Recovery*, October 2011, available at http://www.oecd.org/dataoecd/45/46/44686629.pdf, accessed July 30, 2012.
3. A standard measure of inequality, discussed in chapter 1, is the Gini coefficient. Under that measure, perfect equality has a value of 0; perfect inequality, of 1. Reasonably good countries have a measure of .3. The United States, the worst of the advanced industrial countries, has a measure of around .47, and highly unequal countries have a measure in excess of .5. A country's Gini coefficient usually moves *very* slowly, but Spain's rose from 32.6 in 2005 to 34.7 in 2010. See IMF, "Income Inequality and Fiscal Policy," June 2012, available at http://www.imf.org/external/pubs/ft/sdn/2012/sdn1208.pdf, accessed July 30, 2012.

PART VIII

PUTTING AMERICA
BACK TO WORK

I BEGAN THIS BOOK WITH A SHORT SECTION ON THE making of the Great Recession, focusing on the linkages between that recession and inequality—how it was both consequence and cause. I end by returning to these themes.

By the close of 2009 it was clear that we had saved the banks and that the country had avoided another Great Depression. But it was also clear to me by then that we had not set the economy on a course for a quick recovery. As I noted in the introduction to the prelude, and especially in "How to Get Out of the Financial Crisis," we needed a strong, well-designed, large, and long-term stimulus; we needed a bailout, but one that induced banks to lend to small and medium-size enterprises. The appropriate regulatory reforms would help do this, reducing the scope for them to engage in speculation and market manipulation. We needed a housing policy that would help the millions of Americans losing their homes. We didn't do any of these things. While we had saved the banks, we had not prevented millions and millions of Americans from losing their homes and millions more from losing their jobs. The Obama administration and the Fed seemed more confident than I was that we were about to turn the corner. By the middle of 2011 disillusionment was setting in. Something more was clearly needed to put more Americans back to work. "How to Put America Back to Work" was written for *Politico* to provide an alternative agenda.

It was 2013, and the economy still remained weak. A new national debate was breaking out. Was there a new normal? Should we come to accept a new higher level of unemployment? I continued to believe that the main reason for the weakness in our economy was the lack of demand, and a main reason for that was our inequality—which had become even worse since the beginning of the recession. In "Inequality Is Holding Back the Recovery" I again explain, in some detail, why inequality was so bad for the economy, what we could do to reduce it, and how, accordingly, we could have both better economic performance and less inequality.

As the recovery remained anemic, questions began to be raised about whether the original diagnosis of the economy's problem was correct: Was there something more fundamentally wrong with the economy? At the time of the crisis, the common diagnosis was that the banks had engaged in reckless lending; the banks were bankrupt, and without a functioning banking system, the economy itself could not function. The money provided by the banks was like blood to the body. That's why, it was argued, it was essential to save the banks. It wasn't because we loved the banks and the bankers; it was that we couldn't do without them. The Obama-Bush prescription followed from this diagnosis: put the banks into the emergency room, give them a massive transfusion (or, more accurately, *infusion* of cash), and within a year or two things will be back to normal. The economy would need a short-term boost—a stimulus—in the interim; but since the stimulus was merely a temporary measure, required only while the banks were mending, one didn't have to be too finicky about the details. And so we wound up with a stimulus that was too small, too short, and not particularly well designed.

(Of course, as I explained in *Freefall* and earlier in this book, one could save the banks without saving the bankers and the banks' shareholders and bondholders. The irony was that what we did was unnecessarily expensive to the taxpayer, and less effective than it could or should have been.)

Two years after the collapse of Lehman Brothers, the banks were largely back to health. Lending to small and medium-size enterprises was still markedly below the crisis, but this was partly because we had focused rescue efforts on the big banks, letting hundreds of the smaller, local, and regional banks that are disproportionately engaged in such lending to be shut down. Still, the American economy was not doing well, and especially not if one focused on the average citizen. Indeed, as this book goes to press, some eight years after the breaking of the bubble and the start of the Great Recession, almost seven years after the collapse of Lehman Brothers, median incomes are still below the level attained a quarter-century ago.

"The Book of Jobs" was written to explain what was going on. The basic insight comes from history, looking at the Great Depression and seeing the parallel between what happened then and what is happening now. Increases in productivity in agriculture had contributed to a dramatic fall in incomes in agriculture—down 50 percent and more. These farmers couldn't afford to buy goods made in the cities, and so incomes there declined as well. And farmers with declining income were locked into their farms—they couldn't move elsewhere. Interestingly, those in the city who couldn't get jobs were forced to migrate back to farms; and because of mechanization in the more prosperous farming areas, they were forced to migrate to some of the poorer areas.

What was required was a structural transformation of the economy, from agriculture to manufacturing; but markets don't do this well on their own. Those whose houses had plummeted in value didn't even have the money to move into the cities. Government assistance was required—and it *finally* came, with World War II: we needed to move people to the cities to make the armaments and other things necessary to win the war. And then after the war, we provided everyone who had fought in the war—which was essentially every young man—a free college education, equipping him for the "new economy" that was then emerging.

The article argues that underlying the economy's malaise today are similar events: a growth of productivity in manufacturing that has outpaced growth in demand, so that global employment in manufacturing is declining; changes in comparative advantage and globalization—which we pushed—which imply that the United States will have a smaller share of this declining employment. Like the people then, we are the victims of our own success. And again as then, the markets on their own don't do well in such structural transformations. But things are even worse now: the new sectors that should be growing are service sectors, like health and education, in which government's role is essential. But government, rather than stepping up to help in this transformation, is actually stepping back.

If this analysis is correct, it suggests a bleak future. And in the years since I wrote this article, the predictions have largely been borne out. The mediocre performance of the U.S. economy is in spite of forces that one might have expected to lead to a strong recovery: a high-tech sector that is the envy of the rest of the world, and a boom in shale gas and oil that has brought down prices of gas to new lows. Though as this book goes to press, it appears that growth is at last returning to the economy—a full eight years after the beginning of the recession in 2007—the growth is still barely robust enough to create employment for the new entrants into the labor force. The unemployment rate is down, but mainly because labor-force participation is down, to a level not seen in almost four decades—millions of Americans have dropped out of the labor force.

But as I explain here and elsewhere, this long-term (or as it has sometimes been called *secular*) stagnation into which the United States seems to be descending is a result not so much of underlying laws of economics as of our policies: the failure of government to facilitate the structural transformation and its failure to do anything about our increasing inequality.

The final chapters of this part pursue the implications of changing technology—and the enigmas it seemingly presents—somewhat further. The first two were written before the onset of the Great

Recession, but when it was already very clear to me that there was something wrong with the way our economy was functioning. In "Scarcity in an Age of Plenty" I asked how it could be in this age of plenty, with all the advances of technology that we constantly trumpet, that so many in America and elsewhere seem to have an increasingly difficult time. The answer, in part, was increasing inequality: the fruits of progress were so unequally shared that, in the United States, those in the middle were actually getting worse off.

At the global level, there were two further problems. Some of the policies in the United States were helping the rich in the richest country in the world, at the *expense* of the poorest in the poorest countries: the subsidies to our farmers took badly needed money that could have been used so much better—to invest in infrastructure or technology or education—and gave it to well-off farmers, driving down global prices and further impoverishing poor farmers in developing countries.

And some of our corporate welfare policies were enriching our coal and oil companies at the expense of future generations. We were subsidizing these polluters, which were worsening climate change, again with money that could so much better have been used in other ways. But even worse, it was distorting innovation. Our innovations were directed too much at saving labor—in a world in which there was an abundance of workers relative to jobs—and too little at saving our environment.

Success at improving our standards of living over the long run will depend on growth—the right kind of growth, which means shared prosperity that protects the environment. In "Turn Left for Growth" I explain how this kind of growth can be achieved, why unfettered markets won't on their own create that kind of growth, and what government can do. The crisis showed, to the contrary, that markets are not even efficient or stable. Even when interest rates were very low, the money—and innovation—didn't go to creating well-paying jobs and increasing productivity in key sectors of the economy. It went to building shoddy homes in the middle of the Nevada desert and into speculation. Innovation was directed at creating new financial products that increased risks rather than managing them better. The article presents the outlines of a comprehensive growth agenda—far more promising than the instability and stagnation that we have experienced in recent decades.

In "The Innovation Enigma" I ask, How is it that we claim to be an innovation economy, and yet this innovation doesn't show up in the macroeconomic data, for instance, in GDP per capita? I suggest it is partly because our GDP statistics do not really capture what is going on in our economy (the major theme of the International Commission on the Measurement of Economic Performance and Social Progress, which I chaired).[1] But it is also partly because there has been some hype around innovation. It is important to be able to target advertising more efficiently, as Google and Facebook do, but are these innovations at all comparable to the development of electricity, the computer, the laser, or the transistor?

The flip side of innovation, however, is real: if productivity increases faster than demand, jobs and incomes will decline. This is what happened in the Great Depression. Some 70 percent of the labor force used to be required to produce the food we needed to survive. Now less than 3 percent can produce more than even an obese society can consume. It is not automatic that those who lose their jobs can find jobs elsewhere. Techno-optimists cite the automobile: jobs were lost making buggy whips, but far more jobs were created repairing and making cars. But there is nothing inevitable about this. And the new jobs won't be created if aggregate demand is weak, as it is now.

Note

1. Report available as *Mismeasuring Our Lives: Why GDP Doesn't Add Up*, with Jean-Paul Fitoussi and Amartya Sen (New York: New Press, 2010). For a short discussion, see my column "Towards a Better Measure of Well-Being," *Financial Times*, September 13, 2009.

HOW TO PUT AMERICA
BACK TO WORK[*]

THE COUNTRY IS—OR SHOULD BE—FOCUSED ON JOBS.
Some 25 million Americans who want a full-time job can't get
one. The youth unemployment rate is as much as twice that of the
already unacceptable national average.

America has always thought of itself as a land of opportunity—
but where is the opportunity for our youngsters who face such bleak
prospects? Historically, those who lost their job quickly got another,
but an increasingly large fraction of the unemployed—now more
than 40 percent—have been out of work for more than six months.

President Barack Obama will deliver an address Thursday out-
lining his vision of what can be done. Others should be doing the
same.

Around the country there is growing pessimism. The rhetoric
will be fine. But is there anything that anyone can really do—given
the country's looming debt and deficit?

The answer from economics is: There is plenty we can do to
create jobs and promote growth.

There are policies that can do this and, over the intermediate to
long term, lower the ratio of debt to gross domestic product. There

* *Politico*, September 7, 2011.

are even things that, if less effective in creating jobs, could also pro-tect the deficit in the short run.

But whether politics allows us to do what we can—and should—do is another matter.

The pessimism is understandable. Monetary policy, one of the main instruments for managing the macroeconomy, has proved ineffective—and will likely continue to be. It's a delusion to think it can get us out of the mess it helped create. We need to admit it to ourselves.

Meanwhile, the large deficits and national debt apparently pre-clude the use of fiscal policy. Or so it is claimed. And there is no consensus on which fiscal policy might work.

Are we doomed to an extended period of Japanese-style malaise—until the excess leverage and real capacity works its way out? The answer, I have suggested, is a resounding "no." More accurately: This outcome is not inevitable.

First, we must dispose of two myths. One is that reducing the deficit will restore the economy. You don't create jobs and growth by firing workers and cutting spending. The reason that firms with access to capital are not investing and hiring is that there is insuf-ficient demand for their products. Weakening demand—which is what austerity means—only discourages investment and hiring.

As Paul Krugman emphasizes, there is no "confidence fairy" that magically inspires investors once they see the deficit go down. We've tried that experiment—over and over. Using the austerity for-mula, President Herbert Hoover converted the stock market crash into the Great Depression. I saw firsthand how the International Monetary Fund's imposed austerity on East Asian countries con-verted downturns into recessions and recessions into depressions.

I don't understand why, with such strong evidence, any country would impose this on itself. Even the IMF now recognizes you need fiscal support.

The second myth is that the stimulus didn't work. The purported evidence for this belief is simple: Unemployment peaked at 10 percent—and is still more than 9 percent. (More accurate measures put the number far higher.) The administration had announced, however, that with the stimulus, it would reach only 8 percent.

The administration did make one big error, which I pointed out in my book *Freefall*—it vastly underestimated the severity of the crisis it inherited.

Without the stimulus, however, unemployment would have peaked at more than 12 percent. There is no doubt that the stimulus could have been better designed. But it did bring unemployment down significantly from what it otherwise would have been. The stimulus worked. It was just not big enough, and it didn't last long enough: The administration underestimated the crisis's durability as well as its depth.

Thinking about the deficit, we need to reflect back 10 years, when the country had such a large surplus at 2 percent of GDP that the Federal Reserve Bank chairman worried we would soon pay off the entire national debt—making the conduct of monetary policy difficult. Knowing how we went from that situation to this one helps us think through how to solve the deficit problem.

There have been four major changes: First, tax cuts beyond the country's ability to afford. Second, two costly wars and soaring military expenditures—contributing roughly $2.5 trillion to our debt. Third, Medicare Part D—and the provision restricting government, the largest drug buyer, from negotiating with pharmaceutical companies, at a cost of hundreds of billions of dollars over 10 years. Fourth, the recession.

Reversing these four policies would quickly put the country on the road of fiscal responsibility. The single most important thing, however, is putting America back to work: Higher incomes mean higher tax revenues.

But how do we get America back to work now? The best way is to use this opportunity—with remarkably low long-term interest rates—to make long-term investments that America so badly needs in infrastructure, technology and education.

We should focus on public investments that both yield high returns and are labor intensive. These complement private investments—they increase private returns and so simultaneously encourage the private sector.

Helping states pay for education would also quickly save thousands of jobs. It makes no sense for a rich country, which recognizes education's importance, to be laying off teachers—especially when global competition is so fierce. Countries with a better-educated labor force will do better. Moreover, education and job training are essential if we are to restructure our economy for the 21st century.

The advantage of having underinvested in the public sector for so long is that we have many high-return opportunities. The increased output in the short run and increased growth in the long run can generate more than enough tax revenues to pay the low interest on the debt. The result is that our debt will decrease, our GDP will increase, and the debt-to-GDP ratio will improve.

No analyst would ever look at just a firm's debt—he would examine both sides of the balance sheet, assets and liabilities. What I am urging is that we do the same for the U.S. government—and get over deficit fetishism.

If we can't, there is another, not as powerful but still very effective, way of creating jobs. Economists have long seen that simultaneously increasing expenditures and taxes in a balanced way increases GDP. The amount that GDP is increased for every dollar of increased taxes and spending is called the "balanced-budget multiplier."

With well-designed tax increases—focused on upper-income Americans, corporations that aren't investing in America, or closing tax loopholes—and smart expenditure programs that are focused on investments, the multiplier is between 2 and 3.

This means asking the upper 1 percent of our country, who now garner some 25 percent of all U.S. income, to pay a little more in taxes—or just pay their fair share. Investing this could have a significant effect on output and employment. And because the economy would grow more in the future, again, the debt-to-GDP ratio would come down.

There are some taxes that could actually improve the efficiency of the economy and the quality of life, with an even bigger effect on national output, if we correctly measure output. I chaired an International Commission on the Measurement of Economic Performance and Social Progress, which identified large flaws in our current system of measurement.

There is a basic principle in economics: It is better to tax bad things that generate negative externalities than good things. The implication is that we should tax pollution or destabilizing financial transactions. There are also other ways of raising revenues—better auctions of our country's natural resources, for example.

If, for some reason, such revenue enhancements are ruled out—and there is no good economic reason why they should be—there is still room to maneuver. The government can change the design of tax and expenditure programs—even within the current budget envelope.

Increasing taxes at the top, for example, and lowering taxes at the bottom will lead to more consumption spending. Increasing taxes on corporations that don't invest in America and lowering them on those that do would encourage more investment. The multiplier—the amount GDP increases per dollar spent—for spending on foreign wars, for example, is far lower than for spending on education, so shifting money here stimulates the economy.

There are things we can do beyond the budget. The government should have some influence over the banks, particularly given the enormous debt they owe us for their rescue. Carrots and sticks can encourage more lending to small and medium-size businesses and to restructure more mortgages. It is inexcusable that we have done so little to help homeowners, and as long as the foreclosures continue apace, the real estate market will continue to be weak.

The banks' anticompetitive credit card practices also essentially impose a tax on every transaction—but it is a tax with revenues that go to fill the banks' coffers, not for any public purpose—including lowering the national debt. Stronger enforcement of antitrust laws against the banks would also be a boon to many small businesses.

In short, we are not out of ammunition. Our predicament is not a matter of economics. Theory and experience show that our arsenal is still strong. Of course, the deficit and debt do limit what we can do. But even within these confines, we can create jobs and expand the economy—and simultaneously bring down the debt-to-GDP ratio.

It is simply a matter of politics whether we choose to take the steps we need to take to restore our economy to prosperity.

INEQUALITY IS HOLDING BACK THE RECOVERY*

THE REELECTION OF PRESIDENT OBAMA WAS LIKE A ROR-
schach test, subject to many interpretations. In this election,
each side debated issues that deeply worry me: the long malaise into
which the economy seems to be settling, and the growing divide
between the 1 percent and the rest—an inequality not only of outcomes but also of opportunity. To me, these problems are two sides
of the same coin: with inequality at its highest level since before
the Depression, a robust recovery will be difficult in the short term,
and the American dream—a good life in exchange for hard work—
is slowly dying.

   Politicians typically talk about rising inequality and the sluggish
recovery as separate phenomena, when they are in fact intertwined.
Inequality stifles, restrains, and holds back our growth. When even
the free-market-oriented magazine *The Economist* argues—as it did
in a special feature in October—that the magnitude and nature
of the country's inequality represent a serious threat to America,
we should know that something has gone horribly wrong. And yet,
after four decades of widening inequality and the greatest economic
downturn since the Depression, we haven't done anything about it.

*   *New York Times*, January 19, 2013.

There are four major reasons inequality is squelching our recovery. The most immediate is that our middle class is too weak to support the consumer spending that has historically driven our economic growth. While the top 1 percent of income earners took home 93 percent of the growth in incomes in 2010, the households in the middle—who are most likely to spend their incomes rather than save them and who are, in a sense, the true job creators—have lower household incomes, adjusted for inflation, than they did in 1996. The growth in the decade before the crisis was unsustainable—it was reliant on the bottom 80 percent consuming about 110 percent of their income.

Second, the hollowing out of the middle class since the 1970s, a phenomenon interrupted only briefly in the 1990s, means that they are unable to invest in their future, by educating themselves and their children and by starting or improving businesses.

Third, the weakness of the middle class is holding back tax receipts, especially because those at the top are so adroit in avoiding taxes and in getting Washington to give them tax breaks. The recent modest agreement to restore Clinton-level marginal income-tax rates for individuals making more than $400,000 and households making more than $450,000 did nothing to change this. Returns from Wall Street speculation are taxed at a far lower rate than other forms of income. Low tax receipts mean that the government cannot make the vital investments in infrastructure, education, research, and health that are crucial for restoring long-term economic strength.

Fourth, inequality is associated with more frequent and more severe boom-and-bust cycles that make our economy more volatile and vulnerable. Though inequality did not directly cause the crisis, it is no coincidence that the 1920s—the last time inequality of income and wealth in the United States was so high—ended with the Great Crash and the Depression. The International Monetary Fund has noted the systematic relationship between economic instability and economic inequality, but American leaders haven't absorbed the lesson.

Our skyrocketing inequality—so contrary to our meritocratic ideal of America as a place where anyone with hard work and talent can "make it"—means that those who are born to parents of limited means are likely never to live up to their potential. Children in other rich countries like Canada, France, Germany, and Sweden have a better chance of doing better than their parents did than American kids have. More than a fifth of our children live in poverty—the second worst of all the advanced economies, putting us behind countries like Bulgaria, Latvia, and Greece.

Our society is squandering its most valuable resource: our young. The dream of a better life that attracted immigrants to our shores is being crushed by an ever-widening chasm of income and wealth. Tocqueville, who in the 1830s found the egalitarian impulse to be the essence of the American character, is rolling in his grave.

Even were we able to ignore the economic imperative of fixing our inequality problem, the damage it is doing to our social fabric and political life should prompt us to worry. Economic inequality leads to political inequality and a broken decision-making process.

Despite Mr. Obama's stated commitment to helping all Americans, the recession and the lingering effects of the way it was handled have made matters much, much worse. While bailout money poured into the banks in 2009, unemployment soared to 10 percent that October. The rate today (7.8 percent) appears better partly because so many people have dropped out of the labor force, or never entered it, or accepted part-time jobs because there was no full-time job for them.

High unemployment, of course, depresses wages. Adjusted for inflation, real wages have stagnated or fallen: a typical male worker's income in 2011 ($32,986) was lower than it was in 1968 ($33,880). Lower tax receipts, in turn, have forced state and local cutbacks in services vital to those at the bottom and middle.

Most Americans' most important asset is their home, and as home prices have plummeted, so has household wealth—especially since so many had borrowed so much on their homes. Large numbers are left with negative net worth, and median household wealth fell nearly 40 percent, to $77,300 in 2010 from $126,400 in 2007, and has rebounded only slightly. Since the Great Recession, most of the increase in the nation's wealth has gone to the very top.

Meanwhile, as incomes have stagnated or fallen, tuition has soared. In the United States now, the principal way to get education—the only sure way to move up—is to borrow. In 2010, student debt, now $1 trillion, exceeded credit card debt for the first time.

Student debt can almost never be wiped out, even in bankruptcy. A parent who co-signs a loan can't necessarily have the debt discharged even if his child dies. The debt can't be discharged even if the school—operated for profit and owned by exploitative financiers—provided an inadequate education, enticed the student with misleading promises, and failed to get her a decent job.

Instead of pouring money into the banks, we could have tried rebuilding the economy from the bottom up. We could have enabled homeowners who were "underwater"—those who owe more money on their homes than the homes are worth—to get a fresh start, by writing down principal, in exchange for giving banks a share of the gains if and when home prices recovered.

We could have recognized that when young people are jobless, their skills atrophy. We could have made sure that every young person was either in school, in a training program, or on a job. Instead, we let youth unemployment rise to twice the national average. The children of the rich can stay in college or attend graduate school, without accumulating enormous debt, or take unpaid internships to beef up their résumés. Not so for those in the middle and bottom. We are sowing the seeds of ever more inequality in the coming years.

The Obama administration does not, of course, bear the sole blame. President George W. Bush's steep tax cuts in 2001 and 2003 and his multitrillion-dollar wars in Iraq and Afghanistan emptied the piggy bank while exacerbating the great divide. His party's new-found commitment to fiscal discipline—in the form of insisting on low taxes for the rich while slashing services for the poor—is the height of hypocrisy.

There are all kinds of excuses for inequality. Some say it's beyond our control, pointing to market forces like globalization, trade liberalization, the technological revolution, the "rise of the rest." Others assert that doing anything about it would make us all worse off, by stifling our already sputtering economic engine. These are self-serving, ignorant falsehoods.

Market forces don't exist in a vacuum—we shape them. Other countries, like fast-growing Brazil, have shaped them in ways that have lowered inequality while creating more opportunity and higher growth. Countries far poorer than ours have decided that all young people should have access to food, education, and health care so they can fulfill their aspirations.

Our legal framework and the way we enforce it has provided more scope here for abuses by the financial sector; for perverse compensation for chief executives; for monopolies' ability to take unjust advantage of their concentrated power.

Yes, the market values some skills more highly than others, and those who have those skills will do well. Yes, globalization and technological advances have led to the loss of good manufacturing jobs, which are not likely ever to come back. Global manufacturing employment is shrinking. simply because of enormous increases in productivity, and America is likely to get a shrinking share of the shrinking number of new jobs. If we do succeed in "saving" these jobs, it may be only by converting higher-paid jobs to lower-paid ones—hardly a long-term strategy.

Globalization, and the unbalanced way it has been pursued, has shifted bargaining power away from workers: firms can threaten to move elsewhere, especially when tax laws treat such overseas investments so favorably. This in turn has weakened unions, and though unions have sometimes been a source of rigidity, the countries that responded most effectively to the global financial crisis, like Germany and Sweden, have strong unions and strong systems of social protection.

As Mr. Obama's second term begins, we must all face the fact that our country cannot quickly, meaningfully recover without policies that directly address inequality. What's needed is a comprehensive response that should include, at least, significant investments in education, a more progressive tax system, and a tax on financial speculation.

The good news is that our thinking has been reframed: it used to be that we asked how much growth we would be willing to sacrifice for a little more equality and opportunity. Now we realize that we are paying a high price for our inequality and that alleviating it and promoting growth are intertwined, complementary goals. It will be up to all of us—our leaders included—to muster the courage and foresight to finally treat this beleaguering malady.

THE BOOK OF JOBS*

I T HAS NOW BEEN ALMOST FIVE YEARS SINCE THE
bursting of the housing bubble, and four years since the onset of
the recession. There are 6.6 million fewer jobs in the United States
than there were four years ago. Some 23 million Americans who
would like to work full-time cannot get a job. Almost half of those
who are unemployed have been unemployed long-term. Wages are
falling—the real income of a typical American household is now
below the level it was in 1997.

We knew the crisis was serious back in 2008. And we thought
we knew who the "bad guys" were—the nation's big banks, which
through cynical lending and reckless gambling had brought the
U.S. to the brink of ruin. The Bush and Obama administrations
justified a bailout on the grounds that only if the banks were
handed money without limit—and without conditions—could the
economy recover. We did this not because we loved the banks but
because (we were told) we couldn't do without the lending that they
made possible. Many, especially in the financial sector, argued that
strong, resolute, and generous action to save not just the banks but
the bankers, their shareholders, and their creditors would return

---

* *Vanity Fair*, January 2012.

the economy to where it had been before the crisis. In the meantime, a short-term stimulus, moderate in size, would suffice to tide the economy over until the banks could be restored to health.

The banks got their bailout. Some of the money went to bonuses. Little of it went to lending. And the economy didn't really recover—output is barely greater than it was before the crisis, and the job situation is bleak. The diagnosis of our condition and the prescription that followed from it were incorrect. First, it was wrong to think that the bankers would mend their ways—that they would start to lend, if only they were treated nicely enough. We were told, in effect: "Don't put conditions on the banks to require them to restructure the mortgages or to behave more honestly in their foreclosures. Don't force them to use the money to lend. Such conditions will upset our delicate markets." In the end, bank managers looked out for themselves and did what they are accustomed to doing.

Even when we fully repair the banking system, we'll still be in deep trouble—because we were already in deep trouble. That seeming golden age of 2007 was far from a paradise. Yes, America had many things about which it could be proud. Companies in the information-technology field were at the leading edge of a revolution. But incomes for most working Americans still hadn't returned to their levels prior to the previous recession. The American standard of living was sustained only by rising debt—debt so large that the U.S. savings rate had dropped to near zero. And "zero" doesn't really tell the story. Because the rich have always been able to save a significant percentage of their income, putting them in the positive column, an average rate of close to zero means that everyone else must be in negative numbers. (Here's the reality: in the years leading up to the recession, according to research done by my Columbia University colleague Bruce Greenwald, the bottom 80 percent of the American population had been spending around 110 percent of its income.) What made this level of indebtedness possible was the housing bubble, which Alan Greenspan and then Ben Bernanke, chairmen of the Federal Reserve Board, helped to engineer through low interest rates and nonregulation—

not even using the regulatory tools they had. As we now know, this enabled banks to lend and households to borrow on the basis of assets whose value was determined in part by mass delusion.

The fact is the economy in the years before the current crisis was fundamentally weak, with the bubble, and the unsustainable consumption to which it gave rise, acting as life support. Without these, unemployment would have been high. It was absurd to think that fixing the banking system could by itself restore the economy to health. Bringing the economy back to "where it was" does nothing to address the underlying problems.

The trauma we're experiencing right now resembles the trauma we experienced 80 years ago, during the Great Depression, and it has been brought on by an analogous set of circumstances. Then, as now, we faced a breakdown of the banking system. But then, as now, the breakdown of the banking system was in part a consequence of deeper problems. Even if we correctly respond to the trauma—the failures of the financial sector—it will take a decade or more to achieve full recovery. Under the best of conditions, we will endure a Long Slump. If we respond incorrectly, as we have been, the Long Slump will last even longer, and the parallel with the Depression will take on a tragic new dimension.

Until now, the Depression was the last time in American history that unemployment exceeded 8 percent four years after the onset of recession. And never in the last 60 years has economic output been barely greater, four years after a recession, than it was before the recession started. The percentage of the civilian population at work has fallen by twice as much as in any post–World War II downturn. Not surprisingly, economists have begun to reflect on the similarities and differences between our Long Slump and the Great Depression. Extracting the right lessons is not easy.

MANY HAVE ARGUED that the Depression was caused primarily by excessive tightening of the money supply on the part of the Federal Reserve Board. Ben Bernanke, a scholar of the Depression, has stated publicly that this was the lesson he took away, and the reason he opened the monetary spigots. He opened them very wide. Beginning in 2008, the balance sheet of the Fed doubled and then rose to three times its earlier level. Today it is $2.8 trillion. While the Fed, by doing this, may have succeeded in saving the banks, it didn't succeed in saving the economy.

Reality has not only discredited the Fed but also raised questions about one of the conventional interpretations of the origins of the Depression. The argument has been made that the Fed *caused* the Depression by tightening money, and if only the Fed back then had increased the money supply—in other words, had done what the Fed has done today—a full-blown Depression would likely have been averted. In economics, it's difficult to test hypotheses with controlled experiments of the kind the hard sciences can conduct. But the inability of the monetary expansion to counteract this current recession should forever lay to rest the idea that monetary policy was the prime culprit in the 1930s. The problem today, as it was then, is something else. The problem today is the so-called real economy. It's a problem rooted in the kinds of jobs we have, the kind we need, and the kind we're losing, and rooted as well in the kind of workers we want and the kind we don't know what to do with. The real economy has been in a state of wrenching transition for decades, and its dislocations have never been squarely faced. A crisis of the real economy lies behind the Long Slump, just as it lay behind the Great Depression.

For the past several years, Bruce Greenwald and I have been engaged in research on an alternative theory of the Depression— and an alternative analysis of what is ailing the economy today. This explanation sees the financial crisis of the 1930s as a consequence not so much of a financial implosion but of the economy's underlying weakness. The breakdown of the banking system didn't culminate until 1933, long after the Depression began and long after unemployment had started to soar. By 1931 unemployment was already around 16 percent, and it reached 23 percent in 1932. Shantytown "Hoovervilles" were springing up everywhere. The underlying cause was a structural change in the real economy: the widespread decline in agricultural prices and incomes, caused by what is ordinarily a "good thing"—greater productivity.

AT THE BEGINNING of the Depression, more than a fifth of all Americans worked on farms. Between 1929 and 1932, these people saw their incomes cut by somewhere between one-third and two-thirds, compounding problems that farmers had faced for years. Agriculture had been a victim of its own success. In 1900, it took a large portion of the U.S. population to produce enough food for the country as a whole. Then came a revolution in agriculture that would gain pace throughout the century—better seeds, better fertilizer, better farming practices, along with widespread mechanization. Today, 2 percent of Americans produce more food than we can consume.

What this transition meant, however, is that jobs and livelihoods on the farm were being destroyed. Because of accelerating productivity, output was increasing faster than demand, and prices fell sharply. It was this, more than anything else, that led to rapidly declining incomes. Farmers then (like workers now) borrowed heavily to sustain living standards and production. Because neither the farmers nor their bankers anticipated the steepness of the price declines, a credit crunch quickly ensued. Farmers simply couldn't pay back what they owed. The financial sector was swept into the vortex of declining farm incomes.

The cities weren't spared—far from it. As rural incomes fell, farmers had less and less money to buy goods produced in factories. Manufacturers had to lay off workers, which further diminished demand for agricultural produce, driving down prices even more. Before long, this vicious circle affected the entire national economy.

The value of assets (such as homes) often declines when incomes do. Farmers got trapped in their declining sector and in their depressed locales. Diminished income and wealth made migration to the cities more difficult; high urban unemployment made migration less attractive. Throughout the 1930s, in spite of the massive drop in farm income, there was little overall out-migration. Meanwhile, the farmers continued to produce, sometimes working even harder to make up for lower prices. Individually, that made sense; collectively, it didn't, as any increased output kept forcing prices down.

Given the magnitude of the decline in farm income, it's no wonder that the New Deal itself could not bring the country out of crisis. The programs were too small, and many were soon abandoned. By 1937, FDR, giving way to the deficit hawks, had cut back on stimulus efforts—a disastrous error. Meanwhile, hard-pressed states and localities were being forced to let employees go, just as they are now. The banking crisis undoubtedly compounded all these problems, and extended and deepened the downturn. But any analysis of financial disruption has to begin with what set off the chain reaction.

The Agriculture Adjustment Act, FDR's farm program, which was designed to raise prices by cutting back on production, may have eased the situation somewhat, at the margins. But it was not until government spending soared in preparation for global war that America started to emerge from the Depression. It is important to grasp this simple truth: it was government spending—a Keynesian stimulus, not any correction of monetary policy or any revival of the banking system—that brought about recovery. The long-run prospects for the economy would, of course, have been even better if more of the money had been spent on investments in education, technology, and infrastructure rather than munitions, but even so, the strong public spending more than offset the weaknesses in private spending.

Government spending unintentionally solved the economy's underlying problem: it completed a necessary structural transformation, moving America, and especially the South, decisively from agriculture to manufacturing. Americans tend to be allergic to terms like "industrial policy," but that's what war spending was—a policy that permanently changed the nature of the economy. Massive job creation in the urban sector—in manufacturing—succeeded in moving people out of farming. The supply of food and the demand for it came into balance again- farm prices started to rise. The new migrants to the cities got training in urban life and factory skills, and after the war the GI Bill ensured that returning veterans would be equipped to thrive in a modern industrial society. Meanwhile, the vast pool of labor trapped on farms had all but disappeared. The process had been long and very painful, but the source of economic distress was gone.

THE PARALLELS BETWEEN the story of the origin of the Great Depression and that of our Long Slump are strong. Back then we were moving from agriculture to manufacturing. Today we are moving from manufacturing to a service economy. The decline in manufacturing jobs has been dramatic—from about a third of the workforce 60 years ago to less than a tenth of it today. The pace has quickened markedly during the past decade. There are two reasons for the decline. One is greater productivity—the same dynamic that revolutionized agriculture and forced a majority of American farmers to look for work elsewhere. The other is globalization, which has sent millions of jobs overseas, to low-wage countries or those that have been investing more in infrastructure or technology. (As Greenwald has pointed out, most of the job loss in the 1990s was related to productivity increases, not to globalization.) Whatever the specific cause, the inevitable result is precisely the same as it was 80 years ago: a decline in income and jobs. The millions of jobless former factory workers once employed in cities such as Youngstown and Birmingham and Gary and Detroit are the modern-day equivalent of the Depression's doomed farmers.

The consequences for consumer spending, and for the fundamental health of the economy—not to mention the appalling human cost—are obvious, though we were able to ignore them for a while. For a time, the bubbles in the housing and lending markets concealed the problem by creating artificial demand, which in turn created jobs in the financial sector and in construction and elsewhere. The bubble even made workers forget that their incomes were declining. They savored the possibility of wealth beyond their dreams, as the value of their houses soared and the value of their pensions, invested in the stock market, seemed to be doing likewise. But the jobs were temporary, fueled on vapor.

Mainstream macroeconomists argue that the true bogeyman in a downturn is not falling wages but rigid wages—if only wages were more flexible (that is, lower), downturns would correct themselves! But this wasn't true during the Depression, and it isn't true now. On the contrary, lower wages and incomes would simply reduce demand, weakening the economy further.

Of four major service sectors—finance, real estate, health, and education—the first two were bloated before the current crisis set in. The other two, health and education, have traditionally received heavy government support. But government austerity at every level—that is, the slashing of budgets in the face of recession—has hit education especially hard, just as it has decimated the government sector as a whole. Nearly 700,000 state- and local-government jobs have disappeared during the past four years, mirroring what happened in the Depression. As in 1937, deficit hawks today call for balanced budgets and more and more cutbacks. Instead of pushing forward a structural transition that is inevitable—instead of investing in the right kinds of human capital, technology, and infrastructure, which will eventually pull us where we need to be—the government is holding back. Current strategies can have only one outcome: they will ensure that the Long Slump will be longer and deeper than it ever needed to be.

Two conclusions can be drawn from this brief history. The first is that the economy will not bounce back on its own, at least not in a time frame that matters to ordinary people. Yes, all those foreclosed homes will eventually find someone to live in them, or be torn down. Prices will at some point stabilize and even start to rise. Americans will also adjust to a lower standard of living—not just living within their means but living *beneath* their means as they struggle to pay off a mountain of debt. But the damage will be enormous. America's conception of itself as a land of opportunity is already badly eroded. Unemployed young people are alienated. It will be harder and harder to get some large proportion of them onto a productive track. They will be scarred for life by what is happening today. Drive through the industrial river valleys of the Midwest or the small towns of the Plains or the factory hubs of the South, and you will see a picture of irreversible decay.

Monetary policy is not going to help us out of this mess. Ben Bernanke has, belatedly, admitted as much. The Fed played an important role in creating the current conditions—by encouraging the bubble that led to unsustainable consumption—but there is now little it can do to mitigate the consequences. I can understand that its members may feel some degree of guilt. But anyone who believes that monetary policy is going to resuscitate the economy will be sorely disappointed. That idea is a distraction, and a dangerous one.

What we need to do instead is embark on a massive investment program—as we did, virtually by accident, 80 years ago—that will increase our productivity for years to come, and will also increase employment now. This public investment, and the resultant restoration in GDP, increases the returns to private investment. Public investments could be directed at improving the quality of life and *real* productivity—unlike the private-sector investments in financial innovations, which turned out to be more akin to financial weapons of mass destruction.

Can we actually bring ourselves to do this, in the absence of mobilization for global war? Maybe not. The good news (in a sense) is that the United States has underinvested in infrastructure, technology, and education for decades, so the return on additional investment is high, while the cost of capital is at an unprecedented low. If we borrow today to finance high-return investments, our debt-to-GDP ratio—the usual measure of debt sustainability—will be markedly improved. If we simultaneously increased taxes—for instance, on the top 1 percent of all households, measured by income—our debt sustainability would be improved even more.

The private sector by itself won't, and can't, undertake structural transformation of the magnitude needed—even if the Fed were to keep interest rates at zero for years to come. The only way it will happen is through a government stimulus designed not to preserve the old economy but to focus instead on creating a new one. We have to transition out of manufacturing and into services that people want—into productive activities that increase living standards, not those that increase risk and inequality. To that end, there are many high-return investments we can make. Education is a crucial one—a highly educated population is a fundamental driver of economic growth. Support is needed for basic research. Government investment in earlier decades—for instance, to develop the Internet and biotechnology—helped fuel economic growth. Without investment in basic research, what will fuel the next spurt of innovation? Meanwhile, the states could certainly use federal help in closing budget shortfalls. Long-term economic growth at our current rates of resource consumption is impossible, so funding research, skilled technicians, and initiatives for cleaner and more efficient energy production will not only help us out of the recession but also build a robust economy for decades. Finally, our decaying infrastructure, from roads and railroads to levees and power plants, is a prime target for profitable investment.

The second conclusion is this: If we expect to maintain any semblance of "normality," we must fix the financial system. As noted, the implosion of the financial sector may not have been the underlying cause of our current crisis—but it has made it worse, and it's an obstacle to long-term recovery. Small and medium-size companies, especially new ones, are disproportionately the source of job creation in any economy, and they have been especially hard-hit. What's needed is to get banks out of the dangerous business of speculating and back into the boring business of lending. But we have not fixed the financial system. Rather, we have poured money into the banks, without restrictions, without conditions, and without a vision of the kind of banking system we want and need. We have, in a phrase, confused ends with means. A banking system is supposed to serve society, not the other way around.

That we should tolerate such a confusion of ends and means says something deeply disturbing about where our economy and our society have been heading. Americans in general are coming to understand what has happened. Protesters around the country, galvanized by the Occupy Wall Street movement, already know.

SCARCITY IN AN AGE OF PLENTY*

ROUND THE WORLD, PROTESTS AGAINST SOARING FOOD and fuel prices are mounting. The poor—and even the middle classes—are seeing their incomes squeezed as the global economy enters a slowdown. Politicians want to respond to their constituents' legitimate concerns, but do not know what to do.

In the United States, both Hillary Clinton and John McCain took the easy way out, and supported a suspension of the gasoline tax, at least for the summer. Only Barack Obama stood his ground and rejected the proposal, which would have merely increased demand for gasoline—and thereby offset the effect of the tax cut.

But if Clinton and McCain were wrong, what should be done? One cannot simply ignore the pleas of those who are suffering. In the U.S., real middle-class incomes have not yet recovered to the levels attained before the last recession, in 1991.

When George Bush was elected, he claimed that tax cuts for the rich would cure all the economy's ailments. The benefits of tax-cut-fueled growth would trickle down to all—policies that have become fashionable in Europe and elsewhere, but that have failed. Tax cuts were supposed to stimulate savings, but household sav-

* *Project Syndicate*, June 6, 2008.

ings in the U.S. have plummeted to zero. They were supposed to stimulate employment, but labor-force participation is lower than in the 1990s. What growth did occur benefited only the few at the top. Productivity grew, for a while, but it wasn't because of Wall Street financial innovations. The financial products being created didn't manage risk; they enhanced risk. They were so nontransparent and complex that neither Wall Street nor the ratings agencies could properly assess them. Meanwhile, the financial sector failed to create products that would help ordinary people manage the risks they faced, including the risks of homeownership. Millions of Americans will likely lose their homes and, with them, their life savings.

At the core of America's success is technology, symbolized by Silicon Valley. The irony is that the scientists making the advances that enable technology-based growth, and the venture capital firms that finance it were not the ones reaping the biggest rewards in the heyday of the real estate bubble. These real investments are overshadowed by the games that have been absorbing most participants in financial markets.

The world needs to rethink the sources of growth. If the foundations of economic growth lie in advances in science and technology, not in speculation in real estate or financial markets, then tax systems must be realigned. Why should those who make their income by gambling in Wall Street's casinos be taxed at a lower rate than those who earn their money in other ways. Capital gains should be taxed at least at as high a rate as ordinary income. (Such returns will, in any case, get a substantial benefit because the tax is not imposed until the gain is realized.) In addition, there should be a windfall profits tax on oil and gas companies.

Given the huge increase in inequality in most countries, higher taxes for those who have done well—to help those who have lost ground from globalization and technological change—are in order, and could also ameliorate the strains imposed by soaring food and energy prices. Countries, like the U.S., with food stamp programs clearly need to increase the value of these subsidies in order to ensure that nutrition standards do not deteriorate. Those countries without such programs might think about instituting them.

Two factors set off today's crisis: the Iraq war contributed to the run-up in oil prices, including through increased instability in the Middle East, the low-cost provider of oil, while bio-fuels have meant that food and energy markets are increasingly integrated. Although the focus on renewable energy sources is welcome, policies that distort food supply are not. America's subsidies for corn-based ethanol contribute more to the coffers of ethanol producers than they do to curtailing global warming. Huge agriculture subsidies in the U.S. and the European Union have weakened agriculture in the developing world, where too little international assistance was directed at improving agriculture productivity. Development aid for agriculture has fallen from a high of 17 percent of total aid to just 3 percent today, with some international donors demanding that fertilizer subsidies be eliminated, making it even more difficult for cash-strapped farmers to compete.

Rich countries must reduce, if not eliminate, distortional agriculture and energy policies, and help those in the poorest countries improve their capacity to produce food. But this is just a start: we have treated our most precious resources—clean water and air—as if they were free. Only new patterns of consumption and production—a new economic model—can address that most fundamental resource problem.

TURN LEFT FOR GROWTH[*]

BOTH THE LEFT AND THE RIGHT SAY THEY STAND FOR ECO-
nomic growth. So should voters trying to decide between the
two simply look at it as a matter of choosing alternative management teams?

If only matters were so easy! Part of the problem concerns the
role of luck. America's economy was blessed in the 1990s with low
energy prices, a high pace of innovation, and a China increasingly
offering high-quality goods at decreasing prices, all of which combined to produce low inflation and rapid growth.

President Clinton and then-chairman of the U.S. Federal
Reserve Alan Greenspan deserve little credit for this—though, to
be sure, bad policies could have messed things up. By contrast, the
problems faced today—high energy and food prices and a crum-
bling financial system—have, to a large extent, been brought about
by bad policies.

There are, indeed, big differences in growth *strategies,* which
make different outcomes highly likely. The first difference concerns how growth itself is conceived. Growth is not just a matter
of increasing GDP. It must be sustainable: growth based on envi-

---
[*] *Project Syndicate*, August 6, 2008.

ronmental degradation, a debt-financed consumption binge, or the exploitation of scarce natural resources, without reinvesting the proceeds, is not sustainable.

Growth also must be inclusive; at least a majority of citizens must benefit. Trickle-down economics does not work: an increase in GDP can actually leave most citizens worse off. America's recent growth was neither economically sustainable nor inclusive. Most Americans are worse off today than they were seven years ago.

But there need not be a trade-off between inequality and growth. Governments can enhance growth by increasing inclusiveness. A country's most valuable resource is its people. So it is essential to ensure that *everyone* can live up to their potential, which requires educational opportunities for all.

A modern economy also requires risk-taking. Individuals are more willing to take risks if there is a good safety net. If not, citizens may demand protection from foreign competition. Social protection is more efficient than protectionism.

Failures to promote social solidarity can have other costs, not the least of which are the social and private expenditures required to protect property and incarcerate criminals. It is estimated that within a few years, America will have more people working in the security business than in education. A year in prison can cost more than a year at Harvard. The cost of incarcerating two million Americans—one of the highest per capita rates in the world—should be viewed as a subtraction from GDP, yet it is added on.

A second major difference between left and right concerns the role of the state in promoting development. The left understands that the government's role in providing infrastructure and education, developing technology, and even acting as an entrepreneur is vital. Government laid the foundations of the Internet and the modern biotechnology revolutions. In the 19th century, research at America's government-supported universities provided the basis for the agricultural revolution. Government then brought these advances to millions of American farmers. Small business loans have been pivotal in creating not only new businesses, but whole new industries.

The final difference may seem odd: the left now understands markets, and the role that they can and should play in the economy. The right, especially in America, does not. The new right, typified by the Bush-Cheney administration, is really old corporatism in a new guise.

These are not libertarians. They believe in a strong state with robust executive powers, but one used in defense of established interests, with little attention to market principles. The list of examples is long, but it includes subsidies to large corporate farms, tariffs to protect the steel industry, and, most recently, the mega-bailouts of Bear Stearns, Fannie Mae, and Freddie Mac. But the inconsistency between rhetoric and reality is long-standing: protectionism expanded under Reagan, including through the imposition of so-called voluntary export restraints on Japanese cars.

By contrast, the new left is trying to make markets work. Unfettered markets do not operate well on their own—a conclusion reinforced by the current financial debacle. Defenders of markets sometimes admit that they do fail, even disastrously, but they claim that markets are "self-correcting." During the Great Depression, similar arguments were heard: government need not do anything, because markets would restore the economy to full employment *in the long run*. But, as John Maynard Keynes famously put it, in the long run we are all dead.

Markets are not self-correcting in the relevant time frame. No government can sit idly by as a country goes into recession or depression, even when caused by the excessive greed of bankers or misjudgment of risks by security markets and rating agencies. But if governments are going to pay the economy's hospital bills, they must act to make it less likely that hospitalization will be needed. The right's deregulation mantra was simply wrong, and we are now paying the price. And the price tag—in terms of lost output—will be high, perhaps more than $1.5 trillion in the United States alone.

The right often traces its intellectual parentage to Adam Smith, but while Smith recognized the power of markets, he also recognized their limits. Even in his era, businesses found that they could increase profits more easily by conspiring to raise prices than by producing innovative products more efficiently. There is a need for strong antitrust laws.

It is easy to host a party. For the moment, everyone can feel good. Promoting sustainable growth is much harder. Today, in contrast to the right, the left has a coherent agenda, one that offers not only higher growth, but also social justice. For voters, the choice should be easy.

THE INNOVATION ENIGMA*

AROUND THE WORLD, THERE IS ENORMOUS ENTHUSIASM for the type of technological innovation symbolized by Silicon Valley. In this view, America's ingenuity represents its true comparative advantage, which others strive to imitate. But there is a puzzle: it is difficult to detect the benefits of this innovation in GDP statistics.

What is happening today is analogous to developments a few decades ago, early in the era of personal computers. In 1987, the economist Robert Solow—awarded the Nobel Prize for his pioneering work on growth—lamented, "You can see the computer age everywhere but in the productivity statistics." There are several possible explanations for this.

Perhaps GDP does not really capture the improvements in living standards that computer-age innovation is engendering. Or perhaps this innovation is less significant than its enthusiasts believe. As it turns out, there is some truth in both perspectives.

Recall how a few years ago, just before the collapse of Lehman Brothers, the financial sector prided itself on its innovativeness. Given that financial institutions had been attracting the best and

---

*   *Project Syndicate*, March 9, 2014.

brightest from around the world, one would have expected nothing less. But, upon closer inspection, it became clear that most of this innovation involved devising better ways of scamming others, manipulating markets without getting caught (at least for a long time), and exploiting market power.

In this period, when resources flowed to this "innovative" sector, GDP growth was markedly lower than it was before. Even in the best of times, it did not lead to an increase in living standards (except for the bankers), and it eventually led to the crisis from which we are only now recovering. The net social contribution of all of this "innovation" was negative.

Similarly, the dot-com bubble that preceded this period was marked by innovation—Web sites through which one could order dog food and soft drinks online. At least this era left a legacy of efficient search engines and a fiber-optic infrastructure. But it is not an easy matter to assess how the time savings implied by online shopping, or the cost savings that might result from increased competition (owing to greater ease of price comparison online), affects our standard of living.

Two things should be clear. First, the profitability of an innovation may not be a good measure of its net contribution to our standard of living. In our winner-takes-all economy, an innovator who develops a better Web site for online dog-food purchases and deliveries may attract everyone around the world who uses the Internet to order dog food, making enormous profits in the process. But without the delivery service, much of those profits simply would have gone to others. The Web site's net contribution to economic growth may in fact be relatively small.

Moreover, if an innovation, such as ATMs in banking, leads to increased unemployment, none of the social cost—neither the suffering of those who are laid off nor the increased fiscal cost of paying them unemployment benefits—is reflected in firms' profitability. Likewise, our GDP metric does not reflect the cost of the increased insecurity individuals may feel with the increased risk of a loss of a job. Equally important, it often does not accurately reflect the improvement in societal well-being resulting from innovation.

In a simpler world, where innovation simply meant lowering the cost of production of, say, an automobile, it was easy to assess an innovation's value. But when innovation affects an automobile's *quality*, the task becomes far more difficult. And this is even more apparent in other arenas: How do we accurately assess the fact that, owing to medical progress, heart surgery is more likely to be successful now than in the past, leading to a significant increase in life expectancy and quality of life?

Still, one cannot avoid the uneasy feeling that, when all is said and done, the contribution of recent technological innovations to long-term growth in living standards may be substantially less than the enthusiasts claim. A lot of intellectual effort has been devoted to devising better ways of maximizing advertising and marketing budgets—targeting customers, especially the affluent, who might actually buy the product. But standards of living might have been raised even more if all of this innovative talent had been allocated to more fundamental research—or even to more applied research that could have led to new products.

Yes, being better connected with each other, through Facebook or Twitter, is valuable. But how can we compare these innovations with those like the laser, the transistor, the Turing machine, and the mapping of the human genome, each of which has led to a flood of transformative products?

Of course, there are grounds for a sigh of relief. Although we may not know how much recent technological innovations are contributing to our well-being, at least we know that, unlike the wave of financial innovations that marked the precrisis global economy, they have had a positive effect.

AFTERWORD

The final chapter is different from the others. It is an interview conducted by Cullen Murphy, my editor at *Vanity Fair*, in which I respond to one of the claims made by conservatives, that the rich are net job creators. Taking money away from the rich—or even forcing the rich to pay their fair share of taxes—would, in this view, be counterproductive. Ordinary Americans would suffer. This is just a 21st-century version of the old trickle-down economics, attempting to defend societal inequalities.

My view was that trickle-down economics was *totally* wrong. Around the world there is a wealth of creativity, an abundance of entrepreneurship, *if there is adequate demand* (and if certain other preconditions are satisfied, such as access to capital and adequate infrastructure). In this view, the real "job creators" are consumers; and the reason that the American and European economies have not been creating jobs is that stagnant incomes mean stagnant demand. Indeed, as this book goes to press, wages in many European countries are below their level at the start of the crisis; and, as I have repeatedly pointed out, the income of the typical American family is lower than it was a quarter-century ago. No wonder, then, that demand has been stagnant.

The editors of *Vanity Fair* asked me another question, one that I heard frequently as I traveled around the country: To what time do we date that increase in inequality? And to what do we attribute it? The answer I provided corresponds to what other scholars have found: roughly to the beginning of the Reagan administration. While certain actions that President Reagan took almost surely contributed to this growth in inequality—including tax changes that were of enormous benefit to the very rich—one needs to take a broader perspective, as Thomas Piketty does in his book: an increase in inequality in many advanced countries started around the same time. The "reforms" that were part of the zeitgeist of the 1980s had impacts in country after country. These reforms included not only the lowering of top tax rates but also the liberalization of financial markets.

Thus we end the book repeating themes with which we began: our inequality—the extremes to which it has grown, the forms it has taken—is not inevitable; it is not the result of inexorable laws of economics or physics; it is a matter of choice, of our policies; and these in turn are the result of our politics. We have paid a high price for this inequality, a price we have felt most intensely in the past decade, with the making of the crisis and its aftermath. But it's a price we will pay—in increasing amounts—in the future unless we change the policies that have given rise to it.

Q&A:

Joseph Stiglitz on the Fallacy That the Top 1 Percent Drives Innovation, and Why the Reagan Administration Was America's Inequality Turning Point[*]

* *Vanity Fair*, June 5, 2012.

C ULLEN MURPHY: IN YOUR NEW BOOK, *THE PRICE OF Inequality*, you range very widely both historically and geographically. Looking at American history, what period strikes you as most similar to our own in terms of lack of concern for widening inequality?

Joseph Stiglitz: Two periods come to mind: the Gilded Age of the late 19th century and the boom times of the 1920s. Both were marked by high levels of inequality and corruption, including in the political process (such as the notorious Teapot Dome Scandal that marked the beginning of the 1920s). In fact, until the middle part of the last decade, income inequality had never reached the levels of the 20s. Of course, some of those who made their fortunes in both periods made great contributions to our society—the Robber Barons in building the railroads that transformed the country, or James B. Duke, who was instrumental in bringing electricity to parts of America. But both periods were also marked by speculation, instability, and excess.

There are some, like Edward Conard in his book *Unintended Consequences*, who argue that extreme inequality is

**not only not a sign of deep trouble but in fact is something
to be celebrated. You'll have many bones to pick with that
argument. What are the central flaws?**

Conard argues that greater inequality is good because as rich people
accumulate more money, they will invest it and improve the economy. Further, their wealth is proof positive of their contributions to
innovation. As you mention, there are so many problems with this
view it is hard to know where to begin. Let me highlight three.

First, it is based on the notion of "trickle-down economics," the
idea that if those at the top do well, so will the rest of society. But
the evidence is overwhelmingly to the contrary: the real income
(adjusted for inflation) of most Americans today is lower than it was
almost a decade and half ago, in 1997.

Secondly, it is based on the fallacy that inequality is good for
economic growth, but again, the evidence is to the contrary. Time
and again, inequality has been shown to retard economic growth
and promote instability. These are findings based on mainstream
studies. Even the International Monetary Fund, not known for its
radical economic stances, has come to recognize the adverse effects
of inequality on economic performance.

Thirdly, it is not true that the extremely wealthy use their money
to take innovation-driving risks. What we have seen quite clearly is
that a much more common use of wealth is to gain advantage in "rent
seeking." When small groups of people have disproportionate wealth,
they will use their power to seek special treatment from the government. Some of the wealthiest (historically, and even today) have
gained their riches by the exercise of monopoly, preventing others
from competing with them on a level playing field. Such rent-seeking
behavior is a terribly inefficient use of resources: Rent seekers don't
create value. Rather, they use their privileged positions in markets to
capture larger and larger portions of existing value. They distort the
economy, lowering efficiency and economic growth.

The real drivers of growth and innovation are young businesses and small and medium-size businesses, especially in high-tech areas, typically based on government-supported research. Part of America's problem today is that too many of those at the top don't want to contribute their fair share to these "public goods," with many paying taxes that are but a fraction of the rates paid by those who are much less well off. But it shouldn't be a big surprise that some of the wealthiest Americans are promoting an economic fantasy in which their further enrichment is beneficial to everyone.

In the "recovery" of 2009–2010, the top 1 percent of American income earners captured 93 percent of the income growth. I don't think Conard will persuade the nearly 23 million Americans who would like a full-time job but can't get one to find comfort in that.

If you had to locate a fork-in-the-road moment when we started down the path toward widening inequality, when would that moment be? And what were the precipitating events?

It's hard to pinpoint a single critical moment, but clearly the election of President Ronald Reagan represented a turning point. In the decades immediately after World War II, we had economic growth in which most people shared, with those at the bottom doing proportionately better than those at the top. (It was also the period that saw the country's most rapid economic growth.) Among the precipitating events leading to greater inequality were the beginning of the deregulation of the financial sector and the reduction in the progressivity of the tax system. Deregulation led to the excessive financialization of the economy—to the point that, before the crisis, 40 percent of all corporate profits went to the financial sector. And the financial sector has been marked by extremes in compensation at the top, and has made its profits partly by exploiting those at the bottom and middle, with, for instance, predatory lending and abusive credit card practices. Reagan's successors, unfortunately, continued down the path of deregulation. They also extended the policy of lowering taxes at the top, to the point where today, the richest 1 percent of Americans pay only around 15 percent of their income in taxes, far lower than those with more moderate incomes.

Reagan's breaking of the air-traffic controllers' strike is often cited as a critical juncture in the weakening of unions, one of the factors explaining why workers have done so badly in recent decades. But there are other factors as well. Reagan promoted trade liberalization, and some of the growth in inequality is due to globalization and the replacement of semiskilled jobs with new technologies and outsourced labor. Some of the increase in inequality common to both Europe and America can be ascribed to that. But what's different about America is the remarkable growth in incomes of the very top—especially the top 0.1 percent. This is orders of magnitude greater than in most of Europe and comes partly out of Reagan's deregulatory fervor, particularly in finance, partly out of inadequate enforcement of competition laws, partly out of America's greater willingness to take advantage of inadequate corporate governance laws.

Throughout its history, America has struggled with inequality. But with the tax policies and regulations that existed in the postwar period, we were on the right track toward ameliorating some of that. The tax cuts and deregulation that began in the Reagan years reversed the trend. Income disparities before tax and transfers (help that is given to the poor through, for instance, food stamps) is now larger, and because government is doing less for the poor and favoring the rich, inequalities in income, after taxes and transfers, are even larger.

One of the activities you criticize at length is "rent seeking." Do you see rent seeking at play in the J.P. Morgan fiasco?

The huge losses that J.P. Morgan recently reported show that we have not curbed the excesses of the banks; we have not cured the problems that led to the crisis. There is still a lack of transparency, predatory lending, and reckless behavior—with taxpayers still at risk. The failure to reform the financial sector is a clear manifestation of rent seeking. We have continued with a system where we privatize profits and socialize losses; in effect, the banks have been the recipients of massive (often hidden) subsidies.

The financial industry has used its revolving door with the government first to weaken the regulations that constrain them; and even after it was manifestly clear that they were inadequate, to prevent the imposition of adequate new regulations. We have a deficient regulatory structure because of rent seeking. Banks use their muscle to get special treatment, including bailouts. They have seen that if a loss would put them into bankruptcy, the American taxpayer is there for them with cheap financing (direct injections, zero percent interest rates, propping up the mortgage market, paying AIG's obligations, and so on). In that way, they extract rents from the rest of us. These rents are then paid out in dividends to shareholders and "bonuses" to the management. What upset so many Americans was that those who brought their companies to the brink of ruin still received bonuses. And even as the Fed lent the banks money at close to zero percent interest, and they could make easy money by simply buying a long-term government bond, bankers received bonuses as if the profits were a result of their hard work or genius.

In your book you offer a number of policy options that together, over time, would redress the inequality problem. If you could press a button and achieve only one of them, which one would it be and why? If you could press the button once again, what would the second one be?

There is simply no silver bullet, partly because there are so many different parts to America's inequality: the extremes of income and wealth at the top, the hollowing out of the middle, the increase of poverty at the bottom. Each has its own causes, and each needs its own remedies.

What disturbs me most is the fact that America has ceased to be a land of opportunity, with the chances of those at the bottom making it to the middle or top being much lower even than in old

Europe; in fact, it is worse here than in any of the other advanced industrial countries for which there is data. This lack of equality of opportunity translates, over the years, into increasing inequality, and can lead to the creation of an inherited plutocracy. So for me, the single most important action is to ensure a quality education for all. At the same time, improved education would help Americans compete in the increasingly competitive global market.

The policies that I propose in *The Price of Inequality* follow directly from my diagnosis of the sources of inequality: at the top, excessive financialization, abuses of corporate governance that lead CEOs to take a disproportionate share of corporate profits, and rent seeking; in the middle, the weakening of unions; at the bottom, discrimination and exploitation. Creating good financial regulations, better systems of corporate governance, and laws that curb further discrimination and predatory lending practices would all help. So too would campaign-finance and other political reforms that would curb opportunities for rent seeking by those at the top.

These steps would all reduce the extent of inequality in before-tax incomes. But equally important is a reduction in after-tax income inequality. An easy place to start is with taxation itself—the current system taxes capital gains, which can be profits from speculation, at a much lower rate than salaries and wages. Not only is there no good reason for that, such tax policies distort the economy and increase instability. The wealthy should not be paying a smaller proportion of their incomes in taxes than the middle class. This worsens inequality, further distorts our politics, and makes it harder to restore the country's fiscal health. The increased revenues could, furthermore, help finance the needed public investments in infrastructure, education, and research that will get our economy back on track—and, if well designed, would also increase both equality and equality of opportunity.

There must be voices among the 1 percent who make the same arguments you do about why inequality matters and

why the wealthy have a stake in the welfare of everyone. Who are they?

There are many, including George Soros and Warren Buffett. Hundreds have signed on to a petition coordinated by a group called the Patriotic Millionaires to increase taxes on the rich, which can be found at patrioticmillionaires.org. They understand that a house divided cannot stand; they understand that their own long-term well-being, and that of their children, depends on there being a cohesive American society, one that invests adequately in education, infrastructure, and technology. Many of these are individuals who lived the American dream, who did not inherit their fortunes, and who want others to have the same opportunities that they enjoyed. Above all, I suspect that they believe strongly in certain values—exemplified by Buffett's lifestyle—and they worry that in an increasingly divided America those values will become an increasing rarity. As the Patriotic Millionaires wrote in their petition in support of the Buffett rule, "Our country has been good to us. It provided a foundation through which we could succeed. Now, we want to do our part to keep that foundation strong so that others can succeed as we have."

CREDITS

Grateful acknowledgments are made to the *New York Times* for permission to include the following articles: "Inequality Is a Choice"; "How Dr. King Shaped My Work in Economics"; "Equal Opportunity, Our National Myth"; "Student Debt and the Crushing of the American Dream"; "The One Housing Solution Left: Mass Mortgage Refinancing"; "A Tax System Stacked against the 99 Percent"; "The Wrong Lesson from Detroit's Bankruptcy"; "In No One We Trust"; "Why Janet Yellen, Not Larry Summers, Should Lead the Fed"; "The Insanity of Our Food Policy"; "On the Wrong Side of Globalization"; "How Intellectual Property Reinforces Inequality"; "Inequality is Not Inevitable"; "Singapore's Lessons for an Unequal America"; "Japan Is a Model, Not a Cautionary Tale"; "Inequality is Holding Back the Recovery."

Grateful acknowledgments are made to *Project Syndicate* for permission to include the following articles: "Inequality Goes Global," originally published as "Complacency in a Leaderless World"; "Democracy in the 21st Century"; "Justice for Some"; "Inequality and the American Child"; "Ebola and Inequality"; "America's Socialism for the Rich"; "The Free-Trade Charade"; "India's Patently Wise Decision"; "The Postcrisis Crises"; "The Mauritius Miracle"; "China's

Roadmap"; "Reforming China's State-Market Balance"; "A Light Unto Cities"; "American Delusions Down Under"; "Scarcity in an Age of Plenty"; "Turn Left for Growth"; "The Innovation Enigma."

Grateful acknowledgments are made to *Vanity Fair* for permission to include the following articles: "The Economic Consequences of Mr. Bush"; "Capitalist Fools"; "Of the 1 Percent, by the 1 Percent, for the 1 Percent"; "The 1 Percent's Problem"; "The Book of Jobs"; "Q&A: Joseph Stiglitz on the Fallacy That the Top 1 Percent Drives Innovation, and Why the Reagan Administration Was America's Inequality Turning Point."

Further acknowledgments are made to *Critical Review,* for permission to include "The Anatomy of a Murder: Who Killed America's Economy?"; *TIME,* "How to Get Out of the Financial Crisis"; *Washington Monthly,* "Slow Growth and Inequality are Political Choices. We Can Choose Otherwise"; *Harper's,* "Phony Capitalism"; *Politico,* "The Myth of America's Golden Age," "How to Put America Back to Work"; *The Guardian,* "Globalization Isn't Just about Profits. It's about Taxes Too"; *USA Today,* "Fallacies of Romney's Logic"; the *Washington Post,* "How Policy Has Contributed to the Great Economic Divide"; *Ethics and International Affairs,* "Eliminating Extreme Inequality: A Sustainable Development Goal, 2015–2030"; Tokuma Shoten, "Japan Should Be Alert"; *The Herald,* "Scottish Independence"; Taurus Books, "Spain's Depression."

LONG LOST

LONG LOST

David Morrell

headline

Copyright © 2001 David Morrell

The right of David Morrell to be identified as the Author of
the Work has been asserted by him in accordance with the
Copyright, Designs and Patents Act 1988.

First published in Great Britain in 2002
by HEADLINE BOOK PUBLISHING

10 9 8 7 6 5 4 3 2

British Library Cataloguing in Publication Data
is available from the British Library

ISBN 0 7472 6341 8 (hardback)
ISBN 0 7472 7464 9 (trade paperback)

Typeset by
Letterpart Limited, Reigate, Surrey

Printed and bound in Great Britain by
Antony Rowe Ltd, Chippenham, Wiltshire

HEADLINE BOOK PUBLISHING
A division of Hodder Headline
338 Euston Road
LONDON NW1 3BH

www.headline.co.uk
www.hodderheadline.com

To Jeffrey Weiner:
master of accounts.
A long time ago, you made a promise and you kept it.
Thanks for helping keep distractions from my door
and giving me more time to write.

To the legion of the lost ones,
to the cohort of the damned.

Rudyard Kipling

.

Part One

1

When I was a boy, my kid brother disappeared. Vanished off the face of the earth. His name was Petey, and he was bicycling home from an after-school baseball game. Not that he'd been playing. The game was for older guys like me, which is to say that I was all of thirteen and Petey was only nine. He thought the world of me; he always wanted to tag along. But the rest of the guys complained that he was in the way, so I told Petey to 'bug off, go home.' I still remember the hurt look he gave me before he got on his bike and pedaled away. a skinny little kid with a brush cut, glasses, braces on his teeth, and freckles, wearing a droopy T-shirt, baggy jeans, and sneakers – the last I saw of him. That was a quarter of a century ago. Yesterday.

By the time supper was ready and Petey hadn't shown up, my mother phoned his friends in the neighborhood, but they hadn't seen him. Twenty minutes later, my father called the police. His worst fear (until that moment at least) was that Petey had been hit by a car, but the police dispatcher said that there hadn't been any accidents involving a youngster on a bicycle. The dispatcher promised to call back if he heard anything and, meanwhile, to have patrol cars looking for him.

My father couldn't bear waiting. He had me show him the likely route Petey would have taken between the playground and home. We drove this way and that. By then it was dusk, and we almost passed the bicycle before I spotted one of its red reflectors glinting from the last of the sunset. The bike had been shoved between bushes in a vacant lot. Petey's baseball glove was under it. We searched the lot. We shouted Petey's name. We asked people who lived on the street if they'd seen a boy who matched Petey's description. We didn't learn anything. As my father sped back home, the skin on his face got so tight that his cheekbones stood out. He kept murmuring to himself, 'Oh Jesus.'

All I could hope was that Petey had stayed away because he was mad at me for sending him home from the baseball game. I fantasized that he'd show up just before bedtime and say, 'Now aren't you sorry? Maybe you want me around more than you guess.' In fact, I *was* sorry, because I couldn't fool myself into believing that Petey had shoved his bike between those bushes – he loved that bike. Why would he have dropped his baseball glove? Something *bad* had happened to him, but it never would have happened if I hadn't told him to get lost.

My mom became hysterical. My dad called the police again. A detective soon arrived, and the next day, a search was organized. The newspaper (this happened in a town called Woodford, just outside Columbus, Ohio) was filled with the story. My parents went on television and radio, begging whoever had kidnapped Petey to return him. Nothing did any good.

I can't begin to describe the pain and ruin that Petey's disappearance caused. My mother needed pills to steady her nerves. Lots of times in the night, I heard her sobbing. I couldn't stop feeling guilty for making Petey leave the baseball game. Every time I heard our front door creak open, I prayed it was him coming home at last. My father started drinking and lost his job. He and Mom argued. A month after he moved out, he was killed when his car veered off a highway, flipped several times, and crashed onto its roof. There wasn't any life insurance. My mother had to sell the house. We moved to a small apartment and then went to live with my mom's parents in Columbus. I spent a lot of time worrying about how Petey would find us if he returned to the house.

He haunted me. I grew older, finished college, married, had a son, and enjoyed a successful career. But in my mind Petey never aged. He was still that skinny nine-year-old giving me a hurt look, then bicycling away. I never stopped missing him. If a farmer had plowed up the skeleton of a little boy and those remains had somehow been identified as Petey's, I'd have mourned bitterly for my kid brother, but at least there would have been some finality. I needed desperately to know what had happened.

I'm an architect. For a while, I was with a big firm in Philadelphia, but my best designs were too unorthodox for them, so I finally started my own business. I also decided it would be exciting to change locales – not just move to another East Coast city but move from the East Coast altogether. My wife surprised me by liking the idea even more than I did. I won't go into all the reasons we chose Denver – the lure of the mountains, the myth of the West. The main thing is, we settled there, and almost from the start, my designs were in demand.

Two of my office buildings are situated next to city parks. They not only blend with but also reflect their surroundings; their glass and tile walls act like huge mirrors that capture the images of the ponds, trees and grassland near them, one with nature. My houses are what I was especially proud of, though. Many of my clients lived near megadollar resorts like Aspen and Vail, but they respected the mountains and didn't want to be conspicuous. They preferred to be with nature without intruding upon it. I understood. The houses I designed blended so much that you couldn't see them until you were practically at their entrances. Trees and ridges concealed them. Streams flowed under them. Flat stretches of rock were decks. Boulders were steps. Cliffs were walls.

It's ironic that structures designed to be inconspicuous attracted so much attention. My clients, despite their claims about wanting to be invisible, couldn't resist showing off their new homes. *House Beautiful* and *Architectural Digest* did articles about them, although the photographs of the exteriors seemed more like nature shots than pictures of homes. The local CBS TV station taped a two-minute spot for the ten o'clock news. The reporter, dressed as a hiker, challenged her viewers to a game: 'Can you see a house among these ridges and trees?' She was standing ten feet from a wall, but only when she pointed it out did the viewer realize how thoroughly the house was camouflaged. That report was noticed by CBS headquarters in New York, and a few weeks later, I was being interviewed for a *ten*-minute segment on the *CBS Sunday Morning* show.

I keep asking myself why I agreed. Lord knows, I didn't need any more publicity to get business. So if it wasn't for economic reasons, it must have been because of vanity. Maybe I wanted my son to see me on television. In fact, both he and my wife appeared briefly in a shot where we walked past what the reporter called one of my 'chameleon' houses. I wish we'd *all* been chameleons.

2

A man called my name. 'Brad!'

That was three days after the *CBS Sunday Morning* show. Wednesday. Early June. A bright, gorgeous day. I'd been in meetings all morning, and the rumblings in my stomach reminded me that I'd missed lunch. I could have sent my secretary to get me a sandwich, but what she was doing was a lot more important than running an errand for me. Besides, I felt like going outside and enjoying the sun. Downtown Denver is a model of urban planning – spacious and welcoming, with buildings low enough to let in the light. My destination was a deli across the street, Bagels and More; nothing on my mind but a corned-beef sandwich, when I heard my name being called.

'Brad!'

At first, I thought it was one of my staff trying to catch my attention about something I'd forgotten. But when I turned, I didn't recognize the man hurrying toward me. He was in his mid-thirties, rough-looking, with a dirty tan and matted long hair. For a moment, I thought he might be a construction worker I'd met on one of my projects. His clothes certainly looked the part: scuffed work boots, dusty jeans, and a wrinkled denim shirt with its sleeves rolled up. But I've got a good memory for faces, and I was sure I'd have remembered the two-inch scar on his chin.

'Brad! My God, I can't believe it!' The man dropped a battered knapsack to the sidewalk. 'After all these years! Christ Almighty!'

I must have looked baffled. I like to think people enjoy my company, but very few have ever been so enthusiastic about seeing me. Apparently we had once known each other, although I hadn't the vaguest idea who the guy was.

His broad grin revealed a chipped front tooth. 'You don't recognize me? Come on, *I'd* have recognized *you* anywhere! I did on television! It's me!'

My brain was working slowly, trying to search my memory. 'I'm afraid I don't—'

'Peter! Your *brother*!'

Now everything became totally clear. My brain worked very fast.

The man reached out. 'It's so damned good to see you!'

'Keep your hands away from me, you son of a bitch.'

'What?' The man looked shocked.

'Come any closer, I'll call the police. If you think you're going to get money from—'

'Brad, what are you talking about?'

'You watched the *CBS Sunday* program, didn't you?'

'Yes, but—'

'You made a mistake, you bastard. It isn't going to work.'

On TV, the reporter had mentioned Petey's disappearance. The day after the show, six different men had called my office, claiming to be Petey. 'Your long-lost brother,' each of them cheerily said. The first call had excited me, but after a few minutes' conversation, I realized that the guy hadn't the faintest idea about how Petey had disappeared or where it had happened or what our home life had been like. The next two callers had been even worse liars. They all wanted money. I told my secretary not to put through any more calls from anyone who claimed to be my brother. The next three con men lied to her, pretending to have legitimate business, tricking her into transferring the call. The moment they started their spiel, I slammed down the phone. The day after that, my secretary managed to intercept eight more calls from men who claimed to be Petey.

Now they were showing up in person.

'Stay the hell away from me.' Too impatient to go down to the traffic light, I turned sharply, found a break in traffic, and headed across the street.

'Brad! For God's sake, listen!' the man yelled. 'It really is *me*!'

My back stiffened with anger as I kept walking.

'What do I have to do to make you believe me?' the man shouted.

I reached the street's center line, waiting impatiently for another break in traffic.

'When they grabbed me, I was riding home on my bicycle!' the man yelled.

Furious, I spun. 'The reporter mentioned that on television! Get away from me before I beat the shit out of you.'

'Brad, you'd have a harder time outfighting me than when we were kids. The bike was blue.'

The last statement almost didn't register, I was so angry. Then the image of Petey's blue bike hit me.

'*That* wasn't mentioned on television,' the man said.

'It was in the newspaper at the time. All you needed to do was phone the Woodford library and ask the reference department to check the issues of the local newspaper for that month and year. It wouldn't have been hard to get details about Petey's disappearance.'

'*My* disappearance,' the man said.

On each side, cars beeped in warning as they sped past.

'We shared the same room,' the man said. 'Was *that* ever printed?'

I frowned, uneasy.

'We slept in bunk beds,' the man said, raising his voice. 'I had the top. I had a model of a helicopter hanging from a cord attached to the ceiling just above me. I liked to take it down and spin the blades.'

My frown deepened.

'Dad had the tip of the little finger on his left hand cut off in an accident at the furniture factory. He loved to fish. The summer before I disappeared, he took you and me camping out here in Colorado. Mom wouldn't go. She was afraid of being outdoors because of her allergy to bee stings. Even the sight of a bee threw her into a panic.'

Memories flooded through me. There was no way this stranger could have learned any of those details just by checking old newspapers. None of that information had ever been printed.

'Petey?'

'We had a goldfish in our room. But neither of us liked to clean the bowl. One day we came home from school, and the bedroom stank. The fish was dead. We put the fish in a matchbox and had a funeral in the backyard. When we came back to where we'd buried it, we found a hole where the neighbor's cat had dug up the fish.'

'Petey.' As I started back toward him, I almost got hit by a car. 'Jesus, it *is* you.'

'We once broke a window playing catch in the house. Dad grounded us for a week.'

This time, *I* was the one reaching out. I've never hugged anybody harder. He smelled of spearmint gum and cigarette smoke. His arms were tremendously strong. 'Petey.' I could barely get the words out. 'Whatever happened to you?'

3

Pedaling home. Angry. Feelings hurt. A car coming next to him, moving slowly, keeping pace with him. A woman in the front passenger seat rolling down her window, asking directions to the interstate. Telling her. The woman not seeming to listen. The sour-looking man at the steering wheel not seeming to care, either. The woman asking, 'Do you believe in God?' What kind of question? The woman asking, 'Do you believe in the end of the world?' The car veering in front of him. Scared. Hopping the bicycle onto the sidewalk. The woman jumping from the car, chasing him. A sneaker slipping off a pedal. A vacant lot. Bushes. The woman grabbing him. The man unlocking the trunk, throwing him in. The trunk lid banging shut. Darkness. Screaming. Pounding. Not enough air. Passing out.

Petey described it to me as we faced each other in an isolated booth at the rear of the deli I'd been headed toward.

'You never should have made me leave that baseball game,' he said.

'I know that.' My voice broke. 'God, don't I know it.'

'The woman was older than Mom. She had crow's-feet around her eyes. Gray roots in her hair. Pinched lips. Awful thin . . . Stooped shoulders . . . Floppy arms. Reminded me of a bird, but she sure was strong. The man had dirty long hair and hadn't shaved. He wore coveralls and smelled of chewing tobacco.'

'What did they want with you? Were you . . .' I couldn't make myself use the word *molested*.

Petey looked away. 'They drove me to a farm in West Virginia.'

'Just across the border? You were that close?'

'Near a town called Redemption. Sick joke, huh? Really, that's

11

what it was called, although I didn't find out the name for quite a while. They kept me a prisoner, until I escaped. When I was sixteen.'

'Sixteen? But all this time? Why didn't you come to us?'

'I thought about it.' Petey looked uncomfortable. 'I just couldn't make myself.' He pulled a pack of cigarettes from his shirt pocket.

But as he lit a match, a waitress stopped at our table. 'I'm sorry, sir. Smoking isn't permitted in here.'

Petey's craggy features hardened. 'Fine.'

'Can I take your orders?'

'You're good at giving them.'

'What?'

'Corned beef,' I told the waitress, breaking the tension.

Petey impatiently shoved his cigarettes back into his pocket. 'A couple of Buds.'

As she left, I glanced around, assuring myself that no customers were close enough to hear what we were saying.

'What did you mean, you couldn't make yourself come to us?'

'The man kept telling me Mom and Dad would never take me back.'

'What?'

'Not after what he did to . . . He said Mom and Dad would be disgusted, they'd . . .'

'Disown you? They wouldn't have.' I felt tight with sadness.

'I understand that now. But when I escaped . . . let's just say I wasn't myself. Where they kept me a prisoner was an underground room.'

'Jesus.'

'I didn't see the light of day for seven years.' His cheek muscles hardened. 'Not that I knew how much time had passed. When I got out, it took me quite a while to figure what was what.'

'But what have you been doing?'

Petey looked tortured. 'Roaming around. Working construction jobs. Driving trucks. A little of everything. Just after my twenty-first birthday, I happened to be driving a rig to Columbus. I worked up the nerve to go to Woodford and take a look at our place.'

'The house had been sold by then.'

'So I found out.'

'And Dad had died.'

'I found that out, too. Nobody remembered where Mrs Denning and her son Brad had moved.'

'We were in Columbus with Mom's parents.'

'So close.' Petey shook his head in despair. 'I didn't know Mom's maiden name, so I couldn't track her through her parents.'

'But the police could have helped you find us.'

'Not without asking me a lot of questions I didn't want to answer.'

'They'd have arrested the man and woman who kidnapped you.'

'What good would that have done *me*? There'd have been a trial. I'd have had to testify. The story would have been in all the newspapers.' He gestured helplessly. 'I felt so . . .'

'It's over now. Try to put it behind you. None of it was your fault.'

'I *still* feel . . .' Petey struggled with the next word, then stopped when the waitress brought our beers. He took a long swallow from his bottle and changed the subject. 'What about Mom?'

The question caught me by surprise. 'Mom?'

'Yeah, how's she doing?'

I needed a moment before I could make myself answer. 'She died last year.'

'. . . Oh.' Petey's voice dropped.

'Cancer.'

'Uh.' It was a quiet exhale. At the same time, it was almost as if he'd been punched. He stared at his beer bottle, but his painful gaze was on something far away.

4

Kate's normally attractive features looked strained when I walked into the kitchen. She was pacing, talking on the phone, tugging an anxious hand through her long blond hair. Then she saw me, and her shoulders sagged with relief. 'He just walked in. I'll call you back.'

I smiled as she hung up the phone.

'Where have you been? Everybody's been worried,' Kate said.

'Worried?'

'You had several important meetings this afternoon, but you never showed up. Your office was afraid you'd been in an accident or—'

'Everything's great. I lost track of the time.'

'—been mugged or—'

'*Better* than great.'

'—had a heart attack or—'

'I've got wonderful news.'

'—or God knows what. You're always Mr Dependable. Now it's almost six, and you didn't call to let me know you were okay, and . . . Do I smell alcohol on your breath? Have you been drinking?'

'You bet.' I smiled more broadly.

'During the day? Ignoring appointments with clients? What's gotten into you?'

'I told you, I have wonderful news.'

'*What* news?'

'Petey showed up.'

Kate's blue eyes looked confused, as if I was speaking gibberish. 'Who's . . .' At once, she got it. 'Good Lord, you don't mean . . . your brother.'

14

'Exactly.'

'But . . . but you told me you assumed he was dead.'

'I was wrong.'

'You're positive it's him?'

'You bet. He told me things only Petey could know. It *has* to be him.'

'And he's really here? In Denver?'

'Closer than that. He's on the front porch.'

'What? You left him *outside?*'

'I didn't want to spring him on you. I wanted to prepare you.' I explained what had happened. 'I'll fill in the details when there's time. The main thing to know is, he's been through an awful lot.'

'Then he shouldn't be cooling his heels on the porch. For heaven's sake, get him.'

Just then, Jason came in from the backyard. He was eleven but small for his age, so that he looked a lot like Petey had when he'd disappeared. Braces, freckles, glasses, thin. 'What's all the noise about? You guys having an argument?'

'The opposite,' Kate said.

'What's up?'

Looking at Jason's glasses, I was reminded that *Petey* had needed glasses, too. But the man outside wasn't wearing any. I suddenly felt as if I had needles in my stomach. Had I been conned?

Kate crouched before Jason. 'Do you remember we told you that your father had a brother?'

'Sure. Dad talked about him on that TV show.'

'He disappeared when he was a boy,' Kate said.

Jason nodded uneasily. 'I had a nightmare about it.'

'Well, you don't have to have nightmares about it anymore,' Kate said. 'Guess what? He came back today. You're going to meet him.'

'Yeah?' Jason brightened. 'When?'

'Just as soon as we open the front door.'

I tried to say something to Kate, to express my sudden misgivings, but she was already heading down the hallway toward the front door. The next thing, she had it open, and I don't know what she expected, but I doubt that the scruffy-looking man out there matched her idealized image of the long-lost brother. He turned from where he'd been smoking a cigarette, admiring the treed area

15

in front of the house. His knapsack was next to him.

'Petey?' Kate asked.

He shifted from one work boot to the other, ill at ease. 'These days, I think "Peter" sounds a little more grown-up.'

'Please, come in.'

'Thanks.' He looked down at his half-smoked cigarette, glanced at the interior of the house, pinched off the glowing tip, then put the remnant in his shirt pocket.

'I hope you can stay for supper,' Kate said.

'I don't want to put you out any.'

'Nonsense. We'd love to have you.'

'To tell you the truth, I'd appreciate it. I can't remember when I last had a home-cooked meal.'

'This is Jason.' Kate gestured proudly toward our son.

'Hi, Jace.' The man shook hands with him. 'Do you like to play baseball?'

'Yeah,' Jason said, 'but I'm not very good at it.'

'Reminds me of myself at your age. Tell you what. After supper, we'll play catch. How does that sound?'

'Great.'

'Well, let's not keep you standing on the porch. Come in,' Kate said. 'I'll get you something to drink.'

'A beer if you've got it.' The man who said he was Petey started to follow Kate inside.

But before he crossed the threshold, I had to know. 'Are you wearing contact lenses?'

'No.' The man frowned in confusion. 'What makes you ask?'

'You needed glasses when you were a kid.'

'Still do.' The man reached into his knapsack and pulled out a small case, opening it, showing a pair of spectacles, one lens of which was broken. 'This happened yesterday morning. But I can get around all right. As you know, I need glasses just for distance. Was that a little test or something?'

Emotion made my throat ache. 'Petey . . . welcome home.'

5

'This is the best pot roast I ever tasted, Mrs Denning.'

'Please, you're part of the family. Call me Kate.'

'And these mashed potatoes are out of this world.'

'I'm afraid I cheated and used butter. Now our cholesterol counts will be shot to hell.'

'I never pay attention to stuff like that. As long as it's food, it's welcome.' When Petey smiled, his chipped front tooth was visible.

Jason couldn't help staring at it.

'You want to know how I got this?' Petey gestured toward the tooth.

'Jason, you're being rude,' Kate said.

'Not at all.' Petey chuckled. 'He's just curious, the same as I was when I was a kid. Jace, last summer I was on a roofing project in Colorado Springs. I fell off a ladder. That's also how I got this scar on my chin. Good thing I was close to the ground when I fell. I could have broken my neck.'

'Is that where you live now?' I asked. 'In Colorado Springs?'

'Lord no. I don't live anywhere.'

I stopped chewing.

'But everybody lives somewhere,' Kate said.

'Not me.'

Jason looked puzzled. 'But where do you sleep?'

'Wherever I happen to be, there's always someplace to bed down.'

'That seems . . .' Kate shook her head.

'What?'

'Awfully lonely. No friends. Nothing to call your own.'

'I guess it depends on what you're used to. People have a habit of

17

letting me down.' Petey didn't look at me, but I couldn't help taking his comment personally. 'And as for owning things, well, everything of any importance to me is in my knapsack. If I can't carry it, I figure it holds me back.'

'King of the road,' I said.

'Exactly. You see' – Petey leaned toward Jason, propping his elbows on the table – 'I roam around a lot, depending on where the work is and how the weather feels. Each day's a new adventure. I never know what to expect. Like last Sunday, I happened to be in Butte, Montana, eating breakfast in a diner that had a television. I don't normally look at television and I don't have any use for those Sunday-morning talk shows, but this one caught my attention. Something about the voice of the guy being interviewed. I looked up from my eggs and sausage, and Lord, the guy on TV sure made me think of somebody – but not from recently. A long time ago. I kept waiting for the announcer to say who the guy was. Then he didn't need to – because the announcer mentioned that the guy's kid brother had disappeared while bicycling home from a baseball game when they were youngsters. Of course, the guy on television was your father.'

Petey turned to me. 'As I got older, I thought more and more about looking you up, Brad, but I had no idea where you'd gone. When the announcer said you lived in Denver, I set down my knife and fork and started for here at once. Took me all Sunday, Monday, and Tuesday. Mind you, I tried phoning along the road, but your home number isn't listed. As for your *business* number, well, your secretary wouldn't put me through.'

'Because of all those crank calls I told you about.' I felt guilty, as if he thought I'd intentionally rejected him.

'Three days to drive from Montana? You must have had car trouble,' Kate said.

Petey shook his head from side to side. 'A car's just something else that would own me. I hitchhiked.'

'*Hitchhiked?*' Kate asked in surprise. 'Why didn't you take a bus?'

'Well, there are two good reasons. The first is, in my experience, people who ride buses tend to have the same boring stories, but any driver with the courage to pick up a hitchhiker is definitely someone worth talking to.'

The way he said that made us chuckle.

'If it turns out they're *not* interesting, I can always say, "Let me off in the next town." Then I take my chances with another car. Each ride's a small adventure.' Petey's eyes crinkled with amusement.

'And what's the second reason for not taking the bus?' I asked.

The amusement faded. 'Work's been a little scarce lately. I didn't have the money for the ticket.'

'That's going to change,' I said. 'I know where there's plenty of work on construction projects – if you want it.'

'I sure do.'

'I can give you some pocket money in the meantime.'

'Hey, I didn't come here for handouts,' Petey said.

'I know that. But what'll you do for cash until then?'

Petey didn't have an answer.

'Come on,' I said. 'Accept a gift.'

'I guess I could use some cash to rent a motel room.'

'No way,' Kate said. 'You're not renting any motel room. You're spending the night with us.'

6

Petey threw a baseball to Jason, who was usually awkward, but this time he caught the ball perfectly and grinned.

'Look, Dad! Look at what Uncle Peter taught me!'

'You're doing great. Maybe your uncle ought to think about becoming a coach.'

Petey shrugged. 'Just some tricks I picked up on the road, from Friday nights when I ended up at baseball parks in various towns. All you have to remember, Jace, is to keep your eye on the ball instead of your glove. And make sure your glove is ready to snap shut.'

Kate appeared at the back door, her blond hair silhouetted by the kitchen light. 'It's time for bed, Little Leaguer.'

'Aw, do I have to, Mom?'

'I've already let you stay up a half hour longer than usual. Tomorrow's a school day.'

Disappointed, Jason turned to his uncle.

'Don't look at me for help,' Petey said. 'What your mother says goes.'

'Thanks for the lesson, Uncle Peter. Now maybe the other kids'll let me play on the team.'

'Well, if they don't, you let me know, and I'll go down to the ballpark to have a word with them.' Petey mussed Jason's sandy hair and nudged him toward the house. 'You better not keep your mother waiting.'

'See you in the morning.'

'You bet.'

'I'm glad you found us, Uncle Peter.'

'Me, too.' Petey's voice was unsteady. 'Me, too.'

Jason went inside, and my brother turned to me. 'Nice boy.'

'Yes, we're very proud of him.'

The setting sun cast a crimson glow over the backyard's trees.

'And Kate's . . .'

'Wonderful,' I said. 'It was my lucky day when I met her.'

'There's no getting around it. You've done great for yourself. Look at this house.'

I felt embarrassed to have so much. 'My staff teases me about it. As you saw from the TV show, my specialty is designing buildings that are almost invisible in their environment. But when we first came to town, this big old Victorian seemed to have our name on it. Of course, all the trees in the front and back conceal it pretty well.'

'It feels solid.' Petey glanced down at his calloused hands. 'Funny how things worked out. Well . . .' He roused himself and grinned. 'Coaching's thirsty work. I could use another beer.'

'Be right back.'

When I returned with the beers (inside, Kate, had raised her eyebrows, not used to seeing me drink so much), I also had something in a shopping bag.

'What's that?' Petey wondered.

'Something I've been keeping for you.'

'I can't imagine what you'd—'

'I'm afraid it's too small for you to use if you want to play catch with Jason another time,' I said.

Petey shook his head in confusion.

'Recognize this?' I reached in the bag and pulled out the battered baseball glove that I'd found under Petey's bike so long ago.

'My God.'

'I kept it all these years. I never let it out of my room. I used to hold it next to me when I went to bed, and I'd try to imagine where you were and what you were doing and . . .' I forced the words out. '. . . if you were still alive.'

'A lot of times, I wished I *wasn't* alive.'

'Don't think about that. The past doesn't matter now. We're together again, Petey. *That's* what matters. God, I've missed you.' I handed him the glove, although I couldn't see him very well – my eyes were misted.

7

'So what do you think of him?' I asked Kate, keeping my voice low as I turned off the light and got under the covers. Petey's room was at the opposite end of the hall. He wouldn't be able to hear us. Even so, I felt self-conscious talking about him.

Lying next to me in the darkness, Kate didn't answer for a moment. 'He's had a hard life.'

'That's for sure. And yet he seems to enjoy it.'

'A virtue of necessity.'

'I suppose. All the same . . .'

'What are you thinking?' Kate asked.

'Well, if he didn't like it, he could always have lived another way.'

'How?'

'I guess he could have gone to school and entered a profession.'

'Maybe have become an architect, like you?'

I shrugged. 'Maybe. It wouldn't have been out of the question. I've seen a couple of stories on the news about twins separated at birth and reunited as adults. They discover they have the same job, the same hobbies, wives who look the same and have the same personality.'

'I'm not sure I like being linked with someone's hobby. Besides, you and your brother aren't twins.'

'Granted. Even so, you know what I mean. Petey could have ended up like me, but he chose not to.'

'You really think people have that much choice in their lives? You told me you never would have become an architect if it hadn't been for a geometry teacher you really liked in high school.'

Wistful, I stared at the moonlight streaming through our bedroom window. 'Yeah, I sure was weird – the only kid in high school

22

who liked geometry. To me, that teacher made the subject fascinating. He told me what I had to do, where to go to college and all, if I wanted to be an architect.'

'Well, I seriously doubt that your brother had a geometry teacher. Did he even go to high school?' Kate asked.

'Somebody must have taught him *something*. He's awfully well spoken. I haven't heard a foul word from him.'

Kate turned to face me, propping herself on an elbow. 'Look, I'm willing to do all I can to help. If he wants to stay here for a while until he decides what to do next, that's fine with me.'

'I was hoping you'd feel that way.' I leaned over and kissed her. 'Thanks.'

'Is that the best way you can think of to thank me?' she asked.

I kissed her again, this time deeply.

'Far more sincere.' She drew a hand up my leg.

'Mmm.' It was the last sound for a while. The presence of a stranger in the house made us more self-conscious about being overheard. When we climaxed, our kiss was so deep that we swallowed each other's moans.

We lay silently, coming back to ourselves.

'If we get more sincere than that, I'll need to be resuscitated,' I murmured.

'Mouth-to-mouth?'

'Brings me to life every time.' Getting up to go to the bathroom, I glanced out the window. In the darkness, peering down toward the backyard, I saw something I didn't expect.

'What are you looking at?' Kate asked.

'Petey.'

'What?'

'I can see him in the moonlight. He's down there in a lounge chair.'

'Asleep?' Kate asked.

'No, he's smoking, staring up at the stars.'

'Given everything that's happened, he probably couldn't sleep.'

'I know how he feels.'

'I'll tell you one thing,' Kate said. 'Anyone who's polite enough not to smoke in the house is welcome.'

8

Although Petey had said that he enjoyed his life on the road, I was determined to make sure he enjoyed it even more by paying attention to a few basic matters: his appearance, for example. That chipped front tooth made a terrible first impression. I had a suspicion that Petey had been losing work because contractors he approached to hire him felt he looked like a troublemaker. So, the next morning, I phoned our family dentist, explained the situation, and got him to agree (for double his usual fee) to give up his lunch hour.

'Dentist?' Petey told me. 'Hell, no. I'm not going to any dentist.'

'Just to smooth out that chip in your tooth. It's not going to hurt.'

'No way. I haven't been to a dentist since I needed a back tooth taken out six years ago.'

'*Six years ago?* Good God. All the more reason for you to have a checkup.' I didn't tell him that the hygienist had agreed to give up *her* lunch hour, too.

Before that, I phoned several barbershops, until I found one that wasn't busy. Long hair – my own's hardly what you'd call short – doesn't have to look tangled and scruffy. After the barbershop, we bought some clothes. Not that I deluded myself into thinking that Petey could use dress slacks and a sport coat, but some new jeans and a nice-looking shirt wouldn't do any harm. After that, a shoe store: new work boots and sneakers.

'I can't accept all this,' Petey said.

'I'm glad to do it. If you want, we'll call it a loan. Sometime, when you're flush, you can pay me back.'

Then it was time for the dentist. Afterward, Petey's teeth looked great, although he had several cavities, the dentist said. They'd be taken care of when Petey went back in a couple of weeks. Petey's hair looked stylishly windblown. I was almost tempted to ask a plastic surgeon if anything could be done about the scar on Petey's chin. No matter, a little maintenance had accomplished a lot. He looked like he'd just gotten dressed after playing tennis.

'Hungry?'

'Always,' Petey said.

'Yeah, I get the impression you've been missing a few meals lately. You could use about ten more pounds. Do you like Italian food?'

'You mean spaghetti and meatballs?'

'Sort of. But where we're going, spaghetti's called pasta, and the dishes have names like chicken marsala.'

'Hold on a second.'

'After lunch, I'm going to take you to see a man about a job.'

'Brad . . . Stop . . . Hold it.'

'Why? What's wrong?'

'Don't you have work to do?' Petey asked. 'You took yesterday afternoon off. This morning, you didn't go to work, either. Kate said you had appointments, meetings.'

'None of it's as important as you.'

'But you can't run a business that way, not and spend money on me the way you are. We have a lot to catch up on, but we don't have to do it all at once.'

Petey's worried expression started me laughing. 'You think I'm getting carried away?'

'Just a little.'

'Then what do you suggest?'

'Go to work. There's a park across the street. I'd like to hang out there for a while. Get my mind straight. All these changes. I'll meet you at home for supper.'

'That's really what you want?' I asked.

'You've done enough for me.'

'But how will you get home?'

'Hitchhike,' Petey said.

'What if you don't get a ride?'

'Don't worry. I've got a knack for it.' Petey's teeth looked great when he grinned.

'I have a better idea,' I said. 'Use my car. You can pick me up at the end of the day.'

'Can't. I don't have a driver's license.'

'That's something else we'll take care of.'

'Tomorrow,' Petey said.

'We're going to see about getting your glasses fixed, too.'

'Right,' Petey said. 'Tomorrow.'

9

Petey and Jason were cutting the lawn when I got home. The power mower was awkward for Jason, so Petey was walking beside him, helping him make the turns.

'Hey, look at me, Dad!' Jason yelled to be heard above the motor's roar.

I raised my thumb enthusiastically.

They stopped beside me.

'Can you control it, Jace?' Petey asked.

'I'm pretty sure.'

'Then it's all yours. I'll be over here talking to your dad.'

Jason nodded, concentrating on keeping the mower in a straight line. Its roar diminished as he navigated among trees toward the far side of the yard.

Petey motioned me toward the porch steps, where he picked up a bottle of beer. 'I might've created a monster. If he gets any better at this, you're going to have to raise his allowance.'

'It's the first time he's shown an interest. Could be you've hit on something,' I said. 'Normally, a lawn service does this for me, but it'd be good for him to help a little and learn some responsibility.'

'Can't be too young to learn responsibility.' Petey took a drink of his beer.

'Listen, I appreciate the effort, but you didn't have to mow the grass,' I said.

'No big deal. It looked a little long. I want to do my share.'

'Honestly, it isn't necessary. I'm just glad to have you here. Anyway, since you'll be working next week, take it easy for now.'

Petey cocked his head. 'Working next week?'

'Yeah, I made some calls. I got you a job.'

'You *did*? Great!'

'On a building I designed.'

'Couldn't be better.'

'Uncle Peter!' Jason yelled in panic. At the end of a row, the boy struggled to turn the mower. It veered toward a shrub.

'Hang on!' Petey ran to help him.

10

'No need to help with the dishes.,' Kate said.

'It's the least I can do.' Petey dried another pot. 'I can't remember when I had a tastier beef stew.'

'We don't normally eat this much red meat,' she said. 'I'm trying to put some weight on you.'

'The lemon pie was spectacular.'

Jason eyed a second piece. 'Yeah, we hardly ever get desserts in the middle of the week.'

'Well, you worked hard mowing the lawn,' Kate said. 'You deserve a treat.'

Sitting at the end of the table, I couldn't help smiling. The reality that Petey was actually over there by the sink, reaching to dry another pot, still overwhelmed me.

'Anyway,' he said, returning to an earlier topic, 'it doesn't surprise me that you moved here to Denver.'

'Oh?'

'That camping trip you and I and Dad went on. Remember?' Petey asked.

'I sure do.'

'Out here to Colorado. What a good time. Of course, the long drive from Ohio was a pain. If it hadn't been for the comic books Dad kept buying us along the highway . . . Once we got here, the effort sure was worth it. Camping, hiking, rock climbing and fishing, Dad showing us what to do.'

'The first fish you ever caught, you were so excited that you reeled in before you hooked it good,' I said. 'It jumped back into the lake.'

'You remember that much?'

'I thought about that trip a lot over the years. A month after we got back, school started, and . . .' I couldn't make myself refer to Petey's disappearance. 'For a lot of years, it was the last good summer of my life.'

'Mine, too.' Petey looked down. A long second later, he shrugged off his regret and picked up the last pot. 'Anyway, what I'm getting at is, maybe you came out here because in the back of your mind you wanted to return to that summer.'

'Camping?' Jason broke the somber mood.

We looked at him. He'd been silent for a while, eating his second piece of pie.

'Dad promised to take me, but we never did,' Jason said.

I felt embarrassed. 'We went on plenty of hikes.'

'But we never used tents.'

'Are you telling me you've never actually gone camping?' Petey asked.

Jason nodded, then corrected himself. 'Except, I once slept in a tent in Tom Burbick's backyard.'

'Doesn't count,' Petey said. 'You've gotta be where you hear the lions and tigers and bears.'

'Lions and tigers?' Jason frowned, looking vulnerable behind his glasses.

'It's a joke.' Kate rumpled his hair.

She left some soapsuds. He swatted at them. 'Mom!'

'But that might not be a bad idea.' She looked at Petey and me. 'A camping trip. The two of you can pick up where you left off. Jump over the years. I know it's been hard for you, Peter, but now the good times are starting again.'

'I think you're right, Kate,' Petey said. 'I can feel them.'

'What about *me*?' Jason asked. 'Can't *I* come?'

'We'll *all* go,' Petey said.

'Sorry. Not me, gentlemen.' Kate held up her hands. 'Saturday, I'm scheduled to give a seminar.' Kate was a stress-management counselor; her specialty was advising corporations whose employees were burned out because of downsizing. 'Besides, sleeping in the woods isn't high on my list.'

'Just like Mom.' Petey turned to me. 'Remember?'

'Yeah, just like Mom.'

'Except your mother,' Kate said, 'was afraid of bees, whereas in my case it's a matter of natural selection.'

'Natural selection?' I asked, puzzled.

'You guys are a lot better equipped to crawl out of a tent at night and pee in the woods.'

11

'I've been meaning to ask you something.'

Petey quit studying the map and looked at me. 'About what?'

It was almost eleven o'clock: a radiant Saturday morning. My Ford Expedition was loaded with all kinds of camping equipment. We'd followed Interstate 70 west out of Denver and were now well into the mountains, although Jason wasn't appreciating their snowcaps. He was dozing in a sleeping bag on the backseat.

'After you . . .' I had trouble continuing. 'It suddenly occurs to me that you might not want to talk about it.'

'There's only one way to find out.'

'After you got away from . . .'

'Say it. The sick bastards who kidnapped me. It's a fact. You don't need to tap-dance around the subject.'

'You were sixteen when you escaped. You've talked about roaming the country, working on construction jobs or whatever. But you never mentioned anything about school. When you disappeared, you were in the fourth grade, but you've obviously had more education than that. Who taught you?'

'Oh, I had plenty of education in politeness,' Petey said bitterly. 'The man and woman who kept me in that underground room insisted on a lot of "Yes, sir, yes, ma'am, please and thank you." If I ever forgot, they punched my face to remind me.' The sinews in his neck tightened into ropes.

'I'm sorry. I wish I hadn't raised the subject,' I said.

'It's fine. There's no point in hiding from the past. It'll only catch up in other ways.' Petey's gaze hardened. He took a deep breath, subduing his emotions. 'Anyway, in terms of education, I have better memories. As I wandered from town to town, I learned that

32

an easy way to get a free meal was to show up at church socials after Sunday-morning services. Of course, I had to sit through the services in order to get the free meals. But most times, I didn't mind – the services were peaceful. After so many years of not reading, I'd sort of forgotten how to do it. When members of this or that congregation realized that I couldn't read the Bible, they took steps to make sure I learned my ABCs and, more important, the Good Book. There were always teachers in the congregations. After work some evenings, I'd get private classes at a church in whatever town I happened to be in. There are a lot of decent folks out there.'

'I'm glad to hear it.'

'Hear what, Dad?' Jason asked sleepily from the backseat, where he'd woken up.

'Just that there are decent people in the world.'

'Didn't you know that?'

'Sometimes I wondered. You and your uncle concentrate on the map. Our turnoff isn't far ahead.'

12

We were looking for a place called Breakhorse Ridge. It's odd how some names stay in my memory. Twenty-five years earlier, that was where Dad had taken Petey and me on our camping trip. Somebody at the furniture factory where Dad was the foreman had once lived in Colorado and had described to Dad how beautiful the Breakhorse Ridge area was. So Dad, who'd already committed to taking us camping in Colorado, had decided that would be our destination. But back then, all during the long drive, I'd had a horrifying mental image of somebody breaking horses in half. Not knowing anything about how cowboys 'broke' wild horses so people could ride them. I'd been afraid of what we were going to see. Dad finally got me to tell him what was bothering me. After he explained, my fear turned to curiosity. But when we arrived, there weren't any horses or cowboys, just a few old wooden corrals, and a meadow leading down to a lake and an aspen forest with mountains above it.

I never forgot the name. But as Petey, Jason and I had made plans, I couldn't find the place on a map. I finally had to phone the headquarters for park services in Colorado. A ranger had faxed me a section of a much more detailed map than I was using, showing me the route to Breakhorse Ridge. I'd spread my general map on the dining-room table, put the fax over the section we were interested in, and shown Petey and Jason where we were going.

Now we were almost there, turning to the right onto Highway 9, heading north into the Arapaho National Forest.

'It gets tricky from here on, guys. Keep comparing the map to what's around us,' I said.

34

Jason crawled into the front, and Petey buckled his seat belt over both of them.

'What are we searching for?' Jason asked.

'This squiggly line.' Petey showed him the fax. 'It'll be a narrow dirt road on the right. With all these pine trees, we'll have to watch closely. It'll be hard to spot.'

I steered around a curve. The trees got thicker. Even so, I thought I saw a break in them on the right. But I didn't say anything, wanting Jason to make the discovery. Petey must have read my mind. I saw him look up from the map and focus his eyes as if he'd noticed the break, but he didn't say anything, either.

I drove closer.

The break became a little more distinct.

'There!' Jason pointed. 'I see it!'

'Good job,' Petey said.

'For sure,' I added. 'I almost went past it.'

I steered to the right and entered a bumpy dirt lane. Scrub grass grew between its wheel ruts. Bushes squeezed its sides. Pine branches formed a canopy.

'Gosh, do you think we'll get stuck?' Jason leaned forward with concern.

'Not with this four-wheel drive,' Petey said. 'It'd take a lot worse terrain than this to put us in trouble. Even if it snowed, we wouldn't have to worry.'

'Snowed?' Jason frowned. 'In June?'

'Sure,' Petey said. 'This time of year, you can still get a storm in the mountains.' The trees became sparse. 'See those peaks ahead and how much snow they still have? Up here, the sun hasn't gotten hot enough to melt it yet.'

Taking sharp angles, the lane zigzagged higher. The slope below us became dizzyingly steep. The bumps were so severe that only those cowboys who'd ridden bucking wild horses there years earlier could have enjoyed the ride.

'Who do you suppose built this road?' Jason asked. 'It looks awfully old.'

'The forest service maybe,' I said. 'Or maybe loggers or ranchers before this area became part of the national forest system. I remember our dad saying that in the old days cattlemen kept small herds here to feed prospectors in mining towns.'

'Prospectors? *Gold?*' Jason asked.

'And silver. A long time ago. Most of the towns are abandoned now.'

'*Ghost* towns,' Petey said.

'Gosh,' Jason said.

'Or else the towns became ski resorts,' I said, hoping to subdue Jason's imagination so Petey and I wouldn't be wakened by his nightmares about ghosts.

The road crested the slope and took us into a bright meadow, the new grass waving in a gentle breeze.

'It's the way I remember it when Dad drove us here,' I told Petey.

'After all these years,' Petey said in awe.

'Are we there yet?' Jason asked.

The age-old question from kids. I imagined that Petey or I had asked our dad the same thing. We looked at each other and couldn't keep from laughing.

'What's so funny?' Jason asked.

'Nothing,' Petey said. 'No, we're not there yet.'

13

It took another half hour. The meadow gave way to more pine trees and a slope steeper than the first one, the zigzag angles sharper. We crested a bumpy rise, and I stopped suddenly, staring down toward where the barely detectable road descended into a gentle grassy bowl. Sunlight glinted off a picture-book lake, aspens beyond it, then pine trees, then mountains towering above.

'Yes,' I said, my chest tight. 'Just as I remember.'

'It hasn't changed,' Petey said.

On the right, old corrals were the only variation in the meadow. Their gray weathered posts and railings had long ago collapsed into rotting piles. We drove past them, nearing the lake. There weren't any other cars. In fact, I couldn't find an indication that anyone had been around in a very long time.

We stopped fifty feet from the lake, where I recalled Dad stopping. When we got out of the car, I savored the fresh, pleasantly cool air.

'Look at this old campfire, Dad!'

Petey and he were on the right side of the car. I looked over toward a scorched circle of rocks that had charred hunks of wood in the middle.

'Old is right,' Petey said. 'I bet it hasn't been used in years.' He looked at me. 'I wonder if this is the same place you and I and Dad built *our* campfire?'

'It's nice to think so.'

Jason brimmed with energy. 'Where are we going to put up the tent?'

'How about over there?' I pointed to the right of the old campfire site. 'I think that's where Petey and I helped Dad put up our tent.'

'Can *I* help, Dad?'

'Of course,' Petey said.

There was a moment after I lifted the back hatch and we unloaded our gear when the déjà vu I'd been feeling reached an overwhelming intensity. Everything seemed realer than real. I looked over at Jason and Petey as they pulled the collapsed tent from its nylon sack and tried to figure how to put it together. Jason's glasses and freckles, his sandy hair at the edge of his baseball cap, his baggy jeans and loose-fitting shirt made him look so much like Petey had looked as a boy that I shivered.

Jason noticed. 'What's the matter, Dad?'

'Nothing. This breeze is a little cold is all. I'm going to put on my windbreaker. You want yours?'

'Naw, I'm fine.'

'Big brother,' Petey called. 'You're the expert in how buildings are put together. Do you think you can show us how to put this damned *tent* together?'

The three of us needed an hour to get the job done.

14

By then, it was almost 1:30. Kate had packed a lunch in a cooler: chicken, beef, and peanut butter sandwiches, along with soft drinks, apples and little packages of potato chips. Jason didn't touch the apples. Otherwise, he wolfed everything down, the same as Petey and I did. We saw fish splashing in the lake but decided to get our poles out later. For now, there was plenty to do, exploring. We put our lunch trash in a bag, locked it in the car, and set out, hiking to the left around the lake.

'I remember there was a cave up there.' I pointed above the aspens. 'And lots of places to climb.'

Petey yelled to Jason, who was running ahead of us. 'Do you like to climb?'

'I don't know!' Jason turned to look at us, continuing to run. 'I've never done it!'

'You're going to love it!'

The lake was about a hundred yards across. We reached the other side and found a stream that fed into it. The stream was swift from the spring snowmelt, too wide to cross, so we followed its cascading path up through the aspens, the roar of the water sometimes so loud that we couldn't hear one another.

Even though we were three thousand feet higher than the altitude of five thousand feet we were used to in Denver, the thin mountain air didn't slow us. If anything, it was invigorating. It was like inhaling vitamins. Stretching my legs to climb over fallen trees or to clamber on and off boulders, I felt such pleasure from my body that I criticized myself for not having taken time from work to do this earlier.

Across the stream, above us, a deer moved, its brown silhouette stiffening at our approach, then bounding gracefully away through the white trunks of the aspens. With the noise from the stream, it couldn't have heard us coming, I thought. It must have smelled us. Then another silhouette stiffened and bounded away. A third. Even with the noise from the stream, I heard their hooves thunder.

Soon we reached where the stream cascaded from a high, narrow draw that was too dangerous to go into. We angled to the left, following a steep upward trail that had hoof marks on it. The trail veered farther to the left, maintaining a consistent level along a wooded slope, so predictable that when a sunlit outcrop above us attracted our attention, we decided to explore. Getting to it was more difficult than it appeared. At one time or another, both Petey and I slipped on loose rocks underfoot. We'd have rolled to the bottom, scraping our arms and legs, maybe even breaking something, if we hadn't managed to clutch exposed tree roots. By contrast, Jason scurried up like a mountain goat.

Breathing hoarsely, Petey and I crawled over the rim and found Jason waiting for us on a wide slab of rock that provided a view of the stream below us and the chasm through which it churned. Two hundred feet above it, we were far enough from the roar for me not to need to shout when I warned Jason, 'Stay away from the edge.'

'I will,' he promised. 'But, gosh, this is totally neat, Dad.'

'Beats watching television, huh?' Petey said.

Jason thought about it. His face assumed an expression of 'I wouldn't go *that* far.'

Petey laughed.

'Where's that cave you mentioned?' Jason asked.

'I'm having trouble remembering,' I said. 'Somewhere on this side of the stream is all I know for sure.'

'Can we look for it?'

'Absolutely. After we take a break.'

I settled onto the stone slab, unhooked my canteen from my belt, and took a long swallow of slightly warm, slightly metallic-tasting, incredibly delicious water. The park ranger I'd spoken to on the telephone had emphasized that we needed to take canteens with us and knapsacks containing trail food, a compass and a topographical map (neither of which I knew how to use), a first-aid kit, and a rain slicker in case the weather turned bad. 'Dress in layers,' she'd advised. 'Keep a dry jacket in your knapsack.' I'd already put on my denim windbreaker before we left the car. Now the hike had so warmed me that I took off the jacket and stuffed it into the knapsack.

'Anybody want some peanuts and raisins?' I asked.

'I'm still full from lunch,' Petey said.

Jason looked uncomfortable.

'What's the matter?' I asked.

'I have to . . .'

It took me a moment to understand. 'Pee?'

Jason nodded, bashful.

'Go around that boulder over there,' I told him.

Hesitant, he disappeared behind it.

My parental obligations taken care of for the moment, I stepped forward to admire the chasm. The stream tumbled down a series of low waterfalls. Spray hovered over it. How had Jason described the view? 'Neat?' He was right. This *was* totally neat.

Behind me, he suddenly shouted, 'Dad!'

Something slammed my back with such force that it took my breath away. I hurtled into space.

15

The drop sucked more of my breath away. The little that was left jolted from my mouth when I struck loose stones. Avalanching with them, rolling sideways, I groaned. Abruptly, I hurtled into the air again, plummeting farther, my stomach squeezing toward my throat. I jerked to an agonizing stop, my left arm stretching as if it were about to be ripped from its socket. My arm slipped free of something. I dropped again and hit something hard. Cold mist swallowed me.

Darkness swirled. When my eyelids slowly opened, black turned to gray, but the swirling continued. Pain awoke throughout my body. Delirious, I took a long time to realize that the gray swirling around me was vapor thrown up from the cascading stream. The roar aggravated my dizziness.

I felt that I was breathing through a cold, wet washcloth. Gradually, I understood that my left arm was across my nose and mouth. My shirtsleeve was soaked from the vapor that the thundering stream tossed into the air. Then I trembled, seeing that my sleeve was wet from something besides the mist. Blood. My arm was gashed.

Alarm shot through me. I fought to raise my head and discovered that I was on my back on a ledge. Below was a fall of what I judged to be 150 feet. A series of outcrops led sharply down to the roaring stream.

Jesus, what had happened?

I peered up. The vapor made it difficult for me to see the top of the cliff. Nonetheless, through the haze, I could distinguish a long slope of loose stones below the rim. The slope had saved my life. If I'd fallen directly to where I now lay, my injuries would have been catastrophic. Instead, I'd rolled down the slope, painfully reducing the length of the fall. But beneath the slope of loose stones, there had been a ledge over which I'd tumbled to the ledge I'd landed on, and the distance between them was about twenty feet. A potentially lethal drop. Why wasn't I dead?

My knapsack dangled above me. It was caught on a sharp branch of a stunted pine tree that had managed to grow from the side of the cliff. I remembered stuffing my windbreaker into the knapsack and hanging the knapsack over my left shoulder before I'd walked over to peer into the chasm. The branch had snagged the knapsack. The sharp pain in my left shoulder indicated the force with which I'd been jerked to a stop. My arm had slipped free from the strap. I'd fallen a body length to this ledge. Luck was all that had saved me.

Every movement excruciating, I strained to sit up. My mind tilted, as if ball bearings rolled from the front of my skull to the back. For a moment, I feared that I'd vomit.

'Jason!' I tried to yell. 'Petey!'

But the words were like stones in my throat.

'Jason!' I tried harder. 'Petey!'

The roar of the stream overpowered my voice.

Don't panic, I fought to assure myself. It doesn't matter if they can't hear me. They know where I am. They'll help me.

My God, I hope they don't try to climb down, I suddenly thought.

'Jason! Petey! Stay where you are! You'll fall and get killed!'

My voice cracked, making my words a hoarse whisper.

Straining to see through the haze, I hoped to catch a glimpse of Jason and Petey peering over the rim to try to find me. No sign of them. Maybe they're trying to get a better vantage point, I thought. Or maybe they're hurrying back to the mouth of the chasm, hoping to reach me from below.

I prayed that they'd be careful, that Jason wouldn't take foolish chances, that Petey would make sure he didn't. Trembling, I parted the rip in my sleeve. Wiping away the blood, I saw a gash five inches long between my elbow and my wrist. Blood immediately welled up, obscuring the wound. It dripped from my arm, pooling on the ledge.

Bile shot into my mouth.

Do something, I thought. I can't just sit here and let myself bleed to death.

My knapsack seemed to float over me. I stretched my good arm but couldn't reach it. In greater pain, I mustered the strength to try to stand.

The first-aid kit in the knapsack, I thought.

My legs gave out. I clawed at a niche and barely avoided toppling into the chasm. Despite the cold from the stream, I sweated. Shock made me tremble as I grabbed for a higher niche and wavered to my feet. For a moment, I saw specks in front of my eyes. Then my vision cleared, and I stared up toward the knapsack. Despairingly, it seemed as high as ever. My injured left arm dangled at my side. I extended my right arm upward. Another six inches. All I need is six inches more, I thought.

Pressing my chest against the cliff, standing on tiptoes, wincing from new throbbing pain in my hips, my sides, and my ribs, I stretched as high as I could, then breathed out in triumph as I touched the knapsack's strap.

Vapor from the stream had slicked the nylon. I lost my grip but instantly pawed for the strap again, pushing my tiptoes to their limits, this time clutching with all my strength. I tugged the knapsack to the side, toward the chasm, working to free it from the stout branch it had snagged on. I tugged once, twice, and suddenly felt weightless as the knapsack jerked free.

Falling, I dove toward the ledge. I screamed as my injured arm landed, but I couldn't let myself react. I had to concentrate solely on my good arm hanging over the ledge, the knapsack dangling from my fingers.

Cautiously, I rolled onto my back and placed the knapsack on my chest. The temptation to rest was canceled by the increased flow of blood from my arm. Nauseated, I opened the knapsack, pawed past my windbreaker and rain slicker, pushed the Ziploc bags of trail food aside, and found the plastic case of the first-aid kit.

I clumsily pried it open, dismayed to find only Band Aids and two-inch-square pads along with scissors, antiseptic swabs, antibiotic cream and a plastic bottle of Tylenol. None of that was going to stop the bleeding.

A tourniquet, I thought. I'll use my belt. I'll tighten it around my arm and . . .

But even as I unbuckled my belt, I remembered something I'd read about tourniquets being dangerous, about the risk of blood clots and gangrene if the tourniquet wasn't loosened at proper intervals.

What difference does it make? I thought. I'll bleed to death before I die from gangrene.

A pressure bandage. Whatever I'd read about tourniquets had warned that a pressure bandage was the safe way to stop bleeding, something that put pressure on the wound without cutting off the flow of blood. But where was I going to find something like that?

The bleeding worsened.

Perhaps because I was light-headed, I took more time than I should have to remember something else that might be in the knapsack. Once when Kate had been on a college trip to Paris, she'd sprained an ankle and had limped painfully from drugstore to drugstore, trying to find an Ace bandage, the wide, long elastic material you wrap around a sprain to give the injured area some support. Since then, whenever she traveled, she made sure to carry one in her luggage, and she always took care to pack one for me.

More dizzy, I used my right hand to search through the knapsack. Where *is* it? I thought. It isn't like Kate not to have packed one.

Damn it, this time she hadn't.

Desperate, I was about to dump everything out, when I noticed a bulge at the side of the knapsack. Struggling to clear my mind, I freed a zipper on a pouch and almost wept when I found a folded elastic bandage.

Working awkwardly with one hand, sometimes using my teeth to open packets, I cleaned the gash with antiseptic swabs, spread antibiotic ointment over it, and pressed several two-inch pads onto it. Blood soaked them. Hurrying, I wrapped the elastic bandage around my left forearm. Keeping it tight, circling layer upon layer, I saw blood tint each layer.

I urgently wrapped more layers, applying more pressure, worried about how little of the bandage remained. I prayed that the blood wouldn't soak all the way through. Two more layers. One. I secured the end with two barbed clips that came with the bandage. Then I stared at it, shivering, concentrating to see if blood would soak through. For a moment, I feared that the pale brown of the bandage would become pink, about to turn red. I held my breath, exhaling only when a small area of pink didn't spread.

My watch's crystal was shattered, the hands frozen at ten after two. I had no idea how long I'd been on the ledge, but when I peered up through the vapor from the stream, the sun seemed to have shifted farther west than I would have expected from the brief time since I'd fallen. Evidently I'd been unconscious longer than it seemed.

I stared up at the rim but still didn't see Petey and Jason. Give them time, I thought.

The trouble was, if I didn't get off the ledge soon, I was going to be in a lot worse trouble.

I wasn't an outdoorsman – I'd certainly proven that. But it wasn't possible to live in a mountain state like Colorado without seeing stories in the newspaper or on the TV news about the dangers of hypothermia. Hikers would go into the mountains wearing only shorts and T-shirts. A sudden storm would soak them. If the temperature dropped, if the hikers were more than three hours from warm clothes and hot fluids to raise their rapidly dropping core temperature, they died from exposure.

Lying on the damp, chill ledge, I shivered. My hands and feet felt numb. If I don't get off this ledge soon, I thought, it won't matter that I stopped the bleeding. Hypothermia will kill me.

I tried to calculate how to climb up the almost sheer face to the next ledge and then up the slope of loose stones to the rim. I knew that my injured arm wouldn't support me. The only other way to get off the ledge was . . .

I stared down, trying to judge how the cliff led to the stream. It was a steep slope of outcrops, the ledge below me five feet away, the one after that twice as far. I didn't want to think about the obstacles farther down.

But the sun was already past the rim of the cliff. The bottom of the chasm was in shadow. Even though it was only late afternoon, darkness would come soon. The nearby mountains would block the sun earlier than I was used to. Once it was dark, I couldn't hope to be rescued until morning.

By then, I'd be dead.

The pain of movement was excruciating as I eased the knapsack onto my back, lay on my stomach, and squirmed over the edge. I dangled as far as my good arm would allow, then dropped.

The shock of landing jolted me to the bone. I almost fainted. Crawling over the side of the next outcrop, I ripped my shirt and scraped my chest. My lacerated knees showed through my torn jeans. Straining to control my emotions, I kept struggling downward. A few spots that looked impossible from above turned out to be deceptive, boulders acting like steps. Other spots that looked easy were terrifyingly difficult.

Throughout, the light faded. As the stream's roar grew closer, I descended with greater caution. Testing my footing, I almost fell when a boulder dislodged under my weight and rumbled to the bottom. While the dusk thickened, so did the vapor from the stream, beading my face, soaking my clothes, making me shiver harder. I remembered reading that victims of hypothermia become stupefied near the end, unaware of what's around them. I fought to keep my thoughts clear.

As it was, I struggled to the bottom before I realized, nearly stepping into the raging current, so deadened by its thunder that I hadn't been aware how close I was. Lurching back, I almost twisted my ankle. Unnerved by the surreal contrast between the blue sky above the chasm and the gathering dusk within it, I shifted along the roiling water with delicate care. Spray drenched me. As the chasm sloped toward its murky exit, I worried that I'd break a leg within sight of my escape. I made my way over slick rocks, gripping boulders for support, my mind and body so numbed that it took me a minute to understand that the object I leaned against was an aspen tree, not a boulder, that sunlight was angling toward me, that I'd left the chasm a while ago and now was stumbling through a forest.

It's almost over, I told myself. All I need to do is follow the stream through the trees to the lake. As my steps quickened, I imagined unlocking the car. I anticipated the relief of crawling in and starting the engine, of turning on the heater and feeling hot air

47

blow over me as I changed into warm clothes from my suitcase.

'Jason! Petey!'

I lurched from the aspens to the edge of the lake and squinted through dimming sunlight toward the opposite side.

My stomach sank when I saw that the car wasn't there.

Easily explained. Petey and Jason went for help, I thought. They'll be back soon. All I have to do is crawl into the tent and try to get warm.

The tent was also gone.

'No!' The veins in my neck threatened to burst, but I couldn't stop screaming. '*Noooo!*'

16

Denial's an amazing emotion. During my descent, suspicions had nagged at me, but I'd managed to suppress them, too preoccupied with staying alive. Now I still kept trying to tell myself that I was wrong. After all, six hours previously, the possibility that my brother would push me off a cliff would have been unthinkable, especially given the load of guilt that I'd been carrying around.

My God, what had Petey done with Jason?

Furious, shivering so hard that my teeth clicked together, I yanked off my wet shirt, pulled my denim jacket from the knapsack, and quickly put it over my bare skin. The jacket was damp from having been near the stream, but it felt luxurious compared to what I'd been wearing.

It wasn't going to be enough. I had to get a fire started, had to dry my jeans and socks and shoes. After opening a pouch on my knapsack and confirming that a metal container of matchbooks was as waterproof as the camping-equipment clerk had promised, I went to the aspens to get wood.

A breeze made my wet jeans cold and penetrated my jacket. I hugged myself, trying to generate warmth, but trembled worse than ever. Not knowing what I was doing, I imitated the campfire arrangement on the other side of the lake and put rocks in a circle in a clearing. I placed some twigs and dead leaves in the middle, set some broken sticks over them, and struck a match, but my hand shook so severely that as I brought the match toward the leaves, the flame went out. I tried again, desperate to keep my hand still, concentrating to control my arm muscles, and this time the flame touched the leaves, smoke rising, fire crackling.

A terrible thirst overtook me, but when I reached for the canteen on my belt, it wasn't there. I was dismayed not only that I'd lost it but that I hadn't noticed until now. My tongue was so pasty that it stuck to the roof of my mouth. The roar of the nearby stream tempted me to go to it and scoop water from my hands to my mouth, but I had no idea what kind of bacteria might be in it. I didn't dare risk getting sick. Vomiting or diarrhea would dehydrate me more than I already was.

All the while, sunset dimmed. I needed to pile up all the branches I could. As the last of the sun dipped below the mountains, I worked with greater urgency, dragging back large fallen limbs. Too soon, darkness enveloped me.

But it wasn't as black as my thoughts. Jason. Had Petey hurt him? Please, God, protect my son. *Please.*

The word became my mantra as the night's chill made me huddle closer to the fire. I was caught between the need to get warm and the fear of depleting my fuel supply before the night was over. I picked up the shirt I'd taken off. Holding it to the fire, turning it often, I feared that I'd burn it before I dried it. Although parts of it were in rags, it would provide an extra layer. Hating to expose my chest and back to the cold, I quickly removed my jacket and put on the shirt, then got into the jacket again. I took the rain slicker from my knapsack and put that on as well, pulling its hood over my head, anything to provide more insulation. My hands felt stung by the cold. Rubbing them over the fire, I blamed myself for not having been smart enough to bring gloves.

Hell, if I'd been smart, I never would have invited Petey into my home. But as hard as I tried to find some warning signs from the previous few days, I couldn't think of any.

You bastard! I inwardly screamed, then regretted the word, hating myself for insulting my parents. Every curse I could think of somehow involved them, but what had happened wasn't their fault. It was mine.

The weather forecaster had predicted a low of forty degrees Fahrenheit. If I fell asleep and the flames died, my body might get so cold that I'd never wake up. I thought of the warm sleeping bags that had been in the car. I imagined zipping into one of them and . . .

Awakening with a start, I found myself lying on the cold grass next to the barely glowing embers of the fire. Terrified, I tried to make my right hand work, groped for a handful of twigs, used a stick to poke them into the ash-covered coals, and watched the twigs burst into flame. Clumsily, I added larger pieces, my numbness slowly leaving me, but not the terror of dying from exposure. Dry-mouthed, I tried to chew peanuts and raisins. Praying for Jason helped energize my mind. Guarding the fire, I brooded about Petey.

Hated him.

And stayed awake.

17

At first, the feeling was so soft that I thought I imagined it, an invisible cool feather tickling my face in the darkness. Then I heard a subtle hissing on the hot rocks around the fire. In my confusion, it reminded me of the hiss from our coffeemaker whenever a few drops fell from the unit's spout and landed on the burner. At once, the flurries became a little stronger, the breeze that brought them turning colder.

I straightened from the stupor I'd been in, the gray of false dawn hinting at what swirled around me. My first alarmed instinct was to pile more wood on the fire, but as snow sizzled louder on the hot stones, the sun tried to struggle above the eastern peak, providing sufficient light for me to see the white on the grass around me. Dark clouds hung low. Despite the extra wood I'd thrown on the fire, the flames lessened. Smoke rose.

Panicked, I put on my knapsack. As Petey had told Jason when we'd left the highway, early June wasn't too late for snow in the mountains. On TV, the forecasters sometimes cautioned people that at high altitude, the weather could change for the worse without warning. But snow hadn't been predicted, and I'd figured that with the car and the tent, there wasn't anything to worry about. Now I cursed myself for not making better plans.

The highway was a half hour away by car. Frowning at the thickening, angrier clouds, I tried to calculate how far I'd have to go on foot. The road into the mountains had been so bad, the terrain so rough, that most of the time I hadn't been able to drive more than twenty miles an hour. That meant the highway was about ten miles off. But with my ankle hurting, ten miles might take me five or six hours on foot. In clothes too flimsy for the cold. Besides, as the flurries intensified, preventing me from seeing the lake, I realized that I probably wouldn't be able to find my way to the highway, that I'd risk wandering in circles until I dropped. Of course, if I'd known how to use the compass the camping-equipment clerk had sold me, my chances might have been different. But regret wasn't a survival emotion. Fear for Jason was. Rage at Petey was.

Thinking of Jason, I was suddenly reminded of the last time I'd seen him. The shelf of rock. 'Where's that cave you mentioned?' he'd asked.

The cave.

If I could find it before the storm got worse . . .

Fighting for strength, I lurched into the trees. Abruptly, visibility lessened, and I stumbled to the right toward the stream, not to drink from it but to use it as a guide. A white veil enveloped me as I followed the churning water up through the trees. The flakes became thicker. The snow on the ground covered my tennis shoes.

My tennis shoes. I'd bought a compass, which I didn't know how to use, and yet I hadn't taken the camping-equipment clerk's advice to buy sturdy hiking boots. They weren't necessary, I'd told him. We weren't going to be doing anything heavy-duty.

My feet started to lose sensation. Limping, I worked my way along a slope, worrying that a rock beneath the snow would shift and cause me to fall. Could I rely on my memory of where the cave was? For all I knew, it was on the opposite side of the stream, and it was merely a crevice in a cliff, which, as a thirteen-year-old boy, I had thought was huge.

The slope reached a steep ridge that went to the left. While I plodded along it, the aspens became pine trees. Branches jabbed at my arms and scratched my face. As the snow gusted thicker, I feared that I'd stumble past the cave and never see it. In the summer, hikers would find my body, or what was left of it after the forest scavengers had feasted on it.

I'm an architect, not a survival expert, I thought. I could hardly feel my hands. Why the hell hadn't I put gloves in my knapsack? I was so stupid, I *deserved* to die.

Trying to avoid a pine branch, I lost my footing, fell, and almost banged my head against a boulder on my right. Stupid. Deserve to . . .

18

Architect.

The vague thought nudged my dimming consciousness.

Know how to . . .

Slowly, the thought insisted, making me turn toward the boulder my head had nearly struck.

Build things.

When I struggled to my feet, I discovered that the boulder was as high as my chest. A second boulder, five feet to the left, was slightly less high. The boulders lay against a cliff, which formed a rear wall.

Build things, I repeated.

I stumbled to the pine branch I'd tried to avoid, put all my weight into it, and felt a surge of hope when a *snap* intruded on the smothering stillness. Working as hard as I could, I dragged the branch through the snow to the boulders and hefted it on top, bracing it across them. Staggering, I repeated the process several times, overlaying the needles, trying to form a roof.

The cold made my hands ache so much that tears streamed from my eyes, freezing on my cheeks, but I didn't have time to stick my hands, raw and bloody, under my rain slicker to try to warm them against my chest. There was too much to do. I used football-size rocks to weigh down the edges of the branches.

Delirious, I kicked the snow from the ground between the boulders, adding it to the drift outside the shelter. I stuck two needled branches at the shelter's entrance, forming a further windbreak. No matter how pained my hands were, I couldn't stop. I had to get dead twigs, leaves, and sticks, piling them at the back of the shelter.

I'd left a small hole at the back, where the boulders touched the cliff, hoping that smoke would escape through it. Away from the wind and the falling snow, I felt less assaulted by the cold. But my hands were like paws as I clumsily made a small pile of leaves and twigs, then fumbled to open the container of matches and pull out a book of them. I could hardly peel off one of the matches. My fingers didn't seem to belong to me. The match kept falling. It was finally so damaged that I had to peel off a second match, and this one blessedly caught fire when I struck it. It fell from my hands onto the clump of leaves and twigs, remained burning, and started a small fire. Smoke rose. I held my breath to keep from coughing. Pushed by heat, the smoke drifted toward the hole in the back.

My throat was so dry that it swelled shut, restricting the passage of air to my lungs. Desperate for something to drink, I reached my unfeeling right hand outside and fumbled to raise snow to my mouth. Instantly, I regretted it. The melting snow made my lips and tongue more numb than they already were. Shivering, I felt a deeper cold. I dimly remembered TV news reports that warned hikers caught in a blizzard not to eat snow as a way of getting moisture. They'd use so much body heat melting the snow in their mouths that they had a greater risk of dying from hypothermia.

The small amount of water from the melted snow hadn't done any good. Almost instantly, my lips became dry again. My swollen tongue seemed to fill my mouth. It was a measure of how dazed I'd become that I stared blearily down at the metal container of matches for a long time before my muddled thoughts cleared and I realized what I had to do. Shaking, I put the matches in the first-aid kit. I picked up their metal container, reached outside into the wind, packed the container with snow, and set it near the fire.

Slowly, the crystals melted. Worried about burning my hand, I put my shirtsleeve over my fingers before I gripped the hot container and pulled it away from the fire. It was only half an inch thick and two inches square, but it might as well have been a sixteen-ounce glass, so irresistible was the tiny amount of water in it. I forced myself to let it cool.

Finally, I couldn't be patient any longer. I used my sleeve to raise the container. I brought it close to my lips, blew on it, then gulped the warm, bitter water. My parched mouth absorbed it before I could swallow. I reached greedily outside and packed it with more snow. The lingering heat in the metal reduced the snow to water without my needing to set the container near the fire. Again, I gulped it. Again, the water never got near my throat. I refilled the container, placed it near the fire, and put a few more sticks on the flames.

That became my pattern. When my mouth and throat were moist enough, I pulled a plastic bag of peanuts and raisins from my knapsack, chewing each mouthful thoroughly, making them last. Worrying about Jason, hating Petey, I stared at the fire.

19

I vaguely remember going out to clear a drift from the smoke hole and to find more fuel. Otherwise, everything blurred. A couple of times when I woke, the flames had died out. On those occasions, all that kept me from freezing to death was the heat that the boulders had absorbed.

When I noticed that the pressure bandage around my left forearm was completely pink from the bleeding under it, I didn't react with dismay – the arm seemed to belong to someone else. Even when I saw sunlight beyond the branches and drifts at the entrance to my shelter, I felt oddly apart from it. Eventually, I discovered that an entire day had passed, but while I was trapped in the shelter, time hardly moved.

Probably I'd have lain in a stupor until energy totally failed me, if it hadn't been for water dripping through the roof. The cold drops struck my eyelids, shocking me. The sunlight was painfully bright. I moved my head. The drops fell into my mouth, tasting vaguely of turpentine from the resin on the pine branches. I gagged and spat the water out, sitting up to reach a dry spot.

More drops splashed around me, raising smoke from the almost-dead fire. Coughing, I grabbed my knapsack and stumbled outside, kneeing through the branches and drifts at the entrance. The heat of the sun was luxurious. Snow fell from trees. Rivulets started to form. Standing in the melting snow, my feet and shins became wet again, but it was a different kind of wet, the sun warming me so that I didn't shiver. From the sun's angle in the east, I judged that the time was midmorning. As much as my body didn't want to move, I knew that if I didn't take advantage of the improved weather, I might never have another chance.

I took a long look back at the shelter. It was loose and flimsy, as if a child had put it together, and yet I'd never been prouder of anything I'd designed.

I started down. Light reflecting off the snow lanced my eyes. By the time the sun was directly overhead, much of the snow had melted, the ground turning to mud as I crossed the first meadow. Still, the road remained hidden, and with little to guide me, all I could do was keep heading downward, aiming toward breaks in the trees where the road possibly went through them.

I don't remember reaching Highway 9, or collapsing there, or being found by a passing motorist. Apparently, that was at sunset. I woke up in a small medical clinic in a town called Frisco. By then, a state trooper had been summoned. He leaned over the bed and wanted to know what had happened to me. I later found out that it took him twenty minutes to get a coherent account from me. I kept screaming for Jason, as if my son was within arm's reach and I could help him.

The doctor stitched my left forearm. He disinfected and bandaged my hands, which he was worried might have frostbite.

The state trooper returned from talking on the phone. 'Mr Denning, the Denver police sent a patrol car to your house. The lights were off. No one answered the doorbell. When they aimed a flashlight through a garage window, they saw your Ford Expedition.'

'In the garage? That doesn't make sense. Why would Petey have gone back to the house?' The awful implication hit me. '*Jesus.*'

I tried to scramble out of bed. It took both the doctor and the state trooper to stop me.

'The officers broke a window and entered your house. They searched it thoroughly. It's deserted. Mr Denning, do you have any other vehicles?'

'What difference does . . .' My head pounded. 'My wife has a Volvo.'

'It isn't in the garage.'

That didn't make sense, either. 'The bastard must have taken it. Why? *And where are my wife and son?*' The increasingly troubled look on the trooper's face made me realize that he hadn't told me everything.

58

'The master bedroom and your son's room had been ransacked,' the trooper said.

'*What?*'

'Drawers had been pulled out, clothes scattered. It looked to the Denver officers as if somebody tore through those bedrooms in an awful hurry.'

I screamed.

Part Two

1

No matter how desperately I wanted to get home, the doctor refused to release me until the next morning. The state trooper drove me back to Denver. My right wrist ached from the IV the doctor had given me. After two days without food, I should have been ravenous, but the shock of my emotions killed my appetite. I had to force myself to chew slowly on a banana and take small sips from a bottle of orange juice.

When we turned onto my street, I saw the maple trees in front of our Victorian, a van and a station wagon in our driveway, and a Denver police car at the curb. Farther along were other cars and two trucks from local TV stations.

Getting out of the cruiser, I recognized the female television reporter who stalked toward me, armed with a microphone, a cameraman behind her. Her male equivalent from a rival station wasn't far behind. Reporters scrambled from the other cars.

'How the hell did they find out?' I asked.

'Get in the house.'

Holding out his arms, the state trooper former a barrier while I limped across the lawn. The pants and shirt the doctor had lent me (my own had been rags) hung loosely on me, increasing my sense of frailty. I managed to get inside and shut the door, blocking the noise of the reporters shouting my name. But other voices replaced them. A police officer, several men in sport coats, and others holding lab equipment stood in the living room, talking to one another.

One of the men, heavyset, with a mustache, noticed me in the foyer and came over. 'Mr Denning?'

The motion of nodding made me dizzy.

'I'm Lieutenant Webber. This is Sergeant Pendleton.' He indicated a younger, thinner man, clean-shaven.

'We checked the attic, the basement, and the trees in back. There's no sign of your wife and son,' Pendleton said.

For a moment, I didn't understand what the detective was talking about. The officers who'd entered the house the previous night had said that Kate and Jason weren't home. If Petey had taken them in Kate's Volvo, why would the police now have checked the attic and the . . . I felt sick when I realized that they'd been searching for well-hidden corpses.

'You don't look so good, Mr Denning. You'd better sit down.' Webber guided me into the living room, where the other men shifted to the side. 'I'll get you some water.'

Despite the fluids the doctor had given me, I still felt parched. When the detective came back with a full glass, I had a moment's disorientation, as if this were *his* home and I were a guest. I held the glass awkwardly between my bandaged hands and took a swallow. My stomach protested. I managed to ask, 'You've no idea where my wife and son are?'

'Not yet,' Webber said. 'The state police relayed what you told them, but we need to ask you some questions.' He looked at the scrapes on my face. 'Do you feel strong enough to answer them?'

'The sooner I do, the sooner I'll get my family back.'

A look passed between them, which I understood only later – they weren't as confident as I was that I'd get my family back.

'It would help if . . .' Pendleton glanced at where my fingertips projected from the bandages on my hands. 'We need to take your prints.'

'Take my . . . But why would . . .'

'So we can separate yours from the man who kidnapped your family. Which bedroom was his?'

'Go to the left at the top of the stairs.' I felt out of breath. 'The room's at the end of the hall. On the right.'

'That's the one with the baseball glove on the bed,' Webber told a technician.

'*Baseball glove?*' I tensed. '*On his bed?*'

Pendleton frowned. 'Yes. Is that important?'

'The glove was Petey's a long time ago.'

'I don't understand.'

'He's saying he doesn't want the damned thing anymore. Because he's got something better.'

'Slow down, Mr Denning. We're not following you.'

As a technician pressed my fingertips on an inky pad and then onto a sheet of paper that had a place for each digit, I tried as hard as I could to make them understand.

2

'Long-lost brother?'
'God help me, yes.'
'But how did you know he really *was* your brother?'
'He told me things only my brother could have known.'
The detectives gave each other that look again.
'What's wrong?'
'Just a thought,' Webber said. 'Maybe you heard what you wanted to hear. Some con men are good at making general statements sound specific. The people they're trying to fool fill in the gaps.'
'*No.* I tested him. He got every detail right.'
'They can be awfully clever.'
'But it doesn't make sense. A con man's motive would have been robbery. All he'd have needed to do was wait until Kate and I went to work and Jason was at school. He'd have had all day to loot the house. He wouldn't have needed to try to kill me. That was *personal.* That was Petey getting even!'
Pendleton made a calming gesture. 'We're just trying to get a sense of the man we're after.'
'For God's sake, a con man wouldn't be stupid enough to add murder and kidnapping to a burglary charge.'
'Unless he enjoyed violence.'
The direct look Webber gave me was dizzying in its effect. All along, I'd worked to assure myself that Jason and Kate were alive. Now, for the first time, I admitted to myself that Jason might be dead in the mountains, that Kate's body might be lying in a ditch somewhere.
I almost threw up.

Pendleton seemed to sense my panicked thoughts. His tone suggested an attempt to distract me. 'You don't happen to have a photograph of him, do you?'

'No.'

'With the excitement of the homecoming, you didn't take any pictures?'

'*No.*' I wanted to scream. If only I hadn't let a stranger into my house . . .

But he isn't a stranger, I tried to tell myself.

What the hell's the matter with you? I thought. After twenty-five years, Petey *is* a stranger!

'Mr Denning?'

I looked over at Pendleton, realizing that he'd said my name several times in an effort to get my attention.

'If you're able, we'd like you to walk through the house and tell us if anything's missing.'

'Whatever I have to do.'

They handed me latex gloves and put on their own. Unsteady, I began in the downstairs rooms, and immediately I noticed that the silverware Kate had inherited from her grandmother was no longer on the sideboard in the dining room. A silver tea set was missing also. In the TV room, the DVD and videotape players were gone, along with an expensive audio/video receiver.

'He'd probably have taken the TV, too,' I said bitterly, 'except that it's forty-six inches and wouldn't fit in the Volvo. I don't understand why he didn't keep the Expedition. It's got more room. He could have stolen more things.'

Webber looked uncomfortable. 'We'll talk about it later. Finish checking the house.'

The microwave and the Cuisinart food processor were missing from the kitchen. Numerous compact power tools were gone from the garage. My laptop computer wasn't in my office.

'What about firearms?' Pendleton asked. 'Do you have any in the house? Did he take them?'

'No guns.'

'Not even a hunting rifle?'

'No. I'm not a hunter.'

I made my way upstairs and froze at the entrance to Jason's

room, seeing his drawers pulled out, his clothes scattered on the floor. It took all my willpower to step inside and look around.

'My son saves his loose change in a jar on his desk,' I said.

It wasn't there.

I had an even harder time going into the chaos of the master bedroom. Stepping over some of Kate's dresses on the floor, I stared toward the back of the walk-in closet. 'Four suitcases are gone.'

As the implication hit me, my knees weakened so much that I had to lean against the doorjamb.

I'd assumed that Petey had ransacked the bureaus and closets because he was in a rush to find things to steal. Now, daring to hope, I took a closer look and realized that Kate's and Jason's clothes weren't just scattered – some of them were missing.

'If they're dead, he wouldn't have packed clothes for them,' I told the detectives. 'They're alive. They've got to be alive.'

In a daze, I followed Webber's instructions and kept looking. Some of *my* clothes were gone, too. My emergency stash of five hundred dollars was no longer at the back of my underwear drawer. Kate's jewel box was missing, along with a gold Rolex that I wore on special occasions. None of it mattered; only Kate and Jason did.

Throughout, the technicians kept photographing the chaos in the bedrooms and checking for fingerprints. To get out of their way, the detectives took me downstairs. Again I had the sense that the house no longer belonged to me.

'Why the Volvo?' I managed to ask. My voice seemed to come from far away. 'You said we'd talk about why he took it. The Expedition would have allowed him to steal more things.'

'Yes.' Pendleton spoke reluctantly. 'But the Volvo has something that the four-wheel-drive vehicle doesn't.'

'I don't know what you mean.'

'A trunk.'

'A . . .' Understanding forced me to sit.

'Maybe it isn't a good idea to go into the details.'

'Tell me.' My bandaged hands ached as I clutched the sides of the leather chair. 'I need to know.'

Webber glanced away, as if he couldn't bear to see my eyes. 'The way it looks, he came back here with your son and then subdued your wife. We have to assume they were bound and gagged.'

A rope seemed to cut into my wrists.

'He wouldn't have risked driving with them scrunched down in the backseat. Sooner or later, someone would have noticed,' Pendleton said.

'So he put them in the . . .'

'With the garage door closed, nobody would have seen him do it.'

'Jesus.' Imagining the stench of gasoline and car exhaust, I felt nauseated. 'How could they breathe?' I suddenly remembered Petey's haunted look when he'd described how the man and woman had forced *him* into a trunk.

A shrill beep startled me. Webber reached beneath his blazer and unhooked his cell phone from his belt. As he turned his back and walked toward the piano that Kate enjoyed playing, I barely heard his muted voice.

He put away the phone.

'Something?' I straightened, nervously hoping.

'The Volvo's been found. At a rest stop off Interstate Twenty-five.'

'Kate and Jason? Are they—'

'Not with the car. He left the state. Wyoming troopers found the Volvo north of Casper.'

'*Wyoming?*'

'For all he knew, he had plenty of time, and the Volvo wouldn't have been missed for several days,' Webber said. 'But suppose your wife was expected somewhere Saturday night, or suppose friends were going to arrive, and no matter what he did to persuade her, she wouldn't tell him about it?'

My skin turned cold at the thought of the pain Kate would have suffered.

'His best choice was to get your wife and son away before anyone suspected something was wrong,' Webber said. 'The nearest ATM for your bank has a record of a six-twenty-one P.M. withdrawal of five hundred dollars, the most the machine is allowed to take from an account on any one day. The videotape shows a man making the withdrawal, but his head's bowed so his face is hidden.'

Sweat chilled me when I realized that Petey had forced Kate to tell him our ATM number.

'It looks like he drove until nightfall, then used the cover of darkness to carjack another vehicle at the rest stop outside Casper. The likely target would have been someone traveling alone, but the driver wasn't found near the rest stop, so we assume that he or she is in the car with your wife and son. Until the driver's reported missing, we won't know what kind of car to search for.'

'Three people trying to breathe in a trunk? Jesus.'

Something in the detectives' eyes made me guess what they were thinking. As dangerous as Petey was, it might be only *two* people trying to breathe. He might not have let the driver live.

'Wyoming? But why in hell would he have gone to Wyoming?' At once, I remembered something Petey had said. 'Montana.'

'You sound like that means something to you,' Pendleton said. 'What are you getting at?'

'*Montana's north of Wyoming.*'

They looked at me as if I was babbling.

'No, listen to me. My brother said that when he saw me on the *CBS Sunday Morning* show, he was having breakfast in Montana. In a diner in Butte. Maybe that's why he's heading north. Maybe something in Montana's drawing him back.'

For the first time, Webber was animated. 'Good.' He hurriedly pulled out his phone. 'I'll send descriptions of this guy, your wife and your son to the Montana state police.'

'We'll contact the Butte police department,' Pendleton quickly added. 'Maybe they know something about this guy. If he's been arrested, they'll have a photograph of him that we can circulate.'

'Assuming he called himself Peter Denning up there.' I stared dismally down at the floor.

'There are other ways to investigate. Kidnapping across state lines means the FBI will get involved. The feds will do their best to match the fingerprints we find with ones they have on file. If this guy ever used an alias, we have a good chance of learning what it is.'

I tried hard to believe what they were saying.

'Have you a recent photograph of your wife and son?'

'On the mantel.' I looked in that direction. The beaming faces of

Kate and Jason made me heartsick. I'd taken the photograph myself. Normally, I hardly knew which button to press on a camera, but that day, I'd gotten lucky. We'd been to Copper Mountain, skiing, although falling down was more what Kate and I had done. Jason had been a natural, however. He'd grinned all day. Despite our bruises, so had Kate and I. In the photo, Kate wore a red ski jacket, Jason a green one, the two of them holding their knitted ski caps, Kate's blond hair and Jason's sandy hair glinting in the sun, their cheeks glowing.

'We'll return it as soon as we have copies made,' Pendleton said.

'Keep it as long as you have to.' The truth was, I hated to part with it. The empty place on the mantel reinforced my hollowness. 'Anything else – anything at all – just ask.'

What they need more than anything, I thought, is for God to answer my prayers.

3

Throughout, the phone had rung frequently. I'd been vaguely aware that a policeman had answered it. Now he handed me a list of who'd called, mostly reporters wanting an interview – TV, radio. What had happened would be all over the state by evening.

'Jesus, Kate's parents.' Hurrying, I left Webber and Pendleton in the living room. In the kitchen, my bandaged hand shook when I pressed numbers on the telephone.

'Hello?' an elderly man said.

'Ray . . .' I could hardly make my voice work. 'Sit down. I'm afraid I've got bad news.'

It made me sick to have to tell them, to hear their lives change in a minute. Neither of them was in good health. Even so, they immediately wanted to drive the three hundred miles from Durango through the mountains to Denver. I had a hard time convincing them to stay home. After all, what were they going to accomplish in Denver? Kate's father was breathing so fast that he sounded like he was going to have a heart attack.

'Stay put,' I said. 'All we can do now is wait.' I had a terrible mental image of Kate's father rushing to get to Denver, losing control of his car, and plummeting down a gorge. 'You can wait just as easily at home. I'll let you know the instant I learn anything.'

Setting down the phone, I took a deep breath, then noticed Webber and Pendleton at the entrance to the kitchen.

'What?' I asked.

'We just got a call from the Wyoming state police,' Webber said.

I braced myself.

'A woman from Casper's been reported missing. Saturday

evening, she was en route from visiting her sister in Sheridan, which is about a hundred and fifty miles north of where she lives.'

'You think my brother carjacked her?'

'The timing fits. Just after dark, she would have approached the rest stop where the Wyoming state police found your wife's Volvo. If the woman had to use the rest room . . .'

Inwardly, I flinched as I imagined Petey coming at the woman and how terrified she must have been.

'She was driving a 1994 Chevy Caprice,' Pendleton said. 'Apart from the fact that she was driving alone, her abductor probably singled her out because that type of car has a large trunk. He kept heading north. The Wyoming police gave the license number to the police in Montana, who found the Caprice at a rest stop on Interstate Ninety near Billings.'

'Were my wife and son . . .'

'With the Caprice? No.'

Something about Pendleton's tone made me suspicious. 'What about the woman who owned it?'

He didn't answer.

'Tell me.'

Pendleton glanced at Webber, who nodded as if giving permission.

'Her body was in the trunk.'

'Dear God.' I didn't want to know, and yet I couldn't stop from asking, 'What did Petey do to her?'

'Tied her hands and covered her mouth with duct tape. She' – Pendleton's voice dropped – 'had asthma. She choked to death.'

Thinking about the woman's desperate struggle to breathe, I could barely concentrate as Webber explained that Petey could have driven the Caprice from Casper, Wyoming, to Billings, Montana, that same night. He'd presumably carjacked another vehicle at the Billings rest stop. As the driver got out of the car to go to the bathroom, Petey would have lunged from the shadows.

I imagined how horrifying it would have been for Kate and Jason, pressed next to the dying woman in the dark, the air foul, feeling her thrash, hearing her muffled choking sounds, her frenzied movements, her strangled gasps slowing, getting weaker, stopping.

'It's never going to end,' I managed to say.

'No, we could be close to boxing him in,' Pendleton said. 'You predicted right. He was headed to Montana. Probably back to Butte. Billings is on the interstate that leads there. The local police don't have any criminal record for someone named Peter Denning. But they're searching for a man who matches this guy's description, especially that scar on his chin. The driver of the most recent vehicle he carjacked will soon have somebody report him or her missing. Once the Butte police get the make and license number of the vehicle, they can narrow their search. Meanwhile, they're checking motels and any other places they can think of where your brother might be able to hide your wife and son. Butte's not a big city. Believe me, if he shows himself, he'll be spotted.'

'But what if Petey senses the danger and leaves?'

'We thought of that. The Montana state police have unmarked cars along the interstate, watching for any white male in his thirties who's driving alone. As soon as the FBI processes his fingerprints, we'll have a better idea of who we're dealing with. The way he operates, he's had practice. He's probably got a criminal record, in which case the feds will come up with a recent mug shot we can distribute.'

4

One of the callers on the list the policeman had handed me was from my office, so I had to phone and again explain what had happened. Saying it out loud reinforced the nightmare. Several times, I heard the buzz of call waiting. Twice, I switched to the incoming call in case it had something to do with Kate and Jason, but both times it was a journalist. and after that, I didn't pay attention to call waiting.

The moment I hung up, the phone rang again. We had caller ID, but most times I'd found it was useless, a lot of the calls listed as UNKNOWN CALLER or, in this case, BLOCKED NUMBER. But I answered anyhow, and of course, it was another journalist. After that, I let the policeman answer the phone.

When the lab crew finally left, Webber, Pendleton, and everybody else going with them, the house had never felt so empty. My footsteps echoed off the hardwood floors as I went upstairs. Fingerprint powder smudged furniture, and clothes remained on the bedroom floors. I sat on Jason's bed, inhaling his boy smell. I went into the master bedroom, picked up one of Kate's blouses, and pressed it to my face.

I have no idea how long I remained there. The phone rang again. Ignoring it, I went into the bathroom, took off my borrowed clothes, and tried to take a bath without getting my bandaged hands and my stitched left forearm wet. Dirt and dried blood floated from me. Steam rose, but instead of the water's heat, what I felt was spreading pain as the effect of the pills the doctor had given me began to wear off. The extent of my bruises was appalling. I did my best to shave, then put on fresh clothes, but I begrudged their comfort, telling myself that I didn't deserve it, given the hell that Kate and Jason would be going through.

The doorbell rang. Limping, I needed extra time to get down-stairs. Meanwhile, the bell rang again and then again. *If this is a reporter* . . . I thought. When I opened the door, I saw a straight-backed man in a dark suit, with polished shoes and short, neat, slightly graying hair. His lean face was all business.

'Mr Denning?'

Behind him, out on the street, a camera crew started forward.

'I'm not giving interviews.' I stepped back to close the door.

'No, you don't understand. I'm FBI Special Agent John Gader.' The man showed his ID. 'I kept phoning, but no one answered, so I took a chance and drove over.'

'I was . . . I didn't . . . Please, come in.'

As the reporters neared the house, I shut the door and locked it.

Gader opened his briefcase and took out several small electronic devices. 'These are voice-activated tape recorders.' He linked one to the living room phone. 'Is there a phone in the kitchen?'

He installed a recorder there also. 'We'll deal with the rest of the house later. I've already obtained a court order to have your phone tapped and all calls traced, but it never hurts to have a backup system. If the man who took your wife and son phones to demand a ransom, we'll have a recording of it here, as well as through our intercept at the phone company.'

'There won't be a ransom demand.'

'You never know.'

'I *do* know. My brother doesn't want money. He wants my wife and my son.'

'Your brother?' Gader sounded as if he knew only the general parameters of the case.

So, yet again, I explained what had happened. Gader pulled out a pocket-size tape recorder and took notes as a backup. He assured me that the Bureau would give my case its full attention. After he left, it was as if he'd never been present.

Emptiness again enveloped me.

This can't have happened, I thought, straining to convince myself. I'm having a nightmare. I'll wake up soon. Kate and Jason will be back. Everything'll be perfect, the way it was.

But when I woke in the night, pain racking my body, I reached next to me and was confronted by the emptiness on Kate's side of the bed.

Nothing had changed.

As the days stretched on, the Butte police failed to catch Petey or find any sign of Kate and Jason. The Montana state troopers finally stopped watching the interstate.

5

'**H**e isn't your brother.'
    '*What?*'

'The man who took your wife and son isn't Peter Denning,' Gader said as he stood at my front door. 'His name's Lester Dant.'

I felt as if I'd been shoved. 'You mean Petey used the name Lester Dant as an alias?'

'No. The other way around.'

'For God's sake, what are you talking about?'

'The prints the crime-scene crew found in your house belong to a man named Lester Dant.' Gader stepped inside. 'Here's the file we have on him. Background. Social Security number. Criminal record.'

Bewildered, I sat in the living room and stared at the photograph that came with the documents. Complete with chipped tooth and scarred chin, Petey's face confronted me from a mug shot that had been taken in Butte.

But the file identified the man as Lester Dant. He'd been born in Brockton, Indiana, a year before Petey was born. Over the years, he'd been arrested for, but never convicted of, auto theft, armed robbery, and manslaughter.

'Dant did time for extortion, drug dealing, and rape,' Gader said. 'It's a miracle he didn't kill you all in your sleep. See where the Butte police have a record on him? Lester Dant got in a bar fight and put a man in the emergency ward. He was released from jail a week before the *CBS Sunday Morning* broadcast you were on.'

'But . . .' My sense of unreality intensified so much that the living room seemed to tilt. 'How did he know so much about Petey?'

'They must have crossed paths,' Gader said. 'Maybe your brother saw the *CBS Sunday Morning* show and talked about it with some people he knew, including Dant. Later, in private, Dant got more specifics from him and decided to pay you a visit.'

I raised my voice in dismay. 'My brother hung around with people like *Dant?*'

'Maybe your brother had as rough a life as Dant claimed.'

'But why in God's name didn't Petey come to see me himself?'

Gader stared at me, and I tensed with the realization that Dant might have killed Petey to prevent him from interfering.

'It doesn't make sense,' I told Gader. 'If Dant's this vicious, why would he have packed clothes for my son? Why would he have taken Jason along instead of . . .' The words caught in my throat.

'Killing him?' Gader looked uncomfortable. 'I'm not sure that's a topic you want to get into.'

'Let *me* decide that. *Answer me.*'

Gader exhaled slowly. 'It's probable that Dant took your son to put pressure on your wife. By threatening to hurt Jason, he could force your wife to submit to him.'

I felt as if I'd been struck in the face. 'No.'

'I'm sorry, Mr Denning. You asked me to be candid.'

'Petey . . . Lester Dant . . .'

'Fingerprints don't lie.'

'There's got to be a mistake. What Petey told me about when we were kids and how he was abducted—'

'What *Dant* told you. He probably kept buying your brother drinks to keep him talking, supplying details.'

'But it all felt so *real*. I'm sure he was telling the truth.'

'Listen, some of these con men are good enough actors, they could have won Academy Awards if they'd gone straight.'

'It's just that . . .'

'Everything was a lie. The name of the town in West Virginia where he told you he was held prisoner.'

'Redemption.'

'There's no such place.'

'What?'

'Other parts of his story don't hold together, either. He told you he got the scar on his chin last summer when he fell off a ladder on a roofing project in Colorado Springs.'

'That's right.'

'Well, our agents showed Dant's photograph to all the roofing contractors in that area. Nobody recognized him. The same with the construction contractors. If somebody had gotten a two-inch gash on his face, they'd remember it, they say. It would have required stitches, but the hospitals in the area don't have any record of a construction worker coming in last summer with that kind of injury. However, the Colorado Springs police have a security-camera tape of a man who looks like Dant beating a clerk in a liquor store robbery. A police car chased his vehicle into the mountains. He may have gotten the injury to his face when his car skidded off a curve and tumbled into a draw. There was blood but no driver when officers climbed down to examine the wreckage.'

Bitterness twisted my voice. 'Yeah, Petey has a habit of vanishing.'

'You mean Dant.'

'Sure . . . Dant.'

'We'll get him,' Gader said. 'The money he took from you won't last long. Eventually he'll have to steal gain. One mistake. That's all he has to make, and we'll get him.'

'Eventually.' The word that Gader had used stuck in my throat. I tried not to think about what was happening to Kate and Jason.

6

So a man who was my brother or who *wasn't* my brother but who was pretending to be him had abducted my family and torn my world apart. He'd covered his trail by fooling me and the police into thinking he was going to Butte, Montana. Then he'd vanished off the face of the earth. No other motorists were reported missing for that time period, which meant that the police didn't have a license number and a description of a carjacked vehicle to focus their search. There were numerous reports of stolen cars. Hundreds in Montana, Wyoming, and Colorado. Thousands nationwide. But when any of these were located, Petey (I still couldn't bring myself to call him Dant) was never linked to them. Perhaps he'd switched license plates with another vehicle. The owner of the other vehicle might have taken quite a while to notice that the plates had been switched, by which time Petey might have stolen another car or switched plates again. Or perhaps Petey had taken the money he got for the things he stole from my house to buy an old car and then showed a fake ID to register it under an alias that the police didn't know he had. Perhaps. Could have. Might have.

The local TV stations repeated the story. The networks picked it up, especially CBS, which included excerpts from the *Sunday Morning* segment that Kate, Jason and I had been in. They emphasized the sick twist that a man who claimed to be my long-lost brother had vanished again, this time with my family. I got calls from men who claimed to have taken Kate and Jason. In graphic detail, they described the torture they inflicted. The police traced the calls, but nothing was learned, except that some people love to aggravate the suffering of others. Several of the callers were charged with obstructing the investigation, but none ever went to jail.

Despair and lack of sleep gave me headaches. I went through the motions of working, but my staff ran the business. I spent most of my time in a trance. As the search lost momentum, it became obvious that unless Petey – again I tried to substitute Dant's name, but I couldn't manage to do so – unless Petey stumbled into a policeman, he was never going to be found, especially if he grew a beard to cover the scar on his chin so his mug shot would no longer resemble him.

Blurred photos of Kate and Jason appeared on milk cartons and in mailers. *Have you seen this woman and this boy?* the caption read. But if *I* couldn't recognize the indistinct faces, I couldn't imagine anyone else being able to. I'd never paid attention to the faces on those milk cartons and those mailers when it was someone else's wife or child who was missing. How could I hope that anyone would pay attention when it was *my* wife and child who were missing?

Friends were supportive initially: phone calls of encouragement, invitations to dinner. But after a while, many wearied of my despair. Unable to come up with fresh expressions of sympathy, they kept their distance.

A few remained loyal, though, and it was from my next-door neighbor, Phil Barrow, that I learned how things could get worse. I was listlessly raking dead leaves in my front yard, vaguely aware that autumn had once been my favorite time of year, frost in the air, wood smoke, the rattle of dead leaves, and now it meant nothing, when I happened to look up and see Phil hug his sweater tighter to his chest, then step off the sidewalk and approach me.

'How are you doing, Brad?'

Kate had once told me that no matter how shitty either of us felt, we should always answer 'Never better.'

Phil's shoulders moved up and down as if from a bitter chuckle. 'Yeah, I can see that. You've been raking that same pile of leaves for about an hour.'

'Neatness counts.'

Phil looked down at his hands. 'I don't know if I should tell you this.'

'Oh?' I felt a cold breeze.

'Marge says I shouldn't upset you, but I figure you've got enough trouble without getting *more* trouble from the people who are supposed to be helping you.'

The breeze got colder. 'What are you talking about?'

'An FBI agent came to see me at work yesterday.'

'John Gader?'

'Yeah, that was his name. He asked me if you and Kate got along. If there were a lot of family arguments. If you ever hit your son.'

'*What?*'

'He wanted to know if you lost your temper when you drank. If you had a girlfriend.'

'The FBI suspects *me?*'

'**Y**ou son of a bitch.'

Gader faltered when I stepped in front of his car in the parking garage of Denver's Federal Building. 'Calm down.'

'You think I killed my wife and son!'

'I gather that some of your friends told you I'd been asking them questions about you.'

'Destroying my reputation is more like it!' Fists clenched, I stepped toward him.

'Take it easy,' Gader said.

Its engine echoing, a car drove past in the garage, the driver frowning at us.

'This area has security cameras. It's patrolled,' Gader said. 'You don't even want to *think* about assaulting a federal agent on federal property.'

'It'd be worth it!'

Gader held up his hands in surrender. 'I'm not going to fight you. If you'll calm down and listen . . .'

Behind him, a door banged open. A guard stepped into the garage's harsh lights. His hand was on his holstered gun. 'Is everything all right, Mr Gader?'

'I'm not sure.' Gader's lean face was stern. '*Is* everything all right, Mr Denning?'

I squeezed my fists so tightly that my knuckles ached.

'If you go to prison, how's that going to help your wife and son?' Gader asked.

I trembled, feeling anger burn my face.

'Think about what your family needs,' Gader said.

I relaxed my fists.

'It's going to be fine, Joe,' Gader told the guard. 'You can leave us now.'

'I'll watch the monitor,' the guard said.

'Good idea.' Gader waited until the door rumbled shut.

'How could you possibly think I killed my wife and son?'

'It's a standard part of an investigation. When a family member's missing or killed, a lot of times the person responsible is another family member.'

'Jesus, how could I have driven the Volvo to Wyoming, then stolen a car and abandoned it in Montana, and somehow have gotten back here to maroon myself in the mountains?'

'You could have if this guy Dant had been working for you.'

The depth of Gader's suspicion shocked me. '*Why would I have asked Petey to do that?*'

'Dant. If you had money troubles and needed the payout from a life-insurance policy, or if you had a girlfriend who made your wife an inconvenience.'

I clenched my fists again.

'But there weren't any unusual withdrawals from your bank accounts or your stock portfolio, and there wasn't a hint of scandal about your relations with your family. Besides, I couldn't figure out how you'd have crossed paths with Dant after he got out of jail in Butte and . . . Quit staring at me like that. The investigation wasn't going anywhere. I had to try a different approach.'

'You son of a bitch, you made my friends think I'm responsible for my family's disappearance.'

'It wasn't personal. I told you, I was following standard procedure. The point is, you came through the investigation perfectly. You're in the clear.'

'Thanks. Thanks a fucking lot.'

8

'You seem determined to avoid using Lester Dant's name,' the psychiatrist said.

I didn't answer.

'The FBI did a thorough background check,' the psychiatrist continued. 'They proved that he's not your brother.'

My chest was so tight that I could hardly get the words out. 'They think Dant crossed paths with my brother and learned what had happened to him as a child. He decided to switch places with Petey, possibly killed him.'

I stared out a window toward a pine tree.

'But you don't believe it,' the psychiatrist said.

'I *can't.*'

' "Can't?" ' The psychiatrist evaluated the word.

The tightness spread to my throat. 'If I accepted that Dant kidnapped my wife and son, I'd have to admit that, given his profile, he'd have done whatever he wanted to them and . . .' I couldn't bring myself to say 'killed them'. I kept staring through the window toward the pine tree. 'But if Petey was using Dant as an alias . . .' My voice broke. 'If *Petey* took them, there's a good chance they're still alive.'

The psychiatrist sat forward. 'Why do you think that?'

'I've tried to put myself in his place.' The tree became a blur. 'I've done my best to imagine what Petey must have felt when he came into my house. My loving family, my comfortable surroundings. Petey wouldn't have wanted merely to kill me for destroying his life. He'd have wanted *my* life, the one I'd made for myself.'

I forced myself to continue. 'I've analyzed the moment when Petey pushed me into the gorge. I've relived it again and again. I

86

think Petey's plan was to wait until Jason wasn't around and then kill me, making it look like an accident. Then he intended to sympathize with Kate and Jason, to make himself indispensable, and eventually to take my place. The only problem was, Jason saw him push me.'

I took a deep breath. 'So the plan was ruined. What was Petey going to do? Kill Jason? Make *that* death look like an accident also? Try to take my place with Kate? No. Jason was an essential part of what Petey wanted. Not just my wife but my *family*. Obviously, he couldn't live in my house then, not without Jason telling the police what he'd seen. *But Petey could steal my family.* He could hide them someplace and screw my wife whenever he wanted. He could force my son to treat him like a father.' I squeezed the words out. 'At least they'd be *alive*. If Petey and Dant are the same person. If *Petey* took them. But if Dant's who the FBI claims he is, if he isn't Petey, he probably killed Jason right away and hid his body in the mountains. Then he made the best of a failed plan by looting the house and forcing Kate to go someplace with him, probably the Montana mountains, where he could rape her as much as he wanted before he got bored with her and—' I stopped, unable to admit Kate might be dead.

The psychiatrist narrowed her eyes as if I'd just described hell. But whether it was the hell that Kate and Jason suffered or whether it was the hell of what she considered my delusional mind, I couldn't know.

9

As I swallowed another antidepression pill, I heard the doorbell ring. The FBI with news, I hoped.

But when I opened the door, I frowned at children in costumes on my porch. Trick-or-treaters. It was Halloween, but I hadn't been aware. I didn't have candy. Not that they cared. They stumbled back as if *I* was the one in a scary costume. When I tried to explain, they ran from the porch.

I closed the door and shut off the light. Peering out a darkened window, I saw other costumed children, and as I hoped, they passed the house. I couldn't help remembering that Halloween was one of Jason's favorite holidays. How he'd loved to dress up as a space monster or a mad scientist. How *I* had loved to go out with him. But that wasn't going to happen now. It made me angry that I'd frightened the children. Was my face that twisted with loss? Were my eyes that dark with insanity?

The vial of pills remained in my hand. Cursing, I threw it across the living room. Depression gave way to fury. What was it that Petey had said when he'd first approached me and I'd thought that he was a fake, when I'd told him to get away before I beat the shit out of him? 'Brad, you'd have a harder time outfighting me than when we were kids.' We'll see, I thought. In that moment, as I heard someone on the street shout to warn children away from my porch, I vowed to stop waiting for the police and the FBI to do something. I had to stop hoping that something would happen.

I had to *make* something happen.

10

' A theory of substitution?' Gader asked.

'Yes.' I was so distraught that I stood in front of his desk instead of sitting. 'We know that Petey lied.'

'Dant.'

'But what if the reason he was so convincing is that he based his lies on the truth? He *was* in Butte and Colorado Springs at the times he said, after all. He just wasn't doing what he claimed.'

'What's that got to do with this theory of—'

'You told me that West Virginia doesn't have a town called Redemption.'

'That's correct.'

'But what about the rest of the country? Is there a town called Redemption *anywhere*? Or what about towns in West Virginia whose names have a religious connotation similar to Redemption?'

Gader thought about it. 'Possibly. It would help Dant to keep his stories straight.'

'Could you check?'

Gader leaned back in his chair. His thin face looked even thinner from weariness. 'I'll try. The Bureau has me working double time on . . .' He pointed toward a thick stack of documents on his desk. 'What difference would it make? All that stuff Dant said about his past was a lie to make you sympathize with him.'

'But what if it was only *partly* a lie?'

'It still won't help us find your wife and son. Every lead's been followed. The task force has been disbanded. All we can do is wait for Dant to surface.'

'Petey.' I strained to keep control. 'Damn it, doesn't *anything* you learn about him take you one step closer to understanding his patterns and where he might go?'

'Sure,' Gader said. 'Of course.' He stood and walked me to his frosted-glass door. 'The theory of substitution,' he said without conviction. 'Certainly. I'll definitely do some checking. By all means, if you think of anything else, just let me know.'

11

'Mr Payne will see you now,' the receptionist said.

I set down the three-month-old *Newsweek*, which might as well have been up-to-date, given how little I'd paid attention to what was happening in the world. Crossing the small waiting area, I entered an office that was spacious by comparison, although in my own company it would have been considered tiny.

It was austere: a wooden chair, a desk, a computer, another chair. And a fish tank into which a portly, bespectacled man tapped grains of food. His white hair contrasted with the healthy ruddiness of his cheeks. His sport coat was off. He wore yellow braces over a blue shirt.

'How are you this afternoon, Mr Denning?'

'Not very good, I'm afraid. Otherwise, I wouldn't be here.'

Payne nodded, his puffy chin bobbing slightly. 'It's for sure nobody comes to me with happy news. I used to internalize it all. At the end of the day, I'd be a wreck. But then I remembered the fish tank in my dentist's office and how it calmed me before I went in to have my teeth drilled. These are just garden-variety goldfish. I don't know if they help my clients, but they do wonders for *me*. Would you believe that I used to be a hundred-and-forty-pound bundle of anxiety? But ever since I got these fish, I've' – he spread his arms to his girth – 'blossomed.'

I had to smile a little.

'That's the spirit, Mr Denning.' Payne set down the box of fish food and eased into the chair behind his desk. 'Would you like some coffee? A soft drink?'

I shook my head no.

He laced his fingers over his ample stomach and gave me the

91

most sympathetic look I'd ever experienced. 'Then tell me how I can help you.'

Haltingly, I explained about Kate and Jason.

Payne nodded. 'I read about it in the newspapers and saw the stories on television. A terrible thing.'

'My attorney says you're the best private investigator in Denver.'

'Maybe he doesn't know a lot of private investigators.'

'He says you used to be with the FBI. He says you tracked down a serial killer.'

'That's right.'

'He says you predicted where a team of interstate bank robbers was going to hit next.'

'True.'

'And *when* they were going to do it. He also says you blocked a domestic terrorist attempt to—'

'But that was only on the weekends.'

The joke caught me unprepared.

'Please. All that flattery just makes my cheeks get redder,' Payne said. 'I was part of a team. We each did our share.'

'My attorney says that you did *more* than your share.'

'Did he also tell you that it cost me my first marriage, not to mention a bullet in my knee that forced me to leave the Bureau? I finally got the wisdom to stop having undue expectations of myself. *You* shouldn't have undue expectations either, Mr Denning. I'm good, but only because I often see patterns other don't. For something like this, it's important to your emotional health that you don't count on the impossible.'

With nowhere else to turn, I swallowed my disappointment. 'Fair enough.'

'So let me ask you again: How do you think I can help you?'

'The FBI and the police have given up.' I tried to keep my voice steady. 'It's been six months. I heard somewhere that in missing persons' cases, the more time drags on, the less chance there is of finding the people who are missing.' I could barely add, 'Finding them alive at least.'

'It depends. Every case is different. Statistics are a record of the past, not a prediction of the future.'

'In other words, you've got an open mind. You're exactly the person I need. Name any fee you want. Money isn't an issue.'

'Money isn't an issue with me, either. I charge the same fee to everyone,' Payne said. 'But what do you expect *I* can do that the police and the FBI couldn't?'

'At the moment, they're not doing anything.'

'Possibly because there isn't anything to be learned.'

'I refuse to believe that.'

'Understandably.' Payne spread his hands. 'But you have to realize that I can't duplicate the resources available to the FBI.'

'Of course not. You can listen to new ideas, though. You can . . . I don't think I've made myself clear. I don't want to hire you just to continue the investigation.'

'Oh?' Payne looked mystified. 'Then what *do* you want?'

'I want you to teach me so *I* can continue the investigation.'

12

'I need a handgun,' I said.

'What kind?' The clerk had a beard and a ponytail.

'Whatever's the most powerful and shoots the most bullets.'

'Rounds,' the clerk said.

'Excuse me?'

'They're not called bullets. They're called rounds. The bullet's the part that blows away from the casing and hits the target.'

'Fine. Whatever shoots the most rounds.'

'Is this for target shooting or home defense? The reason I ask is, some people believe a shotgun's the best way to deal with a burglar.'

'How about one of those?'

'A revolver? It only shoots six. These semiautomatics shoot more. But you'll need to decide which caliber you want: nine-millimeter or forty-five.'

'Which is the biggest?'

'The forty-five.'

'I'll take it.'

'Just so you know your options, biggest isn't always best. The forty-five holds seven rounds in the magazine and one in the firing chamber. But this nine-millimeter over here holds *ten* rounds in the magazine and one in the chamber. A lot of power with eight rounds, versus somewhat less power but *eleven* rounds.'

'How much less power?'

'With the nine-millimeter? Let's put it this way, it gets the job done. Actually, the only reason the magazine in this nine-millimeter holds only ten rounds is that in the mid-1990s, Congress passed an antiassault weapon law that limits the capacity of handgun magazines. But *before* the law . . .'

94

'Yes?'

'There's a gun show in town Saturday. I'll introduce you to a friend who's willing to sell a *pre*law Beretta nine-millimeter that holds *fifteen* rounds in the magazine and one in the chamber.'

'That's a lot.'

'You bet. Don't misunderstand. There's nothing illegal about him selling the weapon. The law only forbids manufacturing or importing magazines that hold more than ten rounds. But because my friend bought his before the law was enacted, it's legal. That model doesn't come on the market often, so I expect you'll have to pay extra.'

'Naturally.'

'But after that . . .' The clerk looked uncomfortable.

'After that?'

'No offense. You've obviously new to this. So you don't shoot your foot off, you might want to take some lessons.'

13

In the darkness beyond my window, the first snowstorm of the season gusted, but I hardly paid attention, too busy using Internet addresses that Payne had given me: sites that he said the FBI favored for researching places. Next to my new laptop computer, I had dictionaries and thesauruses to help me find words associated with redemption. Most weren't promising. I couldn't imagine anyone calling a place Atonement, Propitiation, Mediation, Intercession, or Judgment, for example. As it turned out, a village in Utah *was* called Judgment.

On the wall to my right, I'd attached a large map of the United States. Periodically, I got up and stuck a labeled thumbtack where a place's name had a religious connotation. After several hours, there were tacks all over the country, but no pattern. None was in Montana. I was beginning to understand why Gader hadn't wanted to investigate my theory.

My discouragement increased when I suddenly realized how many places had been named after saints. More thumbtacks got added to the map. I soon didn't have any more.

14

'How does a person create a false identity?'

Payne considered my question while tapping fish food into the tank. His chair creaked when he settled his weight into it. 'The way it used to be done, first you pick a city where you've never lived.'

'Why?'

'To prevent your real identity and your assumed one from contaminating each other. If you were raised in Cleveland, you don't want the character you're creating to have come from there, too. Otherwise, someone investigating your new identity might go there, show your photograph around, and find someone who remembers you under your real name.'

I nodded.

'So you go to a different part of the country. But avoid small communities where everybody knows everybody else and can tell an investigator immediately whether someone who looks like you ever came from there. Pick a city, not a town – there's less continuity; memories are shorter. Let's say you choose Los Angeles or Seattle. Go to the public library there and read newspapers that came out a few years after you were born. You're looking for disasters – house fires, car accidents, that sort of thing – in which entire families were killed. That detail's important because you don't want anyone left alive to be able to contradict your story. Study the obituaries of the victims. You're looking for an ethnically compatible male child who, if he had lived, would be the same age you are now.'

'And then?'

'Let's say the victim you choose to impersonate was named

97

Robert Keegan. His obituary will probably tell you where he was born. You send away for a copy of his birth certificate. Not a big deal. People lose copies of their birth certificates all the time. Public record offices are used to that kind of request.'

'But . . .' I frowned. 'If Robert Keegan died, won't there be a note about it on his birth certificate, some kind of cross-reference?'

'Not in the days before computers became an essential part of our society,' Payne said. 'The year that you were born, information wasn't exchanged efficiently. The authorities would send you the copy of Robert Keegan's birth certificate without giving it another thought. Wait a while so that a further inquiry about Robert Keegan won't attract attention. Then contact the hall of records for a copy of Robert Keegan's *death* certificate. The reason I mentioned Los Angeles and Seattle earlier is that the states of California and Washington put Social Security numbers on their death certificates. Many parents apply to get a Social Security number for their children while they're filling out birth certificate forms in the hospital, so the odds are Keegan had one, even though he died young. With his birth certificate and his Social Security number, you can get a driver's license, a passport, and any other major identification that you need. You can get a job, pay taxes, and open a bank account. In short, you can assume his identity.' Payne gave me a long look. 'But we're not talking about you.'

'No, we're talking about my brother. If Lester Dant were dead, could Petey have assumed his identity the way you just explained?'

Payne kept studying me. 'Before your brother was first arrested, photographed, fingerprinted, and booked as Lester Dant? Theoretically.'

'Then I'm not crazy.' I let out a long breath. 'Petey and Dant *could* be the same person. Dant could be Petey's alias.'

'But it didn't happen,' Payne said.

'What?'

'Your brother didn't assume Lester Dant's identity.'

'How can you be so damned sure?'

'Because earlier this morning, I paid a visit to Gader. We knew each other when I was with the Bureau. For old times' sake, I asked to be allowed to review Dant's file.'

I felt uneasy about what Payne was leading up to.

'The file was very revealing,' Payne said. 'You were so insistent that your brother and Dant were the same man, Gader had Dant's background double-checked. There's no death certificate anywhere. Moreover, Dant didn't even apply for a Social Security number until he was a teenager. The signature on the application is consistent with the signatures Dant had to give at the various times he was arrested. Dant and your brother are two different people.'

'*No.*'

'It's the truth,' Payne said.

'That means my wife and son are dead!'

'Not necessarily. Without evidence to the contrary, there's always a reason to hope.'

'Without their corpses, you mean.'

Payne didn't reply for a moment. 'I'm sorry, Mr Denning.'

I stared toward the fish tank. 'You didn't see the look in Petey's eyes when he told me about the goldfish that he and I had buried in the backyard and how the neighbor's cat dug it up. He didn't say it as if he were remembering something he'd heard. His eyes had the clarity of someone who'd been there. *That was Petey talking to me.*'

'Perhaps. But I haven't the faintest idea how you can prove it.'

'I will.' I stood. 'Believe me, somehow I will.'

'Before you go, I've been meaning to ask you something.'

I stopped at the doorway and locked back at him.

'From my years with the Bureau, my nose is sensitive to the smell of cordite. That smell is on my right hand from when we shook hands when you came in. Have you been using firearms, Mr Denning?'

15

'Ready on the firing line!' the female instructor barked.
We straightened.

'Ready on the right!'

We checked in that direction.

'Ready on the left!'

Through safety glasses, we checked in *that* direction, making sure that nobody was doing anything careless.

'*One*,' the instructor yelled, 'grip your holstered weapon! *Two*, draw and aim from the waist! *Three*, raise your weapon to your line of sight! *Four*, press the trigger!'

Eight almost-simultaneous shots filled the long, narrow indoor shooting range. They echoed off the concrete walls, my protective earphones making the reports sound oddly distant.

Although the instructor was directly behind me, she too sounded muffled. 'Aim to the right of the target! To the left!'

We obeyed, not firing, but checking for other targets, which she'd warned could pop up at any time.

'Weapon to your waist! Secure it!'

As one, the eight of us completed the sequence and took our hands from our holstered firearms.

The range became silent.

'Not bad,' she said. 'Let's see if anybody hit anything.'

Each of us stood in a slot, with a ledge in front for ammunition and spare magazines. A button to the left engaged a motorized pulley that brought in the targets.

The instructor studied the results. 'Okay. Nobody hit the bull's-eye, but I don't expect you to at this point. At least none of you missed the target completely. Denning, you hit closest, but you're still a little high and to the left. Practice more dry-firing at home. Stop twisting your wrist when you press the trigger.'

She went on to correct the other students. We put masking tape over the holes in our targets, touched a button that returned the targets to the end of the gallery, and straightened when she shouted, 'Ready on the firing line!'

16

I went to a fitness center every day. I'd never been in top physical condition, but since Petey had taken Kate and Jason, I'd fallen apart. A junk-food diet in combination with too much alcohol and no activity had caused me to put on twenty pounds. No longer. I hired a trainer. Knowing that I had to start slowly, I was nonetheless impatient to get on with it. I progressed from thirty to sixty minutes a day on the machines. I started jogging, at first at the center's indoor track and then outside in the cold. One mile. Two. Five. I lost the weight I'd put on. Fat became muscle.

I took self-defense classes. Angle. Force. Mass. Architect's language. I no longer pretended to try to work. As far as I was concerned, I had only one job, so I disbanded my company, giving my employees a generous severance package. When I wasn't preparing myself by shooting and physical training, I spent my time searching the Internet, using other Web addresses that Payne had given me.

In my former life, I'd always been too busy to explore the Internet. Now I was amazed at how much information I could obtain, provided that, thanks to Payne, I knew where to look. I found Lester Dant's birth information, which was exactly as the FBI had indicated: he'd definitely been born in Brockton, Indiana, on April 24, a year before Petey had been born. I searched the databases for every state in the union but couldn't find corresponding *death* information about Lester Dant. Without proof that Petey had assumed Dant's identity, I grudgingly tested the FBI's theory that Dant had assumed *Petey's* identity, but no matter how far I spread my search, I couldn't find any proof that Petey had died, and, if he had, whether he'd been murdered.

Thanksgiving (the holiday's name made me bitter) had passed. Kate's parents had asked me to spend it with them. I'd refused, hardly in a social mood. But then I'd thought that they were as desolate as I was and we might as well try to console one another. The three of us drank some wine and watched football in the kitchen while we made the dinner, but I never managed a holiday spirit, constantly worrying that the Denver police or Gader and Payne had mislaid the phone number I'd given them in case Kate and Jason were found while I was away.

For Christmas, Kate's parents came to visit. But as soon as I saw Kate's father, I wished that I'd saved them the trouble and had gone to them. I could barely conceal my dismay at how this once tall, robust man had been so stooped by his heart condition, aggravated by worry. As hard as we tried to be festive, we kept remembering former, better Christmases, like when I'd been dating Kate in college and I'd realized I was making progress when she'd invited me to spend Christmas with her and her parents.

Of the many difficult things about the season, choosing the tree had been especially hard for me because Kate and Jason had always joined me – a big family event. As soon as we'd gotten home with it, we'd always begun putting on the decorations, often not finishing until after dark. This time, every ornament that I'd put on the tree racked me with greater loss. Normally, there'd have been plenty of presents under the tree, but this year, Kate's parents and I had agreed not to exchange gifts. After all, there was only one thing we wanted, and it couldn't be put under a tree. As usual, Kate's mother made eggnog. It was as delicious as every other year, but I could hardly get it down. A few days later, they went back to Durango. Kate's father felt so poorly that her mother had to drive.

Phil Barrow invited me next door for a New Year's Eve party. I did my best to be sociable, but for me, the holiday was a wake. I went home an hour before the countdown at midnight. As hard as I tried, I couldn't remember what Kate and Jason sounded like.

Spring came.

May.

June.

They'd been gone a year.

17

'I'm leaving town,' I told Payne.

'Yes, sometimes it's a good idea to get away from bad memories,' he said.

'I was hoping that you wouldn't mind if I had my mail forwarded to you.'

'Sure,' Payne said. 'No problem.'

'I've asked the police and the FBI to leave messages with you in case they learn something new.'

Payne nodded. 'I'll phone you the second I hear anything. Just give me the number where you'll be and—'

'At the moment, that's a little uncertain. I'll have to phone *you*.'

'You don't know where you're going?'

'Not exactly.'

'But you don't just board a plane without having a reservation to someplace.'

'I'm not going on a plane. I thought I'd simply get in my car and drive. See the country. Go wherever the roads take me.'

Payne's eyes narrowed. 'Who are you kidding?'

'I don't understand.'

'Go wherever the roads take you? Give me a break. You're up to something. What is it?'

'I told you. I just need to get away.'

'You worry me.'

I avoided his gaze and looked at the fish tank.

'Don't tell me – you're going out there to try to find him,' Payne said.

I kept looking at the fish tank.

'How the hell do you figure to do it?' Payne demanded. 'It's impossible. You don't have a chance.'

At last, I looked back at him. 'I've done everything else I can think of.'

'Without any leads? It's for damn sure you'll be going where the roads take you. All you'll do is wander.'

'But I *do* have leads,' I insisted.

Payne leaned his ample body forward. 'Tell me.'

'It's hard to explain.'

'Give it a try.'

'Petey wanted to take my place.'

'And?' Payne looked baffled.

'Now I'm going to do it in the reverse. I'm going to take *Petey's* place.'

'What?'

'I'm going to put myself in his mind. I'm going to think like him. I'm going to become him.'

'Jesus,' Payne whispered.

'After all, we're brothers.'

'Mr Denning . . .'

'Yes?'

'I'm as sorry for you as it's possible to be. God help you.'

Part Three

1

Put myself in Petey's mind? Think like him? It was desperation, yes, but what was the alternative? At least it would be motion. It would keep me from losing my *own* mind.

I went to the street where Petey had first approached me outside my office – or what had used to be my office. The time was shortly after 2:00 P.M., as it had been exactly a year earlier. Petey had shouted my name from behind me, which meant that he'd been waiting to the left of the building's revolving door. I walked to a large concrete flower planter, where I guessed that he'd been resting his hips. I studied the front door, trying to put myself in his place. Why hadn't he gone into my office? As I leaned against the planter, feeling invisible to the passing crowd, I understood why he'd done it the way he had. In my office, he'd have been under *my* control, whereas on the sidewalk, yelling my name from behind me, *he* was in charge.

I recalled our initial conversation, this time from *his* perspective as he told me things that only my brother could have known, seeing my amazement, winning me over. I went to the delicatessen across the street, where our conversation had continued. I sat where *he* had sat. I imagined myself from his perspective as he continued to persuade me that my long-lost brother had finally returned. I went home and pretended to be him coming into my house, looking around, seeing all my possessions, the things that he'd never been able to have. Was it at this point that his plan had formed? *I* deserve this, not *you*, he would have thought. Picking up this and that object, he would have worked hard to conceal his anger. *You ruined my life, and this is what you got for it, you bastard.*

Kate would have been easy to look at: her long legs, her inviting waist. But what about Jason? What would Petey really have thought of him? A damned nuisance. Petey's background didn't leave room for paternal instinct. But Jason was part of what Petey would've had if I hadn't destroyed his life by sending him home from the baseball game. Jason went with the package, with the attractive wife and the big house, so Petey wanted him. Petey wanted *everything* that I had.

I recalled the dinner that Petey had eaten with us and how polite he'd been, helping to clean the dishes. Later, he'd played catch with Jason. He must have hated every second of it, just as he'd hated pretending to enjoy reminiscing about our childhood before I ruined his life. But the worst moment of all, the most hateful for him, would have been when I'd brought him the baseball glove that he'd dropped when the man and the woman had grabbed him. He must have wanted to shove the damned glove down my throat.

I went to Petey's room. I lay on his bed. I stared up at the ceiling and discovered that I'd picked up the baseball glove and was slamming my fist into it again and again. He would have wanted a smoke, but he wouldn't have ruined his plan by lighting up in the house and annoying Kate. So he'd crept downstairs, through the French doors off the kitchen, into the moonlit backyard, where he'd sat angrily on a lounge chair and lit a cigarette. I remembered looking from our bedroom window and seeing him down there. I imagined him pretending not to notice when my face appeared. I put myself in his mind. What are you doing up there? he'd have thought. Screwing the wife, are you, bro? Enjoy it while you can. It'll soon be *my* turn.

2

The next morning, I went to the barbershop where I'd taken him. I sat in the chair, feeling the scissors against my head, imagining that he'd festered from the insult that I thought he looked like shit and I was going to make him presentable. Then I went to the Banana Republic where I'd bought him new clothes. Then the shoe store. Then the dentist, where I'd made him feel self-conscious about his chipped tooth, reinforcing his sense that I thought he looked like shit.

When I walked into the dentist's office, the receptionist glanced up in surprise. 'We weren't expecting you today, Mr Denning. We're just about to close for lunch. Is this an emergency?'

'No.' Confused, I realized that I'd almost tricked myself into believing that I could truly repeat the pattern from a year ago. 'I must have gotten my days mixed up. Sorry to have bothered you.'

As I reached unsteadily for the doorknob, I remember waiting in the reception area while Petey had gone in to have his teeth cleaned and the chip in his tooth smoothed away. I tried to project myself into Petey, to imagine him sitting angrily in the dentist's chair. Since he hadn't been to a dentist in years, he would have been nervous, tensing a little as the dentist came at him with . . .

'Actually, there might be a way you can help.' My hand trembling, I released my grip on the doorknob and went over to the counter that separated the receptionist from the waiting area.

She looked at me expectantly.

'A year ago, I was in here with my brother.' My heart pounded from the shock of the idea I'd just had.

'Yes, I remember. I'm terribly sorry about what happened to your wife and son.'

111

'It's been a difficult time.' I fought to keep my voice steady, to hold my emotions in check. 'The thing is, I was wondering . . .' I held my breath. 'Do you know if any X rays were taken of my brother's teeth?'

3

'There!' I told Gader. 'This'll prove it!'

The somber man frowned at what I'd set on his desk. 'Prove what?'

'That my brother and Lester Dant are the same man!'

'Are you still trying to—'

'My brother had dental X rays taken a couple of days before he kidnapped my wife and son. When I was a child, my parents made sure that Petey and I went to a dentist for regular checkups. Show these X rays to our family dentist back in Ohio. He can compare them to his records. He'll prove that the teeth belong to the same person.'

'But a nine-year-old's teeth wouldn't be the same as those of a man in his thirties,' Gader objected.

'Because he wouldn't have had all his permanent teeth by the time he disappeared? No. My dentist says that my brother would have had *a few* permanent teeth, and even if they changed over the years because of work done on them, the *roots* would have kept the same structure. What would it hurt you to look into it?'

Gader set down a thick file he'd been reading. 'All right,' he said impatiently. 'To settle this once and for all. In Ohio, what was the name of your family dentist?'

'I . . . don't remember.'

He looked more impatient.

'But Woodford wasn't a big town,' I said. 'There weren't many dentists. It shouldn't be hard to track down the one we went to.'

'Assuming he's still in business. Assuming he kept records this long.' Gader's phone rang. As he reached for it, he told me, 'I'll get back to you.'

113

'When?'
'Next week.'
'But that isn't soon enough.'
He didn't hear me. He was already speaking into the phone.

4

Saturday morning, I rose from Petey's bed, put camping gear in the Expedition, and packed sandwiches in a cooler. As much as possible, I did everything the same as a year earlier, and at nine, exactly when we'd set out the last time, I took Interstate 70 into the mountains. The peaks were still snowcapped, the same as they had been the previous June. Ignoring their beauty, as Petey would have, I worked to recall our conversation. I squirmed as I sensed a pattern: almost every time Jason had said 'Dad' and asked me something, Petey had answered first. He'd been practicing to take my place, getting used to being called 'Dad'.

When I headed north into the Arapaho National Forest, I imagined him hiding his anticipation. I reached the lake and stopped where the three of us had stopped the previous year. I looked at where Petey, Jason and I had pitched our tent. I hiked around the lake to the stream that fed it, climbing the wooded slope to the gorge from which the stream thundered. All the while, I thought of him looking around for a spot to get rid of me and make it seem like an accident.

I climbed loose stones to the ridge above the gorge. I felt Petey's excitement when Jason went around the boulder to urinate. Now! Brad's back was exposed.

'Dad!'

No, the kid was returning too soon!

Unable to stop, I hurtled my goddamned brother into the gorge, then spun toward the kid, whose face was frozen in terror.

My mental image of Jason's fright shocked me into the present. Snapping from Petey's mind-set, I was nauseated from the darkness of pretending to be him. Despite a chill breeze, sweat soaked me.

115

Working down the loose stones to the trail at the bottom of the ridge, I couldn't help wondering how Petey would have climbed down without falling, given that he had a frightened, struggling boy to contend with. Then I realized that there was only one way he could have done it. The answer made me sick as I imagined what it had been like to carry an unconscious boy through the trees and back to the Expedition.

Since the vehicle didn't have a trunk, Petey would have had to tie and gag Jason, putting him on the back floor, covering him with the tent. As Petey, I drove carefully home through the mountain passes, never exceeding the speed limit, lest a state trooper stop me and wonder about the squirming sounds beneath the tent in the back.

Arriving home, I drove into the garage and pressed the remote control. With a rumble, the door came down. As I got out of the car, I envisioned Kate coming into the garage from the kitchen. She'd have just gotten back from the all-day seminar she'd been conducting. The trim gray business suit she'd been wearing when we'd left that morning made her long blond hair more bright.

'How come you're back so soon?' She frowned. 'Where are Brad and Jason?'

'We had an accident.'

'*An accident?*'

He'd overpowered her, bound and gagged her, gone into the house, found her car keys, then put her and Jason in the Volvo's trunk. The car had a backseat that could be flipped down so the trunk could hold long objects, such as skis. He'd probably opened the seat partway to allow air to circulate into the trunk, using the numerous objects he'd looted from the house to keep the seat from opening completely and allowing Kate and Jason a way to escape. He'd hurriedly packed suitcases, making sure to take some of my clothes. After all, as long as he was replacing me, he might as well look like me.

Around 6:00 P.M., just as Petey had, I got in the Volvo, which the police had returned to me, and drove from the house. At 6:21, exactly when Petey had, keeping my head low from the camera as Petey had, I got money from the same ATM that he'd used. But as I headed north from Denver, following Interstate 25, I realized that, with all the objects Petey had stolen from me, the Volvo would have looked as if he were running an appliance store out of the car. Worried that a policeman might get suspicious, Petey would never have left Denver with all that stuff. He would have sold it as quickly as possible. But he was new in town. When would he have had time to find a fence? Rethinking the previous days, I suddenly remembered that, after the dentist, Petey had wanted some time alone in a park 'to get my mind straight'. The son of a bitch had used the afternoon to arrange to sell what he'd planned to steal from me.

I drove to a rough section of town and imitated the transaction, filling the few minutes that it would have taken. Then I returned to the interstate, and this time, I felt invisible, one of countless vehicles on the road, nothing to make me conspicuous.

5

A road sign informed me that Casper, Wyoming, was 250 miles ahead. I set the Volvo's cruise control to make sure I stayed under the speed limit. When sunset approached and I put on my headlights, I felt even more inconspicuous, blending with thousands of other lights. I passed Cheyenne, Wyoming, able to distinguish little, except that its buildings seemed low and sprawling. Then, four hours after having left Denver, I approached the glow of Casper. For most of the drive, I'd sensed only flat land in the uninhabited darkness around me. Now the shadow of a mountain hulked on my left, blocking stars.

A few miles north of town, I saw a sign for the rest area. Traffic was sparse, most of the vehicles having driven into Casper. An arrow pointed toward a barely visible exit ramp. Following it off the interstate, I approached two squat brick buildings whose floodlights silhouetted three pickup trucks and a minivan.

But Petey would have needed more seclusion, so I took a gravel road that veered to the right from the pavement that led to the rest area. The floodlights at the buildings reached far enough to show picnic tables and stunted trees in back. Satisfying myself that no one had emerged from the rest rooms and seen what might have seemed unusual behavior, I reduced my headlights to parking lights and got just enough illumination to see a redwood-fenced area, behind which the tip of a Dumpster showed.

I parked behind the Dumpster, shut off my parking lights, and walked in front of the fence, verifying that no one, a state trooper, for example, had seen what I'd done and was coming to investigate. Confident that I was hidden, I unlocked the trunk.

What I imagined pushed me back. Kate and Jason on their sides.

Squirming. Terrified. Duct tape pressed tightly across their mouths. Hands tied behind their backs. Ankles bound. Eyes so wide with fright that their whites were huge. Moans that were half apprehension, half pleas. The stench of bodily excretions, of carbon dioxide, of sweat and fear.

Petey would have taken off their gags and allowed them to catch their breath while he'd warned them not to scream. They'd have been too fear-weakened and groggy from the foul air in the trunk to manage much of an outburst. He'd have needed to lift them one at a time from the trunk, loosening their clothes so they could relieve themselves. That unpleasant intimacy would have tested his commitment to his new family. But his obligations were just beginning. For example, they'd have been terribly thirsty. Had he planned ahead and stopped at a fast-food place in Casper to get soft drinks, possibly french fries and hamburgers also? As he regagged them and put them back in the trunk, would he have said any reassuring words?

'I love you.'

I shut the trunk. From the darkness behind the Dumpster, I stared toward the vehicles in front of the rest rooms. I walked in that direction, my footsteps crunching on pebbles. The floodlights at the two buildings made me feel naked the closer I came. By then, most of the vehicles had departed, leaving only a midsize sedan. I went into the men's room and found it empty. I stepped outside. Insects swarmed in the overhead light.

A woman left the other building, pulled keys from her purse, and approached the sedan. She didn't look in my direction. I imagined Petey starting to rush her, then pausing as headlights flashed past on the interstate, not a lot, but enough that there was never a gap, never a moment when somebody driving by wouldn't have seen a man attack a woman.

So Petey had waited for another opportunity, gone into the women's room, and subdued his victim there. He'd watched the interstate until there were just enough gaps between headlights that no one would see him in the few seconds that it took him to carry the unconscious woman around to the darkness. Behind the Dumpster, he'd tied and gagged her. Then he'd returned to the rest area, used the woman's key to start her car (a Caprice, the police had told me). He'd kept the headlights off and driven back to the darkness behind the fence, where he would have had to use a knife to make ventilation holes through the backseats into the Caprice's trunk before he transferred Kate and Jason into it.

But when he'd put the driver in the trunk with them, hadn't it worried him that there might not have been enough air for three people? Why had he risked suffocating Kate and Jason by putting the woman in the trunk with them? As it was, the woman had died. Why hadn't he killed her and hidden her body in the Dumpster? No one would have found her for quite a while, if ever. Again I felt Kate and Jason's horror as the asthmatic woman fought to breathe with the duct tape pressed over her mouth, her frenzied movements, her gagging sounds, her gradual stillness, the release of her bladder, probably her bowels. As the Caprice sped along the interstate, Kate and Jason would have been seized by the out-of-control fear that, if it had happened to the woman, it could happen to *them*.

The question kept nagging at me: *why hadn't Petey just killed her and hidden her body in the Dumpster?* The only answer that made sense to me was that, no matter how indifferent Petey had felt toward the woman, he hadn't intended for her to die. Killing me was one thing. As far as Petey was concerned, I deserved to die for ruining his life. But this woman had merely happened to be in the wrong place at the wrong time. It was the first indication of humanity that I'd detected in him. It gave me hope for Kate and Jason.

He could have left the Volvo behind the Dumpster, where it might not have been discovered for days. Instead, he'd gone to the trouble of moving the Volvo to the front of the rest rooms, where it would be in plain sight. Because he wanted it to be found soon. He wanted it to point the way north, just as abandoning the Caprice outside Billings, Montana, made it seem that he was heading toward Butte. He'd been thinking with frightening control.

6

I drove back to the interstate. A road sign indicated that Billings, Montana, was 250 miles away. My eyelids felt heavy. But I had to keep moving. I had to complete Petey's escape.

Had he slept along the way? Doing that certainly tempted me. But I was afraid that if I steered off the interstate and found a secluded spot – a camping area, for example – where I could get a few hours' sleep, I wouldn't waken until daylight. In Petey's case, the Caprice might have been reported by then. He had to get to Billings. Imitating him, I kept driving.

I played the radio loud. In the middle of the night, it was hard to find a station. The ones I did find broadcast mostly evangelists riddled with static.

A mountain range stretched from north to south on my left. Moonlight glowed off the snowy peaks. My eyelids weakened. To stay awake, I bit my lips. I dug my fingernails into my palms. Interstate 25 became 90. I passed Sheridan, Wyoming, and entered Montana. The signs changed character: Lodge Grass; Custer Battlefield National Monument; Crow Agency . . . At Hardin, the interstate veered west. Meanwhile, as the miles accumulated, I imagined that Petey would have worried that his captives weren't getting enough air. He'd have stopped periodically on deserted roads to check on them. It pained me to think of Kate's and Jason's frightened eyes peering desperately up at him. They flinched when he reached in to touch their brows to calm them. As for the Caprice's driver, he barely looked at her.

When I finally read a sign for Billings, I was troubled that the distance between Casper and Billings should have taken me only four hours, but with frequent stops, pretending to check on my captives, I'd taken ninety minutes longer than I should have.

Even so, it was still dark when I came to the rest stop on the other side of Billings. A sign called it a scenic vista, but with the moon having set, I had only a vague sense of mountains to the north and south. Two vehicles were parked at the rest rooms: a pickup truck and a sedan. Here, too, a service road led behind the buildings. I parked in the darkness. Adrenaline overcame my exhaustion as I got out of the car. The air was surprisingly cold. Two men in cowboy hats came out of one of the concrete-block buildings. I waited while they got in the pickup truck and drove away. At this predawn hour, there was almost no traffic on the interstate. I walked quickly toward the rest rooms and listened for activity in either one. If I heard voices, if there was more than one person, I'd wait for a better opportunity. But if there was only one set of footsteps . . .

At that hour, few women felt safe to drive alone. I assumed that the victim would have been male. Use a tire iron to knock him unconscious in the men's room. Drag him into the darkness. Take his car to the back. Put Kate, Jason and the driver into its trunk.

Would it have been at this point that Petey had discovered that the owner of the Caprice had choked to death from the duct tape over her mouth? He wouldn't have been overwhelmed with sorrow. He'd given her a chance. As far as he was concerned, it wasn't his fault. The penalty for kidnapping was the same as for murder, so with nothing to lose, instead of trying to hide her body, he'd left it with the Caprice. Then he'd gotten into its replacement and driven onto the interstate. But instead of continuing toward Butte, where he wanted the police to think he was going, I was convinced he'd taken the next exit ramp, crossed the overpass, and reaccessed the interstate, reversing direction, heading back toward Billings.

I kept after him. By then, it was dawn. I saw mountains, ranches and oil refineries. Crossing the Yellowstone River, I no longer had the police report to guide me. Petey has been as tired as I was. Where the hell had he gone next?

7

The interstate forked. I had to choose – take 94 northeast through Montana, way up into North Dakota, or else retrace 90 south into Wyoming. I chose the latter. I didn't fool myself that intuitively I was doing what Petey had done. My decision was totally arbitrary.

But as tired as I was, if I didn't soon find a place to sleep, I knew I'd have an accident. Petey must have felt the same. Even charged with adrenaline, he couldn't have kept going much longer. For certain, he wouldn't have dared risk an accident. He didn't have a driver's license, and the car wasn't registered to him. A state trooper questioning him would eventually have gotten suspicious enough to look in the trunk. Meanwhile, as the sun got higher, warming the car's interior, I imagined how hot the trunk must have gotten. No matter how many ventilation holes Petey had made, Kate, Jason and the car's owner would have roasted in that confined space, the sun's heat turning the trunk into an oven, the air getting thicker, smothering. If Petey was going to keep them alive in the trunk, he had to rest by day and drive by night.

Because the Denver detectives had said that duct tape had covered the dead woman's mouth, I presumed Petey had done the same to Kate, Jason and the man whose car he'd stolen. I took my right hand off the steering wheel and pressed it over my mouth, forcing myself to breathe only through my nostrils. My chest heaved. I couldn't seem to get enough air. I had to concentrate to control my heartbeat, to inhale and exhale slowly. I couldn't bear the thought of breathing self-consciously, of taking in a minimum of air for what felt like forever in a hot, closed space.

Definitely, no one in the trunk would have had a chance of

surviving unless Petey drove only when it was cooler – at night. But where could he have stopped? A motel would have been danger-ously public. But what about a camping area? Tourist season was only beginning. Petey might have been able to find a wooded area that didn't have visitors. Listening for the approach of vehicles, he could have risked letting his prisoners out of the trunk. If there was a stream where they could clean themselves, so much the better.

He'd have needed to get food again. At the next exit, I saw a McDonald's, went to the drive-through lane, and ordered an Egg McMuffin, coffee and orange juice. While I waited behind other cars, I frowned at my beard-stubbled image in the rearview mirror. But the beard stubble wasn't what bothered me. I'd been trying to imitate Petey's thoughts, and I'd forgotten one of the most impor-tant things about him: the scar on his chin. It would have attracted attention. I pulled a pen from my shirt pocket and drew a line where Petey's scar would have been. I wanted to know what it felt like to have people staring at my chin.

When I paid for my food, the woman behind the counter pointed toward the ink mark. 'Mister, you've got—'

'Yeah, I know,' I said. 'I can't seem to get the darned thing off.'

I'd intended to ask her if there were nearby camping areas, but feeling conspicuous, I paid for my food and drove away. Squinting from the glare of the morning sun, I decided to let my beard keep growing and hide the streak on my chin.

A likely place for a campground would be along a river, so when I crossed the Bighorn, I took the first exit. There, I debated whether to follow the river north or south. A sign indicated that south would take me to the Crow Indian Reservation. That didn't sound like a place where I'd be invisible, so I headed north.

Traffic was sparse. The land was fenced. In a while, I came to a dirt road that took me to the left, toward the river. It soon curved to the right to parallel the river, although bushes and trees along the bank prevented me from seeing the water. A weed overgrown lane went into the trees. I drove down it, parked behind the trees, walked to the road, and satisfied myself that the car was hidden.

I had no illusions that this was the spot where Petey had stopped, but logic suggested that it was similar. Petey would have ignored the car's owner while he tried to reassure Kate and Jason, saying that he wouldn't hurt them unless they forced him to, that if they did what they were told, there wouldn't be trouble. He would have kept one of them in the trunk while he let the other bathe, making sure that a rope was tied to one and then the other's waist to prevent them from trying to run. He would have allowed them to change clothes. He would have studied them while they ate their fast-food breakfast.

'I'll take care of you.'

They wouldn't have known what to make of that.

As frightened as Kate was, she'd have had all night to analyze the danger they were in. She'd have already decided that their only chance was for her to use her stress-management skills to try to keep him calm. 'Thanks for the food.'

'You like it?'

Despite their fear, Kate and Jason would have been so hungry that they'd have gulped their hamburgers.

'I said, *Do you like it?*'

'Yes,' Kate would have answered quickly.

'It isn't much, but it's better than nothing.'

Was there a threat in the way he said it, that if they gave him trouble, he could make sure that was exactly what they got: nothing? Kate would have taken another deep swallow from her soft drink, knowing that it wouldn't be enough to replenish her fluids. She'd have brushed her tangled hair from her face, aware that she had to try to look as presentable as possible. Make Petey think of you as a human being, not an object. Thank him for courtesies he showed. Behave as if the situation were normal. Make him want to go through efforts for you so he can get the gratification of being appreciated.

But what about Jason? As young as he was, lacking Kate's training, he'd have been nearly out of his mind with terror. Gagged, Kate wouldn't have been able to talk to him in the trunk. She couldn't have coached him. She had to depend on giving him significant looks and hoping that he'd understand her motives, that he'd follow her lead.

'What are you going to do with us?' she'd have asked when the time seemed right.

'I told you, I'm going to take care of you.'

'But why did—'

'We're a family.'

'Family?' Don't react. Make even the outrageous seem normal.

'Brad had an accident.'

'What?'

'He fell off a cliff. I'm taking his place.'

Kate's stomach would have plummeted as if *she* had fallen from a cliff.

'I'm your husband. Jason, you're my son.'

Fighting to keep tears from swelling into her eyes, Kate would have echoed Petey's earlier words, reinforcing their import. 'Take care of us.'

Petey probably wouldn't have been familiar with the term 'the Stockholm principle', but he was a skillful-enough manipulator that he would have understood it. After a period of time, captives grow weary of their roller-coaster emotions. Grateful to be shown small kindnesses, they tend to accept their situation and to bond with their captors.

That would have been Petey's hope. But of course he wasn't accustomed to providing for a wife and son. The breakfast would have quickly disappeared, and then there'd have been the problem of what to do about lunch and supper. Petey wouldn't have thought that far ahead, but even if he had, how was he going to keep hamburgers and fries from spoiling, and what about a way to reheat them? He needed to buy a cooler, a camping stove, pots and pans and . . . What had started as an urge to take my place suddenly didn't have the gratification it had promised. Everything was getting too complicated. Why not admit that he'd made a mistake and chuck the whole business? Why not do what he wanted with Kate and Jason, kill them and the driver in the trunk, hide their bodies, drive into the nearest big town, abandon the car, buy a bus ticket, and adios?

The thought made me shudder. No, that's how Lester Dant would have acted, I tried to assure myself. Lester Dant would have killed Jason right away, then driven Kate to a secret spot and dumped her body down a ravine when he got tired of abusing her. He certainly wouldn't have taken the time and the risk to lay a false trail all the way to Montana. That only made sense if *Petey* had abducted them, if he was determined to take over my life and make Kate and Jason his family.

But his patience would have been sorely tested. The only way he could have felt at ease enough to go to sleep was by putting Kate and Jason back into the trunk so they wouldn't try to escape while he was dozing. The shade of the trees would have prevented the trunk from becoming lethally hot. Still, Petey would have had no idea how long he might sleep. He'd have loved eight hours. Even with numerous ventilation holes, Kate, Jason, and the man whose car he'd stolen probably wouldn't have been able to survive that long in the trunk without the lid being opened periodically to vent carbon dioxide. Two people, though, would have a chance. There'd have been one-third more air for them if . . . That's when I knew that Petey had deliberately killed the second driver, whereas the first death had been an accident.

Sleep. I could barely keep awake. But as I opened a back door, staring at my suitcase, knapsack, laptop computer and printer, I realized that I was going to have to put them in the front seat so I could stretch out in the back. It would have annoyed Petey to move his four suitcases. Another complication. Another nuisance. In addition, I was going to have to disable the car's interior light so I could leave a back door open and stretch my legs while I slept – to prevent the car's battery from dying. One more damned thing to do.

No, this wouldn't have been at all like what Petey had wanted.

8

The sound of a passing vehicle startled me awake. I sat up sharply. Before I checked my watch, the angle of the sun told me that the time was late afternoon. Out of sight from the trees, the vehicle kept bumping along the dirt road. My mouth felt pasty as I got out of the backseat and peered through the trees, seeing that the vehicle was a pickup truck, a rancher in a hurry to get somewhere. My back was sore.

Thus Petey's nervous schedule would have resumed: checking on his captives, lifting them out so they could relieve themselves and wash their faces in the river. At some point, he would have had to take care of himself. His clothes would have felt grimy. Probably he changed them for some of the clothes that he'd stolen from me. Perhaps he'd felt angry as the rumblings in his stomach told him that he had to start thinking about getting more food for everybody. He couldn't go on like this. Either he had to find a place in which to settle or he would have to kill Kate and Jason for creating his problems.

No! The only way I could shove that mind-threatening thought away was by imagining how Kate and Jason might have reacted to Petey's growing impatience. Kate's training would have told her that she had to accommodate Petey as best she could, to make things less complicated for him, to ease the strain he felt.

'I can try to wash these dirty clothes in the river. Tie me to a tree and watch me on the bank. That way, you'll be sure I can't run away. What about these suitcases you moved to the front? Why don't I return them to where they were? There's a lot of housekeeping I can take care of.'

Jason might have caught on by then. He might have understood what Kate was doing and tried his best to appear the obedient son. Reinforce Petey's fantasies. Make him believe that his risk and effort were worthwhile. That was the only way they were going to stay alive. In a way, it was the captives trying to make the *captor* fall into the Stockholm syndrome.

Petey would have been too close to where he'd abandoned the Caprice. The new vehicle he was driving would soon have been reported missing. Maybe it had license plates from several states away, suggesting that the driver had a distance to go before arriving home and wouldn't be reported missing until at least the end of the day. All the same, Petey wouldn't have been able to depend on that. He needed to get on the move. But he didn't dare show the car until darkness made him invisible. That meant waiting to get food for Kate and Jason. But it also meant that Kate and Jason had more time to talk with him, a chance to try to bond with him, to personalize themselves, so that killing them wouldn't be easy.

Petey brought out the rope and the duct tape.

'I need to ask you to do something,' Kate said.

Petey tied her hands behind her back.

'Please, listen,' Kate said. 'I understand why you need to put the duct tape over our mouths. You're afraid we'll yell and make somebody call the police.'

Petey tied her feet.

'Please,' Kate said. 'It's almost impossible to breathe when the trunk gets hot. When you press the duct tape across our mouths, I'm begging you to . . .'

Petey tore off a section of tape.

'*Please.* It won't threaten you if you cut a small hole where our lips are. We still won't be able to yell. But we'll be able to breathe better.'

Petey stared at her.

'You promised you'd take care of us,' Kate said. 'What good are we to you if we're dead?'

Petey's harsh eyes were filled with suspicion. He pressed the tape over her mouth and set her in the trunk. He did the same to Jason. Kate looked beseechingly up at Petey, who reached to close the trunk, paused, then pulled out a knife and slit the duct tape over their lips.

I hoped. But when darkness finally came and I returned to the interstate, I couldn't repress my unease that I was totally wrong about my reenactment of what had happened. In Wyoming, I came to another fork in the interstate. My palms broke out in a sweat as I tried to decide what to do next. I could retrace my route on 25, eventually returning to Denver, or I could veer east on the continuation of 90, heading into the Black Hills of South Dakota. I couldn't imagine Petey returning to Denver. But the Black Hills would surely have appealed to him. Plenty of places in which to hide.

9

Footsteps paused outside the entrance to the men's room. This was at a rest area in South Dakota, shortly after three in the morning. In the harsh overhead light, I stood at a urinal. At that quiet hour, sounds were magnified. That was probably the only reason I noticed the footsteps approaching. Waiting for them to resume, I looked over my shoulder, past the toilet stalls, toward the door on my right. The place had the chill of concrete after the heat of the day had faded.

I waited for the door to swing open. The silence beyond it grew. Still peering over my shoulder, I zipped up my pants. I went over to the sink and washed my hands, fixing my gaze on the mirror before me, which gave a direct view of the door. There weren't any paper towels, only one of those power dryers that force warm air over wet hands. They sound like a jet engine. Needing to hear everything, I didn't press its button.

As my fingers tingled from the water on them, I stared toward the door. The silence beyond it persisted. It's only a tired driver who pulled into the rest area, I thought. He didn't need to relieve himself, just to stretch his legs. He's standing out there, enjoying the stars.

And if I'm wrong?

I told myself I was overreacting. After all, I didn't have any firm reason to believe that someone was out there waiting to surprise me when I opened the door. But I'd been in the foulness of Petey's mind for so long, imitating his movements, re-creating his logic, stalking rest areas; that I couldn't subdue the suspicion. My imagination was so primed that I could *feel* the danger out there as if it were seeping through the wall.

When I'd parked outside, mine had been the only vehicle, an attraction to a predator. He was listening for voices, for more than one set of footsteps, wanting to make sure I was alone. Hearing only me, he'd soon push the door open. I thought of the pistol in the suitcase in my car and cursed myself for being a fool. What good was learning how to use it if I put it where I couldn't get it if I needed the damned thing?

My legs were feathery. I trembled. No! I thought. What if I'd tracked down Petey? What if *he* was outside that door?

I pushed the button on the hand dryer. Its harsh roar obscured my footsteps as I shifted toward the back of the door. Braced against the wall, I felt a spurt of fear in my stomach as the door swung open.

A man in his mid-twenties, wearing cowboy boots, jeans and a cowboy hat came quickly in, holding a tire iron. The door swung shut behind him as he stopped at the sight of the empty rest room. Puzzled, he stared at the roaring hand dryer. He peered toward the toilet stalls.

Abruptly he saw my reflection in the mirror over the sink. He tried to turn. I was already rushing, slamming his back with such force that he hurtled forward, his mustached face hitting the mirror, smashing it into shreds. Blood streaked the mirror as I grabbed him by the back of his collar and his thick belt, ramming him toward the hand dryer, driving his head against it so powerfully that the nozzle on the fan broke off. The dryer kept roaring as I backed him up and drove his head against it even harder. Blood sprayed from the force of the unshielded fan. The tire iron fell from his hand, clanging on the concrete floor. I slammed his head once more and dropped him. He lay like a pile of old clothes. Eyes shut, he moaned. Except for the rise and fall of his chest, he barely moved.

My stomach was on fire. The anger that had brought me close to killing him frightened me. But the emotion that primarily seized me, making me want to shout, was that I'd won.

10

'**F**ederal Bureau of Investigation,' the receptionist said.

'Special Agent Gader, please.' I gripped my cell phone so tightly that my fingers ached.

It was nine in the morning. Sunlight glinted off a secluded lake surrounded by lumpy bluffs studded with pine trees. The ridges were dark gray stone, making it clear how the Black Hills had gotten their name. I'd reached this area before dawn, but when I'd noticed that the map indicated only barren open land beyond them, I'd decided that Petey would have stopped earlier than he'd planned, going to ground for the day.

The beauty of the lake looked odd to me. After what had happened at the rest area, I felt as if I'd stepped into an alternate reality.

'Agent Gader is out of town on an assignment.'

I picked up a rock. Frustration made me hurl it at the lake.

'May I ask who's calling?' the woman asked.

'Brad Denning. I—'

'Agent Gader mentioned that you'd be contacting him. He said that he'd spoken to Mr Payne about the matter you were interested in, and if you'd talk to—'

I broke the connection.

11

'I guess you haven't been back to Woodford in a while,' Payne said.

Pressing the cell phone to my ear, I walked close to the lake. Its cool air drifted over me. My beard stubble scraped against my hand. I worked to calm myself. 'Not since my mother and I moved away when I was a kid.'

'How big was it then?'

'Not very. About ten thousand people.'

'A one-factory town,' Payne said.

'That's right. My dad was a foreman.' I suddenly missed him so much. 'How did you know?'

'Because Gader says the factory shut down and went to Mexico ten years ago. Now Woodford's a bedroom community for Columbus, and its population has doubled to twenty thousand. There are several dentists, but none of them ever heard of the Denning family.'

The air at the lake became colder. 'But surely they know the dentists who worked there before them.'

'Nope. Gader says you don't remember the name of the dentist you went to or his address.'

My head throbbed. 'It was too long ago.'

'Then it's a dead end. Gader says he's sorry.'

'Yeah, I bet.'

'He says if you're relying on dental records to prove that Lester Dant is really your brother using an alias, you're setting yourself up for a big disappointment. Anyway, how's that going to help find your family?'

'I don't know, but I can think of words that are a whole lot stronger than *disappointment*.'

The cell phone's reception became staticky.

'Where are you calling from?' Payne asked.

'South Dakota.'

'Nice there?'

'I didn't come for the scenery,' I said.

'Well, as long as you're determined to be on the road, do you want some advice?'

'Provided it's not "Take it easy and get some rest." '

'No, something else. This might surprise you,' Payne said. 'It'll sound like encouragement.'

'Then go ahead and surprise me.'

'Until I put on all this weight and I got to relying on the Internet,' Payne said, 'I was a hands-on kind of investigator. That's why I noticed things others didn't. When there's time, nothing beats going to the places and people you want to know about.'

' "When there's time." '

'Which you seem to have plenty of.'

'You're suggesting that if I'm determined to find the dentist, I should do it myself?'

'More or less.'

'You're right – it does sound like encouragement. Why the change?'

'Because I'm worried about you.'

The reception became staticky again. I listened hard.

'I'm afraid, if you don't satisfy yourself one hundred percent that you've done everything you can, if you lose hope . . .'

I strained to hear, but the static became worse.

'. . . you'll destroy yourself.'

'I'll get back to you later in the week,' I said.

'What? I can't hear you.'

I broke the connection.

12

As I imagined spending days in secluded places asleep in the back of the car, using my nights to drive as far as I could, I knew that Petey wouldn't have tolerated that routine much longer. The one thing that would have kept him motivated was his discovery – from the widespread news reports on the car radio a couple of days later (the media really loved the story) – that I hadn't died in the mountains. He wouldn't have told Kate and Jason that I was alive, of course. But his secret would have given him resolve, imagining how my fear and longing for my family made me suffer. No crowing midnight phone calls to me, no gleeful postcards, nothing with an inadvertent clue that might have led the police to him. Only taunting, gloating silence.

But, damn it, where would he have taken them? I thought about the South Dakota badlands ahead. In the old days, rustlers used to hide in the maze of sun-scorched canyons, the environment so hellish that posses wouldn't go in after them. It was too desperate a choice, even for Petey. After the badlands, there were hundreds of miles of flat grassland, hardly a tree anywhere, everything exposed. But Petey wouldn't have tolerated being in the open. Hide in plain sight? I doubted it. He wouldn't have felt protected without the shelter of hills and woods.

So had he found a place in the Black Hills? A deserted cabin maybe, or a . . .

I'd come as far as intuition could take me. A dead end, just as Gader had said that the idea about the dentist was a dead end.

The dentist. 'Nothing beats going to the places and people you want to know about,' Payne had said.

Yes.

After sleeping in the back of the car until sundown, I set out toward where I now realized my route had already been taking me, toward where everything had started so long ago.

Toward Petey's lost youth.

Part Four

1

B ROCKTON NEXT EXIT.
The sign caught me by surprise. It was two nights later. I'd gone through Iowa and Illinois and was now on Interstate 70, continuing relentlessly east through Indiana. My destination was Ohio. Just beyond Columbus. Woodford. My hometown.

But as I saw the sign for Brockton, Lester Dant's birthplace, I frowned. Although I'd long ago made myself familiar with Brockton's position on the map, this was the first time I'd realized that it, like Woodford, was close enough to 70 to merit an exit sign. Fixated on the dental records that I hoped to find in Woodford, I hadn't focused on Brockton. But at that moment, my attention rapidly shifted. I made the turn.

A two-land road wound through shadowy farm country. After twenty miles, street lights revealed run-down houses and a bleak main street. Two-story buildings flanked it, some with FOR SALE notices on windows. A sputtering neon sign announced BROCKTON MOTEL, VACANCY. It too looked run-down, but with no other choice, I stopped.

A bell rang when I opened the office door. Harsh overhead lights hummed. A puffy-eyed woman in a robe shuffled from a room behind the office. 'How many nights?'

I said, 'Two,' determined to stick around and learn as much as I could.

The elderly woman seemed puzzled that anyone would have a reason for staying in Brockton more than one night. 'Cash only.' She named an amount, a narrowness in her eyes suggesting that she thought the rate was a fortune, which it wasn't.

When I gave her the money, she looked relieved, handed me a

141

key, yawned, and shuffled back to her room. 'Soft-drink machine's outside next to the candy machine,' she murmured over her shoulder.

'Sorry for waking you.'

'Plenty of time to sleep when I'm dead.'

Outside, in the humid night, a single bulb illuminated the parking area. There weren't any vehicles at any of the ten motel units. The key I'd been given was for number one. Imagining that I was Petey, I noted that all the units were behind the manager's room. In the shadows, I couldn't be seen if I took a bound and gagged woman and child from my trunk.

The room was small, the sheets thin, the mirror dusty. I stared at my thickening beard stubble. My eyes looked haunted. I was a stranger to myself.

2

'**D**o you know this man?'

The manager looked as tired as when I'd wakened her the previous night. Her wrinkled mouth left a trace of lipstick on her coffee cup. Behind the counter, she tilted the police photo this way and that. 'Not exactly flattering. How'd he get the scar on his chin?'

'Car accident.'

'Can't say I recognize him. You another FBI agent?'

'Another?'

'Last year, somebody from the FBI asked me about this guy.'

My optimism sank. If Gader *had* arranged for Dant's background to be double-checked, I was wasting my time.

'He must have done something really bad for you to keep looking for him,' she said.

'Yes. Something really bad. Does the name Peter Denning sound familiar?'

'Nope.'

'How about Lester Dant?'

'Dant.' The woman thought a moment. 'That's the name the other FBI agent asked about. There used to be a couple of families named Dant around here.'

I felt more discouraged.

'The hardware store's named after one of them,' she said, 'but the man who owns it now is Ben Porter.'

Wasting my time, I repeated to myself. Tempted to drive on to Woodford, I decided not to take anything for granted. 'Where's the hardware store?'

3

'I don't know him.' Ben Porter was in his fifties, as was just about everybody I'd passed in the sparsely populated town. His coveralls were flecked with sawdust from boards he'd been cutting. 'But that doesn't mean much.'

'Why not?'

'I never met the store's original owner. I kept the name Dant on the building to maintain tradition.'

In a dying town, the word *tradition* sounded brave. 'You don't know *any* Dants?'

'Like I told the other FBI agent, they're before my time. I moved here only ten years ago.' The expression on his face made it seem that he wished he hadn't.

'Can you think of anybody who might know about them?'

'Sure. The reverend.'

'Who?'

'Reverend Benedict. The way I hear it, he's been in Brockton just about forever.'

4

The white steepled church and the cottage behind it were the only two buildings in town that didn't look in need of repair. On the right, between the church and a graveyard, a path went through a rose garden. Ahead, an elderly man in a short-sleeved blue shirt with a minister's collar had his back to me. He was on his knees, his head bowed in prayer. Then his arms moved and his head bobbed, and I realized he was pruning the roses.

He had a hearing aid tucked behind his right ear. It must have been an excellent model, because he heard me walking across the grass and turned to see who I was.

'Reverend Benedict?'

His wrinkled brow developed more furrows as he came creakily to his feet. His old pants had grass stains on the knees.

'My name's Brad Denning. Ben Porter at the hardware store—'

'A fine man.'

'—suggested I talk to you about a couple of families who used to live around here.'

'Families?'

'The Dants.'

The reverend's eyes had sparkled as if he'd welcomed the opportunity to test his memory. Now they became guarded.

'Do you remember the Dants?' I asked.

'Are you with the FBI?'

'No.'

'Someone from the FBI asked me about the Dants last year,' the reverend said.

'I know that. But I'm not with the Bureau. Did the agent show you this photograph?'

'Yes. That's Lester. I told the agent the same thing.'

'You're sure of that? It's Lester Dant?'

'He was younger. He didn't have that scar on his chin. But there's no doubt it's Lester.'

I felt sick. The theory I'd worked so hard to believe toppled. Lester Dant, *not* my brother, had taken Kate and Jason. He wouldn't have had a reason to keep them alive.

'Why do you want to know about him?'

'It doesn't matter anymore, Reverend,' I managed to say. Hollow, I turned to leave.

' "Just a routine investigation," the FBI agent told me.'

I looked back at him. 'Hardly routine.'

'What's wrong, Mr Denning? You seem in terrible distress.'

I hadn't intended to explain, but something about him invited it. In despair, I started to tell him. I tried to keep my voice steady, but the more I revealed, the more it shook.

The reverend stared. He seemed to hope that I was finished, but then I told him more – and more – and his shocked look turned to pity for someone who, because of a boyhood mistake, had been condemned to the torment of hell.

'*Lester* did all that?'

'Or my brother pretending to be him. That's what I needed to find out.'

'God help him. God help *you*.'

'If only God would.'

'All prayers are eventually answered.'

'Not soon enough, Reverend.'

He seemed on the verge of telling me to have faith. Instead, he sighed and motioned me toward a bench. 'There are several things you need to understand about him.'

' "Understand"? I hope that doesn't mean make excuses or sympathize, because what I really want to do, Reverend, is *punish* him. And please don't tell me to turn the other cheek or let God take care of vengeance.'

'You just said it for me.'

We studied each other.

'You're positive that the man in this photograph is Lester Dant?' I asked.

146

'Yes.'

I felt sicker. Even so, I had to know the truth. 'All right then, Reverend.' Despondent, I sat on the bench. 'Help me "understand" him.'

5

'And his parents,' the reverend said. 'You also have to understand his parents.' He thought for a moment. 'The Dants.' His frail voice strengthened. 'There were six families of them originally. They lived around here for as long as anybody can remember. That's what my predecessor told me, at any rate, when I was assigned here. But they weren't really part of the community. You couldn't even say that they were part of the United States.'

'You've lost me, Reverend.'

'They were separatists. Tribalists. Loners. Somewhere in their history – my predecessor had a theory that it went as far back as the Civil War – something terrible had happened to them. They came from a place that they desperately wanted to forget, and they settled around here, determined to be left to themselves.'

A bee buzzed my face. I motioned it away, fixing my attention on the reverend.

'Of course, to keep their families going, they couldn't be entirely insular. They had to interact with nearby communities, looking for young people to marry. On the surface, they had a lot to recommend them. They knew their Bible. They owned property. They didn't drink, smoke, gamble or swear. For a while, they attracted new members, usually from families so poor that marrying a Dant was a step up. But word got around how severe they were, and the Dants had to look farther, mostly among other strict groups, trying to negotiate marriages. Their options became more limited. By the time my predecessor arrived, the families had dwindled to three.'

I shook my head, puzzled. 'If they were determined to stay to themselves, how come somebody named Dant owned the hardware store?'

'A lifeline. No matter how hard they tried, they couldn't be self-sufficient. Even in a good year, with bountiful crops, there were necessities that they couldn't produce for themselves. To them, Brockton was like a foreign country. The hardware store was their embassy. They exported their excess produce through it and imported lumber, tools, clothing . . .'

'Medicines.'

'No,' Reverend Benedict said, 'never medicines. The Dants were as fundamental religiously as they were politically. To them, sickness was a sign of God's disfavor. They felt it was a sin to use human means to interfere with God's intention.'

'Because of our fallen nature?'

'For which the Dants believed God punished us,' the reverend said.

'With a self-destructive attitude like that, it's a wonder the families survived.'

'That's the point – they're all gone now.' Reverend Benedict pointed a wizened finger toward the photograph. 'Except for Lester.'

'When did you meet him?'

'After the fire.'

'The fire?'

'I'll get to that. First, you need to know that, because the Dants avoided doctors, the town had no idea of the birth and death rate out there. Every so often, emissaries would come to town and get supplies. Mostly men, but sometimes women and children. I suspect that their motive was to show everybody in the family how corrupt the outside world was. It could be that we looked as strange to them as *they* did to us.'

'Strange?'

'The effects of inbreeding were starting to show.'

'The law let them get away with it?'

'Once in a while, a state trooper went out to check on things, but what was he going to charge them with, except wanting to be by themselves?'

'Child endangerment.'

'Difficult to prove if the children are well nourished and can quote their Bible.'

'Isn't there a law that children have to go to school?'

'The Dants hired an attorney who argued that the children were getting an adequate education at home. It came down to religious freedom. These days, I suppose we'd call them survivalists. But they weren't hoarding weapons and they weren't plotting to overthrow the government, so the authorities decided that dragging the Dants into court was worse than leaving them alone. Live and let live became the motto. Until the weekend when Lester's mother was one of the emissaries who came to town.'

I listened harder.

'Her name was Eunice. She was visibly pregnant, but evidently her husband believed that she wasn't far enough along not to travel. She came out of the hardware store. The next thing, she collapsed on the sidewalk, writhing in pain. Her husband, Orval, tried to make light of it, tried to pick her up and put her in the car. But when he saw the blood on her dress and the pool of it around her, he froze in confusion, just long enough for a doctor and a policeman – we had several of both back then – to notice what was happening and rush her to the clinic that served as our hospital. Orval tried to stop them, but suddenly, it was obvious that Eunice wasn't having a miscarriage. She was about to give birth to a premature baby.'

'The creep was willing to risk her life?'

'He didn't do it easily. Orval told the doctor and the policeman that the baby meant more to him than anything else in the world; that he and Eunice had already lost three children to stillbirths; that they'd tried persistently to have another child and finally God had blessed them with this pregnancy. But to rely on a doctor was the same as telling God that they didn't have faith, Orval said. If they interfered with God's plan, the baby would be damned. Orval felt so strongly about this that he actually tried to pick up Eunice and carry her from the clinic. But the doctor warned him that the wife and the baby would die if they didn't stay and receive medical attention. The policeman was more blunt. He threatened to arrest Orval for attempted murder if Orval tried to remove his wife. By then, the baby was on its way, and even Orval realized he was going to have to allow medical help, whether he wanted it or not. Eunice nearly died from loss of blood. The baby nearly died from being so small.'

'The baby was Lester?'

'Yes. Orval and Eunice didn't believe in giving their children names that had religious connotations. They compared it to idolatry. No Matthew, Mark, Luke or John for them. Once you take away the Bible as a source for a name, there aren't many choices. The name Lester was neutral, a default.'

'And then?'

'My predecessor retired. I came here to take his place. Before he left, he explained about the community and told me what I've just told *you*. He said that, despite the doctor's expectations, the baby lived. In fact, a week before I arrived, Orval had brought the child to town to show how healthy the boy was, to prove to the doctor that God's will was the only thing that mattered.'

'But . . .' I felt more puzzled. 'What's this got to do with . . . You said you met Lester after a fire.'

'Years later.'

I leaned forward.

'The smoke woke just about everybody in town. I remember it was a Labor Day weekend. A heat wave had just broken, so most people had their air conditioners off and the windows open, taking advantage of a breeze. My wife and I stepped outside, coughing, wondering whose house was on fire. Then I realized that the fire wasn't in Brockton. Even with the smoke in the streets, I could see a glow on the horizon, to the south, in the direction of where Orval and Eunice had their farm. I knew that it couldn't be any other Dant's place, because by then, Orval, Eunice and Lester were the only Dants left.

'Somebody rang the alarm at the fire station, the signal for volunteers. But when I got there, people had realized that the fire wasn't in town. There was a lot of confusion about whether we should go out to help them or whether we should let Orval and Eunice pay for insisting that they didn't need us. In the end, the town made me proud. The fire brigade had a truck filled with water. They drove it out there, and a whole lot of people went in cars. But even before we got close, it was obvious from the extent of the glow on the horizon that even a *dozen* trucks filled with water wouldn't make a difference.

'It hadn't rained in a month. The wind got stronger. On the left, flames streaked across pastures. Sections of timber were ablaze. Far off, a house and a barn were on fire. We did what we could to stop the flames from spreading across the road. Other than that, we were helpless. By then, it was dawn, and somebody shouted toward a burning field. I looked that way and saw a young man stumble ahead of the flames. He swatted at his smoking clothes, reached a fence, and toppled over it. I got to him first. He was sobbing. I'd never seen eyes so big with fear, but it was obvious that they weren't registering anything. He was blind from hysteria. I tried to stop him, but he lurched to his feet and staggered along the road. It took three of us to get him to the ground and smother the smoke coming off him.'

'That was Lester?'

The reverend nodded. 'He wasn't able to tell us what happened until three days later. After we got him to the ground, something seemed to shut off in him. He became catatonic. We took him to the clinic. He didn't have any serious burns or other obvious injuries, so the doctor treated him for shock. When it was safe to move him, my wife and I brought him here.' Reverend Benedict indicated the cottage behind the church.

His eyes saddened. 'When Lester was alert enough, he told us about the fire, how the smoke and the dogs barking had wakened him. He'd shouted to warn his parents. He'd tried to run down the hall to their room, but the flames were outside his door, and he had to climb out his window. In the yard, he kept shouting to warn his parents. Past the flames in the bedroom, he heard them screaming, but when he tried to get in through the window and pull them out, the heat was like a wall that wouldn't let him through. The breeze had spread the fire beyond the house. The barn and the outbuildings, the fields and the woods – everything was on fire. The only way he escaped was by throwing himself into a cattle trough, soaking himself, and running across a pasture while the fire chased him. In the week that he stayed with us, sometimes he woke screaming from nightmares of hearing his parents' screams.'

Imagining their agony, I shook my head from side to side. 'Did anybody ever learn what caused the fire?'

'Lester said that a light switch had stopped working in the kitchen. His father had planned to fix it the next day.'

'I know about buildings. It sounds like an electrical short,' I said. 'Fire can spread along faulty wires and accumulate behind the walls. When it breaks through, the flames are everywhere at once.'

'According to Lester, it was terrifyingly fast.'

'And *then* what happened? You said that he stayed with you for a week.'

'We wanted him to stay longer, but one morning, my wife looked in on him, and he was gone.'

'Gone?'

'We'd bought some clothes for him. They were missing. A pillowcase was missing also. He must have used it as a duffel bag. Bread, cookies and cold cuts were taken from the kitchen.'

'He left in the middle of the night? *Why?*'

'I think it had something to do with my being a minister and the cottage being next to a church.'

'I don't understand. Lester was raised in a religious family. The church shouldn't have bothered him.'

'Their beliefs were drastically different from mine.'

'I still don't . . .'

'The Dants believed that God turns His back on us because of our sinful nature. What *I* preach is that God loves us because we're His children. I've always suspected that the night before Lester ran away, he overheard me practicing my Sunday sermon. He probably thought he was hearing the words of the Devil.'

'And you never saw him again?'

'Not until last year when the FBI agent showed me that photograph.'

In despair, I peered down at it – at Lester Dant, not my brother. The hope upon which I'd based my search no longer kept me going.

Reverend Benedict looked even sadder. 'My wife and I wanted children, but we weren't able to have any. While Lester recuperated, she and I had talked about becoming his guardians. When he ran away, we felt as if we'd lost a child of our own.' He turned his gaze toward the cemetery beyond the rose garden. 'She died last summer.'

'I'm sorry.'

'Lord, how I miss her.' He looked down at his wrinkled hands. 'The last I heard about Lester . . .' Emotion made him pause. 'A month after he ran away, he was in Loganville. That's a town about a hundred miles east of here. A fellow minister happened to mention a helpless young man who showed up one day and whom members of the congregation were taking care of. I went there to find out if it was Lester and to try to persuade him to come back home, but he was gone by the time I got there. If I'd somehow convinced him to stay with us' – the reverend drew a breath – 'perhaps none of the tragedies he caused would have happened.'

'You did everything possible. *Lester's* the one to blame.'

'Only God can determine that.'

The effort of explaining had obviously tired him. I stood from the bench and shook his hand. 'Thank you, Reverend. This was painful for you. I appreciate the effort.'

'My prayers go with you.'

'I need them. You said that Orval and Eunice lived south of town?'

'About eight miles.'

'Everything's different now, I suppose.'

'An agribusiness wound up farming the land. But not much has changed. If you head that way, you can just make out the burned farmhouse from the road.'

6

I don't remember driving south of town. I was so dazed by what I'd learned that it's a wonder I didn't drift off the narrow road and hit something. I really had no idea why I was going out to where the fire had happened. But the alternative was to drive pointlessly back to Denver, and I refused to do that. Payne's words kept coming back to me: 'Nothing beats going to the places and people you want to know about.' The ruined Dant farm became one of those places.

A sign at the side of the road was weathered, partially overgrown with brush. But something in my subconscious noticed it, bringing me to attention. A large piece of plywood. What I assumed had once been black letters had faded to gray.

REPENT.

That was all, but it was enough to make me realize that I'd entered Dant country. On the right, beyond a pasture, I saw a farmhouse. It was distant, but even from the road, I could tell that it was listing, about to collapse, and that its windows had been broken. The roof on a barn next to it had already caved in.

But the reverend had said that Orval Dant's property had been on the left, so I focused my attention over there and soon noticed scorched stumps bordering fields of knee-high crops. I came to a section of trees, where tall burned timber stood among comparatively shorter, lush new trees. Then the land opened out again, and I saw the weed-covered furrows of a dirt lane stretching back what seemed a quarter of a mile to a wide mound of something near another section of new trees.

A metal gate blocked my way. It had a lock on a chain. I got out and tested the lock, finding it secure. A strengthening breeze carried a hint of moisture. Earlier, the sky had been stark blue, but now it was hazy, darkening on the horizon. The rain wouldn't reach me for a couple of hours. Even so, I reached into the car and got my knapsack, which had trail food, water and a rain jacket, among other things. The jacket was what most concerned me, but the truth was, I'd learned the hard way that even an apparently harmless walk in the woods might not work out as planned. I'd also learned from what had happened at the rest area four nights earlier. My pistol was in the knapsack.

I felt the pack's satisfying weight against my back as I climbed the fence. Dust puffed around my sneakers when I came down on the opposite side. I started at a walk, but as I looked at the bushes around me, I was reminded of something that Kate, Jason and I had done the summer before they'd been kidnapped. An architect friend had bought an old cabin up in the mountains. Trees and undergrowth had almost smothered the log building, so one Sunday he'd invited his friends up to help clear the place in exchange for barbecued steaks and all the beer we could drink. Our families were welcome also. Jason had thought it would be fun working next to me, helping to drag the cut bushes away, and I'd felt my chest swell with pride that the little guy had tried so hard. He made Kate laugh when he objected to her wiping the dirt and sweat from his face and making him look like a sissy.

Now, frustrated that I was no closer to finding them, I increased speed along the lane, anger pushing me. I stretched my legs as far and fast as I could, the sun hot on my face, sweat beading my skin, my jeans and shirt sticking to me.

A quarter of a mile was too short. I felt so infuriated that I could have run for miles, as I'd used to before I'd left Denver. But back in Denver, I'd been hopeful, whereas my frantic speed along that lane was a measure of how strongly I felt defeated.

I reached the end and slowed. The wide mound that I'd seen from the road revealed itself to be the blackened walls of a collapsed wooden structure. Its boards had been reduced to long slabs of charcoal that had toppled into a chaotic pile. Dead leaves were wedged in the gaps. Thorny bushes and vines whose three-leafed pattern warned of poison ivy sprouted from the debris. Beyond, a larger structure (presumably the barn) had similarly burned and collapsed.

Despite the sweat I'd worked up, I felt cold. I told myself that I was only imposing my mood on what I was seeing. All the same, I couldn't ignore what had happened there. Lester Dant's parents had burned to death thirty feet from where I stood. Blackness overwhelmed me.

What the hell am I doing? I thought. I was about to go back to the car, when something beyond the gutted house caught my attention: an area of about thirty by thirty feet enclosed by a low stone wall. The stones had been darkened by the fire. Some had fallen. I passed the ruins, trying to avoid the poison ivy as I approached the walled-in area. It had an opening where a gate had once been, and when I came closer, I saw that the enclosed area, too, was filled with poison ivy, dead leaves and thorny bushes. But, amid the chaos, I noticed regularly spaced clumps. Stepping closer, I realized that they were small piles of rocks arranged in rows. The pattern was too familiar not to be recognized as a graveyard. Instead of mounds, there were depressions, the earth having settled onto decaying wooden coffins and the moldering bodies within them. The depressions were common to most old graveyards. The only reason they didn't appear in modern cemeteries was that coffins were now made from metal, and graves had sleeves of concrete onto which a concrete lid was placed after the coffin was lowered and the mourners had departed.

In that dismal enclosure, generations of Dants had been buried. I imagined the pain and the loneliness with which their loved ones had laid them to rest. What struck me most was how many of the graves were short, indicating the deaths of children.

I don't know how long I stared at the graves, meditating about the independent community that the Dants had hoped to establish and how severely their dreams had failed. At last, I stepped away, going around the back of the ruins.

A small animal skittered through trees behind me. A squirrel perhaps. But because I'd detected no signs of life around the place, the sound startled me. There weren't even any birds.

Sweating from the stark sun, I noticed that the storm clouds were a little closer. Wary of more poison ivy, I continued around the back of the burned house. Abruptly my legs felt unsteady. For an instant, I feared that something was wrong with my brain, that I was having a stroke and my balance was gone. My footing became even more unsteady. My lungs fought for air when I realized in panic that it wasn't my brain or my legs. The ground beneath me parted. I plunged.

With a gasp, I stopped, caught at my hips. My legs dangled in an unseen open area. Heart racing, I pressed my hands against the ground and strained to push myself up through the hole that trapped me.

Immediately my hands felt as unsteady as my legs had. The more I pushed them against the earth, the more they sank into it. I dropped again, but not before I flung out my arms, blocking my fall an instant before the widening hole would have sucked me all the way down.

My legs dangled helplessly, my body swaying in the emptiness beneath me. Only my head and shoulders were above ground, my weight supported by my outstretched arms. Hearing muffled rattles below me, I couldn't make my lungs work fast enough to take in all the air I needed. The ground sagged again. As the rattles got louder, I shouted and plummeted all the way into the hole.

7

With a shock, my feet hit bottom. The impact bent my knees and threw me backward into darkness, jolting me against something. My knapsack jammed against my back, the flashlight, water bottle, and pistol in it walloping against my shoulder blades. I cracked my head and almost passed out. A moldy earthen smell widened my nostrils. The furious whir of rattles made me press harder against what I'd struck.

It felt like a wall. It was made from wood that had turned spongy. Simultaneously, I realized that what I'd fallen onto was the rotted remains of a wooden floor. Concrete showed through. It was pooled with water and had soaked my pants. But none of that mattered. All I cared about were the rattles in the darkness across from me and the rippling movement in the sunlight that came down through the hole in the ground.

Snakes. I scrambled to my feet, pressing into a corner. The flashlight, get the damned flashlight, I thought. Frantic, I tugged the knapsack off my back, yanked at its zipper, and reached in, fumbling for the light. In a rush, I turned it on and aimed its powerful beam at the darkness across from me.

The floor over there was alive with coiled snakes, their angry rattles echoing. A moan caught in my throat. I switched the flashlight's aim toward the scummy water at my feet, fearing that snakes would be coiled there. But the green-tinted water was free of them. It was about two inches deep, and I prayed that something in its scum was noxious to them. The floor tilted down toward the corner I was in, which explained why the water had collected there, but to my right and left and in the corner across from me, the raised part of the floor was dry, which was why the snakes had gathered on that side.

How far can a rattlesnake spring? I thought. Twice its length? Three times? If so, the snakes could fling themselves across the water at me. But my fall had startled them, making them dart back before they coiled. Their writhing mass was on the other side of the enclosure, a sufficient distance to keep me safe for the moment.

The enclosure. What the hell had I fallen into? It was about the size of a double-car garage. To the left of the opposite corner, a portion of the wall had collapsed. Behind its wooden exterior, insulation and concrete had toppled inward, exposing dank earth. A downward channel in the earth showed that whoever had poured the concrete for this chamber had failed to put in adequate drainage behind it. Rain had filtered down, accumulating behind the concrete until its weight had overwhelmed that section of the wall.

The gap explained how water had gotten into the chamber. So did the roof – not concrete, but made of timbers with plywood slabs on top (the hole in the roof showed the layers) and a waterproof rubber sheet above that, with six inches of earth over everything. Nothing prevented mice and other small animals from burrowing through the earth, reaching the rubber sheet and chewing through it. Once rain soaked down to the support beams, the process of rot would have begun, ultimately making the roof incapable of bearing weight.

But the chamber had obviously been built years earlier. During that much time, more than just a few inches of water would have accumulated where I was standing. There had to be a crack in the floor that allowed the water to seep away. That would have caused further erosion, explaining why the floor tilted toward the corner I was in.

I stared toward the fallen section of the wall. In the exposed earth, a channel angled toward the surface – the snakes used it to come and go. I wondered desperately if I could dig up through it, piling the earth in the chamber behind me as I went.

But how was I going to get past the snakes? As the rattles intensified, I braced the flashlight under my right arm and fumbled in my knapsack, gripping the pistol. Immediately I realized the flaw in what I intended. Even with fifteen rounds in the magazine and

one in the chamber, not to mention a further fifteen-round magazine in the knapsack, I couldn't hope to kill every snake. Oh, I
could hit most of them. There were so many that it would be
difficult for me to miss. But *all* of them? Killing them, not merely
wounding? No way. Besides, I had to consider the effect of the
gunshots. The reports would send the surviving snakes into a
frenzy, making them strike insanely at anything that moved, even if
it meant flinging themselves across the water to get at me. And
what about richocheting bullets slamming back at me?

I pressed harder into the corner. Stay quiet, I warned myself,
trying to control my hoarse breathing. Once the snakes realize
you're not a threat, they'll calm down.

I hoped. But I hadn't brought spare flashlight batteries. In a
couple of hours, the flashlight would stop working. A few more
hours after that, the sun would go down. The hole in the roof
would darken. I'd be trapped in blackness, not knowing if the
snakes would disregard the water (which possibly wasn't noxious to
them at all) and slither close to me, attracted by my body heat.

The meager illumination through the hole in the roof would have
to be sufficient. Hoping that my eyes would adjust to the shadows,
I shut off the flashlight, conserving the batteries. Despite the cold
water I stood in, sweat trickled down my face. Fear made me
tremble. Stop moving! I warned myself. Don't attract attention! I
squeezed my muscles, straining to control their reflexive tremors.

At first I wondered if it was my imagination. Long seconds after
I shut off the light and willed myself not to move, the buzz from
the rattles lessened. Slowly, the frenzy subsided. My shadow-
adapted eyes showed me the snakes eventually uncoiling, their
unblinking gaze no longer fixed on me. Their movements became
less threatening. A few went up the channel toward the surface.

But snakes preferred heat. Why had they gathered in the cool
chamber rather than remaining outside and basking in the sun?
What had driven them down? The question made my skin feel
prickly, especially when the few snakes that had gone up returned.
God help me, what didn't they like up there?

The rattling had almost completely stopped, just a few snakes
continuing to coil. Then, except for the hammering of my heart,
the chamber became quiet. Above, I heard sounds past the hole I'd

fallen through. The breeze became a wind, whistling through bushes. I heard a rumble that I hoped was an approaching car but that I suddenly understood was thunder. The light through the hole dimmed.

Lightning cracked. The wind shrieked harder. But none of that was why fear squeezed my chest tighter. No, what terrified me was the *pat pat pat* I heard on the floor, the rain falling through the hole.

8

It came faster. The snakes that were positioned under the hole jerked when the drops hit them. Some slithered toward their companions on the far side of the enclosure. They accumulated on something slightly higher than the floor, a long, flat object that the shadows kept me from identifying. its soft contours having dissolved after years of periodic flooding. But other snakes veered in my direction, the floor seeming to waver as they approached the scummy water.

Some slithered onto it. Rank fumes from the water assaulted my nostrils. I aimed my pistol, trembling, holding fire when I saw that the snakes on the water reversed direction and headed back toward the dry floor. Others had paused at the water and angled away. I'd been right. Something in the water repelled them.

But the rain fell rapidly through the hole, splashing the floor, widening its circle of moisture. A small pool formed, trickling toward my corner. Soon the entire area would be covered. When there wasn't a dry space, the snakes wouldn't have a reason to avoid my corner.

Feeling smothered, I turned on the flashlight and searched for something that I could use to hit the snakes if they came at me. Sections of wood and concrete that had fallen from the opposite wall were too far to reach without putting myself within striking distance of the snakes. As the water spread across the floor, the snakes crowded into a narrower area across from me. It wouldn't be long before they set out in all directions, looking for a place that was dry. I thought about attempting to rip a board from the wall. It might make a club. I had to try it.

Lightning flashed beyond the hole in the roof. The water spread to the snakes across from me, forcing them to pile on top of one another. Some dispersed. They'd soon be everywhere. I shoved the pistol under my belt and aimed the flashlight to my right, looking for a crack in the wall that would give my hands sufficient purchase to yank off a board.

What had been shadows in my peripheral vision were, I saw now, support beams that had fallen from the roof, leaning against the wall. Maybe I could use the beams to build a ramp. Maybe I could climb up and pull down other beams, claw through the earth and reach the surface. I didn't dare worry that the entire roof might collapse and crush me. No matter what, I had to get away from the snakes.

So much rain had fallen through the hole in the roof that the floor was now totally wet. Across from me, more snakes dispersed, rippling over the water. I moved to the right and pressed a shoe against one of the beams that leaned against the wall, to test it. Dismayed, I found that the wood was so rotten that it crumbled under my weight. The sudden lack of resistance threw me off balance. Struggling not to land in the water, I lurched forward and struck the wall behind the beams.

The impact jolted my shoulder. I almost dropped the flashlight. Worse, the noise disturbed the snakes, sending several of them into another frenzy of rattling. I was certain that I'd go crazy, start shooting, and be killed by a dozen bites. My terror so preoccupied me that it took me a moment to register that the wall I'd hit sounded hollow.

More snakes crossed the water toward me. I shoved the other beam to the side and uncovered a door. The nearest snake was three feet away when I gripped the rusty doorknob. I turned it, but the rust had frozen the mechanism. I turned harder, felt it budge, and thrust against the door with all my strength.

It creaked. Another desperate shove, and it suddenly swung inward with a crash, taking me with it. I sprawled on wet concrete, banging my chin but ignoring the pain, concentrating to protect the flashlight. Dazed, I whirled toward the doorway. A snake had coiled, about to strike. I kicked at the door, but its old hinges didn't respond soon enough. The snake leapt. The door banged shut halfway along its body, pinning it, the snake's front half whipping this way and that. The light from the hole in the roof was no longer visible. Only my flashlight. trembling in my hand, showed how the snake was caught. Its agonized movements tore its front half from the door. Its jagged midsection spewed blood as it flopped into the water and thrashed toward me.

I lurched backward. My head banged against something, and as the snake struck the bottom of one of my sneakers, I stood frantically, using my other sneaker to stomp the snake's head, its bones cracking beneath my sole.

The snake's severed body thrashed under my heel, its spastic movements slowing, becoming less violent. When it was finally still, I raised my shoe and aimed the flashlight at the flattened, bloody head. Reminding myself that a prick from its fangs could be poisonous even after it was dead, I kicked the torso toward the door.

When it splashed down, I raised my light to make sure that the door was closed and that no other snakes could get past it. I swung around to find out where I was and if this place, too, was inhabited by snakes. Nothing slithered. No rattling unnerved me. But even though I'd escaped from the first enclosure, I remained trapped.

I was in a tunnel roughly five feet wide and twenty feet long, with a ceiling I could touch if I raised my hand. The end opposite the door was choked with the objects I'd banged against: blackened timbers and other debris from the fire. Unlike in the first chamber, the concrete of the walls and the floor hadn't been covered with wood. The ceiling, though, had the same poor design: timbers with presumably plywood slabs, a rubber sheet, and earth on top. The timbers had not yet fallen, but water seeped between them, and eventually the timbers would rot to the stage of collapse.

As I noticed two rusted metal ducts that went along the ceiling and into the chamber, the rain streamed from the ceiling in greater volume. Rivulets poured down through the wreckage at the end of the tunnel. The water on the floor rose to my ankles. The crack at the door's bottom was too narrow to allow the water to drain. I was trapped in what amounted to a cistern.

How much rain could a strong June storm unload? An inch? Two? That didn't seem a threat unless you considered the expanse of the ground above the tunnel and the square footage of the burned house, both of which collected the water and funneled it into the five-by-eight-by-twenty-foot space that held me. The water probably wouldn't rise all the way to the ceiling, but there was a strong chance it would get high enough that I'd have to dog-paddle to keep my head above the surface. But how long could I do that as the water chilled me and hypothermia set in? Once I started shivering, I'd be dead in three hours.

In fact, I'd *already* started shivering. My flashlight showed wisps of my breath as I splashed toward the debris that blocked the tunnel. I braced the light between scorched boards, its slanted glare making it difficult for me to see as I grabbed a burned timber and strained to tug it loose. The effort made me breathe faster. Inhaling deeply, I coughed from the smoky odor coming off the wet wood.

I pulled harder and freed the timber. With a minor sense of triumph, I was about to shove it behind me, when the debris shifted and caused the flashlight to tumble. I grabbed for it, but my fingers only grazed it. As it flipped from my grasp, I lunged, using my hands like scoops to catch it the instant before it would have fallen into the water. I pulled it to my chest, treasuring it. Almost certainly, it would have stopped working if it had gotten soaked. The panic of nearly having lost my light made me shiver more severely.

The chill water rose to my shins. I tried holding the flashlight with one hand while I used the other to pull at the boards that blocked my way, but I couldn't get a decent grip. Reluctantly, I again tried bracing the flashlight among the debris, but it almost fell the moment I pulled out another board.

My pistol dug into the skin under my belt. It gave me the idea of cramming the flashlight under the opposite side of the belt, but there wasn't room. Think! I told myself. There has to be a way! I took off my knapsack, opened a side pocket, and shoved the flashlight into it. When I resecured the knapsack to my back, the light glared toward the ceiling, but when I leaned forward to grab at the debris, the light did what I wanted, tilting in that direction.

My frenzied movements echoed so loudly that my ears rang. Breathing stridently, I pulled out more boards, thrusting them behind me. Water poured down through the debris and rose to my knees. No matter how hot I felt from my exertions, I couldn't stop shivering. I freed another board and stared at a soot-smeared concrete step that led upward. With greater determination, I pulled two more boards loose, found *another* step, and felt a growing surge of hope. If I could uncover enough steps so I could climb above the water, the danger of hypothermia would lessen. I had food in my knapsack. I'd be able to eat and rest, conserving the flashlight's batteries, using them only while clearing the stairwell.

Desperate, I grabbed a timber and dragged it free, about to shove it behind me, when I heard a crack and gaped up at a huge plug of debris snapping loose. I tried to scramble back, but a jumble of scorched timbers and boards crashed down on me. The force took my breath away, knocking me toward the water. I didn't dare let the flashlight get soaked! Deafened by the reverberating rumble, I fought to raise myself, to keep the knapsack from filling with water. I pushed at the timbers weighing against me. I thrust the boards away. I grabbed something that didn't feel like wood. It was round and soft.

I screamed when I realized that I was holding the snake, its severed body drooping in my hands, the fangs of its crushed head close to my arm. As I hurled it away, a floating timber knocked against me. I fell. The foul water went over my head. It rushed into my ears, crammed my nostrils, and filled my mouth. Gasping, I bolted to the surface, coughing, spitting out soot-tasting water, struggling to breathe. I wiped at my eyes, frantically realizing that my lack of vision had nothing to do with water in them.

The flashlight had gone out.

9

In absolute darkness, my other senses strained to fill the void: the echo of waves splashing and wood thudding against the walls; the feel of my wet clothes clinging to me; the taste of soot and dirt; the stench of the water making me gag. My most extreme sense, though, was terror. Afraid to move lest I touch the fangs of the dead snake floating around me, I stood rigidly, trying to keep balanced in the darkness while I listened to the lapping of the waves slowly subsiding. Soon, all I heard was water streaming from the roof and through the debris in the stairwell.

My wet knapsack was heavy on my back. Blind, I took it off, looped its straps over a shoulder, and carefully took out the flashlight. I shook it. I pressed its on/off button. Nothing. I unscrewed its cap, removed the batteries, dumped the water from the cylinder, and blew on the poles of the batteries to attempt to dry them. After reinserting the batteries, I pressed the button. The darkness remained total. No, I was wrong. My eyes, straining to adapt to the blackness, became sensitive to a slight glow on my left wrist – the luminous coating on the hour marks of my watch. The speckled circled floated, disembodied.

I poured water from the knapsack, put the flashlight in it (and my pistol, which had dug deeper into the skin under my belt). Then I made sure that the pack's zippers were tightly closed and strapped it to my back. Meanwhile, the cold water rose above my knees.

Move! Wading, I groped ahead. I flinched from a chill, clammy, pitted surface, belatedly identifying it as a concrete wall. When I'd lost my balance and fallen, I must have gotten turned around. Now I had to make a choice: right or left. One direction led to the door, the other to the choked stairwell.

I eased to the left, pawing through the darkness. Something pricked my hand. Oh Jesus, I'd touched the snake's fangs. Jerking my hand back, grabbing where I'd been stung, I felt an object stuck in my palm. No. A splinter. Only a splinter. I'd scraped against a board.

I'd found the stairwell. As my watch's luminous dial zigzagged ghostlike in the darkness, I tugged at boards. I yanked at timbers. I pulled and heaved, shoving debris behind me. My hands were in pain, cut and gouged, but I didn't care. I had to clear more space before the water rose fatally higher. My shoulders arched, and my back throbbed. My mouth became dry. I had trouble getting air down my throat and finally had to pause to take my canteen from the knapsack and gulp water, making my mouth and throat feel less swollen, able to get more air.

But the brief rest didn't give me energy. I felt light-headed and realized that carbon dioxide was accumulating in the tunnel, becoming denser as the water rose. I didn't need to worry about hypothermia. I was going to die from suffocation.

With a greater frenzy, I grabbed sightlessly for debris and hurled it behind me. I freed one step after another, working higher, but the water followed, tugging at my hips. I felt unsteady. My mind whirled. Even though I couldn't see, spots wavered in front of my eyes.

The air thickened. My movements slowed. Debris floated against me. When a timber broke in my hands, I jerked backward, almost falling into the water. Then I pulled a chunk of wreckage, releasing not only it but a pool that had gathered in the ruins above me. With the force of a broken dam, it rushed onto me, so strong that it swept me off the steps, knocking me against floating timbers. I was dazed, barely able to keep my head above the surface. I flopped one arm and then the other against the water, trying to swim but remaining in place.

I was so weak, struggling not to sink, that it took me a moment to notice that the air had a hint of sweetness. I stared toward the stairwell and feared that my mind was tricking me, because the darkness was shaded. I saw vague contours of the wreckage. Gray filtered down. Bolstered by the fresh air seeping in, I found the strength to swim to the stairwell. I wavered up the steps and pulled at timbers, the gray beckoning, urging me upward.

When I finally squirmed up through an ooze of soot, squeezing past the jumbled skeleton of the collapsed house, the sky was thick with clouds. The air turned grayer, making me think that the hidden sun was setting and that in my delirium it had taken me all day to burrow up from the stairwell.

The cold rain persisted. It pelted me, but the grime that covered me was like grease and wouldn't come off. I clawed up through wreckage. I strained and dragged myself higher. Several times, boards snapped in my hands, threatening to hurtle me back into the pit. My blood-smeared fingers hooked onto the top of a foundation wall. I pulled myself over, flopping onto mushy ground. It took me several minutes before I could stand. As I plodded through mud, I wondered if I'd have the strength to reach my car.

10

Steam rose around me, but I couldn't get the bathwater hot enough. The cold penetrated to my bones. To my soul.

What use had the chamber served? I kept asking myself. Why had Orval, who'd possessed construction skills, not built the roof with concrete? What had been the purpose of the two ducts that had gone along the roof of the tunnel and into the chamber? If the chamber had been a storage area, there wouldn't have been a need to panel the walls, cover the floor, and use insulation. I couldn't make sense of it. Unless . . .

'*Where they kept me a prisoner was an underground room,*' the man who'd claimed to be my brother had said. Not Petey, God help me, but Lester Dant. Why would Orval and Eunice Dant have kept their only child in an underground room? The horror of it made my mind swirl.

The puzzle of the roof's poor construction now became clear. By working after dark, using no more than the lights from the house, Orval could have dug the space for the tunnel and the underground chamber without anyone who drove by noticing and wondering. Working at night, he could have mixed concrete in small amounts and used a wheelbarrow to transport it for the floor and walls of the tunnel and the chamber.

But the ceiling would have been a problem. To construct it properly, he would have needed to make concrete slabs. Once the slabs were ready, however, he would have needed a small crane to hoist them into place: precision work that would have required more than just standard illumination from the house. Outsiders would have noticed and been curious about so much light in back of his house after dark. Better to be cautious by using wooden beams for the roof, easily and quickly installed. Or maybe there'd been a deadline. Maybe Orval had been forced to compromise with the roof's construction because a timetable was hurrying him.

Sickened, I added more hot water to the tub, but I still couldn't chase the cold from my soul. Making me even colder was my uneasy conviction that I hadn't learned everything I could have out there. I was sure there was something darker. God help me, I didn't want to, but I knew I had to go back.

11

I walked along the lane to the ruin. The time was a little after ten the next morning. My night had been fitful, sleep coming only toward dawn. My nervousness grew as I stepped closer. I removed my pistol from a small camera bag that I'd bought and attached to my belt. Clutching the weapon helped to keep my scraped hands from shaking. The thought of the snakes made bile rise into my mouth.

I paused where I had the previous day. From the lane, I couldn't see the spot where I'd fallen into the chamber. It was as if the earth had sealed itself. But I had a general idea of where the tunnel and the chamber were, and I plotted a direction that avoided them.

I studied the long grass for quite a while, on guard against the slightest ripple. Finally I aimed the pistol and took one cautious step after another. Weeds scraped against my pants. The poison ivy seemed harder to avoid.

I took a wide arc around the back of the house, approaching a group of trees behind the house. The previous night, I'd imagined the design problems that Orval had needed to solve. Insulate the prison chamber. Get heating ducts leading into it. But what about ventilation? One of the ducts would have taken air *from* the furnace in the house. The other duct would have returned air *to* the furnace. A closed system.

That would have been adequate if the chamber had been merely a storage room. But if I was right and the chamber had been a cell, the system would have needed to be modified so that carbon dioxide and other poisonous gases didn't accumulate and kill the prisoner. To prevent that from happening, there would have had to

173

be another duct into the chamber, powered with a fan, to bring in fresh air. The logical place for that duct would have been just below the ceiling, but the snakes had prevented me from noticing the duct if it was there.

The outlet would have had to project above the ground. Otherwise, it would have gotten clogged with dirt. But how had Orval disguised it? The area behind the house was flat. After the fire, the townspeople would have swarmed around the wreckage, hoping to find survivors. They hadn't stumbled over the vent. If they had, they'd have wondered about its purpose and eventually have discovered the underground chamber. So where in hell had Orval hidden the outlet so that nobody had found it back then?

The trees were the obvious answer. Between fallen logs, or inside a stump. Ready with the pistol, I continued through the weeds and long grass. The sun was hot on my head, but that wasn't the reason I sweated. Each time a breeze moved blades of grass, I tightened my finger on the trigger.

I reached the trees, where the grass was welcomely shorter as I crisscrossed the area. Whenever I nudged a log, my muscles cramped in anticipation of finding a coiled snake. I picked up a stick (making sure that it was in fact a stick), then poked through leaves that had collected in hollow stumps. I found nothing unusual.

But the outlet had to be in the area. I turned in a slow circle, surveying the trees. Damn it, where would Orval have hidden the outlet? Ventilation ducts became inefficient the longer they extended. The outlet had to be somewhere among the charred logs and stumps. Everything else in the area was flat.

No, I realised with a chill. Not everything. The graveyard. On my left, about fifty feet from the chamber, it looked so bleak that it discouraged me from going near it. A perfect place to . . .

I stepped from the trees, entering the long grass, and the first rattle took my breath away. I stumbled back, saw the snake under a bush, and blew its head off. The reflex and the accuracy with which I shot surprised me. Hours and hours of practice no doubt explained my reaction. But for over a year, hate and anger had been swelling in me. More than anything, I wanted to kill something. No sooner had I shot the first snake than a second one buzzed. I blew *its* head apart. A third coiled. A fourth. A fifth. I shot each of them, furious that the snakes seemed to be trying to stop me. My shots rang in my ears. The sharp stench of cordite floated around me. Relentlessly, I shifted through the grass. A sixth. A seventh. An eighth. Pieces of snakes flew. Blood sprayed through the grass. Yet more kept rattling, and it seemed that it wasn't my pistol but my raging thoughts that shot them, so directly and instantly did their heads explode the moment I fixed my gaze on them.

The last empty cartridge flipped to the ground. The slide on the pistol stayed back. As I'd done hundreds of times in class, I pushed the button that dropped the empty magazine. I drew a full one from the small camera bag attached to my belt, slammed it into the pistol's grip, pushed the lever that freed the slide, and aimed this way and that, eager for more targets.

None presented itself. Either I'd frightened the rest away or they were hiding, waiting. *Let them try*, I thought in a fury as I picked up the empty magazine and proceeded more relentlessly through the grass. Reaching the graveyard's low stone wall, I climbed over. Brambles and poison ivy awaited me. The place was too foul even for snakes.

The piles of stones in front of each grave made my nerves tighten as I stepped forward. Glancing behind me, I thought I detected a slight furrow in the ground, where earth seemed to have settled. It was so minor that I never would have paid attention to it if I hadn't been looking for it. Faint, it ran from where I'd fallen into the chamber. It went under the graveyard's wall. Even less noticeable, it led to the grave nearest the underground chamber.

A short grave. A child's grave. Angry, I knelt. I pulled away the pile of stones at the head of the grave. For a moment, I couldn't move. The stones had concealed an eight-inch-wide duct sticking up. The duct had a baffle on it so that rain would pour off and not get into the ventilation system.

I was right: the chamber had been a cell. I remembered the long, flat object that the snakes had piled onto to avoid the rising water. Over the years, the object had so deteriorated that, in the shadows, I hadn't been able to identify it. But now I knew what it was. The remains of a mattress. It had been the only object in the room.

175

There hadn't even been a toilet. Had Lester been forced to relieve himself in a pot, contending with the stench until his captors took it away? Their *son*? The horror of it mounted as I stared at the child's grave that they'd desecrated to hide their sin.

12

Reverend Benedict was where I had met him the previous day, kneeling, trimming roses in the church's garden. His white hair glinted in the sunlight.

'Mr Denning.' He stood with effort, shook my hand, and frowned at the scratches on it. 'You've injured yourself.'

'I took a fall.'

He pointed toward my chin, where my beard stubble couldn't hide a bruise. 'Evidently a bad one.'

'Not as bad as it could have been.'

'At the Dant place?'

I nodded.

'Did you find anything to help you locate your family?'

'I'm still trying to make sense of it.' I told him what I'd discovered.

The wrinkles in his forehead deepened. 'Orval and Eunice held their only son prisoner? *Why?*'

'Maybe they thought the Devil was in him. I have a feeling a lot of things happened out there that we'll never understand, Reverend.' My head pounded. 'How did Lester escape from the underground room? When the fire broke out, did Orval and Eunice risk their lives to go down to the basement and free him? Did the parents somehow get trapped? In spite of how they'd treated him, did Lester try but fail to save them, as he claimed?'

'It fits what we know.'

'But it doesn't explain why he didn't tell everybody what he'd suffered. When something outrageous happens to us, don't we want to tell others? Don't we want sympathy?'

'Unless the memory's so dark that we can't handle it.'

'Especially if a different kind of outrage happened out there.'

Reverend Benedict kept frowning. 'What are you getting at?'

'Suppose Lester somehow got out of that room on his own. Or suppose the parents released him every so often as a reward for good behavior. Did *Lester* start the fire?'

'Start the . . . Lord have mercy.'

'One way or another, whether they tried to rescue him or whether he got out on his own, did he trap his parents? Did he stand outside the burning house and listen with delight to their screams? Is that something he'd have wanted to describe to anyone? But that's not all that bothers me.'

'Good God, you don't mean there's more.'

'I'm from Colorado,' I said.

The apparent non sequitur made Reverend Benedict shake his wizened head in confusion.

'Every once in a while, there's a story about somebody who went into the mountains and came across a rattlesnake,' I said. 'Not often. Maybe it's because the snakes have plenty of hiding places in the mountains, and they're not aggressive by nature – they prefer to stay away from us. But Indiana's a different matter. Lots of people. Dwindling farmland. Have you ever seen a rattlesnake around here?'

'No.'

'Have you ever heard of anybody who *has* come across one?' I asked.

'Not that I can think of,' the reverend said. 'A farmer perhaps. Rarely.'

'Because the spreading population has driven them out.'

'Presumably.'

'Then how come there are *dozens* of rattlesnakes on the Dant property? In southern states, in Mississippi or Louisiana, for example, so many snakes might not seem unusual, but not around here. What are they doing on Orval's farm? How did they get there?'

'I can't imagine.'

'Well, *I* can. Do you suppose that the Dants could have been practicing snake handling out there?'

The reverend paled. 'As a religious exercise? Holding them in each hand? Letting them coil around their neck to prove their faith in God?'

'Exactly. If the snakes didn't bite, it meant that God intervened. It meant that God favored the Dants more than He did the people in town. If you've got a bunker mentality, if you've got a desperate "us against them" attitude, maybe you want undeniable proof that you're right.'

'It's the worst kind of presumption.'

'And I suspect it destroyed them.'

'I don't understand.'

'You said that there were three Dant families when Lester was born. By the time of the fire, only *one* family – Orval, Eunice and Lester – remained. You wondered if the other families might have moved away or had gotten deathly ill. But *I'm* wondering if the snakes didn't send the Dants a different message than they expected.'

'You mean the snakes killed them?' the reverend murmured.

'The Dants would never have gone to a doctor for help.'

'Dear Jesus.'

'Snake handling would explain how so many got to be out there. The Dants brought them,' I said. 'What it *doesn't* explain is why the snakes remained. Why didn't they spread?'

'Perhaps they stayed where they belonged.'

At first, I didn't understand. Then I nodded. 'Maybe. That's a foul, rotten place out there, Reverend. I think you're right. If I were in your line of work, I'd say that the snakes are exactly where they feel at home.'

Several bees buzzed my face. I motioned them away.

'Just one more question, and then I'll leave you alone,' I said.

'Anything I can do to help.'

'You mentioned that after Lester ran from your home, he showed up in a town a hundred miles east of here, across the border in Ohio.'

'That's right.'

'What did you say it was called?'

Part Five

1

Loganville was better than I expected: a picture-postcard town with a prosperous-looking main street and a welcoming park in front of its courthouse. I asked directions to the Unitarian church, whose minister I'd phoned to make an appointment. The portly, gray-haired man was stacking hymnals in the vestibule.

'Reverend Hanley?' I'd explained on the phone why I needed to talk with him. I showed him Lester Dant's photograph and asked about the teenager's arrival at the church nineteen years earlier. 'I realize that's a long time ago, but Reverend Benedict seemed to think that you'd remember what happened back then.'

'I certainly do. It's difficult to forget what happened that summer. That boy meant a great deal to Harold and Gladys. They wanted so much to become his guardians.'

'Harold?'

'Reverend Benedict. Their greatest regret was not having children. How *is* Harold, by the way? I haven't seen him in at least a year.'

'He's well enough to get down on his knees and trim roses.'

Reverend Hanley chuckled. 'No doubt saying a few prayers while he's at it.' He studied Lester Dant's photograph and sobered. 'It's hard to . . . Add time and a scar – he could be the same person. The intensity of his eyes is certainly the same. He might be able to help you find your wife and son, you said?'

'He's the one who kidnapped them.'

The minister took a moment to recover from what I'd said. 'I wish I could help you. But I didn't get to know him well. The person you need to talk to is Agnes Garner. She's the member of the congregation who took the most interest in him. And she's the one he most betrayed.'

2

Climbing the porch steps at the address I'd been given, I found a woman in a wheelchair. From her pain-tightened face, I might have guessed that she was almost seventy, if Reverend Hanley hadn't already told me that she'd been thirty-eight when Lester Dant had come into her life nineteen years earlier. 'Ms Garner?'

'*Mrs.*'

'Sorry. Reverend Hanley didn't tell me you were married.'

'Widowed.'

'He didn't tell me that, either.'

'No reason he should have.'

Her abrupt manner made me uncomfortable. 'Thanks for agreeing to see me.'

Her hair was gray. Her dress had a blue flower pattern. She had a cordless telephone on her lap. 'You want to know about Lester Dant?'

'I'd appreciate any information you can give me.'

'Reverend Hanley called and explained about your wife and son. Do you have a photograph of them?'

'Always.' With longing, I pulled out my wallet.

She stared at the picture. Kate's father had taken it when we were visiting Kate's parents in Durango. The magnificent cliff ruins of Mesa Verde aren't far from there. We'd made a day trip of it. The photo showed Kate, Jason and me standing in front of one of the half-collapsed dwellings. We wore jeans and T-shirts and were smiling toward the camera. In the photo's background, next to an old stone wall, a stooped shadow looked like a human being, but there wasn't anything to account for the shadow. Jason had insisted it was the ghost of a Native American who'd lived there hundreds of years earlier.

Ghosts. I didn't want to think I was looking at ghosts.

'A wonderful family.'

'Thank you' was all I could say.

'There's so much sorrow in the world.'

'Yes.' Emotion tightened my throat. 'Mrs Garner, do you recognize this man?' I showed her the photo.

It pained her to look at him. She nodded and turned away. 'It's Lester. I haven't thought about him in years. I try my hardest not to.'

She's going to send me away, I thought.

'Do you honestly believe that what I tell you can help?' she asked.

'I don't know any other way.'

'Hurt him.'

'Excuse me?'

'We're supposed to forgive those who trespass against us, but I want you to hurt him.'

'If I get the chance, Mrs Garner, believe me, I will.'

She gripped the sides of her wheelchair. 'There was a time when I could walk. I was always the earliest to arrive for Sunday services.'

The change in topic confused me.

'I made a point of getting to the church before everyone. Now I wonder if I wasn't too proud and that's why God punished me.'

'Whatever happened, Mrs Garner, it wasn't God's fault. It was Lester Dant's.'

3

H e'd sat at the top of the church steps with his back against the
door.

'A teenager,' Mrs Garner said. 'His head was drooped, but even
without seeing his face, I could tell that I didn't know him. His
clothes were torn, so the first thing I thought was that he'd been in
some kind of accident. The next thing I thought was, the way his
head hung down, he might be on drugs. But before I could make a
decision whether to hurry to help him or run away, he raised his
head and looked at me. His eyes were so direct, there was no way he
could have been on drugs. They were filled with torment. I asked
him if he was hurt. "No, ma'am," he said, "but I'm awful tired and
hungry."

'By then, other members of the congregation had arrived. The
reverend came. But neither he nor anybody else recognized the boy.
We asked him his name, but he said that he couldn't remember. We
asked where he came from, but he couldn't remember that, either.
From the rips in his clothes and the freshly healed burn marks on
his arms, we figured that he must have had something terrible
happen to him, that he was in shock.

'The reverend offered to take him home and get him something
to eat, but the boy said, "No. These people are waiting for the
service to begin." That sounds too good to be true, I know. But
you weren't there. Everybody who came to church that morning
felt so concerned about the boy and so touched by his unselfish
attitude that we had a sense of God's hand among us. We took
him inside. I sat next to him and handed him a Bible, but he
didn't open it. I wondered if he was too dazed to be able to read.
Imagine my surprise when the congregation read out loud from

186

the Scriptures and the boy recited every passage from memory. I remember that the reverend said something in his sermon about keeping compassion in our hearts and helping the unfortunate. He paused to look directly at the boy. Afterward, everybody said that it was one of the most moving services that we'd had in a long time. The reverend took the boy home. He asked me and a couple of other church members to help. We made a big meal. We got the boy fresh clothes. He did everything slowly, as if in a daze.

'Who *was* he? We wondered. What had happened to him? Where had he come from? A doctor examined him but couldn't get him to remember anything. The chief of police got the same results and asked the state police if they knew about anybody who matched the boy's description and had been reported missing. The state police didn't learn anything, either.'

That made sense, I thought. Loganville was in Ohio, but the fire had happened in Indiana. The Ohio police had probably decided that the boy's arrival in Loganville wasn't important enough for out-of-state inquiries. Even if they *had* gone out of state, inquiries to the Indiana state police might have been pointless, the fire having been basically a local matter that the state police wouldn't have monitored.

'Various members of the congregation offered to take the boy in,' Mrs Garner said. 'But the reverend decided that since I'd found him, I had the right to take care of him if I wanted. My husband was the most generous soul imaginable. Five years earlier, we'd lost a son to cancer.' She paused, caught in her memories. 'Our only child. If Joshua had lived, he'd have been the same age as the teenager I'd found on the church steps seemed to be. I couldn't help thinking that God had sent him into our lives for a reason. As a . . .'

Mrs Garner had trouble saying the next word.

'Substitute?' I asked.

She nodded, her pain lines deepening. 'That's another reason I believe I was punished. For vain thoughts like that. For presuming that God would single me out and give me favorable treatment. But back then, I couldn't resist the idea that something miraculous was happening, that I was being given a second son. I told my husband what I hoped for, and he didn't take a moment to agree. If I wanted the boy to live with us while his problems got sorted out, it was fine. My husband loved me so much and . . .'

Her voice dropped. She turned her wheelchair slightly so that she looked even straighter at me. 'The boy came to live with us while the authorities tried to figure out who he was. He was awfully skinny. It took me days of solid home cooking, of fried chicken and apple pies, to put some weight on him. His burns had healed, but the scratches on his arms and legs, where his clothes had been torn, got infected and needed their dressings and bandages changed a lot. I didn't mind. It reminded me of taking care of the son we'd lost. I was pleased to do it. But I couldn't help wondering what on earth had happened to him.

'I left books and magazines on his bedside table so he'd have something to amuse him while he was resting. After a while, I realized that none of them had been opened. When I asked him if they didn't suit him, if he'd like to read something else, he avoided the question, and it suddenly occurred to me that the boy couldn't read.'

I'd taken a seat on a porch swing. Now I frowned. 'But you said that he could recite passages from the Bible.'

'Any passage I asked him.'

'Then I don't understand.'

'I asked him to read the back of a cereal box. I asked him to read the headline of a newspaper. He couldn't do it. I put a pencil and paper in front of him. He couldn't write the simplest words. He was illiterate. As for the Bible passages, there was only one explanation. Someone had taught him the Bible orally, had made him memorize passages that were read to him. It chilled me when I realized that. What on earth had happened to him?'

'That's one of the few questions I have an answer for.'

Her gaze was intense. 'You know?'

Wishing that I hadn't interrupted, I nodded. 'His parents held him prisoner in an underground room.'

'*What?*'

'As much as I've been able to figure out, they believed that the Devil was in him, that the only way to drive Satan out was by filling his head with the Bible.'

Mrs Garner looked horrified. 'But why wouldn't they have let him learn how to read and write?'

'I'm still trying to piece it together. Maybe they believed that reading and writing were the Devil's tools. The wrong kind of books would lead to the wrong kind of ideas, and the next thing, sin would be all over the place. The Bible was the only safe book, and the surest way to guarantee that the Bible was the *only* book Lester knew was to teach it to him orally.'

Mrs Garner's eyes wavered as if she'd become dizzy. She lowered her head and massaged her temples.

'Are you all right?' I asked.

'The things people do to one another.'

'I've told you what Lester did to my family. What did he do to *you?*'

Seconds passed. Gradually, she looked up at me, the pain in her eyes worse. 'He was the politest boy I ever met. He was always asking to help around the house. At the same time, I'd never met anyone so troubled. Some afternoons, he'd lie in bed for hours, staring at the ceiling, reliving God knew what. In the nights, he couldn't go to sleep unless his closet light was on. He often woke screaming from nightmares. They seemed to have something to do with the fire that had burned his arms. I'd go into his room and try to calm him. I'd sit holding him, stroking his head, whispering that he was safe, that nothing could hurt him where he was, that he didn't have to worry anymore.'

She paused, rubbing her temples again.

'Are you sure you're okay?' I asked.

'So long ago. Why does the memory still hurt so much?'

'I don't mean to upset you. If you need to rest for a while, I can come back when—'

'I never spoke about this to anyone. Ever. Maybe I should have. Maybe it wouldn't keep torturing me if I'd told someone, if I'd tried to explain.'

'Do you want to explain it to *me?*'

She looked at me in anguish for the longest while, searching my eyes. 'To a stranger. Yes. Someone whose judgments I'll never have to face again.'

'I don't make judgments, Mrs Garner. All I want is to get my wife and son back. Do you know anything that can help me do that?'

She struggled with her thoughts. 'One night, he kissed me on the cheek. Another night, after one of his nightmares, after I held him and calmed him, he pecked my cheek again. Or tried to. He grazed my lips, as if he'd aimed for my cheek and missed. It was an awkward moment. I stood as soon as I got him settled in bed. I felt uncomfortable, but I kept telling myself that I was imagining things, that the boy hadn't meant anything.'

'Mrs Garner, you don't need to—'

'I have to. Somehow I have to get it out of me. I wanted to take care of the boy so much that I was in denial. Each intimacy seemed innocent. Like when I tried to teach him to read and write. That's what I used to be: a teacher at the high school. This happened at the end of summer. School hadn't started yet. I had time to try to teach him. I used the Bible, since he already knew the words. We sat together at the kitchen table. Our chairs were close. There was nothing wrong. We were just a teacher and a student sitting at a table working on a school problem, and yet, in retrospect, I realize that he sat closer than he needed to. When he helped me make dinner, our hands would touch briefly. I didn't think anything of it. One of the reasons I haven't told anybody about this is that I'm afraid it'll seem as if I took some kind of' – she had trouble saying the word – 'enjoyment . . . That's the furthest thing from the truth. I know that there are a lot of twisted people in this world, Mr Denning. But I'm a churchgoing, Godfearing woman, and I assure you that I am not capable of enjoying the touch of a teenager whom I considered to be like a son.'

An uncomfortable silence gathered. I made myself nod, encouraging her to continue.

'But it's because I wanted so desperately to take care of him that everything happened. One night, after another of his nightmares, when I held him, he grazed my . . .' Self-conscious, she looked down at the front of her dress. 'It seemed accidental, yet I finally admitted that too many accidental gestures like that had happened, and I told him that certain kinds of touching weren't appropriate. I told him that I wanted the two of us to be close but that there were different kinds of closeness. He said that he didn't know what I meant but that if I wanted him to keep a distance, he would.

'The next night . . .' She couldn't get the words out. Her eyes glistened, close to weeping. 'May I see the photograph of your wife and son again, please?'

Puzzled, I took out my wallet.

She studied it even longer than the first time. 'Such a wonderful-looking family. What are their names?'

'Kate and Jason.'

'Are you happily married?'

'Very.' Now *I* was the one who had trouble speaking.

'Is your son a good boy?'

'The best.' My voice became hoarse.

'How will this help you find them?' Moisture filled her eyes.

If Kate and Jason are still alive, I thought. What I'd learned from Reverend Benedict filled me with despair.

'I'm betting that he has habits.' I struggled to hide my discouragement. 'If I can understand him, I might be able to follow his trail.'

'A trail that started nineteen years ago?'

'I don't know where else to go.'

'He raped me.'

The porch became deathly silent, except for her sobs as tears trickled down her cheeks.

I felt paralyzed, trying to get over my shock. 'I'm sorry. I shouldn't have asked you to try to talk about it.'

'Don't talk about it?' Her tears made scald marks on her cheeks. 'God help me, I've been holding it inside all these years. *That's* the torture. My husband was the principal of the school where I taught. Around dark, the janitor called about a water pipe that had burst. My husband hurried down to learn how serious the damage was. I got ready for bed. The boy . . . The rotten son of a bitch bastard—'

The torrent of what for Mrs Garner were the crudest of obscenities shocked me.

'He came into my bedroom while I was undressing, threw me on the floor, and . . . I couldn't believe how strong he was. He was so frail-looking, and yet he overpowered me as if he had the force of the Devil. He kept calling me Eunice, but he knew very well that my

191

first name is Agnes. I tried to fight him off. I scratched. I kicked. Then I saw his fist coming at me. Twice. Three times. I almost choked on my blood, lying there half-unconscious while he . . .'

Her voice faltered. She pulled a handkerchief from her dress, raising it to her cheeks.

'Afterward . . .' Some of her tears dripped from her chin. 'After I vomited . . . After I found the strength to stand, I saw drawers open and realized that he'd stolen anything of value that he could stuff into his pockets. But that was the last thing on my mind. I staggered to the phone to call the police and get an ambulance, and all at once, I realized that I couldn't do that. I thought of the congregation and the town and the high school where my husband and I worked, and I imagined everybody staring at me. Oh, sure, they'd be sympathetic. But that wouldn't stop them from telling everybody they knew about what had happened to Agnes Garner. Being sympathetic wouldn't stop them from staring, and it wouldn't stop word from getting around to the students, who would stare even more than their parents. Rape. Rape.

'I wavered in front of the phone. I remember telling myself that I had to call for help, that I was close to passing out. Instead, I forced myself into the bathroom. I used all my strength to get in the tub and wash myself where he'd . . .' She wiped more tears from her face. '*Then* I got dressed. *Then* I called the police. And no doctor ever had a chance to examine any part of me except my smashed lips and my bruised cheeks. I told everybody that I'd come into the bedroom and found him stealing money and jewelry. Not that I had much jewelry. I'm not that kind of a woman. All told, he took about three hundred dollars, which could be replaced, but a simple necklace that my grandmother had given me could *never* be replaced.

'My husband got home just after the police car arrived. The police searched for the boy but never found him. Maybe he slept in the woods. Maybe he hitchhiked and got a ride out of the area. The next day, Reverend Benedict arrived from Brockton. I learned that the boy's name was Lester Dant. I learned about the fire that had killed his parents. But I never told Reverend Benedict or Reverend Hanley what had really happened in my bedroom. I never told my husband. I never told *anyone*. When word got around, people stared, yes, but it was a kind of staring that I could tolerate. We'd taken a boy into our home. He'd repaid us by beating me and stealing from us. I was the kind of victim that the town could deal with.'

'I can't tell you how sorry I am,' I said.

'Eunice.' She sounded anguished. *'Why on earth did he call me Eunice?'*

I didn't answer.

'You know about the underground room where his parents kept him prisoner. What *else* do you know? Have you any idea why he called me Eunice?'

Her tone was so beseeching that I found myself saying, 'Yes.'

'Tell me.'

'Are you sure you want the answer?'

'The same as *you* need answers.'

I hesitated. 'Eunice was his mother's name.'

Mrs Garner moaned.

'It sounds as if he was punishing . . .'

'His mother. Punishing his *mother*. God help me.' Her voice cracked with despair. 'Hurt him. Remember your promise. When you find him, hurt him.'

'You have my word.'

4

All the way to my car, I tried not to let Mrs Garner see my discouragement. 'When you find him,' she'd said. But I no longer believed that I would. With no information about where Lester Dant had gone that night, I hadn't the faintest idea what to do next. Worse, I didn't see the point of trying. Lester was far more disturbed than the FBI's information about him had revealed. I couldn't imagine him keeping Kate and Jason alive.

Grieving for them, I slumped behind the steering wheel. Hate fought with grief. 'Hurt him,' Mrs Garner had pleaded. Yes, hurt him, I thought. Furious, I drove past well-maintained lawns and neatly trimmed hedges. I reached a four-way stop and turned to the right. At the next four-way stop, I turned to the left. No reason. No direction.

I went on that way, at random, for quite a while, driving through the prosperous farm town until I realized that I was passing certain homes and stores for what might have been the fifth or sixth time. Fatigue finally caught up with me, making me stop at a motel called the Traveler's Oasis on the edge of town.

It was almost five, but for me it felt like midnight as I carried my suitcase and backpack into a room that faced the parking lot. Too exhausted to survey the spartan accommodations, I returned to the car for my printer and laptop computer. I wondered why I'd bothered to bring them. They took up space. I hadn't used them.

Maybe it's time to go home, I thought.

In Denver, it was two hours earlier. I picked up the phone.

'Payne Detective Agency,' a man's familiar voice said.

'Answering the phone yourself?'

194

Payne didn't reply for a moment. 'Ann had a doctor's appointment.' Ann, his receptionist, was also his wife. 'How are you, Brad?'

'Is my voice that recognizable?' I imagined the portly man next to his goldfish tank.

'You've been on my mind. When you called the last time, you were in South Dakota. You said you'd get back to me, but you didn't. I've been worried. What are you doing in . . .' I heard Payne's fingers tapping on a computer keyboard. 'The Traveler's Oasis in Loganville, Ohio.'

'Sounds like you've got a new computer program.'

'It keeps me distracted. What are you doing there?'

'Giving up.'

'I'm sorry to hear that. I figured that as long as you were in motion, you wouldn't do anything foolish to yourself. You didn't learn anything, I gather.'

I sat wearily on the bed. 'The opposite. I learned too much. But it hasn't taken me anywhere.'

'Except to the Traveler's Oasis in Loganville, Ohio.'

Payne tried to make it sound like a joke, but it didn't work. 'I was hoping to find a pattern,' I said into the phone.

'Sometimes a pattern's there. We just don't recognize it.'

'Yeah, well, *my* pattern's been aimless.' Something Payne had said caught up to me – the somber way he'd said it. 'Ann had a doctor's appointment? Is everything okay?'

'We'll see.'

'. . . Oh.'

He hesitated. 'A lump on her breast, but it might just be a cyst. The doctor's doing a biopsy.'

I took a tired breath. 'I'll say a prayer.'

'Thanks.'

'Before all this began, that isn't something I'd have said.'

'That you'd pray for somebody?' he asked.

'The last few days, I spoke to a couple of ministers and a very religious, very decent lady. I guess some of their attitudes wore off on me. The trouble is, I also learned about a man whose parents turned him into a monster. Lester Dant.'

'You believe in him now?'

'Oh, I believe in him all right. God help me.'

'Another prayer,' Payne said.

'I'll be starting home tomorrow. I'll phone as soon as I get back. Maybe you'll have the results of the biopsy by then.'

'Maybe.' Payne's voice sank. 'Have a safe trip.'

I murmured, 'Thanks,' and hung up.

Please, God, keep his wife healthy, I thought.

I lay on the bed and closed my eyes. The draperies shut out the late-afternoon light. I wanted to sleep forever.

Please, God, I hope you didn't let Kate and Jason suffer.

I couldn't help thinking about the good and bad things that religion could do to people. I couldn't help thinking about Lester Dant running from one church and showing up at another and . . .

5

The shock of the idea made me sit up. I found myself standing excitedly, thinking about what Lester Dant, posing as my brother, had told me more than a year earlier.

'*As I wandered from town to town, I learned that an easy way to get a free meal was to show up at church socials after Sunday-morning services.*'

Jesus, I thought, he would have continued doing what worked. He'd have gone to another church in another small town. Payne had been right. The pattern was there. I just hadn't recognized it.

In a rush, I arranged my computer and printer on a table next to the bed. I unplugged the room's phone from the wall and attached my own phone line, connecting it to my computer. Then I turned on the computer and made adjustments to my Internet-access program so I could shift from AOL's Denver phone number to one that it used in the Loganville area.

The next thing, I logged on to an Internet geography site and printed a map for Ohio, along with ones for the surrounding states of Michigan, Indiana, Kentucky, West Virginia and Pennsylvania. What I wanted was a list of towns. Dant would have avoided cities. I was sure of it. After the smothering closeness of having been imprisoned underground, I imagined him recoiling from the congestion of cities.

The maps gave me hundreds of names. Too many to be of use, but a start. I made the list more practical by eliminating the names of towns that were on the extreme reaches of the other states. I further reduced the list by eliminating Indiana, convinced that Dant would have avoided going back to where he'd been imprisoned. That left Ohio, Michigan to the north of it, Kentucky and

197

West Virginia to the south, and Pennsylvania to the east.

But the towns in them weren't what I cared about. What I wanted were the names of *churches* in those towns. I typed 'Churches in Ohio' into the Internet's 'Search For' box. A list appeared, complete with their locations and their Web site addresses. I matched them with the towns on my list. I did the same with churches in Kentucky, West Virginia, Pennsylvania and Michigan. I eliminated any church with a saint's name in it, certain that Dant would have avoided Catholic, Anglican and Greek Orthodox churches. Their theology and ritual would have been alien to him. I need to identify Protestant congregations, I thought, and then I can—

A loud knock on the door distracted me.

I jerked my head in that direction.

Sunlight had long since faded from behind the draperies. I looked at my watch. Almost seven hours had passed. The hands were close to midnight.

The loud knock was repeated. 'Mr Denning?' a man's voice asked.

When I stood, my legs ached from having sat so long. I went to the door, squinted through the tiny lens, and saw an elderly man in a jacket and tie. I kept the security chain on the door when I opened it and peered through the five-inch gap. 'What is it?' The stark floodlights in the parking lot made me blink.

'I just wanted to make sure that everything was all right. Our computer shows that you've been on the phone since around five o'clock, but when I tried to access the line to make sure you hadn't fallen asleep and left the phone off the hook, all I got was static.'

'I've been catching up on office work.'

The man looked puzzled.

'On the Internet,' I said, pointing toward my computer on the corner table, which I later realized he couldn't see.

The man looked more puzzled.

'You have my credit-card number,' I said. 'I'll gladly pay all the phone charges.'

'As long as everything's okay.'

'Couldn't be better.'

'Have a nice night.'

He left, and I became aware of throbbing in my head, of cramps in my stomach. Through the crack in the door, I saw a harsh red-and-blue neon sign across the street. The words it flashed were STEAKS 'N' SUDS. Two eighteen-wheeler trucks were at the edge of the crowded parking lot. Begrudging the time I'd be wasting but telling myself that I couldn't be any use to Kate and Jason if I didn't maintain my strength, I disconnected from the Internet, locked the room behind me, and walked toward country music – a jukebox playing something about a one-man woman and a two-timing man – coming from the restaurant's open window.

6

Forty minutes later, the steak sandwich I'd eaten felt heavy in my stomach. I recalled the strict healthy diet that I'd put myself on in preparation for my search. Tomorrow, I'll rededicate myself, I vowed. Tomorrow.

'Here's your coffee to go,' the waitress said.

'Thanks.'

As I left the restaurant, about to cross the parking lot, a noise made me pause. The jukebox had stopped, but the conversations of the crowd inside were loud enough that I had to strain to listen harder. On my right. Around the side of the restaurant. I heard it again. A groan.

A *woman's* groan.

'Think you can leave me?' A man's muffled voice came from around the corner. 'You're dumber than I always said you were.'

I heard a metallic thump, as if someone had fallen against a car. Another groan.

Inside, the jukebox started playing again: something about lonely rooms and empty hearts. The careful Brad I'd once been would have gone back into the restaurant and told the manager to call the police. But how long would it take the police to arrive, and what would happen in the meantime?

Imagining Petey hitting Kate, I unzipped the small camera bag I always wore on my belt. Knowing that I could draw my pistol if I needed it, I walked to the restaurant's corner. There were only a few windows on that side. Away from the glare of the neon lights, my eyes needed a moment to adjust before I saw moving shadows between two parked cars: a man striking a woman.

'Stop,' I said.

The man spun toward my voice. The minimal light showed a beefy face. A chain on his belt was attached to a big wallet in his back pocket. 'This is a private conversation. Stay out of it.' He shoved the woman to the asphalt. 'You don't want to live with me anymore? Well, either you live with me or you don't live at all.'

'I told you to stop.'

'Get lost, pal, or when I finish my family business, I'll start on *you*.'

'Get lost? You just said the two words I hate the most.'

'You heard me, buddy.' The man jerked the woman to her feet and pushed her into a car. When she tried to struggle out, he struck her again.

'But you're not hearing *me*.' Conscious of the pistol in my bag, I stepped closer.

'All right, I gave you a chance to butt out!' The man spun toward me again. 'Now it's *your* turn.'

'Must be my lucky night.'

He lunged.

The take-out coffee was in my left hand, the liquid so hot that it stung my fingers through the Styrofoam cup. I yanked the lid from the cup and threw the steaming contents at the man's face, aiming for his eyes.

The man shrieked and jerked his hands toward his scalded face.

I drove stiff fingers into his stomach, just below the V of the rib cage, the way I'd been taught.

Sounding as if he might vomit, the man doubled over.

I kicked sideways toward a nerve that ran down the outside of his left thigh.

Paralyzed, his leg gave out, toppling him to the pavement, where he shrieked harder from the pain in his leg.

I yanked his hands from his face and drove the heel of my right palm against his nose, once, twice, three times. Cartilage cracked. I stepped back as blood spurted.

He dropped to the pavement and lay motionless. Ready to hit him again, I shoved him onto his side so the blood would drain from his nose. I felt for a pulse, found one, smelled his sour alcohol-saturated breath, and turned to the woman slumped in the car. 'Are you all right?'

She moaned. I was appalled by the bruises on her face.

'Are you strong enough to drive?' I asked.

'I don't . . .' The woman was off-balance when I helped her from the car. Her lips were swollen. 'Yes.' She took a deep breath. 'I think I can drive. But . . .'

'Do it.'

Behind me, the man groaned.

'Hurry,' I said. 'Before he wakes up.'

Through blackened eyes, the woman looked around in confusion. Bruises that deep couldn't develop in just a few minutes, I knew. They were the consequence of numerous other beatings.

'*Drive?*' she asked plaintively. '*How?* I ran here. I hoped I could borrow money from a girlfriend who works in this place. It turns out she called in sick. *He* was waiting instead.'

Stooping beside the man on the pavement, I satisfied myself that he was still too dazed to realize what was going on. I pulled his car keys from his pants. Then I took his big wallet from his back pocket and removed all the money he had – what looked like a hundred dollars.

'Here,' I told the woman. I pulled out my own wallet and gave her most of the cash I had – around two hundred.

'I can't accept this,' she said.

'My wife would have wanted me to give it to you.'

'What are you talking about?'

'Take this. Please. Because of my wife.'

The woman looked at me strangely, as if trying to decipher a riddle. 'I have a sister in Baltimore,' she said as I gave her the man's car keys.

'No, it's the first place he'll look,' I said. 'If you'd robbed a bank, would you hide at your sister's? Too obvious. You have to pretend you're running from the police.'

'But I haven't done anything wrong!'

'Keep telling yourself that. You haven't done anything wrong. But that son of a bitch over there certainly has. You have to keep reminding yourself that your only goal in life is to stay away from him.' In Denver, when life had been normal, I'd been proud of the volunteer work Kate had done as a stress counselor at a shelter for battered women. I knew the drill. 'Pick a city where you've never

been. Pittsburgh.' I chose it at random. 'Have you ever been to—'
'No.'

'Then go to Pittsburgh. It's only a couple of hundred miles from here. Leave the car at a bus station, and go to Pittsburgh. Look in the phone book under "Community Services". Look for the number of the women's shelter.'

7

I trembled in my motel room, amazed by the rage that had overtaken me. For a moment, as the bastard had come at me, I'd almost shot him. The only thing that had stopped me was the realization that the shot would have sent people scurrying from the restaurant. Someone might have seen me. The police would have come after me. How could I have looked for Kate and Jason if I were in jail?

8

For reasons important to my family and me, my E-mail said, *I'm looking for information about a young man who might have come to your church in the late summer or in the fall nineteen years ago. I realize that it's hard to remember that far back, but I think that the circumstances would have been unusual enough that someone in your congregation would recall him. The boy would have been in his mid-teens. He would have collapsed against the front door of your church early before Sunday services, so that the first person to arrive would have found him there. He would have been wearing torn clothes and would have had scrapes and scratches, suggesting that he'd been in an accident of some sort. He wouldn't have been able to recall his name or what had happened to him or how he had come to be at your church. Members of the congregation would have taken care of him – in particular, women – because something about his eyes invites mothering. He would have been able to quote the Bible from memory but otherwise would have been unable to read or write. Someone, probably a woman, would have tried to teach him. Ultimately, he would have stolen from the people who helped him, perhaps have beaten them also, and have fled town. It may be that near the end he 'remembered' that his name was Lester Dant. If you have any knowledge of someone like this, please send me an E-mail at the above address. I very much need to learn everything I can about this person. A year ago, he kidnapped my wife and son.*

9

The next morning, after a torturous sleep, I sent that message to the E-mail address of every church on my list. Staring at my computer screen, I silently asked God to help me. All I could do now was wait.

The need to urinate finally made me move. But once in motion, I remembered Payne's remark that as long as I stayed in motion, I was less likely to do something foolish to myself. I went for a five-mile run. I returned and checked to see if I had any E-mail. Nothing. I did an hour of exercises, then checked my E-mail again. Still nothing.

What did I expect? That someone at each church would faithfully read the church's E-mail every morning, that word of my message would spread instantly throughout each congregation, that people who remembered something like the events I'd described would immediately send an E-mail back to me? I have to be patient, I warned myself. Even in small towns, news doesn't get around as fast as I want it to. If there's a reply to be had, I probably won't receive it until evening.

So I showered, dressed, and tried to read. I went out and got a sandwich. I took a walk. I watched CNN. But mostly I kept checking to see if any E-mail had arrived. None did. By midnight, I gave up, shut off the lights and tried to sleep.

But unconsciousness wouldn't come, and finally, betraying my resolve of the previous night, I went down the road to a bar and grill, where I wasn't likely to be recognized. If the man I'd beaten was looking for me, the logical place he'd do it was the restaurant across from the motel. This time, it took four beers and shot of bourbon before I felt stupefied enough to go back to my room and try to sleep. I'm going to hell, I told myself.

I *am* in hell.

Around dawn, I woke, but there still wasn't any message. I faced another day of waiting. Time dragged on, until I admitted that I'd been a fool to have hoped. I hadn't been brave enough to identify with Lester Dant as closely as I'd needed to. I'd been wrong in my prediction of where he'd gone nineteen years previously and of what he'd done when he'd arrived there. Vowing that I couldn't persist in leading my life the way I was, wondering if I wanted to lead my life at all, I checked my E-mail and tensed at the discovery of four messages.

10

I was certain that they didn't exist, that I'd tricked myself into seeing things. With a sense of unreality, I stared at them. Unsteady, I printed them out. Each was from a different state: Kentucky, West Virginia, Pennsylvania and Ohio. Initially, their sequence was alphabetic, based on the sender's name, but after I reread them several times, I arranged them so that they formed a geographical and chronological narrative.

Mr Denning, the first began. *Your message so disturbed me that it took me a long time to face up to answering it. My husband told me not to pain myself, but I can't bear the thought that other people have suffered.* The writer identified herself as Mrs Donald Cavendish, and the details of her message paralleled what Mrs Garner had told me. If a rape had occurred, Mrs Cavendish didn't mention it, but I had a disturbing sense of a deeper hurt than even the strong facts of her message accounted for. He hadn't called himself Lester, though. He hadn't used any name at all. The night that he'd disappeared, he'd burned down their house.

This had happened in November, a month after he'd brutalized Mrs Garner. What had occurred in the interval? I checked my maps and found that the town in Kentucky was two hundred miles from Loganville, Ohio. After Lester spent the money that he'd stolen from Mrs Garner, had he wandered, subsisting on the proceeds from house break-ins and liquor-store robberies until his aimless path took him to Kentucky?

The next message (as I arranged them) was from the neighboring state of West Virginia and described events *one year later*, when Lester (he used only his first name) had been welcomed by a churchgoing family whose teenage daughter he eventually victimized. It was the daughter who sent me the E-mail, revealing what she'd hidden from her parents until she was an adult. Lester had warned her that if she told anyone what he'd done, he'd come back one night and kill her. To prove his point, he'd strangled her cat in front of her. The next night, he'd robbed the house, stolen the family car, and disappeared. The police had found the fire-gutted car two hundred miles away, but although Lester was gone, it had taken the daughter a long time before she'd stopped having nightmares about him.

The third message (from Pennsylvania) described events a surprising *eight years* later. He'd shortened his first name to Les. His methods had changed. In his mid-twenties now, he no longer had the air of vulnerability that had made it so easy to portray himself a victim and win the compassion of a small-town congregation. Instead, he'd showed up at the church and offered to do odd jobs in exchange for meals. His amazing ability to quote any Bible passage from memory had endeared him to the congregation. This time, it was the church that he'd burned.

But it was the fourth message that disturbed me most. It was from a man who described events *thirteen years* after the fire in which Lester Dant's parents had been killed. It came from a town in central Ohio. This time when Lester had disappeared, he'd taken the man's wife. She'd never been found. But Lester hadn't used his first name or its abbreviation, Les. He'd used an entirely different first name. It turned me cold.

Peter.

Shivering to the core of my soul, I stared at the maps and the placement of the towns. From Brockton southeast to Loganville in Ohio, then farther southeast to the town in Kentucky, then east to West Virginia, then northeast to Pennsylvania, then northwest to the town in Ohio, a hundred miles from where I was raised in the middle of that state. One month. One year. Eight years. Thirteen years.

He'd been to far-off places in the country during the intervals (his FBI crime report made that clear), but something kept making him return to this general area, and I couldn't help feeling that the placement of towns on the maps wasn't random, that it had a center, that he'd been skirting his ultimate destination, each time getting closer, drawn relentlessly back to where everything had begun.

Part Six

1

It had been more than a quarter of a century since my mother and I had been forced to leave Woodford to live with her parents in Columbus. Payne had told me that the town was now a flourishing bedroom community for the encroaching city. But I hadn't fully realized what that meant. After I steered from the interstate, following a newly paved road into town, I tested my memory. I'd been barely fourteen when Mom and I had left. Even so, from all the times that she and Dad had taken Petey and me to visit her parents, I remembered that there'd been a lot of farmland on the way to the interstate. Much of that was gone now, replaced by subdivisions of large houses on small lots. The panoramic outdoor view that owners had initially been attracted to had been obliterated by further development. Expensive landscaping compensated.

On what had once been the edge of town, I passed the furniture factory where my dad had been a foreman. It was now a restaurant/movie theater/shopping mall complex. The industrial exterior had been retained, giving it a sense of local history. Downtown – a grid of six blocks of stores – looked better than it had in my youth. Its adjoining two-story brick structures had been freshly sandblasted, everything appearing new, even though the buildings came from the early 1900s. One street had been blocked off and converted into a pedestrian mall, trees and planters interspersed among outdoor cafés, a fountain and a small bandstand.

The area was busy enough that it took me a while to find a parking spot. My emotions pushed and pulled me. When I'd been a kid, downtown had seemed so big. Now the effect was the same, but for different reasons – helplessness made me feel small. Despite the passage of years, I managed to orient myself as I passed a comic-book store and an ice-cream shop, neither of which had been in those places when I was a kid. I came to the corner of Lincoln and Washington (the names returned to me) and stared at a shadowy doorway across the street. It was between a bank and a drugstore, businesses that *had* been in those places when I was a kid. I remembered because of all the times my mother had walked Petey and me to that doorway and had taken us up the narrow echoing stairway to our least favorite place in the world: the dentist's office.

That stairway had seemed towering and ominous when I'd climbed it in my youth. Now, trying to calm myself, I counted each of its thirty steps as I went up. At the top, I stood under a skylight (another change) and faced the same frosted-glass door that had led into the dentist, except that the name on the door was now COSGROVE INSURANCE AGENCY.

A young woman with her hair pulled back looked up from stapling documents together. 'Yes, sir?'

'I . . . When I was a kid, this used to be a dentist's office.' I couldn't help looking past the receptionist toward the corridor that had led to the chamber of horrors.

She looked puzzled. 'Yes?'

'He has some dental records I need, but I don't know how to get in touch with him because I've forgotten his name.'

'I'm afraid I'm not the person to ask. I started working for Mr Cosgrove only six months ago, and I never heard anything about a dentist's office.'

'Perhaps Mr Cosgrove would know.'

She went down the hallway to the office that I'd dreaded and came back in less than a minute. 'He says he's been here eight years. Before then, this was a Realtor's office.'

'Oh.'

'Sorry.'

'Sure.' Something died in me. 'I guess it was too much to hope for.' Discouraged, I turned toward the door, then stopped with a sudden thought. 'A Realtor?'

'Excuse me?'

'You said a Realtor used to be in this office?'

'Yes.' She was looking at me now as if I'd become a nuisance.

'Does he or she manage properties, do you suppose?'

'What?'

'Assuming that Mr Cosgrove doesn't own this building, who's his landlord?'

2

'You mean the Dwyer Building.' The bantamweight man in a bow tie stubbed out a cigarette. His desk was flanked on three sides by tall filing cabinets. 'I've been managing it for Mr Dwyer's heirs the past twenty years.'

'The office Mr Cosgrove is in.'

'Unit-Two-C.'

'Can you tell me who rented it back then? I'm looking for the name of a dentist who used to be there.'

'Why on earth would you want—'

'Some dental records. If it's a nuisance for you to look it up, I'll gladly pay you a service fee.'

'Nuisance? Hell, it's the easiest thing in the world. The secret to managing property is being organized.' He pivoted in his swivel chair and pushed its rollers toward a filing cabinet on his right that was marked D.

'Dwyer Building.' He searched through files. 'Here.' He sorted through papers in it. 'Sure. I remember now. Dr Raymond Faraday. He had a heart attack. Eighteen years ago. Died in the middle of giving somebody a root canal.'

After what I'd been through, the grotesqueness of his death somehow didn't seem unusual. 'Did he have any relatives here? Are they still in town?'

'Haven't the faintest idea, but check this phone book.'

3

'. . . a long time ago. Dr Raymond Faraday. I'm trying to find a relative of his.' Back at my car, I was using my cell phone. There'd been only two Faradays in the book. This was my second try.

'My husband's his son,' a suspicious-sounding woman said. 'Frank's at work now. What's this got to do with his father?'

I straightened. 'When my brother and I were kids, Dr Faraday was our dentist. It's very important that I get my brother's dental X rays. To identify him.'

'Your brother's dead?'

'Yes.'

'I'm so sorry.'

'It would be very helpful if you could tell me what happened to the records.'

'His patients took their records with them when they chose a new dentist.'

'But what about patients who hadn't been his clients for a while? My brother and I had stopped going to Dr Faraday several years earlier.'

'Didn't your parents transfer the records to your new dentist?'

'No.' I remembered bitterly that after my father had died in the car accident and it turned out that his life-insurance policy had lapsed, my mother hadn't been able to afford things like taking me to a dentist.

The woman exhaled, as if annoyed about something. 'I have no idea what my husband did with the old records. You'll have to ask him when he gets home from the office.'

4

The baseball field hadn't changed. As the lowering sun cast my shadow, I stood at the bicycle rack where my friends and I had chained and locked our bikes so long ago. Behind me, the bleachers along the third-base line were crowded with parents yelling encouragement to kids playing what looked like a Little League game. I heard the crack of a ball off a bat. Cheers. Howls of disappointment. Other cheers. I assumed that a fly ball, seemingly a home run, had been caught.

But I kept my gaze on the bicycles, remembering how Petey had used a clothespin to attach a playing card to the front fender of his bike and how it had created a *clackclackclackclack* sound against the spokes when the wheel turned. It pained me that I couldn't remember the names of the two friends I'd been with and for whom I'd destroyed Petey's life. But I certainly remembered the gist of what we'd said.

'For crissake, Brad, your little brother's getting on my nerves. Tell him to beat it, would ya?'

'Yeah, he tags along everywhere. I'm tired of the little squirt. The friggin' noise his bike makes drives me nuts.'

'He's just hanging around. He doesn't mean anything.'

'Bull. How do you think my mom found out I was smoking if *he* didn't tell *your* mom?'

'We don't know for sure he told my mom.'

'Then who *did* tell her, the goddamn tooth fairy?'

'All right, all right.'

Petey had nearly bumped into me when I'd turned. I'd thought about that moment so often and so painfully that it was seared into my memory. He'd been short even for nine, and he'd looked even

218

shorter because of his droopy jeans. His baseball glove had been too big for his hand.

'Sorry, Petey, you have to go home.'

'But . . .'

'You're just too little. You'd hold up the game.'

His eyes had glistened with the threat of tears.

To my later shame, I'd worried about what my friends would think if my kid brother started crying around them. 'I mean it, Petey. Bug off. Go home. Watch cartoons or something.'

His chin had quivered.

'Petey, I'm telling you, go. Scram. Get lost.'

My friends had run toward where the other kids were choosing sides for the game. As I'd rushed to join them, I'd heard the *clackclackclack* of Petey's bike. I'd looked back toward where the little guy was pedaling away. His head was down.

Standing now by the bicycle rack, remembering how things had been, wishing with all my heart that I could return to that moment and tell my friends that they were jerks, that Petey was going to stay with me, I wept.

5

U nlike the baseball field, the house had changed a great deal. In fact, the whole street had. The trees were taller (to be expected), and there were more of them, as well as more shrubs and hedges. But those changes weren't what struck me. In my youth, the neighborhood had been all single-story ranch houses, modest homes for people who worked at the factory where my dad had been a foreman. But now second stories had been added to several of the houses, or rooms had been added to the back, taking away most of the rear yards. Both changes had occurred to add space to the living room. The freestanding single-car garage at the end of the driveway had been rebuilt into a double-car garage with stairs leading up to a room.

Parking across the street, seeing the red of the setting sun reflected off the house's windows, I was so startled by the change that I wondered if I'd made a mistake. Maybe I wasn't on the right street (but the sign had clearly said Locust) or maybe this wasn't the right house (but the number 108 was fixed vertically next to the front door, just as it had been in my youth). I felt absolutely no identification with the place. In my memory, I saw a different, simpler house, the one from which my dad and I had hurried that evening, scrambling into his car, rushing toward the baseball diamond in hopes of finding Petey loitering along the way.

A wary man from the property next door came out and frowned at me, as if to say, What are you staring at?

I put the car in gear. As I drove away, I noticed half a dozen FOR SALE signs, remembering that in the old days everyone on the street had been so dependent on the furniture factory that no one had ever moved.

6

M r Faraday had thin lips and pinched cheeks. 'My wife says your brother died or something?'

'Yes.'

'That's why you need the dental records? To identify him?'

'He disappeared a long time ago. Now we might have found him.'

'His body?'

'Yes.'

'Well, if it wasn't something important like that, I wouldn't go to the trouble.' Faraday motioned me into the house. I heard a television from the living room as he opened a door halfway along the corridor to the kitchen. The quick impression I got was of excessive neatness, everything in its place, plastic covers on chair arms in the living room, pots on hooks in the kitchen, lids above them, everything arranged by size.

Cool air rose from the open cellar door. Faraday flicked a light switch and gestured for me to follow. Our descending footsteps thumped on sturdy wooden stairs.

I'd never seen a basement so carefully organized. It was filled with boxes stacked in rows that formed minicorridors, but there wasn't the slightest sense of clutter and chaos.

Two fans whirred: from dehumidifiers at each end of the basement.

'I can't get rid of the dampness down here,' Faraday said. He took me along one of the minicorridors, turned left, and came to a corner, where he lifted boxes off a footlocker.

'What can I do to help?' I asked.

'Nothing. I don't want to get things mixed up.'

He raised the lid on the locker, revealing bundles of documents. 'My wife complains about all the stuff I save, but how do I know what I might need later on?' Faraday pointed toward a stack of boxes farther along. 'All my tax returns.' He pointed toward another stack of boxes. 'The bills I've paid. And *this* stuff . . .' He indicated the documents in the locker. 'My father's business records. The ones I could find, anyway.' He sorted through the bundles and came up with a stack of file folders. 'What was your brother's name?'

'Peter Denning.'

'Denning. Let's see. Denning. Denning. Ann. Brad. Nicholas. *Peter.* Here.' His voice was filled with satisfaction as he held out the file.

I tried to keep my hand steady when I took it.

'What about these others? Do you want yours? Who are Ann and Nicholas?'

'My parents.' I felt heavy in my chest. 'Yes, if it's okay with you, I'll take them all.'

'My wife'll be thrilled to see me getting rid of some of this stuff.'

7

By the time I got back to the car, dusk had set in. I had to switch on the interior lights so I could see to search through Petey's file. No longer able to keep my hand from trembling, I pulled out a set of X rays. I'd never touched anything so valuable.

Back in Denver, when I'd gone to the dentist to get a copy of the X rays he'd taken of the man who claimed to be my brother, I'd made sure to get a duplicate set in case the FBI lost the ones I gave them or in case I needed copies in my search. Now I could barely wait to get to a motel. Driving to the outskirts of town, I picked the first one I saw that had a vacancy. After checking in, I rushed to my room, too hurried to bring everything from my car except my suitcase, which I yanked open, pulling out the X rays from Denver.

A child's teeth and an adult's have major differences, which made it difficult to tell if these X rays came from the same person. For one thing, when Petey had been kidnapped, some of his permanent teeth would not yet have grown in. But *some* of them would have, my dentist had said. Look at the roots, he'd said. On a particular tooth, are there three roots or four? Four are less common. Do the roots grow in any unusual directions?

With the adult's X rays in my left hand and the child's in my right, I held them up to my bedside lamp. But its shade blocked much of the illumination. I almost took off the shade before I thought of the bathroom and the bright lights that motels often have there. Hurrying past the bed, I found that this particular motel had a large mirror in front of a makeup area. When I jabbed the light switch, I blinked from the sudden glare above the mirror. After raising both sets of X rays to the fluorescent lights, I shifted my gaze quickly back and forth between them, desperate to find

223

differences or similarities, frantic to learn the truth. The child's teeth looked so pathetically tiny. I imagined Petey's frightened helplessness as he was grabbed. The adult's. Whose *were* they? Slowly, I understood what I was looking at. As the implications swept over me, as the various pieces of information that I'd found began fitting into place, I lowered the X rays. I drooped my head. God help Kate and Jason, I prayed. God help us all.

8

An organ blared as I opened the church's front door: a solemn hymn I didn't recognize. To the right of the vestibule, stairs led up to the choir loft. They creaked as I climbed them. It was shortly after noon. I'd been to eleven Protestant churches before this one. With only six more to go, I was losing hope.

The choir loft was shadowy except for a light above the organ. As the minister finished the hymn, in the gathering silence my echoing footsteps made him turn.

'Sorry to bother you, Reverend.' I walked nearer, holding out the photograph. 'The secretary at your office said that you were almost done getting ready for choir practice. I'm trying to find this man. I wonder if you recognize him.'

Puzzled, the minister took the photograph, pushed his glasses back on his nose, and studied it.

A long moment later, he nodded. 'Possibly.'

I tried not to show a reaction. Even so, my heart hammered so loudly that I was sure the minister could hear it.

'The intensity of the eyes is the same.' The minister put the photograph under the organ's light. 'But the man I'm thinking of has a beard.' He pointed toward my own.

Beard? I'd been right. He'd grown a beard to hide his scar. 'Perhaps if you put your hand over the lower part of his face.' I tried to sound calm, despite the tension that squeezed my throat.

The minister did so. 'Yes. I know this man.' He looked suspicious. 'Why do you want to find him?'

'I'm his brother.' I managed to keep my hand steady as I shook hands with the minister. 'Brad Denning.'

'No. You're mistaken.'

'Excuse me.'

'Denning isn't Pete's last name. It's Benedict.'

I didn't know what struck me more, that Petey was using his own first name or that he'd taken the last name of the minister who'd wanted to adopt him after the fire. My stomach soured. 'So he still won't use the family name.'

The minister frowned. 'What do you mean?'

My heart pounded harder. 'We used to live around here. But a long time ago, Pete and I had a falling-out. One of those family arguments that cause such bad feelings, it splits the family apart.'

The minister nodded, evidently familiar with what that kind of argument had done to some families in his congregation.

'We haven't spoken to each other in years. But recently, I heard that he'd come back to town. This was the church we used to go to. So I thought someone here might have seen him.'

'You want to be reconciled with him?'

'With everything that's in me, Reverend. But I don't know where he is.'

'I haven't seen him since . . .' The minister thought about it. 'Last July, when Mrs Warren died. Of course, he was at the funeral. And before that, the last time I saw him was . . . Oh, probably two years. I'm not even sure he's in town any longer.'

'Mrs Warren?'

'She was one of the most faithful in the congregation. Only missed one service that I can remember. When Pete showed up two years ago and volunteered to do handiwork for the church for free, Mrs Warren took a liking to him. She was amazed by how completely he could quote Scripture. Tried to trick him several times, but he always won.'

'That was my dad's doing, teaching Pete the Good Book.'

'Well, your father certainly did an excellent job. Mrs Warren finally offered him a handyman's job on her property. Our loss, her gain. When she missed that service I mentioned, I was convinced she must be sick, so I telephoned her, and I was right – she had a touch of the flu. The next time she came to church, Pete wasn't with her. She told me that he'd decided to move on.'

'Yeah, Pete was always like that. But you say he was here for her funeral?'

'Evidently, he'd come back and was working as her handyman again. In fact, the way I hear it, she left her place to him.'

'Her place?'

'Well, she was elderly. Her husband was dead. So were her two children. I suppose she thought of Pete as the closest thing she had to family.'

'Sounds like a kind old lady.'

'Generous to a fault. And over the years, as she sold off portions of the farm her husband had worked – it was the only way for her to survive after her husband died – she made sure to let eighty acres around her house go wild for a game preserve. Believe me, the way this town's expanding, we could use more people like Mrs Warren to preserve the countryside.'

'Reverend, I'd appreciate two favors.'

'Yes?' He looked curiously from behind his glasses.

'The first is, if you see Pete before I do, for heaven's sake don't tell him that we've spoken. If he knows I'm trying to see him, I'm afraid he'll get so upset that he might leave town.'

'Your argument was that serious?'

'Worse than you can imagine. I have to approach him in the right way and at the right time.'

'What's the second favor you want?'

'How do I find Mrs Warren's place?'

9

Two miles along a country road south of town, I reached a T intersection. I steered to the left, and as the minister had described, the paved road became gravel. My tires threw up dust that floated in my rearview mirror. Tense, I stared ahead, hoping that I wouldn't see a car or a truck coming toward me. The countryside was slightly hilly, and at the top of each rise, I was afraid that I'd suddenly come upon an approaching vehicle and that *he'd* be driving it. Maybe he wouldn't pay attention, a quick glimpse of another driver, but maybe he paid attention to everything. Or maybe he wouldn't recognize me with my beard, but if he did, or if he recognized Kate's Volvo (Jesus, why hadn't I thought to bring another car?), I'd lose my chance of surprising him. I'd have even less chance of finding Kate and Jason.

Sweating, my shirt sticking to my chest, I saw the expanse of thick timber and undergrowth that the minister had said would be on my left. I passed a mailbox, a closed gate, and a lane that disappeared into the forest. Mrs Warren's house was back there, the minister had said, where she could watch the deer, the squirrels, the racoons, and the rest of what she'd called 'God's children' roaming around the property. Relieved that I hadn't seen anybody and hence that no one had seen me, I kept driving, more dust rising behind me. At the same time, I couldn't help worrying that the reason I hadn't seen any activity was that Petey wasn't there, that he'd moved on.

Petey.

Yes.

Each X ray had shown a particular tooth with four roots that grew in distinctive directions. The child's had been smaller and less pronounced than the man's. Nonetheless, it hadn't been difficult to see that one had evolved into the other. Not that I'd relied on my opinion. Before going to the various churches, I'd made sure to be at a dentist's office when it opened. With cash I'd gotten from a local bank, I'd paid the dentist a hundred dollars to examine the X rays before he attended to his scheduled patients. He'd agreed with me: man and boy – the X rays had belonged to the same person.

So there it was. The man who'd claimed to be my brother had told the truth. The FBI had been wrong. Lester Dant hadn't assumed Petey's identity. *Petey* had assumed *Lester's*. But that disturbing discovery settled nothing. The reverse. It prompted far more unnerving questions to threaten my sanity.

This was clear. After Petey had tricked the police into thinking that he was heading west through Montana, he'd taken Kate and Jason in the reverse direction – back to Woodford. Because he no longer had to lay a false trail by abandoning vehicles that he'd carjacked, it wouldn't have been hard to avoid capture. All he had to do was carjack a vehicle that had a license for a distant state. The driver wouldn't have been expected for several days. By the time he or she was reported missing, Petey would have reached Mrs Warren's property and hidden the car. Meanwhile, he'd have switched license plates several times and hidden the car owner's body somewhere along the interstate.

Mrs Warren. Petey had been confident that he could intimidate her, because that's what he'd done a year earlier. At the church where I'd learned about Petey and Mrs Warren, the minister had mentioned that Petey was Mrs Warren's handyman, that she never missed Sunday service except for an uncharacteristic absence one Sunday two years earlier, *one* year before Petey took Kate and Jason from me. Petey must have done something so dismaying to Mrs Warren that she found it impossible to go to church that Sunday. When the minister phoned her, certain that only something dire would have kept her away, she'd claimed that she had the flu. The next Sunday, she'd been in church again. Meanwhile, she'd said, Petey had left the area.

The minister's phone call had probably saved Mrs Warren's life. His concern for her must have made Petey think that the minister was suspicious, must have driven Petey away. But when Mrs Warren felt safe, why hadn't she confessed the horrors that had happened out there? The answer wasn't hard to figure. Like Mrs Garner in Loganville, she'd been ashamed to let the other church members know what Petey had done to her. What's more, Petey had no doubt terrified her with a threat to return and punish her if she caused trouble for him.

Maybe she started feeling secure again, but then, to her fright, Petey came back a year later. He might have found a way to hide Kate and Jason from her. No matter – her torment resumed. He intimidated her severely enough to make her put him in her will. 'He feels like a son to me,' she'd have been forced to tell her lawyer, coached to sound convincing. Petey would have stood next to her in the lawyer's office when she signed the document, a reminder of his warning that if she turned against him, he'd make sure that she spent her remaining years in agony. Then he'd have kept her a prisoner at the house while he dropped a word here and there among the congregation that she hadn't been feeling well lately. That way, people would have been prepared when she died. After all, as the minister had said, Mrs Warren was elderly. Maybe one night she passed away in her sleep – with help from a pillow pressed over her face.

As I sped back to town, I used my cell phone to call Special Agent Gader, but his receptionist told me that he wouldn't be in the office for a couple of days. I phoned Payne's office but got a recording that said he wouldn't be in the office for the rest of the week. I had a hollow feeling in the pit of my stomach that told me his wife's biopsy hadn't been good.

That left getting in touch with the local police, but when I parked outside the station (the same brick building from years ago), I had a disturbing image of policemen piling into squad cars and rushing out to Mrs Warren's. I feared that their arrival would be so obvious that if Petey *was* in that house, he'd notice them coming and escape out the back. I might never learn what he'd done with Kate and Jason. Even if the police *did* manage to capture him, suppose he refused to answer questions? Suppose he denied knowing anything about where Kate and Jason were hidden? If they were still alive, they might starve or suffocate while he remained silent. Think it through, I warned myself. I needed more information. I couldn't trust the police to go after him until I knew exactly how they should do it.

10

The pilot said something that I couldn't quite hear amid the drone of the single-engine plane.

I turned to her. 'Excuse me?'

'I said, Woodford's over there.'

I glanced to the right, toward where she pointed. The sprawl of low buildings, old and new, stretched toward the interstate.

She put so much meaning into the statement that I shook my head from side to side. 'I don't understand.'

'You told me you wanted to see how the old hometown looked from the air.'

'More or less.'

'Seems like less. You've barely looked in that direction. What you're interested in are those farms up ahead.'

We flew closer to the eighty-acre section of woods and underbrush. Although the day was sunny, there was a touch of wind. Once in a while, the plane dipped slightly.

'You're a developer, aren't you?'

'What?'

'We've had our share of development the last five years. Seems like every time I look, there's a new subdivision.'

It was an easier explanation than the truth. 'Yeah, too much change can be overwhelming.'

I stared down at the large, dense section of trees. I saw the lane leading into it from the gravel road. I saw a clearing about a hundred yards into it where a brick house was surrounded by grass and gardens.

I'd bought one of those pocket cameras that had a zoom lens. Now I pulled it out and started taking photographs.

11

Back in my motel room, I spread out the eight-by-tens on a table. I'd paid a photographer to stay open after hours and process them. Now it was after dark. My eyes ached. To help keep me alert, I turned on the television – CNN – and as an announcer droned in the background, I picked up a magnifying glass and leaned down over the photographs. They were slightly blurred from the plane's vibration. Nonetheless, they showed me what I needed.

One thing was immediately obvious. No one would have noticed it at ground level, where the front, sides and back of the house couldn't be viewed simultaneously. But when seen from above, the grass and gardens in back of the house looked different from those at the sides and the front. They seemed to have had work done on them recently. The area seemed slightly lower than the others.

Sunken? I wondered. As when ground settles after it's been dug up and then refilled?

In the background, the CNN announcer explained that a distraught man with a gun was holding his ex-wife and his daughter prisoner in a house in Los Angeles. A police SWAT team surrounded it. With greater intensity, I stared through the magnifying glass at the photos, confirming that a section of grass and garden in the back of the house did appear slightly lower than what was around it.

I noticed a blue pickup truck parked next to the house. I studied a stream that wound through the middle of the woods in back. But what I kept returning to was that area behind the house. The grass seemed greener there, the bushes fuller, as if they were getting more attention than those at the front and the sides.

I set down the magnifying glass and tried to calm myself. There

233

was nothing sinister about relandscaping, the police would say. A blighted lawn and old bushes had been replaced with healthy ones. But what if the lawn and bushes had been replaced because something had been built under them?

On the television behind me, the announcer reported that the hostage situation had ended badly. As the police tightened their circle around the building, the man had shot his daughter and his ex-wife, then pulled the trigger on himself.

I stared at the television.

12

When I'd driven past Mrs Warren's property, I'd made the mistake of using Kate's Volvo. Petey might have recognized it. This time I drove only to the outskirts of town, where I left the car among others at a shopping mall. I put on my knapsack and hiked into the countryside.

As in most midwestern farm communities, the road system was laid out in a grid that contained squares or rectangles of land. Avoiding the road that fronted Mrs Warren's property, I took an indirect route that added several miles, coming at the wooded eighty acres from the road behind. Under a bright, hot sun, I hiked past fields, past cattle grazing, past farmers tending their crops. I adjusted my baseball cap and moved the camera bag on my belt to a more comfortable spot on my waist, trying to look as if I didn't have a care in the world, that I was merely out for a pleasant day of walking. In truth, I wanted desperately to run. The adrenaline burning through me needed exertion to keep it controlled. If I didn't do something to vent the pressure swelling inside me, I feared I'd go crazy. To my right, across a field, the woods got larger. Nearer. Kate and Jason. They're alive, I told myself. They have to be.

Worried about being noticed crossing the field toward the woods, I waited until a car went by and there wasn't any other traffic. The stream that I'd seen in the photographs crossed the field and went under the road. I climbed down to it. Its banks were high enough that I was out of view as I walked next to the water. In contrast with the stark sun, the air was cool down there.

After five minutes, the stream entered the trees. I ducked under a fence, climbed the slippery bank, and found myself among maples, oaks and elms. The noise I made in the undergrowth troubled me, but who would hear me? Petey wasn't going to be patrolling his fences, guarding his property against intruders. The logical place for him to be was at the house. Or maybe he'd be off somewhere, committing God knew what crimes.

The forest cast a shadow. A spongy layer of dead leaves smelled damp and moldy. I wiped my sweat-gritted face, took off my knapsack, and pulled out a holster that I'd bought that morning. It was attached to the right side of a sturdy belt. My spare fifteen-round magazine was in a pouch to the left, along with two other newly purchased magazines. A hunting knife went next to it and a five-inch long, thumb-width flashlight called Surefire, which the clerk in the gun shop had shown me was surprisingly powerful for its size. I took the pistol from the camera bag and shoved it into the holster. The weight of the equipment dug into my waist.

Thirsty from nervousness, I sipped water from one of three canteens in the knapsack. I ate a stick of beef jerky and several handfuls of mixed peanuts and raisins. Uneasiness made me urinate. Then I put on the knapsack and pulled a compass from my shirt pocket. Unlike a year ago, I'd taken the time to learn how to use it. Remembering the photographs, estimating the angle that I needed to follow in order to reach the house, I took a southeast direction, making my way through the trees.

All the while, I listened for suspicious noises in the forest. The scrape of a branch might have been Petey creeping toward me, but it turned out to be a squirrel racing up a tree. The snap of a twig startled me, until I realized that it was a rabbit bounding away. Birds fluttered. Wary, I scanned the undergrowth, studied my compass again, and moved cautiously forward.

The next time I stopped to get a drink, I checked my watch, surprised to find that what had seemed like thirty minutes had actually been two hours. The air felt thicker. Sweat stuck my shirt and jeans to me. I took another step and immediately dropped to a crouch, seeing where the trees thinned.

On my stomach, I squirmed through the undergrowth, the moldy smell of the earth widening my nostrils. I crawled slowly, trying not to move bushes and reveal my position. From having designed homes for wealthy clients, I was familiar with intrusion detectors. I watched for anything ahead of me, motion sensors on posts or a wire that might be attached to a vibration detector. Nothing struck me as unusual. In fact, now that I thought about it, an intrusion detector would be useless in the woods. The animals roaming about would trigger it.

Animals? I suddenly realized that for a while I hadn't noticed *any* animals. Nor a single bird. The sense of barrenness reminded me of what I'd felt at the Dant farm.

Snakes? I studied the ground ahead of me. Nothing rippled. Taking a deep breath, I squirmed forward. The trees became more sparse, the bushes less thick. Peering through low branches, I saw a clearing. A lawn. A flower garden.

In the middle was the redbrick house. I'd come at it from its right side. The two-and-a-half-story wall had ivy. White wooden lawn furniture and a brightly colored miniature windmill decorated the lawn.

I took binoculars from my knapsack and made sure that the sun wasn't at an angle that would cause a reflection off the lenses. Then I focused them and studied the downstairs and upstairs windows. All had lace curtains. Nothing moved beyond them. In the photographs I'd taken, the pickup truck had been parked on the opposite side of the house, so to find out if it was still there, I'd have to crawl around to that side.

I stayed as flat as possible while I shifted through the undergrowth. When I came within view of the back of the house, I still didn't see movement in any of the windows. I stared at the open area behind the house, which from ground level seemed to have a natural slope, its slightly sunken outline no longer apparent. An unsuspecting visitor would have noticed nothing unusual about it, except that the lawn and gardens were attractive. If there was indeed a room beneath it, I assumed that Petey watered and fertilized that area frequently to compensate for the shallow roots that the underground structure would cause. If so, today wasn't his day to work in the garden. He wasn't in sight. The place seemed abandoned.

I dared to hope that I'd gotten lucky, that he wasn't home. But as I crept through the bushes toward the other side of the house, my stomach soured when I saw the pickup truck where it had been the previous afternoon. Angry, I continued through the undergrowth on that side of the house, coming to a view of the front, where a roofed porch had a rocking chair and a hammock, homey and inviting.

But no one was visible there, either, and I retreated to a sheltered spot that gave me a view of the side, part of the back, part of the front, and all of the truck. Bushes enclosed me. I eased out of my knapsack, sipped from one of the canteens, ate more beef jerky, peanuts and raisins.

And waited.

13

Hours later, I was still waiting. The sun eased below the trees. Seeing a light come on in a downstairs window, I felt my muscles compact. Then a light came on in an adjacent room, and another farther over. I strained to see movement through the curtains, but the house continued to seem deserted. For all I knew, the lights were controlled by timers. When an upstairs light came on and a shadow moved past a window, I held my breath for a moment.

A *man's* shadow. I was certain of it. I'd caught only a glimpse, but the broad shoulders and forceful stride obviously didn't belong to a female. Several seconds later, the shadow appeared downstairs, going from one room to another. Raising my binoculars, I strained to see through the windows and suddenly focused on a man with a beard. His face was toward me for only a few seconds before he went through an archway into the kitchen.

But a few seconds were all I needed. Regardless of the beard, I couldn't fail to recognize him. Even through binoculars, the solid shoulders and the intense eyes were unmistakable.

The man was Petey.

'Go home,' I'd told him. After a lifetime of being lost, he'd done exactly that. He'd come back to Woodford. Did he ever drive by the house where we used to live? Did he ever go to the baseball field and remember that afternoon, brooding about how different his life would have been if I hadn't preferred my friends over him and sent him away from that baseball game?

Stop thinking like that! I warned myself. Get control! Guilt and regret weren't going to change the past. They were a weakness. They could get me killed. They could get *Kate and Jason* killed.

239

Petey wasn't my brother any longer.

He was my enemy.

My impulse was to crawl from my hiding place, reach the window, wait for him to step into view again, and shoot. But what if I missed? My hand was shaking enough to throw off my aim. Or what if Petey noticed me outside the window before I could pull the trigger? Suppose he ducked out of sight and used Kate and Jason as hostages? Or what if I did manage to shoot him, but Kate and Jason weren't where I suspected they were?

Shoot to wound him? How did I know the wound wouldn't be more serious than I intended? Petey might die before I could question him. I'd have lost the chance to find Kate and Jason.

Stay put. Think it through, I warned myself. If I make a wrong move, it'll be the same thing I was afraid the police would do.

I had to keep watching the house. I needed to get a sense of his patterns. When I phoned the police, it had to be at the right time.

When the situation was in my favor.

Sure. And when the hell will *that* be? I wondered.

In the darkness, the air was damp and chill, making me pull a woolen shirt from the knapsack and put it on. It didn't warm me. As Petey's indistinct shape prepared food in the kitchen, I told myself that I should eat also, but I didn't have any appetite. Acid burned my stomach.

Eat! I told myself. I forced a chunk of beef jerky into my mouth and reluctantly chewed. The side dish was another handful of nuts and raisins, the dessert dehydrated apples. I had thought about bringing sandwiches, but I'd been worried that they would spoil and make me ill. After all, I had no idea how long I'd have to stay in the woods and watch the house. That was why I'd brought three canteens of water. Determined to conserve it, I took only a few sips to help me swallow the dehydrated apples.

How long would the police have been willing to hide like this? I wondered. They'd have swatted at the mosquitoes buzzing around them. They'd have felt the cold seeping through their clothes, the dampness sticking their pants to their legs. They'd have thought about hot coffee and a warm bed, someone to share it with. They'd soon have lost their patience and stormed the house.

I buttoned the woolen shirt all the way to my neck but still felt a chill. Raising the binoculars again, I stared through a window, through an archway toward the kitchen, which was on the far side of the house. There, Petey continued to prepare food. Eventually his silhouette disappeared.

My muscles cramped from not having moved in quite a while. My arms and neck ached from keeping the binoculars raised. Minutes passed. I checked the luminous dial on my watch. A quarter of an hour became half an hour. When a full hour had passed, I couldn't ignore the pressure in my bladder. I crawled back from where I was hiding, stopped among trees, and urinated close to the ground, doing my best to make as little noise as possible.

The moment I returned through the bushes, the light went out in the kitchen. I tensed, watching Petey's shadow move from room to room downstairs, turning off the lights. A minute later, one of the upstairs lights went off also. I spent an hour gazing at the remaining upstairs light. Then it, too, went out.

The sky was overcast, hiding the stars. The house remained dark. I hugged myself, trying to keep warm. My eyelids grew heavy. I fought to keep them open, turning from the house toward the murky lawn and garden in back, under which, I was certain, Kate and Jason were imprisoned. So close. Have to get to them. Have to . . . My eyelids fluttered shut. I sank to the ground and drifted into sleep.

14

A door banged, jolting me from a nightmare of being whipped. My eyes snapped open. I jerked my head up enough to be able to see through low bushes toward the house. The clouds had passed. The sun was behind me, glinting off windows across from me. The reflection stabbed my eyes, aggravating a headache. A breeze from the day before had strengthened, ruffling bushes. The movement of the leaves around me must have been the source of my nightmare about being whipped.

I stared toward the back of the house, where I'd heard the door bang. Petey came into view. He wore a light green shirt, which contrasted with his dark beard. I recognized the shirt. It was one that he'd stolen from me a year earlier. The wind tousled his thick dark hair. He peered around, assessing the woods, then pulled a hose from a hook on the wall and went over to the area behind the house. Watering several bushes, he confirmed my suspicion that something beneath the ground caused shallow roots in need of frequent care. The wind sometimes sprayed the water back at him, eventually annoying him enough that he dropped the hose, went to the back wall to shut off the water, and returned to the house.

The sun's reflection off windows prevented me from seeing what he was doing inside. After a half hour, the wind had parched my lips so much that I reached for a canteen, only to stop when I heard another door bang, this one at the front. Petey came onto the porch. He'd changed his spray-soaked green shirt for a gray one. It, too, had belonged to me. He raised his head, almost as if he was sniffing the breeze. That's what my brother had become: an animal assessing if there was danger. Because of me.

Stop thinking that way! I again warned myself.

He came down the porch steps and rounded the house, making my pulse quicken when he got into the truck and fastened his seat belt. The truck was faced in my direction but away from the sun's glare, so that I saw his beard and his stark eyes through the windshield before he made a U-turn. Dust blew as he drove down the lane, the blue of the truck soon vanishing among the windswept trees.

For a moment, I was sure that my mind had played a trick on me. Had I actually seen what I most wanted to see? Was the sound of the truck actually diminishing in the distance? For several long minutes, I didn't move. Perhaps Petey had only gone to check the mailbox at the road and would soon be coming back. Or perhaps he had somehow suspected that someone was watching the house and had driven away in order to lure an intruder into the open. As soon as I started toward the house, would he shoot me from where he'd sneaked back and was watching from the trees?

The sun rose higher. The wind grew stronger, buffeting the bushes I hid among. But it didn't cool me. Instead, the morning seemed unduly warm. Sweat dried immediately on my dust-caked cheeks. Nervous, I checked my watch and saw that fifteen minutes had passed. If Petey had merely gone to the mailbox, he'd have been back by now, I told myself. I scanned the woods where the driveway disappeared into them. But the wind kept shifting the leaves and prevented me from noticing any movement where he might be hiding, watching for an intruder.

I stared toward the bushes behind the house. The police. Use the cell phone, I thought. But as I reached for it, I worried that if Petey was watching from another part of the forest, he'd hear me. Instead of muffling what I said, the wind might carry my voice directly to him.

Or what if Petey wasn't alone? What if someone else was in the house and would hear my voice? To prevent that from happening, I'd have to retreat several hundred yards into the forest before I felt safe using the phone, but that would mean losing sight of the farmhouse, and there was no telling what might happen while I was away.

The sun rose higher, no longer reflecting off the windows. Nothing moved beyond them. Last night, I'd seen no other silhouette, only Petey's. Was it safe to assume that he was alone? The police wouldn't be able to get here in time before he got back. Damn it, this might be my only chance. I crawled through the undergrowth toward the back of the house. If Petey was watching from the trees in front, he wouldn't be able to see me approach from the rear.

Squirming through low branches, I came to the edge of the clearing. I checked again for any movement behind the lace curtains. Then I drew my pistol and hurried into the open. The wind tried to push me back. I reached a lilac bush, used it for cover, then darted toward a grape arbor, which screened me while I studied the house a final time. I sprinted to the back wall and pressed against its sun-warmed bricks.

Steps rose to the back door. At the top, I raised my head warily to peer through a window. Beyond gauzy curtains, I had an indistinct view of a kitchen, cupboards, a sink, and a stove on the right, an archway and a refrigerator on the left. A small table was in the middle. A single chair suggested that Petey lived by himself.

What I started worrying about now was that Petey might have a dog, a pit bull, for example, trained not to show itself until an intruder entered the house, at which time the dog would tear the intruder apart. It would make sense for Petey to have one, but the more I thought about it, the more I doubted that he did. I'd been watching the house for over twelve hours, and Petey hadn't let a dog out to relieve itself. True, Petey might have done so while I was asleep. But wouldn't the dog have picked up my scent and attacked me? And unless Petey was superscrupulous about cleaning up after his dog, wouldn't I have seen dog droppings on the lawn? Besides, a dog locked in the house would limit Petey's ability to stay away for periods of time. He could leave food for Kate and Jason in their prison. But it would be harder to leave enough for a big dog to survive for any length of time, and that didn't take into consideration the mess that the dog would make in the house.

No, I was increasingly convinced that Petey didn't have a dog. But on the off-chance that he did, I prepared to shoot it.

I tried the back door. No surprise – it was locked. I was going to have to smash the window, reach through, and open the lock from the other side. I changed my position so that I could look down through the window and see the area above the doorknob. The handle of a lock came into view. After I smashed the window, all I needed to do was reach through, twist the lock's handle, and . . .

Maybe only an architect or somebody in construction would be bothered. The lock was a deadbolt, a type that I recommended. On the outside, the only way to get in was to use a key. But on the *inside*, there could be two ways to open the lock, depending on how it was installed. If there wasn't a window through which an intruder could reach, a handle on the lock was both convenient and safe. But in the case of a window, the secure way to install the lock was to use another key arrangement rather than a lock with a handle. That way, even if an intruder broke the window and reached through, he couldn't free the lock unless he had a key.

So, did it make sense for Petey to have a superior lock and an inferior installation? Granted, Mrs Warren might have been the one who'd had the lock put in. But would Petey, with every reason to be cautious, have ignored the security lapse? I doubted it.

As I brooded about the problem, something else troubled me. The door had been installed so that it opened toward the cup-boards on the right rather than toward an open space on the left, an inconvenient arrangement that prevented the door from being opened to its full range and that risked damaging the cupboards if the door was opened forcefully.

Nervous, I used the butt of my pistol to smash the window. With the barrel of the pistol, I carefully pulled the curtains toward me. Once they were outside the window, I yanked them loose, gaining a clear view of the kitchen, at least of the parts that I could see. I went back down the steps. Exposing myself to the wind, I found a dead branch rather than a live one because I needed the branch to be stiff. I climbed the steps again and peered down through the gap in the window. Careful not to show my head or hands, I put the branch through the broken window and pressed down on one side of the lock's handle, which was horizontal rather than round and thus could be manipulated with the stick. Moving, the lock made a scraping sound. Ready with my pistol, I turned the doorknob, stayed where I was, and pushed inward.

The shocking blast made me flinch as a ten-inch jagged hole appeared in the opened door. My ears hurt as if they'd been slapped. The stench of gunpowder widened my nostrils.

Taking a deep breath to steady myself, I inched my head forward and peered cautiously through the doorway. To the left, I saw a pantry area, where hinges on a doorjamb showed that a door had been taken off. In the pantry, a shotgun had been mounted to a worktable. A strong cord had been attached to its trigger. The cord went around a pulley behind the shotgun, then up to another pulley, and finally overhead to a metal hook at the top of the door on the inside. The tension on the cord had been adjusted so that the shotgun would go off only when the door was opened a certain distance, allowing for the intruder to show himself before the shotgun detonated.

The massive hole in the door made me wonder what the blast would have done to my midsection. Sickened, I warned myself not to get distracted. I still couldn't be sure that Petey didn't have a dog.

Uneasy, I aimed toward the only other entrance to the kitchen: the archway on the left. The ringing in my ears prevented me from hearing anything else. I saw no movement.

I stepped into the house.

15

The wind strengthened. When I shut the door, the gusts came through the broken window and the jagged hole beneath it. As urgent as I felt, I moved slowly. When I passed the kitchen table, my architect's training again warned me about something. The archway on the left was the only other entrance to the kitchen. That didn't make sense. There should have also been a door straight ahead that would give easy access to what I assumed were stairs in front leading up to the second story. The way the rooms on the ground floor were laid out, someone coming down from the second story had to take an indirect route from the front hall, through the rooms on the other side of the house, and finally into the kitchen. Mrs Warren, who was elderly, wouldn't have tolerated the inconvenience. The wall straight ahead wasn't being used for anything. It would have been easy and logical to install a door there. Why hadn't it been done?

Maybe there *had* been a door in that wall at one time, I thought. I stepped closer, noticing a slight difference between the top molding on the wall in front of me as opposed to the molding on the wall to my left. The white paint on the wall ahead of me looked slightly brighter than the white paint to my left. The plaster felt smoother. Someone had put a new wall over the doorway, preventing access to the front hall.

Had Petey done it? Why? Even for a young man, the indirect route into the kitchen would be a nuisance. Why had he deliberately wanted it?

The only answer I could think of was that Petey had blocked the other door because he wanted to force an intruder to go the long way through the house. He'd set other traps.

Of course. The kitchen didn't have a door that led down to the basement. The entrance to it must be in the front hall. But to reach it, an intruder would have to go through the other rooms.

As the wind howled, I stared through the archway toward the room on my left. I noticed a broom next to the refrigerator and waved it through the archway, moving it up and down and from side to side, checking that there weren't any other triggering devices (electronic beams, for example) linked to weapons.

Nothing happened.

I pressed the hard end of the broom onto a carpet that led through the archway.

The floor was solid. I entered the dining room, scanned its long table, chairs and sideboard, saw no obvious further traps, and stepped toward another archway. Through it, I could see old padded chairs and a sofa in what Mrs Warren would probably have called the parlor.

I tested another section of carpet and stepped toward the front room.

Crack! The floor gave way. My stomach surged toward my heart. Plummeting, I lurched forward, slamming my chest against the edge of the trapdoor. As the pistol and the broom flew from my hands, I clawed at the wooden floor. My hands slid. I hooked my fingers over the edge and dangled. Frantic, I peered down at a section of the basement that had been enclosed. Through a wooden platform below me, knives protruded, four inches apart in every direction, so that it wasn't possible to land among them and not be injured. One end of the carpet was attached to the floor, dangling rather than falling onto the points below and preventing them from impaling me. I'd have bled to death if I hadn't died instantly.

My arms ached as I strained to pull myself up. But I tested the floor! I thought. How the hell did I get fooled? The trapdoor must have been rigged to spring open only if a certain amount of weight was applied to it. Petey must have stepped over it when he passed through the archway. I strained harder to pull myself up and managed to prop my elbows on the trapdoor's edge. Slowly, I squirmed into the parlor. On my back on the floor, I breathed deeply. Trying to steady myself, I listened to the wind.

Petey might come back any minute, I thought.

I reached for the pistol and the broom, which had flown from my hands when I'd fallen. But caution instantly controlled me. Trying to subdue my too-fast breathing, I scanned the faded furniture, the ceiling, the corners. Nothing seemed to threaten me. Through the front windows, I studied the lane leading into the windblown forest. Staying to the edge of the room, I pushed a chair ahead of me, wary of other traps.

To the right of the front windows, an archway led to a corridor. Stairs went up. On a landing beyond the front door, another shotgun had been rigged. As before, a cord was attached to the trigger. The cord looped back through two pulleys and connected to a hook on top of the door. When the door was opened and someone stepped through, the shotgun would blow the intruder in half. It wouldn't have been difficult for Petey to attach the cord to the hook as he pulled the door shut, or for him to unhook the cord when he returned and opened the door just enough for him to reach his hand up. For anyone who didn't suspect, though, death would have been instantaneous.

Had I found all the traps? Straining my eyes, I studied the corridor. I fixed my gaze on a door beneath the stairway. I was sure that it would take me down to the basement. Kate and Jason were only a couple of hundred feet away.

The floor had no carpet. It looked solid. Nonetheless, I stayed to the edge of the hallway and inched along. When I came to the door beneath the stairs, I tested the knob. It turned freely in my hand. But another trap might be behind it. So I pulled the flashlight from my belt, gently opened the door an inch, and scanned the light up and down, looking for a cord.

The area beyond was totally dark. Warily opening the door a few inches farther, I smelled something bitter, like camphor.

Mothballs.

I opened the door farther, aimed the flashlight, and saw coats and dresses on a rod. A closet! No! Furious, I used the blunt end of the broom to prod among the clothes. I tapped the floor. The walls. Nothing sounded hollow. Where the hell was the entrance to the basement?

Hurry! I thought.

I remembered the previous night when I'd watched Petey's

249

silhouette through the window. He'd been cooking. Then his silhouette had disappeared. I'd assumed that he'd been eating in an area of the kitchen that was out of my view.

But what if he'd taken the food to Kate and Jason?

In the kitchen? *How?* There wasn't a door to the basement.

A shock of understanding hit me. Trying not to let my eagerness make me careless, I returned the way I'd come. I paused only once: to look through the front windows, past the windswept shrubs, and check if Petey's truck was returning. Then I stepped over the open trapdoor between the parlor and the dining room, rushing into the kitchen.

The pantry. I tapped the walls behind the canned goods on the shelves. They sounded solid. I glanced down at the floor, realized what Petey had done, and grabbed the workbench upon which the shotgun had been secured. Tugging it away, I saw the outline of another trapdoor. This one had a ring. I pulled upward and stared down at wooden steps descending into darkness.

16

'**K**ate! Jason!'
     The names echoed back to me.
No one shouted in return.

I tilted the trapdoor back so that it rested against the shelves behind it. I positioned the workbench so that if the trapdoor accidentally fell, it would be stopped before it slammed down and possibly locked. Then I aimed my flashlight into the darkness, saw a switch on a post about five steps down, and tested the first step as I eased down to turn on the basement lights.

No, I warned myself. Petey wouldn't booby-trap the ground floor and not do something to the basement as well. I'd gotten this far because I'd put myself in his place. I thought like him. What would Petey have done to protect the basement?

The broomstick remained in my hand. I tilted it downward, flicked the switch . . .

And stumbled back from an arc of electricity that shot from the switch, blackening the stick. The flash was blinding, the force so great that it knocked the stick from my hand. I felt a tingle in my palm where the current had started to reach me.

Smoke rose from the fake switch. Smelling burned wires, I aimed the flashlight again and went cautiously down a few more steps. I eased my weight onto each of them, always gripping one behind me for support in case a step broke away. The lower I got, the less I heard the wind. I scanned the flashlight across the basement, seeing boxes, a handyman's bench, tools on the wall above it, shelves of preserves, a washing machine, a dryer, an oil furnace, a laundry tub and a water heater. A window above the laundry tub had been boarded over. The walls and floor were old concrete. The ceiling

251

had pipes, wires and joists exposed. Everything smelled of mold.

I eased lower and saw a switch on another post, this one at the bottom. Reaching it, I picked up the broomstick where it had fallen. Once more, I flicked with the stick, and this time, the switch was real. Lights glowed in the basement's ceiling: dim lights – sixty-watt bulbs – but nonetheless they made me squint.

'Kate! Jason!'

Again, my shouts echoed.

Again, no muffled voices answered me.

I oriented myself. The wall that faced the area behind the house was on my left. There wasn't a door, only a tall object like a bookshelf on which there were jars of preserved peaches and pears. I studied it from various angles, looking for another trap. I stepped protectively to the left and pushed with the broomstick.

The shelves slid away.

I inched my head around the corner, peering into the opening. The tunnel was about fifteen feet long. Its concrete was smooth and new-looking. Petey had imitated the arrangement that Orval Dant had used, with the difference that instead of a wooden ceiling, Petey had chosen concrete.

At the end was a metal-covered door. It had a deadbolt lock, but *this* one didn't have a knob that needed to be turned. Instead, it had a slot for a key, and I didn't have a doubt in the world that the door was locked.

I wanted to rush it, but I hesitated. Why had Petey gone to the extra effort of building the tunnel instead of putting the cell directly next to the house? The latter setup would have been quicker and easier. Had Petey merely been imitating the arrangement that Orval had used? Or did the tunnel contain an additional trap?

I studied the bare floor, the walls, and the ceiling, unable to see a threat. About to yell to Kate and Jason again, I abruptly understood the purpose for the tunnel. If a stranger came down to the basement, Kate and Jason would be too far away to hear or be heard.

But how was I going to open the door? Noticing that its hinges were on the tunnel side, I turned to the right, toward the workbench. I grabbed a hammer and a chisel . . .

And stopped, a sound paralyzing me.

Something dripped. In the stillness of the basement, the slight noise seemed magnified. I focused on the laundry tub, but its taps were secure. No water leaked from them.

Drip. I turned, trying to identify the direction from which the sound came. *Drip. Drip.* Steady. Relentless.

My attention focused beneath the stairs. On a pipe projecting from the wall. *Drip. Drip.* Then I smelled it. *Drip.* Gasoline. Trickle. Gasoline was coming from the pipe, spreading across the concrete floor. The flow must have been activated when I'd pressed the fake switch on the stairs. Petey's final trap. If all else failed, when enough fuel emptied onto the floor, a detonator would ignite it. The house and the intruder, the evidence against Petey – everything would be obliterated. I could try to plug the pipe with a cloth, but when the cloth became saturated, the gasoline would continue to drip.

Clutching the hammer and the chisel, I raced into the tunnel. My frenzied movements echoed as I tried the doorknob and confirmed that it was locked. I held the chisel beneath the head of a hinge pin and hammered upward, freeing it. The pin clanged onto the floor. I did the same to the two other pins and pulled at the hinges, straining to free the door.

'Kate, I'm here!' I pounded on the door. 'Jason, it's Dad! I'll get you out!'

But they didn't pound on the other side of the door. I didn't hear any muffled shouts answering me.

The door wouldn't budge. I stared at the key mechanism, hoping that I could unscrew its plate and disassemble the lock, but Petey had drilled the heads off the screws.

I used the chisel and the hammer to pound at the concrete next to the lock. Chunks flew. My arms ached as I pounded harder. Larger chunks fell away. I worried about causing sparks that might detonate the fumes, but I didn't have a choice. I had to do something, *anything*, before the house exploded. I hoped to expose the lock's bolt, but what I came to was a stout metal sleeve into which the bolt had been seated. For all I knew, the metal sleeve went several feet into the side of the wall. It would take me all day to pound away that much concrete.

I ran back to the workbench and scanned the tools above it, looking for a crowbar. There wasn't one. I swung toward a shovel and a hoe next to the bench, looking for an ax with which I could try to chop through the metal covered door.

There wasn't one.

The smell of the gasoline was stronger. I saw a three-foot section of pipe on the floor, probably left over from a trap. I ignored it, stared again at the tools above the workbench, looked back at the pipe, and grabbed it. Gagging on fumes, I raced along the tunnel. I used the chisel and the hammer to pound at the concrete next to the middle hinge. Again, chunks flew. My arms cramped. Ignoring the pain, I hammered more fiercely against the chisel. My aim missed. I struck my fist, screamed, ignored the blood oozing from my knuckles, and pounded the chisel with greater force. When a hole opened, I dropped the hammer and chisel, rammed the pipe into the hole, and levered with all my weight. Sweating, I pushed relentlessly against the pipe. Suddenly the door budged. I strained. The gap widened. I stumbled, nearly falling as the door popped loose, leaving me sufficient space to squeeze through.

17

Please, God, let them be alive, I prayed.

I lurched into a room the size of a garage. A woman and a boy cowered, straining to get away from me. Each had a five-foot-long chain that led from a shackle on a wrist to a metal ring secured to the wall.

'Kate! Jason!'

They looked dazed. The pupils of their eyes were unnaturally large, black squeezing out the white around them. I could think of only one thing that would do that. Gader had told me that one of Lester Dant's numerous crimes had been drug dealing. I looked down at something I'd knocked over when I broke in. A waste can. Empty vials and used syringes had tumbled from it.

You son of a bitch, you drugged them! I inwardly screamed.

Kate and Jason kept cowering. They wore the kind of clothes that I associated with going to church. Kate had dark pumps, a knee-long modest blue dress, and a matching ribbon in her hair. Jason had black Oxfords, black trousers, and a white shirt topped with a bow tie. Their hair was meticulously combed, with the not-quite-natural look when someone else does the job. Their faces were pale, with hollows under their eyes. Kate wore lipstick, which was smeared.

The only furniture was a bed they'd been slumped on until the noises I'd made crashing into the room had terrified them.

'Kate, it's me! It's Brad!'

They cringed, desperate to keep a distance from me.

'Jason, it's Dad!'

Moaning, the boy squirmed back to the limit of his chain.

They'd never seen me with a beard. The drugs had so fogged

their minds that they didn't recognize me. All they knew was that the violence of my entrance made me a threat.

'Listen to me! You're safe!'

I returned to the tunnel for the hammer and chisel. When I rushed toward Kate and Jason, they thrust their arms over their heads to protect themselves.

'You don't have to be afraid anymore!'

Their whimpers were obscured by the clang of the hammer against the chisel as I struck next to one of the metal rings embedded in the wall. Concrete flew. The fumes from the gasoline hadn't yet reached the chamber. For the moment, the danger of sparks didn't worry me as I slammed harder at the ring and the concrete around it. No longer whimpering, Kate and Jason were speechless with terror. Suddenly the ring to which Jason was anchored thumped onto the mattress.

I redirected the chisel toward the ring that held Kate. As I struck concrete above her head, she trembled. She reminded me of a dog that had been intimidated so often that it cowered at the sight of its owner.

My God, that's what she thinks, I realized. I imagined the drugged haze through which she and Jason must have been seeing me. My beard was the most pronounced thing about my appearance. *Petey's* beard was the feature they'd have most noticed in the swirl of their half-consciousness. Sweet Jesus, they thought I was Petey.

In outrage, I realized what had happened. Petey had tried to condition them, to make Kate call him Brad and Jason call him Dad – more important, to make them believe it. He'd drugged them until they didn't know who they were. Day after day, he'd persisted in the same routine, determined to take away their will and resistance, to mold them into the obedient, worshipful wife and son of his fantasies. He didn't want a wife and son who had minds of their own. What he needed were puppets who acted out his delusions.

'It's me! It's really me!' I pounded the chisel against the wall. 'It's Brad!'

Their eyes widened with greater terror.

'Jason, I'm not who you think I am! I really am your father!'

I didn't have time to explain. I had to get them outside before the fumes spread farther and the house exploded. With one last frantic blow, I knocked away the ring that held Kate to the wall.

She and Jason were too frightened to move.

I grabbed their chains and dragged them toward the gap in the doorway. I squeezed into the tunnel and used their chains to pull them through one at a time. Immediately, I felt light-headed, realizing that the fumes were starting to suffocate me. Tugging Kate and Jason along the tunnel, I was again reminded of dogs that refused to go with their master. I reached the basement, seeing smoke billow from the fake light switch that had almost electrocuted me. The detonator. When it burst into flame, the house would blow up.

Daylight gleamed through the open trapdoor.

'You're almost free, Kate! Jason, you'll soon be out of here!'

But as we started up the stairs, Jason gaped and jerked back. He screamed. Above us, a shadow loomed into view, blocking part of the light. Then the light was blocked totally as Petey slammed the trapdoor shut.

18

Smoke billowed thicker from the fake light switch. I coughed but couldn't clear my lungs. A rumble above the trapdoor warned me that Petey was sliding the heavy workbench onto it. I drew my pistol and shot toward the noise. As four bullet holes appeared in the trapdoor, I realized in dismay that the muzzle flashes from my pistol might detonate the fumes.

My ears rang from the shots. Gasoline now covered most of the floor. Frantic, I looked around for a way to get out. Above the laundry sink, the boarded-over window caught my attention. I ran back for the hammer, raced toward the laundry sink, and pried the boards from the window.

It was the type that had to be pulled up on an angle and held in place by a hook in the ceiling. When I opened it, I heard the wind, which had become even stronger since I'd entered the house. Feeling a gust hit my face, I lifted Jason. He struggled as I pushed him through the opening. I lifted Kate, shocked by how little she weighed. The sight of the outdoors, of freedom, gave her some life. With greater energy, she squirmed through the window's opening, desperate to get away from me.

Any moment, I feared, a searing blast would rip me apart. I climbed onto the sink, and just as I shoved my chest through the opening, the sink pulled away from the wall, crashing under my weight. I grabbed a branch on a shrub and dangled. The branch bent. I sank.

I clawed at the earth, kept slipping back into the basement, braced my elbows against each side of the window, and stopped. Below me, the concrete wall tore my jeans as I kneed against it, struggling to squirm upward. Even with the wind at my face and the smoke coming past me through the window, I smelled the gasoline.

I grabbed another branch and pulled myself hand over hand through the opening. But the buckle on my gun belt wedged against the sill. I tried to raise my hips, working to ease the buckle over the sill. I heard it scrape on the concrete. I sucked in my stomach, raised my hips as high as I could, felt the buckle slip free, and tugged forward harder, inching through the opening. My hips came through. My thighs. As soon as I was on my hands and knees, I surged up.

Adrenaline burned my muscles as I raced from the bushes at the side of the house. I saw Petey's truck, which the boards over the window had prevented me from hearing when he'd returned to the house. I didn't see Kate and Jason, but I was certain that, even dazed, they'd have known enough to run in the opposite direction of the truck. I whirled to charge after them toward the back of the house, to cross the clearing and reach the cover of the forest . . .

And found myself ten feet from Petey, who aimed a shotgun at my chest.

He trembled with rage.

I couldn't draw my pistol and shoot before he pulled the trigger. Even if I hit him, my 9-mm bullet might not kill him, but with a shotgun at ten feet, he was sure to blow my chest apart.

'Stop, Petey!' With my beard, I couldn't be sure he recognized me. 'It's me! It's Brad!'

Even before I shouted, his eyes had narrowed. He looked startled. Straining to see past my beard, he realized who I was.

The wind buffeted us so hard, I could barely hear him murmur, 'Brad.'

'Listen to me! *Did they tell you who Lester was?*' I yelled, doing the only thing I could think of to distract him from shooting. '*Do you know why they took you?*'

'Lester,' he murmured.

'*Did they tell you Lester was Orval and Eunice's only child?*'

Smoke poured from the basement window.

Moving away from it, I had to keep distracting him. '*Did they tell you he died, that they went crazy with grief?*'

The house would soon explode.

'They'd already lost three children to stillbirths!' I kept my voice raised, inching toward the trees. 'The rest of the Dants were dead! Eunice couldn't conceive any longer. Lester was their only chance of continuing the family line.'

Petey sighted along the shotgun's barrel. 'Lester.'

As smoke billowed, I moved closer to the trees. 'They were desperate to replace him. But they couldn't do it in Brockton. That was too close to home. They might have been recognized.'

Petey kept pace with me, the shotgun aimed at my chest.

'So they set out on the interstate, driving from one town to another. They waited for God to direct them, to put a boy of the same age before them. They tried one town after another. They crossed from Indiana to Ohio. They passed Columbus. They came to Woodford.' I spoke faster, more intensely. 'We'll never know what made them leave the interstate and pick our town. Something must have seemed a sign from God. As they drove this way and that, they turned a corner, and there you were, all by yourself, pedaling down a street that seemed deserted.'

' "Can you tell us how to get to the interstate?" ' Petey said it with such bitterness. ' "Do you believe in God? Do you believe in the end of the world?" '

The smoke worsened. I tasted it as I neared the trees.

He moved with me, his finger looking tighter on the shotgun.

'They took you, and they put you in that underground room, and they told you your name was Lester, and they punished you if you didn't act like their son.'

'Lester.'

I thought I saw flames beyond the smoke at the basement window.

' "*This my son was dead, and is alive again; he was lost, and is found.*" Luke, fifteen, twenty-four,' Petey said.

'When you told me you'd been molested, I thought you meant sexually.'

I took another step.

So did Petey.

The wind gusted harder.

'But you didn't mean sexually. You meant molested in your *mind.*

In your *soul*. They wanted you to be Lester so much that they beat you and starved you; they treated you like an animal, until you didn't know who you were. It was so awful that in the end you were ready to be anybody they wanted you to be as long as they didn't hurt you, as long as they took away your bodily wastes and gave you something to eat.'

'They taught me the good book,' Petey said. ' "*The truth shall make you free.*" John, eight, thirty-two.'

'The truth is, you *can* be free. I'll get help for you, Petey! It's not too late! Once the police understand why you did what you did, *they'll* want you to get help, too. I promise you, life can be better. Don't let Orval and Eunice destroy you again. Stop being what they made you into, Petey.'

'Don't call me Petey!'

My voice broke. 'I can't tell you how sorry I am. I know that your life changed because of me, that everything would have been different if I hadn't sent you home from that baseball game! But, damn it, we were just kids. How was I to know that the Dants were going to grab you? *Nobody* could have known about them. You were just my little brother tagging along. I didn't mean for it to happen, Petey.' Tears streamed down my face. 'There wasn't a night since you disappeared that I didn't beg God to bring you back safe, that I didn't plead for a second chance. Let me make it up to you, Petey. Please, let me try to give you the life that Orval and Eunice took from you.'

'Stop calling me Petey!'

'You're right. When you came to my house, you asked to be called Peter, but I didn't. We're not kids anymore. You're Peter.'

'No! Don't call me that, either!'

Staring at the shotgun's trigger, I made a placating gesture. 'Okay. Whatever you want, Lester.'

'I'm *not* Lester!'

'Then I don't understand. Who *are* you?'

'*Brad.*'

The dark intensity in his eyes made clear how serious he was. I'd ruined *his* life. Now *he'd* stolen *mine*. Taking my wife and son, he'd convinced himself that he was also taking my identity. In his mind, he *was* me. As the depths of his insanity became obvious, my legs felt unsteady. 'I'm so sorry. God help you,' I murmured.

'No.' His tone left no doubt that he was going to pull the trigger. 'God help *you.*'

19

The blast hurtled me into the bushes. Not from the shotgun. The blast from the house. As the building exploded, the shock wave lifted me off my feet and threw me into the undergrowth. Wreckage flew, chopping tree branches, shredding leaves.

Dimly, I became aware enough to smell smoke and hear the crackle of flames. In pain, I slowly sat up. I felt dizzy, sick to my stomach. The ringing in my ears was unbearable.

I'd been thrown into a hollow. That was the only reason I'd survived the shrapnel from the blast. Chunks of smoking, burning wreckage lay around me. Bushes were on fire. The wind thrust the flames from tree to tree.

Coughing from the smoke, I staggered to my feet. I stared around, searching for Petey. I faced the burning crater of the house. He wasn't on the ground where we'd last stood. He must have been thrown into the undergrowth the same as I had been.

Flames crowded me. Kate and Jason. I had to find them. As I stumbled deeper into the forest, I prayed that they'd kept running, that they were far enough away that the fire wouldn't reach them.

And that Petey wouldn't. He'd do everything in his power to get them back.

Unless he was dead. Unless the blast had killed him.

Then where was his body? After the explosion, there was so little cover that I should have been able to see his corpse. Where *was* he?

The wind hurled smoke at me, making me cough harder as I lurched through the forest. While I'd been unconscious, the fire had spread rapidly, leaping from tree to tree. Bushes burst into flames. I zigzagged, trying to avoid flames on my right, only to discover that a new section of the forest was suddenly afire on my left.

I wanted to shout, 'Kate! Jason!' But they'd been so afraid of me in the house that I doubted they'd answer me. If anything, I'd throw them into a greater panic. On the off chance that they did answer my shouts, Petey would hear them, would go to them.

Plus, if I shouted to Kate and Jason, Petey would hear *me*, would know where *I* was.

The fire roared around me. The smoke whirled past, driven by the wind. Fighting for breath, I stumbled into a clearing. Again, the fire leapt into the trees ahead of me.

How far had Kate and Jason managed to go? I remembered the stream that I'd followed into the forest. If I could reach it, if Kate and Jason could reach it, we had a chance.

Reach it? *How?* I'd been so distracted by my need to avoid the fire that I'd lost my bearings. The same with Kate and Jason. They might be fleeing in a circle.

I fumbled for the compass in my shirt pocket. Squinting in the smoke, I aligned myself in a northwest direction, the opposite of the southeast line that I'd used to approach the house. I put the compass back in my shirt, dodged a flaming branch falling toward me, and ran toward untouched trees northwest of me.

The noise from the fire was filled with pops and cracks as wood ignited. Dry stumps exploded from the heat. A huge chunk of bark and wood blew away from a tree on my right, and I dove to the ground, realizing that one of the blasts was from Petey's shotgun.

I drew my pistol, dismayed by how violently my hand shook. In Denver, my instructor had warned that no matter how good a shooter was at target practice, nothing prepared one for controlling a gun in a kill-or-be-killed situation. When fear took charge, skill collapsed.

The fire swept closer. I couldn't stay where I was. But as soon as I moved, Petey would shoot again. I thought of everything that Kate and Jason had suffered, of everything that I'd been through to find them. I thought of Petey leaving me to die in the mountains. Fury compacted my muscles. My hand stopped shaking.

I raced toward another tree. A shotgun blast tore a chunk from it. Immediately I did what Petey would have least expected, charging back toward the flames, toward the tree where I'd hidden. I had a sense of where he'd shot from, a clump of bushes that I now put three bullets into. Smoke enveloped me. I held my breath and used the smoke for cover, rushing toward those bushes, angrily putting three more bullets into them. But when I crashed through, what I found wasn't a body, only an empty shotgun shell.

I crouched, breathing hoarsely, scanning the undergrowth for movement. But everything was in motion as the heat from the flames added to the force of the wind. The empty shotgun shell. How many times had Petey shot at me? Two that I knew of. How many shells did a shotgun hold? In the gun store where I'd taken lessons, I recalled hearing that most held four in the magazine and one in the chamber. Petey's shirt pockets hadn't bulged from spare shotgun shells. As far as I knew, he had only three shots left.

My back felt so scorched that I had to rush toward farther cover. Staying low, I reached more bushes, took advantage of the smoke around me, and raced toward another tree stump. *Blam!* The top of the stump disintegrated. The shocking pain in my left shoulder felt as if hornets had stung me at enormous speed. I lurched back, shooting as I fell. I hit the ground, hoping that what had struck me were chunks of wood from the stump. But the blood on my shoulder warned me that I'd been struck by metal pellets. The only reason that my arm hadn't been separated from my shoulder was that Petey had shot from a distance. In the confusion of the smoke and the flames, his aim had been thrown off. Only part of the spray had hit me.

The wound throbbed. I had trouble moving that arm. But I had no trouble moving the rest of me. I was so primed with fear and adrenaline that I rolled toward a fallen tree, knowing that I didn't stay where I'd fallen. The fire again scorched my back. Its wind-driven smoke enveloped me. But it had to be enveloping Petey also. He wouldn't be able to see me.

I pulled the compass from my shirt and checked it again. Straining not to cough and let Petey know where I was, I aligned the compass on a northwest route and shifted forward through the fast-moving haze. I couldn't see more than five feet ahead of me. Prepared to shoot the instant I saw a threatening shadow, I worked farther through the forest, checking the compass frequently.

Blood dripped from my left shoulder. I felt light-headed. The fire was about to get ahead of me. Heat shoved me, urging me to move faster.

I was so busy watching the blowing smoke for a sign of Petey that I didn't pay attention to the ground. The slope to the stream was about six feet deep. I'd have fallen into it if a deer hadn't charged from the flames on my right. It startled me, crashing past me and down, splashing through water, then bounding up the opposite side.

I squirmed down to the water, feeling cool air. The stream was shallow. I crossed it, oblivious to my hiking boots and socks getting wet, concentrating on where Petey might be. On my right, farther along the stream, a shadow moved amid the smoke. I started to shoot but stifled the impulse, realizing that the shadow might belong to Kate as easily as to Petey.

I kept aiming. The smoke made my eyes water as I strained to see along the barrel. I stared at the smoke, waiting for the shadow to become more distinct.

The shadow disappeared. Whoever it was had climbed from the stream and continued through the forest. Keeping pace with it, I struggled up the slope and passed through smoky undergrowth, watching for the shadow to come into view again.

I kept thinking, If it was Kate, wouldn't I have seen a smaller shadow with her: Jason?

Not if he was on the other side of her.

I had to be certain before I pulled the trigger. Creeping farther through the trees, I blinked tears from my smoke-irritated eyes and stared toward the indistinct forest on my right. Something moved. For an instant, I caught a glimpse of Petey's beard. He raised his shotgun. I pulled the trigger.

Abruptly I was almost blinded as a gust of wind tossed flames overhead. Trees and bushes erupted into fire ahead of me. Feeling the explosion of heat singe my hair, I stumbled backward and this time did lose my balance. When I fell down the bank of the stream, I landed on my wounded shoulder. I strained not to cry out, rolling down to the water, coming to a painful stop.

It took all my effort to stand. I'd dropped my compass. I couldn't find it. Not that I could get any help from it now. With the fire ahead and behind me, with Petey possibly on my right, the only safe direction was to the left along the stream. I had no idea if I'd hit him. But if I hadn't, he'd need to take shelter in the stream, which meant that he'd stalk along it in my direction. All I had to do was find a curve in the stream, hide, and ambush him.

I couldn't remember how many times I'd shot. My pistol might have been almost empty. Trying to keep my hands steady, I pressed a button on the side, dropped the magazine, grabbed the fifteen-round spare from the pouch on my belt, and slammed it into the grip, ready to shoot again.

My vision grayed. As the smoke thickened, I fought for air, realizing that the fire was sucking away oxygen. The flames squeezed closer. Afraid that I'd pass out, I worked along the stream, trying to stay on the bank, to avoid making noise in the water. But loss of blood added to my dizziness. I couldn't control where my hiking boots landed, sometimes splashing in the water, sometimes slipping through mud.

Hot air seared my nostrils. I rounded a curve, its slope protecting me from the flames above me on my right. I lurched around another curve, and cool air struck my face. I'd reached a section of the stream that wasn't yet bounded by fire. The coolness was the most luxuriant thing I'd ever felt. I sucked it into my lungs, hoping to clear my thoughts, to get rid of the spots that wavered in my vision.

As the fresh air took the gray from in front of my eyes, I staggered to a halt at the sight of footprints in the mud. Two sets of them. An adult's. A child's. They were following the stream, as *I* was.

Kate. Jason.

I whirled toward urgent footsteps splashing through the stream behind me. But as I aimed, it wasn't Petey, but a panicked dog that scrambled into view. It raced out of sight along the stream. The air became hot again. The flames drew closer.

I ran in the direction of the footprints. A tree had fallen across the bank. I ducked under it, straightened on the other side, and groaned as something heavy walloped across my forehead. The blow sent me reeling back against the tree. Dazed, I sank to my knees in the water. Blood trickled down my face. I tried to clear my blurred vision.

Her eyes frantic from the drugs, Kate stood over me, a clublike branch raised to hit me again. Jason cowered behind her.

'No, Kate.' I was appalled by how distant my weakened voice sounded. 'Don't. It's me.'

'You bastard!'

I managed to raise my right arm before she struck me again. The club whacked below my elbow, deflecting the blow, but the pain that shot through my arm made me fear that she'd broken it.

My pistol thudded onto the bank.

'No, Kate, it's really me! Brad!'

'*Brad!*' Kate shrieked and struck again with the club.

I dove to the right, barely avoiding the blow. It smashed into the stream. She swung again. I rolled as she kept swinging.

She gaped at something behind me.

I followed her gaze.

Petey's face showed above the tree that spanned the stream. His forehead was covered with soot. His hair and beard were singed. His shirt was blackened by smoke. Blood flowed from his left shoulder, where I'd evidently hit him the last time I'd pulled the trigger.

His shotgun rested on the horizontal tree, its barrel facing us.

Jason backed away.

'If you know what's good for you, son, don't take another step,' Petey told Jason.

I was on my back in the stream. My right arm was useless, probably broken from when Kate had struck it. My buckshot-punctured left arm was in similar agony, but at least it was mobile. Sweating from effort, I groped for the knife on my belt.

Jason kept backing away.

'Listen to your father,' Petey said. 'Stay put.'

Jason opened his mouth in a silent wail.

Then *Petey* wailed as I rolled under the tree and plunged the hunting knife into his thigh. The blade scraped bone. When he lurched back, his shotgun went off. The pellets whistled past my head. No! Afraid that the blast had hit Kate and Jason, I stabbed Petey's thigh again. As his blood spurted over me, I redirected my aim toward his side.

But he rammed down with the butt of his shotgun, hitting my

wounded shoulder. I almost passed out, able to do only one thing, to throw my weight against his legs and bring him down with me into the stream. I crawled onto him, stabbing toward his face, but he pushed me to the side and grabbed my throat, choking me so hard that I feared my larynx would break.

Smoke reached us. The fire crackled nearer. I plunged the knife into his wounded shoulder. In agony, he fell back, landing where he'd dropped his shotgun. He grabbed it, pumped out an empty cartridge, and pulled the trigger.

I lurched back from the blast that would blow my chest apart, but the shotgun made only a clicking sound. It was empty. Roaring, Petey swung it like a club, but loss of blood weakened him. The blow glanced off my leg. My left arm was in greater agony, much less mobile, as I thrust with the knife and missed.

A shot kicked up dirt.

We spun toward it.

Kate had crawled beneath the trees. Wavering to her feet, she held the pistol that I'd dropped. Doing her best to keep it steady, she looked as if, throughout her ordeal, a small part of her mind had remained lucid enough to fantasize about getting even. Normally, at close range, there wasn't any trick to using the gun. Even though she knew nothing about pistols, all she had to do was look down the barrel and pull the trigger.

But she was drugged, and she'd already missed once, and now she mustered her concentration, her eyes dark above her hollow cheeks. The twin vision of her nightmare – two Peteys, two Brads – must have threatened the little sanity she had left.

'Help me,' Petey said. 'I came here to save you. Shoot him.'

She hesitated, then turned the gun toward me.

'Please, Kate, don't,' I said.

I watched her finger tighten on the trigger.

'Shoot him,' Petey said.

'I love you, Kate.'

'I'm your husband. Do what I tell you,' Petey said.

She turned toward Petey and shot him in the face.

She took a step closer, pulled the trigger, and this time missed. So she stumbled closer, until she was on top of him. At point-blank range, she shot him in the chest. The next bullet burst his throat.

She didn't aim at those parts. They just happened to be where the barrel wavered. She shot and kept shooting, too close not to hit him somewhere, his shoulder, his knees, his groin, riddling his body, until all fifteen bullets in the magazine had been expended and the slide on top of the pistol stayed back.

Tears rolled down her face.

I managed to stand.

But as I approached her, wanting to hold her, she staggered back in fright. She raised the pistol again and pulled the trigger repeatedly. Nothing happened. The gun was empty. But if there'd been any rounds left, she'd have killed me.

I tried to make a reassuring gesture. 'It's okay. You're safe now. I'm not going to hurt you.'

But the dark frenzy in her eyes told me that she didn't believe me.

'I won't touch you,' I said. 'But please let me help you. Please.' I felt heat behind me. I heard a crackling roar and looked over my shoulder at the fire. 'We have to get out of here.'

I took another step forward. In response, she backed away toward the tree across the stream.

'Jason?' I asked. 'Where's Jason? *My God, was he shot?*'

As I stared frantically under the tree toward where I'd last seen Jason, Kate scrambled under it, trying to get away from me. I lurched after her, rising on the other side. Fearful that I'd see Jason's body blown apart from Petey's last shotgun blast, I breathed out in relief when I found him standing next to the stream.

He threw a rock.

It struck my chest, but I was far beyond pain. All I wanted was to get him out of there.

'It's okay, Jason. You've got nothing to be afraid of now.'

I took a step toward him. Covered with blood, singed by the fire, I must have looked indistinguishable from Petey.

He scrambled up the bank and into the forest.

Off balance from my injuries, I struggled after him. Heat and smoke almost succeeded in pushing me back as I stumbled through the underbrush.

I saw bright flickers within the smoke. The heat intensified. A tree exploded into flames. A wall of fire reached bushes.

'Jason!' Smoke clogged my throat. I bent over, coughing, forced myself to straighten, and veered past more trees.

The wind cleared the smoke for an instant. Ahead, Jason was blocked by the approaching fire. He turned, desperate to run from it, then stopped when he saw me. I must have been more threatening than another wall of fire. He dodged to my left and raced toward an opening in the blaze. As I leapt, the wind hurled flames toward him. I knocked him down an instant before a fiery gust flashed above our sprawled bodies. With the remaining strength in my wounded arm, I dragged him back from the flames. He kicked and hit me. Then Kate was hitting me. 'Let him go!' she screamed.

The three of us tumbled down the bank and landed in the water. They kept hitting and kicking, but I didn't resist. Their punches weakened. Finally, they collapsed, staring at me, their gaunt chests rising and falling.

'I love you,' I said.

They stared.

Something slowly changed focus in their eyes, as if they dimly remembered a time when those words had been familiar.

'Stay here. There's something I have to do,' I managed to say.

As the fire approached the top of the bank, I splashed water over me. Then I ducked under the tree that spanned the stream. I came to where Petey lay. His body was almost totally covered with blood from the number of times he'd been shot.

But that wasn't good enough. He'd come back once. I needed to be absolutely certain that he was dead, that he could never come back again, not even in my nightmares.

I grabbed his feet, but my injured arms had stiffened too much, causing too much pain for me to drag him up the bank. I tried as hard as I could but was about to give up, when Kate's hands came into view. I looked at her, startled, but she didn't say a word, just helped me tug Petey up the slope.

We threw him toward the fire. His corpse burst into flames. Only then did we stumble back down to the stream. At the bottom, Kate fell, but she wouldn't let me touch her to help her get up. Keeping a wary distance from me, she and Jason ran.

Epilogue

The three of us were in hospital for quite a while. The police and the district attorney questioned me, demanding to know why I hadn't let the authorities go after Petey. I did my best to tell them that events had overtaken me. How could I explain that I was afraid the police would have gotten Kate and Jason killed instead of saving them? Despite my repeated denials, they insisted that my motive had been rage, that I'd been determined to get even with Petey.

So I had to appear before a grand jury, and the way my attorney explained it to me, I could have been charged with what amounted to taking the law into my own hands. But I doubt there was a person on the jury who, after looking at my broken arm in a sling and the burns on my face, didn't think that I'd gone through enough. Certainly Kate and Jason had gone through plenty. Their eyes had the haunted expression of war refugees.

It took three weeks before we were allowed to leave. I paid someone to drive the Volvo back to Denver while Kate, Jason and I flew home from Columbus. Our friends welcomed us back. They phoned. They visited. They had a party for us. We thanked them. But the truth was, we were too traumatized to be sociable. Smiles and small talk were difficult to manage, and as for 'large talk', when we were asked details about what had happened, we weren't ready to discuss it yet. After a while, the newness of our return wore off. The phone calls, visits and invitations declined. Finally, we were left to ourselves.

Jason remained so silent that the parents of his friends didn't feel comfortable having him around their children. For her part, Kate got nervous whenever she had to leave the house. She finally gave up trying to do so. The only good thing was, as soon as I shaved my beard, as soon as the drugs wore off and Kate and Jason distinguished me from Petey, they no longer considered me a threat, although I'm always careful to let them see when I'm going to touch them.

I've tried to be honest with myself. I've done my best to understand what happened, hoping to adjust to it. But sometimes I wonder if it's *possible* to adjust to what Petey . . . Lester . . . did to us. Odd how I struggled so hard to deny that Petey was Lester and now I accept that the two were the same. My brother died a long time ago. Because of *me*.

Sometimes when Kate and Jason aren't aware of it, I study them, trying to decide if they're getting better. Without being obvious, I try to see beyond their eyes. I look in the mirror and try to see beyond my own. Do we carry darkness in us?

Payne came over the other day, a welcome visitor.

I asked him about his wife. 'Is she well? What was the result of the biopsy?'

'The lump on her breast turned out to be a cyst, thank God.'

Only then did I realize that I'd been holding my breath. 'I'm glad to hear good things can happen,' I said.

In the backyard, Payne eased his weight onto the lounge chair where Petey had sat the previous year, peering up at our bedroom window.

Kate brought us two glasses of iced tea.

We pretended not to notice that her hands shook and the ice rattled.

'Thanks,' I said.

When I touched her shoulder, she actually smiled.

Payne watched her return to the house. 'Has she been seeing anyone?'

'A psychiatrist? Yes,' I said. 'All three of us have.'

'Is it doing any good?'

'My own guy has me writing a journal, describing what happened and how I feel about it. I talk to him about it once a week. Is it doing any good?' I shrugged. 'He claims that it is but says that I don't have the objectivity to know it yet. He also says that because the trauma we went through lasted a long time, it isn't reasonable to expect to get over it quickly.'

'Makes sense.'

'Kate went into the supermarket all by herself today.'

Payne looked puzzled.

'It's a big step,' I explained. 'She has trouble being near crowds and strangers.'

'What about *you*? Do you plan to go back to work?'

'I'm going to have to soon,' I answered. 'Our insurance doesn't cover all the medical expenses. Certainly not the *legal* expenses.'

'But how are you feeling? Are you *ready* to go back to work?'

I sipped my iced tea and didn't answer.

'When I was with the Bureau, I had to shoot somebody,' Payne said.

'Kill him?'

He concentrated on his glass. 'I got shot in the process. Three months medical leave. A lot of counseling. I think I told you that's when I put on all this weight and left the Bureau. It took me a long time to feel normal again.'

'*Normal*'s a complicated word,' I said. 'I wonder if I *can* feel normal again. In my previous life, it's like I was blundering around in a world of hurt but was too stupid to realize it.'

'And now?'

'I think Kate's right to be careful of what's going on around her. Anything can happen. One moment, I was standing on a ridge, admiring the scenery. The next moment, my brother shoved me into a gorge.'

'Caution's a virtue.'

'So I've learned. You asked me if I planned to go back to work. I *am* at work.'

'Oh?' Payne studied me.

'Taking care of my family. It's my job to love Kate and Jason as hard as I can, to thank God for every moment I have with them, to hold them and cherish them and do my damnedest to keep them safe.'

Payne's concentration was powerful. 'You know what, Mr Denning?'

'Please call me Brad.'

'The more I get to know you, the better I like you.'